TWENTIETH-CENTURY BRITAIN

CASSELL'S COMPANION TO

TWENTIETH-CENTURY BRITAIN

Pat Thane

GENERAL EDITOR · DEREK BEALES

CASSELL&CO

First published in the United Kingdom in 2001 by Cassell & Co.

Distributed in the United States of America by
Sterling Publishing Co., Inc., 387 Park Avenue South, New York, NY 10016–8810

A CIP catalogue record for this book is available from the British Library

ISBN 0-304-34794-9

Designed by Gwyn Lewis
Printed and bound in Finland by WS Bookwell

Cassell & Co., Orion House, 5 Upper St Martin's Lane, London WC2H 9EA

FRONTISPIECE Ramsay MacDonald (1866–1937), the first Labour Party prime minister, addressing the House of Commons, painted by Sir John Lavery (1856–1941). © *Scottish National Portrait Gallery, Edinburgh/Bridgeman Art Gallery*

Contents

General editor's introduction

Knowledge of the history of one's own country is necessary for an understanding of its present situation. Hence English, Welsh, Scottish and Northern Irish men and women have become more interested in the history of their own countries – both of the larger unit, the United Kingdom, and of the nations within it – even as the significance of these nations and their histories has apparently been diminished by the dismantling of the Empire, devolution, the development of European integration and globalization. At the same time, the richness of recent historical writing has made it more difficult than ever for the non-specialist reader to keep up-to-date with current scholarship.

For many outside Britain, too, British history must have a special appeal. Large parts of the world have been deeply influenced, for good or ill, by British rule, commerce, industry, religion and example, and by the English language and its literature.

The object of these dictionaries is to make readily accessible the necessary basic information about the history of the United Kingdom and its constituent nations together with some account of the results of historians' new research and thinking. It is intended to appeal to VI Form and University students and libraries and to the reader generally interested in British history. Each volume will be the work of one, or at most two, distinguished historians so that each book, while fulfilling the necessary functions of a work of reference, will reflect the individual approach of its author(s). I believe that the series will be found both practically useful and intellectually stimulating.

Professor Derek Beales

SIDNEY SUSSEX COLLEGE, CAMBRIDGE, 2001

Author's introduction

We cannot consider the history of twenthieth-century Britain in isolation
from that of the rest of the world. Throughout the century Britain was
closely bound to other countries through a multiplicity of shifting interests,
alliances and conflicts, arising from trade, war, politics, migration, sport,
travel, intellectual exchange and the export and import of culture of all
kinds, from TV programmes to opera.

The century can readily and accurately be portrayed, for Britain as for
other countries, as a time of unparalleled barbarism in which weapons of
mass destruction more terrible than ever before killed on a scale and with
an efficiency beyond the nightmares of earlier generations. Equally
important, it was a century in which, for the first time in human history,
most people lived to old age, in better conditions, healthier and more
literate than ever before; and when more people than ever before gained
the opportunity to participate in political decision-making. The spectacular
advances in science and technology in the century led both to the H-bomb
and to immense improvements in living standards and in the capacity of
medicine to cure. One certain outcome of this contradiction between the
good and the evil that marked the century was the destruction of the
belief, still widespread in intellectual circles at the beginning of the century,
in the likelihood of steady, progressive, all-embracing improvement in
human behaviour.

The other major, over-arching change was that the world in 1900 was dominated by the nation states of Europe, the most powerful of which (Britain, France, Russia) directly controlled large areas of the rest of the world, which formed their empires. London was at the heart of the largest empire and the world centre also for international finance. By the year 2000 Europe no longer dominated the world and, internally, it was more united and peaceable than it had been for centuries. No formal empires remained. The international importance of London, and of Britain, had declined. Nation states were said to have less autonomy than before in relation to regional groupings of states (such as the European Union), which were formed in the second half of the century. Powerful international institutions, international business and the internationalizing forces of 'globalization', were said to be the defining feature of the late twenthieth century. The term 'globalization' means that the world has become a single unit for all manner of public and private transactions: businesses move their operations around the world, regardless of the boundaries of nation states; individuals travel and communicate with each other across national boundaries with ease.

Yet it is possible to overestimate the speed and character of such changes. One reason for surveying the whole history of twenthieth-century Britain is to gain an informed perspective on the extent of change and the influences upon it. The world of 1900 was highly mobile. The years before 1914 saw the greatest period of mass international migration in recorded history, much of it from Europe to the United States, though hundreds of thousands of people left Britain, mainly to settle in the colonies. Most of these would now be described as 'economic migrants', searching for a better life and often finding it. Migration into and out of Britain declined in the years of economic depression between the first and second world wars, but revived after 1945. The world in 2000 saw still greater movement: migrants in search of economic betterment, refugees from persecution, business people, tourists; though the formal, legal barriers to any but temporary movement had become much greater as the volume of movement grew.

Similarly, though globalization was said to be erasing national and cultural differences, awareness of such differences remained extremely strong and politically powerful internationally. In Britain the movements for autonomy for Scotland and Wales, which existed throughout the century, resulted in devolved government only in 1999, whilst the particular, distinctive, problems of Northern Ireland remained unresolved.

The two world wars dominated the first half of the century, killing large numbers of civilians as well as service-people. The killing power of weapons of war mounted, until it became so destructive, with the dropping of the atomic bombs which ended World War II, that powerful states agreed – tacitly at first, then openly – to restrain it. This did not mean an end to severe antagonism and tension between powerful nations, but it prevented localized conflicts escalating to threaten world peace. Shortly after World War II global warfare was replaced by the global 'Cold War' between the two dominant post-war powers, the USA and USSR and their allies (Britain being a supporter of the USA), which dominated international politics until the collapse of communism in eastern Europe from 1989. The second half of the century saw no global war, though there were many local wars, which were waged with increasing technological expertise often with support from the global superpowers. Some were wars of independence, such as that in Malaya (Malaysia) from 1948–60, which were part of the process of decolonization that was an important feature of British and international history between the end of World War II and the 1970s; others were struggles for national control between communists and non-communists as in Korea (1950–53) and Vietnam (1959–75).

Though British forces were involved in these and other wars to the end of the century, either as primary protagonists (as in the Falklands, 1982) or as part of the United Nations (as in Bosnia, 1990) or NATO (as in Serbia, 1999) forces, war and the armed forces were less significant in British life in 2000 than in 1900. The fact that a Ministry of 'Defence' replaced the 'War' Office as the senior government department responsible for the armed services from 1947 symbolized the difference between the two halves of the century in this respect. By the end of the century senior figures in the armed services were no longer household names, as they had once been, and defence/warfare claimed a declining proportion of government expenditure.

War and defence were replaced as central concerns of government and as objects of government expenditure by growing government responsibility for the well-being of the population. Social issues, such as health and education, came to dominate political debate as international affairs had once done. Another novel feature of the twentieth century, especially the second half of the century, was that most modern states became 'welfare states'. It was recognized that healthy, secure populations were socially and politically stable and economically productive. The 'welfare' role of the British state grew steadily over the first half of the century. As in other west European countries it was reconstructed and expanded significantly immediately following World War II. Expansion continued through what is increasingly regarded as a 'golden age' of high levels of employment and rising living standards, until the 'oil shock' of 1973 destabilized the national and international economy. Even then, however, public and private expenditure in Britain on health, welfare and education continued to rise to the end of the century, despite efforts to cut it back. This was partly because of the cost of supporting large numbers of unemployed people, who were the casualties of economic recession, and there were compensating reductions in other areas of social expenditure, such as housing and social services. Yet, despite the desires of some and the fears of others, the welfare state did not wither away, though by the end of the century, with unemployment much reduced, it was much in need of, and was beginning to receive, fundamental reconstruction.

Government expenditure played a major role over the first half of the century in diminishing the extensive poverty and high infant mortality rates that prevailed at the beginning of the century, but much real poverty remained by the time of World War II. The welfare state was only one reason for the marked general improvement in living standards in the second half of the century. The full employment and increased family incomes of the decades between World War II and the 'oil shock' owed much to international as well as national efforts to stabilize the world economy. Leading politicians, particularly in the USA and Britain, sought to establish international economic and political organizations that would stabilize and expand world trade by removing trade barriers (the General Agreement on Tariffs and Trade – GATT), by supporting faltering economies with loans and advice (the World Bank and the International Monetary Fund) and by expanding purchasing power in non-communist countries (Marshall Aid).

An important outcome of economic stabilization was a great improvement in living conditions for most people in Britain and the elimination of the severest poverty. An excellent indicator is the change in life expectancy. Life expectancy at birth in 1901 was 51 for men and 58 for women; by 1991 it was 76 and 81 respectively. Before 1920 an average of 74 people each year reached their hundredth birthday, but in the 1990s 3000 did so each year; and people were reaching old age in a far better state of fitness than in earlier decades, as a result, above all, of improved diets and health care.

This was just one of many ways in which Britain changed over the twentieth century. Most strikingly, at the opening of the twentieth century, Britain was a major player in the world economy and in world politics and was the leading imperial power. From World War II this role was much diminished and the colonies directly dependent upon Britain dwindled to a handful of small islands scattered across the globe. The full effects of these changes in role and status remain difficult to assess, though some are evident. The memory that Britain had a world role not so long ago makes it difficult for some, even at the beginning of the twenty-first century, to accept the status of one country among equals in Europe. The comment of US Secretary of State, Dean Acheson, in 1962, that 'Britain has lost an Empire but has not found a role' has all too often rung all too true. The legacy of the empire is evident in the multicultural character of Britain at the beginning of the twenty-first century, largely the result of migration from former colonies from the 1950s. The population of London in 2000 looked very different from the overwhelmingly 'white' city of 1900.

There were other obvious ways in which Britain changed over the century. Women became more prominent in public life and in a wider range of occupations, though equal opportunities between men and women had certainly not been achieved. Many of the greatest inequities between the social classes had diminished, but striking differences remained between the incomes, states of health, life expectancy and levels of education achieved by those born at the top and bottom of the social heap.

Changes in the recent past can be more difficult to assess than those of distant centuries because they are still incomplete. The outcome of Margaret Thatcher's long premiership, for example, cannot yet be fully assessed because, among other things, it is not yet clear whether it brought about a permanent or a transient change in public attitudes towards the respective roles of the individual and the state. It is easy to overestimate the significance of events that loom large in the present and easy to overlook how many events, which seemed similarly important in the past, are now forgotten: the details of the London mayoral election seemed massively important while much of this volume was being written in London during the campaign; just a year later their significance has faded. A purpose of this volume is to help readers make up their own minds about what changed in twentieth-century Britain and what was significant and why.

ACKNOWLEDGEMENTS

For assistance in compiling this volume I am grateful to Hera Cook, Kristin Doern, Jennifer Morawiecki, John Shepherd, Rob Skinner and Selina Todd.

A–Z of 20th-century Britain

A

Abbey Theatre. *See* YEATS, W.B.

abdication crisis (November–December 1936), crisis precipitated by the determination of King EDWARD VIII to marry his companion, Mrs Wallis Simpson, which led to the king's abdication.

On 16 November 1936 Edward notified the prime minister, Stanley BALDWIN, that he wished to marry Mrs Simpson (1896–1986), an American whose second divorce had recently been finalized. Baldwin, supported by the cabinet and by many other influential political figures, opposed Edward's wishes on the basis that marriage to a divorcée – scandal aside – would seriously undermine the king's position as supreme governor of the CHURCH OF ENGLAND and could thus provoke a constitutional crisis. A 'morganatic' marriage – in which a private act would be passed in Parliament allowing Edward and Mrs Simpson to marry but denying her the status of queen – was also rejected after Baldwin's consultation with the governments of the dominions. From 3 December 1936 the British press broke its self-imposed silence on the issue. Edward, faced with the decision either to remain king or to give up Mrs Simpson, chose to abdicate on 10 December. In a historic broadcast to the nation the following evening he pledged his allegiance to his brother, the new king GEORGE VI, and spoke of his inability 'to carry the heavy burden of responsibility and to discharge my duties as king as I would wish to do without the help and support of the woman I love'. The couple immediately went into voluntary exile in France, marrying on 3 June 1937.

FURTHER READING Lord Beaverbrook (M. Aitken), *The Abdication of King Edward VIII* (1966); F. Donaldson, *Edward VIII* (1974); P. Ziegler, *King Edward VIII* (1991).

Aberfan, coal-mining village in Mid Glamorgan, South Wales, scene of one of the century's worst industrial disasters. At approximately 9.15 a.m. on 21 October 1966 some 2 million tons of coal slag slid off the side of Merthyr Mountain, demolishing a farm and a row of terraced houses before engulfing Pantglas Junior School. The children had just settled into their classrooms after morning assembly. A teacher at the school remembers, 'I could feel the room shaking and I could see the room filling up. What was happening I just didn't know. And then it stopped. And there was such an eerie silence, there was nothing just this deadness.' In all 116 children and 28 adults died.

What had happened at Aberfan could have happened anywhere in the coalfield. What was the cause? The immediate explanation of Lord Robens, chairman of the National Coal Board (NCB), was that 'recent heavy rainfall had soaked through the tip and washed away the base'. There had been warnings from miners that the NCB was tipping on top of a hidden spring, but Robens insisted 'it was impossible to know that there was a spring in the heart of this tip which was turning the centre of the mountain into sludge'. Ten months later the independent tribunal of inquiry set up immediately by the Labour government concluded that 'The blame for the disaster rests with the NCB and its personnel', which it criticized severely, especially Robens. The NCB did not admit responsibility and no one faced criminal charges or was dismissed. The government refused Robens's half-hearted offer to resign. It – as well as most Labour backbenchers – was reluctant to criticize either a nationalized industry or a long-time leader of the National Union of Miners, as Robens was. In the Commons the new Conservative shadow minister of power, Margaret THATCHER, criticized the failure of anyone in the NCB to take responsibility. Robens worked hard to deflect press criticism. The NCB refused even to pay the full cost of removing the remaining six coaltips above Aberfan. After prolonged negotiation it contributed £350,000 to the removal and the Treasury another £350,000, while £150,000 came from the £1.75 million raised for the Aberfan Disaster Fund from voluntary donations.

SEE ALSO COAL MINING; NATIONALIZATION.

FURTHER READING I. McLean, 'On Moles and the Habits of Birds: The Unpolitics of Aberfan' in *Twentieth Century British History*, 8, 3, (1997), 285–309.

abortion. Abortion was illegal in Britain until 1967. There had been growing concern that this was leading to large numbers of illegal and often highly unsafe abortions, which endangered the lives or health of the mothers. It was unknown how many such abortions there had been throughout the century: 68,000 was the number calculated by an academic demographer for 1935 alone, and it was estimated that in 1933 500 women died as a result of abortion. Campaigners for BIRTH CONTROL in

the interwar years, such as Marie STOPES, argued that access to birth-control knowledge and techniques was necessary to prevent illegal abortions. The Abortion Law Reform Association (ALRA) was founded in 1936 by seven women, campaigning for legal abortion to be available to safeguard women's health. In the following year the British Medical Association recommended reform of the law to legalize abortion. In the later 1930s a series of prosecutions of abortionists led to acquittals and judgements that abortion was legal to preserve the mental or physical health of the mother. In opposition was the ROMAN CATHOLIC CHURCH, and those who feared that legal abortion would encourage promiscuity.

The ALRA became more active in the 1960s, when popular support for safe legal abortion grew, especially among women. In 1967 the Liberal MP David STEEL introduced the Abortion Reform Bill as a private member's bill. The Labour government ensured that the bill had parliamentary time and it passed into law (although it did not apply in NORTHERN IRELAND). It required that two doctors should certify that abortion was necessary on medical or psychological grounds. Abortions could be performed on the NATIONAL HEALTH SERVICE. Medical workers could refuse to attend such cases on grounds of conscience. The time limit was not clearly defined in the 1967 act, but it was generally taken that abortions performed within the first 28 weeks of gestation were legal. For the remainder of the century there were persistent, unsuccessful, attempts to limit or destroy the act. The 1990 Human Fertilization and Embryology Act included a clause that removed the gestation limit where the health or life of the woman or the future health of the unborn child were at stake (this had always been so in Scotland). Other abortions were now legal only within the first 24 weeks of gestation, although, in practice, non-urgent abortions had hardly ever been performed after 24 weeks. Legal abortions in Britain rose from 90,000 in 1970 to almost 200,000 in 1990; about 50% were performed on the National Health Service.

Abyssinian crisis (1935), international crisis arising out of Italy's invasion of Abyssinia (Ethiopia), launched on 3 October 1935. The Italians used a minor border incident on the frontier with Eritrea (then an Italian colony) as a pretext, but in reality the invasion was in pursuit of Mussolini's ambitions to heighten his international reputation and create an empire. The conquest was carried out with considerable brutality. Emperor Haile Selassie of Abyssinia appealed for the protection of the LEAGUE OF NATIONS.

France and Britain, however, were pursuing a policy of APPEASEMENT towards Mussolini in the hope of retaining him as an ally against Hitler's Germany. They had recently agreed with Italy to form an anti-German front and they refused to condemn the invasion, though under pressure of public opinion the British government reluctantly endorsed economic sanctions imposed on Italy by the League. In Britain the PEACE BALLOT organized by the League of Nations Union had recently demonstrated that of 11.5 million participants, 10 million supported the League and believed that it should employ economic sanctions against any nation that attacked another. The government still sought a compromise. In December the foreign secretary Sir Samuel HOARE and his French counterpart Pierre Laval concluded the HOARE–LAVAL PACT, proposing to allow Italy to take half of Abyssinia. The pact was leaked to the French press and there was an outcry in Britain; Hoare was forced to resign.

The German reoccupation of the Rhineland in March 1936 diverted attention from Abyssinia, allowing Italy to complete the conquest. League sanctions were discontinued during the summer of 1936. The crisis made clear that the League was incapable of maintaining international order.

Adams, Gerry (1948–), Northern Ireland politician; president of SINN FÉIN (1983–). In the 1970s Adams was twice interned, and then imprisoned, as a suspected IRA terrorist. In 1978 he became vice president of Sinn Féin, then president in 1983. He was elected Sinn Féin MP for Belfast West in the 1983 election, serving until 1992 despite a ban on media appearances imposed by prime minister Margaret THATCHER (although Adams could be filmed, his voice had to be over-dubbed by an actor). His links with the Provisional IRA made him an important figure in the clandestine, and later public, negotiations for a Northern Ireland peace settlement in the late 1980s and the 1990s. He regained Belfast West for Sinn Féin in 1997 and became a member of the Northern Ireland Assembly in 1998. As a signatory of the Good Friday Agreement (see NORTHERN IRELAND), Adams – like his Ulster Unionist counterpart David TRIMBLE – was committed to the nonviolent resolution of Northern Ireland's political conflict. At the end of the century he continued to face difficulties in his attempts to balance on the one hand Sinn Féin's obligations to the peace process and the decommissioning of IRA arms, and on the other the suspicions and concerns of hardline Republicans. Strains within the Republican movement were evidenced by the split from the IRA of dissident Republicans to form the 'Real IRA' in 1997 (see OMAGH BOMB).

Addison, Christopher (1869–1951), Liberal politician who subsequently became a prominent figure in the LABOUR PARTY. Addison was educated at Trinity College, Harrogate, Sheffield Medical School and St Bartholomew's Hospital Medical School, London, obtaining his medical qualification in 1892. He was professor of anatomy at the University of Sheffield, 1897–1901, then lecturer in anatomy at Charing Cross Hospital, London, from 1901. He was elected Liberal MP for Hoxton, east London, in January 1910 and advised David LLOYD GEORGE on the national health insurance measure of 1911 and on other welfare legislation. He became parliamentary secretary to the Board of Education in 1914, and minister of munitions in 1915. He canvassed support for Lloyd George's coup against ASQUITH in 1916 and continued as minister of munitions in the Lloyd George government that followed. He became minister of reconstruction in July 1917, then president of the Local Government Board in January 1919. As such he was responsible for bringing into being the new Ministry of Health and in June 1919 he became the first minister of health. This ministry was also responsible for HOUSING. His Housing and Town Planning Act, 1919, provided the first large government subsidies to house-building. This later suffered temporary cuts, but the act transformed housing provision in Britain, especially for poorer people.

Addison lost his parliamentary seat in the general election of 1922 and wrote two volumes of memoirs: *Politics from Within* (1924) and *Practical Socialism* (2 vols., 1926). He then joined the Labour Party and was elected as Labour MP for Swindon, 1929–31. He was parliamentary secretary to the Ministry of Agriculture in 1929 and minister of AGRICULTURE, 1930–1. He refused to support the NATIONAL GOVERNMENT. He was re-elected as Labour MP for Swindon, 1934–5. He was elevated to the House of LORDS in 1937 as a baron and became leader of the Labour peers in 1940.

In 1939 Addison published *A Policy for British Agriculture* with the LEFT BOOK CLUB, advocating NATIONALIZATION of agricultural land in order to maximize food production and minimize food prices, and also stressing continuity with the radical Liberal land campaigns earlier in the century. The book opened with the words: 'At the General Election of January 1910 we went round singing "God gave the Land for the People". We called ourselves Radicals in those days and I am not sure that we had not more of the real democratic stuff in us than some who call themselves Socialists these days.' Such ideas represented an important strand in the Labour Party in the 1940s.

Addison became a viscount in 1945. As leader of the House of Lords, 1945–51, at a very advanced age, he played an important part in guiding Labour's innovative and controversial legislation through a Conservative-dominated House. He was also secretary of the state for the dominions, 1945–7, during a sensitive period that included the lead-up to independence in the Indian subcontinent. He was lord privy seal, 1947–51, a cabinet post without specific duties.

Aden, a volcanic peninsula in Arabia at the southern entrance to the Red Sea, annexed by the British in 1839 and administered by the British government in INDIA until 1 April 1937, when Aden became a crown colony, together with the islands of Perim and Kamaran in the Red Sea and Sokotra in the Indian Ocean. Britain also assumed a protectorate over more than 260,000 square km (100,000 square miles) of the Arabian hinterland. The port of Aden was a valuable fuelling station on the route to India and an oil refinery was developed there, but its importance declined in the 1950s as British trade and naval activity in the Indian Ocean lessened. In 1959 Britain established the hinterland protectorate as the South Arabian Federation of Arab Emirates, to which Aden acceded in 1963. This was seen by Britain as a first step to independence for the Federation within the COMMONWEALTH. However, Arab nationalist sentiment had been growing in Aden. A republican movement developed in neighbouring Yemen, backed by Nasser's Egypt, and from September 1965 there was a state of warfare in and around the port of Aden. In the following two years 129 British servicemen were killed there. Britain gave up sponsorship of the Federation and withdrew from Aden in November 1967. The former colony and the protectorate were established as the independent People's Republic of South Yemen. It was unified with North Yemen in 1990.

adoption. Adoption of children by those who were not their natural parents had occurred throughout British history, but it became legally permissible and regulated only in 1926. Pressure for legal regulation arose in the later 19th century because of fears that orphan children were being harmed and exploited and even killed following what were sometimes cash transactions. Bona fide charities that arranged adoptions of orphans or the children of unmarried mothers also wished their activities to gain the protection and respectability of legal status. The campaign was assisted by the experience of WORLD WAR I, which gave rise to an increase in the numbers of unmarried mothers, orphans, childless widows who wished for children, and parents who had lost their child. The war was immediately followed by the INFLUENZA PANDEMIC, which further increased the number of orphans and widows.

Following the 1926 Adoption Act, widows and unmarried people were allowed to adopt. An important change incorporated in the act was confidentiality: adoptive children thereafter could trace their natural parents only by court order, which could only be obtained with great difficulty. Adoption came to be shrouded in secrecy and a certain shame. Attitudes changed in the later 20th century, however, and adopted children were enabled to trace their natural parents.

FURTHER READING G.K. Behlmer, *Friends of the Family: The English Home and its Guardians, 1850–1940* (1998).

adult education. Institutions providing adult EDUCATION had their origins in the 19th century. Adult education was normally in the evenings, supported sometimes by residential courses of varying lengths. It was aimed mainly but not exclusively at the working and lower middle classes, and did not generally lead to formal qualifications. In London the Working Men's College (founded 1854) and Morley College (founded 1899) survive into the 21st century. A number of such foundations in London (Birkbeck College), Manchester, Birmingham, Leicester and elsewhere evolved into or joined universities. Organizations formed for other purposes also offered education. For example, TOYNBEE HALL, the world's first settlement house, founded in 1884, provided social support and opportunities for cultural improvement to the poor of London's East End. It sponsored classes,

concerts, literary societies and (from 1901) the Whitechapel Art Gallery, all of which attracted lower-middle-class female schoolteachers at least as much as male workers. By 1914 there were at least 46 settlement houses in UK cities, most of them offering courses. The COOPERATIVE MOVEMENT and its women's wing, the Women's Cooperative Guilds, organized lectures, libraries and classes in some places until at least the 1960s, as did the YMCA and YWCA. Some TRADE UNIONS also supplied education, most impressively the worker-run miners' institutes in South Wales, which provided libraries, courses, lectures and concerts, together with debating, theatrical, choral, operatic and film societies. These had also declined by the 1970s owing to the contraction of coal mining combined with competition from local authorities and from the entertainment industry.

Offering more formal education, the Workers' Educational Association (WEA) was founded in 1903 by Albert Mansbridge (1876–1952). It was active throughout the country, and was initially mainly aimed at working people. WEA courses included three-year courses that strove to supply reading, discussion and essay-writing at university level, as well as shorter courses and university-based summer schools. In 1899 two Americans, Walter Vrooman and Charles Beard, established Ruskin College in Oxford to provide residential courses for working men. Similar colleges were founded in the Midlands (Fircroft in Birmingham, in 1909), in Wales at Coleg Harlech (1927) and in Scotland at Newbattle Abbey (1937). Hillcroft, founded in 1920 in Surbiton, Surrey, was the first residential college for working women. All survived to the end of the century, though facing increasing competition from state-sponsored further and higher education. Throughout the century local authorities expanded their provision for evening and part-time education in a range of vocational and nonvocational subjects. Some subsidized WEA classes.

The University Extension movement was founded in the late 19th century to provide lectures by university academics for the wider public.

They especially attracted middle- and upper-class women who had been deprived of a university education. Many university teachers were also WEA lecturers. University College, Hull, established the first department of adult education in 1928. By 1939 most English universities had a department of extramural studies, as they continued to do to the end of the century, while admitting increasing numbers of mature and part-time students to their regular degree courses. During WORLD WAR II many academics and teachers joined the Army Educational Corps, which organized compulsory classes in current affairs and other topics for the armed forces. It gained a not wholly justified reputation for left-wing bias and for influencing the large 'soldiers' vote' for the LABOUR PARTY in the general election of 1945.

The BRITISH BROADCASTING CORPORATION (BBC) introduced educational broadcasting from 1924, with greater coverage and impact after World War II. The OPEN UNIVERSITY was founded in 1971 to provide degree- and sub-degree-level courses for adults through the medium of radio and television with a success that continued into the 21st century.

FURTHER READING T.A. Kelly, *A History of Adult Education in Great Britain* (3rd edn, 1992).

Agadir, small port on the Atlantic coast of Morocco, scene of an international incident in 1911. On 1 July 1911 a German gunboat was sent to Agadir, allegedly to protect German commercial interests against French expansion in Morocco. This aroused British fears that the Germans aimed to establish a naval base at Agadir, close to GIBRALTAR and vital British trade routes. On 21 July David LLOYD GEORGE, then CHANCELLOR OF THE EXCHEQUER, gave a strong warning to Germany in a speech in London. The Germans denied any desire to annex Agadir, and entered negotiations with the French. In November Germany agreed to recognize French rights in Morocco in return for the cession of territory in the French Congo. The Agadir crisis confirmed British suspicions of German expansionism, and prompted for the first time close cooperation between the Admiralty and the War Office in preparing for a possible war.

agriculture. Following the prosperity of the mid-19th century, parts of British agriculture suffered depression in the later 19th century, with falling prices, wages, land values and employment caused by increased international competition. However, the suffering of farmers was less than the vocal complaints of many of them suggested. Some sectors that catered for the growing urban market and general rise in living standards, such as market gardening and much livestock rearing, prospered. On average the incomes of farmers – both owners and tenants – rose by 10% between 1861 and 1911. Farm workers decreased in number by 23% in England and Wales between 1871 and 1911, and by 36% in Scotland, pulled away from the land by new opportunities in mining, industry or in the colonies as often as they were pushed off the land by the problems of agriculture. In 1911, 1.4 million men were employed in British agriculture, compared with 6.5 million men in industry; an unknown number of farmers and labourers' wives and daughters were employed in agriculture for no pay or worked irregularly and unrecorded. Output per worker rose by 26% between 1871 and 1911, and incomes rose by more than 50% on average. However, incomes were still lower than those of regularly employed urban workers, and between 1902 and 1914 farm workers' wages lagged behind the rise in prices. Government refrained from anything other than minor interventions in the sector and – unlike a number of European states – refused to protect agriculture with TARIFFS.

WORLD WAR I brought a temporary revival. There were growing fears before the war about the potential danger arising from the dependence of England, Wales and Scotland on imported foodstuffs, but these were slow to translate into official action. In August 1914 the president of the Board of Agriculture announced that he saw 'no occasion whatever for public alarm over food supplies'. Tens of thousands of men were recruited into the armed services from agricultural districts before the introduction of selective recruitment in 1915. IRELAND remained primarily agricultural and indeed became a major source of food for the remainder of the United Kingdom during the war. But food production in the other countries of the UK also gradually expanded as the government came to recognize the emerging problems of food supply and the possible length of the war. By the summer of 1915 retail food prices had risen by one-third over their 1914 level. In May 1915 the government appointed a committee, chaired by Lord MILNER, to report on the measures needed to increase food output in England and Wales if the war were to continue beyond the harvest of 1916. The committee reported in July 1915 and recommended that greatly increased output was possible but that effective measures would require government guarantees of prices and markets. The government declined to act and simply exhorted farmers to produce more, with little effect, until the 1916 harvest turned out to be poor and the German submarine blockade intensified. Then the new government, headed by David LLOYD GEORGE, appointed a 'food controller' (initially Viscount Devonport, then Lord Rhondda) with a brief to increase home food production and supply. To encourage output, farmers were guaranteed minimum prices for six years, to be reviewed after four years, in 1920. Over the same period there were to be MINIMUM WAGES for agricultural workers, enforced by wages boards. Rents of agricultural land were controlled and measures were introduced to ensure maximum use of agricultural land. The Corn Production Act, 1917, embodied the price guarantees and established the Agricultural Wages Board, which fixed minimum wage rates at 25 shillings a week for England and Wales; voluntary wage negotiation appeared to be effective in Scotland. The 1917 act also controlled rents. In fact, neither the minimum prices nor the minimum wages operated, since wartime shortages forced prices and wages above these levels, though wages rose more slowly

than prices, failing to keep pace with inflation for the first three years of the war. The use of the Women's Land Army and prisoners of war for agricultural work undercut the bargaining position of agricultural workers. Full employment and rising household incomes, combined with reduction of imports, led to increased home demand and higher prices. Farmers' costs (including wages and rents) did not rise as quickly as prices, resulting in greatly increased profits. The area of tillage increased from 4.2 million hectares (10.3 million acres) in 1913 to 5 million hectares (12.4 million acres) in 1918, mostly in England and Wales. Britain was the only European country involved in the war to take effective steps to maintain food supplies, which greatly benefited morale in wartime Britain. No serious rationing of food was required until 1918, and Britain avoided the serious food shortages suffered in Germany and elsewhere in central Europe during and after the war. This had much to do with the success of the convoy system in keeping up supplies across the Atlantic and the greater effectiveness of Britain's blockade of Germany than Germany's of Britain, but increased home production played a part.

The boost to agriculture did not long outlast the war. There was little confidence that pre-war conditions would not return and many landowners had sold their land during the war, while prices were high and the going was good (*see* ARISTOCRACY). High prices and profits continued after the war, as disruption to international trade continued. Farmers, like the TRADE UNIONS, became more effectively organized during the war: the National Farmers' Union (NFU), founded in 1908, had 80,000 members by 1918 and was recognized as a body with the status to negotiate with government. It opposed the minimum wage for farm workers. In 1921 massive grain imports from Argentina, Canada, Australia and India resumed, pushing down prices. As the worsening international economic situation began to hit and UNEMPLOYMENT to rise, the government abandoned price guarantees to farmers (which it had confirmed in the Agriculture Act, 1920), though compensation grants were given in 1922. Farmers had complained about the controls as being too restrictive. They soon came to criticize the abandonment of controls as a 'betrayal' when they experienced the reality of falling world prices. There were increasing sales of land – perhaps a quarter of the land in England changed hands between 1918 and 1921 – encouraged by demand from urban businessmen who had made money during the war and wanted a rural retreat. But sales were often to sitting tenants, during the prosperous years before 1921, who were then saddled with high mortgages during the Depression. Prices continued to fall through the 1920s, though they were higher than before 1914, and farmers continued to bewail their plight, though again with perhaps some exaggeration. The crisis was certainly not sufficient to cause a widespread exodus from farming: there were 306,000 farmers in Great Britain in 1921, 294,000 in 1931. The numbers of both the smallest and the largest farms tended to decline, while those with 80–120 hectares (200–300 acres) expanded. By the time of the next census in 1951 there were 302,000 farms. The abolition of the Central Agricultural Wages Board in 1921 enabled farmers to cut costs by reducing their employees' wages. They fell from a national minimum of 42 shillings a week in 1921 to an average of about 28s in 1922, provoking a serious strike in 1923 in East Anglia where wages were lowest (about 25s). In consequence the first LABOUR government restored statutory wage regulation in agriculture in the Agricultural Wage (Regulation) Act, 1924. Average wages rose to 31s 5d in 1925 and thereafter remained steady, rising to 34s 9d in 1939. SCOTLAND had no wages legislation until 1934 and wages continued at low levels. Many farmers maximized their chances by diversifying production, in particular into livestock and vegetables for the home market, but they were vulnerable in a fluctuating world economy in which many of their competitors were protected by tariffs, while the home market was not buoyant. They were assisted by the abandonment of the GOLD STANDARD in 1931, which led to reduced interest rates and increased import prices.

From 1932 world prices recovered but British agriculture continued to lose workers: the number fell from 729,000 to 601,000 in the ten years before WORLD WAR II, again partly pulled by the recovery of other forms of employment. Mechanization increased, with more use of tractors, combine harvesters, crop sprayers, milking machines and other innovations, though productivity did not advance spectacularly. Farmers were assisted in the 1920s by the reduction (in 1923) and then the removal (in 1929) of their obligation to pay rates (local taxes) on their land; otherwise the government kept intervention in farming to a minimum. This policy was reversed in the 1930s, when government assistance to farming came to exceed anything previously offered in peacetime, even in the early 19th century, though all governments were reluctant to move away from cheap foodstuffs and farmers were never satisfied with the extent of assistance. From November 1931 tariffs were gradually introduced, though IMPERIAL PREFERENCE, as finalized at the OTTAWA CONFERENCE of 1932, meant that some of British agriculture's main competitors in the empire were wholly or partly exempted. Indeed the main effect of tariffs was to shift trade towards the EMPIRE and away from other countries. Under the Agricultural Marketing Acts, 1931 and 1933, any branch of farming could produce an approved marketing scheme which would qualify for price and import controls and, eventually, subsidies. Some of these schemes, such as the Milk Marketing Board, greatly improved the efficiency of a chaotic market. They replaced the voluntary cooperative schemes that operated successfully elsewhere in European agriculture but had never appealed to British farmers. The various forms of relief added up to an estimated subsidy to agriculture of £45 million in 1933.

However, at the outbreak of the World War II Britain was still dependent upon imports for 60–65% of its food requirements, including more than half of meat supplies and about 90% of cereals and fats. More than half of the total came from the empire. When the war began the government had plans in place for the expansion and subsidy of home production, price controls, RATIONING and the use of convoys to maintain a flow of imports. Again this was successful in keeping up adequate food supplies – and morale – and in boosting farming incomes.

After the war, the Labour government maintained controls on prices and supplies, but from the 1950s farming had again to face world competition, though one in which tariffs were much diminished and regulated (*see* GENERAL AGREEMENT ON TARIFFS AND TRADE) and in which it had to work within new international trading units, first the EUROPEAN FREE TRADE AREA, then from 1973 the European Community (EC; *see* EUROPEAN ECONOMIC COMMUNITY). Farms, except in upland areas, became much larger and more specialized, and made greater use of machinery and chemicals and less of labour. In consequence output in 1993 was more than three times the level of 1900 and more than twice that of 1955. The agricultural labour force in Great Britain had fallen from 1.4 million in 1911 to 352,000 in 1981. Under pressure of competition farming had become highly efficient. Governments continued to subsidize farming (unlike other declining industries), conscious of its importance in times of national crisis, and under constant pressure from the NFU to do so. Farming gained very substantially from subsidies from the EC, within which agriculture was a very powerful lobby. The EC's Common Agricultural Policy existed to subsidize unprofitable small farmers elsewhere in Europe, and this also benefited smaller British farmers. There were still greater gains from access to the protected European market for efficient farmers who adjusted output to European demand, especially since competition from elsewhere in the world was much restricted. Wheat imports were cut by half and British wheat-growing increased by half during the 1970s: at 1.5 million hectares (3.6 million acres) in 1980, the acreage under wheat exceeded the wartime peak

of 1943 and was the highest figure since 1874. Modern techniques increased yields to twice the level of ten years earlier and were ten times as high as fifty years before. British consumers, on the other hand, paid food prices inflated by EC controls on output and pricing, designed to keep farmers in business. By the end of the century many British farmers were receiving substantial 'set-aside' subsidies not to use their land in order to avoid overproduction and uncommercially low prices, but to keep it available for agricultural use in case of need. At the end of the century British farmers suffered a series of crises, such as the epidemic of BSE ('mad cow disease') in cattle, which necessitated the slaughter of large numbers of cattle and considerably restricted exports for some time. They received substantial government compensation for their losses and it was unclear by the end of the century whether agriculture was indeed in serious decline or whether, once more, the vocal complaints of farmers overstated the real extent of the crisis. Modern farming techniques also faced mounting public criticism arising out of fears of the effects of the extensive use of chemicals. Increasing numbers of consumers preferred to buy 'organic' vegetables (produced without the use of chemicals) and growing numbers of farmers found this a profitable area into which to diversify.

FURTHER READING B.A. Holderness, *British Agriculture since 1945* (1985); R. Perren, *Agriculture in Depression, 1870–1940* (1995).

air raid precautions (ARP). *See* BLITZ.

Alanbrooke, Alan Francis Brooke, 1st Viscount (1883–1963), field marshal, the most senior British officer in WORLD WAR II. Brooke was the son of an Irish baronet from Fermanagh, a member of the Protestant ascendancy. Educated in France and at the Royal Military Academy, Woolwich, Brooke went on to serve in Ireland and India, and with distinction on the Western Front in WORLD WAR I. He subsequently became an instructor at the Staff College, Camberley, and at the Imperial

Defence College; promoted to brigadier, he was commander of the School of Artillery, Larkhill (1929–32), then became lieutenant general in command, Anti-Aircraft Corps (1938), and commander in chief, Southern Command (1939). In World War II he was a corps commander in France, organizing the evacuation of troops in 1940 (*see* DUNKIRK), then became commander in chief of home forces. In 1941 he was appointed chief of the Imperial General Staff and chairman of the Chiefs of Staff Committee. In these roles he organized the British military contribution to the Allied war effort from the time of the defeats of 1941 to the end of the war. He worked well with CHURCHILL, CUNNINGHAM (chief of naval staff) and PORTAL (chief of air staff), and is credited with the successful appointments of ALEXANDER, MONTGOMERY and SLIM to key army commands. Brooke was made a viscount in 1946. After the war he held various posts: master gunner of St James's Park, 1946–56; director of the Midland Bank (1949–63); lord lieutenant, county of London, and constable of the Tower (1950); and president of the Zoological Society (1950–4).

alcohol. Alcohol consumption peaked in Britain in the late 1870s, then declined. Convictions for drunkenness in England and Wales fell from 207,000 in 1905 to 152,000 in 1910. During WORLD WAR I taxes on alcohol were greatly increased and the opening hours of public houses were restricted for the first time, especially in areas of munitions manufacture, in order to maximize war production. After the war drink consumption continued to drop. Beer was overwhelmingly the drink of working-class men in England (in SCOTLAND they drank whisky also). Beer consumption fell throughout the interwar period. The middle and upper classes more often drank spirits, port, sherry and wine, and their consumption did not noticeably decline. In WORLD WAR II the drink trade was again strictly regulated. Although beer was left unregulated for reasons of morale, prices rose, and wine imports were prohibited. From the 1950s

the range of alcoholic products available grew and there was a significant rise in the consumption of wine and spirits, while beer consumption declined relatively. By the mid-1970s drunkenness convictions formed 25% of non-motoring offences in MAGISTRATES' courts (*c.*105,000). The proportion declined to 7% in 1997 (*c.*29,000). Such statistics, however, may say more about POLICE priorities than about the use of and abuse of alcohol. Over the century, and especially after World War II, drinking by women became more visible and socially acceptable. The opening hours of public houses and restrictions on the sale of drink were greatly relaxed in the 1980s and 1990s.

Aldermaston. *See* CAMPAIGN FOR NUCLEAR DISARMAMENT.

Alexander, Harold (Robert Leofric George)

(1891–1969), field marshal, one of the most successful British commanders in World War II. Alexander was the third son of the 4th earl of Caledon, and was born in the family home in County Tyrone, Ireland. He was educated at Harrow School and the Royal Military College, Sandhurst. He was commissioned in the Irish Guards and served with distinction as a battalion commander in France in WORLD WAR I. Immediately after the war he was a member of the Allied Relief Commission in Poland, and fought against the Bolsheviks in Latvia, leading a Baltic-German unit. Between the wars he saw active service as a brigadier general on the northwest frontier of INDIA, following rapid promotion. He held a variety of army posts and was promoted to major general in 1937, the youngest general in the British army. He commanded the first division of the British Expeditionary Force in 1939–40 and was the last officer evacuated from DUNKIRK. In 1942 he was flown to BURMA to command the final withdrawal from Rangoon to Assam in the face of much superior Japanese air power; he was almost captured.

Churchill appointed Alexander commander in chief, MIDDLE EAST, in August 1942. In North

Africa Alexander oversaw the preparations for the second and the decisive third battle of EL ALAMEIN, and directed the advance to Tunis, working well with General MONTGOMERY, who served under him as commander of the 8th Army. Alexander was appointed deputy commander in chief to General Eisenhower and was always on good terms with the American allies. He commanded the Allied armies that landed in Sicily and Calabria and was appointed commander in chief, Mediterranean, but then suffered from the diversion of men and material to other fronts. The ANZIO landing was not a success, but his forces reached Rome by the first week of June 1944 and a vigorous offensive from the Po valley northward was maintained until the end of the war in Europe. He was appointed field marshal in December 1944 and made a viscount in 1946.

From 1946 to 1952 Alexander served as the last British governor general of CANADA, returning to London as minister of defence in Churchill's Conservative cabinet, 1952–4. He was created Earl Alexander of Tunis in 1952, and became a director of a number of companies in his retirement. He had a reputation for elegance and imperturbable confidence, for amenability and for reconciling opposing points of view. Churchill described him as possessing 'an easy, smiling grace', while MOUNTBATTEN believed that he had 'only the average brain of an average English gentleman'.

FURTHER READING N. Nicolson, *Alex: The Life of Field Marshal Earl Alexander of Tunis* (1976).

Allenby, Edmund (Henry Hynman) (1861–1936), army commander in the MIDDLE EAST in WORLD WAR I. Educated at Haileybury and Sandhurst, he was commissioned in the Inniskilling Dragoons and served with distinction in the BOER WAR. In World War I he commanded a cavalry division of the British Expeditionary Force in France in 1914 and the Third Army in the battle of Arras, 1917. In June 1917 he was appointed commander in PALESTINE. Advancing against the Turks, he captured Jerusalem on 9 December 1917, then pushed the Turks back through Syria until they signed an armistice at Mudros on 30 October 1918. The following year he was created Viscount Allenby of Megiddo (after his decisive victory over the Turks in September 1918), and was made high commissioner in Egypt (1919–25).

Amery, Leo(pold Charles Maurice Stennett) (1873–1955), Conservative politician. Born in India, Amery was educated at Harrow School and Balliol College, Oxford, gaining a first-class degree in classics and becoming a fellow of All Souls from 1897 until his death. He worked as a journalist on *The Times* (1899–1909) and was in SOUTH AFRICA, 1899–1900, during the BOER WAR. He became a passionate advocate of British imperialism, and edited and largely wrote *The Times'* history of the South African War (7 vols., 1900–9). Called to the Bar in 1902, he then embarked on a career in politics, sitting as the Conservative MP for South Birmingham (Sparkbrook) from 1911 to 1945. He joined the cabinet secretariat in 1916, and went on to hold a number of government positions: parliamentary undersecretary, Colonial Office, 1919–21; parliamentary and financial secretary, Admiralty, 1921; privy councillor, 1922; first lord of the Admiralty, 1922–3; and colonial secretary, 1924–9. As colonial secretary, he zealously advocated IMPERIAL PREFERENCE, but with less success than he had hoped, since it was not negotiated with all the colonies; he also established the Empire Marketing Board. As secretary of state for INDIA (1940–5) he worked to bring the country to independence within the COMMONWEALTH. He is best remembered for leading the attack in the Commons that ousted Neville CHAMBERLAIN from the premiership on 7 May 1940, quoting Oliver Cromwell: 'You have sat too long for any good you have been doing. Depart, I say, and let us have done with you. *In the name of God, go!*' He was made a Companion of Honour in 1945. His eldest son John was executed for treason in 1945, having admitted that, while living in wartime Germany, he had tried to persuade British prisoners of war to join a

British Free Corps to fight alongside the Germans against the Soviets.

FURTHER READING L. Amery, *My Political Life* (3 vols., 1953–5).

Amritsar massacre (April 1919), incident in the Punjab city of Amritsar in which British troops opened fire, without warning, upon a peaceful crowd of demonstrators, killing 379 and wounding 1200. The outcome was a stimulus to nationalism in INDIA and the emergence of GANDHI as its leader. Most Indian nationalists had supported Britain in WORLD WAR I, hoping that dominion status for India and a higher degree of independence would be their reward (*see* EMPIRE). They were encouraged in this by British officials, but in 1919 the government of India extended its emergency wartime powers, causing serious protests, especially in the Punjab, where martial law was declared. The local military commander, Brigadier General R.E.H. Dyer, ordered his troops to open fire upon protesters in Amritsar. The massacre that resulted led to the establishment of a commission of inquiry and to Dyer's enforced resignation. However, he was regarded as a hero by some in Britain. Indian public opinion was horrified and the nationalist movement radicalized. The Indian National Congress established its own committee of inquiry with Gandhi as a key member. This helped to establish him as a leader of the movement.

FURTHER READING J.M. Brown, *Gandhi's Rise to Power: Indian Politics 1915–22* (1972).

Anglicanism. *See* CHURCH OF ENGLAND.

Anglo-Irish agreement (1985). *See* IRELAND; NORTHERN IRELAND.

Anglo-Irish treaty (1921). *See* IRELAND.

Angry Young Men. *See* DRAMA; FILM INDUSTRY; NOVELS.

Anti-Apartheid Movement (AAM), organization that campaigned for the abolition of the racist apartheid system in SOUTH AFRICA. The AAM emerged in 1960 as a continuation of the boycott campaign against South African goods that began in 1959, inspired by a number of leading anti-colonialist activists such as Julius Nyerere (later president of independent Tanzania) and a well-known campaigner against racism in South Africa, the Anglican priest Trevor HUDDLESTON. The British AAM was the world's largest anti-apartheid organization (other than the South African liberation movements), and possibly the most successful British single-issue extra-parliamentary campaign of the 20th century. The movement focused on the campaign to boycott South African goods, disinvestment in the country and the imposition of economic sanctions. Other British-based organizations, such as Canon John Collins's Defence and Aid, helped to support the South African liberation movements. The AAM also helped to promote public support for a cultural boycott of South African sports teams and the country's isolation from the world of the arts and entertainment. When the South African Springbok rugby team toured the UK in 1969–70 it was met by mass demonstrations. The tour was completed, but the summer's visit of the South African cricket team was called off, and South Africa was banned from competing in international cricket.

During the 1970s international opposition to apartheid increased, especially after the Soweto uprising of 1976 and the death in custody of the Black Consciousness leader Steve Biko the following year. After the election of Margaret THATCHER as prime minister, the British government seemed to move closer to the government in Pretoria, and when the South African president P.W. Botha visited Thatcher in 1984, the AAM helped to organize a demonstration of over 50,000 people, bringing central London to a standstill.

The previous year saw the establishment of Trevor Huddleston as president of the AAM. In 1985 Archbishop Huddleston – alongside the African National Congress (ANC) president Oliver Tambo and the Reverend Jesse Jackson – led a

100,000-strong march through London. In addition to its ability to organize mass protests, the success of the AAM's campaign was acknowledged by the chairman of Barclays Bank when it pulled out of South Africa in 1986.

In 1988 the AAM organized a major tribute to Nelson Mandela on his 70th birthday, attracting leading international musicians to perform to a packed Wembley Stadium. When the situation in South Africa began to change rapidly after President F.W. de Klerk lifted the ban on the ANC and released Mandela in 1990, the AAM attempted to keep pace with official ANC policy, calling for the maintenance of sanctions until all apartheid legislation had been rescinded. As the ANC entered into negotiations that led to the first fully democratic election in South Africa in April 1994 the role of the AAM became less clear, and in the June following the South African elections its members voted to disband, handing over its resources to a new organization, Action for Southern Africa.

ANZAC. *See* AUSTRALIA; GALLIPOLI.

Anzio, small port on the west coast of Italy, 56 km (35 miles) south of Rome. In January 1944, during WORLD WAR II, it was the site of Allied landings intended by General ALEXANDER to force a German withdrawal from the strongly defended Gustav line 100 km (60 miles) to the south (*see* MONTE CASSINO). The landings, of a 50,000-strong Anglo-American force, took place on 22–23 January and were at first a complete success, taking the enemy by surprise. However, following a decision by the American commander, General Lucas, to dig in rather than to advance, the Germans mobilized reinforcements (diverted from the Eastern Front, given the seriousness of the assault) sufficient to prevent the planned break-out towards Rome. The Anzio area withstood German counter-attacks until the last week of May, when the Germans withdrew and the Allied force was able to join the main body of the 5th Army, which reached the suburbs of Rome on 4 June. Although the Anzio landing failed to bring the quick and effective results that were intended, it seriously damaged German defences and made an important contribution to the victory of the Allies in Italy.

appeasement, foreign policy pursued by the British government (though most notably associated with Neville CHAMBERLAIN) in the late 1930s. The term has come to acquire overwhelmingly negative connotations. Broadly speaking, appeasement was a policy adopted by both the British and the French when dealing with the expansionist aims of Nazi Germany and Fascist Italy. Both governments opted to avoid confrontation over issues such as the Italian invasion of Ethiopia in 1935 (*see* ABYSSINIAN CRISIS) and the 1936 German reoccupation of the Rhineland (which had been made a demilitarized zone by the treaty of VERSAILLES). In Britain there was a belief among many politicians that the aims of Hitler and Mussolini were limited in scope, and that stability in Europe could be maintained if the demands of the dictators were met in the wider interests of peace. In addition, there was strong anti-war sentiment among the British public in the mid-1930s, not to mention a lack of fiscal and military preparedness for war. Many also believed that the reparations levied on Germany, as laid out in the Versailles treaty, were too harsh. In fact, as early as the 1920s the British government had practised a form of economic appeasement in reducing the level of financial reparations Germany owed Britain.

However, a series of events in 1938 alarmed many observers and caused Neville Chamberlain (who had become prime minister the year before) to seek further assurances from Hitler. First, Germany had annexed Austria in the Anschluss (March 1938), an action strictly prohibited by the treaty of Versailles. Later that year, Germany announced its intention to reclaim the Sudetenland region of Czechoslovakia, with its majority population of ethnic Germans. Chamberlain flew to meet Hitler, Mussolini and Edouard Daladier of France to discuss the situation a number of times. Their meetings resulted in the MUNICH AGREEMENT (September 1938). Chamberlain sought assurances and believed that if Hitler were appeased in his desire to reclaim the Sudetenland a possible war would be averted and Germany's ambitions would be satisfied. Chamberlain's efforts were initially praised and he was hailed on his return to Britain as a peacemaker, but Hitler soon proved, after ordering his troops to occupy the rest of Czechoslovakia (March 1939), that the agreement was a sham. Chamberlain's efforts to placate the dictators were soon being scorned rather than praised, particularly by Winston CHURCHILL and his supporters in the CONSERVATIVE PARTY.

Historians are divided in their assessment of the policy of appeasement. Many have suggested that, as Churchill believed, it was cowardly of Chamberlain to have sacrificed Czechoslovakia for what turned out to be an empty promise from Hitler. Had Britain and France stood up to the dictators from the beginning, it is argued, war might have been averted and Nazi/Fascist ambitions nipped in the bud. However, other historians have claimed that Chamberlain had little choice other than to pursue the policy of appeasement. First and foremost, he believed (if naïvely) that the dictators were men of their word and would stand by the agreements made. A dreadful and costly war in Europe could thus be averted. However, he also believed that Britain was in no position, either financially or militarily, to go to war at that time. It is argued that the Munich agreement, as the culmination of the appeasement policy, bought Britain valuable time in which to re-arm and introduce CONSCRIPTION when it became obvious that war was imminent in early 1939.

FURTHER READING F. McDonough, *Neville Chamberlain, Appeasement, and the British Road to War* (1998).

architecture. A persistent theme of 20th-century British architecture has been competition between traditional and innovative styles. Influenced by the Arts and Crafts movement, the leading architects at the beginning of the century, notably Sir Edwin Lutyens (1869–1944) and William Lethaby (1857–1931), combined the two in domestic and church architecture. They drew on traditional designs, but made innovative use of colour and of materials, emphasizing craftsmanship and individuality of expression. C.F.A. Voysey (1857–1941) and, in Scotland, Charles Rennie MACKINTOSH (1868–1928, a pioneer of Art Nouveau) shared these preferences but moved further towards MODERNISM in their use of modern materials and simplified forms. Popular domestic architecture (as in Hampstead Garden Suburb, begun 1907) was much influenced by these approaches. At the same time public buildings – such as Belfast City Hall (built 1897–1906) and government buildings in Parliament Square in Westminster (1898–1912) – exhibited a more elaborate baroque influence.

Modernist use of new methods and materials (such as concrete and steel), and the more functionalist style deemed appropriate to them, began to spread from continental Europe before 1914, resulting in John Burnet's (1857–1939) Kodak building in Kingsway, London, in 1910–11 and Heal's Furniture Store in Tottenham Court Road in 1916. Modernism spread fastest in the 1920s and 1930s. Notable examples include Berthold Lubetkin's designs for the Gorilla House (1933–4) and the Penguin Pool (1934–5) at London Zoo, and a number of private houses and flats (such as Wells Coates's Isokon Flats in Hampstead, 1933) and commercial buildings (such as Charles Holden's designs for London Transport, including Arnos Grove station, 1932–3). There was some influence from exiles from the German Bauhaus school, such as the De La Warr Pavilion, Bexhill, Sussex, built in the mid-1930s by the Bauhaus architects Erich Mendelsohn and Serge Chermayeff. The strand of modernism influenced by Art Deco produced more exuberant buildings, including cinemas and Wallis Gilbert and Partners' Hoover Factory in Perivale, west London (1932–5). More traditional styles were still powerful: Sir Giles Gilbert Scott's (1880–1960) Liverpool Anglican cathedral, started in 1910 but not completed until the 1950s, was an outstanding example of Gothic revival. In contrast, the Anglican cathedral in Guildford designed in 1933 by Sir Edward Maufe (1883–1974) shows a restrained form of modernism. Meanwhile, the fastest spreading popular domestic form was the semi-detached house, often employing modern methods of construction to recreate versions of traditional styles.

After WORLD WAR II modernism continued to be highly influential in both domestic and public building. Examples of the latter include Frederick Gibberd's (1902–84) Heathrow Airport (1951) and the Royal Festival Hall (1949–51), built for the FESTIVAL OF BRITAIN, and Basil Spence's (1907–76) Coventry Cathedral (1956–62), which was also widely seen as a symbol of post-war renewal. Other examples include the stark concrete blocks that compose the external forms of the Queen Elizabeth Hall and the Hayward Gallery (1964) on London's South Bank, designed by the Architecture and Civic Design department of the Greater London Council, led by Geoffrey Horsefall. There were growing opportunities for a generation of younger British architects, influenced by Le Corbusier and Mies van der Rohe and attracted by the possibilities of steel and glass and innovative use of concrete and brick. Such materials also found expression in the wave of university building in the 1960s. Examples include Denis Lasdun's (1914–) University of East Anglia at Norwich, Spence's University of Sussex and James Stirling's History Faculty Building at Cambridge (1965–7). Gibberd designed a distinctly, and controversially, contemporary Roman Catholic cathedral for Liverpool (1960–7), in contrast to its stately Anglican neighbour.

In the same period high-rise building began to change the urban skyline. A notable example in central London was Seifert and Partners' Centrepoint Tower, but there were also many publicly built blocks of high-rise flats, as modernism came to influence mass domestic architecture. These high-rise flats were all too often cheaply built and unpopular with their occupants. By the end of the century disillusion or boredom with modernism bred a fashion for eclectic postmodernism (a remarkable example of which is the headquarters of MI6 on the river Thames in London). Postmodernism coexisted with a surviving, modified modernism and the hi-tech style of such architects as Richard Rogers (1933–) and Norman Foster (1935–), for example Rogers' Lloyd's of London building, built 1981–6.

FURTHER READING A. Jackson, *The Politics of Architecture: A History of Modern Architecture in Britain* (1970); P. Murray and S. Trombley, *Modern British Architecture since 1945* (1984).

Ardennes offensive. *See* BULGE, BATTLE OF THE.

aristocracy, a term for a particular social stratum, derived from the Greek word *aristokratia* ('rule by the best'). Somewhat fluid in its definition, the aristocracy is generally assumed to include members of the hereditary peerage and their families, but not always the gentry. Their rank was signified by a bewildering array of hereditary titles. At the apex were dukes, followed by marquesses, earls, viscounts and barons. Men with such titles are often known as 'Lord so-and-so'. At the lowest level of title were the baronets, known as 'Sir so-and-so'. The latter were generally of lesser status, though baronets were often prominent landowners and wielders of influence in their own localities and of long lineage; they predominated among the gentry. Some families inherited an accumulation of titles that could be used as 'courtesy titles' for male heirs. It was rare and difficult to transmit a title to a daughter. As the century went on, titles were scattered with increasing liberality among everyone from businessmen (honest or otherwise) to rock stars, sometimes by politicians, such as David LLOYD GEORGE, willing to award peerages in return for cash donations to their political parties. However, following the introduction of life peerages in 1958, very few new creations were hereditary.

At the beginning of the 20th century, membership of the aristocracy required a peerage and ownership of substantial amounts of land and at least the appearance of 'respectable' ancestry, although the British were less concerned about ancestry, and the rules of membership of the aristocracy were more fluid, than in some other European countries. About 360 landowners held estates of 4000 hectares (10,000 acres) or more – a sound basis for aristocratic status. The history of the British aristocracy in the 20th century has largely been about consolidation, decline and shrewd marketing of its trappings in order to ensure survival, while its smartest members diversified their assets and their skills into new channels. The prestige if not always the wealth of the land-owning aristocracy plummeted over the century. In the late 19th century, they enjoyed as a whole unrivalled wealth, power and status as leaders of government and of society. The wealthiest men and the biggest landowners in Britain were among their ranks. They socialized with royalty and young women from wealthy families. Female members of the aristocracy 'came out' (joined adult society – the term changed its resonance by the end of the century) by being presented to the monarch at an annual ball. The last such presentation of 'debutantes' occurred in 1958. In national government, members of the aristocracy usually made up at least half of the members of cabinets in the 19th century: in 1886, for example, 10 out of a total of 15 members of Salisbury's cabinet were aristocrats. The House of LORDS had almost as much political power as the House of COMMONS.

The decline of the aristocracy in the 20th century was precipitated by the disappearance, in the earlier part of the century, of the aristocracy in IRELAND as that country's governing, land-owning and social elite. Two other factors were significant, both as an outcome and a reinforcement of the decline of the aristocracy. The first was the introduction of taxation on the unearned increment of land values, which the aristocracy had long resisted. The second was the curbing of their political

powers by the 1911 Parliament Act (*see* LORDS, HOUSE OF). The taxation assault began in 1894 with the modest death duties on inheritors of large estates introduced by a LIBERAL government. This was taken further by the duty on land sales and the increased rates of taxation on higher incomes introduced in the 1909 'People's Budget', which finally went through in 1911 (*see* LLOYD GEORGE). The financial impact of these taxes was, as yet, small, but they were perceived as a blow to the power of the aristocracy.

Between 1910 and 1922 a great sale of land by aristocrats took place. It constituted the greatest transfer of property in Britain for centuries, rivalled in the second millennium only by the Norman conquest in the 11th century and the dissolution of the monasteries in the 16th. Between 1919 and 1921 alone, one quarter of rural land in England changed hands. To some extent this can be attributed to the effects of WORLD WAR I, during which more members of the aristocracy were killed than in any other conflict since the Wars of the Roses in the 15th century. This led to the sale of some estates that did not have a male heir. However, the scale of the transfer was only partly due to the deaths of heirs. Rural land was profitable during and immediately after the war. Tenant farmers were eager to buy, and large landowners sought to maximize profit and to consolidate sometimes scattered landholdings. Not all aristocratic families were disadvantaged by the sales, especially since rural land values plummeted during the agricultural depression of the interwar years (*see* AGRICULTURE). Some, such as the dukes of Westminster and Devonshire, managed to remain, to the end of the century, extremely wealthy, largely because of their ownership of valuable urban land. In 1873, 54 landowners owned estates of 8000 hectares (20,000 acres) or more. In 1973, 33 of these families still lived on their still substantial estates.

But some of the aristocracy were hit hard by falling incomes based on agriculture, the escalating costs of maintaining their ancestral homes and estates, and the crippling effects of taxation and death duties, which increased from World War I onwards. Some aristocrats were compelled to sell their homes and estates, with the result that many COUNTRY HOUSES were converted into schools, luxury hotels or conference centres, or even demolished. Particularly after WORLD WAR II, many of those who retained their properties opened their houses to the public in order to survive, and subsequently styled themselves conservators of the NATIONAL HERITAGE. This led to a thriving and competitive stately-homes business in Britain, led by organizations such as English Heritage and the NATIONAL TRUST. Others successfully diversified in different ways, finding alternative investments for their capital, or taking up lucrative employment, sometimes, though not always, trading on their names and titles. Up to the mid-1960s, members of aristocratic families continued to be strongly represented in CONSERVATIVE governments, but there was a striking change thereafter. In the final third of the century merely being an aristocrat still conferred social prestige but carried less power in itself, wealthy and powerful though many of them remained as individuals.

FURTHER READING D. Cannadine, *The Decline and Fall of the British Aristocracy* (1990).

armistice, an agreement between belligerents to suspend a war until a peace settlement is agreed. The most prominent example of an armistice in 20th-century European history – consequently referred to as *the* Armistice – is the document signed in a railway carriage at Compiègne, 65 km (40 miles) northeast of Paris, France, by representatives of Germany and the Allied powers on 10 November 1918, ending WORLD WAR I as from the following day, at 'the eleventh hour of the eleventh day of the eleventh month'. Earlier armistices had been signed by the Allies with Bulgaria (at Salonika, on 29 September 1918), Turkey (at Mudros, on 30 October 1918) and Austria-Hungary (at Padua, on 3 November 1918). The final, fragile 'peace settlement' between the Allies and Germany was agreed in the treaty of VER-SAILLES in June 1919. On 22 June 1940, following the German defeat of France in WORLD WAR II, Hitler required French representatives to sign an armistice with Germany in the same railway carriage, at the same spot, as in November 1918.

army. As the century opened, the British army was engaged in the BOER WAR. This conflict exposed unexpected inadequacies, and after the war there were speedy moves towards reform. In 1902 the Committee of Imperial Defence was established to survey the military needs of the EMPIRE and to improve forward planning. In 1904 the War Office (Reconstitution) Committee (the Esher Committee) recommended a reconstruction of the command structure and of the War Office. These and other reforms were implemented by the secretary for war, R.B. HALDANE. New weaponry, tactics and training methods were introduced. In 1908 Haldane established the TERRITORIAL ARMY in place of the previous militia, to provide both additional reserve forces and a corps for home defence. On the eve of WORLD WAR I the regular army numbered 247,432. There were also 209,280 reserves, and an additional 268,777 in the Territorial Army. Much of the regular army was based – as it had long been – in INDIA. Large numbers of soldiers from the subcontinent fought in the British army until independence in 1947, as, in smaller numbers, did men from other colonies. Gurkhas, from Nepal, continued to play a role in the British army throughout the century.

At the outbreak of World War I it was not foreseen that Britain would have to commit large numbers of soldiers to fighting in continental Europe. It was expected that, as in the Napoleonic Wars, Britain's main contribution to the war would be naval. But fighting in France quickly absorbed such large numbers of regular soldiers and Territorials that by December 1914 Lord KITCHENER – who had become secretary for war on the outbreak of hostilities – established a mass volunteer army, known as 'Kitchener's Army'. There were almost 1.2 million volunteers by the end of 1914. In

February 1916 CONSCRIPTION was introduced, following an act of Parliament in the previous month. The army's training, transport, supply, medical and welfare systems had great difficulty in coping with the unforeseen scale, length and brutality of the conflict. The army command and the government faced severe criticism, some of it justified, and there were improvements later in the war.

In 1917 the Women's Army Auxiliary Corps (WAAC) was founded to help solve the service manpower problem by transferring non-combatant work behind the lines to women. It was the first time such a service had been established. A small number of women had received voluntary military training before the war by women-organized groups, and in 1915 the Marchioness of Londonderry founded the Women's Legion to provide cookery and transport services for the military, one of many similar organizations set up by women active in the pre-war WOMEN'S MOVEMENT. The Women's Legion became the core of the WAAC, which was greeted with enthusiasm by some women, though others opposed the idea of women's direct involvement in war. It met strong resistance from some men, especially senior members of the armed forces who accepted it only due to manpower shortages. About 80,000 women were enrolled by the end of the war. The WAAC was re-named Queen Mary's Army Auxiliary Corps in 1918. It was disbanded between the wars.

After World War I no major conflict was expected for at least a decade and, amid cuts in government expenditure with the onset of the Depression, the army reverted to a small force whose chief task was suppressing civil disturbances in various parts of the EMPIRE, including IRELAND and INDIA. The government opted to build up the ROYAL NAVY and ROYAL AIR FORCE, aiming to make them the key to British defence strategy rather than the army. Despite limited resources the army built up its expertise in TANK WARFARE. After the MUNICH AGREEMENT (1938) cabinet policy changed and the army was built up again. The same year the Auxiliary Territorial Service (ATS)

was founded for women, and male conscription was introduced in May 1939, following legislation of the previous month. By the beginning of WORLD WAR II the army numbered 237,736 regulars, 212,000 reserves and 249,000 territorials. Once more the army was not fully prepared for war, but it was in a better state than in 1914 and adapted more rapidly, assisted by modern COMMUNICATIONS (radio replaced telephone and telegraph) and use of air power. However, the larger geographical scale of the war created problems of strategy, supply and communications. The ATS provided invaluable support to combatant men throughout the conflict. It was awarded full military status in 1949, becoming the Women's Royal Army Corps (WRAC).

After 1945 the army was kept at full stretch. It played a part in the occupation of Germany until the early 1950s. The COLD WAR brought new imperatives, and a British army brigade fought with UNITED NATIONS forces in the KOREAN WAR in 1950–3. The army was also involved in the conflicts associated with DECOLONIZATION, notably in PALESTINE until 1948, in MALAYA 1948–58, in CYPRUS 1954–9 and in KENYA in the late 1950s. To maintain the necessary strength a two-year period of CONSCRIPTION was retained for all young men. This continued until 1960, when the last men began their national service (ending in 1962). Such a conscript army was unprecedented in peacetime in modern British history.

By the late 1950s the process of decolonization, combined with the development of NUCLEAR WEAPONS, led governments to revert to a long-term strategy of diminishing the role of the army and relying upon the nuclear threat and the ROYAL AIR FORCE for defence. The SUEZ CRISIS of 1956 exposed Britain's relative weakness in international military terms and speeded up the process of change. From 1960 the regular army was reorganized and limited to 185,000 regulars, the Territorial Army to 123,000, with a reserve of about 70,000. In 1966 the last two were merged into the Territorial and Army Reserve. From the 1970s

in particular the army, like many other publicly funded institutions, faced government cost-cutting and frequent reorganization, as well as problems of recruitment. Most of the historic regiments disappeared in the new structures. At the end of the century the army continued to be regularly deployed in NORTHERN IRELAND and as part of UN and NATO forces in crises in various parts of the world, notably in Iraq in 1990–1 (*see* GULF WAR) and the Balkans through much of the 1990s (*see* KOSOVO), but it was as a much smaller, more flexible, mobile and more highly trained force than at the beginning of the century. A notable development towards the end of the century was the disbanding of the WRAC and the integration – after much opposition – of women into the regular army as combatants rather than just auxiliaries. For much of the century officer status was the preserve of aristocrats and former public schoolboys – except in wartime – and a natural career for many of them. Male and female members of the royal family held honorific titles of command in various regiments. By the end of the century, however, the army was somewhat more ready to admit non-elite officers.
FURTHER READING C. Barnett, *Britain and Her Army, 1509–1970: A Military, Political and Social Survey* (1970); J. Gould, 'Women's Military Service in First World War Britain' in M. Higonnet et al., *Behind the Lines. Gender and the Two World Wars* (1987), 114–125; J. Strawson, *Gentlemen in Khaki: The British Army, 1890–1990* (1989).

Army Territorial Service (ATS). *See* ARMY.

Arnhem, battle of (17–26 September 1944), in WORLD WAR II, part of 'Operation Market Garden', an Anglo-American plan masterminded by General MONTGOMERY to outflank the German defences along the Rhine by a massive turning movement through the Netherlands into northern Germany. The British 1st Airborne Division (including a brigade of Polish parachutists) sought to capture the road bridge over the lower Rhine at Arnhem, while American airborne units were to seize bridges at Nijmegen and Grave (the airborne element of the operation was code-named 'Operation Market'). The British 2nd Army was then intended to advance 94 km (59 miles) to link up with the airborne forces, taking advantage of the bridges they had seized (the 'Garden' element). By ill chance for the Allies two much-battered German Panzer divisions were in the area, refitting, and had just completed a military exercise on how to repel an airborne landing. Montgomery had been warned of the presence of this German armour by Ultra (*see* BLETCHLEY PARK), but chose to ignore the intelligence. The British forces were prevented from securing the bridge. Some 6000 of the 9000 airborne force at Arnhem were taken prisoner and almost half of these were wounded; 1400 were killed. The failure at Arnhem destroyed Allied hopes of an early victory on the Western Front.
FURTHER READING G. Powell, *The Devil's Birthday: The Bridges to Arnhem 1944* (1984); C. Ryan, *A Bridge Too Far* (1976).

Arts Council of Great Britain, arts-funding organization that grew out of the COUNCIL FOR THE ENCOURAGEMENT OF MUSIC AND THE ARTS (CEMA) following World War II. It was founded in 1946, funded by the Treasury. Its members were to be appointed by the government for their knowledge of one or more of the arts, unpaid and for fixed terms. Separate, autonomous committees were established for SCOTLAND and WALES, and a separate Arts Council for NORTHERN IRELAND. Specialist advisory panels were established on a similar basis, initially for music, drama, art and poetry, later for dance, literature, photography and film. The Arts Council was founded under a royal charter, which defined its objectives as follows: to develop and improve knowledge, understanding and practice of the arts; to increase their accessibility to the public; and to advise and cooperate with government, local authorities and other public bodies to achieve these aims. Its grant-in-aid from the Treasury in its first year was £235,000;

in 1992–3 it was £221.2 million. Its grant was voted annually by Parliament.

The first chairman of the Council was Sir Ernest Pooley, who was succeeded by Sir Kenneth (later Lord) CLARK in 1952. In 1965 Jennie Lee became Britain's first minister for the arts, and in 1967 the Council received a new royal charter. It was expanded in size, and the Scottish and Welsh committees were redesignated councils. The scope of the Council's work became more ambitious, and expenditure rose: £3.9 million in 1965–6, £28.8 million in 1975–6, £106 million in 1985–6. It supported major national, London-based, institutions with annual subsidies: the Royal Opera, the Royal Ballet, the Royal NATIONAL THEATRE, the ROYAL SHAKESPEARE COMPANY. It also increasingly supported major regional companies: Welsh National Opera, Scottish Opera, major symphony orchestras in London, Liverpool, Manchester, Birmingham, Bournemouth and Glasgow, and a network of regional drama companies. Through the 1970s and early 1980s it placed especial emphasis upon supporting the work of creative artists, playwrights and composers. Thereafter the emphasis shifted, as in many government-funded bodies, to a greater concern for cost-effectiveness and encouragement of commercial rather than government sponsorship of the arts. Increasingly responsibility was delegated to newly created regional arts boards.

FURTHER READING R. Shaw, *The Arts and the People* (1987); E.W. White, *The Arts Council of Great Britain* (1975).

Ashdown, Jeremy John Durham (known as **Paddy**) (1941–), Liberal, then Liberal Democrat politician; leader of the Liberal Democrat Party (1988–99). The oldest of seven children, Ashdown was born in New Delhi, INDIA, into a family of soldiers and colonial administrators who spent their lives in India. When he was aged four his family returned to Britain and bought a farm in Northern Ireland. He was educated in England, at Bedford School, where his Irish accent gained him the enduring nickname 'Paddy'. From 1959 to 1972 he served as an officer of the Royal Marines and saw active service as a commando officer in Borneo and the Persian Gulf. After special-forces training in Britain in 1965 he commanded a Special Boat Section in the Far East. A gifted linguist, he went to Hong Kong in 1967 to undertake a full-time course in Mandarin Chinese. He returned to Britain in 1970 and was given command of a commando company in Belfast.

In 1972 he left the Royal Marines and joined the Foreign Office. He was posted to the British mission to the UNITED NATIONS in Geneva, where he was responsible for Britain's relations with a number of UN organizations and took part in the negotiation of several international treaties and agreements between 1974 and 1976. In 1976 he left the Foreign Office and worked in industry in the Yeovil area of Devon, in southwest England, until 1981. In 1981 the firm for which he worked closed and he experienced four months' unemployment. Then he obtained a post as a youth worker with Dorset County Council Youth Service, where he was responsible for helping the young unemployed. He stood unsuccessfully as Liberal candidate for Yeovil in 1979, then won the seat at the 1983 election, holding it until he retired from Parliament in 2001. He increased his majority in the 1987 election. He was elected leader of the Liberal Democrats in July 1988, and was made a privy councillor in January 1989. He stood down as party leader in 1999 and was succeeded by Charles Kennedy. Ashdown left Parliament at the election of June 2001.

Asian immigration. *See* IMMIGRATION.

Asquith, H(erbert) H(enry) (1852–1928), Liberal politician; PRIME MINISTER (1908–16). Son of a Yorkshire wool merchant who died when he was eight, Asquith had a disrupted, insecure early life. He attended City of London Boys' School, then Balliol College, Oxford, where he gained a first-class degree in classics and was president of the

Oxford Union (the university debating society). He was called to the Bar and married Helen Melland, the daughter of a leading Manchester doctor. Fourteen years and five children later she died. By this time he was Liberal MP for East Fife. He married Margot Tennant, a socialite whose style, contacts and wealth were better suited to his growing ambitions. He entered Gladstone's last government as home secretary in 1892. He was effective as a minister and in Parliament. When the LIBERAL PARTY returned to government in 1905 with a large majority, after ten years in opposition, he was appointed chancellor of the exchequer. On 5 April 1908 the prime minister Sir Henry CAMPBELL-BANNERMAN resigned owing to ill health and Asquith succeeded him.

One of the most notable achievements of Asquith's pre-war government was the breaking of the power of the House of LORDS. This followed the constitutional crisis arising from an equally notable achievement, David LLOYD GEORGE's 1909 'People's Budget'. His government also introduced an innovative flow of social-reform legislation that laid the foundation of the WELFARE STATE. In addition, Asquith, as chancellor, had begun a fundamental reform of the tax system with the introduction of a graduated income tax in 1907. His government also had to deal with increasing tensions both abroad (*see* AGADIR) and at home. On the domestic front there was, above all, serious conflict in IRELAND arising from the demand for HOME RULE. There were also increasingly public and angry demands by women for the vote (*see* SUFFRAGETTES; SUFFRAGISTS) – to which Asquith was quite unsympathetic. There was also increasing TRADE UNION action, including strikes, and quarrels in Parliament about defence expenditure. Asquith led the government successfully through these crises and developments – and through two GENERAL ELECTIONS, both in 1910. These were fought on the issue of the House of Lords' rejection of the People's Budget. In the two elections the Liberals lost the large majority gained in 1906, and the Irish nationalists and the Labour Party subsequently

held the balance of power. Eventually overshadowing all of this was the onset of WORLD WAR I.

Asquith coped less well with the difficulties of managing a war that turned out to be longer, on a larger scale and to require different strategies than had been anticipated. Apart from the difficulties posed by the war itself, he faced opposition in his party to the coalition that was formed with the Conservatives in May 1915; he also faced opposition to CONSCRIPTION and to the economic controls that were introduced, which were contrary to the principles of many Liberals. His capacity for management declined and his drinking problem (which had earned him the nickname 'Old Squiffy') grew. He had come to rely on his war secretary, Lord KITCHENER, who died in June 1916. Still more traumatically for Asquith, his eldest son Raymond was killed in action in September 1916. He faced increasing criticism for the conduct of the war. In December 1916 he was forced to resign by a group of senior Liberals led by LLOYD GEORGE, who succeeded him as prime minister. Asquith refused to remain a member of the government and the Liberal Party became split between supporters of the two leaders – Asquith's followers becoming known as 'Squiffites'.

Asquith lost his parliamentary seat in 1918, returning to the Commons in 1920 to lead a much depleted party. After the fall of the Lloyd George coalition in 1922 there was an uneasy reconciliation of the Liberal factions. Asquith remained titular leader of the party after losing his seat again in 1924 and accepting a peerage, as earl of Oxford and Asquith. He resigned from the leadership in 1926 and was succeeded by Lloyd George. He died two years later.

FURTHER READING R. Jenkins, *Asquith* (rev. edn, 1978); S. Koss, *Asquith* (1976).

Astor, Nancy (Witcher) (*née* Langhorne) (1879–1964), Conservative politician, the first woman to sit in the House of COMMONS. Born in the United States, she moved to Britain in her twenties with a small child, having divorced an alcoholic, abusive husband. She then married the wealthy Conservative politician Waldorf Astor. He was forced to retire from the House of Commons in 1919 on inheriting his father's title and seat in the House of LORDS, and she became Viscountess Astor of Hever Castle.

It had become possible for women to vote and to stand for Parliament only in the previous year (*see* SUFFRAGETTES; SUFFRAGISTS) and Nancy stood as a Conservative candidate for Plymouth in the resulting by-election, not as a feminist seeking to promote the cause of women, which at this stage she was not, but as a stop-gap while Waldorf sought to divest himself of the unwanted title. He failed to do so and she remained the MP for Plymouth through seven elections, until 1945, developing into an able politician and an active promoter of women's rights. Repelled by the misogynistic atmosphere of the House of Commons, she welcomed and supported women of all parties who followed her there. She worked for equalization of the voting age for men and women (achieved in 1928), defended the right of married women to work, which was widely opposed at the time, and supported equal pay, widows' pensions (introduced 1925), provision of nursery schools, the raising of the school-leaving age, the recruitment of women to the police force, child protection, temperance (because male drunkenness was a major contributor to violence against women and children), and reform of the law on prostitution to remove the double standard that punished women for soliciting but not men for employing prostitutes. However, she was reluctant to support either gender equality in access to DIVORCE or the promotion of BIRTH CONTROL – both important issues at the time – for fear that they would encourage sexual laxity. Her political priorities were influenced both by the experience of her first marriage and by her religious belief as a Christian Scientist.

In the 1930s Nancy became alienated from many in the WOMEN'S MOVEMENT owing to the support she and her social circle, known as the CLIVE-DEN SET, gave to APPEASEMENT. After the outbreak of war she acknowledged her misjudgement and became a strong supporter of Winston CHURCHILL, despite their long-standing antipathy. During the war she worked hard to bolster morale in her Plymouth constituency, which suffered heavily in the BLITZ. Nevertheless she lost her seat in the LABOUR PARTY landslide in 1945. She did not re-enter politics thereafter.

FURTHER READING J. Grigg, *Nancy Astor: A Lady Unashamed* (1980); B. Harrison, 'N. Astor: Publicist and Communicator' in *Prudent Revolutionaries* (1987), 73–97.

Atlantic, battle of the, name invented by Winston CHURCHILL in March 1941 for the struggle throughout WORLD WAR II to control supply routes to Britain. German SUBMARINES ('U-boats') first successfully attacked two convoys on 18–19 October 1940, sinking 32 ships. Improved air cover checked the attacks, until the construction of longer-range U-boats enabled them to reach the US coast and cause serious damage. An average of 96 Allied ships a month were sunk during 1942. From mid-1943 the use of special escort aircraft carriers and RADAR – together with the decipherment of German naval signals at BLETCHLEY PARK – cut Allied losses to an average of 12 vessels over the last year and a quarter of the war in Europe.

Atlantic Charter (14 August 1941), a statement of fundamental principles for the post-war world issued to the press after the first of the CHURCHILL–Roosevelt meetings, which took place aboard warships in Placentia Bay, Newfoundland, 9–12 August 1941. The United States was still technically at peace at this time. Agreeing to the charter was part of Churchill's strategy to draw the USA into WORLD WAR II. It emphasized British and American opposition to further territorial expansion and to any territorial changes contrary to the wishes of the inhabitants. It asserted that people should choose their own form of government and live free from fear and want. It supported post-war economic collaboration and proposed that the aggressor nations should be disarmed pending the establishment of an international security system. The Americans did not, as Britain hoped, commit to joining a successor organization to the LEAGUE OF NATIONS after the war. A month later it was announced that the Charter had been endorsed by the Soviet Union and the 14 other countries at war with Germany and Italy. The principles of the Charter formed the basis of the UNITED NATIONS.

atom bomb. *See* NUCLEAR WEAPONS.

ATS. *See* ARMY.

Attlee, Clement (Richard) (1883–1967), Labour politician; PRIME MINISTER (1945–51). Born in Putney, London, the second child of a successful upper-middle-class family, Attlee was educated at Haileybury and University College, Oxford, where he took a degree in history in 1904. After an unenthusiastic period in a law office he became a voluntary social worker at the Haileybury House Settlement in Stepney, east London, which prompted his conversion to socialism. He joined the INDEPENDENT LABOUR PARTY in 1907, becoming parliamentary candidate for Limehouse, east London. In WORLD WAR I he joined the East Lancashire regiment, reaching the rank of major and serving with distinction at GALLIPOLI and in Mesopotamia, where he was wounded, .

From 1919 to 1920 Attlee was mayor of Stepney, the LABOUR PARTY having taken control of the local council. In the general election of 1922 he won Limehouse for Labour and became parliamentary private secretary to the party leader, Ramsay MACDONALD. When Labour formed its first government in January 1924 he was appointed undersecretary at the War Office. In 1927, on MacDonald's recommendation, he was appointed to the Simon Commission on constitutional reform in INDIA, from which he gained experience of India and became committed to a gradual move towards self-government for the subcontinent. This role disqualified him from office when Labour formed

its second government in 1929, but when Oswald MOSLEY resigned as chancellor of the duchy of Lancaster in May 1930 Attlee replaced him. In February 1931 he became postmaster general. In 1931 the government fell apart (*see* LABOUR PARTY). In the election that followed in October 1931 Attlee held his Limehouse seat with a majority of only 551, being one of only two cabinet ministers in the Labour administration to hold their seats as Labour Party candidates. Attlee became deputy to the new leader, George LANSBURY, and worked hard throughout the country to rebuild the party. When Lansbury resigned in 1935 Attlee replaced him first on a temporary, then on a permanent basis after defeating Herbert MORRISON and Arthur Greenwood in a ballot. He gave clear expression to his view of Labour Party socialism in two books, *The Will and the Way to Socialism* (1935) and *The Labour Party in Perspective* (1937). He was a strong opponent of APPEASEMENT.

It was Attlee's role in WORLD WAR II that consolidated and strengthened his position within the party, though he continued to face criticism, especially from the left for his lack of explicit commitment to their causes. From May 1940 Labour participated in CHURCHILL's coalition government. Attlee served as lord privy seal, lord president, secretary for the dominions and – at first unofficially, then officially from February 1942 – as deputy prime minister, which enabled him to prove his ability to run the CABINET and to contain the tensions within the coalition and within his party. He played an important role in managing the home front while Churchill managed the war. He helped to shape post-war reconstruction policy on such issues as India and foreign policy.

Attlee's success in government during the war and his calm demeanour compared with that of Churchill contributed to Labour success in the election of 1945, though it did not protect him from an unsuccessful attempt by Morrison to displace him as leader after the election. As prime minister from 1945 to 1951 he again showed his skills of leadership of the cabinet, making shrewd choices of ministers and encouraging younger talent such as Hugh GAITSKELL and Harold WILSON. In foreign affairs he shared his foreign secretary Ernest BEVIN's antipathy to the Soviet Union and preference for alliance with the United States, neither of which stances won favour with the left of the party. He was committed to the establishment of NATO in 1949 and to building up the UNITED NATIONS. In this connection he committed Britain to participation in the KOREAN WAR in 1950. In 1947 he took, with Bevin, a controversial, secret decision to build a British NUCLEAR WEAPON. He acted personally to speed up the independence of India, which came about – perhaps too speedily in view of the blood-soaked partition that followed – in August 1947. This was followed by independence for BURMA in 1948.

In domestic policy Attlee presided over and supported an impressive series of social-policy measures that established the post-war WELFARE STATE, notably the foundation of the NATIONAL HEALTH SERVICE (NHS) and a reconstruction of the system of social security. In economic policy Labour was responsible for the NATIONALIZATION of industries that were vital to economic reconstruction but were malfunctioning: COAL MINING, RAILWAYS and road haulage. Nationalization of the iron and STEEL INDUSTRY in 1949 was more controversial. The government had considerable success in rebuilding the economy, restraining consumption by retaining RATIONING (which was not universally popular) and holding back on welfare spending in order to prioritize investment in manufacturing export industries. Its economic policies, however, were shaken by a largely externally induced economic and financial crisis in 1947 and by continuing high defence costs, exacerbated by the KOREAN WAR. Labour only narrowly won the election of February 1950. An ageing administration that had few new ideas staggered through an uncomfortable 20 months, marked by the death of Bevin and party conflict over participation in the Korean War and the decision to introduce charges for NHS prescriptions in order to fund rearmament, which led

to the resignation of Aneurin BEVAN. Attlee called another election in October 1951; Labour narrowly lost, despite gaining more votes than the CONSERVATIVE PARTY (*see* GENERAL ELECTIONS).

Attlee remained leader of the Labour Party, mainly preoccupied with seeking to minimize conflict between the right (broadly supporters of Gaitskell) and left (broadly supporters of Bevan). He resigned in 1955 and took a peerage as Earl Attlee of Walthamstow. Until his death in 1967 he devoted himself to promotion of the idea of world government.

FURTHER READING K. Harris, *Attlee* (1982); N. Tiratsoo (ed.), *The Attlee Years* (1991).

Auchinleck, Claude (John Eyre) (1884– 1981), army commander, affectionately nicknamed 'the Auk'. Educated at Wellington College and the Royal Military College, Sandhurst, Auchinleck joined the Indian army in 1914. He served in Egypt, Palestine and Mesopotamia in WORLD WAR I, and in India for most of the interwar period. In WORLD WAR II he commanded the British force at Narvik in 1940, and then was sent to INDIA as commander in chief in 1941, exchanging commands with WAVELL as commander in chief, MIDDLE EAST, in July of the same year. He launched a major desert offensive in November 1941 and, despite setbacks, his forces reached Benghazi and controlled all of Cyrenaica by the end of the year. However, Rommel won back all the territory for the Axis forces in the following year. In June 1942 Auchinleck took personal command of the 8th Army and won the first battle of EL ALAMEIN. However, CHURCHILL underrated him and replaced him with ALEXANDER as commander in chief, Middle East, and MONTGOMERY as commander of the 8th Army in August 1942. Auchinleck became commander in chief in India again in 1943, and served as supreme commander in the subcontinent during the difficult period leading up to independence. He was promoted to field marshal in 1946. Regarded by some Indian leaders as too favourable to Pakistan, he was asked to resign by the viceroy, MOUNTBATTEN, in 1947. He refused a peerage. In retirement he became president of the London Federation of Boys Clubs (1949–55) and chair of the Armed Forces Art Society (1950–67). He lived in Marrakesh from 1968 till his death.

Auden, W(ystan) H(ugh) (1907–73), English poet. Auden was the youngest son of a doctor and was brought up in Birmingham. He was educated at Gresham's School, Holt, Norfolk, then at Oxford University, where he studied English literature – thus becoming probably the first major English poet to study English literature at university level. At Oxford he became excited by the forms of Anglo-Saxon and Middle English poetry. A first pamphlet of his *Poems* was published in 1928, the year that he graduated. He then spent ten months in Germany writing and reading widely in psychology, and in 1930 he published a full-length volume of poems, again titled *Poems*. It was well received and established him as a talented poet. These cryptic, free-verse poems were mostly about love.

After 1930 Auden began to write more political poetry, critical of British public life. This was expressed in *The Orators* (1932). He shared a rather ill-defined left-wing response to the international crisis of the period with a group of other poets: Louis MacNeice, Cecil Day Lewis and Stephen Spender. Auden taught in a private school from 1932. In 1935, though homosexual, he married Erika Mann, daughter of the German novelist Thomas Mann, to provide her with a passport, so enabling her to leave Nazi Germany. In the same year he gave up teaching to concentrate on writing. He also worked with the GPO film unit (a leading documentary film unit at this time), where he became friendly with the composer Benjamin BRITTEN, who set many of his poems to music – their most famous collaboration was on the soundtrack for the documentary *Night Mail* (1936). A second collection of lyric poetry, *Look Stranger* (1936), extended Auden's fame. In the later 1930s he and one of his lovers, Christopher Isherwood, produced a string of successful dramas: *The Dog Beneath the Skin* (1935), *The Ascent of F6* (1936) and *On the*

Frontier (1938). At this time Auden also travelled widely. His 1936 trip to Iceland with MacNeice produced their joint *Letters from Iceland* (1937), and in 1937 he went to observe the Spanish Civil War. His poem that followed, 'Spain', expressed a certain disillusion with the politics he had previously supported. In the following year he travelled with Isherwood to China, then fighting invading Japanese forces. Together they wrote *Journey to a War* (1939), which expressed further disillusion and the difficulties of politically engaged writing.

Auden moved to the United States on the eve of World War II. In the USA he fell in love with Chester Kallman, a younger American writer, who became his lifelong companion. Auden was also increasingly attracted to Christianity and became a practising member of the Church of England in 1940. His volume *Another Time* (1940) represents a transition between his older and newer sentiments. It includes the poem 'September 1, 1939', which tried to come to terms with what he called the 'low dishonest decade' of the 1930s, a view reinforced in another volume, *The Double Man*, published in London as *New Year Letter* (1941). His religious faith influenced his later writing and led him to rewrite some of his earlier work and to his disowning some of his political pieces. His mother had also been a devout Anglo-Catholic. She died in 1941, and it was to her he dedicated *For the Time Being: A Christmas Oratorio* (1944). Auden faced much criticism in Britain for his wartime absence, and his reputation fell. In 1946 he became an American citizen, though from 1948 he spent much time in Italy. This inspired new poetry, culminating in the collection *Homage to Clio* (1960). He also wrote opera libretti. He and Kallman collaborated on the words for Stravinsky's *The Rake's Progress* (1951) and a number of further operas. By this time his reputation had been rehabilitated in Britain. In 1956 he was elected professor of poetry at Oxford for three years. He spent much of his later years in Oxford and died suddenly in Vienna.

FURTHER READING H. Carpenter, *W.H. Auden: A Biography* (1981).

Australia, a former 'white dominion' of the British EMPIRE, later an independent nation and member of the COMMONWEALTH. Australia's form of government at the end of the century was that of a constitutional monarchy. The 20th century witnessed the country's transformation from a loose collection of underdeveloped territories to successful united nationhood.

By the late 19th century, there were a number of separate colonies established on the Australian continent. The original colony, New South Wales, had been settled since the late 18th century. Tasmania was founded in 1812, Western Australia in 1827, South Australia in 1834, Victoria in 1851, and Queensland in 1858. By the end of the 19th century the idea of federal union was being seriously touted, and on 1 January 1901 the Australian Commonwealth Act came into effect. This united all the separate colonies as the Commonwealth of Australia, with a federal Parliament located at Canberra in the newly formed Australian Capital Territory. The new Parliament became responsible for federal issues such as trade, defence, the economy and the postal service.

Australian soldiers fought for Britain during the BOER WAR as well as in WORLD WAR I (as part of ANZAC (the Australia and New Zealand Army Corps) and WORLD WAR II. In particular they distinguished themselves at GALLIPOLI in 1915, despite suffering heavy casualties. The experience of Gallipoli, which many Australians felt was a betrayal by incompetent British commanders, was a formative moment in Australian national consciousness. World War II proved a further turning point in Australia's relations with Britain. As Singapore fell in 1942 and the British withdrew from the Pacific, Australians became increasingly alarmed by the inability of Britain to protect them, and angry that while the Japanese were bombing Darwin, Australian soldiers had been sent to fight in Europe and the Middle East. Australia began turning to the United States when it came to matters of defence. In 1951 it formed the ANZUS defence pact with the USA and New Zealand.

The population of the young nation grew substantially in the 20th century. Until the 1950s there was a large amount of immigration from Britain, but thereafter more immigrants came from other European countries, such as Italy and Greece, as well as Southeast Asia. From a population of 5 million in 1920, immigration swelled these figures to over 12 million by 1970 and 19 million by the end of the century.

The nationwide celebrations surrounding the 200th anniversary of the landing of the British fleet at Botany Bay in 1788 proved a focal point for two issues that most heavily impacted on Australia later in the century. The first was the contentious relationship between white Australians and the Aborigines, who marked the bicentennial with protests to highlight the fact that the arrival of Europeans had been the beginning of their own demise as a people. Enfranchised only in 1967, and the victims of racist attitudes and policies, the Aborigines had been ignored for decades by governments and denied rights to their traditional lands. Tension, especially over land rights, continued to the end of the century.

The second issue to which the bicentennial drew attention was the Australian republican movement. This first found widespread expression in the post-war period. The presence of Prince CHARLES representing the queen at the bicentennial celebrations was viewed as questionable by some. The republican movement reached its apogee with the election of Paul Keating as prime minister in 1992. An ardent republican, he sought to replace the queen with an elected president as head of state and reasserted the long-held belief that Australia's future lay with prosperous Asia, not with Britain or the Commonwealth, especially since a high proportion of the population was no longer of British origin. Although initially popular, Keating's campaign began to lose steam as his views became more extremist and Anglophobic, and he was soundly defeated in the 1996 election. A proposal to replace the queen with a president appointed by the Australian Parliament was narrowly defeated in a referendum in 1999, but republicanism itself did not disappear as an issue.

FURTHER READING G. Bolton, *The Oxford History of Australia, Vol. 5, 1942–1995: The Middle Way* (1996); S. MacIntyre, *The Oxford History of Australia, Vol. 4, 1901–1942: The Succeeding Age* (1997).

aviation. Britain took an early lead in the development of both commercial and military aircraft. Following a certain amount of experiment before the war, WORLD WAR I gave a major impetus to aircraft development. Britain produced war planes such as the Sopwith Camel, the De Havilland DH-4 and the Bristol F-2 Fighter. The ROYAL AIR FORCE was formed in 1918 out of the Royal Naval Air Service and the Royal Flying Corps. In 1919 the British aviators John Alcock and Arthur Brown became the first to make a nonstop flight across the Atlantic.

Commercial aviation began soon after the war, with the first regular service operating between London and Paris from 1919. Croydon airport, on the edge of London, was opened in 1920. Air travel became fashionable in the 1920s and new small airlines were established, many of which combined into Imperial Airways as Britain's major airline in 1924. By the 1930s this connected Britain with its colonies in the Middle East, INDIA, AUSTRALIA, NEW ZEALAND, and East and SOUTH AFRICA.

After a period of experimentation between the wars, rearmament in the late 1930s, followed by WORLD WAR II, gave another impetus to aircraft design. The Hawker Hurricane, which entered RAF service in December 1937, displaced the biplane fighter, and the Supermarine Spitfire (1938) became the leading fighter plane internationally. War needs led to the design of bombers such as the De Havilland Mosquito and the Avro Lancaster. The first British jet fighter, the Gloster Meteor, was introduced in 1944.

British commercial flying was largely suspended during the war. In 1939 Imperial Airways combined with a smaller firm to form a new national airline, the British Overseas Airways Corporation (BOAC), which reintroduced commercial services after the war. The Labour government in 1945 established two new national airline companies, as a boost to the industry: British European Airways (BEA) and British South American Airways (BSAA). Thereafter Britain led the way in developing new types of aircraft, which were flown by the national airlines. The most innovative product was the De Havilland Comet, the first jet-powered aircraft in the world to enter commercial service, with BOAC in 1952. A series of fatal crashes led to its grounding in 1954. An improved version was successfully launched in 1958, but by this time it had been overtaken by US designs.

Until the 1960s Britain was highly competitive in aircraft production, supported and encouraged by both Labour and Conservative governments. In an attempt to rationalize the industry the British Aircraft Corporation was formed from a number of smaller private companies in 1960. It amalgamated with most of the remaining independent companies to form British Aerospace in the late 1970s. Governments also supported collaborative projects with France, including the Jaguar fighter-bomber (1970s) and the Concorde supersonic airliner, which began development in the 1960s but did not enter commercial service until 1976 because of technical problems and vast cost overruns. It became the prestige aircraft of British Airways, which was formed out of BOAC and BEA in 1973. Later major British aircraft projects tended to be in cooperation with European partners in order to compete with powerful US producers.

Government involvement in the aircraft and airline industries, as in other sectors of the economy, diminished in the 1980s. British Airways was privatized in 1987. British Aerospace remained to the end of the century a successful military and commercial producer, and British commercial aviation remained buoyant.

FURTHER READING K. Hayward, *The British Aircraft Industry* (1989).

B

baby boom. *See* POPULATION.

Bacon, Francis (1909–92), artist. He was born in Dublin, Ireland, of English parents, a descendant of the Elizabethan and Jacobean writer and statesman of the same name. As a child he suffered from severe asthma and had little conventional education. His father was a racehorse trainer, puritanical in personality, who sent his son away from home at the age of 16 when he was discovered trying on his mother's underwear. Bacon then spent a short time in Berlin, followed by 18 months in Paris, where he was impressed by an exhibition of Picasso's work. Then, in 1929, he settled in London where he made a living designing furniture and rugs. Although he had no formal training as an artist, he began to produce drawings, watercolours and later oils, receiving some advice from his friend, the painter Roy de Maistre. In 1933 he began exhibiting in commercial galleries in London, but he then destroyed much of his early work and in the late 1930s he virtually gave up painting, supporting himself with various jobs, including running an illegal casino. He returned to painting during World War II, during which he worked for a while in the Civil Defence, having been excused military service because of his asthma. He made his reputation in April 1945 when his triptych *Three Studies for Figures at the Base of the*

Crucifixion (1944) was exhibited in a group exhibition at the Lefevre Gallery in London. It was seen as deeply shocking – above all for the distorted, damaged images of human bodies that he represented – at a time when British art was dominated by the neo-romanticism of Graham SUTHERLAND and John PIPER.

From 1946 to 1950 Bacon lived mainly in Monte Carlo and thereafter in London. He associated with other painters, including Lucian FREUD, in what has been loosely termed the 'London School', though stylistically they had little in common. From 1949 he had fairly regular one-man exhibitions, first in London, then in New York, Paris and elsewhere. He developed a distinctive use of paint, by means of which he presented twisted, violated, fantastical male faces and bodies. Portraits were a major part of his work and he made numerous self-portraits, but his paintings sought to convey not straightforward likenesses, but his pessimistic perceptions of the nature of existence. Characteristically, his figures were set in isolated, empty spaces, at times accompanied by cuts of raw meat. His work was novel and unsettling for critics and public alike, but he grew in stature. In 1962 a retrospective exhibition of his paintings was held at the Tate Gallery in London, and later toured several galleries elsewhere in Europe. This firmly established his international reputation, which then grew rapidly, though critics and public were divided between admiration and revulsion of his negative perception of human existence. A second major retrospective exhibition of his work was held at the Tate in 1985, which confirmed his international standing as a major figure in 20th-century art. He probably achieved greater international recognition than any other British painter of the century, though his work showed little development after the 1960s. He also acquired notoriety for promiscuous homosexuality, hard drinking and heavy gambling. His work had relatively little direct effect upon other artists, though he may have contributed to the desire to shock of younger, later 20th-century British artists (see BRITART).

FURTHER READING J. Russell, *Francis Bacon* (rev. edn, 1993).

Baden-Powell, Olave. *See* BADEN-POWELL, ROBERT.

Baden-Powell, Robert (Stephenson Smyth)

(1857–1941), soldier and founder of the Boy Scouts and Girl Guides movements. Baden-Powell was born in Oxford, where his father, who died when he was aged three, taught geometry. He attended Charterhouse School, then entered the 13th Hussars, serving in INDIA 1876–83. He fought in the 1888 Zulu War, the 1895 Ashanti War in west Africa and the 1896 Matabele uprising in what is now ZIMBABWE. In 1897 he was promoted to colonel, commanding the 5th Dragoon Guards, a cavalry regiment based in India. He was then ordered to SOUTH AFRICA to raise cavalry and organize the police forces along the frontier of Cape Colony. During the BOER WAR he commanded the besieged garrison at Mafeking 1899–1900 for seven months before being relieved. In Britain he was hailed as the 'hero of Mafeking'.

After the war Baden-Powell devoted himself (full-time after his retirement from the army in 1910) to a scheme for building up the character of the boys of the British EMPIRE: the Scout movement. This started with a trial camp for boys of mixed social origins at Brownsea Island, off Poole, Dorset, in 1907. It was inspired by the interest shown by young boys in his army training manual *Aids to Scouting* and the example of the Boys' Brigade, which was associated with NONCONFORMIST churches, whose main aim, however, was religious rather than patriotic revival. In 1908 he published *Scouting for Boys*, which remained in print throughout the century, a major best seller for most of it. In 1910, assisted by his sister Agnes, he founded the Girl Guide movement, primarily to prevent girls from forming troops in direct imitation of Scout troops, as some 6000 had done by 1909. His view of the purpose of scouting was that it should provide the physical and moral training and the sense of patriotism appropriate for the manly defence of the empire, which he felt was under threat in the early 20th century, due in part to physical and moral decline within Britain. Such training he thought inappropriate for girls; in *Girl Guides: A Suggestion for Character Training for Girls* (1909), he and his sister Agnes wrote that girls were to be trained to become 'guides' of men through learning sewing, cooking, first-aid and nursing, together with moral instruction.

Both movements became highly successful internationally. By 1910 there were 100,000 Scouts, and by 1913 140,000. In 1914 a junior branch of the Scouts, the Wolf Cubs, was founded, as was a junior branch of the Guides, the Rosebuds (renamed Brownies in 1918; this name derived from a book of 1870 by Juliana Ewing, in which Brownies were elf-like creatures who, at night, finished the housework for humans). In 1919 a senior wing of the Scouts, the Rover Scouts, was established. In these early years the movements gained from the financial support of Sir Arthur Pearson, the newspaper publisher. They continued in being throughout the century, Scouts having around 16 million members in 150 countries by the 1990s, representatives of whom came together for regular international jamborees; there were also about 8.5 million Guides in over

100 countries holding regular international Guide conferences.

Baden-Powell married, at the age of 55, Olave Soames (1889–1977), who was 32 years his junior. She became the figurehead of the Girl Guide movement, for which she worked for the remainder of her life. He became a baronet in 1922 and Baron Baden-Powell of Gilwell in 1929. The Baden-Powells spent the later years of his life in Kenya, where he died.

FURTHER READING T. Jeal, *The Boy-Man: The Life of Lord Baden-Powell* (1990); J. Springhall, *Empire and Society: British Youth Movements, 1883–1940* (1977).

Baird, John Logie (1888–1946), pioneer of an early television system. Born in Scotland, Baird studied electrical engineering in Glasgow. He began his television research with makeshift equipment in 1922, and first demonstrated his system on 26 January 1926. In 1928 he made the first transatlantic TV transmission and demonstrated colour and stereoscopic television. His system was used by the BRITISH BROADCASTING CORPORATION, experimentally from 1929, and then in its public television service from 1936 to 1937, when his mechanical scanning system was overtaken by electronic rivals. He demonstrated a big-screen television in 1930, and made the first ultra-short-wave transmission in 1932. He continued to experiment with stereoscopic and large-screen television until his death.

balance of payments, the net surplus or deficit of exports over imports of a country. Britain's international trading position can best be illustrated by looking at the changing balance over the century. Figures comparable with the remainder of the century are not easily available until 1919.

The years listed in the table on the right have been selected to illustrate trends. Throughout the century Britain imported more merchandise than was exported (known as 'visible trade'), and ran a surplus on income from overseas investments, loans and other financial transactions, such as providing insurance services (known as 'invisible trade'). Hence the importance of the CITY OF LONDON to the British economy since it was at the centre of these 'invisible' transactions. The pattern of each form of trade and the balance between the two fluctuated. The table illustrates the relative stability of the period before WORLD WAR I, especially when the economy recovered from the costly effects of the BOER WAR, after 1902. Accurate statistics are hard to find for the period of World War I, which severely disrupted normal patterns of trade. The table illustrates the relative prosperity of the immediate post-war period, then the fluctuations of the unstable inter-war international economy, when manufacturing exports fell to low levels, especially in the 1930s. WORLD WAR II was again highly disruptive to trade and left Britain with large overseas debts. The table illustrates the success of the post-war Labour government in bringing about a recovery of the exporting industries, despite the setback caused by the acute fuel shortage, followed by the convertibility crisis of 1947 (*see* DALTON, HUGH). The consumer boom of the 1950s, encouraged by Conservative government policy, spurred the import of manufactured goods and a growing deficit. The post-1964 Labour government had some success in controlling this deficit until it was hit by the sterling crisis of 1966. Recovery thereafter was followed by the effects of the 'OIL SHOCK' from 1973, which greatly increased the cost of oil imports, creating an unprecedented deficit in peacetime. Recovery in the later 1970s and early 1980s was followed by a slump to Britain's worst-ever trade deficit in November 1988, which lasted until 1992. This was a product of over-optimistic management of the British economy by Margaret THATCHER's Conservative government, prolonged by a mistaken and short-lived attempt to tie sterling to the European Exchange Rate Mechanism (ERM; *see* EUROPEAN MONETARY SYSTEM) amid general world economic slowdown. Recovery followed to the end of the century.

Net balance of payments

Year	£m	Purchasing value of £ (1900 = £1)
1900	+37.9	20s
1905	+81.5	19s 4d
1910	+167.3	18s 1d
1913	+181	17s 3d
1920	+235	7s
1923	+169	10s
1925	+72	9s 11d
1926	−15	10s 1d
1927	+82	10s 5d
1929	+103	10s 7d
1931	−104	11s 10d
1934	−77	12s 4d
1935	+32	12s 2d
1936	−18	11s 10d
1939	−250	10s 10d
1940	−804	8s 11d
1945	−875	6s 10
1948	+26	5s 9d
1949	−1	5s 7d
1950	+307	5s 5d
1951	+1369	5s
1954	+117	4s 7d
1955	−155	4s 5d
1956	−208	4s 2d
1960	−244	3s 11d
1963	−358	3s 7d
1966	+109	3s 3d
1967	−294	3s 2d
1970	+731	2s 8d
1974	−3278	9p
1978	+1162	5p
1985	+2888	3p
1986	−2265	3p
1989	−23,491	2.5p
1994	−1458	1.5p
1997	+6303	1.5p
1998	+474	1.4p

Sources: B.R. Mitchell and P. Deane, *British Historical Statistics* (2nd edn, 1981); *Annual Abstracts of Statistics.*

Baldwin, Stanley (1867–1947), leader of the CONSERVATIVE PARTY (1923–37); PRIME MINISTER (1923–4, 1924–9, 1935–7). Baldwin grew up in Worcestershire, where his family owned an ironworks of moderate size and prosperity. He was educated at Harrow School and Cambridge University, then entered the family business. On his father's death in 1908 he was elected to succeed him as MP for their local constituency of Bewdley. He made little impact during his first ten years in Parliament. In 1917 he became a junior minister in the coalition government and in 1921 entered the CABINET as president of the Board of Trade. In 1922 he was the only cabinet minister to join the revolt against David LLOYD GEORGE as leader of a coalition government now composed primarily of Conservatives. He made the key speech at the meeting of Conservative backbenchers at the Carlton Club that brought down Lloyd George and the coalition in October 1922. The Conservative leader, Bonar LAW – who was in poor health and had at the last minute agreed to lead the revolt – became prime minister and invited Baldwin to become CHANCELLOR OF THE EXCHEQUER. In May 1923 Bonar Law's ill-health forced him to retire. Baldwin succeeded him as prime minister and as leader of a still divided party. In October 1923 he called an election, soliciting from the voters support for protective TARIFFS as a solution to the gathering Depression (*see* UNEMPLOYMENT), a solution that grew out of his industrial experience. The bid was unsuccessful and the LABOUR PARTY formed its first government (January 1924).

Thereafter Baldwin abandoned tariffs and successfully established himself as a sound and reassuring figure in his party and in the country, presenting an image of an honest, reliable countryman seeking social and industrial harmony. He himself had donated one-fifth of his private fortune during WORLD WAR I to reduce the war loan, in contrast to the 'hard-faced men ... who look as if they had done very well out of the war', as he was said to have described many occupants of the post-war Conservative benches in Parliament. As prime minister from November 1924 to May 1929 he ably controlled a cabinet that had been constructed to reconcile the conflicting party factions. Winston CHURCHILL, newly recruited to the party after a long sojourn with the Liberals, was made CHANCELLOR OF THE EXCHEQUER, to appease the supporters of FREE TRADE. In his first budget, in 1925, Churchill returned Britain to the GOLD STANDARD, which pleased certain patriots and many in the CITY OF LONDON, but was of doubtful assistance to the economy. The appointment of Neville CHAMBERLAIN as minister of health was more obviously successful, and delivered a succession of social-reform measures. To the dismay of many in his party Baldwin sought to buy time to resolve the conflict in the COAL-MINING industry by providing a subsidy in 1925. When this was unsuccessful and the conflict spread to cause the GENERAL STRIKE in 1926, he rejected the urging of King GEORGE V and some of his cabinet to order a military assault on the strikers. By keeping calm and relying on the reluctance of most TRADE UNION members to become involved in conflict, and urging the population to do likewise, he emerged from the crisis with his reputation enhanced. He failed, however, to restrain his party colleagues from passing the punitive Trade Disputes Act, 1927, which sought to undermine both the unions and the LABOUR PARTY and alienated many voters. He led the Conservatives into the election of May 1929 under the slogan 'Safety First'. This failed to inspire voters, who returned Labour as the largest party in the Commons.

Between 1929 and 1931 Baldwin faced sustained attack from the 'Empire Crusade', a campaign for a tariff wall around the EMPIRE (*see* IMPERIAL PREFERENCE) waged by the press barons Lords BEAVERBROOK and Rothermere. He fought back and survived, and in August 1931, in order to enable Britain to survive the financial and economic crisis of the GREAT CRASH, he agreed to serve as lord president of the council under Ramsay MACDONALD in a NATIONAL GOVERNMENT. The Conservative Party made up the largest part of the

coalition, and Baldwin succeeded MacDonald as prime minister of the National Government in 1935; before that he did much to hold the coalition together and worked to achieve a compromise in the constitutional negotiations with INDIA, thus provoking the hostility of Winston Churchill and others in the party who opposed any concessions to the movement for Indian independence. On becoming prime minister he called an election in November 1935, winning comfortably.

The hostile public reaction to the HOARE-LAVAL PACT of December 1935 shook the government, and Baldwin suffered a breakdown early in 1936. He recovered in time to handle the ABDICATION CRISIS with tact and skill, winning public approval. In 1936 he also speedily pushed through the Public Order Act, to curb the activities of the BRITISH UNION OF FASCISTS. He decided to retire at the coronation of GEORGE VI in May 1937 and accepted an earldom, becoming Earl Baldwin of Bewdley. His reputation fell after his death, but was revived late in the century when some Conservatives grew nostalgic for his 'one-nation' touch.

FURTHER READING R. Jenkins, *Baldwin* (1987); K. Middlemas and J. Barnes, *Baldwin* (1969).

Balfour, Arthur James (1848–1930), Conservative politician; leader of the CONSERVATIVE PARTY (1902–11), PRIME MINISTER (1902–5) and, as FOREIGN SECRETARY (1916–19), the author of the BALFOUR DECLARATION. Balfour was born at Whittingehame in East Lothian, the son of James Maitland Balfour, a Conservative MP, and the former Lady Blanche Cecil. He was educated at Eton and Trinity College, Cambridge. He remained a bachelor all his life, perhaps as a result of the grief he experienced after the death in 1875 of the young woman he had wished to marry, May Lyttelton. As a young man he demonstrated no burning desire for any particular occupation. He had a lifelong interest in philosophy, and in 1879 published an original work, *In Defence of Philosophic Doubt*, but did not choose to devote himself to scholarship. Instead, he followed his family tradition and entered politics. Balfour learned the politician's craft under the patronage of his uncle Robert Cecil, the marquess of SALISBURY. However, the philosopher Balfour's approach to politics was largely cerebral, and he was never fully able to come to terms with the reality of mass democracy and the contact with the 'man on the street' that this necessitated.

Balfour was first elected MP for Hertford (a borough in which the Cecil family influence was strong) in 1874. His earliest major accomplishment was being named chief secretary for IRELAND, a post he held from 1887 to 1891. An opponent of HOME RULE, he ordered instances of rebellion and disorder to be ruthlessly suppressed, and thus earned himself the nickname 'Bloody Balfour'. However, he also intervened to improve the conditions of Irish life, and implemented policies such as selling land at favourable rates to tenant farmers and investing in transport and agricultural infrastructure.

After leaving his post in Ireland, Balfour returned to Westminster where, through Salisbury's intervention, he was made leader of the Conservative Party in the House of COMMONS. This set him up to replace Salisbury as prime minister in 1902. The central achievements of his premiership included the passage of the 1902 Education Act, to which he was strongly committed. Under the act the school-board system was abolished and local education authorities set up (*see* EDUCATION). Other major achievements included the ENTENTE CORDIALE of 1904, and the creation of the Committee of Imperial Defence. However, during his premiership the Conservative Party was racked by division over TARIFF REFORM, an issue that eventually split the party even after its main proponent, Joseph CHAMBERLAIN, resigned from the cabinet. Balfour himself advocated something of a fence-sitting position on the issue, a position he termed 'retaliation'. This involved threatening the erection of tariffs if other nations did not reduce or eliminate their own tariffs on British goods. However, Balfour was unsuccessful in promoting this position and it earned him the scorn of support-

ers of FREE TRADE and IMPERIAL PREFERENCE alike. Balfour resigned in December 1905, and the damage the party sustained over the issue led to a catastrophic loss at the polls in the election of January 1906 (*see* GENERAL ELECTIONS), during which Balfour himself lost his seat. He soon returned to Parliament, but led the party to two further defeats in the elections of 1910, and he resigned the leadership of the Conservatives in 1911.

Nevertheless, Balfour did not fade into obscurity after his resignation. He joined the wartime coalition government of LLOYD GEORGE and served as foreign secretary from 1916 to 1919. It was in this capacity that he issued the BALFOUR DECLARATION, touting the creation of a Jewish state in Palestine. After the war he continued to serve in various roles, which included representing Britain at the LEAGUE OF NATIONS (1920–2), but never again did he play an active role in government. In 1922 he was created 1st earl of Balfour of Whittingehame. Balfour was among the last of a dying breed of aristocratic Victorian career politicians.

FURTHER READING R.F. Mackay, *Balfour: Intellectual Statesman* (1985).

Balfour Declaration (November 1917), a statement of support by the British government for 'the establishment in PALESTINE of a national home for the Jewish people'. It was issued in the form of a letter to Lord Rothschild, a leading figure among British Jews, from the former prime minister A.J. BALFOUR, who was foreign secretary in LLOYD GEORGE's wartime coalition government. Historians have suggested that the motivation for the Declaration stemmed not from sympathy for the Jewish position, but rather from the desire to attract influential American Jewish support for the Allied effort in WORLD WAR I.

The terms of the Declaration, which also safeguarded the rights of non-Jewish peoples in Palestine, were incorporated into the mandate for Palestine granted to Britain by the LEAGUE OF NATIONS in 1920. As a direct result there was a very large amount of Jewish immigration (mainly from Europe) into Palestine in the interwar years, which raised the ire of the mainly Arab population already in situ. The conflict created between the Jewish immigrants and the Palestinian Arabs resulted in increasing violence and resentment, as the Arabs wanted the Jews ejected from Palestine and the Jews expected the British to make good their pledge to establish an independent Jewish state.

FURTHER READING E. Friesel, *The Balfour Declaration in Historical Perspective* (1988).

ballet. At the beginning of the century ballet was a popular entertainment in Britain, having a role in music hall and drawing large crowds to the Alhambra and Empire theatres in London. Before 1914 Anna Pavlova and Mikhail Mordkin brought a small Russian ballet troupe to London and Sergei Diaghilev brought the exotic Ballets Russes on a long-term basis. Diaghilev's troupe provided a seed-bed for the founders of major British ballet companies: Ninette de Valois (born Edris Stannus), Alicia Markova (Alicia Marks), Anton Dolin (Patrick Healey-Kay) and Marie Rambert (Cyvia Rambam) all worked with him. Rambert opened her ballet school in 1920; de Valois followed in 1926.

The Association of Teachers of Operatic Dancing was formed in 1920, becoming the Royal Academy of Dancing in 1936. Throughout the 1920s the main performing opportunities for British dancers were in commercial pantomime and revues, where two of Diaghilev's choreographers, Leonide Massine and George Balanchine, found work. A native British repertory began to emerge with the work of Frederick Ashton from 1926 and, later, with that of Anthony Tudor. The first public performances by Rambert students from 1930 were the first steps towards a native company. In 1931 Lilian Baylis, the theatre producer and manager of the Old Vic Theatre in London, supported de Valois in moving her school into the Sadler's Wells Theatre as the nucleus of a new company devoted exclusively to ballet. Markova was principal ballerina until 1935, when

she was succeeded by Margot Fonteyn, in the same year that Ashton became resident choreographer. De Valois built a company of international stature at Sadler's Wells, devoted to classical ballet, culturally somewhat distant from music hall and pantomime.

Before World War II British ballet had to compete with glamorous visiting companies from overseas, especially from Russia, but during the war (although new companies, such as the Anglo-Polish Ballet, were formed by refugees) there was no such competition, and British ballet flourished. Ballet Rambert performed in workplaces around the country and sought wider audiences in London. The Sadler's Wells Ballet, as it was known from 1940, also travelled to military and civilian theatres throughout the country and found a new choreographer in Robert Helpmann when Ashton joined the Royal Air Force. Under the direction of the economist John Maynard KEYNES (who was married to the ballerina Lydia Lopokova) the government-funded COUNCIL FOR THE ENCOURAGEMENT OF MUSIC AND THE ARTS (CEMA) assisted ballet. CEMA (from 1945 renamed the ARTS COUNCIL OF GREAT BRITAIN) financed and managed Rambert from 1943 to 1947, following 18 months of closure. CEMA/the Arts Council also supported de Valois's Sadler's Wells Ballet in making the Royal Opera House, Covent Garden, its permanent home when the Opera House reopened after the war in 1946. Its activities were popularized by the resident ballerina Moira Shearer's starring role in Michael Powell's film *The Red Shoes* (1948). In 1956 it became the Royal Ballet, going from strength to strength, nurturing the choreography of Kenneth MacMillan, the 1960s partnership of Fonteyn and Rudolf Nureyev, and a range of younger stars.

Markova and Anton Dolin had spent the war years dancing in America. In 1948 they returned as guest dancers at Covent Garden. They formed a small touring company which in 1950 took the name Festival Ballet, in anticipation of the FESTIVAL OF BRITAIN of the following year. They achieved success by offering a wide-ranging repertoire combining classical with innovative works at popular prices. Dolin remained artistic director until 1960. The company was renamed the English National Ballet in 1989, continuing to pursue its established approach. In 1966 Ballet Rambert abandoned classical ballet and successfully transformed itself into a contemporary dance company.

The Arts Council encouraged the development of regional ballet companies, such as the Western Theatre Ballet, formed in Bristol in 1957. This moved to Glasgow in 1969 and took the name Scottish Theatre Ballet, becoming in 1974 Scottish Ballet, blending traditional with more daring works. The classical Northern Dance Theatre was formed in Manchester in 1969, becoming the Northern Ballet Theatre in 1977 and basing itself in Halifax. In 1990 an offshoot of the Royal Ballet transferred to Birmingham and became the Birmingham Royal Ballet. Influences from overseas, especially from Russia, continued, and tours by Russian ballet companies, both before and after the collapse of the Soviet Union, were widely popular. At the end of the century ballet still had much appeal, if in a less popular form than at the beginning.

FURTHER READING A. Bland, *The Royal Ballet: The First Fifty Years* (1981); J.W. White (ed.), *20th Century Dance in Britain* (1985).

Bank of England, the British central bank. The Bank of England was founded in 1694 as a private company, and it remained as such at the beginning of the 20th century, though its activities had long been closely regulated by government statute. By the 19th century it had become the central bank and the currency manager for the British state. It was managed by a governor, who was appointed by and responsible to a court of directors, composed of leaders of major CITY OF LONDON institutions, overwhelmingly partners in merchant banks. The Bank saw its role as maintaining the stability of sterling and managing the government debt, while being independent of politics. It assumed that by providing a well-ordered monetary system it created a secure structure within which the broader economy could operate successfully. While Britain was on the GOLD STANDARD (until World War I, and from 1925 to 1931), the Bank controlled flows of gold into and out of the country.

The Bank operated uncontroversially until World War I. During the war it took on the crucial role of responsibility for raising loans, mainly from the United States, from both public and private sources, to meet the costs of the war. The Bank had performed this role previously but not on such a large scale. Thereafter, until it was nationalized in 1946, the history of the Bank was powerfully influenced by Montagu NORMAN, who became deputy governor in 1918 and governor from 1920 until 1944. Norman developed the principles of central banking. Central banks, he believed, should be independent entities entrusted with financial and fiscal questions, while governments should take care of budgetary and political issues. Above all, he believed that all currencies must first be stabilized and then returned to the gold standard. Together with the governors of the US Federal Reserve Bank and the governors of the German Reichsbank, he set out to make this a reality. At first the policy seemed to be successful. After the return of Britain to the gold standard in 1925, the currencies of France, Germany and Belgium were stabilized, but the British economy suffered because the value of the pound could be maintained only by the Bank fixing interest rates at higher levels than the sluggish state of the economy warranted. The system collapsed in the GREAT CRASH of 1931 and Norman's approach was discredited. Norman and the Bank were less influential in the 1930s, though he sought, with no great success, to take on the new role of directly assisting British industry by encouraging rationalization of declining sectors. From 1931 the Treasury took greater control of international financial transactions and played the major role in financing World War II.

In 1946 the LABOUR government nationalized the Bank of England. This move was influenced by the belief that Norman and the Bank had played a role in bringing down the Labour government in 1931 and that the crisis of that year could have been less catastrophic had the Bank been answerable to government. But more important was the belief of KEYNES that the government should have direct control of interest rates and of the money supply in order to guide the economy and maintain full employment. An independent Bank had a role in a more or less *laissez-faire* economy but not in the more government-controlled economy envisaged by Labour. The structure of the Bank remained unchanged, but successive governors were appointed by government and in general cooperated with it. This relationship was unexpectedly changed when one of the first acts of the incoming Labour government in 1997 was to hand over to the Bank the responsibility for setting interest rates, which it was believed had been manipulated for political motives by successive Conservative governments.

FURTHER READING D. Kynaston, *The City of London, Vol. 2, 1890–1914* (1995); *Vol. 3, 1914–45* (1999); *Vol. 4, 1946–2000* (2001); D. Kynaston and R.W. Roberts (eds.), *The Bank of England: Money, Power and Influence, 1694–1994* (1995); R.S. Sayers, *The Bank of England, 1891–1944* (3 vols., 1976).

Baptists. *See* NONCONFORMISTS.

Battle of Britain. *See* BRITAIN, BATTLE OF.

BBC. *See* BRITISH BROADCASTING CORPORATION.

Beatles, the. The first British popular music group to make a major international impact. They first became well known in 1963 (*see* SIXTIES, THE), and their work remained popular and influential to the end of the century and beyond, when they continued to be imitated by successful bands. They built on the market for popular music that had expanded in the 1950s. The 'Fab Four' – John Lennon (guitar, vocals), Paul McCartney (bass, vocals), George Harrison (guitar, vocals), Ringo Starr (drums, vocals) – came from Liverpool. They boosted the morale of an economically depressed region and brought fame to the Cavern Club, where they played early in their career (though it was subsequently demolished). Their first record was 'Love Me Do' in 1962, followed by a succession of worldwide hit singles and albums. They were managed by Brian Epstein through their early successes (until his suicide) and inspired by the arrangements and production of George Martin. They played regular live tours only until 1966, subsequently concentrating on song-writing, recording and involvement in films, such as *Magical Mystery Tour* and *Let It Be*.

There was increasing conflict within the group by the end of the 1960s, and they broke up in 1970. Their last public performance as a group was a free concert played on the roof of the offices of their company, Apple, in 1970. They never played together again and were involved in a series of court cases over their financial affairs. All four remained wealthy and followed solo careers of variable success. Most successful was the song-writing and entrepreneurial career of Paul McCartney, who was knighted in 1997. John Lennon moved to the United States in the 1970s with his second wife Yoko Ono and devoted himself to performance art rather than music. In 1980 he recorded a come-back album but shortly after was shot dead in New York.

FURTHER READING G. Stokes, *The Beatles* (1988).

Beatty, David (1871–1936), one of Britain's leading admirals during WORLD WAR I. Beatty was born in Cheshire, of Irish ancestry. He joined the ROYAL NAVY at the age of 13 in 1884 on *Britannia*. He was decorated (DSO) in 1896 for daring leadership of a gunboat force on the Nile, was promoted to commander in 1898 following further action on the Nile, then to captain in 1900 following service in China in the Boxer Rising. He became rear admiral in 1910, the youngest man to reach this level for over a century; then was naval secretary to Winston CHURCHILL at the Admiralty, 1912–13. He commanded the battle-cruiser squadron in the Grand Fleet, 1913–16, a key post in the naval battles of World War I. He led the squadron in the engagement at the Dogger Bank (January 1915) and at the battle of JUTLAND (May 1916), where three of his ships were lost but the battle was won with much credit to Beatty's command. He became commander in chief of the Grand Fleet, 1916–19. In this role he encouraged senior officers to use their initiative, and was a strong believer in the convoy system (merchant ships travelling in groups, escorted by warships), and operated one between Britain and Norway. He accepted the surrender of the German High Fleet in November 1918. He became admiral in January 1919, admiral of the fleet in April 1919, and was created Earl Beatty in the same year.

As first sea lord, 1919–27, Beatty was responsible for the post-war reorganization of the navy and was a member of the British delegation that helped to draft the Washington naval treaty that prevented a naval arms race between Britain and the USA after the war. He opposed attempts to reduce expenditure on the navy in the depression of the 1920s, advocated a strongly defended naval base at Singapore and supported Admiralty control of the Fleet Air Arm against the claims of the ROYAL AIR FORCE. He encouraged scientific research on the part of the Royal Navy and established the Admiralty Experimental Laboratory at Teddington. He was reputed to be a man of great courage, demonstrative and flamboyant in his younger days (in World War I), but reflective and of sound judgement, thinking with great clarity in a crisis.

FURTHER READING S. Roskill, *Admiral of the Fleet Earl Beatty: The Last Naval Hero* (1980).

Beaverbrook, Max Aitken, 1st Baron (1879–1964), newspaper proprietor and politician. Lord Beaverbrook was born William Maxwell Aitken in Ontario and grew up in New Brunswick, Canada. An early career as a successful financier had made him a good deal of money by the time he met Bonar LAW, a fellow Canadian who went on to become British prime minister. In 1910 Aitken decided to seek a new life in Britain and, with the help of Bonar Law, he won a seat as a Conservative MP that year. His success in politics and business stemmed from his ability to befriend almost anyone who he thought might be of benefit to him. He served in the coalition government of LLOYD GEORGE during WORLD WAR I, becoming minister of information and chancellor of the duchy of Lancaster in February 1918. He was awarded a baronetcy, under somewhat questionable circumstances, in 1916, and was made a peer in 1917 as 1st Baron Beaverbrook.

After the war Beaverbrook became very interested in journalism and began buying newspapers. Most notably he bought the *Daily Express* in 1919 and the London *Evening Standard* in 1923. He went on to use his newspapers as a sounding board from which to promote his views on issues that concerned him. These included imperial unity and IMPERIAL PREFERENCE, and support for EDWARD VIII during the ABDICATION CRISIS and for Neville CHAMBERLAIN's policy of APPEASEMENT.

Despite his support of Chamberlain, however, when WORLD WAR II began Beaverbrook worked closely with Winston CHURCHILL and became one of the most powerful men in Britain. In 1940 he was made minister for aircraft production, and with his keen business sense performed this job admirably, increasing production and enabling the ROYAL AIR FORCE to win the battle of BRITAIN. He went on to serve as minister of supply (1941–2), minister of production (1942) and lord privy seal (1943–5). Early in the war he was also involved in negotiations with the USA for the LEND-LEASE programme.

After 1945 Beaverbrook continued managing his newspaper empire and expounding his views on various political issues, retaining a particularly strong commitment to the EMPIRE. Late in life he reasserted his Canadian origins and began transferring many of his interests and assets back to Canada, probably in order to avoid British taxes and death duties. He died in 1964 and was buried in New Brunswick.

FURTHER READING A. Chisholm and M. Davie, *Beaverbrook: A Life* (1992).

Beeching Report. *See* RAILWAYS.

Bell, Vanessa (1879–1961), artist and designer. She was a member of a distinguished literary family and was the elder sister of Virginia WOOLF. She studied at the Royal Academy Schools of Art from 1901 to 1904 and in 1905 founded the Friday Club as an informal discussion group for artists. In 1907 she married fellow artist Clive Bell and their house became one of the focal points of the BLOOMSBURY GROUP. Her early work was fairly traditional, but from 1910 she was influenced by Roger FRY, with whom she had a close relationship, and through him by post-impressionism and the use of bright colours and bold and abstract forms. From 1913 to 1919 she was co-director with Fry of the Omega Workshop in Bloomsbury, which sought to improve the standard of design of everyday objects, such as chairs, tables and rugs, in Britain. Her first solo exhibition was mounted by Omega in 1916. In the same year she moved to Charleston farmhouse at Firle, Sussex, to live with another artist, Duncan Grant, with whom she had a daughter in 1918. Grant was a CONSCIENTIOUS OBJECTOR in World War I. He worked on the land and they both continued to paint and to redesign the farmhouse. She remained married to and on good terms with Clive Bell, who praised both her and Grant's work. Her work was less innovative between the wars and fell from favour after World War II, though she continued to be productive.

FURTHER READING Q. Bell and A. Garnett, *Vanessa Bell's Family Album* (1981); H. Lee, *Virginia Woolf* (1996).

Benn, Tony (Anthony Wedgwood) (1925–), Labour politician. The son of Viscount Stansgate,

a Labour MP and cabinet minister under Ramsay MACDONALD, Benn served in the RAF Volunteer Reserve and Royal Navy Volunteer Reserve before becoming the Labour MP for Bristol South East in 1950. He held no major party posts during the 1950s, but found himself in the spotlight when he refused to accept the peerage he inherited in 1960. When his seat was declared vacant, he successfully fought a by-election before an electoral court overturned the result. His return to the House of COMMONS was made possible by the 1963 Peerage Act, which permitted peerages to be disclaimed. Benn was re-elected MP for Bristol South East in 1963, and held the seat until 1983. He was Labour MP for Chesterfield from March 1984 until his retirement in 2001. He served in Harold WILSON's 1964–70 government, first as postmaster general and then (from 1966) as minister for technology. Between 1970 and 1974 he was opposition spokesperson on trade and industry, and he became secretary of state for industry after Labour returned to power in 1974. During the 1970s Benn's politics moved increasingly to the left, and his shift to opposition to British membership of the EUROPEAN ECONOMIC COMMUNITY brought about his move to secretary of state for energy in 1975. Along with his leftward move in politics, he simplified his name from Anthony Wedgwood Benn to the more demotic Tony Benn.

In opposition again after 1979, Benn's relations with the parliamentary party became increasingly hostile. Popular in the party outside Parliament, and a member of Labour's National Executive Committee from the 1960s, Benn was a leading figure in moves to 'democratize' the party, which resulted in the establishment of an electoral college, dominated by extra-parliamentary party members, to elect party leaders. In addition, Benn's vocal criticism of Labour policies during the 1970s, together with his insistence that the party's lack of electoral success in the 1980s was due to a lack of commitment to socialist ideals, combined to make him a divisive voice in the party. He was closely defeated by Denis HEALEY in the 1981 election for deputy leader of the party, and was to become marginalized under the successive leaderships of Neil KINNOCK, John SMITH and Tony BLAIR. His reputation as a dedicated diarist resulted in the publication of five volumes of political diaries in the late 1980s and 1990s. His integrity and support for unpopular causes won him respect in some quarters, even among those who, like Harold Wilson, viewed him as 'a kind of ageing, perennial youth who immatures with age'. He stood down as a member of Parliament in 2001.

FURTHER READING T. Benn, *Out of the Wilderness: Diaries 1963–7* (1987); T. Benn, *Office Without Power: Diaries 1968–72* (1988); T. Benn, *Against the Tide: Diaries 1973–6* (1989); T. Benn (ed. R. Winstone), *Conflicts of Interest: Diaries 1977–80* (1990); T. Benn (ed. R. Winstone), *The End of an Era: Diaries 1980–9* (1992); T. Benn (selected, abridged and introduced by R. Winstone), *The Benn Diaries* (1995).

Bennett, (Enoch) Arnold (1867–1931), English novelist. Bennett was born in Burslem, Staffordshire, in the Potteries, into a family originally of potters, although his father, Enoch, became a solicitor and wanted Arnold also to enter the legal profession. Arnold, however, abandoned the law and at the age of 21 went to London, where he began to publish, beginning with a short story 'A Letter Home' in the avant-garde periodical *The Yellow Book*. He became assistant editor of a penny paper called *Woman*, and began to write at the fast pace that was to characterize his career, often drawing on his background in the Potteries.

By 1900 Bennett was still working for *Woman*, and had published a sensational novel and his first serious novel, *A Man from the North* (1898). He had also begun the novel that was to make his name, *Anna of the Five Towns* (1902), published a nonfiction work, *Journalism for Women*, and three one-act plays called *Polite Farces,* collaborated on another play with his friend Arthur Hooley and helped dramatize Eden Philpotts'

novel *Children of the Mist*. In 1903, after the death of his father, he moved to Paris, became fluent in French, gained a mistress and associated with artists. At the age of 39 he married his secretary, Margaret Soulie. This was ultimately disastrous. They separated in 1921, but she would not agree to a divorce. Meanwhile, however, he completed in ten months the 200,000-word *The Old Wives' Tale* (1908), which won critical acclaim. The book compares the lives of two sisters, one of whom lives conventionally at home, while the other elopes to an exciting life in France. He also wrote two shorter farcical novels and many essays, short stories and items of drama within a short time. He wrote for prestigious journals, such as Ford Madox Ford's *English Review* and the *New Age*. His articles introduced English readers to new Russian and French writers, placing him among the avant-garde and offering inspiration to younger writers. In 1911 he wrote an acclaimed play, *The Honeymoon*, published *Clayhanger*, the first novel of his Clayhanger trilogy, another novel, *The Card*, and collaborated in writing another play, before publishing the second novel of the Clayhanger trilogy, *Hilda Lessways*. Also in 1911 he visited the United States, where he was celebrated. He wrote of his experiences in *Those United States* (1912). Bennett was now wealthy enough to buy a country estate in Essex and a yacht. He wrote of his voyages at sea in *From the Log of the Velsa* (1914).

During World War I Bennett was closely associated with Lord BEAVERBROOK, who recruited him into the Ministry of Information. He wrote a series of weekly war articles for the *Daily News*, became a director of the *New Statesman* and toured the Western Front. During the war he also completed his Clayhanger trilogy (with *These Twain*, 1915) and wrote five more minor novels and three plays. From 1922 he lived with a young actress, Dorothy Cheston, who took his name by deed poll. In 1923 he published *Riceyman Steps*, a psychological study of miserliness, for which he won the James Tait Black prize for the best novel of that year. In 1926 his only child, Virginia, was born and he published *Lord Raingo*, a depiction of the war cabinet in action and of a good man in melancholic decline. His final years were marked by ill-health and a need for money to sustain his lifestyle and his wife's unsuccessful theatrical career. He travelled in Germany and Russia with Beaverbrook and completed his last novel, *Imperial Palace* (1930), a study of the hotel world and a sympathetic portrait of the 'new woman'. He died of typhoid.

Bennett was immensely popular and also critically well regarded in his day. Posters advertising his novels were posted on London buses. He was offered and refused a knighthood. He played an important role in the transition from the realist to the modernist NOVEL in Britain. But he was attacked by a new, yet more advanced, generation of novelists – notably by Virginia WOOLF in 1924 – and his critical reputation did not long outlive him, though it revived a little later in the century.

FURTHER READING O.R. Broomfield, *Arnold Bennett* (1984); M. Drabble, *Arnold Bennett* (1974).

Berlin airlift (1948–9), an early crisis between the Western Allies and the USSR, marking a freezing of the COLD WAR. Berlin was entered by the Red Army on 21 August 1945 and the Soviets held the entire city by 1 May. Subsequently, in accordance with the YALTA agreements, the three main Western Allies – the USA, Britain and France – were given zones of occupation in the city and allowed access along specific corridors from western Germany. In 1946–7 tension mounted between Britain, France, the United States and the USSR, initially over elections in Berlin, then over the introduction of a new currency in West Germany, which the Soviets refused to accept in Berlin. They insisted that these developments did not accord with wartime agreements, and to emphasize their control of Berlin they imposed restrictions on rail traffic to the city from the west on 30 March 1948. Three months later they blocked road traffic, effectively blockading Berlin from the west. The Americans and

British organized an airlift of food, mail and personnel through the winter of 1948–9. The continuation and success of the airlift convinced the Soviets that they could not unilaterally control the future of Berlin without risking war. In February 1949 they began talks with the Western Allies and the blockade was lifted in May, though the airlift continued until September in case the Soviets reimposed restrictions.

FURTHER READING A. and J. Tusa, *The Berlin Blockade* (1988).

Bevan, Aneurin ('Nye') (1897–1960), Labour politician, founder of the NATIONAL HEALTH SERVICE (NHS) and informal leader of the left wing of his party. Born in Tredegar, South WALES, Bevan was educated at elementary school and Nonconformist Sunday school before following his father into the mines at the age of 13. He worked as a miner during a period of industrial conflict and then through World War I before winning, in 1919, a South Wales Miners' Federation scholarship to the Central Labour College, London, where he studied politics and economics for two years. He opposed the war and did not serve – not because he was a CONSCIENTIOUS OBJECTOR, but because he suffered from an eye disease contracted in the mines, and this exempted him from service. He returned to Tredegar in 1921 and became active in the miners' union, and chaired the Tredegar Council of Action during the GENERAL STRIKE of 1926. Involving himself in local politics, he became a member of his local district council in 1922 and of Monmouthshire County Council (1928–9). From 1929 until his death in 1960 he was MP for the mining constituency of Ebbw Vale. In Parliament he was an early opponent of fascism and of APPEASEMENT and, in domestic politics, of the household MEANS TEST. In 1934 he married Jennie Lee, also a left-wing Labour MP (and destined to be Britain's first minister of the arts, in the 1960s). In 1939 he was expelled from the LABOUR PARTY along with Stafford CRIPPS for advocating a POPULAR FRONT. During WORLD WAR II

Bevan kept party politics alive, relentlessly opposing Winston CHURCHILL when the leaders of the Labour Party joined the coalition government.

When Attlee chose Bevan as minister of health following the general election of 1945 it was to general surprise, as Bevan had no experience as a minister. He is best remembered as the architect of the NHS, which he brought into being by cajoling and compromising with reluctant senior medical men, and also by compromising with Labour Party policy by accepting the doctors' terms: the continuation of private practice and considerable independence for the medical profession. 'I stuffed their mouths with gold,' he is famously reported as saying. In January 1951 he became minister of labour and national service. Shortly thereafter GAITSKELL imposed charges for dental and ophthalmic treatment in what Bevan had envisaged as a free health service, in order to contribute to the costs of the KOREAN WAR. Bevan and others, including Harold WILSON, resigned from the government.

When Labour went into opposition in 1951 Bevan became the figurehead of a loosely defined left wing of the party, opposed in often bitter battles to an equally loosely defined 'right wing' grouped around Gaitskell. Bevan opposed the party leadership's support for manufacture of the hydrogen bomb (*see* NUCLEAR WEAPONS). He was defeated by Gaitskell for the post of party treasurer in 1954 and for the leadership in 1955. Thereafter he effected a reconciliation with Gaitskell and was much less clearly identified with the left. He became shadow colonial secretary, supported the party in the SUEZ CRISIS in 1956, the year in which he became party treasurer, and denounced unilateral nuclear disarmament at the party conference of 1957. He became shadow foreign secretary in 1957 and deputy leader in 1959. In 1960 he died of cancer. His robust style led Churchill to describe him as a 'merchant of discourtesy', whereas Churchill's fellow Conservative 'Rab' BUTLER rated him 'the greatest parliamentary orator since Charles James Fox'.

FURTHER READING J. Campbell, *Nye Bevan and the Mirage of British Socialism* (1987); M. Foot, *Aneurin Bevan, 1897–1945* (1962); M. Foot, *Aneurin Bevan, 1945–60* (1973).

Beveridge, William Henry (1879–1963), economist and social reformer whose 1942 report laid the foundations of the modern WELFARE STATE, set up after World War II. Beveridge was born in India, son of a senior member of the colonial civil service. He was educated at Charterhouse School and Balliol College, Oxford, where he was influenced by the prevailing concern for liberal social reform and by friends such as his contemporary R.H. TAWNEY. After leaving Oxford he lived and undertook voluntary work at the social-work settlement TOYNBEE HALL in London's East End. At the same time he worked as leader writer on social issues for the Conservative newspaper the *Morning Post*, and was actively involved in contemporary debates about social reform. He became convinced of the need for careful investigation and analysis of social problems. His *Unemployment, a Problem of Industry* (1909) was the first serious British analysis of the causes of UNEMPLOYMENT. He believed that reorganization of the labour market and maximization of employment opportunities was the key to elimination of the severe poverty of the period. In the previous year he had been recruited by Winston CHURCHILL, then president of the Board of Trade, as adviser on unemployment policy. He played a major role in the introduction of labour exchanges in 1909 and unemployment insurance in 1911.

During WORLD WAR I Beveridge worked in the Ministry of Munitions and the Ministry of Food. In 1919 he was knighted and became director of the London School of Economics and Political Science (LSE), which had been founded by his associates Beatrice and Sidney WEBB in 1895. Beveridge played an important role in establishing the LSE as a major institution in the social sciences, despite conflicts with colleagues. He remained actively engaged with social policy, publishing *Insurance for All and Everything* (1924), a proposal for reform and integration of the national insurance schemes. In 1925–6 he was a member of the Samuel Commission on the COAL-MINING industry and chairman of the Unemployment Insurance Statutory Committee (1934–44), which administered unemployment insurance in the later stages of the Depression. In 1937 he became master of University College, Oxford.

At the outbreak of WORLD WAR II Beveridge hoped to be put in charge of manpower administration, but his rather difficult personality prevented this. He was placed in charge of a relatively insignificant Ministry of Labour manpower survey. Anxious to be rid of him, the minister of labour, Ernest BEVIN, recommended in 1941 that he become chairman of an inquiry into the reorganization of social insurance and allied services, which were part of the post-war reconstruction programme. The report that resulted in 1942, *Social Insurance and Allied Services* (usually just called 'the Beveridge Report'), was very much Beveridge's own work, though advice and evidence were taken from others. Its impact went far beyond the expectations of the coalition government. It recommended the integration and expansion of the systems of health and unemployment insurance to cover the entire population, and a similar expansion of pensions for widows, the elderly, the blind and other disabled people, all of which had previously been confined to the lower paid. It also recommended the addition of new benefits such as death benefits. The report built on proposals by Beveridge himself and by others in the pre-war years. It proved immensely popular, fuelling hope for a better world after the war, assisted by Beveridge's astute use of the mass media, to the discomfiture of Winston Churchill, who was not anxious to commit the government to extensive post-war social reform. The LABOUR PARTY's support for the proposals played a role in the party's success in the 1945 general election, and the Beveridge Report supplied the basis for the ATTLEE government's recon-

struction of the social-insurance system in 1948.

Beveridge still regarded full employment as the key to national welfare. His recommendations, of a broadly 'KEYNESian' kind, were published in *Full Employment in a Free Society* (1944). He had hoped to be commissioned by the government to carry out this further inquiry. When he was not, he carried out the investigation with private finance and the advice of a group of younger economists, who were all to have distinguished careers: Barbara Wootton, Joan Robinson, Nicholas Kaldor and E.F. Schumacher. Beveridge himself became Liberal MP for Berwick-upon-Tweed in 1944, but lost the seat in the 1945 general election. He accepted a peerage in 1946 (becoming Baron Beveridge of Tuggal) and became leader of the Liberals in the House of LORDS. Also in 1946 he commenced the study that was published in 1948 as *Voluntary Action*, an expression of his enduring belief in mutuality and voluntary action as essential for social cohesion and as necessary complements to the safety net provided by the welfare state. He continued to be an active and sometimes controversial public figure, chairing two NEW TOWN corporations and a public inquiry on the future of broadcasting, travelling widely, speaking on social questions and increasingly, with the advance of the COLD WAR, on world peace and nuclear disarmament (*see* CAMPAIGN FOR NUCLEAR DISARMAMENT).

FURTHER READING J. Harris, *William Beveridge* (2nd edn, 1997).

Bevin, Ernest (1881–1951), trade-union leader and Labour politician who as FOREIGN SECRETARY (1945–51) aligned Britain with the USA in the early years of the COLD WAR. Born in Somerset to an unmarried village midwife who died when he was eight, Bevin experienced poverty and insecurity in childhood. He left school aged eleven and became a farmworker for two years. He then moved to Bristol and worked as a deliveryman. He became active in the Baptist Church and retained his religious faith thereafter, while also taking up socialism. As a consequence of his work on behalf of the unemployed he was asked in 1910 to organize the carters for the Dock, Wharf, Riverside and Labourers' Union (the dockers' union), then progressed to become a regional, then a national, organizer of the union.

Bevin became a well-known figure in the TRADE UNION movement. He was a strong supporter of greater concentration and coordination of the movement, and played a decisive role in the formation in 1922 of the Transport and General Workers' Union (TGWU) out of 14 different unions. Bevin became its first general secretary. He supported the GENERAL STRIKE in 1926, but its failure convinced him that negotiation from strength was more effective than direct action. He also came to believe that government economic and social policy was crucial to the well-being of working people and became increasingly active in the LABOUR PARTY, especially after the crisis of 1931. Through the 1930s he played a central role in coordinating relations between the Trade Union Congress (TUC) and the Labour Party and in shaping Labour's domestic and foreign policies, supporting rearmament and opposing APPEASEMENT. His speech at the 1935 party conference played an important role in removing George LANSBURY from the party leadership.

In May 1940 CHURCHILL appointed Bevin minister of labour, and he entered Parliament for the first time as MP for Central Wandsworth in London. For the rest of WORLD WAR II he made an outstanding contribution in mobilizing and organizing labour to maximize war production (young men conscripted to go down the mines became known as 'Bevin boys'). He also achieved greater recognition of trade unionism. After the 1945 election he became a powerful figure in the Labour government, and was the closest confidant of the prime minister, Clement ATTLEE. As foreign secretary, despite his lack of experience in the field, he played a central role in developing the British alliance with the United States against the Soviet Union as the COLD WAR progressed. He supported

the MARSHALL PLAN, the construction of a British atomic bomb (*see* NUCLEAR WEAPONS) and the creation in 1949 of NATO. He was criticized by the Labour left for his close association with the United States, and by Labour moderates for his lack of interest in building alliances in Western Europe, but his grasp of Britain's role in world politics at this time was broadly realistic.

Bevin was unusual among leading politicians of this period in keeping his pronounced working-class accent. This made him the object of snobbish condescension in some quarters, but he was unabashed, and his accent made him popular with many working-class voters. His health was poor throughout the 1940s. He reluctantly gave up office in 1950 and died shortly after.

FURTHER READING A. Bullock, *The Life and Times of Ernest Bevin* (2 vols., 1960–7); A. Bullock, *Ernest Bevin: Foreign Secretary, 1945–51* (1983).

Big Bang, the name given to the changes in the London Stock Exchange system that occurred on 27 October 1986. These led to one of the most important transformations in the history of the CITY OF LONDON, and hence in the centrally and internationally important financial sector of the British economy. The immediate cause was threatened litigation by the Office of Fair Trading against restrictive practices in the Stock Exchange, though an important long-term cause was overseas competition, especially from New York. An agreement between the trade and industry secretary, Cecil Parkinson, and the chairman of the Stock Exchange in 1983 led to the dropping of litigation in return for changes in Stock Exchange practices, to be implemented by the end of 1986. Fixed commissions for stock transactions were abandoned, the Stock Exchange opened to outside members, and the separation between a stock broker who dealt on behalf of clients with a stock 'jobber' or trader was ended. The outcome was increased automation of transactions, huge investment in information technology and the purchase of most brokers' and jobbers' firms by British and foreign banks.

Many firms incurred severe losses, but overall the position of the City of London as an international financial centre was strengthened.

FURTHER READING D. Kynaston, *The City of London, Vol. 4, 1946–2000* (2001); M. Reid, *All Change in the City: The Revolution in Britain's Financial Sector* (1988).

Birkenhead, Lord. *See* SMITH, F.E.

birth control. When the 20th century began, birth control was socially unacceptable. The churches declared it immoral, while the medical profession insisted that contraception could damage women physically. Even in the 1920s, working-class women complained bitterly that doctors who told them it would be dangerous for their health to have another child would then refuse information on how to prevent births. Nonetheless, fertility rates had been declining for several decades by 1900, especially among middle-class couples, in spite of the fact that no reliable, safe methods of birth control existed. The most widely used methods were ABORTION, which was illegal and dangerous, and withdrawal before ejaculation, which was unreliable at preventing pregnancy but good at lessening sexual pleasure. Men appear to have used condoms (first readily available when issued to soldiers during WORLD WAR I) mainly for protection against venereal disease (*see* SEXUALLY TRANSMITTED DISEASES). The available sources of information also promoted methods that were completely ineffective, such as coughing after intercourse, or 'holding back', which referred to the woman preventing herself having an orgasm. It is probable that many couples prevented pregnancy by having sexual intercourse very infrequently or not at all. By World War I this was changing rapidly.

In 1921 Marie STOPES opened the first birth-control clinic in Britain. Her clinics, and the others that followed, only ever reached a tiny percentage of working-class women, but they created enormous publicity and stimulated research. By the mid-1930s clinic researchers were able to state clearly how the methods could best be used. Laboratory investigation had distinguished effective spermicides, and rubber technology had improved radically, leading to growing use of the cheaper, improved condoms and, to a lesser extent, caps. It is probable that illegal abortion rates also rose sharply. As late as the 1950s contraception was rarely mentioned in public, and it was only after the introduction of the birth-control pill in 1961 that open discussion became possible.

In 1930 the Lambeth Conference of CHURCH OF ENGLAND bishops issued a statement accepting the use of contraception for 'morally sound' reasons. Then in 1931, following pressure from a wide variety of women's groups, the minister of health permitted local authorities to provide birth-control services for married women whose health would be damaged by further births. The five existing birth-control societies had joined together in 1930 and in 1939 they renamed themselves the Family Planning Association. They pressured local authorities to provide facilities, and also established clinics and continued testing contraceptives. Following a vigorous campaign, in 1975 birth control was made available free through the NATIONAL HEALTH SERVICE to all women and men, married or unmarried, although access to abortion differed regionally, as was still the case at the end of the century. At the century's close, access to safe, reliable birth control was taken for granted, but control over their own fertility had done more to increase the choices available to women than had any of the other apparently momentous transformations of modern life.

FURTHER READING P. Fryer, *The Birth Controllers* (1965); A. Leathard, *The Fight for Family Planning: The Development of Family Planning Services in Britain 1921–74* (1980).

Black and Tans, nickname for a supplementary police force specially recruited in Britain and NORTHERN IRELAND in 1920–1 to reinforce the Royal Irish Constabulary, which was beleaguered by the Anglo-Irish War (*see* IRELAND). Many members of the Black and Tans were unemployed ex-soldiers, and were not to be confused with the more elite Auxiliary Force, which recruited among former British army officers. The Black and Tans were so named for their distinctive uniforms of dark green and khaki; 'black and tan' is also a breed of Irish hound, and the name is associated with the Black and Tan hunt in Munster. Characterized by Irish republicans as ill-trained hooligans, the force soon gained a reputation for drunkenness, lack of discipline and excessive brutality, although members claimed that they were often provoked by the IRISH REPUBLICAN ARMY (IRA) into counter-terrorist reprisals. One such incident occurred on 21 November 1920, known as 'Bloody Sunday', when the IRA assassinated 11 suspected British intelligence officers, many at home. In response, the Black and Tans opened fire on a crowd at a Gaelic football match at Croke Park, Dublin, later that afternoon, killing 12 and wounding 60. They were also involved in acts of murder, arson and the destruction of public property. Such incidents provoked a major outcry both in Britain and in other nations. The actions of the Black and Tans were viewed as embarrassing at best and criminal at worst. Historians have suggested that their acts of savagery may well have helped speed up the process of negotiations that resulted in the ending of the Anglo-Irish War and the signing of the treaty to create the Irish Free State.

FURTHER READING R. Bennett, *The Black and Tans* (2nd edn, 1976).

Black Friday (1921). *See* GENERAL STRIKE.

Black Monday (19 October 1987). *See* THATCHER, MARGARET.

Black Wednesday (16 September 1992). *See* MAJOR, JOHN.

Blair, Tony (Anthony Charles Lynton) (1953–), Labour politician; PRIME MINISTER (1997–). Born in Edinburgh, Blair was educated at Fettes Col-lege, Edinburgh, and St John's College, Oxford. He was called to the Bar in 1976 and married fellow barrister Cherie Booth in 1980. Elected as a Labour MP for the safe seat of Sedgefield in 1983, he became a member of the shadow cabinet in 1988, speaking on energy and employment. When John SMITH was elected leader of the LABOUR PARTY in 1992, Blair became spokesperson on home affairs, refuting the accusation that Labour was 'soft' on crime. After Smith's death in 1994 Blair was elected party leader by a huge majority, and set about the 'modernization' of the party. Having achieved the abolition of CLAUSE FOUR of the party's constitution – which had committed Labour to a policy of public ownership – Blair began to shift the party to the political centre. He began to refer to the party as 'New Labour' and sought to appeal to the voters of 'Middle England'.

Blair managed successfully to capture the votes of both the middle class and Labour's traditional 'core supporters' in the May 1997 general election, winning with the biggest majority (240 seats) in the history of the Labour Party. His first term as prime minister was characterized by attempts to promote a sense of a young and innovative government, associated with 'Cool Britannia', 'radical' and yet committed to the cautious economic spending limits of the previous Conservative government (*see* BROWN, GORDON). After an initial period in which he was the most popular prime minister on record, concerns over Blair's autocratic approach to party management and policy-making began to surface, particularly over his attempts to control the party's choice of leader in the devolved legislatures of Scotland and Wales and over the issue of the Labour Party's candidate for London mayor (*see* LONDON GOVERNMENT).

In June 2001, however, Blair led his party to a second landslide election win, thereby becoming the first Labour prime minister to win a second term of office with an unassailable parliamentary majority.

FURTHER READING K. Jefferys (ed.), *Leading Labour. From Keir Hardie to Tony Blair* (1999).

Bletchley Park, country house some 80 km (50 miles) north of London, the centre for tracking and intercepting German radio communications in WORLD WAR II. It recruited large numbers of academics, including mathematicians and linguists. From early in the war they were highly successful in breaking German, Italian and Japanese codes, including the supposedly unbreakable German Enigma code. This remained unknown to the Germans, and information from Enigma, code-named Ultra, played an important role in the Allied victory. Bletchley Park was also home to one of the world's first computers, the 'Colossus'.

FURTHER READING P. Calvocoressi, *Top Secret Ultra* (1980); F.H. Hinsley and A. Stripp (eds.), *Codebreakers* (1993); N. West, *GCHQ* (1986).

Blitz, the, popular name for the bombing attacks on British towns during WORLD WAR II by the Germans, mostly at night, mainly from September 1940 to May 1941. The term was derived from the German *Blitzkrieg*, meaning 'lightning war'. The effect, however, was not a swift German victory. Towns important for the war effort, principally Belfast, Coventry, Manchester, Sheffield, Glasgow, Hull, Liverpool and Plymouth, suffered, but London bore the worst attacks, being bombed every night except one for over two months. Casualties were fewer than feared, though about 42,000 were killed and 50,000 seriously wounded in London. Damage to property was considerable. However, neither the war effort nor morale was destroyed; rather the Blitz emerged as an emblem of stoical survival, which sustained British resistance. In June 1941 Hitler turned his attention to the attack on the USSR.

The Blitz prompted British bombing raids on German towns (in addition to those on military targets). These raids were initially retaliatory, but later designed to force the German into submission; the most controversial was the heavy bombing of DRESDEN in February 1945.

FURTHER READING A. Calder, *The People's War* (1969).

Bloody Sunday (1920). *See* BLACK AND TANS.

Bloody Sunday (30 January 1972), a pivotal event in contemporary Irish history, during which 13 unarmed Catholic protesters were killed and 17 wounded by British soldiers of the First Battalion Parachute Regiment. The day began with a banned, and thus illegal, march in the working-class Bogside area of Derry/Londonderry by the Northern Ireland Civil Rights Association, protesting against anti-Catholic discrimination in the province. After the march ended, protesters gathered to hear speeches under the watchful eyes of British soldiers, suspicious that the IRISH REPUBLICAN ARMY (IRA) was involved in the day's events. Gunfire broke out; the British paratroopers claimed that they were fired upon first by suspected IRA snipers and thus were forced to return fire in self-defence. Many of the protesters and other witnesses, however, claimed that the soldiers had opened fire on the unarmed crowd with no provocation whatsoever. Many of those wounded and killed were shot in the back as they attempted to flee the scene, and it was later established that none of the victims were members of the IRA.

Bloody Sunday, as the day came to be known, had immediate repercussions both in the Republic and in NORTHERN IRELAND. Days later the British embassy in Dublin was burned by an outraged crowd. The unrest and sectarian violence that erupted in the wake of the day's events eventually resulted in the HEATH government's repeal of HOME RULE in Northern Ireland, the dissolution of its parliament at Stormont and the imposition of direct rule from Westminster. Bloody Sunday also led to serious resentment in the Catholic community towards the deployment of British troops in Northern Ireland. A widely criticized inquiry conducted soon after exonerated the paratroopers from blame and concluded that they had fired in self-defence. A further inquiry was in progress in 2000–1.

FURTHER READING J. Bowyer Bell, 'Bloody Sunday: January 1972' in *The Irish Troubles:*

A Generation of Violence 1967–1992 (1993);
R. McClean, *The Road to Bloody Sunday* (1983).

Bloomsbury group, a group of intellectuals and artists, active mainly between the wars, named after an area of central London where many of them lived for much of their adult lives. At the heart of the group were the sisters Virginia WOOLF (1882–1941) and Vanessa BELL (1879–1961), daughters of a prominent late Victorian intellectual, Sir Leslie Stephen, who provided them with a very limited formal education but much exposure to an intellectual environment. Virginia became pre-eminent in British modernist literature and was also the author of trenchant and influential feminist works, notably *A Room of One's Own* (1929). Vanessa became an appealing but less successful painter and designer. Many of their associates were friends of their brother Thoby (who died in 1906) at Cambridge University. They included John Maynard KEYNES; the writers Lytton Strachey (1880–1932) and (more marginal to the circle) E.M. FORSTER (1879–1970); the publisher, writer and Labour political activist Leonard Woolf (1880–1969), who married Virginia; and the art critic Clive Bell (1881–1964), who married Vanessa. Vanessa was later to form close relationships with the painter and influential art critic Roger FRY (1866–1934), then with the painter Duncan Grant (1885–1978), with whom she had one of her three children, her only daughter, Angelica. T.S. ELIOT was also associated with the group at various times.

As a group they were devoted, characteristically of their time, to developing a 'modern', post-Victorian approach to their various enterprises. From 1913 to 1919 Vanessa Bell, Fry and Grant formed the Omega Workshop in Bloomsbury, to apply modernist design to everyday objects, such as chairs, rugs and curtains. Some, but not all, of the group also took a free approach to sexual relationships, an approach that they also believed to be 'modern'. They were important shapers of British MODERNISM.

FURTHER READING M.Holroyd, *Lytton Strachey:*

A Biography (1971); H. Lee, *Virginia Woolf* (1997).

Blunt, Anthony (1907–83). *See* CAMBRIDGE SPIES.

Boer War (1899–1902), conflict in southern Africa between Britain and the Boer (Afrikaner) republics, resulting in the creation of a united SOUTH AFRICA under British rule. The conflict is also known as the Second Boer War (the first having been fought in 1880–1), the Anglo-Boer War, or the South African War.

The independence of the Boer republics of southern Africa, the Orange Free State and the Transvaal, had been recognized by Britain in the 1850s, but British ambitions to create a federated South Africa led to the annexation of the Transvaal in 1877. An uprising led by Paul Kruger in 1880–1 restored the independence of the Transvaal, subject to British conditions. Following the discovery of major gold deposits on the Witwatersrand in the Transvaal in the late 1880s, large numbers of mainly British immigrants entered the republic. Despite their large numbers these immigrants, or Uitlanders, were denied political rights – allowing British imperialists an excuse to revive their territorial interests.

Following the failure in 1896 of the Jameson Raid (a plot instigated by Cecil Rhodes and given covert support from the British government), tensions in the region escalated. Encouraged by Sir Alfred MILNER, high commissioner in South Africa since 1897, Uitlanders on the Witwatersrand called for British intervention in the republic. Meetings between the British and Transvaal governments brought no compromise, and, having decided that the British were determined to take control of the Boer republics, Kruger declared war. In October 1899 Boer forces from the Transvaal and Orange Free State invaded Natal and the northern Cape, laying siege to the towns of Ladysmith, Kimberley and Mafeking. British reinforcements arrived in late 1899, but their advances were slowed by Boer forces at Magersfontein in the west, and

Colenso and Spion Kop in the east. Yet the numerically superior British forces began to reverse Boer successes, recapturing Ladysmith, Kimberley and Mafeking. When General Roberts took control of Johannesburg and Pretoria by early June 1900, it seemed that the war was over, and the Conservative-Unionist government in London took the opportunity to hold what became known as the 'khaki election'. With the Liberal opposition split over the war, the Conservatives returned to power.

However, the Boer generals – whose forces had been allowed to retreat largely unscathed from the British advance – turned to guerrilla tactics, attacking supply lines and small detachments of British troops. The British commander, General (later Lord) KITCHENER, resolved to round up the remaining Boer 'commandos' by depriving them of supplies. Farms were destroyed, Boer families transported to large camps near railway lines, and lines of 'blockhouses' (small forts linked by barbed wire) were established during 1901. The Boer forces' ability to fight was gradually undermined, and in May 1902 the remaining Boer commanders accepted the terms of surrender at Vereeniging in the Transvaal. It was a less than overwhelming victory for Britain, however. The war raised serious questions about the strength of British imperial power, both in terms of the 'fitness' of British adult men and in terms of the ability of Britain to sustain a major imperial war.

What had been envisaged as a brief imperial engagement ended as the longest and most costly British military endeavour for half a century, with consequences that would have significant effects in the 20th century. Part of the strategy against the guerrilla tactics of the Boer commandos was to remove Boer families en masse to encampments, usually close to railway junctions. Poorly administered and under-resourced, these 'concentration camps' were soon rife with disease and starvation. The subject of much controversy both in Britain and abroad, the concentration camps characterized the Boer War's role as a precursor of the kind of warfare that would be experienced over the next century, blurring the distinction between civilian and combatant. The camps would, later in the century, become a defining moment in the construction of Afrikaner nationalism, and a continuing focus of tension between the English- and Afrikaner-speaking populations of South Africa.

FURTHER READING T. Pakenham, *The Boer War* (1979).

Bonar Law. *See* LAW, (ANDREW) BONAR.

Bondfield, Margaret (1873–1953), trade-union leader and Labour politician, the first female cabinet minister in British history. Born in Somerset, by the age of 14 she had left school and was working as a shop assistant. Her experiences led her later to join the National Union of Shop Assistants, of which she became assistant secretary in 1898. She also became interested in the socialism of the INDEPENDENT LABOUR PARTY (ILP) and the FABIAN SOCIETY. In 1899 she was the only female delegate to the annual conference of the Trades Union Congress (TUC).

Until World War I Bondfield continued her involvement with both the ILP (eventually becoming one of its national leaders) and the TUC. In 1918 she was elected to the general council of the TUC, and in 1923 was made its first female chair. She was also heavily involved in women's issues, defending the rights of working women and promoting universal, not just limited, female suffrage. This brought her into conflict with many middle-class feminists.

Bondfield's growing involvement with the fledgling LABOUR PARTY and later with the NATIONAL GOVERNMENT was eventually to draw her away somewhat from her leftist, working-class roots. She was elected as the MP for Northampton in 1923, served until 1924 and then again from 1926 to 1931. In the first Labour minority government of 1924 she served as parliamentary secretary to the minister of labour, but in the second Labour minority government of 1929–1931 she herself became minister of labour, with a seat in the cabinet. Her political convictions were by this point moving further towards the right, and within the Labour Party she supported both Ramsay MACDONALD and the fiscally conservative Philip SNOWDEN, who introduced cuts to UNEMPLOYMENT benefit in 1931.

Bondfield's increasing conservatism led to a decline in her earlier influence and political power. She lost her parliamentary seat in 1931, and later her position within the TUC and many leftist organizations. She worked until the 1940s in public organizations such as the National Council for Social Service. However, she is perhaps best remembered for her role as the first woman cabinet minister, and for her work with the TUC and women's organizations such as the Women's Cooperative Guild, the Women's Labour League and the National Federation of Women Workers.

FURTHER READING M.A. Hamilton, *Margaret Bondfield* (1924).

Boundary Commission, body charged with reviewing the boundaries of parliamentary constituencies. The first Boundary Commission was established in 1917 to devise a scheme for the redistribution of seats in accordance with the forthcoming expansion of the electorate. This expansion would result from the REPRESENTATION OF THE PEOPLE ACT (1918), which was to extend the franchise to all adult men and most women. There were no further changes in constituency boundaries until World War II, despite major population shifts.

In 1944 a Speaker's Conference was established to consider this and other electoral matters. It recommended the establishment of a permanent Boundary Commission to ensure that constituency boundaries were regularly reviewed, at intervals of not less than three or more than seven years, and maintained at approximately equal sizes. There were to be separate commissions for England, WALES, SCOTLAND and NORTHERN IRELAND, with the Speaker chairing each. Their recommendations were to be agreed by Parliament. This recommendation became law in 1944. The system continued to operate on these principles for the remainder of the century. Commissioners consulted the electorate of each constituency before proposing changes.

FURTHER READING D. Butler, *The Electoral System in Britain since 1918* (1963).

Bowen, Elizabeth (Dorothea Cole) (1899–1973), novelist. Bowen was born in IRELAND, a member of the land-owning, Protestant, Anglo-Irish ascendancy. Her early years were spent between Dublin and the family estate, Bowen's Court in County Cork (which she described in *Bowen's Court*, 1942). She settled in London in her early 20s and, encouraged by the novelist Rose Macaulay, began to write short stories. In 1923 she published her first volume of stories, *Encounters*, and married Alan Cameron, who worked for the BBC. They lived for ten years in London, becoming part of a wide literary circle, and Bowen evoked London vividly in much of her work. She published a succession of short stories and novels, establishing herself with *The House in Paris* (1935) and *The Death of the Heart* (1938), written in a traditional narrative rather than modernist style. These novels expressed her view of the world and the people in it as treacherous and dangerous, whether in personal or public affairs. She was an early enthusiast for film as a cultural medium, and wrote film reviews in the 1930s, when this was still unfashionable in high cultural circles.

During WORLD WAR II she worked as an air-raid warden in London (her own home was bombed) and for the Ministry of Information. In the latter capacity she made frequent trips to neutral IRELAND to assess the state of Irish opinion about Britain. These experiences made their way into her short-story collections *Look at All Those Roses* (1941) and *Ivy Gripped the Steps* (1941) and her outstanding novel of wartime love and espionage in London and Ireland, *The Heat of the Day* (1949). During the war she also wrote *Seven Winters* (1942) about her own childhood.

In 1930 Bowen had become the first woman to inherit Bowen's Court. Her Anglo-Irish identity was important to her and after the war she and her husband lived there. She continued to write reviews and essays, and struggled to keep up the estate, which she was forced to sell in 1959. Her husband died in 1952 and thereafter she travelled widely, spending her last decade in England. Her final novel, *Eva Trout*, was published in 1968.
FURTHER READING V. Glendinning, *Elizabeth Bowen: Portrait of a Writer* (1977); H. Lee, *Elizabeth Bowen: An Estimation* (1981).

Boy Scouts. *See* BADEN-POWELL, ROBERT.

Bragg, W.H. and **Lawrence.** *See* SCIENCE.

Britain, battle of (July–September 1940), protracted aerial engagement between the Luftwaffe (German air force) and Fighter Command of the ROYAL AIR FORCE (RAF), commanded by Air Chief Marshal Dowding (1882–1970), mostly fought over the Channel and southern England. It frustrated Germany's plan for an invasion of Britain by sea, which was much feared in Britain early in WORLD WAR II. It followed CHURCHILL's refusal to negotiate with Hitler following the French surrender and the evacuation of DUNKIRK in June 1940. The Germans hoped to use their air power to destroy British shipping and airfields to such an extent that it would knock out effective resistance to an invasion.

The Luftwaffe was superior in numbers to the RAF. Initially it had almost 1400 bombers and 1020 fighters, against about 700 British Hurricane and Spitfire fighters. But the Germans were inferior in AVIATION technology and, most importantly, the British had a well-developed RADAR system, which the Germans did not fully understand, backed up by a sophisticated code- and cipher-breaking system (*see* BLETCHLEY PARK). The Germans also made a number of miscalculations. Their intelligence and targeting were poor, and they underestimated the extent of British fighter

production, which, at about 100 new planes a month, was double that of Germany by the summer of 1940. Hermann Goering (the Luftwaffe commander) and his staff also made tactical errors. In view of these disadvantages, the Luftwaffe performed well, but there probably never was a realistic possibility that Germany could have invaded Britain against the combined force of the RAF and the formidable ROYAL NAVY. By September 1940 the effort was abandoned, and the bombing of civilian as well as military targets (the BLITZ) was adopted as an alternative strategy. During the twelve-week battle 1733 German aircraft were destroyed, against the loss of 915 British fighters and the lives of 449 British fighter pilots.

The battle of Britain became one of the symbols of British courage and defiance of the enemy during the war. It was popularly represented as a victory of 'the few' over a stronger opponent, and hence helped to sustain popular morale – although, in fact, the RAF had advantages over the Germans that outweighed just numbers of aircraft. The British victory also helped shift the views of American opponents of participation in the war.
FURTHER READING P. Addison, J. Addison, A. Crang (eds.), *The Burning Blue: A New History of the Battle of Britain* (2000); R. Overy, *The Battle of Britain* (2000).

BritArt, the name given at the end of century to the varied work of a number of younger British artists of the 1980s and 1990s (known earlier as YBAs). They rejected traditions of painting and sculpture in favour of installation art, which might incorporate objects of any conceivable kind, or performance art incorporating a variety of activities including the use of video. There was no organized group and the activities involved were highly diverse, though they united in the desire to shock and to shift popular perceptions of the everyday. Many of the most celebrated practitioners were products of Goldsmiths' College, London, and they were represented in a series of exhibitions, most famously *Sensation* at the Royal Academy in

1997, and as candidates for the annual Turner Prize award. Many of them were supported by the patronage of Charles Saatchi, who made a fortune out of advertising and established a gallery in north London. The best-known artists of their generation, both winners of the Turner Prize, in 1993 and 1995 respectively, were Rachel Whiteread (1963–) and Damien Hirst (1965–). They were preceded, however, by the Turner prize winners of 1986, the rather older Gilbert and George. Gilbert (Proesch, 1943–) and George (Passmore, 1942–) met at St Martin's School of Art in 1967 and from 1968 they lived and worked together as self-styled 'living sculptures'. They first attracted notice in 1969 with their work of Performance Art (*see* VISUAL ARTS) *Underneath the Arches*, in which they dressed (as always) in neat suits, with their hands and faces painted gold, and mimed mechanically to the music-hall song of that name. They gave up such 'living sculpture' performances in 1977 and concentrated rather on photo-pieces (large arrangements of photographs), but they continued to present their whole life together as a work of art.

Whiteread was a sculptor, trained at Brighton Polytechnic and the Slade School, who from 1993 made a novel kind of sculpture consisting of casts of domestic features or the spaces around them, such as the space under a bed. She won the Turner Prize with a cast of an entire house in the East End of London, of a representative terraced type, which was then demolished, leaving her cast standing in commemoration, though in time it was also demolished. The work gave rise to much derision in the popular press. Whiteread, however, did not court publicity as some other younger artists did and she survived with dignity. In 1997 she became the first woman to represent Britain with a solo show at the Venice Biennale.

The outstandingly notorious figure of this generation, who nurtured his reputation as *enfant terrible*, was Damien Hirst. He studied at Goldsmiths' College. He long had a fascination with death and his best-known, and popularly derided, work consisted of dead fish or mammals floating in preserving fluid. The work with which he won the Turner Prize, *Mother and Child Divided*, consisted of four tanks containing the severed halves of a cow and a calf. Tracey Emin (1963–) won the Turner Prize in 1999 by displaying her unmade bed, with surrounding debris, and produced work that represented aspects of her own disturbing life about which she was quite open in public. These and other younger artists in Britain and elsewhere formed a new avant-garde, revolting against social and artistic conventions as their predecessors had done.

British Broadcasting Corporation (BBC), broadcasting organization founded in 1922 as a private monopoly regulated by the Post Office. The BBC became a public corporation providing the new mass medium of radio in 1927. Its tone in its early years was set by John REITH, its first director general. He was guided by a notion of public service, which incorporated a belief that the role of the BBC was to encourage cultural self-improvement, rather than giving people what they believed they wanted. He sought to counter the influence of American mass culture, and was determined that the new medium would be 'respectable' (which he achieved) and a force for good – as he saw it. Classical music, opera and intellectual discussion had a prominent role in radio output, though no musical programmes were broadcast on Sunday, which was dominated by religious programmes. Announcers spoke with upper-class accents and even wore evening dress while broadcasting. This approach attracted criticism as the audience grew: by 1935, 98% of the population had access to radio (or 'wireless' as it was then called). The BBC grew in size and in 1932 moved to its new headquarters, Broadcasting House, a classic of British modernist architecture in central London.

The BBC's own network of regional programming provided one source of challenge to Reith's approach. There was also increasing competition from commercial stations broadcasting from the continent, such as Radio Luxembourg, which broadcast popular music that attracted a considerable British audience – especially among younger people and especially on Sundays, despite often poor reception. During the 1930s the BBC responded by increasing the number of variety and light-entertainment programmes. It began to undertake systematic listener research and to pay attention to it. At the same time technology, quality and range of reception greatly improved. Radio increasingly became part of everyday life. *Radio Times*, the BBC weekly magazine that listed programmes along with articles about them, sold over 3 million copies a week, and the *Listener*, which printed versions of talks and other programmes, became a large-selling intellectual weekly.

Broadcasting to the EMPIRE began in 1932, greatly extending the BBC's range. For the first time the king's voice could be heard around the COMMONWEALTH and empire, most dramatically during the ABDICATION CRISIS in 1936. In 1938 foreign-language broadcasts began, in response to initiatives elsewhere in Europe, though with less overtly propagandist content than German and Italian broadcasts. Programmes were being broadcast in 14 languages by 1939. Increasingly the BBC became an important source of news, freed from earlier restrictions. Especially during the GENERAL STRIKE of 1926 the BBC had been accused of siding with the government. In the 1930s a code evolved that sought to achieve strict neutrality and political balance in the presentation of news, politics and current affairs. In 1938 Reith resigned to became chairman of Imperial Airways (*see* AVIATION), a decision he immediately regretted.

WORLD WAR II extended the national and the international role of the BBC, and its staff more than doubled in size. By 1944 it was broadcasting in 44 languages. Its news and overseas broadcasts in a variety of languages became valuable sources of information and sometimes of intelligence messages, including those to resistance movements in occupied countries. The war also removed competition from continental stations such as Radio Luxembourg. A Forces Programme aimed at ser-

vicemen was eventually adopted and became popular with a wide audience. The BBC became an important instrument both for providing information and for building morale. CHURCHILL took full advantage of it to broadcast to the nation. The novelist J.B. Priestley gave regular talks stressing national unity and resilience. Comedy shows, such as *It's That Man Again* (*ITMA*), and other entertainment shows were immensely popular, as, less predictably, was the regular question-and-answer programme *The Brains Trust*, which transformed some intellectuals into celebrities.

In 1944 William Haley became director general and committed himself to continuing Reithian principles. In 1946 the radio was split into a range of services. The Light Programme focused on entertainment and popular music, and became the most popular. The Home Service emphasized the spoken word, and provided news, current affairs and middlebrow drama and discussion programmes; it acquired a substantial and loyal following. The Third Programme provided high culture, with an especial concentration on music; it gained about 1% of the audience. In 1949 a committee chaired by William BEVERIDGE reviewed the BBC's charter and recommended that the monopoly continue despite growing arguments for competition. Overseas broadcasting was cut back after the war but expanded again as a weapon in the COLD WAR, though broadcasting to the Commonwealth and empire diminished with the process of DECOLONIZATION. In 1965 external broadcasting was redefined as the World Service, with the aim of projecting the British image abroad. In the late 1990s World Service and domestic programmes were increasingly integrated, which aroused criticism.

The role of the BBC was extended by the growth of television. Pioneer John Logie BAIRD began to cooperate with the BBC in 1929, but his mechanical scanning system was overtaken by electronic rivals. In 1936 the BBC began broadcasting the first regular television service in the world, and televised the coronation of King GEORGE VI in the following year. Audiences remained tiny until 1939, when operations were suspended throughout the war. In June 1946 services resumed. Rapid technological development, reduced costs and greater prosperity ensured television's more rapid spread; the broadcast of the coronation of Queen ELIZABETH II gave it an especial boost. As TV spread so did criticism of the BBC's monopoly, notably among the CONSERVATIVE PARTY, which was now in government. In 1955 competing commercial TV companies were authorized, funded by advertising rather than, as the BBC was, by an annual licence fee paid by all owners of radio and TV equipment. The Independent Television Authority was established in 1954 to award franchises to commercial television companies, each of which would control a new commercial TV channel in a different region of the country. Independent television (ITV) was heavily regulated to ensure that it did not seriously transgress the cultural norms still upheld by the BBC. But it was more disposed to give the audience what its directors believed, and audience research reported, that they wanted, and it put the BBC under pressure.

Through the 1960s the BBC, directed by Hugh Greene, diversified its output, giving outlets to a wider range of talent, and also reflecting social change with series that were controversial as well as entertaining. A notable example – broadcast at the height of controversy over race relations (*see* IMMIGRATION) – was *Till Death Us Do Part*, which featured a racist central character who is challenged by his children. In 1964 the BBC was allocated a second channel, BBC2, with a brief to focus on more intellectually and culturally demanding programmes, leaving BBC1 to cater for a more popular audience. In 1982 ITV acquired a second channel, Channel 4, also more up-market in purpose. In 1983 morning programmes – 'breakfast TV' – were introduced for the first time on all channels. A fifth commercial channel, Channel 5, was added in 1997 in response to the competition from cable and satellite broadcasters, who were providing a massive increase in the number of channels available. At the end of the century, with the advent of digital broadcasting, television viewing was in process of further transformation, and the BBC was facing greater competitive pressure than at any time in its history.

This was as true of radio as of television. In the early days of mass television, the demise of 'steam radio' as anything but an outdated minority pursuit was confidently predicted. But a greater range of stations, commercial and BBC, national, international and local, provided for a great variety of tastes. The BBC and the government were reluctant to adapt, but in 1964 Radio Caroline, a pirate (unlicensed) commercial company operating offshore, broadcast a steady output of popular music and captured audiences and the popular imagination. The government closed down Radio Caroline and other pirate stations, but the BBC adapted by expanding its popular-music programming with the introduction of Radio 1, which was devoted to popular music. In the early 1970s commercial radio was introduced. Technological changes enabled people to carry light radios around with them and to listen in their cars. Radio continued to hold mass audiences to the end of the century.

FURTHER READING A. Briggs, *The BBC: The First Fifty Years* (1985); A. Briggs, *The History of Broadcasting in the United Kingdom* (4 vols., 1961–79); C. Seymour-Ure, *The British Press and Broadcasting since 1945* (1991).

British Empire. *See* EMPIRE.

British Legion. *See* ROYAL BRITISH LEGION.

British National Party. *See* NATIONAL FRONT.

British Union of Fascists (BUF), fascist movement founded in 1932 by Sir Oswald MOSLEY. Fascism had a very limited influence in Britain compared with many other European countries. A group of British *fascisti* had been formed in 1923, influenced by events in Italy. One member was William JOYCE, later notorious as Lord Haw-Haw for his pro-Nazi broadcasts in English from Germany during WORLD WAR II. The Imperial Fascist League was formed in 1928. These were small groups, and others, such as the overtly anti-Semitic Nordic League, emerged in the early 1930s. There was wider sympathy for Italian and later for German forms of fascism in Britain, especially before their more virulent aspects became evident, though it was unorganized and its extent difficult to gauge.

The British Union of Fascists – formed in 1932 and propelled by Mosley's charismatic oratory – was a somewhat more important organization. Initially it had support from the *Daily Mail* and from a variety of people disillusioned with the state of inter-war Britain. Support ebbed following a violent meeting at Olympia in London in June 1934. Its main support thereafter was in the East End of London, where there was a substantial Jewish population. The demonstrations and violence by black-shirted supporters of the BUF that followed led the government to pass the Public Order Act (1936), which banned the wearing of political uniforms. The coming of war destroyed support for the BUF, though a fascist fringe lingered in existence.

Mosley sought to revive the movement after the war as the Union Movement, but election defeats in 1959 and 1966 showed that he had minimal support. In the 1960s racist groups tried to build on hostility to black and Asian IMMIGRATION. Such groups included the National Socialist movement led by Colin Jordan, which was briefly active in the early 1960s, and the NATIONAL FRONT, formed in 1967. The involvement of the latter in violent street incidents in the 1970s suggested that it might be gaining support, but its failure to achieve any success in the election of 1979 was followed by its disintegration. Tiny racist, nationalist groups survived to the end of the century, but with little public impact.

FURTHER READING R. Skidelsky, *Oswald Mosley* (1981); R. Thurlow, *Fascism in Britain 1918–1985* (1987).

Brittain, Vera (Mary) (1893–1970), feminist and pacifist. Daughter of a successful Staffordshire paper manufacturer, Brittain vividly described her upbringing in *Testament of Youth* (1933), writing that her education was designed to fit her for 'provincial young ladyhood'. But she rebelled and, after considerable parental opposition, went to Somerville College, Oxford, in 1914. She left after one year to serve as a Voluntary Aid Detachment (VAD) nurse in France in WORLD WAR I. At the beginning of the war she had fallen in love with Roland Leighton, a school friend of her brother. *Testament of Youth* describes their love, the devastating effect on her of Leighton's death in action, and the subsequent deaths of her brother and two other close friends. After the war she returned to Oxford and completed her degree in history. She then shared a house with Winifred Holtby, a friend from Oxford and a fellow writer and feminist.

In 1925 Brittain married the political scientist George Catlin, but, unusually for that time, she kept her own name, and for many years they lived apart for substantial periods of time, while Catlin was a professor at a North American university. They had a son and a daughter who, as Shirley Williams (1930–), was to become a prominent Labour politician and one of the founders of the SOCIAL DEMOCRATIC PARTY. Brittain continued to share a house with Holtby until the latter's premature death in 1935. Together and separately they were active in a number of feminist and peace organizations, Brittain in the feminist Six Point Group and Open Door Council in the 1920s, then with the LEAGUE OF NATIONS Union and the PEACE PLEDGE UNION. She was a pacifist in WORLD WAR II, which brought her much criticism. Apart from the best-selling *Testament of Youth* (first published by the LEFT BOOK CLUB), Brittain was a prolific author and journalist. Her books include the further volumes of autobiography *Testament of Friendship* (1940), a memoir of Holtby, and *Testament of Experience* (1957).

FURTHER READING D. Gorham, *Vera Brittain: A Feminist Life* (1996).

Britten, (Edward) Benjamin (1913–76), one of the leading British composers of the 20th century. Born in Lowestoft, the son of a dentist, Britten began composing at the age of 5 and produced *Quatre Chansons Françaises* at the age of 15. In his early years his most influential teacher was Frank Bridge. He felt that his period at the Royal College of Music (1930–3) was unhelpful, though John Ireland's composition classes may have been more useful than he acknowledged. He secured a handful of prestigious performances while still at the college. In 1935 he began writing incidental music for documentary films for the General Post Office (GPO), then for the theatre. He collaborated with W.H. AUDEN on several projects, including the famous GPO films *Coal Face* (1935) and *Night Mail* (1936). When Auden moved to the United States, Britten (a pacifist) followed in 1940. He spent a highly productive two and a half years there, and during this time his lifelong partnership with the singer Peter Pears was established. The importance to him of Suffolk, where he had grown up, inspired him to write the opera *Peter Grimes* in 1942, the first performance of which, on 7 June 1945, has been said to mark the rebirth of English opera. In 1942 he returned to Britain, registered as a CONSCIENTIOUS OBJECTOR and was exempted from military service on condition that he took part in concerts for the COUNCIL FOR THE ENCOURAGEMENT OF MUSIC AND THE ARTS (CEMA). In 1947 Britten, with John PIPER and Eric Crozier, formed the English Opera Group, which was responsible for the artistic direction of the Aldeburgh Festival from its start in 1948 and with which Britten was closely associated until his death. He was at his peak of output and success in the 1950s and 1960s, and his most celebrated works are his operas, such as *Albert Herring*, *The Turn of the Screw*, *Billy Budd* and *A Midsummer Night's Dream*. His oratorio *War Requiem* (1961), written for the rededication of Coventry Cathedral in 1962, combines the liturgical text with poems by the war poet Wilfred Owen (*see* POETRY). In 1976 Britten became the first person from the world of MUSIC to become a life peer.

FURTHER READING H. Carpenter, *Benjamin Britten: A Biography* (1992); E.W. White, *Benjamin Britten: His Life and Operas* (2nd edn, 1983).

broadcasting. *See* BRITISH BROADCASTING CORPORATION.

Brown, George (Alfred) (1914–85), Labour politician, a colourful figure in the Labour governments of the 1960s. A Londoner, Brown became an official of the Transport and General Workers' Union after leaving school at 15. He became Labour MP for Belper in Derbyshire in 1945, and served as a junior minister in the government of Clement ATTLEE. He opposed the left-wing 'Bevanites' in the Labour party during the 1950s (*see* BEVAN, ANEURIN) and was elected deputy leader of the party in 1960. After being defeated by Harold WILSON in the Labour party leadership election in 1963, Brown went on to become secretary of state for economic affairs in Wilson's first government. His disagreement with the rest of the cabinet over economic policy led to a transfer to the Foreign Office in 1966. As foreign secretary Brown oversaw unsuccessful negotiations for British entry into the EUROPEAN ECONOMIC COMMUNITY. He resigned in 1968 after further conflict with the cabinet, and lost his seat in the 1970 election. After the election defeat, he ceased to be deputy leader of the Labour Party, but was created a life peer. Brown resigned from the Labour Party in 1976 in protest at the Wilson government's support for TRADE UNION 'closed shops'. He remained in the House of LORDS, and joined the SOCIAL DEMOCRATIC PARTY in 1982. FURTHER READING G. Brown, *In My Way: The Political Memoirs of Lord George-Brown* (1971).

Brown, (James) Gordon (1951–), Labour politician; CHANCELLOR OF THE EXCHEQUER (1997–). Brown was educated at Kirkcaldy High School and Edinburgh University. He worked in the late 1970s and 1980s as a university lecturer and journalist. After his election as Labour MP for Dunfermline

East in 1983, he served as opposition chief secretary to the Treasury, and deputized for the shadow chancellor John SMITH while the latter recovered from a heart attack. Brown then worked as shadow trade and industry secretary and became shadow chancellor when Smith became leader of the Labour Party in 1992. Despite being disappointed by the election of Tony BLAIR as leader of the party following John Smith's death, Brown worked closely alongside Blair on the modernization of the party. As shadow chancellor, Brown pledged to keep strict control on government spending, announcing before the 1997 general election that Labour would accept the Conservative government's spending plans and not increase income tax. He became chancellor of the exchequer in 1997, following Labour's election victory. One of his first acts as chancellor was to give greater independence to the BANK OF ENGLAND, thus reducing the susceptibility of interest rates to political manipulation. By the end of the century Brown had built up a reputation as a competent chancellor, maintaining tight control over government spending and successfully keeping inflation down. He also played a role in social welfare policy (*see* WELFARE STATE) unprecedented in a 20th-century chancellor. He introduced cautious but potentially effective redistributive policies by, among other measures, stopping tax loopholes that benefited the rich, and introducing the working families' tax credit, which was targeted at low earners – 'the working poor', as he described them.

Bulge, battle of the (December 1944–January 1945), an attempt by Hitler to counter-attack against the advancing Allied forces in France and Belgium, aiming to move through the Ardennes and retake the port of Antwerp. This was unsuccessful but its unexpectedness was a shock to the Allies and gave rise to criticisms of Allied intelligence or of the willingness of military commanders to heed it. Also known as the Ardennes offensive, it was the last significant German offensive on the Western Front in WORLD WAR II.

Burgess, Guy. *See* CAMBRIDGE SPIES.

Burma, former British colony in Southeast Asia, now known as Myanmar. Upper Burma was established as a province of British INDIA in 1885. Following anti-British riots in the 1930s, the Government of India Act (1935) constituted Burma as a British crown colony with a degree of self-government. When, during WORLD WAR II, the Japanese invaded Burma in February 1942, some Burmese welcomed them as liberators from the British. The Japanese assisted a section of Indian nationalists, led by Subhas Chandra Bose, to establish an Indian National Army to fight against the British in Burma. Both captured Allied servicemen and Burmese people were brutally treated during the Japanese occupation. Most notoriously, 46,000 servicemen were forced to work on the construction of the Burma–Thailand railway; 16,000 died of starvation, disease, gross neglect and brutality, as did 50,000 Burmese forced labourers. This episode was represented – not wholly accurately – in the film *Bridge On the River Kwai* (1957). A puppet government was established, led by Aung San and U Nu. However, both assisted the British, Indian and Gurkha units to defeat the Japanese. The successful assault was spearheaded by Major General Orde Wingate, who died in an air crash in 1944 before victory was complete. Thereafter Sir William SLIM led an assault which was successful in the spring of 1945, while US and Chinese troops put pressure on the Japanese forces in the north. Aung San was invited to London by Prime Minister ATTLEE in 1946 and independence for Burma was agreed. Shortly after his return to Rangoon Aung San was assassinated and U Nu completed negotiations for independence on 4 January 1948. A lengthy civil war followed.

Butler, R(ichard) A(usten) (1902–82), Conservative politician who held a succession of top government posts, but failed in his two bids for the party leadership and premiership. Commonly known as 'Rab', Butler was born in India, where his father was a senior civil servant. He was educated at Marlborough College and Cambridge University. He became a Conservative MP in 1929 for the safe seat of Saffron Walden, and a junior minister in the India Office in 1932. He was an undersecretary at the Foreign Office during the period of APPEASEMENT, and his career never fully recovered from this association. As minister of education in the coalition government in WORLD WAR II he was responsible for the major Education Act of 1944 (*see* EDUCATION).

In opposition between 1945 and 1951 Butler played a key role in reshaping the CONSERVATIVE PARTY, and was seen as one of its more progressive figures. As CHANCELLOR OF THE EXCHEQUER from 1951 to 1955 he was seen, with Hugh GAITSKELL, as one of the symbols of the supposed post-war 'consensus' between the major political parties on economic and social policy, which was known as 'BUTSKELLISM'. His tax-cutting budgets contributed to Conservative electoral success, as did the abandonment of economic controls and RATIONING, which had had important roles in Labour economic policy. He was a reforming home secretary from 1959 to 1961, chairman of the Conservative Party (1959–61), leader of the House of COMMONS (1955–61), lord privy seal (1955–9), deputy prime minister (1962–3) and foreign secretary (1963–4). In both 1957 and 1963 he was widely expected to become party leader and prime minister, but on both occasions was thwarted by Harold MACMILLAN (who became leader in 1957, and who in 1963 made sure the leadership went to Alec DOUGLAS-HOME). Butler's failure to become leader was due partly to his record on appeasement, though his vacillating approach to the SUEZ CRISIS in 1956 did not enhance his reputation. Harold WILSON is said to have described him as 'the best prime minister we never had'. In 1965 Butler accepted a life peerage as Baron Butler of Saffron Walden, and became master of Trinity College, Cambridge, until 1978.

FURTHER READING P. Cosgrave, *R.A. Butler: An English Life* (1981); A. Howard, *RAB: The Life of R.A. Butler* (1987).

Butskellism, name given by commentators in the 1950s to apparent, broadly KEYNESian, similarities in the policies followed as chancellor of the exchequer by the Labour chancellor Hugh GAITSKELL (1950–1) and his Conservative successor R.A. BUTLER (1951–5).

C

cabinet, a small body of senior government ministers responsible for directing the administration of the country. It is the executive committee of the government, technically appointed by the monarch but in practice appointed by and answerable to the PRIME MINISTER. Its members are normally drawn from the majority party in the House of COMMONS, together with some members of the House of LORDS. They link the legislative part of the state with the executive. They head the executive departments and effectively provide the leadership of the party. The decisions of cabinet are the decisions of the government. In principle, whatever disagreements there may be within the cabinet, all of its decisions are binding upon its members. Disagreements may not be expressed outside meetings of cabinet and all members accept collective responsibility for all decisions. However, especially later in the 20th century, dissent within the cabinet was not always kept secret.

The role of the cabinet was transformed during the 20th century owing to the growth of government work. During World War I, for the first time, a cabinet secretariat was appointed to take minutes of cabinet decisions (*see* CABINET OFFICE), which previously had been left to trust and memory. Increasingly, especially from World War II, much of the detailed work of the cabinet was delegated to cabinet committees, chaired by the prime minister or another senior minister and, where appropriate, including junior ministers from outside the cabinet. By 1995 there were 19 cabinet committees or subcommittees, including a committee on domestic and economic policy presided over by the prime minister, and a committee on public expenditure chaired by the CHANCELLOR OF THE EXCHEQUER. Committees consisted of ministers whose departments were most closely involved, with a brief to resolve as many issues as possible, in order to keep the cabinet's workload to manageable proportions and to enable it to focus upon central issues of state. Some decisions, however, throughout the century, were taken by the prime minister alone, or with a small group of cabinet colleagues.

Despite the increasing demands upon government, the cabinet remained stable in size through the century, though wartime cabinets, from December 1916 to October 1919 and throughout World War II, were smaller. There were 19 members in most years from 1900 to 1960, 21 by 1970 and 22 from 1980 to 2000. However, the number of ministers without cabinet rank, often working with cabinet ministers within their departments, grew steadily from 10 in 1900 to 34 in 1999. From 1974 ministers were allowed to appoint 'special advisers' – experts from outside Parliament. By the end of 1974 there were 28 such advisers; in July 1999, 72.

Cabinet Office, department within the civil service formed in 1938 to coordinate government business, servicing the CABINET and its many committees. It built on the cabinet secretariat first established by David LLOYD GEORGE when he became prime minister in 1916. Its head (equivalent in rank to a permanent secretary in the civil service), the cabinet secretary, advises the PRIME MINISTER. The first cabinet secretary was Sir Maurice (later Baron) Hankey (1877–1963), who held the post from 1918 to 1938. He headed the smaller War Cabinet secretariat from 1916. He placed the secretariat on a permanent footing and did much to shape its role and to develop the idea of the cabinet office. The office grew in size from 186 staff in 1938 to 393 in 1950, 580 in 1980, 1484 in 1990 and 1548 in 1998. From 1997, under Tony BLAIR's premiership, it took on for the first time an explicit role of developing, and advising the government on, policy.

Callaghan, (Leonard) James ('Jim') (1912–), Labour politician who held a number of senior government posts before becoming PRIME MINISTER (1976–9). Educated at elementary and secondary schools, Callaghan became a tax officer after leaving school and also worked for the TRADES UNION CONGRESS (TUC) before war service in the naval intelligence. He entered Parliament in 1945 as MP for Cardiff, which he represented until his retirement from the Commons in 1987. He held junior posts in ATTLEE's government of 1945–51. He became shadow chancellor in 1961 and stood as a candidate for party leader following the death of GAITSKELL in 1963. He became CHANCELLOR OF THE EXCHEQUER after the Labour election victory of 1964. Callaghan, like Harold WILSON, opposed the devaluation of sterling, and when the pound was eventually devalued in November 1967 Callaghan offered his resignation and was appointed home secretary. While at the Home Office Callaghan ordered British troops to NORTHERN IRELAND in 1969, following violent clashes in the summer of that year.

When Labour returned to power in 1974 he became foreign secretary, a post he held until Harold Wilson's resignation in March 1976. Callaghan won the subsequent leadership election and became the first British prime minister to be elected by MPs, as well as the first person to hold that post after serving as home secretary, foreign secretary and chancellor. Callaghan's three years as prime minister were beset by economic and political difficulties. By the autumn of 1976 a rapid fall in the value of sterling meant entering into negotiations with the International Monetary Fund (IMF) for a loan. The conditions of the IMF package, which included stringent cuts in spending on public services, caused conflict within both the LABOUR PARTY and the CABINET. When the government's parliamentary majority vanished in 1977 it was protected by the support of the LIBERAL PARTY in the 'Lib-Lab pact'. Instead of calling an election after the Lib-Lab pact ended in mid-1978, Callaghan decided to continue his government, attempting to combat rising inflation with a renewed prices-and-incomes policy. As industrial action in opposition to pay policy spread rapidly over the 'winter of discontent' (*see* TRADE UNIONS), Callaghan's government appeared increasingly impotent. His popular image at this time is exemplified by media reports of his reaction to the industrial turmoil as 'Crisis! … What crisis?' upon his return from an international summit in Guadeloupe in January 1979. What in fact happened is that he was asked by a journalist at the airport: 'What … of the mounting chaos in the country at the moment?' To which Callaghan replied, 'I don't think that other people in the world share the view that there is mounting chaos.'

With the withdrawal of Liberal support in the Commons, Callaghan had to rely on the support of Scottish National Party (SNP) MPs. However, his government had agreed to an amendment to the 1978 bill on devolution for SCOTLAND that insisted that 40% of registered voters in the referendum of 1 March 1979 should vote 'yes' for devolution to come about. When only a narrow majority in a relatively small turnout voted in favour, the devolution proposal was defeated, and the SNP members proceeded to propose a vote of no confidence in the House of COMMONS. After Callaghan's government lost the vote, a GENERAL ELECTION was called, bringing the CONSERVATIVE PARTY under Margaret THATCHER into power. Callaghan remained leader of the Labour Party until the following year, when he was replaced by Michael FOOT. He remained a Labour MP until 1987, when he was given a peerage as Baron Callaghan of Cardiff.

FURTHER READING K.O. Morgan, *Callaghan: A Life* (1997).

Cambridge spies, the, group of high-ranking British officials who engaged in espionage for the Soviet Union during WORLD WAR II and the early years of the COLD WAR. Guy Burgess (1911– 63), Donald Maclean (1913–83), 'Kim' Philby (Harold Adrian Russell Philby; 1912– 88) and Anthony Blunt (1907–83) met in the 1930s at Trinity College, Cambridge, where they were recruited by the Soviet secret service. All four took up influential posts in the British establishment. Burgess was in MI6, 1939–41, and the Foreign Office from 1944. Philby was recruited into MI6 in 1940 by Burgess. Maclean joined the Foreign Office in 1934 after Cambridge, and worked in the British embassy in Washington between 1944 and 1948. His knowledge of the US atomic weapons programme, in particular, was of utmost importance to the USSR, as was his information on the formation of NATO and Western policy in the KOREAN WAR. Burgess, as secretary to the deputy foreign minister, and later from a post in the Washington embassy, routinely supplied the Soviets with copies of sensitive documents. The journalist Kim Philby also worked for MI6, and so was able to supply the USSR with highly important information about the activities of Western agents within the Soviet bloc.

As the liaison officer between MI6 and the CIA in Washington, Philby became aware that the FBI had discovered the activities of a Soviet agent in the British embassy in Washington. Guessing that this was Maclean, Philby arranged for Burgess, then living in Philby's Washington apartment, to return to London to warn their comrade. Burgess did so, but, instead of discreetly aiding Maclean's defection to the USSR, he fled alongside Maclean in May 1951, casting suspicion upon Philby. Philby was able to refute allegations that he was the 'third man', but was forced to resign from MI6. In 1955 the allegations against Philby were raised again, this time in Parliament. Foreign secretary Harold MACMILLAN exonerated Philby, who moved to Beirut, where he worked again for MI6 and continued to pass information to the Soviets. After Philby was identified as the 'third man' by a Soviet defector in 1963, he too fled to the USSR, where he worked as an adviser to the KGB.

Anthony Blunt, who had served in MI5 during the war, became director of the Courtauld Institute of Art and was appointed surveyor of the queen's pictures in 1956. He recruited Soviet spies and acted as a go-between for Philby, Burgess and the Soviet intelligence service. Suspicion fell on Blunt in 1964, and, after being assured of immunity from prosecution, Blunt admitted his role as the 'fourth man'. Despite confessing to espionage, Blunt continued to work for the queen until 1979, when the newly elected prime minister Margaret THATCHER publicly exposed his activities. In 1991 John Cairncross – who had been a contemporary of the four spies at Cambridge and who had served in the Treasury, at BLETCHLEY PARK and with MI6 during World War II – admitted to being the 'fifth man'.

FURTHER READING C. Andrew, *Secret Service. The Making of the British Intelligence Community* (1984); C. Andrew and O. Gordievsky, *KGB. The Inside Story of its Foreign Operations from Lenin to Gorbachev* (1990).

Camden Town Group (1911–13), a group of British artists who took their name from a then drab district of north London. It had a brief existence but the name came to characterize a distinctive strain in British painting from *c.*1905 to 1920. The leading influence on the group was Walter SICKERT, who settled in Camden Town after a period in France. With the aim of creating a 'Salon d'Automne milieu in London' where progressive artists could discuss, exhibit and sell their work, he held regular open house at his studio in Fitzroy Street, Bloomsbury, less than a mile from his lodgings in Camden Town. Among the artists who met there was Lucien Pissarro (1863–1944), son of the famous French impressionist Camille Pissarro. Life in the domestic interiors, music halls and urban spaces of Camden Town became the subject of Sickert's painting and that of several of his associates, for example his *The Camden Town Murder* series of 1909 and Spencer Gore's paintings of Mornington Crescent, the area of Camden Town where Sickert lived.

In 1911 the artists who met in Fitzroy Street decided to form a distinct Camden Town Group as they found existing organizations not progressive enough. Membership was limited to 16 and it was decided to exclude women from membership, although at least two women artists, Ethel Sands and Nan Hudson, had associations with the painters who were accepted into the Group. The members (most of them not obviously more memorable than the excluded women) were: Walter Bayes, Robert Bevan, Malcolm Drummond, Harold Gilman, Charles Ginner, Spencer Gore (president), J.D. Inness, Augustus JOHN, Henry Lamb, Wyndham Lewis, Maxwell Gordon Lightfoot, J.B. Manson, Lucien Pissarro, William Ratcliffe, Walter Sickert and John Doman Turner. Lightfoot soon resigned and was replaced by Duncan Grant. These artists varied considerably in their purpose and style, but their paintings were generally small, unpretentious representations of everyday life, including street scenes in Camden Town, landscapes, informal portraits, still lifes and nudes.

The main function of the Group was to organize the exhibition of the paintings of its members, who feared exclusion from mainstream galleries. They held three shows at the Carfax Gallery in June and December 1911 and December 1912. These were financially disastrous. In 1913 the Group expanded into a larger exhibiting group, the London Group, which did admit women, including Vanessa BELL, and which survived until 1950. Lewis, Lamb, Gore and Grant showed in Roger FRY's post-impressionist exhibition of 1912–13. Most of the members of the original Camden Town Group exhibited in the *Post-Impressionists and Futurists* exhibition at the Dore Galleries in October 1913 and the *English Post-Impressionists, Cubists and Others* exhibition at the Brighton Art Gallery in 1913–14.

FURTHER READING W. Baron and M. Cormack, *The Camden Town Group* (1979).

Campaign for Nuclear Disarmament (CND),

organization that campaigned for unilateral British, and ultimately total global, nuclear disarmament. It was founded in 1958 as a result of growing alarm at the progress of the COLD WAR, and counted many prominent intellectuals among its early membership, including J.B. Priestley, E.P. Thompson, Michael FOOT and Bertrand RUSSELL (who served as its first president). It was a loosely structured, broadly based coalition employing, not without dispute, a variety of tactics, the leaders initially preferring those of a conventional lobbying group. It attracted most publicity for its annual Easter marches from the Atomic Weapons Research Establishment at Aldermaston, Berkshire, to Trafalgar Square in London (initially in the reverse direction). In the early 1960s crowds of up to 150,000 were attracted to its marches and rallies.

CND scored a major victory in 1961 when it influenced the LABOUR PARTY at its annual conference to support unilateral nuclear disarmament, but this decision was reversed the following year when the party adopted a policy of multilateralism. In 1963 much of the wind was taken out of CND's sails when Britain, the USA and the USSR signed the Nuclear Test Ban treaty. Its fortunes flagged for several years, but revived after 1979, when the USA began siting cruise missiles in

Britain and Europe, leading to increased US–Soviet tensions. CND's membership swelled to about 100,000 in 1984, mostly from the left-leaning middle class. It also had a large network of offshoots and affiliates, including Christian CND and various green, pacifist and youth groups. Its best-known leaders included Bruce Kent (a Roman Catholic priest when he became prominent, but he later left the priesthood) and Joan Ruddock (who later became a Labour MP). Notably, the most famous anti-nuclear protest of the 1980s in Britain, the women's 'peace camp' at GREENHAM COMMON, was not affiliated with CND. Another active group, in which E.P. Thompson was prominent, formed European Nuclear Disarmament (END), an attempt to work with dissidents in communist Eastern Europe; others in CND disapproved of this development.

Opinion polls throughout the period of anti-nuclear activism suggested that most of the population believed that Britain should retain a nuclear arsenal. Nevertheless, in the 1980s the CONSERVATIVE PARTY allocated a budget of £1 million to countering what Michael Heseltine (defence secretary, 1983–6) repeatedly referred to as 'one-sided disarmament'. The Conservatives were concerned to counter the growing unilateralist campaign and to embarrass the Labour Party, which in 1982 finally gave a majority at its annual conference to unilateralism. Labour went into the 1983 election (in which the recent FALKLANDS war figured prominently) pledged to cancel the Trident missile (*see* NUCLEAR WEAPONS) and remove all nuclear bases within Britain within five years. After their failure in the election, Labour moved away from this stance. Support for nuclear disarmament dwindled still further in the 1990s, mainly because of the ending of the COLD WAR.

FURTHER READING P. Byrne, *The Campaign for Nuclear Disarmament* (1988).

Campbell-Bannerman, Henry (1836–1908),

Liberal politician; PRIME MINISTER (1905–8). Born in Glasgow, the son of Sir James Campbell (a wholesale draper), he added his mother's maiden name, Bannerman, to his own in 1872. He was educated at Glasgow High School and at Glasgow and Cambridge universities. He worked for twelve years in the family firm before entering the House of COMMONS for the Stirling Burghs in 1868. From 1871 he held various junior government positions, before becoming chief secretary for Ireland (1884–5) and secretary of state for war in 1886 and 1892–5. He favoured the progressive causes supported by the radical wing of the LIBERAL PARTY, including HOME RULE for IRELAND, Scottish devolution, church disestablishment, women's suffrage, labour representation and the curbing of the power of the House of LORDS. In 1895 he was knighted, and in 1899 he became leader of the Liberals in the Commons when ASQUITH declined. He proved an effective and popular leader of a party divided over Irish home rule and the BOER WAR, and led it into office in December 1905, the king having invited him to form a government on the resignation of Arthur BALFOUR. He became prime minister despite the manoeuvres of rivals, and his position was reinforced by the Liberal success in the general election of January 1906.

Campbell-Bannerman's government included not only Asquith and LLOYD GEORGE, but also John Burns, the first working-class man to sit in a British cabinet. Much of his reforming legislative programme was blocked by the House of Lords, but he did manage to get through the 1906 Trades Disputes Act (*see* TRADE UNIONS), and his government also granted self-government to the former Boer republics in SOUTH AFRICA, which helped the process of reconciliation after the Boer War. However, ill-health forced Campbell-Bannerman's resignation in April 1908, and he died less than three weeks later. He was succeeded as premier by Asquith, who carried on the process of reform and took on the power of the House of Lords.

FURTHER READING J. Harris and C. Hazlehurst, 'Henry Campbell-Bannerman' in J.P. Mackintosh (ed.), *British Prime Ministers in the 20th Century, Vol. 1, Balfour to Chamberlain* (1977),

43–77; G.R. Searle, *The Liberal Party: Triumph and Disintegration, 1886–1929* (1963).

Canada, a constitutional monarchy and member of the COMMONWEALTH occupying almost all of the northern half of the North American continent. In 1900 Canada had firm ties to Britain, and as one of the 'white dominions' served as a cornerstone of the EMPIRE. Despite its large French-speaking minority, located mainly in Quebec province, and the large numbers of European immigrants settling the central and western regions of the country, Canada at this stage still had a strong British-influenced character. Between 1902 and 1912 over 1.5 million Britons emigrated to Canada.

Canada entered WORLD WAR I in support of Britain and its allies almost immediately. Of 425,000 Canadian troops sent overseas, some 60,000 were killed, most famously at YPRES, Vimy Ridge and PASSCHENDAELE. Initially under British command, the troops began to come under Canadian command after 1917, partly in response to the widespread resentment of French Canadians who were conscripted to serve a foreign nation to which they felt no ties. A growing sense of nationhood and autonomy was expressed during the war and in the years after; in 1919 Canada represented itself at the Paris Peace Conference (*see* VERSAILLES, TREATY OF).

Further steps towards autonomy were taken in the 1920s under the premiership of the Liberal prime minister William Lyon Mackenzie King, who argued for the right of Canada (as well as the other 'white' dominions) to determine its own foreign and legislative policies during the IMPERIAL CONFERENCE of 1926. These rights were enshrined in the Statute of Westminster, passed in the British Parliament in 1931, which gave Canada greater legislative independence. During WORLD WAR II Canada exercised its right to choose whether or not to join the war effort, and waited a week after Britain's declaration of war on Germany before itself declaring war (10 September 1939). None-

theless, Canada again sent a large number of soldiers overseas and suffered many casualties. There was a greater Canadian command presence than there had been in World War I, but many soldiers still fought under the command of British generals and this sometimes caused great resentment and controversy, as in the disastrous raid on Dieppe in August 1942, an experiment in landing techniques in which a largely Canadian force was decimated.

The immediate post-war years in Canada were prosperous. As in the United States, there was a boom in manufacturing, the extraction of natural resources and the building of infrastructure. Some 1.5 million new immigrants, many of them from Britain, helped fuel the economy. However, the post-war period also saw the erosion of ties with Britain, whose decline in status was rapidly accelerating, and the forging of new links with the new superpower to the south, the USA. The new relationship between Britain and Canada (as well as other members of the old empire/new Commonwealth) was best illustrated by the SUEZ CRISIS of 1956, when Britain's role was condemned by many of the Commonwealth governments, including that of Canada, whose prime minister, Lester Pearson, was awarded the Nobel Peace Prize for his role in brokering a settlement to the crisis.

Full independence came in 1982, when a new constitution (the Canada Act) was passed into law and received the personal and official sanction of Queen ELIZABETH II. For the first time Canada was enabled to amend its own constitution. Quebec was the only province that refused to ratify it, on the basis that it did not provide sufficient recognition and protection of the French minority. This intensified the problems that had long existed between the Francophone and Anglophone communities, which at the end of the 20th century remained the greatest threat to Canada's nationhood. Quebec separatist movements started in the 1960s and continued to be highly active throughout the rest of the century. In addition, there were long-standing tensions between the western agrarian provinces and the more industrialized east.

Despite joining the North American Free Trade Agreement with the USA and Mexico in 1993, Canada also felt threatened by the cultural, economic and political influence of the United States. This was at least partly responsible for Canada's continuance of ties with Britain, via the Commonwealth. Though most Canadians felt no great affinity with Britain, there was nevertheless no serious republican movement, comparable with that in AUSTRALIA.

FURTHER READING J.M. Bumsted, *The Peoples of Canada: A Post-Confederation History* (1992); R.D. Francis et al., *Destinies: Canadian History Since Confederation* (1992).

Cape Matapan, battle of. *See* CUNNINGHAM, ANDREW.

capital punishment. The number of crimes punishable by death fell during the 19th century to four by the beginning of the 20th: murder, treason, piracy and sabotage, including arson in the king's/queen's dockyards. A death sentence was mandatory following a conviction for murder: judges had no discretion, although clemency from the home secretary might commute the sentence to one of life imprisonment. A total of 657 people were executed by hanging between 1900 and 1949, and between 1949 and 1964 a total of 143 executions took place in England, Wales and Scotland. The last hanging in England took place on 13 August 1964. (For details of executions between 1949 and 1964, *see* table.)

Throughout the century surveys of public opinion showed strong support for capital punishment. However, the death penalty was abolished in the end as a result of effective lobbying. In 1921 the Howard League for Penal Reform made repeal a principal objective. In 1925 the National Council for the Abolition of the Death Penalty was established as a coordinating body for opponents. But the issue did not become prominent in British politics until 1955, as a result of several notable cases.

Hangings in Great Britain, 1949–64

Year	England and Wales executions	Scotland executions	Total
1949	17	0	17
1950	14	2	16
1951	18	1	19
1952	17	3	20
1953	16	0	16
1954	12	2	14
1955	9	0	9
1956	0	0	0
1957	3	0	3
1958	5	1	6
1959	4	0	4
1960	7	1	8
1961	4	0	4
1962	2	0	2
1963	2	1	3
1964	2	0	2

Source: Parliamentary Papers, 1950–1965/6. *Criminal Statistics England and Wales.*

In December 1952 two youths, Christopher Craig and Derek Bentley, were surprised when breaking into a warehouse in Croydon. Craig, aged 16, shot and killed a policeman. Bentley, aged 19 and in terms of mental capacity a good deal younger, had been in police custody for 15 minutes at the time of the shooting. He was convicted and hanged while Craig was sentenced to life imprisonment because he was too young for execution. This led to a long campaign led by Bentley's family for his exoneration from the murder, which was finally granted by the Labour home secretary, Jack STRAW, in 1999. In 1953 John Christie was found guilty of murdering six women. This brought to light the fact that four years earlier Timothy Evans, who had lived in the same apartment house, had been convicted and executed for murdering his wife and child. Christie had testified against Evans but it seemed highly likely that he had committed these murders also.

It was the recognition that innocent people were being executed that most fiercely fuelled the campaign to abolish capital punishment. This was led by the National Campaign for the Abolition of Capital Punishment. The Homicide Act of 1957 created separate categories of capital and non-capital murder; capital murder included the killing of a police officer. In 1965 the Abolition of Capital Punishment Act suspended the death penalty completely for five years; Parliament made this permanent in 1969. Subsequent attempts to reintroduce the death penalty failed.

FURTHER READING L. Blom-Cooper (ed.), *The Hanging Question* (1969).

Caribbean immigration. *See* IMMIGRATION.

Carrington, Peter (Alexander Rupert) Carrington, 6th Baron (1919–), Conservative politician. Born into an aristocratic family, Carrington was educated at Eton and Sandhurst. He served as an officer in the Grenadier Guards during World War II before taking an active role in the House of LORDS. During the early 1950s he was parliamentary secretary to the Ministry of Agriculture and the Ministry of Defence, before being appointed high commissioner in Australia in 1956. On his return to the UK in 1959 he was made first lord of the Admiralty, and was leader of the House of Lords from 1963 to 1964. He acted as leader of the opposition in the Lords from 1964 to 1970, whereupon he was made defence secretary and for a short time secretary of state for energy in the government of Edward HEATH. After serving again as opposition leader in the House of Lords he was made foreign secretary by Margaret THATCHER in 1979. He chaired the Lancaster House conference that led to the creation of independent ZIMBABWE in 1981. Although supportive of Thatcher, he was not a zealous Thatcherite, and found himself a scapegoat for the Argentinian invasion of the FALKLAND ISLANDS in 1982. He resigned from his post, and took a step back from UK parliamentary politics. He continued to hold prominent positions in international organizations, however, being secretary general of NATO from 1984 to 1988, and led an unsuccessful peace mission to the Balkans in the early 1990s.

FURTHER READING Lord Carrington, *Reflection on Things Past* (1988); P. Cosgrave, *Carrington: A Life and a Policy* (1985).

Carson, Edward Henry (1854–1935), lawyer and politician who led the Protestant resistance to HOME RULE for IRELAND, earning him the nickname the 'uncrowned king of Ulster'. Born and educated in Dublin, Carson became Unionist MP for Dublin University (1892–1918) and then for the Duncairn division of Belfast (1918–21). A formidable barrister, Carson was appointed solicitor general for Ireland in 1892, and in the following year was called to the English Bar. His devastating cross-examination of Oscar Wilde in Wilde's libel suit against the marquess of Queensberry (1895) led to Wilde's conviction for sodomy and confirmed Carson's reputation. His defence in 1910 of a naval cadet accused of theft was the subject of Terence Rattigan's play *The Winslow Boy* (1946).

From 1900 to 1905 Carson was solicitor general in the conservative governments of SALISBURY and BALFOUR. In 1910 he organized Protestant resistance to home rule in Ireland, and led the Irish Unionists in the house of COMMONS, leading the movement for a provisional government in Ulster from 1911 (*see* ULSTER UNIONIST PARTY). In 1910 he also refused to stand for the CONSERVATIVE PARTY leadership. In 1913 he established the ULSTER VOLUNTEERS, a private army of 100,000 men pledged to resist home rule; at the outbreak of WORLD WAR I he offered the volunteers as a division to the British army, which accepted them. In May 1915 Carson became attorney general in ASQUITH's wartime coalition government, but left the government in October 1916 and became a leader of the dissident Conservatives. In December 1916 he assisted Bonar LAW and LLOYD GEORGE to overthrow Asquith, and became first lord of the Admiralty (December 1916–July 1917), then minister without portfolio in the war cabinet for six months. He left the cabinet on learning that Lloyd George intended to introduce home rule for the whole of Ireland. After the war he sought a compromise solution to Irish government, and did not oppose the Government of Ireland Bill (1920). The following year he resigned the leadership of the Ulster Unionists, but continued to watch over their interests. He was created a baron in 1921 as Lord Carson of Duncairn, and became a lord of appeal (1921–9).

FURTHER READING H. Montgomery Hyde, *Carson* (1953).

Casement, Roger (David) (1864–1916), diplomat and Irish nationalist. Casement entered the British consular service in 1892, and reported with distinction on the corrupt administration of the Congo Free State (1903) and atrocities committed by agents of the Peruvian Amazon Company (1910). He was knighted in 1911, and retired to IRELAND in 1913. A fervent nationalist, he joined the committee of the Irish National Volunteers. In November 1914 he visited Berlin, via the United States, to secure German aid for Irish independence, and vainly tried to recruit Irish prisoners of war for the German army. He landed from a German submarine in Tralee, southwest Ireland, on the eve of the EASTER RISING in 1916. A trawler accompanying the submarine and carrying 20,000 guns was scuttled after being intercepted. Casement told his MI5 interrogators that he knew that the Easter Rising was doomed to failure when Germany reneged on its promises to send troops to support the rebels, and that he was all too likely to be caught. He was hoping to warn the rebels of the hopelessness of their situation. He was arrested and hanged as a traitor in Pentonville prison on 3 August 1916, despite a campaign for clemency by prominent men, including Sir Arthur Conan Doyle, Joseph CONRAD and T.E. LAWRENCE, which greatly alarmed the civil servants. His so-called 'black diaries', containing homosexual passages, were circulated by British agents to discredit him and to discourage any campaign for a reprieve. It remains uncertain whether they were forgeries. Casement was subsequently regarded as a patriotic martyr in Ireland, nationalists insisting that the diaries were forgeries – an allegation that is still the subject of debate among historians.

Castle, Barbara (Anne) (*née* Betts) (1910–), Labour politician. Educated at state schools and Oxford University, she worked in the civil service during World War II. She became MP for Blackburn in the 1945 election, and was a leading figure on the LABOUR PARTY's National Executive Committee from 1950 until 1979. Castle was party chairman for a time in the late 1950s, and became minister for overseas development in Harold WILSON's first government in 1964. She became minister of transport the following year, and held the post until 1968. As secretary of state for employment and productivity (1968–70), Castle produced a white paper, *In Place of Strife* (1969), outlining proposals for TRADE-UNION regulation. The paper was rejected by the cabinet, but Castle achieved greater success with the 1970 Equal Pay Act, introducing improvements for the rights of women at work. After Labour's return to power in 1974, she was appointed secretary of state for health and social services. She successfully introduced child benefit (*see* FAMILY ALLOWANCES), but faced problems in her attempts to phase out pay beds in NHS hospitals. She lost ministerial office when James CALLAGHAN, with whom she always had a tense relationship and little political sympathy, became prime minister in 1976, and she retired from the Commons in 1979. Despite her earlier opposition to British membership of the EUROPEAN ECONOMIC COMMUNITY, Castle served for ten years in the European Parliament, leading the British Labour group (1979–85) and becoming vice chair of the European Parliament's socialist group (1979–86). Thereafter she was active in the House of LORDS as Baroness Castle of Blackburn, and was a determined campaigner for improved OLD-AGE PENSIONS.

FURTHER READING B. Castle, *Fighting all the Way* (1993); B. Castle, *The Castle Diaries, 1964–76* (1990).

Cat and Mouse Act (1913), legislation designed to frustrate hunger strikes by SUFFRAGETTES in prison. In the early years of the 20th century, the militant suffragettes of the Women's Social and Political Union (WSPU), led by Emmeline and Christabel PANKHURST, frequently found themselves arrested for their violent and disruptive tactics. Almost all, when sent to prison, promptly began hunger strikes to protest against the government's refusal to extend the franchise to women. Fearful of the repercussions should a suffragette die while in custody, the government ordered that hunger strikers should be force-fed, a dangerous and painful procedure in which rubber tubes were inserted through the nose or mouth. Public opinion quickly condemned the practice as shocking and barbaric.

The ASQUITH government's subsequent solution to the problem was to pass the Prisoners' Temporary Discharge for Ill-Health Act in 1913. It was commonly known as the 'Cat and Mouse' Act after the WSPU produced a poster depicting a helpless mouse (the suffragettes) being held in the jaws of a large and vicious-looking cat (the government). The act released from prison suffragettes whose health was in danger, but they were to be immediately re-arrested once they had recovered. Emmeline Pankhurst herself was re-arrested some twelve times under the act, but other suffragettes proved elusive once released from prison. Special homes were established around the country where suffragettes could go to recover from their ordeal.

FURTHER READING D. Atkinson, *The Suffragettes* (1993); P. Bartley, *Votes for Women, 1860–1928* (1998).

Cavell, Edith (Louisa) (1865–1915), English nurse whose execution at the hands of the Germans during WORLD WAR I made her a national heroine. Cavell was born at Swardeston, near Nor-

wich. She started her working life as a governess, in 1886. Two years later she went to Belgium for the first time to work as a governess to a Belgian family. In 1895 she returned to England, and the following year decided to change career and began training as a nurse at the London Hospital. Later she engaged in POOR LAW nursing. In 1907 the contacts she had made while in Belgium resulted in her being invited to Brussels to help establish the first Belgian school of nursing, of which she became matron. Over the next six years she worked to establish the school and raise money for its operation.

In 1914 Cavell was on holiday in Norfolk when the war broke out. She quickly returned to Brussels, where the nursing school had been turned into a Red Cross hospital. She worked tirelessly at her job, nursing both German and Allied soldiers. In private, however, she began helping to establish an escape network for Allied soldiers on the run from the German offensive. In August 1915 her efforts were exposed and she was arrested by the Germans and charged with having sheltered some two hundred Allied soldiers in her home and then helping them escape from Belgium. Her trial began on 7 October 1915; she was found guilty within days and sentenced to execution by firing squad. Despite many appeals made on her behalf by government officials from several neutral nations, including Spain and the United States, she was shot at dawn on 12 October 1915. Her execution, carried out without deference to her gender or her humanitarian motives, provoked a national outcry in Britain, and she was instantly proclaimed a heroine and martyr. British propagandists seized upon the story as yet another German atrocity in Belgium, and ensured that it had a particular impact in the neutral United States. Cavell's body was finally returned to England in 1919 and she was buried outside Norwich Cathedral. Her memorial service was held at Westminster Abbey and attracted huge crowds. The stone memorial to her outside the National Portrait Gallery in London bears her last words: 'I realize

that patriotism is not enough. I must have no hatred or bitterness towards anyone.'
FURTHER READING S. Grant, *Edith Cavell, 1865–1915* (1995); N. Richardson, *Edith Cavell* (1990).

Cavendish Laboratory, building housing the department of physics of the University of Cambridge for many years. It was the site of some of the most important scientific work of the century, including the discovery of the electron (1897), the artificial splitting of the atom and the discovery of the neutron (1932), the elucidation of the structure of DNA (deoxyribonucleic acid; 1953) and the discovery of pulsars (1967). It was opened in 1874 and founded by the 7th duke of Devonshire, chancellor of the university, who gave it his family name. Ernest Rutherford (1871–1937), Cavendish professor of physics from 1919 until his death, did much to consolidate and strengthen the influence of the laboratory and to maintain the high quality of those who worked there. During WORLD WAR II many Cavendish physicists contributed to the development of RADAR and NUCLEAR WEAPONS. After the war new lines of research were developed, notably in molecular biology and radio astronomy. The laboratory was at the forefront of research in physics at the end as at the beginning of the century, with research concentrated in condensed-matter physics, radio astronomy, high-energy physics, laboratory astrophysics and energy research.
SEE ALSO SCIENCE.
FURTHER READING J.G. Crowther, *The Cavendish Laboratory, 1874–1974* (1974).

CEMA. *See* COUNCIL FOR THE ENCOURAGEMENT OF MUSIC AND THE ARTS.

censorship. Censorship was an issue in relation to many forms of COMMUNICATION in the 20th century. The 1904 Wireless Telegraphy Act placed the licensing of broadcasting in the hands of the government, giving it the potential power to control content. Sir John REITH as director general of the BRITISH BROADCASTING CORPORATION in its early years imposed strict cultural censorship, owing to his belief that the BBC should promote 'high' rather than 'low' culture and should not give a voice to values that challenged the political or religious mainstream. Control over the content of radio and television relaxed in the later 20th century, but did not disappear, the Home Office retaining ultimate control over content; for example, British terrestrial television channels were forbidden from showing sexually explicit material when children might be watching, before the 9 p.m. 'watershed'.

Theatre censorship in various forms had existed for centuries. Under legislation enacted in 1737 the lord chamberlain (the controller of the royal household) had the power to license stage plays, and hence to withhold a licence from those deemed unsuitable or to demand changes in return for licensing. This power was abolished by the Theatres Act of 1968, although the Home Office retained the right to ban or demand changes in stage performances, and local authorities retained the right to prevent stage performances believed to be offensive to morality.

Publications were controlled by the Obscene Publications Act, 1857, under which James Joyce's novel *Ulysses* was seized in 1923. The act was modified by the Obscene Publications Act of 1959, which allowed a defence of artistic or literary merit. This was tested in 1960 when *Lady Chatterley's Lover*, the previously banned novel by D.H. LAWRENCE, was cleared for publication, after a high-profile test case in which a succession of prominent witnesses testified to its combination of literary value and moral integrity.

From its earliest days, the British FILM INDUSTRY regulated itself, establishing the British Board of Film Censors in 1912, to restrict what could be seen on film and who could see it. Standards shifted over the century, but children continued to be excluded mainly from films thought to be sexually explicit or excessively violent. Local authorities could also refuse the showing of a film within their jurisdiction.

Censorship of news and other information disseminated by any means was most severe in wartime, but present at all times. In WORLD WAR I the 1914 DEFENCE OF THE REALM ACT (DORA) extended the OFFICIAL SECRETS ACT (1911), rendering it an offence to publish information of value to the enemy. This legislation remained in force to the end of the century and was used for example to prevent former British intelligence agents, such as Peter Wright in the 1980s and David Shayler in the late 1990s, from publishing information. It also underpinned the D (Defence) Notice system whereby (also for the remainder of the century) such notices could be issued to prevent publication of any information deemed harmful to British national security. In both world wars journalists learned to impose self-censorship and to work with the controls.

Various other pieces of legislation imposed censorship in one form or another: the 1917 Venereal Disease Acts suppressed publications about SEXUALLY TRANSMITTED DISEASES; the 1934 Contraceptives Act restricted the advertisement of contraceptives, for fear of encouraging immorality (*see* BIRTH CONTROL); the 1955 Harmful Publications Act was intended to protect children from violent or obscene material, for example in strip-cartoon form; the 1968 Race Relations Act prohibited any publication that expressed racial discrimination or incited racial hatred. The variety of this list suggests the difficulty and sensitivity of the issue of censorship.

FURTHER READING D. Tribe, *Questions of Censorship* (1973).

census. The UK census to count the size of the population was started in 1801, and in the 20th and 21st centuries was carried out by government representatives every ten years from 1901 to 2001, with the exception of 1941, which fell during wartime. In addition to establishing numbers of people, various questions were asked; some of these varied from census to census, such as those regarding religion or ethnic origin, while some did not,

such as occupation and place of residence on the night of the census. It was compulsory to complete the census questionnaire, but every decade a minority of conscientious objectors refused to do so and an uncertain number of people went unrecorded, especially in areas of high population turnover such as urban centres.

SEE ALSO POPULATION.

Chadwick, James. *See* SCIENCE.

Chamberlain, (Joseph) Austen (1863–1937), Conservative politician. The eldest son of Joseph CHAMBERLAIN and half-brother of Neville CHAMBERLAIN, Austen Chamberlain was born in Birmingham and educated at Rugby School and Cambridge University. He was groomed for politics from an early age, entering Parliament in 1892, representing East Worcestershire as a Liberal Unionist (the Liberal faction that opposed William Gladstone's plans for HOME RULE for IRELAND). The Liberal Unionists were increasingly fused with the CONSERVATIVE PARTY from 1895, and formally merged in 1912. After 1914 Chamberlain held his father's seat, Birmingham West, for the Conservatives; he also shared his father's support for TARIFF REFORM.

Chamberlain entered the cabinet as postmaster general in 1900, and was twice CHANCELLOR OF THE EXCHEQUER, first in BALFOUR's Conservative government (1903–5), and then in LLOYD GEORGE's coalition (1919–21). He contended for the leadership of the Conservative Party in 1911, but withdrew in favour of Bonar LAW. During WORLD WAR I he was secretary of state for INDIA (1915–17), resigning over the failure of the Mesopotamian campaign, which was conducted by an Anglo-Indian force controlled by the British government in India. He returned to the war cabinet in 1918–19. After his second stint as chancellor he became lord privy seal (1921–2). As foreign secretary (1925–9) under BALDWIN he negotiated the LOCARNO PACT, for which he received the Nobel Peace Prize and a knighthood.

Chamberlain was leader of the Conservative Party in the Commons (1921–2). He lost his chance to become prime minister, and the party leadership, because of his continued support for the Lloyd George coalition when it was rejected by the Conservative backbenchers in 1922. Such loyalty was characteristic of him. When the NATIONAL GOVERNMENT was formed in 1931 he was offered the post of first lord of the Admiralty, rather than the Foreign Office as expected. After the 1931 general election that followed the formation of the National Government he withdrew to the back benches. As the 1930s progressed, Chamberlain became one of the earliest of British politicians to warn of the dangers from Hitler's Germany. Following the debacle of the HOARE–LAVAL PACT in 1935 Baldwin offered him the Foreign Office, but he declined. He died two years later.

FURTHER READING D. Dutton, *Austen Chamberlain: Gentleman in Politics* (1985).

Chamberlain, Joseph (1836–1914), Liberal, then Liberal Unionist, politician; father of Austen and Neville CHAMBERLAIN. The son of a shopkeeper, Joseph Chamberlain was born in London and educated at University College School. He made his fortune as a manufacturer in Birmingham, and gained national recognition as a radical lord mayor of Birmingham (1873–6). In 1876 he entered Parliament as a LIBERAL, switching to the anti-HOME RULE Liberal Unionists when William Gladstone committed his government to home rule for IRELAND in 1886. He continued to be a campaigning social reformer, supporting the introduction of OLD-AGE PENSIONS among other reforms. From 1895 to 1903 he was colonial secretary in the Conservative government, working especially for expansion in Africa and closer integration of the EMPIRE. This led him, after the BOER WAR, to campaign for TARIFF REFORM and IMPERIAL PREFERENCE, which led to his resignation and to splits in the Conservative Party. In 1906 he suffered a serious stroke and withdrew from politics.

FURTHER READING P. Fraser, *Joseph Chamberlain. Radicalism and Empire, 1868–1914* (1964).

Chamberlain, (Arthur) Neville (1868–1940), Conservative politician; PRIME MINISTER (1937–40). The son of Joseph CHAMBERLAIN by his second wife (and half-brother of Austen CHAMBERLAIN), Neville Chamberlain was educated at Rugby School and Mason Science College, Birmingham. He was expected to enter a business career. He worked first as an accountant, and then was sent by his father to the Bahamas for seven years to recoup the family fortune through a sisal-growing venture. This was a disaster because of poor soil and the low market value of sisal. He returned to Britain in 1897 and successfully managed a number of Birmingham companies. In 1911 he was elected to Birmingham City Council at the age of 42 and four years later became lord mayor. He acquired a reputation for innovation and reform in the areas of public health and town planning, and established Britain's first, and only, municipal savings bank. His success led to his appointment by David LLOYD GEORGE to the control board established to oversee the liquor trade in WORLD WAR I; in December 1916 he became director general of National Service, in charge of mobilizing the civilian workforce for industry. The duties of the post were ill-defined and Chamberlain did not get on with Lloyd George. He resigned in August 1917, and there was lifelong animosity between them thereafter.

Chamberlain was aged almost 50 when he entered Parliament for Ladywood, Birmingham, as a Conservative (December 1918). He supported the CONSERVATIVE PARTY opposition to Lloyd George's coalition government in 1922 and advanced rapidly under the party leaderships of Bonar LAW and BALDWIN. Between 1922 and the loss of office by the Conservatives in January 1924 Chamberlain served, successively, as postmaster general, paymaster general, minister of health and CHANCELLOR OF THE EXCHEQUER, gaining a strong reputation. He chose to return to the Ministry of

Health when the Conservatives returned to power in November 1924, having mapped out a programme of reform while out of office, which he proceeded to implement with great efficiency. Among his achievements were the introduction of pensions for widows and orphans; the reduction to 65 of the age of eligibility for OLD-AGE PENSIONS (1925); the Rating and Valuation Act (1925), which gave relief from local RATES to agriculture and industry; and the Local Government Act (1929), which finally abolished the POOR LAW, transferring its powers and institutions to the county and county borough councils. He also facilitated an expansion of public and private house building.

While the Conservatives were out of office between 1929 and 1931 Chamberlain reorganized the Conservative Central Office and established a research department. During Baldwin's absence abroad he represented the party in the negotiations that led to the formation of the NATIONAL GOVERNMENT in 1931. He was chancellor of the exchequer in that government, persuading it to abandon FREE TRADE and to place a duty of 10% on almost all imports except those from within the EMPIRE. He reversed cuts in UNEMPLOYMENT payments, following riots, and in 1937 levied a tax on business profits to finance defence expenditure. He succeeded Baldwin as prime minister and Conservative Party leader on 28 May 1937 without serious opposition.

As prime minister Chamberlain was mainly concerned with international relations. He sought to avoid war mainly because he was all too well aware of Britain's limited capability and resources to defend a global empire. He followed the policy that became known as APPEASEMENT by seeking to renew good relations with Japan and to separate Hitler and Mussolini. In 1938, after Germany's absorption of Austria and Hitler's demand for self-determination for Germans in the Sudetenland region of Czechoslovakia, Chamberlain made a series of trips to meet Hitler in order to find a peaceful resolution of the crisis, convinced that Britain was not prepared for war and uncertain that sup-

port would be forthcoming from the EMPIRE or from the isolationist United States. The MUNICH AGREEMENT of 30 September 1938, brokered by Mussolini, achieved peace by ceding the Sudetenland to Germany. The agreement was widely applauded in Britain. However, after Hitler went on to occupy the rest of Czechoslovakia in March 1939, Chamberlain came to realize that appeasement was impossible, and sought to guarantee other nations of central and eastern Europe – notably Poland – against aggression. With the outbreak of WORLD WAR II he continued to serve as prime minister, though neither the LABOUR PARTY nor the LIBERAL PARTY would join him in a coalition government. His defensive rather than proactive approach to the war, influenced by his continuing belief that Britain was ill-prepared (a belief that had some foundation), led to heated criticism (*see* AMERY, LEO) and his resignation on 10 May 1940. He was succeeded by CHURCHILL. Chamberlain continued as leader of the Conservative Party and lord president of the council, despite failing health, until his death from cancer in November 1940.

FURTHER READING D. Dilks, *Neville Chamberlain: Pioneering and Reform, 1868–1940* (1984); R.A.C. Parker, *Chamberlain and Appeasement: British Policy and the Coming of World War II* (1993).

Chanak crisis (September–October 1922), crisis in Anglo-Turkish relations. It arose from the victory of Mustapha Kemal (Atatürk) over the Greeks at Smyrna (now Izmir) in August 1922, and his apparent intention to carry the war into the European territories assigned to Greece in 1920 by the abortive treaty of Sèvres (which Kemal had never accepted). The British government feared that Kemal would also attack the Allied army of occupation guarding the approaches to Constantinople (Istanbul). Prime minister LLOYD GEORGE favoured the reinforcement of British detachments serving at Chanak on the Asiatic shore of the Dardanelles. The crisis was averted by an Anglo-Turkish agreement at Mudania on 11 October

1922; this pledged the return to Turkey of eastern Thrace and Adrianople, provided that the Turks accepted the neutralization of the Bosphorus. This agreement formed the basis of the treaty of Lausanne in July 1923. The crisis precipitated the break-up of the Lloyd George coalition because Conservative leaders were alarmed by what they perceived as his irresponsibility in bringing Britain to the brink of war with Turkey. He was ousted from office within two weeks of the Mudania convention.

chancellor of the exchequer, the name given to the post of the head of the Treasury, the department of government which supervises government income ('revenue') and expenditure. The department and the office became increasingly important through the 20th century owing to increasing government involvement in economic affairs and the great increase in the ratio of public spending to national income. Immediately after World War I the chief civil servant at the Treasury, the permanent secretary, was recognized as head of the civil service. This had much to do with the personal power exerted by Sir Warren FISHER (1879–1948), who was permanent secretary to the Treasury and head of the civil service, 1919–39. The role of the Treasury as controller of the expenditure of other departments thus became entrenched.

In general, throughout the century, the Treasury was perceived, with some justice, as playing a conservative role, anxious to restrain levels of taxation and of expenditure. This led to conflict with other government departments, though, as with most offices of state, the reality varied with the policies and the personalities of individual chancellors, as Roy JENKINS, himself a Labour chancellor (1967–70), put it in his magisterial survey of the role, *The Chancellors* (1998): 'The attempt to draw patterns is a tenuous and even sterile exercise. It is like trying to break a cipher from an imperfect text. Perhaps happily, chancellors do not come as die stampings.' This comment might equally be applied to all other CABINET positions throughout the 20th century.

SEE ALSO BALANCE OF PAYMENTS; STOP-GO.

Channel Islands, all that remained in the 20th century of the British monarchy's once extensive possessions in France. They were retained when King John lost the remainder of the duchy of Normandy in 1204. They consist of the four larger islands of Jersey (population 84,000 in 1991), Guernsey (59,000), Alderney (2300) and Sark (570), plus a number of smaller islands. Alderney lies closest to France – about 16 km (10 miles) from the French coast. The official languages are English and French, with some Norman-French patois still in use. Under the constitution introduced in 1948, the British monarch appoints a lieutenant governor as her representative in the two bailiwicks of Jersey and Guernsey (which includes Alderney and Sark and the smaller islands of Herm and Jethou). The lieutenant governors are appointed for five years. All communications between the UK government and the islands pass through their offices. A bailiff, also appointed by the crown, presides over the local elected legislatures, known as the States, and over the sittings of the Royal Court. The islands have their own courts of law, but there remains leave to appeal to the Judicial Committee of the Privy Council. The States may initiate legislation, but they must petition the sovereign in council to give these measures force of law. Acts of the UK Parliament do not apply to the Channel Islands unless by express provision or necessary application. As a general rule the UK Parliament refrains from legislating on matters with which the States can deal, unless for some reason a UK act must be preferred to local legislation. The public revenues of the islands are raised by duties on imported goods, and by income taxes and other taxes. Proposals made by the States for raising revenue require authorization by order in council, but responsibility for determining how the revenue shall be spent is, in practice, left to the States. Immunity from taxation for crown purposes has been a privilege of the islands since the time of Edward VI in the

16th century. The islands have their own currency.

The Channel Islands were the only part of the British Isles to be occupied by the Germans during WORLD WAR II. They were liberated on 9 May 1945. The period of the occupation was still, at the end of the century, shrouded in a certain silence and mystery, in what remained tightly knit communities. After the war the islands profited from tourism and as a tax haven, owing to their low rates of income tax.

Channel Tunnel. Proposals to build a tunnel linking Britain and France beneath the Channel were made at intervals from the early 19th century. These proposals foundered for technical and financial reasons, and there was also a strategic reason – fear of invasion from Europe. The Suez Canal Company gave the project serious investigation in 1957. Both British and French governments approved the project in 1964, and in 1966 gave an estimated completion date of 1975. Rising costs led to the abandonment of the scheme in 1975. Interest returned when the heads of European Community governments met in Bonn in 1985. In February 1986 a treaty was signed between the British and French foreign ministers at Canterbury providing for government cooperation in the construction by a private consortium of a twin-tunnel rail link between Cheriton, Kent, and Frethun, Pas-de-Calais. It was hoped that the tunnel would be in use by 1993. The first passenger rail service began on 14 November 1994, the reason for the delay being mainly financial. Two rail tunnels were constructed, to convey cars, freight and passenger trains, with a smaller service tunnel. The tunnel is 50 km (31 miles) long. By the end of the century the train service to Paris and Brussels and the car-transporter and freight service to France had proved highly successful and popular.

SEE ALSO RAILWAYS.

Charles, prince of Wales (1948–), the current heir to the British throne. He was born to Princess Elizabeth and the duke of Edinburgh (later Queen ELIZABETH II and Prince Philip) on 14 November 1948 and educated at Cheam School, Gordonstoun School and Trinity College, Cambridge. Created prince of WALES in 1958, he was invested during a ceremony at Carnarfon Castle in July 1969. He learned to fly with the RAF before attending the Royal Naval College, Dartmouth, in 1971, and served with the Royal Navy until the end of 1976, when he left to pursue full-time royal duties. He married Lady Diana Spencer (later DIANA, PRINCESS OF WALES) on 29 July 1981; they separated in 1992 and divorced in July 1996. He is the father of two sons: Prince William, born in 1982 (second in line to the throne), and Prince Henry ('Harry'), born in 1984.

Prince Charles's public image has undergone a considerable shift over time. He gained some notoriety for his vehement disapproval of modern architecture in a speech to the Royal Institute of British Architects in May 1984. His most significant public achievement, however, was his foundation of the Prince's Trust in 1976, which funds community and self-improvement schemes for young people, largely from deprived inner-city backgrounds. Gradual public awareness of the unhappiness of his marriage to Diana, and then of his long-term attachment to Camilla Parker-Bowles, created some unpopularity for him, but it was not universal. His supportive relationship with his sons after their mother's death in 1997 restored some sympathy for him. Prince Charles does not receive any money from the State. Instead, as the duke of Cornwall, he receives the annual net revenue of the Duchy to meet all the costs of his public and private commitments.

FURTHER READING J. Dimbleby, *The Prince of Wales: A Biography* (1994).

Charter 88, pressure group formed in 1988, consciously echoing the Chartist movement that had sought constitutional reform in early 19th-century Britain and the Charter 77 civil-rights movement in communist Czechoslovakia. It also commemorated the bicentenary of the Revolutionary settlement of 1688. Its aim was constitutional reform: minimally PROPORTIONAL REPRESENTATION (PR) to replace the 'first-past-the-post' electoral system; maximally the introduction of a written constitution for Britain. It gained much publicity in its early years as part of a wider movement for PR (an important aim of the LIBERAL PARTY), and remained in being to the end of the century, though it was little noticed in later years. It may have had some effect in persuading the Labour Party to consider electoral reform, but its influence, if any, is difficult to assess.

Chequers, a country house in the Chiltern Hills, near Wendover, Buckinghamshire. In 1917 it was donated by Lord Lee of Fareham as a country house for the PRIME MINISTER, which it remained throughout the century. Lee was a Conservative MP, first elected in 1900, who came to admire LLOYD GEORGE and served in his government of 1916–22. He received a barony in 1922. Lloyd George was the first prime minister to make use of Chequers, in 1921. Successive prime ministers used it, to varying degrees, for relaxation and for political gatherings.

child benefit. *See* FAMILY ALLOWANCES.

Childers, (Robert) Erskine (1870–1922), novelist and Irish nationalist. Childers was born in London and educated at Haileybury and Trinity College, Cambridge. His father, a distinguished oriental scholar, died when he was six, and Childers was brought up by his mother, whose family came from Ireland. He was a clerk of the House of Commons, 1895–1910. During this time he volunteered to fight in the Boer War and wrote two books about his experiences. In 1903 he published *The Riddle of the Sands,* a spy thriller that centred on German preparations to invade Britain. Grippingly written, it touched British fears of Germany and became a bestseller. From 1910 Childers became increasingly involved with Irish nationalism, and in 1914 he ran a quantity of arms to

Howth, near Dublin, in his yacht. At this point he was committed to HOME RULE for IRELAND. Despite this, he was employed by the Royal Naval Air Service during World War I, 1914–19. After the suppression of the EASTER RISING in 1916, like many Irish nationalists he was converted to the cause of full independence for Ireland, to which he devoted himself after the war. He accompanied Irish envoys to the Paris Peace Conference in 1919; was elected as the SINN FÉIN member for County Wicklow (whence his mother came) in the self-constituted Dáil Éireann (Irish parliament) in 1921, and was principal secretary to the Irish delegation that negotiated the treaty with the British government in 1921. However, in 1922 he joined DE VALERA in opposing the treaty, became a member of the IRISH REPUBLICAN ARMY and was arrested for possession of a revolver, court-martialled and shot by the government of the Irish Free State. He died with composure after shaking hands with the firing squad. His son Erskine was president of the Republic of Ireland from 1973 to 1974.

FURTHER READING A. Boyle, *The Riddle of Erskine Childers* (1977).

Child Poverty Action Group. *See* FAMILY ALLOWANCES.

Churchill, Winston (Leonard Spencer) (1874–1965), Liberal, then Conservative, politician and writer; PRIME MINISTER (1940–5, 1951–5). He was an inspiring leader of the British people during WORLD WAR II, although his peacetime record was less impressive.

Born at Blenheim Palace, one of Britain's grandest country houses, Churchill was the elder son of Lord Randolph Churchill, a controversial, radical Conservative politician, and an American heiress, Jennie Jerome; he was a grandson of the 7th duke of Marlborough. Educated at Harrow School and the Royal Military Academy, Sandhurst, Churchill was commissioned in 1895 and served with the army in INDIA and Africa (1896–8), at the same time working as a journalist, in which role he had sent back despatches from the war of independence in Cuba (1895). Resigning his commission in 1899, he became a war correspondent in SOUTH AFRICA during the BOER WAR and was briefly captured by the Boers. Churchill enjoyed wars and was to become the first British prime minister since the duke of Wellington (in 1815) to have fought in battle.

Churchill became Conservative MP for Oldham, Lancashire, in 1900, proving to be an awkward, critical backbencher. In 1904 he crossed to the LIBERAL PARTY on the issue of FREE TRADE, which he strongly supported. This earned him the undying hostility of some Conservatives. He was elected to the Commons as a Liberal in 1905 and became undersecretary to the colonies under the premiership of Henry CAMPBELL-BANNERMAN. In 1908 he married Clementine Hozier. When ASQUITH became prime minister in 1908 he entered the cabinet as president of the Board of Trade. In this role he was responsible for the introduction of unemployment insurance, labour exchanges and other measures to alleviate UNEMPLOYMENT and low pay (*see* MINIMUM WAGE). From February 1910 to October 1911 he was home secretary, in which role he gained a reputation for authorizing the use of troops against striking workers, and for enforcing more rigorously the practice of force-feeding militant SUFFRAGETTES who were on hunger strike in prison. In 1911 he became first lord of the Admiralty, in charge of the ROYAL NAVY, and fought for increased funding for warships as vigorously as he had opposed this when he had been a social reformer in 1908–9. When WORLD WAR I came, his interference in operational decisions in the navy caused tensions with the naval professionals. This came to a head when Churchill masterminded the disastrous GALLIPOLI campaign in 1915. This forced Asquith to form a coalition government with the Conservatives, who refused to work with Churchill. He resigned and served as a battalion commander on the Western Front.

In July 1917 Churchill was recalled by David LLOYD GEORGE – with whom he had worked closely in the Liberal Party before the war and who was now prime minister – to be minister of munitions, in which role he continued until January 1919. He was secretary for war and air until February 1921, and responsible for the peaceful demobilization of the armed forces and a drastic reduction in the size of the ROYAL AIR FORCE. He failed to persuade the cabinet to seek to overthrow the Bolshevik government in Russia. He then became colonial secretary, negotiating the treaty with IRELAND that brought the Irish Free State into being, until the fall of the coalition government in 1922 (*see* BALDWIN, STANLEY). He lost his parliamentary seat at Dundee in the election of 1922.

Churchill then began work on his history of World War I, the first volume of which was published in 1923, the last in 1931. During this period he reverted to support of the CONSERVATIVE PARTY and was elected as 'Constitutionalist' (then Conservative) MP for Epping in 1924. Baldwin appointed him CHANCELLOR OF THE EXCHEQUER, to the surprise of many. He remained in this post until the election of 1929, during which time he returned Britain to the GOLD STANDARD, in the budget of 1925, with almost certainly harmful consequences for already ailing British exports. He was prevented from running down the navy as drastically as he had the air force only by the threatened resignation of the entire Board of Admiralty; nevertheless the navy was severely cut. His robustly reactionary response to the GENERAL STRIKE in 1926 further reinforced the hostility of organized labour towards him.

After the fall of the Baldwin government in 1929 Churchill was out of office for more than ten years, during which time he was at odds with the Conservative leadership on a succession of issues. He resigned from the shadow cabinet in January 1931 because he opposed Baldwin's support for moves towards greater self-determination for INDIA, a cause that he continued to abhor. He supported EDWARD VIII in the ABDICATION CRISIS, admired Mussolini, and sympathized with Franco during the SPANISH CIVIL WAR. He spent little time in Westminster, devoting himself to travel, journalism and other writing, and building up his family fortune, which had suffered in the crash of 1929. He did, however, oppose Nazi Germany, APPEASEMENT and the MUNICH AGREEMENT – partly because he hoped to avert war by the formation of an international alliance to force Hitler to back down. At the outbreak of war Neville CHAMBERLAIN was forced to offer him a key post and he returned to the Admiralty.

When Chamberlain fell on 10 May 1940 Churchill succeeded him partly because Labour refused to join a coalition with his rival, Lord HALIFAX. Churchill proved an inspirational leader in WORLD WAR II. Despite making numerous mistakes, he brought many skills to the role, including his ability to boost the nation's morale with his oratory. Many Conservatives remained uneasy with him, however, and he had little interest in home affairs, leaving these to ATTLEE and other Labour ministers in the coalition; he even failed to recognize the importance of the BEVERIDGE Report of 1942. This was one reason why, to his astonishment, the electorate rejected him as a peacetime leader in July 1945, despite respecting his wartime role. This defeat was a great blow to Churchill, but he remained Conservative leader. He continued to take little interest in home affairs, which were left to others, such as R.A. BUTLER, while he concentrated on his role as world statesman. He opposed British withdrawal from EMPIRE, and he gave an early warning of the onset of the COLD WAR in a famous speech at Fulton, Missouri, USA, in March 1946, in which he coined the term 'Iron Curtain' for the division between Soviet-controlled Eastern Europe and the West – a division he had done much to plan in the later stages of the war (*see* YALTA). Churchill had already become a 'Cold War warrior' by the end of the war in Europe.

From October 1951 Churchill served a second term as prime minister, continuing to give most attention to international affairs. He was aged 77 in 1951, had suffered two strokes and would suffer two more. He retired from the premiership, unwillingly, on 5 April 1955, being succeeded by Anthony EDEN. He remained an MP until 1964, and died the following year. He had refused to retire to the House of Lords, but was knighted in 1953. He was given a state funeral.

FURTHER READING P. Addison, *Trust the People: Winston Churchill in Home Affairs 1900–1955* (1992); M. Gilbert, *Churchill: A Life* (1991); H. Pelling, *Winston Churchill* (2nd edn, 1989).

Church in Wales, Anglican church that came into being on 31 March 1920 as the result of a 1914 act of Parliament that 'disestablished' the CHURCH OF ENGLAND as the official church in Wales, though it retained this status in England. The four dioceses in Wales became a self-governing church within the Anglican communion. The bishop of St Asaph, Alfred George Edwards, became the first archbishop of Wales. Welsh bishops lost their right to sit in the House of LORDS. This change was an outcome of the early phase of Welsh nationalism (*see* HOME RULE) and of long-term pressure by the Liberal Party (*see* WALES). It also arose from the fact that by the beginning of the 20th century NONCONFORMIST religious groups, such as METHODISM and the Baptist Church, had more adherents in Wales than the Church of England. Following the Parliament Act, 1911, the necessary legislation could at last pass the House of Lords. The act marked the victory of the disestablishmentarians over antidisestablishmentarianism.

Church of England, the nationally established church of England throughout the century, and of Wales until 1920 (*see* CHURCH IN WALES). It is also known as the Anglican church. It had its origins in the 16th century and emerged as a hybrid between western Europe's two main ecclesiastical forms, Protestantism and Roman Catholicism, since it rejects papal jurisdiction but retains a clerical hierarchy of bishops and archbishops. The monarch is formally head (or 'supreme governor') of the church, though in practice the archbishop of Canterbury is the church's spiritual leader and heads its administration from his offices in Lambeth Palace, London. He is advised on church policy by a representative body established in 1919, known as the Church Assembly (*see* TEMPLE, WILLIAM), which was replaced in 1969 by the more powerful General Synod. This is composed of 53 bishops, 259 elected clergy and 258 elected lay members of the church. The church plays a highly visible role in state ceremonies, such as Remembrance Day (*see* HAIG, DOUGLAS), and the archbishop of Canterbury crowns each new monarch. The archbishops and 26 senior bishops had the right to sit and to vote in the House of LORDS to the end of the century, but clergy were banned from seeking election to the House of COMMONS. The church also controlled throughout the century a substantial network of state-funded primary and secondary schools.

The church is divided into two provinces, Canterbury and York, each headed by an archbishop, Canterbury (the 'primate of all England') taking precedence. Formally they are appointed by the monarch, though in practice this falls to the PRIME MINISTER, who acts through a patronage secretary. In 1977, as part of a wider process of granting the church a greater degree of self-government, a crown Appointments Commission was formed, in which the church was given a voice in composing a shortlist (of a maximum of two names). However, the prime minister still makes the final decision and need not observe the recommendations. Within the two provinces are 43 dioceses (bishoprics), in turn subdivided into archdeaconries (led by archdeacons), then deaneries (led by rural deans). The basic organizational unit is the parish, about 13,100 of which covered the whole of England at the end of the century. All have at least one parish church, administered by a priest, sometimes supported by a deacon or deaconess, though increasingly over the century such clergy ministered to more than one parish.

In 1992, after a long and sometimes bitter battle, it became possible for women to be ordained priests. Women had long served as deaconesses (487 did so in 1989). The decision to ordain women led a minority of Anglicans to transfer to the ROMAN CATHOLIC CHURCH, which was intransigently opposed to the ordination of women. By the end of the century there were no female Anglican bishops.

Over the century the church experienced a loss of influence, despite considerable (though not always efficiently administered) ownership of land, a certain amount of patronage, and close connections with elite institutions (such as public schools and some Oxford and Cambridge colleges). The church also experienced a significant decline in its membership, and in the numbers of men coming forward for ordination. Earlier in the century it was referred to as the 'Tory Party at prayer' in view of its associations. This was never wholly true, and during the century members of the church repeatedly challenged establishment orthodoxy. For example Robert Runcie (archbishop of Canterbury, 1980–91) disagreed publicly with Margaret THATCHER's triumphalism over the outcome of the FALKLANDS War. Defence policy was scrutinized critically in a publication, *The Church and the Bomb* (1982), and urban policy in *Faith in the City* (1985). Nevertheless, the church remained primarily identified with conservatism, and it lost popular support. Church statistics indicate that numbers of baptisms and confirmations dropped by more than half over the course of this century, though there is some evidence that this decline stabilized in the 1970s. Anglicanism declined from its position as the single largest religious denomination in England. In 1996 it was estimated to have 1.3 million practising members, while the Roman Catholic Church was estimated to have over 1.9 million. In 1930, 699 in every 1000 children born in England were baptized in the Church of England; in 1989 the number was 288. Church membership was slightly higher in the countryside than in the towns. However, as befitted its historic position as the national church, a substantial number of English people (estimated at around

40%) identified themselves as Anglicans, even if they did not practise. Despite the small number of people actively involved in the life of the church, it remained an important and visible body in national cultural and political life, and played an important social and pastoral role at local level.

Increasingly over the century the church drew much strength from its overseas organization. Of the 28 provinces comprised by the Anglican Communion worldwide, only two were in England itself. Most, though not all, were located throughout the former British EMPIRE. Globally, the church was estimated to have some 70 million members at the end of the century. Bishops from the entire Communion gather in England every ten years for the Lambeth Conferences, to discuss theological, social and cultural matters affecting the church throughout the world.

FURTHER READING R. Lloyd, *The Church of England 1900–1965* (1966); P.A. Welsby, *A History of the Church of England, 1945–1980* (1984).

Church of Scotland, the principal, and culturally highly influential, church in SCOTLAND since the Reformation. From 1559 it developed on Calvinistic, Presbyterian lines in fierce opposition to Anglican episcopalianism; in other words it was sternly opposed to the hierarchy of bishops and archbishops, ceremony and religious imagery, which were regarded as undesirable Roman Catholic residues in the CHURCH OF ENGLAND. In the 19th century it experienced a number of sectarian divisions, most notably the secession of many members in 1843 over the issue of patronage to form the Free Church of Scotland. These were largely reconciled following the Church of Scotland Act, 1921, which declared the church's spiritual freedom and diminished conflict over aspects of religious belief. It also declared that the Church of Scotland was the 'national state church' in Scotland, but not the 'established church'. A General Assembly was established composed equally of ministers and elders (lay members of the church chosen by local church members). Following the act, the Free Church of Scotland, which had joined the United Presbyterian Church to become the United Free Church in 1900, reunited with its parent body in 1929, although a rump of dissenters formed a new and strongly sabbatarian Free Church of Scotland, nicknamed the 'Wee Frees'. Moves to affiliate the main Church of Scotland with the Church of England were defeated in 1959 and 1971. Women were admitted to the eldership in 1966 and to the ministry in 1968. Membership was 662,000 in 1900, rising to 1.2 million in 1930 (largely due to the 1929 reunification) and remaining at that level until the 1960s, then falling to 680,000 in 1998.

cinema. *See* FILM INDUSTRY.

City of London, the pre-eminent world financial centre throughout the 20th century. At the beginning of the century it was the capital of international banking, with more overseas bank branches than any other city, and also the leading world centre for the issue of foreign loans and equities, with over 40% of the total exported capital of the world raised on its markets. British insurance companies were also spreading around the world, their dominance owing much to the unique role of Lloyd's, which dominated the world marine-insurance market. This financial supremacy was due to three factors above all: Britain's large share of world trade (14% in 1913); its possession of a worldwide EMPIRE; and the importance of the pound sterling in the functioning of the international GOLD STANDARD. The City had developed an efficient network of financial institutions: the clearing banks in 1913 held about two-thirds of deposit accounts in England and Wales and could supply credit, while the merchant banks financed world trade. The London Stock Exchange was the cheapest in the world for dealing in securities.

The City began to face competition from the United States during WORLD WAR I. Britain had to sell overseas investments to pay for the war and went off the gold standard; the dollar began to replace sterling as the means of payment for international trade. The City regained much, though not all, of its international position during the interwar years, building on its experience, and became increasingly involved with the home economy. Its prominence increased further in the 1960s and 1970s as it developed new markets and took advantage of US government restrictions that made London a more attractive centre in which to deposit dollars. In the 1970s and 1980s Britain had the highest share of international banking activity, holding 20% of the world's foreign assets, and was the principal market in foreign exchanges. The City also had strong international positions in various commodity markets, in insurance and in services such as accountancy, law and funds management. The difference from the position up to World War II was that few of these transactions took place in sterling and much of this activity was undertaken by foreign banks, of which there were still more branches in London than in any other centre. The London equities market was smaller in volume than its main rivals, New York, Frankfurt and Tokyo, but it was more international.

The City was also a unit of local government within London, with a tiny resident electorate. It was presided over by a lord mayor, chosen from among the banking elite. However, its significance in British culture and economy was as a financial centre. At the end of the century it was poised uncertainly between closer integration with European financial centres and a wider world role.

SEE ALSO BANK OF ENGLAND; BIG BANG.

FURTHER READING D. Kynaston, *The City of London, Vol. 2, 1890–1914* (1995); *Vol. 3, 1914–45* (1999); *Vol. 4, 1946–2000* (2001); H. McRae and F. Cairncross, *Capital City: London as a Financial Centre* (2nd edn, 1991); R.C. Michie, *The City of London: Continuity and Change since 1850* (1992).

civil list, the annuities payable to the sovereign and members of the royal family. The civil list is granted by Parliament upon the recommendation of a select committee. Specific sums are allocated to named members of the royal family. In 1981 Queen ELIZABETH II undertook to bear the cost of the civil list payment to three of her cousins (the duke of Kent, the duke of Gloucester and Princess Alexandra) by refunding to the exchequer the equivalent sum from her considerable private fortune. On 11 February 1993, as the royal family were facing increasing criticism and satire, it was announced that thereafter the queen would also refund civil-list payments to all other members of the royal family apart from the queen mother, the duke of Edinburgh and herself. It was also announced that the queen had agreed that her personal income from investments and other sources would henceforth be taxed.

The sum voted for the civil list was £385,000 in 1900. In 1931 it was reduced by £50,000 by order of King GEORGE V, in view of the economic crisis. It stood at £475,000 in 1952, £4,249,200 in 1981(of which the queen retained £3,964,200), and £10,420,000 in 1993 (of which she retained £8,900,000).

SEE ALSO MONARCHY.

civil service, the body of people directly employed by central government to enable it to carry out its functions and policies. Their numbers grew throughout the 20th century, as the functions of government grew, though this growth was disguised, at some times more than others, by the transfer or delegation of government work to non-governmental bodies – sometimes, as in the period of Margaret THATCHER's government, in order to cut direct government costs. The total size of the civil service in 1900 is not available. For 1 August 1914, the total is given as 779,520 staff. In 1938 it was 580,891, rising to 972,174 in 1950 and 996,274 in 1960. Thereafter the total fell, largely owing to the rundown of the 'industrial' civil service, such as workers in defence industries including the Royal Ordnance factories that manufactured ammunition.

The civil service was strictly hierarchical, recruiting separately to different grades, according to educational and vocational qualifications, with limited internal mobility between grades. At the beginning of the century the higher-status departments – the Treasury, the Home Office, above all the Foreign Office – were only slowly and reluctantly opening their higher ranks to 'open' competition, as distinct from the exercise of patronage by influential people that had previously been the normal method of recruitment; but it was still open mainly to men from elite universities, primarily Oxford and Cambridge. Women were only slowly admitted to the lower and middle ranks of some ministries and until World War II they were obliged to leave on marriage. The first woman to be appointed head of a department was Dame Evelyn Sharp (1903–85), who became permanent secretary at the ministry of housing and local government in 1955. Between 1955 and the end of the century only seven women were appointed to equivalent positions, mostly in social-service ministries.

There was, especially in the 1980s, a further reduction in the numbers of official civil servants, as government functions were dispersed, where possible, to semi-autonomous agencies managing themselves outside the main civil-service structure (so saving the government the very considerable costs of paying the pensions to which established civil servants were entitled). The main moves in this direction followed the recommendations of a report into civil-service reform, commissioned by Prime Minister Margaret Thatcher in 1987 and published in 1988, *Improving Management in Government: The Next Steps* (the Ibbs Report). Its recommendations were embodied in the Government Trading Act, 1990. The total number of civil servants, on the old definition, was 704,903 in 1980, 562,388 in 1990 and 494,173 in 1998. In 1998, 383,290 civil servants were working in 'Next Steps' agencies, as they were referred to. These included workers in the Passport Agency and the Office for National Statistics, among many others.

Strong doubts were expressed as to whether the changes increased the efficiency of the government service.

The civil service had for much of the century a deeply entrenched tradition of neutrality between political parties: civil servants remained in office as governments changed and gave politically neutral advice. There were suggestions that this began to change in the 1980s as more overtly political appointments, promotions and dismissals were alleged to have been made. The service was also criticized – increasingly so from the 1960s – for the limited range of experience on which it drew, especially at its more senior levels, where incumbents were still overwhelmingly male, white and products of a limited range of elite schools and universities. It was assumed that higher civil servants required no specialized training – indeed it was a matter of pride that they were talented 'generalists' rather than specialists. This concept had been especially encouraged by Sir Warren FISHER, permanent secretary at the Treasury and head of the civil service during its period of rapid expansion in the interwar years. It was the practice to move them at regular intervals among ministries requiring different bodies of knowledge. The Plowden Committee on the civil service reported in 1961 that the Treasury had no adequate system for forecasting or controlling expenditure. The Fulton Committee in 1968 was more comprehensively critical, calling for specialist expertise in the civil service related to contemporary needs (for example, in economics and science) and for more movement between the civil service and other occupations, such as industry. As one result the Civil Service College was established in 1970 in order to provide further training, as required, for senior civil servants.

Increasingly from the 1970s, ministers appointed 'special' or 'political' advisers from outside the civil service to supplement, or counterbalance, official advice. During the Conservative administration of 1970–4 some ministers had such advisers, paid from party funds. When Harold

WILSON's Labour government came to power in 1974 it was agreed that any cabinet minister could appoint two advisers for the term of her or his period of office. In 1979 Margaret Thatcher limited ministers to one adviser, except for the most powerful ministries: the Treasury, the Home Office, the Foreign Office and the Department of the Environment. In May 1997 the incoming Labour government agreed that each cabinet minister could have two advisers, and there was a significant increase in the number employed in the prime minister's office; two of the latter (Alastair Campbell and Jonathan Powell) were dispensed from the previous rule that special advisers had no authority over civil servants.

FURTHER READING D.N. Chester and F.M.G. Wilson, *The Organization of British Central Government 1914–56* (1960); E.W. Cohen, *The Growth of the British Civil Service 1780–1939* (1941); G.K. Fry, *Statesmen in Disguise. The Changing Role of the Administrating Class of the British Home Civil Service, 1853–1966* (1969); G.K. Fry, *Reforming the Civil Service: The Fulton Commission on the British Home Civil Service* (1993); R. Pyper, *The British Civil Service* (1995).

Clark, Kenneth (Mackenzie) (1903–83), art historian. Born to a family who had made a considerable fortune from manufacturing cotton thread, he had a neglected childhood and an undistinguished career at Winchester School and Oxford University. He then spent two years apprenticed to Bernard Berenson, the art historian and collector, and entered a career in the world of fine art. In 1931 he was appointed keeper of the Ashmolean Museum, Oxford, then, again at a remarkably young age, in 1934 became director of the National Gallery, London, where he remained until 1946, at the same time holding the position of surveyor of the king's pictures (until 1944). At the National Gallery he greatly improved the hanging, lighting and decoration, and made some notable acquisitions, though he was unpopular with staff. During World War II the collection was evacuated to North Wales, but one great picture was returned to London each week during the BLITZ, to console the public who attended free lunchtime concerts in the galleries. Clark also worked during the war in the film division of the Ministry of Information. After resigning from the National Gallery, Clark became Slade professor of fine art at Oxford (1946–50), chairman of the ARTS COUNCIL (1953–60) and chairman (1954–7) of the new Independent Television Authority (ITA; *see* BRITISH BROADCASTING CORPORATION). He was also at various times a trustee of the British Museum, member of the Advisory Council of the Victoria and Albert Museum, and vice chairman of the Royal Opera House and of the National Theatre.

After resigning from the ITA he embarked upon a career as a television performer, successfully popularizing great art, most notably in the 13-part series *Civilization*, first shown by the BBC in 1969 and often repeated (which suggests a different side to the SIXTIES from the popular one). He wrote a number of books, also characterized by a talent for high-quality popularization, notably *Landscape into Art* (1949) and *The Nude* (1956). He assembled a fine personal art collection and was a key patron of such modern British artists as Victor PASMORE, Graham SUTHERLAND, John Piper and Henry MOORE.

He was knighted in 1938, made a companion of honour in 1959, received a life peerage in 1969 and the Order of Merit in 1976. His son, Alan Clark (1928–99), became a colourful Conservative politician, remembered for the indiscretions of his published diaries.

FURTHER READING K. Clark, *Another Part of the Wood: A Self-Portrait* (1974); K. Clark, *The Other Half: A Self-Portrait* (1977); M. Secrest, *Kenneth Clark: A Biography* (1984).

class. *See* SOCIAL CLASS.

Clause Four. Clause Four, Section Four of the 'Party Objects' section of the LABOUR PARTY's constitution, adopted in 1918, committed the party 'To secure for the workers by hand or by brain the full fruits of their industry, and the most equitable distribution thereof that may be possible, upon the basis of the common ownership of the means of production, [distribution and exchange] and the best obtainable system of popular administration and control of each industry or service.'

The phrase 'distribution and exchange' was added by the 1929 Labour Party conference, acknowledging that production was not the only important activity of the economy. The clause was drafted by Sidney WEBB, a leading FABIAN and party intellectual, and Arthur HENDERSON, the party secretary. It caused less controversy when it was first drafted than later, when it came to symbolize, to some, the party's commitment to wholesale NATIONALIZATION. In fact, it was deliberately phrased in such general terms as to be capable of a variety of interpretations, and was chiefly intended to signal the party's openness to a variety of views and to people of a variety of backgrounds, hence the reference to workers 'by brain' as well as 'by hand'.

Controversy over Clause Four erupted in the 1950s, when there were divisions in the party about how far nationalization should be taken. In 1959 Hugh GAITSKELL, then party leader, attempted to amend the clause on the grounds that it was a source of misunderstanding and of electoral unpopularity. He was forced to withdraw by opponents at the 1960 party conference.

When Tony BLAIR became party leader in 1994 he aimed to amend the clause on the grounds that Labour had long, in practice, been committed to a mixed economy and the clause had become anachronistic. Following a ballot of all party members in 1995 a special party conference voted to amend Clause Four to read: 'The Labour Party is a democratic socialist party. It believes that by the strength of our common endeavour we achieve more than we achieve alone, so as to create for each of us the means to realize our true potential and for all of us a community in which power, wealth and opportunity are in the hands of the many not the few, where the rights we enjoy reflect the duties we owe, and where we live together freely, in a spirit of solidarity, tolerance and respect.'

FURTHER READING K. Jefferys, *Leading Labour. From Keir Hardie to Tony Blair* (1999); R. McKibbin, *The Evolution of the Labour Party 1910–24* (1974); P. Williams, *Hugh Gaitskell: A Political Biography* (1979).

Clean Air Act (1956), the first effective legislation to prevent or reduce air pollution. The act arose from the increasing incidence of severe 'fogs' in urban areas, and recognition that they caused deaths. It came to be realized that these were not normal fogs. The term 'smog' was invented to convey the phenomenon in which normal fog (water vapour) was mixed – to lethal effect – with unhealthy smoke emissions from coal fires, both industrial and domestic, and from steam railway engines. A smog in London that lasted from 26 November until 1 December 1948 was accompanied by a death rate 20–30% higher than in the preceding four weeks (about 700–800 additional deaths). Such smogs continued through the early 1950s, securing especial publicity when they occurred in London. Medical experts commented on the association with death and illness, especially following the London smog of 5–9 December 1952, which was responsible for about 4000 deaths, probably the worst smog the country had experienced.

Government response was slow, partly because it took time to gather evidence of the effects of the smog. Harold MACMILLAN, the minister responsible as minister for housing and local government, refused for six months to hold an inquiry, then, under mounting pressure in the press and in Parliament, agreed to do so in May 1953. The inquiry was chaired by Sir Hugh Beaver, managing director of Guinness, and included a range of experts. It reported in November 1954. It unanimously recommended 'smokeless zones' and financial assistance to enable house owners to comply. The government was pushed into action by one of its own backbenchers, Gerald Nabarro, who had been campaigning on the issue and who was successful in the annual Commons ballot to introduce a private member's bill. He chose to introduce a measure incorporating all the Beaver recommendations. He withdrew the bill when the government agreed to introduce its own legislation. It did so in good time for the election of 1955 and it passed into law in 1956, dispelling smog and much reducing the grime of inner cities – which in turn encouraged many middle-class people to return to and 'gentrify' parts of inner cities, London in particular. Although coal smoke was no longer a problem, the increase in vehicle exhaust emissions towards the end of the century led to the return of smogs in large cities from time to time.

FURTHER READING P. Hall et al., *Change, Choice and Conflict in Social Policy* (1975), 371–409.

Cliveden set, term applied in the 1930s to the group of friends around the Conservative MP Nancy ASTOR and her husband Waldorf, Viscount Astor, who met at the Astor's Buckinghamshire country house, Cliveden. The term was coined by the left-wing journalist, Claud Cockburn, who asserted that the policy of APPEASEMENT, which he strongly opposed, was devised at house parties at Cliveden. The facts that Waldorf Astor owned the *Observer* newspaper and his brother controlled *The Times* and that the Astors did hold regular house parties for politically influential people made it plausible that important political matters were decided there. However, although the Astors supported appeasement, there is no evidence to support Cockburn's accusations. The set was also known as 'God's Truth Ltd', and LLOYD GEORGE spoke of 'a very powerful combination – in its way perhaps the most powerful in the country'.

FURTHER READING N. Rose, *The Cliveden Set: Portrait of an Exclusive Fraternity* (2000).

CND. *See* CAMPAIGN FOR NUCLEAR DISARMAMENT.

coal miners' strikes. *See* MINERS' STRIKES.

coal mining. In the 19th century coal mining was central to Britain's industrialization, and coal was its main source of fuel and power. By the time of WORLD WAR I it accounted for one-third of British exports and employed almost 10% of the male labour force. There were some 3000 coal-mining firms, many of them small. Miners were strongly organized in TRADE UNIONS and engaged in a number of strikes in the years before the war. The outcome of one such strike was the introduction in 1912 of a MINIMUM WAGE in the industry. During the war, labour, wages and prices in this as in other industries came under government control.

After the war the miners pressed for improved wages and conditions, resulting in the SANKEY COMMISSION (1919). However, the industry suffered from the decline in world trade and increased foreign competition, many firms finding it difficult to compete because of outdated equipment. They had limited resources with which to invest for improvement; wage costs were relatively high, and relations between employers and workers poor. The industry suffered especially from the Depression: there was widespread UNEMPLOYMENT and industrial unrest as employers sought to resolve the problems by reducing wages and increasing hours of work. The miners went on strike, and there was a short-lived GENERAL STRIKE (May 1926) in support of the miners' demands. The miners remained on strike for six months after the General Strike collapsed, but were ultimately defeated and accepted wage cuts. The crisis continued throughout the 1920s, unemployment reaching a peak in 1929–32, at 40–60% in some districts. There was a small recovery in the 1930s, assisted by rearmament and by government assistance, encouraging the rationalization of the industry by mergers among firms.

During WORLD WAR II coal was essential to the war effort, and it received both government support and control. The underlying problems of the industry remained after the war and in 1946 the coal mines were nationalized by the Labour government (*see* NATIONALIZATION) with little opposition. It was widely believed that this was the only means to reconstruct this vital industry, which came under the control of a public corporation, the National Coal Board (NCB). Massive investment and organizational changes streamlined the industry and increased productivity, but the large scale and monolithic structure of the NCB meant that, in contrast to the previous situation, the industry could be too unwieldy for efficiency. More importantly, coal faced competition from cheaper alternative fuels, especially oil, used to run heating systems, transport and machinery. Again the industry went into decline. Industrial relations deteriorated once more, as miners felt their jobs threatened. There were major strikes in 1972 and 1974, the latter playing a role in bringing down Edward HEATH's Conservative government (*see* MINERS' STRIKES).

This increased the determination of the next Conservative government, elected in 1979 and led by Margaret THATCHER, to reduce the power of the miners' union and the size of the industry, which seemed excessive in relation to the demand for coal. This led to the major, violent miners' strike of 1984–5. The miners claimed that the government was determined to close large numbers of mines. The government denied this, though later events seemed to justify it. The miners were defeated owing to a number of factors: the government's careful advance planning, including stockpiling of coal; the reduced importance of coal to the economy; and the refusal of a large number of miners to join the strike. By the end of the 1980s the number of miners had fallen by 50%, but productivity improved and output remained the same. The industry continued to decline, without support from government. By 1994 it was reduced to about a dozen mines and 10,000 miners, and it was mainly privately owned.

FURTHER READING B. Supple, *The History of the British Coal Industry, Vol. 4, 1913–1946* (1987); W. Ashworth, *The History of the British Coal Industry, Vol. 5, 1946–1982* (1986).

Cod War (1972–6), period of increased tension between Britain and Iceland, prompted by the latter's extension of its fishing limit to 80 km (50 miles) in 1972. Clashes between Icelandic gunboats and British trawlers brought about the intervention of ROYAL NAVY frigates to protect the fishing vessels. The 'Cod War' ended in 1976 when a compromise was struck allowing a limited number of British trawlers in Icelandic waters.

Cold War, period of diplomatic and ideological tension between the West and the Soviet bloc (more specifically, the USA and the USSR) between the late 1940s and 1991. It was characterized by an arms race between the superpowers and the threat of nuclear war, particularly during the Cuban missile crisis of 1962.

Historians are divided in their assessment of Britain's role in the initial stages of the Cold War. Some have suggested that, as a second-class power and American ally, Britain did not have any significant role to play. Others have suggested that Britain neglected to seize the opportunity to serve as a bridge between the USA and the USSR, or to lead a united Europe as a 'third force' that might have come to match the superpowers. These possibilities, it is posited, were abandoned in the 1940s so that Britain could continue to receive American financial aid (via the MARSHALL PLAN) as well as military protection against the Soviet threat. This then enabled Britain to rebuild its own economy, shattered by WORLD WAR II, and turn more attention to the doomed task of trying to sustain its EMPIRE.

In 1945, Britain was still recognized as a force to be reckoned with, as witnessed by Winston CHURCHILL's participation in the 'Big Three' conferences along with Franklin D. Roosevelt and Joseph Stalin (*see* YALTA). It was Churchill who most famously brought attention to the Cold War in March 1946 when, during a speech given in the USA, he referred to an 'Iron Curtain' descending across Europe, dividing East from West. He also called for an Anglo-American alliance against the forces of Soviet communism. In 1948–9 Britain played a key role in the BERLIN AIRLIFT, an episode that marked the rapid freezing of relations with Eastern Europe, which was now largely controlled by the communist USSR. Britain was among the original member states of NATO, formed in 1949. With the creation of NATO, America committed itself to the security of Western Europe against the perceived Soviet threat. Britain at this time still hoped to play a prominent role, developing its own NUCLEAR WEAPONS programme while also providing America with a base for military operations in Europe. British scientists had been involved in the development of the atom bombs dropped on Japan in 1945, and into the 1950s Britain continued to develop its own project to build a hydrogen bomb and thus establish itself as a nuclear power. In 1963 Britain, along with the USA and USSR, signed the Nuclear Test Ban treaty. This was a direct result of the Cuban missile crisis which had threatened to bring the USA and USSR to the brink of nuclear war. However, by this time the nuclear programmes of the superpowers had been developed to such a degree that it was obvious that Britain could no longer compete.

In 1954 Britain had signed the treaty that established the South East Asia Treaty Organization (SEATO), with Australia, France, New Zealand, Pakistan, the Philippines, Thailand and the USA. It provided for collective action if any of the signatories should be attacked or should be weakened by internal subversion. Britain, however, like France, evaded any long-term commitments under this treaty. In 1955 Britain also joined the Central Treaty Organization (CENTO), an alliance with the USA, Iran, Turkey, Pakistan and Iraq, which, among other things, sought to defuse tension between India and Pakistan over Kashmir, and in the 1960s between Greece and Turkey over CYPRUS. By the 1950s it had become apparent that the USA and the USSR were now the world's great powers, and Britain had been relegated to a distinct second-power status. This was most visibly and embarrassingly demonstrated by the SUEZ debacle of 1956. In the end, any role that Britain played in the Cold War was to support America, as a member of NATO. Its obligations towards the latter included the supply and maintenance of troops in mainland Europe, primarily in northern West Germany. British soldiers were sent to fight in the KOREAN WAR of 1950–3 against the communist threat there. The British also suppressed a communist-led rebellion in MALAYA – the so-called 'Malayan Emergency'. However, it did not send troops to fight alongside the USA in the Vietnam War in the 1960s, probably in contravention of its SEATO obligations, though British military advisers, drawing in particular on their experience in Malaya, did give considerable assistance to their US allies in Vietnam.

Even as the Vietnam War continued, the period 1969–71 witnessed the negotiation of détente (relaxation of tension) between the superpowers. This was brought on, above all, by the emergence of China as the third world superpower, a rival to the USSR in the communist world, and a potential ally of the USA against the USSR if that should turn out to be in its own interests. This new configuration of power rendered violent international conflict too great a risk for any of the powers. What followed was a lengthy, heavily armed truce, in the course of which further US nuclear forces were positioned in Britain. Although the Cold War ended in 1991, after the demise of the communist regimes of Eastern Europe, the reunification of Germany and the collapse of the Soviet Union itself, Britain continued to ally itself with America and NATO, as witnessed by its staunch support during the 1991 GULF WAR and the 1999 conflict in KOSOVO.

FURTHER READING D. Reynolds, *One World Divided. A Global History since 1945* (2000); J.W. Young, *The Longman Companion to Cold War and Détente, 1941–91* (1993).

Collins, Michael (1890–1922), Irish nationalist leader. Born in County Cork, Collins was the son of a farmer. He worked in London as a postal clerk and bank cashier before returning to IRELAND as an active nationalist, and assisted in organizing the EASTER RISING (1916). He was imprisoned for short terms in 1916 and 1918. He was a leading military figure in the IRISH REPUBLICAN ARMY in the war of independence against the British from 1919. As a member of the first Dáil Eireann (Irish parliament) he went as a delegate to the Anglo-Irish Conference in London in 1921, which gave southern Ireland dominion status in the COMMONWEALTH as the Irish Free State. Collins became chairman of the provisional government of the Free State in January 1922. A civil war, however, was initiated by dissident anti-treaty Republicans, one of whose groups assassinated him in August 1922.

Commission for Racial Equality. *See* IMMIGRATION.

Committee on Finance and Industry. *See* MACMILLAN COMMITTEE ON FINANCE AND INDUSTRY.

Committee on National Expenditure. *See* MAY COMMITTEE ON NATIONAL EXPENDITURE.

Common Agricultural Policy. *See* AGRICULTURE.

Common Market. *See* EUROPEAN ECONOMIC COMMUNITY.

Commons, House of, the lower house of the UK Parliament. In the 20th century, in contrast to previous centuries, the House of Commons, rather than the House of Lords, was the dominant body through which legislation had to pass. This was particularly so following the Parliament Act, 1911, which reduced the powers of the Lords (*see* LORDS, HOUSE OF). In 1912 there was a further significant reform, when members of Parliament (MPs) were paid for the first time, opening up politics to those without a private income or sponsorship from any other source.

Unlike the Lords, the Commons is wholly elected, although GENERAL ELECTIONS were not fully democratic until 1928, when all women gained the right to vote at age 21 (*see* EQUAL FRANCHISE ACT), a right gained by only some women but all men in 1918 (*see* REPRESENTATION OF THE PEOPLE ACT). Until the REPRESENTATION OF THE PEOPLE ACT of 1948 certain university graduates had two votes, one for their home constituency, one for a university seat. By the 1969 Representation of the People Act, the voting age was lowered to 18.

There were 670 MPs in 1900. This fell to 615 following the formation of the Irish Free State in 1922, which removed Irish members from Westminster, other than those from NORTHERN IRELAND. The number rose to 640 in 1945, and was 659 by the end of the century.

The major function of the Commons is to debate, amend and pass legislation. Debates are chaired by the speaker, who is deemed to be neutral in party politics for the period of his or her office. The bulk of legislation is initiated by the leadership of the government of the day rather than by rank-and-file members (known as 'backbenchers', because they sit behind the 'front benches' on which the leading members of the main parties sit and face one another across the floor of the House).

The increasing control of the parties over members' voting, exercised through the WHIPS, has further diminished the independent power of MPs. An annual ballot selects a small number of backbenchers to put forward their own 'private member's bills', which are allotted ten days for discussion. But any bills that would increase public expenditure must obtain government backing and, in reality, private member's bills have little chance of success without government support. The influence of backbenchers over the government of the day is greatest when the government majority is small. When it is large their power is extremely limited.

From the 1960s backbenchers sought to increase their influence through the extension of the long-established system of select committees.

Originally these were set up on an ad hoc basis to deal with specific issues or pieces of legislation. Following reforms introduced by Richard CROSS-MAN in 1966, select committees were appointed for a whole parliamentary session to consider a particular subject area (e.g. race relations and immigration) or a department (e.g. education and science). In 1979 a new structure of select committees was introduced to cover the work of each major department. Their membership is proportionate to party representation in the Commons. They can investigate widely within their area of interest and have the power to summon persons, papers or records as required, sometimes to the embarrassment of governments. They have increased the knowledge and power of backbenchers and have become the chief means by which ministers are made accountable, especially in view of the publicity given to their reports.

Since 1945 the Commons has sat for about 37 weeks each year, normally with breaks of about three weeks at Christmas, one week at Easter and one week in late May, with a summer break from late July until mid-October. The working period was somewhat shorter earlier in the century. The working day in the Commons has also varied: in 1902 the House met from 2 p.m. until 11.30 p.m., but in 1906 this was changed to 2.45 p.m. to 11.30 p.m., to allow more time for lunch. From 1945 the normal hours of sitting became 2.30 p.m. until 10.30 p.m. on every weekday except Friday, although the House may sit much later, even throughout the night if there is urgent business or if members choose to prolong debate for tactical reasons. There have been recurrent complaints about the working hours, most strenuously at the end of the century from some of the exceptionally large number of younger women who were elected as Labour members in 1997, some of them mothers of young children, who could see no good reason why Parliament could not work similar hours to the bulk of the electorate. They received little sympathy, though there were sporadic attempts to tinker with the hours of work. In 1967 there was a short-lived experiment with morning sittings on two days each week. In 1997 the Commons began to meet on Wednesdays at 9.30 a.m. and in 1999 on Thursdays from 11.30 a.m. to 7.30 p.m. In November 1999 experimental sittings began in Westminster Hall to provide extra time for debates and for discussion of select committee reports.

FURTHER READING D. and G. Butler, *Twentieth-Century British Political Facts 1900–2000* (2000), 185–232.

Commonwealth of Nations, a loose federation of states whose sole common characteristic is that they were once colonies of the British EMPIRE. (An exception is Mozambique, formerly a Portuguese colony, which was admitted to the Commonwealth in November 1995 as a 'unique and special case' with the backing of its Commonwealth neighbours, including SOUTH AFRICA.) All member states accept that the British monarch is the symbolic head of the Commonwealth, but not all recognize the monarch as their own head of state, as some member states are republics.

The term 'Commonwealth' first appeared in this context in the late 19th century, but was later more widely used to refer to the 'white' dominions in their newly evolved and more egalitarian relationship with Britain. The IMPERIAL CONFERENCE of 1926 had defined the nature of dominions as 'autonomous communities within the British Empire, equal in status and freely associated as members of the British Commonwealth of Nations'. In 1931 those so recognized – CANADA, Newfoundland, AUSTRALIA, NEW ZEALAND, the Irish Free State (*see* IRELAND) and SOUTH AFRICA – were granted legislative autonomy under the terms of the Statute of Westminster. However, the admission of the newly independent republics of INDIA and Pakistan – as non-white former colonies – to the Commonwealth (no longer termed 'British') in 1947 set the tone for the Commonwealth's future growth and qualifications for admission.

Early supporters of the Commonwealth had

many hopes and plans for it, many of which never came to fruition. Some hoped that the metamorphosis of the old empire into the Commonwealth would help Britain regain some of its former global power and influence. But many members were very protective of their hard-won independence and had no desire to assist Britain in this way. The scheme of IMPERIAL PREFERENCE, which was put into place in the 1930s, was touted as a partial solution to Britain's economic problems, but proved a stumbling block in the post-war world where the United States held financial sway; all imperial trade preferences were of necessity dropped by 1973 when Britain joined the EUROPEAN ECONOMIC COMMUNITY. Historians have suggested that the unrealized faith of some influential British people in the potential of the Commonwealth may have helped contribute to Britain's fractious relationship with Europe in the 1960s and after. It had been hoped that the Commonwealth would serve Britain's interests, but in practice member states were far more interested in pursuing their own agendas and finding out what the Commonwealth could do for them.

The Commonwealth has thus evolved into a somewhat different organization from that which many of its early proponents envisioned. The Commonwealth Secretariat was established in London in 1965 to facilitate political, economic and cultural cooperation among the member states, with a good many other institutions undertaking special Commonwealth projects. Perhaps the most visible manifestations of the Commonwealth at the end of the 20th century were the biennial conferences, during which all Commonwealth leaders gather to discuss issues of mutual interest, and the Commonwealth Games, which are held every four years and provide young athletes with valuable competition experience while training for other sporting events such as the Olympic Games.

At the end of the century the Commonwealth had some fifty member states located all over the globe. Almost all of Britain's former colonies were

members. There were some notable exceptions, however, such as the United States. BURMA (Myanmar) never joined, though it was offered membership. Nigeria was suspended from 1995 to 1999, following serious human-rights violations by its government. Other nations left and then rejoined: for example, Fiji left in 1987 but returned in 1997; and Pakistan withdrew in 1972 in protest at the recognition of Bangladesh (formerly East Pakistan), but rejoined in 1989. Most famously, South Africa was forced out in 1961 because of its apartheid policy, and for a number of years the Commonwealth became an important site of anti-apartheid lobbying. Following its first fully democratic elections South Africa was welcomed back in 1994. Interestingly, the Republic of Ireland, which left the Commonwealth when it became a republic in 1949, began to consider rejoining in 1998, perhaps a testimony to the Commonwealth's appeal as a loose-knit, diverse and modern organization.

FURTHER READING M. Beloff, *Dream of Commonwealth 1921–42*, Vol. 2 of *Imperial Sunset* (1989); N. Mansergh, *The Commonwealth Experience* (2nd edn, 1982).

Common Wealth Party, short-lived moderately left-of-centre party formed in 1942. It was a merger of the Forward March movement founded by Sir Richard Acland, then Liberal MP for Barnstaple, Devon, and the 1941 Committee established by the playwright J.B. Priestley. It was formed as a protest against the wartime electoral truce whereby the established political parties did not oppose each other in by-elections because they had formed a coalition government for the duration of the war. The leaders of the new party argued that fundamental political differences did not disappear in wartime. Common Wealth was an idealistic, moderate, socialist grouping, strongly middle class in composition. Its main themes were common ownership and active, participatory democracy, both of which had been important causes for interwar liberals. Its immediate aim was to contest all by-elections in which a candidate unsympathetic to such ideals (i.e. most Conservatives) was not opposed by a Labour, Liberal or other 'progressive' candidate. It won three seats, all from Conservatives, between 1943 and 1945. In 1943 the Labour Party refused an application from Common Wealth to affiliate to it, and members of the Labour Party were forbidden to join Common Wealth. In the general election of 1945, Common Wealth put up 23 candidates, but were only successful in Chelmsford, where there was no Labour candidate. The victor, E. Millington, then joined the Labour Party, as did Acland as soon as the 1945 election results were known. He called for the party to dissolve and for members to become individual members of the Labour Party.

communications. Technological innovations in the 19th century had laid the foundations for the sweeping changes in communications media that were to occur over the course of the 20th century. By 1900 the telegraph was already established as an important form of long-distance communication. The first major 20th-century development was wireless telegraphy (sending Morse-code messages via radio waves), dramatically publicized in 1901 when Guglielmo Marconi sent the first transatlantic message via wireless telegraph. Even more dramatic was the use in 1910 of the wireless telegraph to apprehend the poisoner Dr Crippen as he attempted to escape to Canada by ship.

Radio technology capable of transmitting and receiving speech and other sounds resulted in an even more significant development following World War I, which had seen a rapid expansion in the use of communications technology. Wartime developments in radio transmitters and receivers meant that, by the 1920s, the 'broadcast' of a single message to a mass audience – which had developed through mass-circulation newspapers, the theatre and cinema – was brought, potentially, into every home. State control over wireless communications in Britain was established through the licensing of wireless telegraphy and radio transmission. The

General Post Office (GPO) had a virtual monopoly over telegraph communications from the late 19th century, and radio was monopolized for decades by the British Broadcasting Corporation, established in 1922. By the 1930s the broadcast of moving pictures as well as sound had become possible, but it was not until after World War II that television was available to a wide audience. The arrival of television further established the power of mass communications, and was exploited by an increasingly powerful and sophisticated advertising industry in the second half of the century. (For further details about radio and television, *see* BRITISH BROADCASTING CORPORATION.)

In addition to the development of mass media, the 20th century also saw huge changes in personal communications. By World War I the GPO had a monopoly over telephone operation in the UK, and responsibility for telecommunications within Britain remained with the GPO until 1969, when the WILSON government introduced a Post Office Act that created a separate telecommunications division within the nationalized Post Office. In 1981 a separate corporation, British Telecommunications, was established, and the 1984 Telecommunications Act provided for the privatization of the company – the first major privatization of the THATCHER government. Further government shares in the company were sold in 1991 and 1993. By the end of the century, conventional communications were challenged by the rapid spread of the mobile (cellular) phone, and the whole telecommunications industry had been opened up to competition.

The telephone system, still relatively undeveloped at the turn of the century, expanded rapidly after World War II when it became possible to send voice signals over extremely long distances by cable. The first transatlantic telephone cables came into service in the mid-1950s, followed by a gradual upgrading of the telegraph system that had linked the British EMPIRE since the late 19th century. British dominance of an international cable system based upon the old imperial network prompted the USA to develop a rival system of satellite communications. Although satellites were unable to compete with cables, particularly after the introduction in the 1980s of fibre-optic cables capable of carrying tens of thousands of simultaneous telephone calls, they did form the foundation of the network of global satellite television broadcasters (such as Rupert Murdoch's BSkyB) that would challenge the dominance of the existing terrestrial television networks in the last decade of the century.

What many regarded as the most significant development in the area of communications networks in the late 20th century was the Internet, a series of interconnected computer networks. The development of computers, stimulated by the needs of the military during World War II and after, followed by the introduction of the integrated circuit ('silicon chip') in the 1970s, meant that by the 1980s small 'personal computers' were available for domestic use, although their relatively high cost made them a mainly middle-class possession. The development of computer networks began in the USA in the 1970s with the establishment of the ARPANET, a project sponsored by the US Department of Defense. The opening-up of computer networks to commercial use in the 1980s and the establishment of the World Wide Web in the early 1990s brought electronic communications into the home.

FURTHER READING B. Winston, *Media Technology and Society – A History: From the Telegraph to the Internet* (1998).

Communist Party of Great Britain (CPGB),

left-wing political party founded in 1920 in the aftermath of the 1917 October Revolution in Russia by a small group of British workers and intellectuals who considered themselves the advance guard of the proletarian revolution. They aimed to affiliate to the LABOUR PARTY, but were refused; after 1924 dual membership of the two parties was banned by the Labour Party.

The CPGB was affiliated to the Communist International (Comintern), whose policies and activities were largely dictated by Moscow. It remained small, with a high turnover of members, and was marginal to British politics. It was critical of Parliament as an institution, although it ran a small number of candidates in elections, with only occasional success. It was active in the unemployed workers' movement of the interwar years (*see* HUNGER MARCHES; UNEMPLOYMENT), but was less influential than it sometimes claimed. It was most influential in certain TRADE UNIONS, especially in the 1930s and particularly among the miners, and in a few districts such as Clydeside. The role of communists in the opposition to Franco in the SPANISH CIVIL WAR and also in the broad anti-fascist cause (*see* POPULAR FRONT) attracted many intellectuals, including scientists and literary figures – although many such people were only briefly members, in their youth. The Hitler–Stalin pact of 23 August 1939 was a shock to many anti-fascist communists, and the party lost some of its 18,000 members. Some of the remainder took a pacifist stance. When Germany attacked the Soviet Union in June 1941 and Britain and the USSR became allies, the CPGB became a keen supporter of the war. It benefited from popular admiration in Britain of the Soviet Union's war effort, and following the German defeat at Stalingrad membership rose, briefly, to a peak of 100,000. Two Communist Party candidates were successful in the 1945 GENERAL ELECTION, but no others were elected in any Westminster election to the end of the century. As the COLD WAR became established, the CPGB supported the USSR unwaveringly and became even less popular, though it remained influential in a few trade unions, notably the electricians' union and the National Union of Mineworkers. The Soviet invasion of Hungary (1956) and the revelation at the 20th Congress of the Communist Party of the Soviet Union (also in 1956) of the atrocities committed under the leadership of Joseph Stalin (who had died in 1953) caused general hostility and a number of high-profile defections from the CPGB, which never recovered such support as it had had. Its membership declined from 34,000 in 1964 to under 20,000 in 1977. Young people preferred to join other, mainly Trotskyite, left-wing parties (*see* MILITANT). The CPGB tried several times to reinvent itself in the 1970s and 1980s, but continued to shrink. It retained a public profile through its theoretical journal, *Marxism Today*, which acquired a certain vogue in the 1980s among intellectuals hostile to THATCHERism and despairing of the Labour Party. The CPGB retained some prestige from the high public profiles of certain intellectuals (such as the historian Eric Hobsbawm) and trade unionists (such as Mick McGahey of the miners). In 1990 it decided to drop Marxism-Leninism in favour of democratic socialism. The collapse of the Soviet Union in 1991 led the remnants of the party to adopt the new name of Democratic Left.

FURTHER READING G. Andrews, N. Fishman and K. Morgan, *Essays on the Social and Cultural History of British Communism* (1995); N. Branson, *History of the Communist Party of Great Britain 1927–1941* (1985); D. Childs, 'The Cold War and the "British Road" 1946–53' in *Journal of Contemporary History*, Vol. 12 (1977), 237–53.

community charge, LOCAL GOVERNMENT tax, popularly and pejoratively known as the 'poll tax' throughout its short history. The community charge was introduced by act of Parliament in 1988 for implementation in 1990 (1989 in Scotland) by the Conservative government led by Margaret THATCHER – and very much with her blessing, with minimal CABINET discussion or consultation with local authorities. It was an attempt to reform the long-established system of local taxes – the RATES – which were calculated on the basis of the value of domestic and business property and paid by the principal owner or tenant of the property. In the case of tenants, for example in local-authority housing, rates were often incorporated within rents. This system was uncontentious among most rate payers, and evasion was difficult and rare.

The purpose of the change was to increase popular interest in local government (which had long been flagging, evidenced by low turnouts in local elections) by making every adult personally responsible for paying a local tax. This, it was thought, would make individuals more alert to expenditure by their local authority and inclined to use their votes to curb it when they thought it excessive – as the Conservatives believed the expenditure of some (mainly LABOUR-controlled) councils to be. The tax was immediately attacked as being socially inequitable, since every adult in a local-authority area was liable for the same level of tax regardless of income (although there were reductions for certain people on low incomes), whereas the rating system was perceived to be broadly fair because it was related to the value of the property inhabited by the taxpayer. The community charge also proved impossible to collect, especially from more geographically mobile sections of the population, such as young workers and students. Significant numbers of people openly refused to pay, and when prosecuted aroused wide public sympathy. Unknown numbers simply did not pay and could not be traced. Also unknown numbers were disenfranchised because they feared that by placing their names on the electoral register they would reveal their whereabouts and eligibility for the tax. The fact that it had been introduced in Scotland before England and Wales had the further effect of increasing the disaffection of many in SCOTLAND towards government from Westminster.

On 30 March 1990 a demonstration against the community charge in Trafalgar Square in central London led to 300 injuries and 308 arrests. The failure of the tax contributed to disillusionment with Margaret Thatcher in her own party and in the country at large, and to her downfall in November 1990. The Conservative government led by her successor, John MAJOR, abolished the community charge in 1993, replacing it with a local 'council tax' levied on the value of property, which operated successfully.

Community Relations Commission. *See* IMMI-
GRATION.

comprehensive schools. *See* EDUCATION.

Concorde. *See* AVIATION.

Congregationalists. *See* NONCONFORMISTS.

Conrad, Joseph (Józef Teodor Konrad Korzen-
iowski) (1857–1924), novelist. Conrad was born of
Polish parents in the Russian-dominated Ukraine.
His father's political sympathies caused the family
to be exiled to northern Russia, where Conrad's
mother died when he was seven. After their return
to Poland, his father died and Conrad was raised
by an uncle who was to be a continuing influence
on his life. In 1874 he went to sea, on a French
vessel, embarking on a career as a sailor that was
to supply much material for his writing. In 1886
he became a British subject and qualified as a
master mariner. In 1894 he settled in England and
devoted himself to writing.

Conrad began writing his first novel, *Almayer's
Folly*, in 1889; he wrote in English, which was at
least his third language. In 1895 he married Jessie
George; they were to have two sons. In the same
year he published *Almayer's Folly*, followed by *An
Outcast of the Islands* (1896). In these works he
was still struggling with technique and with the
English language. His talent emerged with *The
Nigger of the Narcissus* (1897) and *Lord Jim*
(1900). The sea provided the setting for his novels
and short stories, but his chief preoccupations were
human corruptibility and vulnerability, demonstrated most vividly in his famous story *Heart of
Darkness* (1902). His narratives used techniques
such as breaks in time sequence, speech with lay-
ered meanings and studied non-answering in dia-
logue, which were to influence modernist writers.
After a brief period of collaboration with Ford
Madox Ford, Conrad produced *Typhoon* (1903)
and the major work *Nostromo* (1904), more clearly
political than his earlier novels, or, rather, con-

cerned with political psychology, set amid the revolutionary politics of the fictional South American country of Costaguana. Like his other work,
it also described realistically both work and
acquisitiveness. *The Secret Agent* (1907) and *Under
Western Eyes* (1911) again had political themes,
the former set among another group of unsuccessful revolutionaries in London, the latter a
daring, sceptical revision of Dostoyevski's *Crime
and Punishment*, set among yet more unsuccessful revolutionaries, this time Russian students in
Switzerland. Though warmly praised by fellow
authors, including GALSWORTHY and BENNETT,
Conrad's work was poorly received by critics and by
the public, and he struggled financially. His first
popular and financial success was *Chance* (1913),
the story of the lonely daughter of a crooked financier, which had a sea background but a theme
of romantic love and more female interest than
was common in his work. *Victory* (1915) also sold
well during World War I, which itself seemed to
bear out some of his doubts about human nature.
By the time of his death Conrad was established
as one of the leading modernist writers.

FURTHER READING J. Baines, *Joseph Conrad:
A Critical Biography* (1960); Z. Najder, *Joseph
Conrad: A Chronicle* (1983).

conscientious objection, principled objection
to participation in war. Conscientious objection is
as old as history, but in Britain it was the introduction in WORLD WAR I, for the first time, of universal male CONSCRIPTION that made it a public
issue. Britain's first statutory conscription measure, the Military Service (No. 2) Act (1916), included a hastily drafted clause that recognized that
some might have a principled objection to service. This was a response to the strong opposition in
the CABINET and in the country to conscription,
rooted in liberal objections to state coercion. There
was confusion over its meaning and inadequate
administrative machinery for its enforcement, both
of which caused serious difficulties for both conscientious objectors (COs) and the government.

For all its inadequacies, however, the clause was an attempt to safeguard moral as well as religious objections to war.

The problems arose because adjudication on pleas of conscientious objection was left to untrained, voluntary, local tribunals whose role was to adjudicate on all pleas for exemption from service, including ill health and essential civilian occupation. They were not well briefed by the government nor assisted by the presence on each committee of a military representative whose role was to question the authenticity of applications.

Between early 1916 and the end of the war over 16,000 men applied for exemption on grounds of conscientious objection; about 6000 were not exempted or refused to recognize the authority of the tribunal. At first they were called up to the army; if they did not respond they were arrested and handed over to the military, who generally court-martialled and imprisoned them. After several highly publicized cases in which COs were severely mistreated under military discipline, the army issued Order X, which provided that COs should be handed to the civil authorities for imprisonment. The Home Office became concerned that the prisons were being filled up with these (probably difficult) political prisoners, and created special 'work centres' for COs. These did not operate satisfactorily, but constituted less of a problem than that caused by 1300 'absolute' objectors, who refused any compromise with war regulations and who were sentenced to hard labour, sometimes repeatedly. A few died or became seriously ill as a result. Publicity about these cases, skilfully disseminated by their supporters, especially the No-Conscription Fellowship, caused the government great embarrassment.

The problems were not resolved before the end of the war, but lessons were learned that were put into operation in WORLD WAR II. When compulsory military service was reintroduced in 1939, local tribunals excluded the military and included members with legal training and experience. They also received clear guidelines. Tribunals were appointed by the Ministry of Labour and National Service, which, under the control of Ernest BEVIN, acted with sensitivity. The voluntary Central Board for Conscientious Objectors, which spoke for them, cooperated with the state – unlike the generally hostile No-Conscription Fellowship in the previous war. As a result, cases of serious injustice or ill treatment were rare. Only 10% of COs suffered any period of imprisonment in World War II, compared with 33% in World War I. Conscription was abolished in 1962 and was not reintroduced for the remainder of the century.

FURTHER READING R. Barker, *Conscience, Government and War: Conscientious Objection in Great Britain 1939–45* (1982); J. Rae, *Conscience and Politics: The British Government and the Conscientious Objector to Military Service, 1916–1919* (1970).

conscription, mandatory military service. Unlike many other European countries, Britain did not use conscription between the end of the Napoleonic Wars and WORLD WAR I. Britain relied upon a strong ROYAL NAVY and a volunteer army to police the EMPIRE and to protect its perceived interests. There was strong opposition in the country and in Parliament, on civil-libertarian grounds, whenever conscription was proposed (most notably by the Wantage Commission in 1892).

World War I unexpectedly required the deployment of larger numbers of British troops than could be supplied by volunteers. Despite strong opposition in the LIBERAL PARTY, matched by strong support in the CONSERVATIVE PARTY, ASQUITH brought in Britain's first mandatory service bill in January 1916. This 'bachelor's bill' applied only to unmarried men between the ages of 18 and 41. It came into effect in February 1916. The intake was still insufficient and in May 1916 a general conscription bill was introduced, which included married men. Even this was not enough, and before the end of the war the upper age limit was raised to 50 and conscription was extended to IRELAND, which previously had been excluded because of the tensions between Britain and Ireland over HOME RULE. This tension had grown following the EASTER RISING in 1916, and so conscription was virtually unenforceable in Ireland. Conscription also created the problem of CONSCIENTIOUS OBJEC-TION among men who had a principled objection to participation in war.

Conscription ceased in April 1920. As the danger of war grew in the 1930s its reintroduc-tion was proposed but successive prime ministers refused, aware of its unpopularity. But by April 1939 it was clear that it was needed in order to maintain the necessary expansion of the armed services. Neville CHAMBERLAIN introduced the first peacetime conscription law in modern times, call-ing only for six months' service for men aged 20 and 21. The law came into effect in May 1939. In June 1940, with WORLD WAR II well under way and with a German invasion threatening, a bill was passed making all persons and property liable to wartime service – a far more sweeping measure than any previous legislation. The government had learned an important lesson from the mistakes of World War I and was determined to prevent the enlistment of workers in occupations essential to war production, such as mining. The legislation gave Ernest BEVIN, as minister of labour and national service, power to regulate the whole labour market and to retrain workers for civilian occupations as necessary. This was smoothly accomplished. By the end of 1941 more than 90% of males aged 14–64 were in the services or in nec-essary civilian employment, but there was still a labour shortage. In December 1941 another un-precedented piece of legislation introduced manda-tory national service of some kind for all persons, regardless of sex, aged 18–50. This was success-fully applied, with restraint and flexibility. Military conscription of young men continued after the war. Men served for a period of 18 months, extended to two years in September 1950 because of the KOREAN WAR. 'National service' remained in place until 1962, the last conscripts having begun their service in 1960. British conscripts fought in Korea, Malaya, Cyprus, Kenya and other struggles of DECOLONIZATION. It was not reintro-duced for the remainder of the century.

FURTHER READING R.J.Q. Adams and P. Poirier, *The Conscription Controversy in Great Britain 1900–1918* (1987); P. Dennis, *Decision by Default: Peacetime Conscription and British Defence 1919–1939* (1972); T. Royle, *The Best Years of Their Lives: The National Service Experience* (1986).

Conservative Party, the principal force on the right of British politics throughout the 20th cen-tury. The party was officially known as the Union-ist Party from *c*.1895 to 1925, signifying its support for the union of Great Britain and IRE-LAND. It is also often referred to informally as the Tory Party, a name deriving from its origins in the late 17th century. The Conservative Party was in government for more years than any other party during the 20th century. It produced no explicit, generally agreed code of beliefs, and was some-times seen as motivated primarily by the desire to win power, though certain beliefs – including the right to own private property, a preference for the free market, a belief in the necessity for social hier-archy – were widely held among its supporters.

The party's support tended to come from the upper and middle classes, but not exclusively so. It consistently though unevenly attracted working-class voters, and the intellectual and public-service middle class inclined rather to parties further to the left. It has often been asserted that the capac-ity of the Conservatives to attract a majority of women voters was a major reason for their con-tinued success; but the statistical evidence that this was consistently so is weak – for example, women moved sharply against the party during the period of Margaret THATCHER's premiership. From the time that women obtained the vote in 1918, how-ever, they were substantially represented among party members and activists, although they were poorly represented in the parliamentary party.

Throughout the century the party had a strong, well-funded organization. It consisted of a national, voluntary organization, the National Union, founded in 1867, consisting of party members. It had an association in each constituency, and many associations employed full-time paid agents whose chief role was to organize election campaigns (an asset that other parties were not able to afford in such numbers). There was also a regional tier of organization, an executive that met regularly and an annual conference. The National Union had influence, but little formal power. Policy was decided by the party leader, who from 1965 was selected by a ballot of MPs. Previously he (as it always was) emerged as a result of soundings taken by senior party figures among influential sections of the party. The other important element of the party organization was the body of salaried officials located in Conservative Central Office (founded 1870), close to the Houses of Parliament in central London. Central Office was responsible to and controlled by the leader. Its primary role was to help local associations to win elections, although in principle it could not dictate to these associations, which regarded themselves as autonomous.

From 1911 a party chairman, usually a prominent parliamentarian, was appointed to oversee party organization at the local level and to keep in touch with the rank and file. This post was introduced when the party reorganized itself following the GENERAL ELECTION defeats of 1906 and 1910. Such reorganization became the party's characteristic response to defeat or major constitutional change. Following the extension of the franchise to include all men and some women in 1918, branches were developed for women and for working-class men. After the defeat of 1945 Central Office was reorganized under the chairmanship of Lord Woolton and the party gave increasing attention to establishing what voters wanted, by use of opinion polls and advertising to target selected categories of voters, such as middle-class women. Following its unprecedentedly heavy defeat in the May 1997 and June 2001 general elections, the party appeared to be searching for a means to reorganize itself again to appeal to voters. In the leadership election that followed the resignation of William Hague the unexpected elimination of Michael POR-TILLO left the Conservatives facing a choice between the Europhile Kenneth Clarke (1940–), a former cabinet minister under both Thatcher and Major and the Eurosceptic right-winger Iain Duncan Smith (1954–).

For details of party policy *see* entries for: Lord SALISBURY (to 1902); Arthur BALFOUR (1902–11, 1922–3); Andrew Bonar LAW (1911–21, 1922–3); Austen CHAMBERLAIN (1921–2); Stanley BALDWIN (1923–37); Neville CHAMBERLAIN (1937–40); Winston CHURCHILL (1940–55); Anthony EDEN (1955–7); Harold MACMILLAN (1957–63); Alec DOUGLAS-HOME (1963–5); Edward HEATH (1965–75); Margaret THATCHER (1975–90); John MAJOR (1990–7); William HAGUE (1997–2001).

FURTHER READING R. Blake, *The Conservative Party from Peel to Thatcher* (1985); J. Ramsden, *A History of the Conservative Party, Vol. 3, The Age of Balfour and Baldwin 1902–1940* (1978); A. Seldon and S. Ball (eds.), *Conservative Century: The Conservative Party since 1900* (1994).

cooperative movement, social (and subsequently political and cultural) movement that arose out of a number of societies founded in the 19th century with the aim of buying and selling goods for the benefit of their members. The British cooperative movement was established in 1844, when 28 weavers subscribed £1 each to start the Rochdale Cooperative Society. From its inception, the cooperative movement differed from other retailers by distributing profits to customers. Customers became members of a cooperative society by paying a small fee, entitling them to a 'dividend' on purchases. Cooperative societies emerged across Britain, and by 1914 the cooperative movement ('the Co-op', as it was popularly known) was the country's major retailer, boasting almost 3 million members, mostly in working-class communities. Cooperative stores, aided by the establishment of the Cooperative Wholesale Society in 1863, were followed by the Cooperative Insurance Society

(1867) and the Cooperative Bank (1872). The movement gained a national, democratic structure through the introduction of an annual Cooperative Congress (1869) and the Cooperative Union (1873). Women members' representation was facilitated by the Cooperative Women's Guild (1883). Cooperative societies used a portion of their profits to develop educational and cultural provision in working-class communities. The movement's internationalism inspired the International Cooperative Alliance (1895), and the export of cooperative ideas to the Americas and Australasia by 1914.

During World War I membership increased to over 4 million and the movement entered mainstream politics through the Cooperative Political Party (1917). One Cooperative MP was elected in 1918. Thereafter the party worked closely with the LABOUR PARTY. The two parties did not run candidates against one another and in 1926 local cooperative parties became eligible for affiliation to the Labour Party. The Cooperative Political Party gained its peak number of seats, 23, in the election of 1945.

The interwar cooperative movement asserted its political and cultural identity, developing educational and youth programmes and close links with the TRADE UNIONS and, through the Cooperative Women's Guild, with the WOMEN'S MOVEMENT. In 1922 it established the Cooperative College for ADULT EDUCATION, which ran correspondence courses in such subjects as bookkeeping. From 1929 the movement owned the weekly newspaper *Reynolds News*. In 1938 membership had risen to 6.5 million; at this time the Cooperative Women's Guild had 90,000 members. By 1946 membership had increased to 9.73 million, largely owing to the movement's position in World War II as Britain's largest grocer, and as an emphatic opponent of fascism and profiteering.

The post-war political climate was less favourable to 'Co-operation'. The intensification of the COLD WAR caused suspicion of labour organizations with international links, and the economic boom of the 1950s benefited the Co-op's competitors, multiple retailers such as Marks and Spencer and Woolworth. The amalgamation of smaller cooperative societies could not halt the movement's decline after 1958, when membership peaked at 12,594,000. As multiple retailers reduced profit margins to remain competitive in the 1970s and 1980s, cooperative societies abandoned the dividend to survive. In the mid-1990s the future of the movement, faced by takeover bids from entrepreneurs, was in doubt. However the cooperative movement retained its independence, and by 2000 had reintroduced the dividend in a fresh attempt to emphasize its distinctive nature as a cooperative venture in a capitalist society. The Co-operative Bank continued to be successful to the end of the century, and distinguished itself from other banks by introducing an 'ethical' investment policy in the 1990s.

FURTHER READING A. Bonner, *British Co-operation* (2nd edn, 1970); J. Gaffin and D. Thomas, *Caring and Sharing. The Centenary History of the Cooperative Women's Guild* (1983).

Council for Racial Equality. *See* IMMIGRATION.

Council for the Encouragement of Music and the Arts (CEMA), the first scheme of state sponsorship of the arts and the forerunner of the ARTS COUNCIL OF GREAT BRITAIN. CEMA was established in 1939 with the aim of keeping the arts in being during WORLD WAR II. Theatres and concert halls were closed and the contents of museums and art galleries removed in anticipation of heavy bombing. At the same time potential audiences were evacuated from, or voluntarily left, urban centres, and musicians and actors were conscripted. The government decided that it was essential for the morale of the population and for Britain's image abroad to maintain cultural life through the war.

The Treasury, via the Board of Education, provided financial assistance through CEMA to voluntary organizations, notably the Pilgrim Trust, initially to encourage amateur activity in the arts, mainly through the further education system. Over time its focus shifted from encouraging adult education and amateur performance to support of professionals and maintaining high standards in the arts in wartime. CEMA funded concerts in works canteens and tours by professional acting companies. During the BLITZ musicians were sent to play in air-raid shelters, centres for homeless victims of bombing and munitions factories, sometimes in rivalry with the ENTERTAINMENTS NATIONAL SERVICE ASSOCIATION (ENSA). The latter generally provided popular entertainment, while CEMA sponsored high culture, especially classical music. The funding and administration of CEMA shifted increasingly into government hands.

In 1942 John Maynard KEYNES was appointed to the chair of CEMA by R.A. BUTLER, president of the Board of Education; Keynes retained the post for four years despite his demanding Treasury responsibilities. Under his direction the annual Treasury grant grew to over £200,000, and the ramshackle administrative structure was overhauled. CEMA began to encourage the arts in London, in contrast to the earlier anti-metropolitan bias – though other regions were not neglected. Keynes also demanded strict financial accountability from sponsored organizations. Keynes oversaw CEMA's transition into a permanent peacetime organization for state patronage of the arts, which in 1946 was established as the Arts Council. CEMA succeeded in its aim of keeping cultural activities alive during the war, and revealed a much higher level of public enthusiasm for the arts than had previously been suspected.

FURTHER READING R. Hutchinson, *The Politics of the Arts Council* (1982); F.M. Leventhal, '"The Best for the Most": CEMA and State Sponsorship of the Arts in Wartime 1939–1945' in *20th Century British History*, Vol. 1 (1990), 289–317.

country houses. At the beginning of the century most of rural Britain was divided into large estates, most of them centring upon a country house – which might be anything from a grand palace, such as Blenheim (Oxfordshire), where Winston CHURCHILL was born, to a relatively modest manor house. Such houses could accommodate family, servants and parties of friends staying for weekends or longer, and often contained the estate offices; they also served as expressions of the landlord's status and power. Some would be opened on occasion to the local population, or to 'respectable' tourists in limited numbers.

Many such estates were in economic decline from the 1870s as British AGRICULTURE became less profitable. Increased taxation introduced in the budgets of LLOYD GEORGE between 1908 and 1914 and, worse still, the effects of death duties (taxes levied on property possessed at death) as younger owners were killed in WORLD WAR I, made many estates less viable financially and enforced many sales. In the interwar years, however, such estates found buyers, often among newly rich businessmen for whom access to the countryside was eased by the spread of the motorcar. Some country houses were demolished by their owners in order to build smaller, more manageable houses. WORLD WAR II drove many owners from their houses – at least temporarily – owing to shortages of servants, fuel, building materials or government requisition of the houses for military use, evacuated schools, convalescent homes and so on. After the war there was another wave of sales and demolitions, as owners were reluctant to return to them in conditions of austerity. Many country houses became schools, offices, hotels or nursing homes.

It seemed as though country houses had had their day. Evelyn WAUGH's *Brideshead Revisited* (1945) was a best-selling elegy for the way of life that they epitomized. But the very fact that the book sold so well suggested that there was a popular interest in them. The Labour prime minister Clement ATTLEE set up a government inquiry into historic houses, which recommended in 1950 that the government should provide a subsidy to help preserve up to 2000 of the finest houses still in private ownership. A limited grant system was established by 1953. The voluntary NATIONAL

TRUST, which had initially focused on the preservation of open spaces, had during the war begun to acquire country houses, by gift or bequest, in order to open them to the public, and did so increasingly after the war. Some owners began themselves to open their houses on a commercial basis, beginning with the marquess of Bath at Longleat (1949) and Lord Montagu at Beaulieu (1952). The spread of the motor car and the motor coach combined with greater affluence provided a growing market of consumers for such attractions. By the early 1960s some 600 houses – now popularly described as 'stately homes' – were opened to over 10 million visitors per year, and the owners wooed them with safari parks, funfairs and much else. This popularity was undiminished at the end of the century. Also at the end of the century, hundreds of country houses remained comfortably in private ownership without entering the commercial market-place, maintained on agricultural, inherited or business incomes, either by families who had held them for many generations, or by newcomers.

SEE ALSO ARISTOCRACY; NATIONAL HERITAGE.
FURTHER READING H. Clemenson, *English Country Houses and Landed Estates* (1982); P. Mandler, *The Fall and Rise of the English Country House* (1998).

Crick, Francis. *See* SCIENCE.

cricket. *See* SPORT.

crime. It is possible to provide a clear picture only of those crimes that are reported to the police and so appear in government statistics. Some 90% of all reported crimes throughout the century were crimes against property, mainly theft or handling of stolen goods. By contrast violent and sexual crimes were only 5% of those reported.

At the beginning of the century the homicide rate was about one crime per 100, 000 of the population per annum. This fell to 0.3 per 100,000 in the early 1950s, then began to rise and just exceeded the level at the beginning of the century

in the mid-1980s. As a whole, serious crime (primarily murder and serious assault to persons or to property) was fairly level between 1900 and 1914, at around 249 crimes per 100,000 of the population, then rose steadily, slackened off in the decade following WORLD WAR II, then rose sharply from the mid-1950s: 2374 per 100,000 were reported in 1965, 6674 in 1984 and about 10,500 in 1994.

The problem, however, is to know whether these statistics describe a rise in crime or increased reporting of crime and more efficient police records. Rape, for example, was reported more frequently during the 1980s, a time when there was greater public awareness and sympathy for victims, who in consequence may have been more willing to report a crime that previously had been kept secret out of misplaced feelings of shame. High levels of reporting of rape continued thereafter. From 1981 *The British Crime Survey* attempted to monitor crime statistics by comparing officially recorded crime with responses from a sample of the population to questions about the level of crime they had experienced. This consistently showed that most crime was petty, that violent crime was rare, and that burglary had not risen as fast as official records suggested. Throughout the century most offenders were young males, often under the age of 20, sometimes in gangs, often not. Young men were also the most frequent victims of violent crime. Organized professional crime was also rare, though great publicity surrounded such examples as the 'Great Train Robbery' of 1963 and the activities of the Kray brothers in the 1960s. The Krays, like other professional criminals before them, were active mainly in the world of pornography, the sex trade, gambling and, increasingly, drugs, all of which played a major role in organized crime by the end of the century – often, like other business activities, on a global scale.

Crime is often assumed to be the preserve of the socially marginal, but the growth in legislation regarding taxation and business and financial regulation – with the attendant opportunities for evasion and fraud – extended the definition of crime later in the century, together with the social backgrounds of those involved. Such crimes, however, were often viewed more sympathetically than the crimes of marginal people.

FURTHER READING V.A.C. Gatrell, 'Crime, Authority and the Policeman-State' in F.M.L. Thompson (ed.), *The Cambridge Social History of Britain, Vol. 3, 1750–1950* (1990), 243–310; R. Hood and A. Roddam, 'Crime, Sentencing and Punishment' in A.H. Halsey and J. Webb (eds.), *Twentieth Century British Social Trends* (2000), 675–710.

Cripps, (Richard) Stafford (1889–1952), Labour politician. Cripps was educated at Winchester School and University College, London, where he studied chemistry. Despite success as a chemist, he followed his father and grandfather into the law, becoming a barrister in 1913. During World War I, owing to the ill health that would afflict him throughout his life, he served as assistant superintendent at the Queensbury Explosives Factory (1915–18). After the war he established a successful legal career, becoming Britain's youngest king's counsel in 1927. His legal work for the London County Council impressed its leader, Herbert MORRISON, who persuaded him to join the LABOUR PARTY. Cripps's father, Alfred, previously a Conservative MP, then a peer (as Lord Parmoor), had joined Labour in 1924 and was lord president in the first Labour government. Both father and son were committed Christians; Stafford was actively involved in Christian peace organizations.

Cripps was appointed solicitor general in the second Labour government in October 1930, and was knighted. He was elected to Parliament in 1931, one of only 52 successful Labour candidates following the party split in 1931 (*see* MACDONALD, RAMSAY). He was on the left of the party, and in 1938 was expelled for supporting a POPULAR FRONT with the COMMUNIST PARTY OF GREAT BRITAIN. In May 1940 Winston CHURCHILL unexpectedly appointed him ambassador to Moscow,

believing that the USSR must be persuaded to join the war against Hitler and that an ambassador sympathetic to communism could best achieve this. Cripps was successful as an ambassador, and returned to Britain in January 1942 to such acclaim that Churchill had little choice but to appoint him to the CABINET as lord president. In March 1942 he was sent to INDIA to negotiate with nationalist leaders, with whom he was sympathetic, but he had no brief to offer acceptable terms and nothing was achieved. His relations with Churchill were poor and he was removed from the cabinet (in which he had served as leader of the House of Commons) and was given the important, if politically marginal, role of minister for aircraft production, in which he was highly effective.

Cripps was readmitted to the Labour Party in 1945, and in the Labour government elected that year he was appointed president of the Board of Trade, with primary responsibility for RATIONING. A lean, moralistic vegetarian with a simple lifestyle, unsympathetic to frivolity, he came to embody austerity in the public mind, and he was unpopular, despite (or because of) his efficient performance of his duties (Churchill nicknamed him 'Christ and Carrots').

In 1947 the government faced widespread criticism, partly owing to the economic difficulties arising from an exceptionally cold winter. Cripps and others tried to engineer a coup to replace Clement ATTLEE with Ernest BEVIN as prime minister. Attlee responded shrewdly by appointing Cripps to the newly created Ministry of Economic Affairs, to try to sort out the economic crisis. Cripps showed his usual efficiency, further reinforcing his austere image by repeatedly exhorting the population to hard work. When Hugh DALTON was forced to resign as CHANCELLOR OF THE EXCHEQUER later in 1947 the two ministries were combined, with Cripps in charge as the new chancellor. He was an ardent supporter of a mixed, planned economy, rather than of wholesale NATIONALIZATION. He played an important role in improving the state of the economy over the next two years, partly by maintaining controls and restricting both public expenditure and private consumption. In October 1950 he resigned owing to the ill health that had long affected him, partly because of overwork, and he died 18 months later. **FURTHER READING** R. Eatwell, *The 1945–51 Labour Governments* (1979); K.O. Morgan, *Labour in Power 1945–51* (1984).

Crosland, (Charles) Anthony (Raven) (also known as **Tony**) (1918–77), Labour politician. Crosland was educated at Highgate School, London, and Trinity College, Oxford, where he became a lecturer in economics in 1947. In 1950 he gave up his academic career and became Labour MP for South Gloucestershire. He lost the seat in 1955 and was re-elected in 1959 for Grimsby, the seat he held until his death. In the interim he wrote *The Future of Socialism* (1956), the principal exposition of Labour 'revisionism'. He argued, optimistically, that Western capitalism had been fundamentally modified since 1945 and that the chief challenges now facing socialists were social and ethical: how to redistribute the fruits of the modern mixed economy to achieve greater equality and justice. He placed great emphasis on educational reform to equalize opportunities and on redistributive taxation. He was a close ally of Hugh GAITSKELL, supporting his attempt to repeal CLAUSE FOUR and also his stance against unilateral disarmament. Throughout his political career, Crosland had a reputation as a *bon viveur*, while priding himself on his easy relationship with his working-class constituents in Grimsby.

In Harold WILSON's first government Crosland was secretary of state for education and science (1964–7), in which role he had a major influence on the shape of education for the remainder of the century, being responsible for the introduction of comprehensive schools (*see* EDUCATION), polytechnics (to provide higher technical education, theoretically of equal esteem and status with university education), and a number of wholly new UNIVERSITIES, which were intended both to in-

crease the number of university places and to develop imaginative new approaches to higher education. From 1967 to 1969, in Wilson's second government, he was president of the Board of Trade. In the Labour government formed in 1974 he was secretary of state for the environment, 1974–6, then foreign secretary until his sudden death in 1977.
FURTHER READING S. Crosland, *Tony Crosland* (1982); D. Lipsey and D. Leonard, *The Socialist Agenda: Crosland's Legacy* (1981).

Crossman, Richard (Howard Stafford) (1907–74), Labour politician. Crossman was educated at Winchester and New College, Oxford, where he studied classics and philosophy. He became a fellow of New College in 1930, then spent a year in Germany. He was concerned to communicate his intellectual concerns to a wider audience outside Oxford and, with that aim in mind, published *Plato Today* in 1937, *Socrates* in 1938 and *Government and the Governed* in 1939, and also lectured for the Workers' Educational Association (*see* ADULT EDUCATION). He was involved with the politics of the non-communist left and in 1938 he became assistant editor of the left-wing weekly, the *New Statesman*. During World War II he joined the staff of the Ministry of Economic Warfare in 1940, then was assistant chief of psychological warfare, 1944–5. In 1945 he was elected Labour MP for Coventry East, a seat he retained until his death.

During the 1950s Crossman supported Aneurin BEVAN against Hugh GAITSKELL during the battles in the LABOUR PARTY and wrote a number of essays and pamphlets seeking to define the way forward for Labour, which was much divided after the successes of the ATTLEE governments, though the impact of Crossman's writing was limited. He devoted much time to proposals to revise the party's social-security policy, recognizing the inadequacy of the post-BEVERIDGE legislation. He was a close supporter of Harold WILSON and played an important role in Labour's election victory in 1964, in part by working hard to communicate with workers in the fields of modern science and technology, to convince them that Labour saw development of their skills and ideas as essential to the future prosperity of the British economy. This was a policy that was central to Wilson's election campaign and in which Crossman sincerely believed, since he was convinced (with good reason) that the British economy was failing to keep up with modern technology.

To his disappointment Crossman was made minister of housing and local government in 1964, a field about which he knew little, rather than minister for social security, on which he had become expert. As a minister he became very critical of the CIVIL SERVICE, which he felt obstructed policy innovation, and of the working practices of the House of COMMONS, which had changed little since the 19th century, despite social change and the increasing load of work. He made one successful change by originating, in 1966, the system of specialized select committees of MPs, each appointed for the duration of a parliament, to examine in depth specific subject areas, such as race relations or education. He failed in his ambition to reform the House of Lords. He was at last appointed to the Department of Health and Social Security in 1968, but failed to get his pension reform through the Commons before Labour lost the 1970 election.

Crossman was editor of the *New Statesman* from 1970 to 1972, and spent his retirement thereafter preparing for publication the diaries he had kept while in office. These were published, after his sudden death, as *The Diaries of a Cabinet Minister* in three volumes in 1975, 1976 and 1977, followed by *The Backbench Diaries of Richard Crossman* in 1981. The diaries provide useful perspectives on the period. He was a clever, thoughtful, impatient politician, whose talents were underused.

Cunningham, Andrew (Browne) (1883–1963), one of the most successful admirals of WORLD WAR II. Cunningham was the son of a professor of anatomy at Edinburgh University and was edu-

cated at the Edinburgh Academy and Stubbington House, Fareham. He entered the ROYAL NAVY in 1897 as a cadet, then spent the period from 1911 and through WORLD WAR I as captain of the destroyer *Scorpion*, serving at the DARDANELLES, being promoted to commander and being awarded the DSO.

Following steady promotion, by the outbreak of World War II he was an acting admiral and commander in chief of the Mediterranean Fleet, an especially important role once Italy joined the war in 1940. In November 1940 Cunningham directed a carrier-based air attack on the harbour of Taranto, disabling three out of four Italian battleships and forcing the Italian fleet to withdraw northwards. In March 1941, in a night attack, Cunningham led his fleet to a decisive victory over the Italians off Cape Matapan, reinforcing British naval domination of the eastern Mediterranean. He remained at his Mediterranean command during the Allied landings in North Africa (1942) and Sicily (1943), following which he was appointed first sea lord and chief of naval staff. In 1945 he was given a barony, and he was created Viscount Cunningham of Hyndhope in 1946. He was lord high commissioner of the General Assembly of the Church of Scotland in 1950 and 1952, and lord rector of Edinburgh University, 1945–8.

Curragh incident (March 1914), incident arising out of the issue of HOME RULE for IRELAND. The threat of Ulster Protestant opposition to home rule became so acute in the spring of 1914 that the British government feared that it would be necessary to use troops to keep order in the north of Ireland. Officers stationed at the Curragh, near Dublin, were told they might resign their commissions if their consciences would not permit them to fire on Ulstermen. In response, 58 of the 71 officers of the 3rd Cavalry Brigade, including their commander, said they would prefer dismissal if ordered north. Senior military authorities sympathized, and the officers received a written assurance that they would not, after all, be required to enforce home rule in the north. The threat of resignation was then withdrawn. Technically the incident was not a mutiny (as it is sometimes described). It was a rare incidence of the British officer class putting pressure on the government.

Curzon, George Nathaniel (1859–1925), Conservative politician and imperial administrator, best known for his roles as viceroy of INDIA (1899–1905) and foreign secretary (1919–24). The son of Baron Scarsdale, Curzon was educated at Eton and Balliol College, Oxford. In 1895 he married an American heiress, Mary Leiter, by whom he had three daughters: Irene, Cynthia (who married Sir Oswald MOSLEY) and Alexandra. Mary died in 1906, and Curzon later married Grace Duggan in 1917. He was created Baron Curzon of Kedleston in the peerage of Ireland in 1898, and was made an earl in 1911 and a marquess in 1921.

From 1886 to 1898 Curzon served as the Conservative MP for Southport, and during this time undertook several world tours, concentrating on the East. In 1891–2 he worked as parliamentary undersecretary for India. In 1895 he was made parliamentary undersecretary for foreign affairs. As a result of his intellectual capabilities and his remarkable knowledge of Eastern political affairs, he was appointed as viceroy and governor general of India in 1898, at the age of 39 – the youngest man ever to hold the post. Curzon's viceroyalty is widely regarded as having marked the apogee of the British Raj in India, and was noted for its high ceremonial and splendour. The Delhi Durbar of 1902 was referred to by Curzon's critics as the 'Curzonation'. Certainly Curzon was known for his arrogant and somewhat haughty manner, which did not endear him to all (even when he was at Oxford a rhyme had circulated: 'My name is George Nathaniel Curzon,/I am a most superior person,/My cheek is pink, my hair is sleek,/I dine at Blenheim once a week.') His viceroyalty was characterized by many changes. Some were well received, such as administrative and agricultural reform and the extension of the railways, but others, such as the partition of Bengal in 1905, were not. He was also responsible for the creation of the Northwest Frontier Province. Curzon accepted a second term as viceroy in 1904 but resigned the following year. The reasons were complex, but the catalyst was his disagreement with Lord KITCHENER over the running of the Indian army. Kitchener had been made commander in chief of the army in 1902 and had his own designs on the viceroyalty. Curzon left India in 1905 both disappointed and bitter over the outcome of his political career in the subcontinent, and was upset by Westminster's declining interest in India and its affairs.

Curzon kept a low profile after his return to Britain; he served in the House of LORDS from 1908 but did not return to politics in any substantial capacity until 1915 when ASQUITH made him lord privy seal. From 1916 to 1919 he was part of LLOYD GEORGE's war cabinet. From 1919 to 1924 he served as foreign secretary, and fully expected in 1923 to become prime minister after Bonar LAW's resignation. He was passed over in favour of Stanley BALDWIN, however, mainly on account of his somewhat pompous personality which, it was felt, would not make him an effective leader. This was one of the most crushing disappointments of his life, but still he pledged his loyalty to Baldwin and served as foreign secretary for another year. Curzon died in 1925, one of the last of a dying breed of upper-class imperialist statesmen, whose seemingly inexhaustible capacity for work made him one of the most notable politicians of his time.

FURTHER READING D. Gilmour, *Curzon* (1994).

Cypriots. *See* IMMIGRATION.

Cyprus, island in the eastern Mediterranean that was under Turkish sovereignty from 1571 to 1914. The Cyprus Convention of 1878 permitted Britain to station troops on the island. From the point of view of Turkey, this provided it with some protection against Russia. For the British Cyprus was a crucial base, both to contain Russia and to safe-guard the Suez Canal. Greek Cypriots – who out-numbered Turkish Cypriots by four to one – demanded *enosis*, or union with Greece. Britain refused, while giving Cyprus limited autonomy. In 1914, when Turkey entered WORLD WAR I as an ally of Germany, Britain declared Cyprus a pos-session, which was confirmed by the treaty of Lau-sanne in 1923. In 1925 Cyprus became a British crown colony.

Greek nationalist hostility to Britain simmered thereafter, with a serious explosion in 1931. It was muted during WORLD WAR II, when British troops defended Cyprus and the Greek government in exile was based in London. Demands for *enosis* revived after the war. Britain refused because Greece was in a state of civil war and Britain feared a communist victory; Cyprus was also strategically useful during the COLD WAR, especially after Britain evacuated Egypt in 1954. Britain made it clear that – as the minister of state at the Colonial Office, Henry Hopkinson, declared in 1954 – Cyprus 'can never expect to be fully independent'.

The Greek nationalist movement continued, led by Lieutenant Colonel George Grivas – who established the National Organization of Cypriot Fighters (EOKA) – and by the spiritual leader of the Greek Cypriots, Archbishop Makarios. The movement, which was supported by the Greek government, became increasing violent. Turkish Cypriots opposed *enosis* and advocated partition of the island should it become independent of Britain. Large numbers of British troops were deployed in the guerrilla war waged by EOKA, and in March 1956 Makarios was deported to the Seychelles. The SUEZ CRISIS later in 1956 demon-strated Cyprus's limited strategic value to Britain. The British government decided that, provided that it could keep two air bases on Cyprus, it would withdraw. In April 1957 Prime Minister Harold MACMILLAN allowed Makarios to return to Athens, and later to plead the Greek-Cypriot cause at the UNITED NATIONS. He also appointed a liberal gov-ernor, Hugh Foot. Violent conflict between Greek and Turkish Cypriots followed. Britain negotiated with Greece and Turkey, resulting in a settlement whereby Britain would withdraw, and Greeks and Turks would share power in proportion to their numbers.

Cyprus became an independent republic within the COMMONWEALTH in August 1960, with Makar-ios as president, and a Turk, Fazil Küçük, as vice president. But conflict between Greeks and Turks continued. British troops remained as peacekeep-ers until replaced by a UN force in 1964. Pro-*enosis* extremists forced Makarios into exile in England in 1974, whereupon Turkey occupied northern Cyprus. The island remained partitioned for the rest of the century.

FURTHER READING N. Crawshaw, *The Cyprus Revolt: An Account of the Struggle for Union with Greece* (1978); G. Horton Kelling, *Countdown to Rebellion: British Policy in Cyprus 1939–1955* (1990).

D

Dalton, (Edward) Hugh (John Neale) (1887–1962), Labour politician. Born in Glamorgan, South Wales, Dalton was the only son of an Anglican clergyman who had been tutor to the sons of Queen Victoria. He was educated at Eton College, then studied economics at King's College, Cambridge, where he was taught by John Maynard KEYNES. At Cambridge he joined the FABIAN SOCIETY and came to regard himself as a socialist. He served through WORLD WAR I in the Army Service Corps and then the Royal Artillery, describing his experiences in *With Guns in Italy* (1919). He then became a lecturer in economics at the London School of Economics and was active in the LABOUR PARTY.

In October 1924 Dalton was elected as Labour MP for Peckham in south London. In 1929 he transferred to the seat of Bishop Auckland, County Durham, which he lost in 1931 but held again from 1935 until 1959, when he left the House of COMMONS. He was a member of the National Executive Committee (NEC) of the Labour Party from 1925 and undersecretary at the Foreign Office, 1929–31. In the 1930s he helped to shape Labour's commitment to economic planning, and his views were expressed in his *Practical Socialism for Britain* (1935). He also encouraged younger socialist intellectuals such as Hugh GAITSKELL, Evan Durbin and Douglas Jay.

In the WORLD WAR II coalition formed in May 1940 Dalton was appointed minister of economic warfare. In February 1942 he became president of the Board of Trade, responsible for RATIONING, reconstruction and the location of industry, among other things. Following Labour's election victory in 1945 he became CHANCELLOR OF THE EXCHEQUER, playing an important role in the successful reconstruction of the post-war economy but retaining controls and restraining domestic consumption and housing construction while boosting manufacturing industry. The economy faced a temporary crisis in 1947, largely due to the terms imposed in return for a loan from the United States. In November 1947, minutes before introducing the annual budget to the House of Commons, Dalton casually revealed its contents to a journalist. Traditionally, this has been regarded as a major indiscretion in Britain and Dalton was forced to resign. He remained active on the NEC and returned to the CABINET in October 1948 as chancellor of the duchy of Lancaster, with special responsibility for European affairs; then between 1950 and 1951 he was minister of town and country planning, but he was never again so influential within the Labour Party. He lost his seat on the NEC in 1952, being identified with Gaitskell and opposed by the BEVANites. He then concentrated on promoting his protégés, such as Gaitskell and Anthony CROSLAND. He was made a life peer in 1960.

FURTHER READING B. Pimlott, *Hugh Dalton* (1985); B. Pimlott (ed.), *The Political Diary of Hugh Dalton* (1986); B. Pimlott (ed.), *The World War II Diary of Hugh Dalton* (1986).

Dardanelles, the, a channel in the eastern Mediterranean, between the Aegean Sea and the Sea of Marmara, the first stretch of the waterway linking the Mediterranean and the Black Sea. In January 1915 the War Council in London accepted the proposals of Winston CHURCHILL for an Anglo-French naval assault on Turkey via the Dardanelles with the aim of capturing Constantinople (now Istanbul), centre of the Ottoman empire. The fleet suffered such heavy losses early in the engagement that the naval attack was abandoned in favour of a land attack to seize the Turkish forts at GALLIPOLI. This was equally disastrous.

Dawes Plan. *See* REPARATIONS.

D-Day (6 June 1944), the code name given to the first day of the Normandy landings that opened the Allied invasion of German-occupied northwest Europe in WORLD WAR II; this was the Western powers' major contribution to the Allied victory in the war. US, British and Canadian troops landed on the Normandy coast, under the supreme command of General Eisenhower (US) and the immediate command of General MONTGOMERY.

FURTHER READING M. Hastings, *Overlord* (1984).

decimalization (1971), the introduction of a decimal currency in the UK. The currency was changed from its historic system of pounds, shillings and pence (12 pence = one shilling, 20 shillings = £1) to match the decimal-based currencies of all other major players in the world economy and especially of the EUROPEAN COMMUNITY. The change was announced in December 1966 to be implemented in 1971. The changeover occurred on 15 February 1971.

decolonization, in Britain's case, a term usually used to describe the rapid transfer of power and the granting of independence to most of the former colonies of the EMPIRE from the late 1940s to the 1970s. Many supporters of empire claimed that it had always been Britain's intention to shepherd its imperial possessions towards eventual self-government; however, by the early 1940s the only real efforts toward this end had been made in the dominions, which were colonies of white settlement. The 1931 Statute of Westminster (*see* IMPERIAL CONFERENCES) had formally granted legislative autonomy to CANADA, Newfoundland, AUSTRALIA, NEW ZEALAND, the Irish Free State (*see* IRELAND) and SOUTH AFRICA, nations that had already had responsible government for some time. The dominions, along with Britain, were now increasingly referred to as the British COMMONWEALTH – a term that would later encompass most of the former colonies of the old empire, not just those that were colonized by whites.

The events of WORLD WAR II clearly demonstrated to the world that Britain no longer had the financial means or the military might necessary to keep its empire together. Britain was also under increasing pressure from the United States (to which it was heavily in debt by the end of the war) to abide by the terms of the ATLANTIC CHARTER (1941) and allow its colonial peoples to choose for themselves the government under which they would live. The humiliation of the SUEZ CRISIS of 1956 further pushed Britain into accepting that it was no longer a major world power.

INDIA was the first of the non-white colonies to demand independence from Britain. By 1945 it had become clear to the Labour government that the demands of Indian nationalists could no longer be resisted. Independence was granted to India in August 1947, and amid terrible turmoil the nation was partitioned along religious lines with Pakistan, in the northwest and northeast of the subcontinent, becoming a Muslim state. The independence of India opened the doors for the advance of general decolonization in the next few decades. In Asia, both BURMA (later renamed Myanmar) and Ceylon (later renamed Sri Lanka) followed suit in 1948. MALAYA became independent in 1957, and was joined in 1963 by Sarawak, Sabah (formerly North Borneo) and Singapore to form the new nation of Malaysia. Singapore dropped out of the federation in 1965 to stand on its own.

The many colonies of Africa were to decolonize en masse in the 1960s. The Gold Coast, renamed Ghana under the leadership of Kwame Nkrumah, was Britain's first sub-Saharan African colony to become independent, in 1957 (although Sudan, an Anglo-Egyptian condominium, had been granted independence in 1956). Prime Minister Harold MACMILLAN realized that Ghana had set the African precedent, and in 1960 his reference in a speech to the 'wind of change' blowing through Africa proved prophetic, as African nationalism bloomed in the 1960s. Nigeria became independent in 1960, Tanganyika and Sierra Leone in 1961, Uganda in 1962, Zanzibar (which united with Tanganyika in 1964 to form Tanzania) in 1963, Northern Rhodesia (Zambia) and Nyasaland (Malawi) in 1964 and the Gambia in 1965. KENYA, which was also settled by Europeans and Asians, gained independence in 1963, but this followed conflict with a violent nationalist movement, the Mau Mau, in the 1950s. Another colony with a substantial non-African minority, Southern Rhodesia (ZIMBABWE), did not gain its independence until 1980, following the white minority government's illegal declaration of independence in 1965 and a long anti-colonial war throughout the 1970s.

The 1960s also saw the beginning of widespread decolonization in the Caribbean. In 1962 Jamaica and Trinidad and Tobago withdrew from the fledgling West Indian Federation (*see* WEST INDIES) and Barbados became independent in 1966. In the following two decades many other Caribbean islands followed suit.

By the 1980s decolonization of the old empire had slowed to a trickle. Indeed, evidence that independence was not a universal objective among the remaining British colonies was seen in the 1982 war between Britain and Argentina over the FALKLAND ISLANDS. The end of the century saw the last significant instance of decolonization when HONG KONG reverted to China in July 1997; many viewed the handover of Hong Kong as symbolizing the last gasp of the old empire.

By the end of the 20th century Britain retained only a handful of far-flung colonies – the Falklands, GIBRALTAR and various islands in the South Pacific and Caribbean. But it still maintained loose constitutional, economic and cultural ties with most of its former imperial possessions in the form of the Commonwealth, which included some fifty nations in its ranks at the end of the 20th century.

FURTHER READING J. Darwin, *Britain and Decolonization: The Retreat from Empire in the Post-War World* (1988); J. Darwin, *The End of the British Empire: the Historical Debate* (1989); J. Gallagher, *The Decline, Revival and Fall of the British Empire* (1982).

Defence of the Realm Act (DORA) (1914),

legislation that empowered the government to make temporary regulations 'for securing the public safety and the defence of the realm' during WORLD WAR I. The initial legislation was passed on 8 August 1914, and it was amended and extended several times thereafter.

The act authorized the death penalty for offences 'committed with the intention of assisting the enemy'; it was under this dispensation that the executions following the 1916 EASTER RISING in IRELAND were carried out. The act also regulated wartime activities in a wide variety of ways: it banned the showing of lights at night in large cities and the shooting of pigeons in case a carrier of official messages was brought down; the press and international mail were censored; and it was illegal to write or to speak anything that might harm recruiting or cause disaffection in the armed forces. In 1918 the pacifist Bertrand RUSSELL was sentenced to six months in jail under DORA for denouncing the presence of American troops in Britain. The opening hours of public houses were restricted, to discourage heavy drinking that might undermine the war effort. It became illegal for a woman suffering from venereal disease to have sexual intercourse with a member of the armed services. DORA enabled the state to increase control over the economy in unprecedented ways to meet war needs: the government could, and did, authorize controls of prices and supplies and requisition land, buildings and materials. Most of the regulations ended with the ARMISTICE, and all of them were rescinded on 31 August 1921.

Democratic Unionist Party. *See* PAISLEY, IAN.

Department of Economic Affairs. *See* BROWN, GEORGE; LABOUR PARTY; NATIONAL ECONOMIC DEVELOPMENT COUNCIL.

Depression. *See* GREAT CRASH; UNEMPLOYMENT.

de Valera, Eamon (1892–1975), Irish nationalist politician. Born in New York of a Spanish father and an Irish mother, de Valera was educated in Ireland, becoming a lecturer in mathematics at Maynooth college. He joined SINN FÉIN, distinguishing himself as a battalion commander in the EASTER RISING, 1916. He was captured by the British and sentenced to death but not executed, serving a year's imprisonment at Lewes instead. On returning to Ireland he was elected president of Sinn Féin, a post he held from 1917 to 1926. He was again captured by the British and imprisoned at Lincoln (1918–19), but escaped and travelled to the United States where in 1919–20 he raised more than £1 million for the IRISH REPUBLICAN ARMY. He was president of the Irish Republic declared in 1919 until 1922, when his hostility to those such as Michael COLLINS – who were prepared to accept partition and dominion status for southern IRELAND as the Irish Free State within the Commonwealth – led him to conduct a civil war against them in 1922–3.

In 1926 de Valera changed his tactics, recognizing the Irish parliament (the Dáil) and forming a political party, Fianna Fáil. Following the general election of 1932 he formed a government of Fianna Fáil and Labour. He was prime minister for 16 years, formally cutting ties with Britain, though keeping up informal contacts. A new constitution in June 1937 created the sovereign democratic state of Eire, and in 1948 Ireland became a republic and left the Commonwealth. De Valera was committed to a united Ireland, and he gave this as his reason for maintaining strict Irish neutrality during World War II. He was forced into opposition in 1948, returning as prime minister in 1951–4 and 1957–9. In 1959 he stood successfully for president, being re-elected, by only 10,000 votes, in 1966. He retired at the age of 90 in 1973.

devolution. *See* HOME RULE; SCOTLAND; WALES.

Diana, princess of Wales (1961–97), former wife of CHARLES, PRINCE OF WALES, noted for her extensive charity work. She was born Lady Diana Spencer on 1 July 1961, to Viscount and Viscountess Althorp (later the 8th Earl Spencer and Mrs Frances Shand-Kydd). Educated both in England and at a Swiss finishing school, she was briefly employed as a nanny and kindergarten teacher before becoming engaged to Prince Charles at the age of 19. The marriage took place on 29 July 1981, after which she became HRH the princess of Wales. She was the mother of two sons, Prince William, born in 1982 (second in line to the throne), and Prince Henry ('Harry'), born in 1984. The couple separated in 1992 and divorced in 1996, after which she became formally known as Diana, princess of Wales, and devoted increasing energy to her charity work. She was killed along with her companion Dodi Fayed in a car accident in Paris on 31 August 1997, at the age of 36.

From the announcement of her engagement to Prince Charles, Diana quickly grew to become a highly popular member of the royal family and was rarely out of the media spotlight for the rest of her life. Her beauty, love of fashion and unique style meant that by the mid-1980s she had become the most photographed woman in the world. She broke with royal protocol when in November 1995 she gave an interview to the BBC programme *Panorama*. Speaking with unprecedented frankness, she confirmed persistent rumours concerning her eating disorders, her depression and both her own and her husband's extramarital affairs, and discussed her hopes for the future. She devoted much of her time to her work with charities, displaying a natural empathy with children, the elderly and the sick. Most notably, she helped change public perceptions of AIDS by being photographed in 1987 shaking the hand of an AIDS patient. In the summer of 1997 she travelled to Angola and Bosnia to publicize the plight of landmine victims and lent her support to the campaign for a global ban on landmines. Such was her celebrity that her premature death provoked a remarkable public outpouring of shock and grief, not only in Britain but across the globe.

SEE ALSO ELIZABETH II.

FURTHER READING A. Morton, *Diana: Her True Story, in Her Own Words* (rev. edn, 1997).

Dirac, Paul. *See* SCIENCE.

disestablishment. *See* CHURCH IN WALES, CHURCH OF SCOTLAND.

divorce. From 1901 to 1905 an average of 812 divorce petitions a year were filed in England and Wales, most of them successfully, 53% of them by husbands, 47% by wives. The numbers rose to an average of 7535 in 1931–5 (45% by husbands, 55% by wives), to 32,168 in 1951–5 (44% by husbands, 56% by wives), 121,772 in 1971–5 (34% filed by husbands, 66% by wives). In 1994 158,200 divorces were granted in England and Wales. These increases were influenced by cultural shifts, by changes in POPULATION and in the law, and by the effects of war; divorce rates peaked during the two world wars.

At the beginning of the century it was more difficult in law for a wife than for a husband to obtain a divorce. A wife could be divorced for adultery alone, whereas a man was required to have committed an additional offence, such as cruelty or desertion. A strong social stigma attached to divorced people, especially women, which discouraged petitions for divorce. In 1923 women were enabled to obtain a divorce on the same grounds as men, although adultery was the only ground recognized by law. Immediately the number of wives seeking divorces outstripped the number of husbands doing so. In 1937 the range of legally recognized grounds for divorce was extended to include desertion for at least three years, cruelty and incurable insanity. Again this led to a rise in the number of petitions. In 1969 the principle of marital fault was abandoned, the concept of 'irremediable breakdown' was introduced and legal processes were simplified. The annual number of petitions more than doubled. Extensions in the provision of legal aid to poorer people in 1914, 1920, 1949 and 1960 made divorce available to many who had previously been unable to afford it. Changes in the law resulted from pressures from within the legal profession and from women's organizations throughout the century. The stigma attached to divorce diminished as the number of divorces grew. The number of marriages broken by divorce increased along with the decline in the numbers broken in middle life by death and as life expectancy increased over the century.

FURTHER READING A.J. Hammerton, *Cruelty and Companionship* (1992); R. Phillips, *Putting Asunder: A History of Divorce in Western Society* (1988); L. Stone, *Road to Divorce: England, 1530–1987* (1990).

DNA. *See* CAVENDISH LABORATORY.

dole, the, pejorative term applied to cash benefits for unemployed people during the period of high UNEMPLOYMENT in the GREAT CRASH of the interwar years. (The term is still used informally.) The scheme of unemployment insurance introduced in 1911 (*see* WELFARE STATE) was extended after World War I to cover most manual workers. As unemployment grew in the 1920s increasing numbers of people were unemployed for longer periods than were covered by the provisions of the national insurance scheme. A succession of schemes was introduced to provide for the unemployed, all making regular provision for their basic needs but incorporating conditions; the most important, and the most hated, of these was the 'means test', whereby the unemployed had to prove the inadequacy of their household income, taking account of the earnings of partners and children and of the value of household possessions, and also that they were 'genuinely seeking work' with due assiduity. These conditions were often felt to be demeaning, especially in areas where there was very little work to be sought.

FURTHER READING W.R. Garside, *British Unemployment, 1919–1939: A Study in Public Policy* (1990).

domestic service. At the beginning of the century domestic service was the largest female occupation, employing about 1 million. Only the grandest households employed male servants – as butlers, footmen and coachmen – although more employed gardeners and, with the spread of motor transport, chauffeurs. Employment of live-in domestic servants was a feature of the lives of middle- and upper-class people that was taken for granted.

The experience of service could vary immensely, from being part of the complex hierarchy of grand households to being the sole, poorly paid general servant of a much less affluent household. Many households also employed daily cleaners and laundrywomen. At the top level there was the possibility of career progression, from maid to cook to housekeeper, or from valet to butler, but for most female servants it was a limited, closely controlled work environment, which many longed to leave. They did so in large numbers in WORLD WAR I, when new occupations opened up for young women, though many found themselves forced to return to service after the war when the opportunities disappeared.

But the numbers of servants did not return to pre-war levels, and they declined again throughout the interwar years, especially in the 1930s as new industries opened up. In addition, the falling size of middle-class families and houses, together with the development of new technologies that eased the burden of housework for those who could afford new gadgets such as vacuum cleaners, meant that many middle-class families could dispense with servants, often thankful to be rid of the additional cost and of an intrusive presence in the household.

WORLD WAR II saw a decisive decline in the employment of servants in private households. Whereas in 1911 10% of British families employed live-in servants, by 1951 the proportion had fallen to 1% and by 1981 to 0.1%. Improved working-class living standards and a greatly extended range of employment opportunities for women reduced the supply of servants. The expansion of the welfare state increased demand for forms of service that were seen as less demeaning, for example in hospitals and schools or as 'home helps' employed by local authorities to perform domestic tasks for people who were in need of help, such as older and disabled people, rather than just for those who could afford it.

However, unknown numbers of households continued to employ cleaners for a fixed number of hours each week, and the foreign resident au pair became an established provider of childcare in many middle-class households from the 1960s. From the 1980s the combination of high unemployment and the increasing numbers of high-earning two-income households led to an increase in the availability and employment of people to care for children and other forms of service, although precise statistics are difficult to establish. The number of servants shrank and the nature of their work declined over the century, but they never disappeared, and there were signs of a resurgence at the end of the century.

FURTHER READING F.V. Dawes, *Not in Front of the Servants: Domestic Service in England, 1850–1939* (1973); R. Schwarz Cowan, *More Work for Mother: The Ironies of Household Technology from the Open Hearth to the Microwave* (1983).

dominions. *See* AUSTRALIA; CANADA; COMMONWEALTH; IMPERIAL CONFERENCES; NEW ZEALAND; SOUTH AFRICA.

Donovan Commission on Industrial Relations (1965–8). *See* TRADE UNIONS.

doodlebugs. *See* V1S AND V2S.

Douglas-Home, Alec (1903–95), Conservative politician, PRIME MINISTER (1963–4) and FOREIGN SECRETARY (1960–3 and 1970–4). From a landed, non-political Scottish family, Douglas-Home was educated at Eton College and Christ Church, Oxford. In 1918 he inherited the title of Lord Dunglass, a courtesy title that did not entitle him to sit in the House of LORDS. He was Conservative MP for Lanark, 1931–45, when he lost the seat, returning 1950–1. He was Neville CHAMBERLAIN's parliamentary private secretary, 1936–40, but otherwise not prominent. Because of illness 1940–3 and electoral defeat in 1945 he was largely outside politics. He was minister of state at the Scottish Office, 1951–5. In 1955 he inherited his father's title as 14th earl of Home and entered the House of Lords. He joined the CABINET in the same year as Commonwealth secretary, a post he retained until 1960. He was deputy leader of the Lords, 1957, leader, 1957–60, lord president of the council, 1957 and 1959–60, and foreign secretary, 1960–3, a role in which he emerged as strongly anti-Soviet. In all these roles he was competent but inconspicuous.

Home emerged, to the surprise of the public, as leader of the CONSERVATIVE PARTY, and prime minister, following Harold MACMILLAN's sudden resignation in 1963. The party was divided over the other possible contenders and he became leader following inner-party consultations; there was not at that time an open voting system for the party leadership. Iain MACLEOD and Enoch POWELL refused to serve in the cabinet with him. It was necessary for Home to take the previously impossible step of renouncing his earldom and standing for election to the House of COMMONS. The renunciation was made possible by the Peerage Act, 1963 (*see* LORDS, HOUSE OF), and he re-entered the House of Commons as Sir Alec Douglas-Home, following a by-election in Kinross and West Perthshire, which he represented until 1974. In April 1964 Douglas-Home announced an election in the autumn. His background made it difficult for him to compete with the modernizing election message of Harold WILSON, and he did not present himself well on television; the Conservatives narrowly lost the election. There was opposition to Douglas-Home in the party and he resigned as leader in 1965. He remained as shadow foreign secretary, 1965–70, and supported Harold Wilson's unsuccessful 1969 plan to reduce the House of Lords to 250 nominated peers. When the Conservatives regained power in 1970 he once more became foreign secretary, 1970–4. He supported entry to the European Community, and sought moderation in Rhodesia (*see* ZIMBABWE). He also chaired a party committee that in 1970 called for an elected Scottish Convention with limited powers (*see* DEVOLUTION). In 1974 he returned to the House of Lords as life peer, with the title Baron Home of the Hirsel.

FURTHER READING R.S. Churchill, *The Fight for the Tory Leadership* (1964); Lord Home, *The Way the Wind Blows* (1976); D.R. Thorpe, *Alec Douglas-Home* (1996).

Dowding, Hugh. *See* BRITAIN, BATTLE OF; ROYAL AIR FORCE.

Downing Street declaration (1993). *See* NORTHERN IRELAND.

drama. The two leading British dramatists at the beginning of the century were Arthur Wing Pinero (1855–1934) and Henry Arthur Jones (1851–1929), but they were overtaken in public esteem and influence by George Bernard SHAW. The plays of John GALSWORTHY (1867–1933) were also successful. Both he and Shaw had plays performed at the Royal Court Theatre under the management of Harley Granville-Barker (1877–1946). Barker himself both acted and wrote plays, mainly concerned with moral and political issues, as were those of Galsworthy and Shaw. Closer to fantasy, though not lacking in social comment, were the plays of J.M. Barrie (1860–1937), notably *Peter Pan* (1904). The Irishman J.M. Synge (1871–1909) wrote distinguished work, rooted in Irish life, such as *The Playboy of the Western World* (1907). There was a strand of poetic drama running through the work of his compatriot William Butler YEATS (1865–1939), and through that of John Masefield (1878–1967), T.S. ELIOT and Christopher Fry (1907–). In comedy, large audiences were drawn from the Edwardian period into the interwar years to the work of Somerset Maugham (1874–1965), then to the plays of Noël Coward (1899–1973), such as *Hay Fever* (1925) and *Private Lives* (1930), and the farces of Ben Travers (1886–1980). In the newly independent Irish Free State of the 1920s, Sean O'Casey (1884–1964) critically examined the nature of Irish nationalism in *The Shadow of a Gunman* (1923), *Juno and the Paycock* (1924) and *The Plough and the Stars* (1926).

Revivals and escapism predominated during World War II, as for a time after the war did drawing-room comedy, farces and popular thrillers. Terence Rattigan (1911–77) used the form of the drawing-room drama to explore serious personal issues, as in *The Winslow Boy* (1946) and *The Browning Version* (1948). John Osborne (1929–64) created a sensation in 1956 with his first play, *Look Back in Anger*, performed at the Royal Court Theatre, which became the home of innovative and controversial drama. For his attempt at realistically portraying the seediness of everyday life in this 'kitchen sink' drama, and his criticism of contemporary culture, Osborne came to be defined as one of an emerging group of 'Angry Young Men' (many of the others were novelists, such as John Braine, whose *Room at the Top* was published in 1957, and Alan Sillitoe, with *Saturday Night and Sunday Morning*, 1958). Arnold Wesker (1932–) also wrote plays in more proletarian settings than the British theatre had previously been accustomed to, as did the Irishman Brendan Behan (1923–64) and Shelagh Delaney (1939–). These last two were promoted by Joan Littlewood's East London Theatre Workshop, which sought out radical new playwrights. Littlewood's most famous production was *Oh, What a Lovely War!* (1963), a Brechtian attack on World War I and implicitly on all war (Littlewood was a prominent member of CND).

Most influential, however, were Samuel Beckett (1906–89), from the London opening in 1955 of his *Waiting for Godot*; and Harold Pinter (1930–), whose first play to appear was *The Birthday Party* (1958). The 1960s was an especially productive time for British theatre, with Robert Bolt (1924– 94), Peter Shaffer (1926–), Peter Nichols (1927–), Tom Stoppard (1937–), Joe Orton (1933–67) and Christopher Hampton (1946–) all producing new plays, varied in style and content, many of them at the NATIONAL THEATRE (formed in 1963). The abolition of stage CENSORSHIP in 1968 took the shackles off the theatre. The following decade saw the emergence of a generation of politically and socially radical dramatists: David Hare (1947–), Howard Brenton (1942–), Howard Barker (1946–) and the 7:84 Theatre Company of John McGrath (1935–). More conventional and more popular contemporary dramatists to the end of the century were Michael Frayn (1933–), Simon Gray (1926–) and Alan Ayckbourn (1939–). There were strikingly few successful female dramatists, a notable exception being Caryl Churchill (1938–).

FURTHER READING C. Innes, *Modern British Drama* (1992); J.R. Taylor, *Anger and After: A Guide to the New British Drama* (2nd edn, 1977).

Dreadnought, HMS, the first modern battleship, which revolutionized naval warfare. At the beginning of the century the ROYAL NAVY, as the leading naval force internationally, felt threatened by advances in gunnery technology, which it feared might render the armaments of existing battleships redundant. In 1905 the first sea lord, Sir John FISHER, ordered the construction of a new battleship that made full use of modern gunnery. The outcome was HMS *Dreadnought,* built at the Royal Dockyard at Plymouth within a year in 1905–6. It was not only better equipped but also faster than any existing battleship. It forced rival navies to build ships of the new type, which became known generically as 'dreadnoughts'. By the time of WORLD WAR I all of the major world battle fleets consisted of dreadnoughts. HMS *Dreadnought* itself fought through World War I, after which it was decommissioned and sold for scrap.

FURTHER READING R. Hough, *Dreadnought: A History of the Modern Battleship* (2nd edn, 1968).

Dresden, bombing of (1945). The city of Dresden in eastern Germany was bombed by an Anglo-American force on 13–14 February 1945. 774 British bombers struck by night, and 450 American bombers on the following day. Most of Dresden's anti-aircraft guns had been sent to the Ruhr to assist defence there, where it was thought to be more urgent. The dead in Dresden were overwhelmingly civilians, a high proportion of them women, children and older people who had fled from bombing elsewhere to Dresden, which had not previously been bombed. The total number of deaths is unknown; it was not less than 60,000 and was probably higher. The city, until then one of the most beautiful in central Europe, was destroyed. The raids were carried out to support the Soviet offensive on the Eastern Front (since Dresden was a major communications centre), to assert Allied authority over Germany and, in the case of Britain, in revenge for the bombing of British civilians, especially the attack on Coventry in 1940. It has also been suggested that it was intended to show

the advancing Soviets the strength of British and US air power. For the remainder of the century it was debated in Britain whether such slaughter of civilians was justified when the war was almost won by the Allies.

SEE ALSO HARRIS, ARTHUR.

FURTHER READING M. Connelly, *Reaching for the Stars* (2001); R. Neillands, *The Bomber War* (2001).

drug addiction. Drug addiction was not a highly visible or a serious problem at the beginning of the century. The state paid little attention to it, although it had long existed on a limited scale, and the concept of addiction was not recognized until around the time of World War I. At this time Britain introduced controls under pressure from the United States, which was concerned about the trade in drugs from East Asia. Also during the war (unjustified) fears arose of an epidemic of cocaine addiction among British soldiers mixing with prostitutes, and this led to the introduction of narcotics regulation in 1916 under the DEFENCE OF THE REALM ACT (DORA). International drug control was incorporated in the Versailles settlement that followed the war.

Thereafter Britain followed a penal approach to drug control, inaugurated by the Dangerous Drugs Act, 1920, which located control in the Home Office rather than the Ministry of Health, which might have emphasized prevention and support. The medical profession reasserted their role in the Rolleston Report, 1926, which permitted medically controlled 'maintenance prescribing' to addicts who would otherwise be unable to function. This remained the British approach, under Home Office supervision, until the 1960s. Throughout this time the numbers of addicts were small.

Numbers of addicts grew from the SIXTIES as the non-medical use of drugs such as heroin and cocaine spread, and cannabis especially was increasingly used as a recreational drug. Other drugs, in particular amphetamines, were also in wider use. The Dangerous Drugs Act, 1967, controlled the prescribing of amphetamines and banned prescription of heroin and cocaine by general practitioners, placing it in the hands of specialists working in drug-dependence units. All addicts were to be formally notified to the Home Office. Numbers of addicts seemed to stabilize in the 1970s, but availability of a variety of drugs increased and levels of addiction rose in the 1980s and 1990s.

Drug trafficking (supplying illegal drugs) became a notifiable offence in 1982. Between 1987 and 1997 these offences, which are regarded as serious by the courts, increased from about 7000 to over 23,000. The spread of drug dependency had a serious impact on the amount of crime, especially robbery. Use of heroin and cocaine was estimated to have increased crime rates by one-third by the end of the century.

The government continued to seek means to control and punish the sale and use of harmful drugs and to educate people in the dangers of drug abuse, with no evident success. A campaign, begun in the 1960s, for a distinction to be drawn between seriously harmful substances, such as heroin and cocaine, and less harmful drugs, in particular cannabis, continued, but was resisted by government on the grounds of conflicting evidence as to whether cannabis was indeed harmful. There were also growing pressures to legalize cannabis for the use of those suffering from certain medical conditions – such as multiple sclerosis and the effects of certain cancer therapies – for whom the drug appeared to provide relief.

FURTHER READING V. Berridge, 'Drugs and Social Policy: The Establishment of Drug Control in Britain, 1900–1930' in *British Journal of Addiction*, Vol. 79 (1984) 17–29; G. Stimpson

and E. Oppenheimer, *Heroin Addiction: Treatment and Control in Britain* (1992).

Dunkirk, port town in northern France from which a mass evacuation of Allied troops took place during WORLD WAR II, from 27 May to 4 June 1940. Earlier that spring the British Expeditionary Force had landed in France to help the French and Belgian armies counter a brilliantly successful German offensive. The Allies were soon trapped, however, when an unexpected and swift German advance sent forces southwest past Dunkirk to the English Channel. A counter-offensive kept the Germans in check briefly while the Allies considered their position. Realizing the futility and danger of the situation, the British government ordered the evacuation of troops on 26 May. A hastily established flotilla of some 850 boats – including everything from navy vessels to small civilian pleasure craft – was despatched, and, remarkably, some 330,000 troops were rescued and taken back to England. About 233,000 of these were surviving members of the British Expeditionary Force. The cooperative efforts made to pull off the evacuation were inspirational to many, and what became known as the 'spirit of Dunkirk' proved to be a morale booster to Britons throughout the war. Although all of the Allies' heavy weaponry and equipment had of necessity to be left behind, many historians have suggested that the evacuation may have been a vital factor in Britain's eventual winning of the war, as it saved its only large contingent of trained troops.

FURTHER READING R. Jackson, *Dunkirk: The British Evacuation 1940* (1976); P. Turnbull, *Dunkirk: Anatomy of Disaster* (1978).

E

Easter Rising (24–29 April 1916), armed rebellion in Dublin aimed at striking a blow for Irish independence. The timing of the rising was designed to take advantage of Britain's attention being turned while it fought World War I in Europe. The rebellion was led by Patrick (Padraig) Pearse of the Irish Republican Brotherhood and James Connolly of SINN FÉIN. The nationalist rebel forces established themselves in several centres around the city, but their headquarters were located at the General Post Office in Sackville (now O'Connell) Street. It was on the steps of the GPO that Pearse proclaimed the birth of the Irish Republic, with himself as president of its provisional government. After five days of fighting British troops the rebels were forced to surrender. They had been unsuccessful in their attempt to obtain arms from Germany, which partly explained the failure of the rebellion to spread nationwide as its leaders had planned. Pearse, Connolly and twelve other leaders were summarily shot, while over 2000 others were interned.

In its immediate aims the rebellion was a failure, partly due to the fact that the nationalist rebels received little support from an Irish public more supportive of HOME RULE than the establishment of a republic (*see* IRELAND). However, the heavy-handedness of the British in punishing all those involved, including the execution of its leaders, shocked the nation. The rising and its aftermath were key factors in the subsequent rapid growth of Irish nationalism.

SEE ALSO CASEMENT, ROGER; CONSCRIPTION; MARKIEWICZ, CONSTANCE.

FURTHER READING M. Caulfield, *The Easter Rebellion* (1995).

Ecology Party. *See* ENVIRONMENTALISM.

Eden, (Robert) Anthony (1897–1977), Conservative politician; PRIME MINISTER (1955–7). Educated at Eton College and Oxford University, Eden was elected MP for Warwick and Leamington in 1923 at the age of 27 and continued to represent this constituency until his retirement from the House of COMMONS in 1957. He was parliamentary private secretary, 1926–9, to Austen CHAMBERLAIN during the latter's period as foreign secretary; parliamentary undersecretary at the Foreign Office, 1931–4; lord privy seal, 1934–5; minister for League of Nations affairs, with a seat in the cabinet, 1935; and foreign secretary from 1935 until his resignation in 1938 in protest against the APPEASEMENT of Italy. Biographers have suggested that he was less critical of Germany, and that his attitude even to Italy was equivocal since he supported the lifting of LEAGUE OF NATIONS sanctions against Italy following the ABYSSINIAN CRISIS.

It is suggested that the resignation was motivated less by principle than by pique at being overruled by Neville CHAMBERLAIN in foreign affairs.

Eden returned to government as dominions secretary, 1939-40, and then in CHURCHILL's coalition he was secretary of state for war (May–December 1940) and then foreign secretary again until 1945. He emerged as Churchill's principal lieutenant, although they often disagreed, for example over relations with the Soviet Union, which Eden was more anxious to appease. Privately he strongly disagreed with Churchill's outspoken anti-Soviet stance after the war, and he appears to have resented the fact that Churchill did not hand over leadership of the party to him after the war or after the Conservative election defeat of 1950. He became a knight of the Garter in 1954, and was foreign secretary again from 1951 to 1955, although his relationship with Churchill was now openly hostile.

In 1955 Eden succeeded Churchill as prime minister and led the Conservatives to an immediate election victory. Shortly after, the government faced economic problems and more serious difficulties in Egypt, where Gamal Abdel Nasser was leading a campaign against continuing British influence in the region. The remainder of Eden's period as prime minister was dominated by the SUEZ CRISIS. This began when Nasser nationalized the Suez Canal. Eden wished to resist this with military force and made a catastrophic attempt to do so, which was opposed by sections of his own government, by the United States, the COMMONWEALTH, the UNITED NATIONS and the LABOUR PARTY. A humiliating withdrawal followed. Eden's health had been failing for some time, partly because of an operation in 1953 that had gone wrong. He resigned as prime minister and as a member of Parliament in January 1957. He accepted a peerage in 1961 and became earl of Avon.

FURTHER READING D. Carlton, *Anthony Eden: A Biography* (1981); A. Eden, *The Eden Memoirs* (3 vols., 1960–5); R. Rhodes James, *Anthony Eden* (1986).

education. Education in Britain underwent considerable change in the 20th century. In 1900, secondary and higher education were still mainly confined to the middle and upper classes. The 1870 Education Act had ensured that all children could receive what was known as an 'elementary education' from the age of 5, but the school-leaving age was set at just 10. Compulsory attendance was established in 1880, and state education became free of charge in 1891. The leaving age was raised to 12 by 1899, but most working-class children still left school as soon as they were able, in order to begin work.

The 1902 Education Act (often known as the Balfour Act since it owed much to the work of Arthur BALFOUR) abolished the separately elected local school boards set up by the 1870 act and replaced them with local education authorities (LEAs), which were subcommittees of elected local borough and county councils. LEAs were responsible for providing state-school education in their areas, and also gave grants to local voluntary (church) schools. In 1907 state grants were made to fee-paying secondary schools to admit free of charge a limited number of elementary school pupils, selected by examination. The 1918 Education Act (often called the Fisher Act after H.A.L. Fisher, the Oxford historian who was president of the Board of Education at the time) raised the school-leaving age to 14. It also aimed to provide limited secondary education for 14- to 18-year olds, but this was never enacted because of postwar budget restrictions.

It was the next Education Act, in 1944, that did most to shape schooling into a form recognizable today. The act (also known as the Butler Act, since R.A. BUTLER played a major role in bringing it into being), raised the school-leaving age again, to 15. (It was raised again in 1973 to 16, where it remained until the end of the century and beyond.) Most importantly, the 1944 act provided for free, compulsory secondary education. Thereafter state secondary education began for all from the age of 11 (12 in Scotland); state schools for children below this age became known as primary schools. There were serious efforts after World War II to improve conditions and standards in primary schools, in particular to reduce class sizes: classes of 50 or 60 pupils had not been uncommon in pre-war elementary schools. In secondary education, the 1944 act introduced the 'tripartite' system whereby pupils were to be streamed into one of three types of schooling, depending on their performance in a qualifying exam taken at age 11 (the 'eleven-plus' as it came to be known). Those with good academic ability who performed well in the 'eleven-plus' were admitted to grammar schools, some of which also admitted fee-paying pupils. Pupils who were judged to possess practical, vocational abilities were to enter technical schools. The remaining pupils attended 'secondary modern' schools.

The tripartite system never developed fully: in particular, few technical schools were provided. Social research in the 1950s indicated that the 'eleven-plus' was socially selective, with better-off children having a greater chance of success and hence of entry to grammar schools. Nationally, about 25% of all pupils attended grammar schools; however, it also became apparent that the ratio of grammar-school places to potential pupils was highly variable from place to place, for historical reasons: the old fee-paying grammar schools had not been evenly distributed around the country, and few new schools were built for some years after the war. There were also more of such schools for boys than for girls (most grammar schools were single sex). Consequently girls had fewer opportunities of gaining grammar-school places than boys and had to achieve higher scores in the 'eleven-plus' to receive a place: a discriminatory process compounded by the fact that girls on average gained higher scores in the tests than did boys. There was also concern about the quality of secondary modern schools, a high proportion of whose pupils left school at the minimum age without formal qualifications. In consequence the system came under increasing criticism, and from 1965 Harold WILSON's Labour government initiated the establishment of 'comprehensive' schools, which did not select on the basis of ability. Such schools were already operating successfully in some rural areas. It was hoped that the comprehensive system would eventually become universal, and by the early 1980s many state secondary schools had become comprehensives. The system of school-leaving examinations, known from the early 1980s as General Certificates of Secondary Education (GCSE), was extended with the aim of providing a measure of attainment for all school-leavers. Local authorities retained a high degree of independent control over the form and content of education in their areas and were allowed to retain selection at age 11 if they wished. A minority did so, and the grammar schools never wholly disappeared. They were given a further lease of life in the 1980s and 1990s when successive Conservative governments promoted the right of parents to choose which type of school their children would attend.

In 1988, concerns about falling standards in state schools led to the passage of the Education Reform Act, which provided for the establishment of a National Curriculum. This laid down the subjects to be taught and the content of courses, according to different age groups, known as 'key stages'. There was also a standardized system of testing. After much criticism and protest from teachers concerning the scope of the National Curriculum, it was revised in 1994. The 1988 Education Reform Act also attempted to undo the levelling effects of the comprehensive system by allowing state schools to opt out of local council control and become grant-maintained. The Labour government elected in 1997 did not reverse these changes and took further steps to raise standards, focusing initially on primary schools by introducing compulsory periods of literacy and numeracy teaching into the curriculum.

Although the vast majority of British children in the 20th century attended state schools, private options continued to exist. These included some grammar schools as well as the confusingly named 'public' schools, some of which had been in existence for centuries. Traditionally used by the wealthy and the upper classes, all public schools charge fees and most also board their pupils. In addition to the elite minority of high-status public schools (e.g. Eton and Winchester for boys, Benenden and Cheltenham for girls), which provided high standards of education in return for high fees, there were also throughout the century large numbers of fee-paying private schools, both day and boarding, of highly variable quality and cost, some excellent, some very poor. Throughout the century approximately 5–8% of children attended fee-paying (or, as they increasingly chose to call themselves in the later 20th century, 'independent') schools.

The majority of students educated privately went on to universities, but numbers of state-educated students going on to higher education rose sharply in the 1990s with the conversion of many polytechnics and other institutions of higher education into universities after 1992, and the consequent rapid expansion of university places.

SEE ALSO ADULT EDUCATION; OPEN UNIVERSITY; UNIVERSITIES.

FURTHER READING: H. Silver, *Education as History: Interpreting Nineteenth- and Twentieth-Century Education* (1983); G. Smith, 'Schools' in A.H. Halsey and J. Webb (eds.), *Twentieth Century British Social Trends* (2000), 179–220.

Education Acts (1902, 1918, 1944). *See* EDUCATION.

Education Reform Act (1988). *See* EDUCATION.

Edward VII (1841–1910), king of Great Britain and Ireland and emperor of INDIA (1901–10). The eldest son and second child of Queen Victoria and Prince Albert, he was born Prince Albert Edward and created prince of WALES a month after his birth. Educated at Edinburgh University, Christ Church College, Oxford, and Trinity College, Cambridge, Edward showed little aptitude for intellectual pursuits and later joined the Grenadier Guards. He married Princess Alexandra of Denmark, daughter of the future King Christian IX of Denmark, in 1863. They had six children: Prince Albert Victor, known as Eddy (who died in 1892); Prince George (the future King GEORGE V); Princess Louise, the princess royal; Princess Victoria; Princess Maud; and Prince Alexander (who died in infancy).

As prince of Wales Edward had a somewhat hedonistic reputation and was at the epicentre of fashionable society in the late Victorian age. His predilections for horseracing, theatre-going, foreign travel and extramarital affairs made many observers, including his own mother, worry that he possessed a character unfit for kingship. As a result Victoria assigned him almost no constitutional duties and did not allow him access to state documents until very late in her reign.

Edward was 60 years old by the time he ascended the throne in 1901, but surprised many by quickly becoming a popular and competent monarch. The state visit he made with Queen Alexandra to France in 1903 was widely regarded as having paved the way for the ENTENTE CORDIALE between Britain and France. As king, Edward gained a reputation as a kind of 'uncle' to all of Europe, who could exert control over his wayward relatives such as the German Kaiser, although historians have since downplayed his influence in British foreign policy during his reign. Edward is also notable for having restored and to some extent created more of the pomp, pageantry, glamour and excitement of the MONARCHY after the rather austere reign of Victoria. He attended more state events (which his mother had found burdensome), invented others, and presided over all with relish. By his death in 1910 'Good Old Teddy' was a much-loved king genuinely mourned by his subjects.

FURTHER READING C. Hibbert, *Edward VII: A Portrait* (1976).

Edward VIII (1894–1972), king of Great Britain and Ireland and emperor of INDIA (1936). The eldest son of the duke and duchess of York (later King GEORGE V and Queen Mary), he was educated at the Royal Naval Colleges of Osborne and Dartmouth and at Magdalen College, Oxford. Christened Edward but known as David to his family, he was created prince of WALES in 1911, and went on to achieve much public popularity due to his charm, informal manner and modern playboy image. He undertook several foreign tours in the 1920s, representing his father George V in the EMPIRE and beyond, and expressed concern for the plight of the unemployed in the 1930s. His brief reign in 1936, during which he styled himself Edward VIII, was troubled. His determination to marry the American divorcée Wallis Simpson (1896–1986), in spite of disapproval from both the government and the royal family, brought about the ABDICATION CRISIS, which resulted in his voluntary exile with Mrs Simpson to France and the accession of his younger brother to the throne as King GEORGE VI. He was created HRH the duke of Windsor after the abdication. Edward and Mrs Simpson married in June 1937 and went on to lead lives devoted mainly to fashionable leisure, though Edward did serve as governor of the Bahamas from 1940 to 1945. He died in 1972 and his body was returned to Britain for royal burial.

Edward's romantic public image was that of a fashionable playboy prince, who gave up the material trappings of royalty in order to marry the woman he loved. His decision to abdicate, however, deeply wounded the royal family, who considered his actions a selfish betrayal of his birthright and duty. Future generations of the family were also hurt by persistent suggestions that he may have been a traitor to Britain, precipitated mainly by his trip to Germany and subsequent meetings with Hitler in 1937. It has been suggested that it was because of suspicions about his loyalty that he was despatched to the Bahamas during WORLD WAR II, to prevent him becoming a figurehead in any puppet government should Britain be defeated.

Notwithstanding these suspicions, he and Mrs Simpson remained celebrity figures throughout the 20th century, as demonstrated by the great public interest in the 1998 auction of their personal belongings in New York.

FURTHER READING Lord Beaverbrook (M. Aitken), *The Abdication of King Edward VIII* (1966); P. Ziegler, *King Edward VIII* (1991).

Eire. *See* IRELAND.

El Alamein, battles of (1942), three important WORLD WAR II engagements to the south of El Alamein, a town on the Mediterranean coast of Egypt, west of the Nile. The battles stopped the Axis (Italian-German) drive into Egypt, led by General Erwin Rommel. The Axis onslaught on Egypt began in the spring of 1942 and was initially successful against British forces, who retreated to a defensive line between El Alamein and the Qattara Depression to the south. In the first battle (1–3 July) the British 8th Army, under the commander in chief, Middle East, General Sir Claude AUCHINLECK, stopped the Axis drive towards the Nile Delta. The British reinforced their positions through the summer, and in August Auchinleck was replaced as commander in chief, Middle East, by General Sir Harold ALEXANDER, while General Sir Bernard MONTGOMERY took over the 8th Army. In the second battle of El Alamein (30 August–6 September) the British stopped another Axis advance. In the third, decisive battle (23 October–4 November) the 8th Army advanced against Rommel's forces, forcing them to retreat westwards into Libya. The 8th Army was supported by British naval attacks on Italian supply convoys, American supplies and by the increasing German absorption in the Eastern Front. On 8 November Allied forces landed in northwest Africa, and Rommel found himself between two advancing Allied armies.

FURTHER READING C. Barnett, *The Desert Generals* (1982).

electoral reform. *See* EQUAL FRANCHISE ACT (1928); REPRESENTATION OF THE PEOPLE ACTS, 1918, 1948, 1969.

electoral system. *See* EQUAL FRANCHISE ACT (1928); GENERAL ELECTIONS; LOCAL GOVERNMENT; PROPORTIONAL REPRESENTATION; REPRESENTATION OF THE PEOPLE ACTS, 1918, 1948, 1969.

Elgar, Edward (William) (1857–1934), composer. Born near Worcester, the son of a Roman Catholic, Elgar received some formal instrumental tuition but was largely self-taught as a composer, absorbing much from books and scores in his father's music shop. He earned his living as a violin teacher in the Midlands and gained experience in performing and conducting at local musical events. He joined W.C. Stockley's orchestra in Birmingham, which performed his *Serenade Mauresque* in 1883. In the following year his *Sevillana* was performed in London. His marriage in 1889 to (Caroline) Alice Roberts, the daughter of a major general, enhanced his security and social status. Thereafter he gradually gained national and international respect, such compositions as the orchestral *Variations on an Original Theme* ('Enigma') of 1899, the oratorio *The Dream of Gerontius* (1900) and the first march of *Pomp and Circumstance* (1901) making him Britain's leading composer by the beginning of the 20th century. The music of the first *Pomp and Circumstance* march was linked with Arthur Benson's words 'Land of hope and glory …' to become a popular patriotic anthem. This was followed by the overture *Cockaigne (In London Town)* (1901), the oratorios *The Apostles* (1903) and *The Kingdom* (1906) and the *Introduction and Allegro* for strings (1905).

Elgar was the first Peyton professor of music at Birmingham University, 1905–8. Thereafter he produced two popular symphonies, in A flat major (1908) and E flat major (1911), a violin concerto (1910) and the 'symphonic study' *Falstaff* (1913). World War I slowed his output, though he produced *The Spirit of England* in 1917, in part a lament for the fallen, his last major work for soloists, chorus and orchestra. Immediately after the war he produced a number of chamber works and a cello concerto (1919). Following the death of his wife in 1920 he produced no further major works, but was active in conducting his own music in the concert hall and in the recording studio.
SEE ALSO MUSIC.
FURTHER READING M. Kennedy, *Portrait of Elgar* (1982); B. Maine, *Elgar: His Life and Works* (2 vols., 1933); J. Northrop Moore, *Edward Elgar: A Creative Life* (1984).

Eliot, T(homas) S(tearns) (1888–1965), poet, dramatist and critic. Eliot was the grandson of a New Englander, who moved to St Louis, Missouri and founded a Unitarian church and Washington University. His father was a successful brick manufacturer, who did not encourage his literary interests; his mother was a poet who did encourage him. Eliot was educated at Harvard University, the Sorbonne and Merton College, Oxford, where he completed a PhD dissertation in philosophy. His collection *Prufrock and Other Observations* (1917) is regarded as a landmark of modernist writing. This was followed by *Poems* (1919) and *Poems, 1909–25*, which included 'The Hollow Men' (1925). In 1915 he married an Englishwoman, Vivien Haigh-Wood, who was to suffer a succession of physical and emotional illnesses; the marriage ended in 1932. Eliot himself had a breakdown in 1921. While recovering he wrote *The Waste Land* (1922), which seemed to express the dislocation of Europe after WORLD WAR I. In 1925 he became a director of the London publishing house of Faber and Faber, building up a list of MODERNIST poets. He became a British subject in 1927, and continued to publish through the 1930s and 1940s; works from this period include 'Ash Wednesday' (1930), which expresses his conversion to Anglo-Catholicism (in 1927), the poetic dramas *Murder in the Cathedral* (1935) and *The Family Reunion* (1939), the *Four Quartets* (1936–42) and a book of verse for children, *Old*

Possum's Book of Practical Cats (1939), which was turned into the highly successful stage musical *Cats* in 1981. After World War II he produced further successful plays: *The Cocktail Party* (1950), *The Confidential Clerk* (1954) and *The Elder Statesman* (1959). He was awarded the Nobel Prize for literature and the Order of Merit in 1948. In 1957 he married Valerie Fletcher, his long-time secretary at the publishing house of Faber and Faber.
FURTHER READING C. Behr, *T.S. Eliot: A Chronology of his Life and Works* (1983).

Elizabeth II (1926–), queen of Great Britain and Northern Ireland and head of the Commonwealth (1952–). The eldest daughter of the duke and duchess of York (later King GEORGE VI and Queen Elizabeth), she was born in London as Princess Elizabeth Alexandra Mary of York, and was privately educated. She became heir presumptive to the throne in 1936, with the abdication of her uncle EDWARD VIII and the accession of her father. In 1945 she worked briefly for the war effort and trained to drive ambulances. In 1947 she married her cousin Lieutenant Philip Mountbatten, who was created duke of Edinburgh on the eve of their wedding and was styled Prince Philip in 1957. They have four children: CHARLES, PRINCE OF WALES; Princess Anne, the princess royal; Prince Andrew, duke of York; and Prince Edward, earl of Wessex.

Elizabeth became queen upon the death of her father on 6 February 1952. She was in KENYA on a state visit at the time and immediately flew back to London. Her coronation in June 1953 was the first to be televised, and was seen by a worldwide audience of millions. Politically her reign has seen the rapid DECOLONIZATION of the British EMPIRE, but the queen has consistently shown great interest in retaining and strengthening old imperial ties in the form of the revamped COMMONWEALTH of nations. Thanks to developments in modern transportation, she has been able to travel more widely than any previous monarch, both within Britain and throughout the world.

Elizabeth's reign has also been characterized by increasingly intrusive media scrutiny, particularly of her children and their spouses. Any restraint the British press had exercised early in her reign dissolved in the 1980s and 1990s, with a stream of salacious coverage of the royal family's private lives. The queen has retained a good deal of respect and popularity, particularly among older members of the British public. However, she was not immune to growing criticism in the 1980s and 1990s that the royal family was out of touch with the mass of the British public and that their lifestyles were too ostentatious. In the wake of the death of DIANA, PRINCESS OF WALES in 1997 and the resulting backlash of ill feeling towards the MONARCHY, the queen initiated further reforms, including the decommissioning of the royal yacht *Britannia* and the relaxation of some forms of protocol.
SEE ALSO CIVIL LIST.
FURTHER READING B. Pimlott, *The Queen: A Biography of Queen Elizabeth II* (1996).

emigration. During the 19th century large numbers of British people emigrated, mainly to the United States and the countries of the EMPIRE. Emigration diminished somewhat from the beginning of the 20th century, partly because, with rising living standards in Britain, it became less enticing. Other countries were also less willing to accept migrants in the Depression of the interwar years, and they had fewer economic opportunities to offer.

About 1,816,000 migrants left Great Britain and Ireland between 1901 and 1910, half of them for the dominions of the empire (principally AUSTRALIA, CANADA, NEW ZEALAND and SOUTH AFRICA); and a further 1,811,553 left between 1920 and 1929, over 65% bound for the dominions. In the Depression years 1930–9 the number fell to 334,467 and for the first time for many decades immigration exceeded emigration; numbers of emigrants rose again to 652,000 in the period 1950–9. Emigrants tended to be young (mainly under 45) and in the 20th century included more women and children than in the previous century; migration from IRELAND was unusual in that women generally outnumbered men. The rate of emigration from Ireland and SCOTLAND was consistently higher than from England and WALES.

The British government encouraged migration to the colonies in order to ensure the cultural predominance of 'British stock' and to retain British control of the empire. For example, former soldiers were encouraged by favourable land settlements to migrate to South Africa following the BOER WAR – although they did not do so in the numbers hoped for. After World War I the government financed low-cost assisted passages for migrants to the dominions; initially, in 1919, this scheme was for ex-servicemen and their families, as part of the strategy for preventing unrest in Britain if former servicemen faced UNEMPLOYMENT and POVERTY, as it was feared they would. This measure was followed by the Empire Settlement Act, 1922, which provided for the funding of land-settlement schemes and assisted passages, in cooperation with the dominion governments. Between 1922 and 1936 this scheme assisted the passages of 405,230 people, about 36% of all migrants to the empire in these years. Most of them went to Canada or Australia, and only 1226 to South Africa. The act was renewed in 1937, 1952, 1957, 1962 and 1967 and expired in 1972, but the government never succeeded in spending all the money allocated to the scheme.

By the 1970s the British government no longer had an incentive to retain cultural control of an empire that had largely vanished. In addition, the former colonies were unwilling to encourage migrants unless they had skills necessary to their economic success, and were increasingly ready to welcome migrants from countries other than Britain. By the end of the century the EUROPEAN UNION had eased movement for work within Europe, and increasing numbers of British people took advantage of this opportunity.

FURTHER READING N.H. Carrier and J.A. Jeffrey, *External Migration, 1814–1950: A Study of the Available Statistics* (1953); S. Constantine (ed.), *Emigrants and Empire: British Settlement in the Dominions between the Wars* (1990).

empire. In the 20th century the British empire reached its zenith, in physical terms, becoming the largest empire the world had ever known. By the end of World War I it encompassed a quarter of the globe's land area, and was claimed to be populated by one-fifth of the world's people. It was proudly referred to by Britons as an empire on which 'the sun never set'. Nevertheless, in its apparent strength and glory were already sown the seeds of its demise. The history of the British empire from 1900 was largely characterized by its slow decline, and historians have argued that the roots of this downward movement stretch back into the late 19th century.

The imperial history of the 20th century began with Britain's Pyrrhic victory in the second BOER WAR (1899–1902). It was a humiliating experience for the British ARMY, which had confidently expected to rout a peasant rabble but found difficulty in resisting the Boers' guerrilla tactics. The recruitment process for the war had also brought the precarious state of health of the British working class into public view, and provoked fears that the British 'race' was degenerating into feebleness (*see* MEDICINE; STANDARDS OF LIVING). The 'high imperialism' and general optimism of Britons in the late Victorian age gave way to pessimism after the turn of the century, and there was a growing sense that British domestic affairs were of greater importance than the empire.

The struggles of WORLD WAR I reinforced these fears. Though colonial troops, particularly those from the 'white' dominions and INDIA, rallied to Britain's cause, the tenacity of the Germans confirmed fears concerning Britain's position as an imperial power. Although the empire grew after the war ended, through its acquisition of 'mandates' over former German and Turkish possessions (*see* VERSAILLES, TREATY OF), there were now very real concerns that Britain could not hold on to the empire in its existing form much longer. Britain struggled on throughout the 1920s and 1930s, but its inability to protect its imperial interests was made plain during WORLD WAR II, when its Australasian dominions and colonies were left to fend for themselves against the Japanese as the British struggled to keep the Germans from their own shores.

Agitation came from within the colonies as well as from external forces. Although there had been nationalist movements in various colonies before World War II, most notably in India, the experience of war subsequently gave nationalism enormous impetus. The fact that the British colonial masters had been ousted from colonies such as Burma and Malaya by the Japanese, an Asian people, demonstrated to many subject peoples that the British were not all-powerful and had failed to protect them. The costs of war meant that Britain could no longer afford to support and administer a vast empire. Britain also came under pressure to decolonize from its US ally. The movement towards the general DECOLONIZATION of the empire began in India, where Britain handed over power in 1947. In the 1950s and 1960s a torrent of other colonies in Asia, Africa and the Caribbean followed in demanding independence.

With neither the power to keep the empire together by force, nor the support of an increasingly inward-looking British public behind them, supporters of the empire soon realized that it had to change in some way if any semblance of it was to be retained. The answer lay in the foundation, promotion and growth of the COMMONWEALTH. The term 'British Commonwealth of Nations' had been used as early as World War I to describe the relationship between Britain and the 'white' dominions, but it only began to be used to replace the term 'empire' after 1947 and the independence of India. In that year 'emperor of India' was dropped from King GEORGE VI's list of titles and the designation 'head of the Commonwealth' was added –

a clear sign that the empire as Britain had known it for over three hundred years was no more.
FURTHER READING T.O. Lloyd, *The British Empire, 1558–1995* (2nd edn, 1996); P.J. Marshall (ed.), *The Cambridge Illustrated History of the British Empire* (1996); B. Porter, *The Lion's Share: A Short History of British Imperialism 1850–1995* (1996).

Empire Windrush. *See* IMMIGRATION.

Employment Policy White Paper (1944). *See* UNEMPLOYMENT.

Enigma code. *See* BLETCHLEY PARK.

ENSA. *See* ENTERTAINMENTS NATIONAL SERVICE ASSOCIATION.

Entente Cordiale (French, 'friendly understanding'), the agreement made in 1904 between Britain and France, mainly to support each other's colonial policies. (The term is less commonly used to describe Anglo-French agreements in the 19th century.) The state visit of EDWARD VII to France in 1903 helped to prepare for greater Anglo-French cooperation. The 1904 agreement resolved past problems over colonial issues; for instance, France recognized Britain's influence in Egypt, while the British supported French interests in Morocco. However, the underlying reason for the Entente Cordiale was the growing suspicion of the two countries concerning the motives of Germany. In a mutual understanding of defence issues, the Entente was expanded in 1907 to include Russia (France and Russia had formed an entente in 1893), and from then on was known as the Triple Entente. Although the agreements were informal and none of the countries were bound by any treaty to protect anyone else, the Triple Entente formed the basis of the Allied forces in WORLD WAR I and helped to bring Britain into the conflict.
FURTHER READING P.J.V. Rolo, *Entente Cordiale* (1969).

Entertainments National Service Association (ENSA), organization formed in 1938 to provide entertainment to British and Allied armed forces in anticipation of the outbreak of WORLD WAR II. During the war it employed about 4000 artists and provided the full range of entertainment from symphony concerts and full-length plays to stand-up comedy acts. There was also an ENSA film unit, which gave up to 500 shows a week (*see* FILM INDUSTRY). ENSA was initiated by a London theatrical director, Basil Dean; it failed to secure War Office backing but received funding from the Navy, Army and Air Force Institutes (NAAFI). At the beginning of the war black-out restrictions caused many entertainment venues to close and performers were free to join ENSA. It was supported by composers and conductors such as Sir Henry Wood, Sir Malcolm Sargent and William Walton, and actors such as John Gielgud. Celebrated entertainers, including the popular singer Gracie Fields, came out of retirement to entertain the troops. The Theatre Royal, Drury Lane, in central London, became ENSA's headquarters, where rehearsals took place. Performers and films were despatched to every accessible theatre of war.
FURTHER READING R. Fawkes, *Fighting for a Laugh: Entertaining the British and American Armed Forces, 1939–1946* (1978).

environmentalism. Concerns regarding the effects of industrial society upon the environment were first voiced in the late 19th century: two of the 20th century's most popular conservation groups, the Royal Society for the Protection of Birds (1889) and the NATIONAL TRUST (1895), emerged in the last two decades of the 19th century. This largely upper- and middle-class movement continued to develop in the first half of the 20th century and preferred to pursue its aims though established political channels. It was given official recognition in 1949 with the establishment of the Nature Conservancy, a government agency for the protection of plants and wildlife. The 1940s also saw the establishment of the Soil Association,

an organization devoted to organic farming as the way to national revival. Despite links with fascism in its formative years, the Soil Association became by the end of the century the established authority on organic AGRICULTURE in Britain, setting the standards by which farms and farm products could be marketed as 'organic'.

While the more conventional political lobbying of the various conservation movements continued to be immensely popular throughout the second half of the 20th century, the final decades of the century saw a significant shift in the form of what became known as the environmental or 'green' movement. Unconventional political protest over countryside issues had been seen in the interwar period, when disputes over access to the countryside led to mass trespasses on private land, most notably on Kinder Scout in the Peak District in 1932. From the 1970s, however, new organizations concerned with ecological issues began to emerge. The intellectual foundations of this movement came from scientific critiques of industrialized society such as Rachel Carson's book *The Silent Spring* (1962). The 'counter-cultural' movements of the late 1960s found the arguments of ecologists attractive, resonating with their own anti-materialist politics (*see* SIXTIES,THE).

The environmental movement produced one group that aimed to participate in the political system – the Green Party. Set up in 1973 as the People Party, renamed the Ecology Party in 1975, and finally the Green Party in 1985, the party fielded candidates in GENERAL ELECTIONS from 1974. However, it achieved little success, except in the 1989 European Parliament elections in which it managed to capture 15% of the vote. Unlike some other European green parties, the British party failed to exert significant influence upon mainstream national politics, although an environmental conscience was recognized by the end of the century as an element of policy by the major political parties.

The 1970s also saw the establishment of British branches of international environmental organizations, which became household names by the end of the century. The first of such groups was Friends of the Earth (FOE), a US organization that set up in the UK in 1970. Highlighting problems of pollution and nuclear power, with a loose and decentralized structure, FOE-UK undertook direct-action ecological campaigns underpinned by a critique of the economic and political foundations of modern society. By the end of the century, FOE had established itself as an authoritative source of data on environmental issues, adept at conventional lobbying and campaigning. Similar aims and unconventional tactics were employed by Greenpeace, established in Canada in the early 1970s. By the 1980s it had become one of the best-known international environmentalist groups. With a more rigid organizational structure than FOE, Greenpeace concentrated on direct action designed for maximum publicity through mass media, illustrated by its campaign against the oil company Shell's decision to dump the Brent Spar installation at sea in 1995.

While Greenpeace and FOE illustrate the 'mainstream' of environmental campaigning, the late 20th century also saw the emergence of a number of smaller and more radical groups. Groups concerned with animal welfare had been part of the conservation movement since the 19th century, such the Royal Society for the Prevention of Cruelty to Animals (RSPCA, 1840), but from the late 1970s more extreme groups of animal-rights campaigners appeared. The Hunt Saboteurs Association, which was formed in the mid-1960s by defectors from the RSPCA, brought direct action into anti-fox-hunting protests. In 1976 more extreme hunt saboteurs formed the Animal Liberation Front (ALF), whose tactics included the release of laboratory animals as well as attacks upon laboratories, factory farms and laboratory staff. Less extreme groups campaigning for cruelty-free consumer products and farming methods have been successful in changing public opinion, exemplified by the commercial success of companies such as the Body Shop. The potential for animal-welfare campaigns to bring together a broad cross-section of British society was illustrated by the widespread local support for demonstrations against the export of live animals at Shoreham, Brightlingsea and Coventry airport in 1995.

Another important issue of the late 20th century was that of road construction, which became the focus of protests from the early 1990s. Associated with these protests were a new group of 'disorganizations', movements without official membership or organizational structure that espoused direct action combined with an uncompromising stance. Protests against road building, in particular at Twyford Down in Hampshire, Newbury, east London and Manchester airport, took place between 1992 and 1996. While many of these campaigns, like those against live exports, successfully brought together middle-class local residents with radical protesters, it was the more radical groups that found themselves at the forefront of direct action against construction companies, bailiffs and the police. Prominent among these 'disorganizations' was Earth First!, whose UK arm was set up in 1991. A similar organization, Reclaim the Streets, was responsible for a variety of demonstrations against society's reliance upon motor vehicles.

SEE ALSO NATIONAL HERITAGE; TOWN AND COUNTRY PLANNING

FURTHER READING P. Byrne, *Social Movements in Britain* (1997).

Episcopal Church in Scotland, the Scottish offshoot of the Anglican communion (*see* CHURCH OF ENGLAND). It is a minority church in Scotland and its membership dwindled from 116,000 in 1900 to 54,000 in 1998.

Epstein, Jacob (1880–1959), Britain's most outstanding and innovative sculptor during the first half of the 20th century. He is held to have established MODERNISM in sculpture. Epstein was born to a Polish-Jewish family on the Lower East Side of New York City, the second son of eight surviving children. His father was a successful tailor who then moved into property. As a result of childhood illness, Epstein became isolated and concentrated upon reading and drawing. Having discovered a love of sculpture he attended courses and acquired experience in New York before moving to Paris in 1902, where he studied at the École des Beaux Arts and became interested in ancient and ethnographic sculpture through visits to the Louvre. He moved to London in 1905. There he executed his first important commission: 18 naked male stone figures for the façade of the British Medical Association headquarters in the Strand, London. These aroused much criticism from those who considered them obscene, but they survived until 1937 when the building was taken over by the High Commission for Southern Rhodesia (*see* ZIMBABWE). The statues were by then decaying as a result of neglect and were dismantled. Epstein also faced an outcry over his tomb of Oscar Wilde in the Père Lachaise Cemetery, Paris (1912), which featured a hovering angel with male sexual organs. He created a further shock in London with *The Rock Drill* (1913–14), a robot-like figure mounted upon an enormous real mechanical drill, which he said symbolized 'the terrible Frankenstein's monster we have turned ourselves into'. The original does not survive, though casts are exhibited in Tate Britain in London and elsewhere.

Thereafter Epstein's work was less audacious, but it continued to provoke adverse reaction in Britain. *Rima,* a stone memorial to the naturalist W.H. Hudson in London's Hyde Park (1922), was daubed with green paint, and a number of prominent figures, including the novelist Sir Arthur Conan Doyle, petitioned for its removal, but without success. Increasingly thereafter he concentrated on bronze portrait busts, mainly of famous men and women, but also of children including his own. These were perceptive and expressive and aroused much praise and far less controversy.

After World War II Epstein began to achieve public acceptance. He was given a retrospective exhibition at the Tate Gallery in 1952 and in the same year his *Madonna and Child* (far more 'respectable' than his earlier pieces) was sited at the Convent of the Holy Child Jesus, Cavendish Square, London. He received honours (including a knighthood in 1954) and major commissions, including *Lazarus* for New College Chapel, Oxford (1947–8), the TRADES UNION CONGRESS War Memorial, London (1956–7) and the huge *St Michael and the Devil* (1956–8) for Coventry Cathedral.

FURTHER READING S. Gardiner, *Jacob Epstein: Artist against the Establishment* (1992).

Equal Franchise Act (1928), legislation that gave women, for the first time, the vote on exactly the same terms as men, i.e. any person over the age of 21 could vote (*see* REPRESENTATION OF THE PEOPLE ACT, 1918). The electorate thereby grew from 21,731,320 in 1924 to 28,850,870.

Equal Opportunities Commission. *See* EQUAL PAY.

equal pay. For the whole century British women workers received lower pay than men, and they protested about it. At the beginning of the century protest came most vocally from women in the civil service and teaching, where it was clear that women and men were doing equal work for unequal pay, though they had support among women in the private and industrial sectors. The government defence of inequality was that women were less productive than men, were absent from work more often and had higher turnover rates. These differences were shown not to be significant. Nevertheless a report by the Royal Commission on the Civil Service in 1915 recommending equal pay was ignored.

The campaign continued and widened during the interwar years, receiving the support of TRADE UNIONS in the Trades Union Congress (TUC) and of the WOMEN'S MOVEMENT. These supported equal pay for work of equal value, aware that the labour force was strictly gender-divided and that men and women rarely did identical work. The chief argument against equal pay at this time was that men required larger incomes because they had families to support. This overlooked the numbers of men without dependants, and the very large number of women workers who were widowed single mothers, wives of disabled or unemployed men, or who were responsible for ageing parents. The House of Commons voted in 1936 for equal pay for civil servants and in 1944 for teachers, but in both cases the government refused to accept it. Some women who temporarily took over men's jobs during WORLD WAR II were paid the male wage, while other women initiated strikes for equal pay, some of them successful.

In 1944 a Royal Commission on Equal Pay was appointed. It reported in 1946, giving detailed evidence of unequal pay for closely similar work in most sectors of employment. It did not recommend immediate equalization for fear of the cost implications for the post-war economy. The LABOUR PARTY government of 1945–51 endorsed this position throughout its period of office. The feminist Equal Pay Campaign and the trade-union-led Coordinating Committee on Equal Pay conducted separate campaigns that culminated in the presentation of petitions to Parliament in March 1954. The Conservative chancellor of the exchequer R.A. BUTLER had already initiated a review of government policy and persuaded the cabinet to accept equal pay in the public service, noting that Labour had pledged to introduce equal pay if they won the forthcoming general election. This suggests the electoral importance of working women at this time. There was little change in the private sector.

From the early 1960s organizations of working- and middle-class women, including women in trade unions, increasingly demanded equal pay. There was a flurry of strikes for equal pay, most famously at Ford's Dagenham plant in 1968. The Labour Party won a clear majority in the general election of 1966, supported by the highest proportion of female voters they had obtained since 1945. In 1967 Labour set up a committee to investigate discrimination against women. In 1970 Barbara CASTLE, as secretary of state for employment, introduced the Equal Pay Act. It was hurriedly prepared and rushed through Parliament before the election of 1970 and so was deeply flawed, as Castle was well aware. Many employers were extremely reluctant to concede equal pay. After-Labour returned to government in 1974 it introduced in 1975 the Sex Discrimination Act, which established the Equal Opportunities Commission among other procedures to remove a range of inequalities in the workplace, such as opportunities for training and promotion, as well as unequal pay. Again, this legislation had only limited results. During the 1980s equal-pay regulations introduced by the EUROPEAN UNION enabled some women to achieve equal pay through the European Court. The outcome was a slight narrowing of pay differentials between men and women by the end of the century.

FURTHER READING E. Meehan, *Women's Rights at Work: Campaigns and Policy in Britain and the United States* (1985); H.L. Smith, 'The Politics of Conservative Reform: The Equal Pay for Equal Work Issue, 1945–1955' in *Historical Journal*, Vol. 35 (1992) 401–415; P. Thane, 'Towards Equal Opportunities? Women in Britain since 1945' in T. Gourvish and A. O'Day (eds.), *Britain since 1945* (1991).

eugenics, the 'science' of effecting the physical improvement of human populations by altering the genetic make-up of a population. It emerged in the later 19th century and was influential in most developed countries, especially from the 1920s to the later 1940s. The leaders of the eugenics movement in Britain were Francis Galton (1822–1911) and Karl Pearson (1857–1936), whose research appeared to show that the lower social classes were more prone to produce children who were physically and mentally unfit. This was thought to be alarming at this time because the birth rate was falling faster among the more affluent classes than

among the lower classes (*see* POPULATION). It was predicted that a national physical decline would result, and it was suggested that this could only be remedied by selective breeding. This might involve inducements to the 'superior stock' (such as tax reliefs or FAMILY ALLOWANCES) to breed in larger numbers or restrictions on breeding among the 'inferior' (for example by institutionalizing or sterilizing them). Such ideas were promoted by the Eugenics Education Society, which was founded in 1907 and soon became the Eugenics Society. But it had only a limited influence in Britain, where the strong environmentalist tradition upheld the argument that the physical inferiority of poor people was as likely to be due to low incomes and poor environmental conditions as to heredity. Despite repeated efforts up to World War II to introduce legalized segregation and sterilization, for example of 'mental defectives', this was resisted in Parliament and elsewhere, though some covert sterilization occurred. The Eugenics Society provided a forum for the discussion of a wide range of population issues in relation to social reform, which attracted a number of progressive reformers through the interwar years. By the 1950s eugenic ideas were discredited by the gradual revelation of the extent of eugenic experimentation in Nazi Germany. In the late 1990s renewed support for the influence of heredity upon human physical condition and behaviour, and belief in the possibility of manipulating genetic inheritance in order to perfect the species, came from international research on genetics. Interest in genetics was as fashionable among a limited group of intellectuals at the end of the century as at the beginning.
FURTHER READING R. Dawkins, *The Selfish Gene* (1976); P. Mazumdar, *Eugenics, Human Genetics and Human Failings: The Eugenics Society, Its Source and Its Critics in Britain* (1991); R.A. Soloway, *Demography and Degeneration: Eugenics and the Declining Birth Rate in 20th-Century Britain* (1990).

Euro, the. *See* EUROPEAN MONETARY SYSTEM.

European Atomic Energy Commission (Euratom). *See* EUROPEAN ECONOMIC COMMUNITY.

European Community. *See* EUROPEAN ECONOMIC COMMUNITY.

European Economic Area (EEA). *See* EUROPEAN FREE TRADE ASSOCIATION; EUROPEAN UNION.

European Economic Community (EEC), free-trade organization, often referred to as the Common Market. It was formally established in 1957 when the treaty of Rome was signed by six European nations: France, West Germany, Italy, Belgium, the Netherlands and Luxembourg. It was an outgrowth of the European Coal and Steel Community (ECSC), which had been established in 1951. The ECSC arose out of the concern of several European countries, especially France, for European security after World War II, and the ECSC marked a concerted effort by these countries to aid West Germany's economic reconstruction, while at the same time keeping it in check militarily. Britain opted not to join the ECSC because of the supranational character of the organization. It was anxious to preserve its own sovereignty and its relations with the COMMONWEALTH and the USA. Also, as the Labour government had just nationalized Britain's coal and steel industries, TRADE UNIONS required reassurance that Britain's industries would remain under British control.

Formed at the same time as the EEC in 1957 was the European Atomic Energy Community (Euratom), which in the long term proved largely ineffective as it became clear that individual nations wanted to develop their own nuclear-power programmes.

When the EEC was formed it expanded the economic cooperation between the original six member states of the ECSC to include a wide variety of industrial produce in addition to raw materials. Among other changes that it implemented over a period of time were the removal of trade barriers among member states and the development of a common tariff policy for imports. Again, the supranational character of the EEC made Britain nervous, and although it participated in talks about membership in 1955, it opted not to join two years later. Instead, it led the way in the formation of the rival EUROPEAN FREE TRADE ASSOCIATION (EFTA) in 1960.

Britain proved fickle in its allegiance to EFTA, however, and the following year it began negotiations to become a member of the evidently more successful EEC. This process was made difficult by European – particularly French – resentment over Britain's ambivalence towards any federation, and its continued reliance on both the USA and the COMMONWEALTH rather than its continental neighbours. The French president Charles de Gaulle vetoed Britain's membership bids in 1963 and 1967.

That same year, 1967, was a year of expansion and change, as the EEC, Euratom and the ECSC were united under the umbrella of one organization, the European Community (EC). With the resignation of de Gaulle in 1969 the way was opened once again for Britain to reapply for membership. This time it was successful, and in 1973 Britain, Ireland and Denmark became members (*see* HEATH, EDWARD); Greece joined in 1981 and Spain and Portugal in 1986. But even after joining, Britain's relationship with the EC continued to prove fractious. Although a 1975 referendum showed that the majority of Britons were in favour of EC membership, many chafed at certain aspects of EC policy. Farmers, for instance, resented the imposition of the Common Agricultural Policy (*see* AGRICULTURE), which had been implemented across the EC but into which Britain had had no input. There was also discontent over the level of the nation's monetary contributions to the EC and whether it was good value for money; Margaret THATCHER renegotiated Britain's EC dues in 1984. Under her leadership Britain cemented its reputation for ambivalence and uncooperativeness within the EC. In 1993, by the treaty of MAASTRICHT, the EC became the EUROPEAN UNION.

FURTHER READING D. Dinan, *Ever Closer Union? An Introduction to the European Community* (1994); D. Weigall and P. Stirk (eds.), *The Origins and Development of the European Community* (1992).

European Free Trade Association (EFTA), trade bloc established in 1960 as a rival to the EUROPEAN ECONOMIC COMMUNITY (EEC) by seven nations who had decided against EEC membership. The founder-members were Britain, Austria, Denmark, Norway, Portugal, Sweden and Switzerland. Finland became an associate member in 1961, Iceland joined in 1970 and Liechtenstein in 1991. The aim of EFTA was to facilitate better economic cooperation across Western Europe, including the member nations of the EEC, but without the worries of supranational structures. Tariffs among the member states were all removed by 1967. However, the effectiveness of EFTA as a rival to the EEC was blunted almost from the beginning when in 1961, just a year after its founding, Britain, Denmark and Norway applied for EEC membership. Britain and Denmark left EFTA in 1973 when they were finally successful in becoming full members of the European Community (EC). Portugal left to join the EC in 1986. While EFTA still exists as an organization, it is now of marginal importance as in 1991 it made an agreement with the EC to create a Europe-wide free-trade zone, the European Economic Area (EEA). The EEA came into being in 1994.

SEE ALSO EUROPEAN UNION; MAASTRICHT, TREATY OF.

FURTHER READING M.J. Dedman, *The Origins and Development of the European Union 1945–95: A History of European Integration* (1996).

European Monetary System (EMS), the set of arrangements for coordinating currency values and money supply among members of the EUROPEAN UNION. The EMS was introduced in 1979, after an earlier attempt at Economic and Monetary Union (EMU) had foundered. The Exchange Rate Mechanism (ERM) was the most important feature of the EMS, although a state could be a member of the EMS without being in the ERM; this was the case with the UK until October 1990, and again from September 1992 ('Black Wednesday'; *see* MAJOR, JOHN) when the UK joined Greece and Portugal outside the ERM. The ERM was based on an agreed-European Currency Unit (ECU). The value of the ECU was calculated from that of a basket of member-nation currencies, weighted according to each country's gross domestic product (GDP), trade and short-term credit position. Each currency had a fixed rate against the ECU from which it might deviate only slightly.

In 1991 the treaty of MAASTRICHT included proposals for gradual economic and monetary union, to be prepared by a European Monetary Institute (EMI), which was established in January 1994 as a prototype central bank for the EU. Mistrust of the EMU by national parliaments and voters, wary of interference with the economic and financial policies of the governments of member states, delayed further action. At the Madrid heads-of-government conference in December 1995 it was agreed to seek the completion of the EMU by 1 January 1999, when a single currency, the euro, was introduced. The purpose of these arrangements was to ensure stability and to prevent international currency speculation. It was also agreed in Madrid that the founding members of the EMU would not be chosen until 1998, and that their economic performance would have to meet certain criteria: (1) a budget deficit of less than 3% of GDP; (2) a government debt not exceeding 60% of GDP; (3) inflation rates not more than 11.5% and interest rates of not more than 2% above the three best performing economies in the EU. In March 1998 an EU report indicated that every member state except Greece had met these criteria. However, Britain, Sweden and Denmark chose to join Greece in staying outside the 'Eurozone', as it came to be known, until it was clear whether or not the euro system was sound and stable. This was not clear at the end of the century.

European Union (EU), the successor to the European Community (EC; *see* EUROPEAN ECONOMIC COMMUNITY). The EU came into being on 1 November 1993 after the passage of the treaty of European Union (commonly called the treaty of MAASTRICHT). It comprised all the member states of the former EC. In 1995 Austria, Finland and Sweden became members, and CYPRUS, MALTA, Switzerland and Turkey had applications pending at the end of the century. It was likely that in future many of the nations of the former Soviet bloc would also join the EU; tentative agreements had been made with Poland, Romania, Slovakia, the Czech Republic, Hungary and Bulgaria.

The EU has its headquarters in Brussels, and its administrative structures consist of the European Commission, an elected European Parliament, the Council of Ministers (who actually make final policy decisions) and a European Court of Justice. The EU is responsible for administering the common policies on agriculture and the fisheries, which it inherited from the EC, as well as the common currency, the euro, which came into use in eleven of the member states in January 1999. There was greater economic cooperation and freer trade in Europe than ever before after the European Economic Area (EEA) came into being in 1994. This was the result of negotiated cooperation between the EU and the nations of the EUROPEAN FREE TRADE ASSOCIATION (EFTA).

The EU's increased movements into non-economic policy made some people in member states, including Britain, uneasy. Britain's relations with Europe, always contentious, became even more so in the 1990s in the wake of the proposals made by the treaty of Maastricht. The 'Eurosceptic' faction of the CONSERVATIVE PARTY emerged in 1992 and berated the then prime minister John MAJOR for his signing of the treaty, although he had secured opt-out clauses for Britain for two of the treaty's most controversial features: the single currency and the so-called 'Social Chapter'. Many in Britain, politicians and members of the public alike, feared the loss of national sovereignty and subsequent rule from Brussels. After Tony BLAIR's Labour government swept into office in 1997, there were hopes in Brussels that Britain's traditional ambivalence towards the EU might come to an end. While Labour certainly had a more positive attitude towards Britain's membership of the EU, they did not, for instance, reverse the Major government's decision not to adopt the euro.

FURTHER READING M.J. Baun, *An Imperfect Union: The Maastricht Treaty and the New Politics of European Integration* (1996); M.J. Dedman, *The Origins and Development of the European Union 1945–95: A History of European Integration* (1996); D. Dinan, *Ever Closer Union? An Introduction to the European Community* (1994).

Euston Road School. 'A New School for a limited number of pupils of Drawing and Painting' was established at 12 Fitzroy Street, Bloomsbury, London, in 1937, under the direction of Claude Rogers (1907–79), Victor PASMORE and William Coldstream (1907–87). The organizing secretary was Thelma Hulbert (1913–95), whose work included landscapes and pictures of birds and flowers.

In February 1938 the School moved to larger premises at 314–316 Euston Road where it became known as the Euston Road School. Associated teachers included Vanessa BELL, Augustus JOHN and Duncan Grant. Though the number of students was small, the School acquired a powerful reputation in a short time. Its prospectus, paid for by Sir Kenneth CLARK, then director of the National Gallery, stressed direct contact with teachers who were themselves practising painters and 'training the observation'. The aim was to encourage skills in representational painting in order to end the isolation of artists from the public that other avant-garde art movements had experienced. The School also opposed what they described as 'the pseudo-realism of the Royal Academy and kindred societies'. Coldstream, with the painter and critic Graham Bell (1910–43), who was also asso-

ciated with the School, had for some time advocated painting of 'actual experience' with contemporary relevance. They were in tune with other left-wing movements of the time, such as MASS-OBSERVATION. Bell wrote about art for the left-wing weekly journal the *New Statesman* and since 1934 Coldstream had been employed by the General Post Office Films Department, which produced both films and advertising. Financial support from Kenneth Clark and Samuel Courtauld, the textile manufacturer and patron of the arts, enabled both Coldstream and Bell to take up full-time painting and teaching in 1937. Clark's patronage also liberated Pasmore from working full-time in the Public Health Department of the London County Council.

The outbreak of World War II in 1939 caused the School to close, but the term 'Euston Road' was used for a decade or so longer for painting in the style advocated by the School. The tradition was upheld by the founder members and teachers, especially by Coldstream who taught at Camberwell School of Art in London before his appointment to the prestigious position of Slade professor of fine art at University College, London. Pasmore and Rogers also taught at Camberwell. Rogers became professor of fine art at Reading University and in the 1950s Pasmore was director of painting at Newcastle University.

FURTHER READING B. Lawton, *The Euston Road School* (1986).

evacuation of children in World War II.

Before WORLD WAR II massive bombing of the major cities of Britain was anticipated at the outbreak of war. The government therefore planned for the dispersal to the countryside of vulnerable groups – especially children, whose survival would be essential for the rebuilding of Britain after the war. The evacuation of the cities began just before the outbreak of war on 1 September 1939. Those who could afford it made their own arrangements to remove themselves and/or their children from the cities, either to the countryside or abroad. Many children spent the war years with relatives and family friends in the United States, the dominions or the colonies. Other, mainly poorer, children, some with their mothers, were removed in school-based groups, often with little warning or briefing, and billeted with strangers. About 1.5 million people moved in the first few days; about 4 million over the entire war.

The outcome was mixed. Some children settled happily into supportive new surroundings and valued the experience. Others were ill-treated and some seriously abused. There were cultural conflicts as country people encountered for the first time the serious deprivation of very poor children from the inner cities (sometimes verminous, under-fed and suffering from skin conditions); and many children in turn were bewildered by the unfamiliar expectations of their hosts. Understanding of psychology was limited at this time, and its influence on policy apparently nonexistent. There was little awareness of the likely behavioural effects upon children of sudden separation from their parents and familiar environments. The evacuation jolted some people into greater awareness of poverty; others had prejudices confirmed. The heavy bombing did not immediately occur and about 80% of evacuees had returned to the cities by the time the BLITZ in fact began in late 1940. Another wave of evacuation then began with similar results.

FURTHER READING A. Calder, *The People's War* (1969); T.L. Crosby, *The Impact of Civilian Evacuation in World War II* (1986).

F

Fabian Society, association of socialist intellectuals, launched on 4 January 1884 at the home of Edward Pease (1857–1955), its general secretary from 1890 to 1913. The purpose of the society was to promote a gradual, peaceable achievement of socialism by means of conducting research into – and recommending policy solutions to – social and economic problems, and by persuading politicians of all parties to follow its recommendations. The title was a reference to Quintus Fabius Cunctator (d.205BC), the Roman general who supposedly defeated Hannibal by using gradualist tactics.

Prominent early Fabians included George Bernard SHAW and Sidney WEBB. Sidney and his wife Beatrice WEBB were to become particularly closely identified with the Fabians. The society included socialists with a variety of views. Its ideas were first widely promoted in *Fabian Essays in Socialism* (1889) edited by Shaw. The Fabians became particularly associated with 'municipal socialism' as the first step towards socialism on a national and international scale: 'municipal socialism' meant public ownership at local-authority level of services and businesses so that they would operate for the social and economic good of all, rather than the profit of a few. The Fabians believed strongly in public ownership, and that private ownership of wealth was the fundamental cause of social and economic inequality. In 1892 six Fabians,

including Webb, were elected to the London County Council (LCC; *see* LONDON GOVERNMENT) on a municipal-socialist platform. In the 1890s the Webbs established the London School of Economics, and contributed to the establishment of Imperial College of Science and Technology (also in London) to promote research and teaching in areas they thought essential.

Fabians attended the founding conference of the INDEPENDENT LABOUR PARTY in 1893 and of the LABOUR REPRESENTATION COMMITTEE in 1900, which gave birth to the LABOUR PARTY, but they were not yet committed to the idea of a new political party and preferred to try to 'permeate' the CONSERVATIVE and LIBERAL parties with their ideas. When the Webbs failed in 1912 to persuade the Liberal government to 'break up' the POOR LAW and replace it with modernized social services, they came to support the Labour Party. This view was not shared by all Fabians, and the society underwent a series of factional disputes and divisions over ideology and tactics.

The society established a junior branch (for those under 28) and also, in 1908, a Fabian Women's Group. The latter was successful in promoting social and economic reforms affecting the lives of women, notably the Trades Boards Act, 1909, which established a MINIMUM WAGE for women in some of the lowest-paid trades. In 1912 the Webbs established the Fabian Research Department, headed by G.D.H. Cole (1889–1959) – who became one of Britain's leading social scientists – and William Mellor (1888–1942). In the same year they founded the *New Statesman*, which for the remainder of the century was the leading weekly journal of the British intellectual left.

The society became increasingly identified with the Webbs, and Sidney Webb became increasingly influential within the growing Labour Party. In 1918 he played a large part, with Arthur HENDERSON, in drafting the party's first constitution, including the important CLAUSE FOUR. Webb was also a member of the first two Labour governments, in 1924 and 1929–31.

The Fabian Society continued in existence as a Labour think-tank to the end of the century, publishing a nonstop flow of publications on a wide range of domestic and international political issues. Between the 1940s and 1960s its Colonial Bureau was prominent in arguing that Britain had an obligation to promote self-government for its colonies, but that DECOLONIZATION should be a gradual process linked to the promotion of economic development. A high proportion of Labour MPs in the years after World War II were members of the Fabian Society, but it is hard to assess the direct impact of the society upon the Labour Party, partly because its ideas and campaigns were often shared by non-Fabians. Probably its impact varied over time and was generally less than its critics and its strongest supporters have believed.

FURTHER READING A.M. McBriar, *Fabian Socialism and British Politics, 1884–1918* (1962); P. Pugh, *Educate, Agitate, Organize: One Hundred Years of Fabian Socialism* (1984).

Falkland Islands, British colony in the south Atlantic, comprising the islands of East and West Falkland as well as several other dependencies including South Georgia. Their ownership had long been disputed, mainly by Britain and Argentina. The Argentinians, who refer to the islands by their Spanish name, Las Malvinas, claimed that sovereignty of the Falklands was passed to them by the Spaniards after they withdrew from their possessions in South America in the early 19th century. Argentina formally claimed this sovereignty in 1829. Britain, which had maintained a small settlement on West Falkland between 1765 and 1774, did not recognize the claims of either Spain or Argentina, and in 1833 sent a small force to expel the Argentinian presence. In 1840 the islands were made a crown colony and at that time were populated with British settlers.

Although Argentina raised its objections to the British presence periodically over the next 150 years, no serious action was taken over what it perceived as the illegal takeover of its territory until the early 1980s. By this time there was a military junta, led by General Galtieri, in government. On 19 March 1982 a party of civilian scrap-metal dealers landed without permission on South Georgia and raised the Argentinian flag. They were followed on 2 April by a military force, which seized the main Falkland Islands and declared them to be the property of Argentina. Humiliated by how quickly the islands, with only one detachment of marines to protect them, had fallen, the government of Margaret THATCHER responded swiftly, justifying its actions to retake the Falklands by citing the clear determination of the local population to remain British. The US secretary of state, Alexander Haig, attempted to negotiate a peaceful settlement between the two states, but was unsuccessful.

The invasion of 2 April was followed by ten weeks of what historians have termed the Falklands War or the Falklands conflict. It was Britain's last, and perhaps most peculiar, colonial war of the 20th century. A British task force was quickly established, consisting of 44 warships and supporting ships, together with aircraft, and a fighting force numbering 10,000. By 25 April South Georgia was recaptured. On 2 May, the turning point of the war, the Argentinian cruiser *General Belgrano* was torpedoed by a British submarine and 323 seamen aboard lost their lives (*see also* OFFICIAL

SECRETS ACT). This event served to destroy the peace plan then being proposed by the Peruvians. On 4 May the Argentinians retaliated for the loss of the *Belgrano* by firing an Exocet missile at the British destroyer HMS *Sheffield*; 20 seamen were killed and the ship was left to sink. British troops landed on the islands themselves on 21 May, and by 14 June they had surrounded the capital, Port Stanley, and forced the surrender of the Argentinian garrison there. The following day General Menendez surrendered on behalf of all the Argentinian forces in the Falklands. The conflict had resulted in the deaths of 236 members of the British forces and 750 Argentinians.

It is significant that the Falklands War, predicated on historical issues of sovereignty and the self-determination of the islanders themselves, also served the political ends of the governments involved. In Argentina the initial invasion of 2 April was calculated to appeal to national pride and focus the attention of Argentinians away from the domestic problems and unrest afflicting the country under the rule of a military junta. With the capitulation of the Argentinian forces on the Falklands, however, came the fall of Galtieri's government. In Britain the conflict's imperialistic nature was also well timed to revitalize the flagging fortunes of Margaret Thatcher's Conservative government, plagued by UNEMPLOYMENT and other domestic social problems. Some Britons, depressed by the economic and social state into which the country had fallen by the early 1980s, warmed to Thatcher's suggestion that the war showed Britain still possessed those qualities that had once made it the most powerful nation on earth. Aspects of jingoism not seen for decades resurfaced in the media, most notoriously when the *Sun* shrieked 'GOTCHA!' on its front page the day after the sinking of the *General Belgrano*. The Falklands War was a strangely old-fashioned colonial war, taking place at a time when the EMPIRE had long ceased to be a reality, but when nostalgia for it had begun to reappear in British popular culture.

FURTHER READING L. Freedman, *Britain and the Falklands War* (1988); M. Middlebrook, *The Falklands War, 1982* (1985).

family allowances, state payments to families to help support children. A universal system of state-funded children's allowances was introduced by the World War II coalition government in the Family Allowances Act, 1945. State aid to mothers and young children was first proposed before World War I, notably by the Women's Group of the FABIAN SOCIETY. New forms of state support for poorer children were granted by the LIBERAL governments of this time, notably the introduction of free school meals for needy schoolchildren in 1906 and school medical inspections in 1907, but family allowances remained controversial.

The campaign was taken up actively by the WOMEN'S MOVEMENT after World War I. The introduction for the first time during the war of state-funded dependants' allowances and pensions for the widows and orphans of men killed in action demonstrated the effectiveness of such payments in improving child and maternal health. Research revealing the extent of malnutrition among women and children, especially in areas of high UNEMPLOYMENT during the interwar years, gave further impetus to the campaign, which was conducted most prominently by Eleanor RATHBONE, with other members of the Family Endowment Society (founded in 1917). Her aim was not only to improve conditions for children but also to provide full-time mothers with an independent income as a reward for their work in the home. Her arguments were most clearly expressed in her book *The Disinherited Family* (1924). Some feminists opposed family allowances on the grounds that they reinforced the notion that women's roles were confined to the family. Many workers, including those in TRADE UNIONS and the LABOUR PARTY, feared that allowances would provide employers with an excuse to keep wages low, as they believed was occurring in France, where family allowances had been introduced earlier in the century. Partly for this reason, and partly owing to the cost, the

Labour Party in the interwar years advocated improving state-funded health, education and other welfare services as the most effective means to help the neediest families. Fears in the 1930s about the falling birth rate (*see* POPULATION) led some, in Britain and elsewhere, to advocate family allowances as an inducement to increased births, although research indicated that this had nowhere been successful.

The social reformer William BEVERIDGE had long supported family allowances, and he endorsed them in his famous report of 1942. They were introduced in 1945 partly due to this recommendation, and also because trade-union and Labour resistance had diminished. There was also a widespread and serious determination not to return after the war to the poverty of the interwar years; and some still believed that family allowances could reverse the fall in the birth rate. From 1945 five shillings a week was paid for all children other than the first in each family. The initial proposal was to pay them to fathers through the pay packet. Eleanor Rathbone's last campaign before her death in 1946 was to persuade the House of Commons to vote to have them paid directly to mothers through the Post Office.

Family allowances were helpful to poorer families but never widely popular. They declined in value over the next 20 years, until in the 1960s the social scientists Peter Townsend and Brian Abel-Smith revealed the surprising extent of child poverty in what was widely believed to be an increasingly prosperous WELFARE STATE. The Child Poverty Action Group was founded in 1964 to campaign on the issue, as it continued to do for the remainder of the century. Support for more comprehensive and generous benefits grew and led to the Child Benefit Act, 1975, which eventually abolished both the family allowance and child income-tax allowance (introduced in 1910), replacing it with 'child benefit', a tax-free, flat-rate benefit for all children, which was introduced in 1977. Its value declined during the 1980s since the Conservative government was critical of the universal

character of the benefits and preferred to build up new benefits targeted at low-income groups, such as the 'family income supplement', introduced in 1971, which was replaced by 'family credit' in 1988. John MAJOR's government raised child benefit substantially in 1991. The Labour government elected in 1997 again raised child benefit substantially (by 22% between 1997 and 1999), and also developed new, relatively generous benefits targeted at all low-earning families, in particular the 'working families' tax credit', initiated by the chancellor of the exchequer, Gordon BROWN.

FURTHER READING J. Macnicol, *The Movement for Family Allowances, 1918–1945* (1980); S. Pedersen, *Family, Dependence and the Origins of the Welfare State: Britain and France, 1914–1945* (1993); N. Timmins, *The Five Giants. A Biography of the Welfare State* (1996).

family credit. *See* FAMILY ALLOWANCES.

family income supplement. *See* FAMILY ALLOWANCES.

farming. *See* AGRICULTURE.

fashion. For much of the 20th century, high fashion, or *haute couture*, was mainly dictated by the designers of Paris, although this influence diminished from the 1960s. There had been previous instances in which aspects of particularly British design were brought to worldwide attention. Fashion historians generally agree that British designers made two significant contributions to international style in the earlier 20th century: the romantic, formal evening/ball/wedding gown, and the tailored suit. The romantic formal gown, usually full-skirted and made from a variety of glamorous fabrics, appeared from the 1930s to the 1950s in the collections of designers such as Norman Hartnell (who frequently dressed Queen ELIZABETH II), Hardy Amies, John Cavanagh, Victor Stiebel and Michael Sherrard. The style was revived again in the early 1980s when DIANA, PRINCESS OF WALES chose the relatively obscure designer Elizabeth Emmanuel to create her wedding gown.

Britain also has a well-deserved international reputation for faultless tailoring, with the Savile Row men's suit setting standards of excellence. This influence was seen in the British government's choice of styles for both men and women in their UTILITY SCHEME clothing, introduced during World War II when textile supplies were short. Linked to this tradition of quality tailoring was the development and marketing of so-called 'country' clothing, a distinctive British style that enjoys consistent popularity in Britain and increasingly elsewhere. Developed to suit the British climate and rural activities such as hunting, fishing and riding, it relies on native natural fibres such as wool, as well as on cotton corduroy.

From the 1900s to the 1950s, high fashion was limited mainly to the upper classes and was produced in a few small houses in the Mayfair district of London. British couturiers made clothes to be worn either at court or during the many events of the London social season, and for the most part they were copies of the latest fashions from Paris (such as the 'New Look', which, with its ample use of fabrics, celebrated the end of wartime restrictions in supplies of material in the later 1940s). The decline of the London season from the 1950s, especially after the ending in 1958 of the annual presentation of 'debutantes' to the monarch (*see* ARISTOCCRACY), prompted the decline of this older-style British *couture*. The SIX-TIES saw the decline of a number of conventions of everyday dress. The wearing of hats declined, and the male bowler hat – once *de rigeur* for the office worker – almost vanished. It ceased to be shocking for women to wear trousers in public, and became normal. Jeans began to be worn by both sexes and moved in and out of a series of fashion roles for the remainder of the century.

British design came into its own in the 1960s, with such innovations as the miniskirt. Well into the 1970s designers such as Mary Quant, Ossie Clarke and Barbara Hulanicki at Biba helped to set the fashion trends of a generation. However, these new designers were not, for the most part, selling *couture*, but ready-to-wear clothing from chic boutiques in Soho and Chelsea in London. Fashionable, affordable clothing was soon available to all through high-street shops. The later development of street styles (such as punk) from the 1960s onward has been a major influence on fashion designers internationally. At the same time rising living standards combined with the introduction of a steadily widening range of low-cost fabrics meant that modified versions of high fashion could be made widely available to the not so young and trendy, for example through such chain stores as Marks and Spencer. Such stores also catered for men, although chains selling mass-produced, moderately priced men's suits and other garments, such as Burton and John Collier, had flourished from the 1920s. Such mass-produced clothes were falling out of favour by the end of the century, displaced by preferences for somewhat more individual styles made possible by new, more flexible methods of production developed by new chains such as Benetton. Clothing costs were kept low by the increasing use of cheap textiles and labour, especially in a number of Asian countries.

British fashion was given a boost in the 1980s and 1990s by Diana, princess of Wales, who developed a stylish image and used it to promote British designers internationally. At the end of the century British design – such as that of Vivienne Westwood – was still exerting great international influence. London Fashion Week was a major event, and *couture* houses in Paris and Milan clamoured for the talents of graduates from London art colleges. Most notably, two major Parisian houses were run by British designers, with Alexander McQueen at Givenchy and John Galliano at Christian Dior.

FURTHER READING A. Mansfield and P. Cunnington, *Handbook of English Costume in the 20th Century, 1900–1950* (1973); E. Wilson and L. Taylor, *Through the Looking Glass: A History of Dress from 1860 to the Present Day* (1989).

Fawcett, Millicent Garrett (1847–1929), feminist and leading suffrage campaigner. Millicent Garrett was born in Aldeburgh, Suffolk, the daughter of a merchant in corn and coal. Her sister, Elizabeth Garrett Anderson, in 1865 became the first woman to qualify as a doctor in Britain. Millicent met her future husband, Henry Fawcett, in 1865. He was professor of economics at Cambridge and MP for Brighton, and was blind. They married in 1867, and the following year their only child, Philippa, was born.

While at Cambridge the Fawcetts moved in Liberal circles, counting such figures as the philosopher John Stuart Mill – a leading advocate of women's rights – among their friends. They became involved in university reform, including the founding of women's colleges. Millicent later became a member of Newnham College's management council. She spent a good deal of time aiding her husband in his work by reading and writing for him; this fostered her interest in politics and economics, and she published a number of books and essays, including *Political Economy for Beginners* (1870) and *Essays and Lectures on Political Subjects* (1872). But she was also by this time working for the cause for which she became best known: woman suffrage, as it was normally described at the time. She was a member of the first women's suffrage committee, founded in 1867, and also helped campaign for the Married Women's Property Act, passed in 1882. She was devastated by the death of her husband in 1884, but continued her work. After 1885 she began supporting the Vigilance Society, which campaigned against so-called 'white slavery', but came to believe that any attempts women made at reform would be far easier and faster if they had the right to vote. She became increasingly alienated from the LIBERAL PARTY owing to Gladstone's opposition to women's suffrage, and she also opposed him on HOME RULE. At heart, however, she remained a Liberal, committed to FREE TRADE and individualism. She opposed free state education on the grounds that

it diminished parental responsibility, and also opposed factory legislation that restricted women's hours and places of work. She supported the BOER WAR, and in 1901 led a ladies' commission of inquiry into concentration camps in South Africa.

In 1897 she began her most visible work, on a national scale, when she became president of the National Union of Women's Suffrage Societies (NUWSS). The NUWSS comprised many independent women's suffrage groups who cooperated on matters of policy and propaganda. Millicent worked tirelessly for the NUWSS for many years, taking part in processions and demonstrations and speaking about the issue of female suffrage whenever the opportunity arose. She was noted as a serious, hardworking, efficient and diligent leader, with her competence compensating for a lack of eloquence and charisma. These qualities were more famously epitomized by the PANKHURSTS, former NUWSS members who broke away in 1903 to form the militant Women's Social and Political Union (WSPU), out of frustration that reform was not occurring quickly enough. During the early years of the WSPU Millicent admired the spirit of the Pankhursts and their followers (who came to be known as the SUFFRAGETTES), but she quickly disassociated herself from them when they launched their campaign of violence against property and began being arrested by the police. Millicent strongly believed that such actions did nothing but harm the movement as a whole and that suffrage campaigners had to be seen to respect law and order. Soon NUWSS members were being referred to as SUFFRAGISTS to differentiate them from their more militant sisters.

Like the WSPU, the NUWSS suspended its campaign upon the outbreak of World War I in 1914. In 1918, after the war's end, suffrage campaigners were rewarded when many women over the age of 30, subject to property and educational qualifications, were given the vote in the REPRESENTATION OF THE PEOPLE ACT. After this victory, Millicent retired from the presidency of the NUWSS and was replaced by Eleanor RATHBONE, but she continued to be involved in women's issues. She supported the campaign for full female suffrage, which was granted in 1928, as well as DIVORCE reform and attempts to open the legal profession and the civil service to women. In 1925 she was made a dame of the British empire. She died in London in 1929.

FURTHER READING M.G. Fawcett, *What I Remember* (1924); S.S. Holton, *Feminism and Democracy: Women's Suffrage and Politics, 1900–1918* (1986); D. Rubenstein, *A Different World for Women: The Life of Millicent Garrett Fawcett* (1991).

fellow travellers, colloquial term for close sympathizers with the COMMUNIST PARTY who were not actual party members. The term was in use from the 1930s to the 1960s, but rarely used thereafter.

feminism. *See* WOMEN'S MOVEMENT.

Festival of Britain (May–September 1951), government-sponsored national celebration to mark the centenary of the Great Exhibition of 1851. It was planned by the Labour government, particularly by Herbert MORRISON, in order to raise the spirits of the nation, which was just emerging from a period of austerity following WORLD WAR II, though preparations were constrained by shortages of materials and of labour. The focal point of the festival was the South Bank Exhibition in London, but there were also exhibitions elsewhere in London (for example at the Science Museum in South Kensington) and around the country. Although many of the exhibitions were temporary, a permanent concert venue, the Royal Festival Hall, was built on the South Bank. The festival was seen as a showcase for talent (especially new talent) in the sciences and the arts, and as an opportunity for enjoyment. It proved immensely popular.

FURTHER READING M. Banham and B. Hillier (eds.), *A Tonic to the Nation: The Festival of Britain 1951* (1976); M. Frayn, 'Festival' in M. Sissons and P. French (eds.), *The Age of Austerity, 1945–51* (1964), 330–52.

film industry. The British film industry made a start before World War I, most actively in Brighton, but the war caused a setback and there were few major developments in the 1920s. The government sought to encourage the industry by requiring exhibitors to show British films on programmes alongside the American films that dominated the medium. Large numbers of these British 'B-feature' films were produced. Cinema-going was increasingly popular with working-class audiences, especially young people and women, but the cultural elite largely held aloof.

An accomplished documentary film tradition was also established, notably by John Grierson (1898–1972), who coined the term 'documentary'. Grierson was influenced both by Russian film technique and American mass media. He persuaded both government and business in Britain that they could serve their own interests by sponsoring films, as propaganda and advertising. His most famous film was *Night Mail* (1936), commissioned by the Post Office, and with a verse commentary by the poet W.H. AUDEN. The most commercially successful British film of the 1930s, and the first to find a substantial overseas market, was *The Private Lives of Henry VIII* (1933), directed by the Hungarian immigrant Alexander Korda. New directors emerged, notably Anthony Asquith, Walter Forde and Alfred HITCHCOCK. Another successful genre was musical comedy, in which the most popular stars were Gracie Fields and George Formby, who had established reputations in music hall.

World War II gave the industry its greatest boost. The supply of American films was restricted and the United States agreed to show British films. British films could represent the war and popular feelings about it in Britain as American films could not, and the Ministry of Information funded and influenced the content of feature films, recognizing their importance for morale, notable examples being *In Which We Serve* (Noël Coward, 1942) and *The Life and Times of Colonel Blimp* (Michael Powell and Emeric Pressburger, 1943). The Ministry of Information supplied generous funding for documentaries, such as *Fires Were Started* (1943), also with the aim of boosting civilian morale. Film-going was not rationed and was relatively cheap. It offered escape from war in the warm and comfortable – even glamorous – surroundings of the cinema, which drew in increasing numbers of the middle classes. Cinema attendance peaked in 1946, with 1.6 billion visits. ENSA (the ENTERTAINMENTS NATIONAL SERVICE ASSOCIATION) took films to the troops. Laurence OLIVIER directed and starred in a film version of Shakespeare's patriotic *Henry V* (1944), which evoked Britain's past greatness in war. Directors such as Carol Reed (*The Way Ahead*, 1944) and David Lean (*This Happy Breed*, 1944) represented an image of everyday British stoicism in the face of war. During this period the Rank Organization, controlled by J. Arthur Rank, came to control the industry.

After the war American competition returned and the government provided financial support to the industry as a potential export earner. British film production was very active in the decade after the war and attracted a wide audience. There were successful adaptations of plays and novels, such as David Lean's film version of Charles Dickens's *Great Expectations* (1946) and *Oliver Twist* (1947). Olivier appeared in screen versions of Shakespeare's *Hamlet* (1949) and *Richard III* (1955). Anthony Asquith directed versions of stage plays, including Terence Rattigan's *The Winslow Boy* (1949) and Oscar Wilde's *The Importance of Being Earnest* (1952). Powell and Pressburger had a major success with *The Red Shoes* (1948), while Carol Reed directed the classic COLD WAR thriller *The Third Man* (1949) scripted by Graham GREENE. However, the bulk of British cinema production consisted of mainstream films for a mass audience. Popular films were made by Roy and John Boulting, such as Graham Greene's *Brighton Rock* (1947). The Ealing Studios, part of the Rank empire, produced a stream of films, with various

directors, which humorously evoked life in post-war Britain: notable Ealing comedies include *Passport to Pimlico* (1949), *Kind Hearts and Coronets* (1949) and *The Lavender Hill Mob* (1951).

A new generation of filmmakers with different preoccupations emerged as the 1950s turned into the 1960s. The plays and NOVELS of the social-realist 'Angry Young Men' (*see* DRAMA) were adapted for the screen, including Tony Richardson's version of John Osborne's *Look Back in Anger* (1959), Jack Clayton's version of John Braine's *Room at the Top* (1959) and Karel Reisz's version of Alan Sillitoe's *Saturday Night and Sunday Morning* (1960). Less sombre and realist and equally successful were the films of John Schlesinger, such as *Far from the Madding Crowd* (1967), and Richard Lester's BEATLES films, *A Hard Day's Night* (1964) and *Help!* (1965). The exiled American director Joseph Losey also made an impact with his art-house psychological films such as *The Servant* (1963) and *Accident* (1967), both with screenplays by the playwright Harold Pinter. In the 1960s American finance became increasingly important for the British industry and enabled the production of more lavish films, such as David Lean's *Lawrence of Arabia* (1961) and the James Bond series, starting with *Dr No* (1962).

As television spread in the 1960s and 1970s cinema audiences declined, from 1.2 billion admissions a year in 1955 to 510 million in 1960 and 190 million in 1970. The lowest point was reached in 1987 with 67 million. It was feared that the British film industry was doomed, despite the success of the quintessentially British *Carry On* comedy series. However, from its foundation the commercial television Channel 4 (*see* BRITISH BROADCASTING CORPORATION) funded innovative feature films, such as Stephen Frears's *My Beautiful Laundrette* (1985), which led to a new wave of British filmmaking. In the 1980s there also emerged a generation of highly intellectual filmmakers with strong, international, minority followings, such as Peter Greenaway, who first made an impact with *The Draughtsman's Contract* (1983), and

Derek Jarman (with films such as *Caravaggio,* 1986). To the end of the century Britain produced a succession of talented young filmmakers, often working on low budgets, some achieving major international success, such as Sam Mendes, whose first movie, *American Beauty,* gained five Oscars in 2000. By the end of the century cinema audiences were rising again.

FURTHER READING C. Barr (ed.), *All Our Yesterdays: Ninety Years of British Cinema* (1986); M. Landy, *British Genres: Cinema and Society, 1930–1960* (1991).

First World War. *See* WORLD WAR I: HOME FRONT and WORLD WAR I: MILITARY.

Fisher, Geoffrey (1887–1972), archbishop of Canterbury (1945–61). Fisher was born in Leicestershire, of a clerical family, and educated at Marlborough College and Exeter College, Oxford, where he studied classics. He taught at Marlborough, 1911–12, and was ordained as deacon of the CHURCH OF ENGLAND in 1912, then priest in 1913. He then succeeded William TEMPLE as headmaster of Repton school, where he remained until 1932. He became bishop of Chester in 1932, bishop of London in 1939, then archbishop of Canterbury following Temple's sudden death in 1945. As bishop of London he was remembered for working hard to support the population during the BLITZ. As archbishop he achieved the most substantial reform of canon law since the 16th century. He travelled more extensively among the worldwide Anglican communion than any previous archbishop, assisted by improved international communications, and he was the first since the Reformation to visit the pope. He took a central position between the High and Low Church of England and helped to lessen antagonisms. He retired from the archbishopric in 1961 and became an active parish curate in Dorset.

Fisher, John (Arbuthnot) (1841–1920), admiral of the fleet, largely responsible for Britain's naval build-up in the early years of the century. Born in Ceylon, he entered the ROYAL NAVY in 1854. He qualified in the gunnery school *Excellent* and joined *Warrior,* the first iron-clad. He was on the staff of *Excellent,* 1864–9 and 1872–6, and devoted himself to the development of the torpedo. He was promoted to captain in 1874 and spent 1876–82 at sea, gaining a CB for services in Egypt in 1882. He was captain of the gunnery school at Portsmouth, 1883–6, then director of ordnance and torpedoes at the Admiralty, 1886–90. He was appointed rear admiral in 1890, third sea lord and controller of the navy, 1892–7, KCB 1894, vice admiral 1896, and commander in chief of the North America and West Indies station, 1897. He commanded the Mediterranean fleet, 1898–1902, greatly increasing its efficiency. He was promoted to admiral in 1901 and was awarded the GCB in 1902. In 1902–3 he was second sea lord with charge of fleet personnel. In this capacity he introduced important reforms, notably the common entry scheme for the training of naval officers at Osborne, Isle of Wight. He became commander in chief, Portsmouth, in 1903, and was a member of the war office Reconstruction Committee, 1903–4. He was awarded the OM in 1904.

As first sea lord 1904–10, Fisher reorganized the fleet to meet the growing strength of the German navy, and advocated the design of the DREADNOUGHT type of battleship and battle cruiser. He was obliged by the Liberal government elected in 1906 to reduce the naval programme; nevertheless he increased the number of battleships by eight in 1909–10. He was created 1st Baron Fisher in 1909. He returned to the admiralty as first sea lord at the outbreak of WORLD WAR I and masterminded the British victory in the battle of the Falkland Islands, 1914. He opposed the attempt to force a naval passage through the DARDANELLES in 1915 and resigned from the navy.

Fisher, Sir (Norman Fenwick) Warren (1879–1948), head of the CIVIL SERVICE (1919–39). He was educated at Winchester and Hertford College,

Oxford, where he studied classics. Fisher entered the Board of Inland Revenue in 1903, becoming a commissioner of the Board in 1913, deputy chairman in 1914 and chairman in 1918. He became permanent secretary to the Treasury and the first person to be appointed head of the Civil Service in 1919, an office that he held until 1939. He was knighted in 1919. He played the major role in establishing the Treasury as the dominant department of the service and established the principles on which the service operated thereafter. Higher (administrative class) civil servants – rather than being specialists attached to one board or ministry, as had been the tradition – became generalists, moving among ministries in the course of their careers. He strove for a conception of the service as a unity and for the highest standards among civil servants, both of conduct and of political neutrality; and for independence of mind in relation to ministers. He was closely involved with preparations for WORLD WAR II, in particular with rearmament. He was defence commissioner, northwestern region, 1939–40, and special commissioner organizing services and clearance in London, 1940–2.
FURTHER READING E. O'Halpin, *Head of the Civil Service: A Study of Sir Warren Fisher* (1989).

Fitt, Gerry (Gerald) (1926–), NORTHERN IRELAND Nationalist politician; leader of the SOCIAL DEMOCRATIC AND LABOUR PARTY (SDLP) (1970–9). After serving in the merchant navy during World War II, Fitt returned to Belfast where he became a city councillor in the late 1950s. He served as an MP for a variety of left-wing political parties in the Northern Ireland Parliament (later Assembly) in the 1960s and 1970s, and served on the 1975–6 Constitutional Convention. After being elected as a Republican Labour MP for Belfast West in 1966, he helped found the SDLP, becoming party leader and serving as a MP from 1970 to 1979. In 1979 he resigned the party leadership (being replaced by John HUME), but retained his seat in the House of Commons as an independent socialist MP from 1979 to 1983, when he became a life peer.

Fleet Air Arm. *See* ROYAL AIR FORCE.

Fleming, Alexander (1881–1955), microbiologist who discovered penicillin. The son of a farming family in Ayrshire, Scotland, Fleming began to study medicine in 1901, at St Mary's Hospital Medical School, London. After qualifying in 1906 he worked at the same hospital on the diagnosis and treatment of syphilis. During World War I he worked on the problem of the failure of current antiseptic techniques to heal wound infections. He continued this research on his return to St Mary's after the war. In 1928 he discovered penicillin, almost by accident, when a spore of mould contaminated a plate in which he was growing staphylococci, a form of bacteria. The mould appeared to destroy the bacteria, but Fleming failed to identify the active agent. In 1940 Howard Florey and Ernst Chain in Oxford purified enough of the agent, called penicillin, for clinical trials, which confirmed that penicillin had remarkable powers to cure infections without ill effects. Fleming was knighted in 1944, and in 1945 Fleming, Florey and Chain shared the Nobel prize for the discovery of penicillin.
FURTHER READING G. Macfarlane, *Alexander Fleming: The Man and the Myth* (1985).

flying bombs. *See* V1S AND V2S.

flying pickets. *See* TRADE UNIONS.

Foot, Michael (Mackintosh) (1913–), Labour politician; leader of the LABOUR PARTY (1980–3). Foot was born into a family of middle-class radical Liberal intellectuals in the southwest of England, where Liberalism remained strong for longer than in any other region. Educated at the Quaker Leighton Park School and Oxford University, Foot became a journalist, then MP for Plymouth Devonport 1945–55. He was on the left of the party in the disputes of the 1950s. He lost his seat in 1955, returning as MP for his hero Aneurin BEVAN's old seat of Ebbw Vale, South Wales, in 1960. He remained MP for Ebbw Vale until 1983, when boundary changes transformed the constituency into Blaunau Gwent, which he represented until his retirement in 1992. His main interests were literature, nuclear disarmament and his devoted marriage to the feminist filmmaker Jill Craigie.

In 1970 Foot showed a previously hidden ambition within the Labour Party and was elected to the shadow cabinet; a year later he was elected to the party's deputy leadership. He was encouraged by the left of the party who had lacked a leader since the death of Bevan and who respected his independent, dissenting stance. In 1974 he entered the CABINET for the first time as employment secretary. In 1976 Harold WILSON resigned as prime minister. Foot was the most successful challenger to James CALLAGHAN for the succession, and was appointed deputy leader and leader of the House of Commons. He worked effectively to hold together the left and right wings of the party.

When Callaghan resigned in 1980 following Labour's defeat in the 1979 GENERAL ELECTION Foot narrowly defeated Denis HEALEY to become party leader. His leadership coincided with the worst of times, when the party was at a low point electorally and much divided. He did not have the skills to heal the rifts and his image as an unworldly, radical intellectual exposed him to pillorying by journalists. He was an intelligent man of principle who took over by default a party in crisis. After Labour's election defeat in 1983 he was replaced as party leader by Neil KINNOCK.

FURTHER READING S. Hoggart and D. Leigh, *Michael Foot: A Portrait* (1981); K.O. Morgan, *Labour People* (1987).

football. *See* SPORT.

foreign secretary, the government minister at the head of the department of state responsible for foreign affairs. This department was originally the Foreign Office, but in 1968 it amalgamated with the Commonwealth Office to form the Foreign and Commonwealth Office. Initially the foreign secretary was second in authority only to the PRIME MINISTER, but, especially from the 1960s, the number-two position was increasingly taken over by the CHANCELLOR OF THE EXCHEQUER, as Britain's influence in world affairs diminished and the running of the economy became increasingly dominant in domestic politics. In the 20th century foreign secretaries exercised less independence than those of the 19th century, such as Lord Palmerston, and were more subordinate to general government policy.

Forster, E(dward) M(organ) (1879–1970), novelist. Forster, known as Morgan, was the only son of Alice (known as Lily) Whichelo (1855–1945) and Edward Morgan Forster, an architect. He died when Forster was 22 months old and Forster was raised by his mother and grandmother, with much input from his father's aunt, Marianne Thornton, daughter of Henry Thornton, a member of the Clapham Sect, a group of early 19th-century evangelical Anglicans who were devout philanthropists. When she died in 1888 she left Forster £8000, which gave him financial security until he began to make a comfortable living from his writing. He wrote her biography, *Marianne Thornton* (1956), which concluded : 'She and no one else made my career as a writer possible and her love, in a most tangible sense, followed me beyond the grave.' Money's ability to confer freedom became a theme of his writings, for example in the novel *Howards End*.

Forster had a happy childhood, living from 1883 to 1893 at a house called Rooksnest, at Stevenage in Hertfordshire, which became a model for the house in *Howards End*. He was much less happy at boarding school, to which he was sent from the age of eleven: first to Kent House, Eastbourne, then to Tonbridge School, which he was to pillory in *The Longest Journey* (1907), his second novel. He went to King's College, Cambridge, in 1897, where he was very happy. His academic career was undistinguished, but he made close friends and literary contacts and was elected to the semi-secret, elite society of intellectuals, the Apostles, through whom he became associated with the BLOOMSBURY GROUP. Visiting Italy with his mother, he became convinced of his vocation as a novelist.

Forster's first novel, *Where Angels Fear to Tread*, was published in 1905. In this, Italy stands for liberation, contrasted with the constricted emotions of the English, another theme of much of his writing. The novel describes a marriage between a young English widow and an Italian of lower social status; transgression of rigid British social boundaries was another of Forster's preoccupations. Similar themes emerged in his third novel, *A Room with a View* (1908). He made his name, however, with the publication of *Howards End* (1910), which interweaves a number of themes: the differences between people who live to make money or live for the arts, and those who have access to neither; the opportunities open to men as opposed to those closed to women; and the conflicts experienced by liberal idealists, such as himself.

From 1906 Forster lived with his mother in Weybridge, Surrey, and became tutor to Syed Ross Masood, an Indian Muslim patriot, with whom the homosexual Forster fell in love. Masood did not reciprocate, but they became close friends and he guided Forster on a visit to INDIA in 1912–13. Also in 1913 Forster paid a visit to Edward Carpenter, a socialist and open homosexual, which inspired him to write a novel of homosexual love, *Maurice*, but such was the taboo about the topic in Britain that it was not published until 1971, after Forster's death. He published a collection of short stories, *The Celestial Omnibus*, in 1911, and began to write stories with erotic themes. These also were only published posthumously, in 1972. During World War I he worked for the National Gallery, then for the Red Cross in Alexandria, where he met the poet Constantine Cavafy, whose work he helped introduce to Britain on his return in 1919. He also had his first serious sexual relationship, with Mohammed el Adl, after which his personal life was more fulfilled, though el Adl died in 1923.

Forster's time in Alexandria inspired two books: *Alexandria: A History and Guide* (1922) and *Pharos and Pharillon* (1923).

In 1921–2 Forster re-visited India, serving as secretary to the Maharajah of Dewas, an experience commemorated in *The Hill of Devi* (1953). He had started to write a novel about India before the war, but the war represented to him the defeat of many of his ideals and arrested his capacity to write. After the war he completed *A Passage to India* (1924). It is bleaker in tone than his earlier novels, but it is his greatest work. It explores again how difficult it is for different social, sexual and, this time, racial groups (the Indians and the English) to follow the maxim that prefaces *Howards End*: 'Only connect' – a maxim that is a presence in all Forster's work. The book also contrasts the sexual openness of India with the constraints of English culture. The novel was a great success, but it was Forster's last. He wrote a work of literary criticism, *Aspects of the Novel* (1927), originally given as lectures in Cambridge, and two volumes of essays, *Abinger Harvest* (1936) and *Two Cheers for Democracy* (1951). The remainder of his life was devoted to support of literature and opposition to CENSORSHIP. He became the first president of the National Council for Civil Liberties, and campaigned in 1928 against the suppression of Radclyffe Hall's lesbian novel *The Well of Loneliness*. In 1960 he appeared as a witness for the defence in the *Lady Chatterley's Lover* trial. In 1946 King's College awarded him an honorary fellowship, and he remained in Cambridge until his death.

FURTHER READING N. Beauman, *Morgan: A Biography of E.M. Forster* (1993); P.N. Furbank, *E.M. Forster: A Life* (2 vols., 1977–8).

Franklin, Rosalind. *See* SCIENCE.

free trade, the absence of all, or nearly all, artificial restrictions such as quotas and tariffs on the amount or content of international trade or the price at which goods are exchanged. There are very few historical examples of this being put into practice in its pure form, but Britain in the late 19th and early 20th centuries came close, with tariffs at a minimum. Britain at this time was a major player in the world economy and the pound sterling was the dominant currency. The British economy profited exceptionally from exports, overseas trade, loans and investment. Britain had everything to gain from free trade and both the major political parties were committed to it. At the end of the 19th century and in the early years of the 20th growing competition from other countries raised doubts, especially in parts of the CONSERVATIVE PARTY, and proposals for TARIFF REFORM were put forward, though the Liberals remained firmly committed to free trade. The effect of WORLD WAR I and the depressed state of the world economy in the 1920s destroyed Britain's favourable balance of trade and payments with the rest of the world. In 1932 free trade was abandoned by the NATIONAL GOVERNMENT with the introduction of a general 10% import tariff, but allowing preferential treatment to COMMONWEALTH countries in return for concessions on British exports (*see* IMPERIAL PREFERENCE). Britain subsequently joined two European free-trade zones, the EUROPEAN FREE TRADE ASSOCIATION in 1960 and the EUROPEAN ECONOMIC COMMUNITY in 1973.

FURTHER READING A.C. Howe, *Free Trade and Liberal England, 1846–1946* (1997).

French, John (Denton Pinkstone) (1852–1925), commander of the British Expeditionary Force (BEF) on the Western Front (1914–15) during WORLD WAR I. French commanded a cavalry division with distinction during the BOER WAR, in which he led the relief of Kimberley. He was commander in chief, Aldershot (1902–7), and inspector-general of forces (1907), responsible for a total reform of military manoeuvres. In 1912 he was appointed chief of the imperial general staff, and became a field marshal in 1913, but resigned in support of fellow officers in the CURRAGH INCIDENT, 1914.

As commander of the BEF in France and Flan-

ders in the first two years of World War I he showed that he was a charismatic cavalryman (a quality that turned out to have little use) but poor at leadership, organization and diplomacy. His relations with his French allies were distant and his only solution to the stalemate of trench warfare was to call for ever more shells. When they ceased to be forthcoming, in May 1915 he secretly encouraged *The Times* and the *Daily Mail* to blame KITCHENER for failing to supply enough shells, creating a 'shell scandal' that rebounded on him, exposing his own inadequacies more than those of others. French barely survived this scandal and was dismissed in December 1915 following another failure at Loos in September–October 1915. He became commander of home forces, then lord lieutenant of IRELAND (1918–21), during the period of violent turmoil that preceded Irish independence. He was knighted in 1900, made a viscount in 1916, and created 1st earl of Ypres in 1922.

Freud, Lucian (1922–), figurative painter, widely regarded as one of the greatest British artists of the 20th century. He was born in Berlin; his father was an architect and his grandfather was the psychoanalyst Sigmund Freud. In 1932, he and his Jewish family moved to England, away from the growing anti-Semitism in Germany. He was educated at progressive boarding schools. In 1939, the year in which he became a naturalized British subject, he enrolled briefly at the East Anglian School of Painting and Drawing, with Cedric Morris, who encouraged pupils to allow feelings to prevail over objective observation. This was his only formal training. He joined the Merchant Navy in World War II but was invalided out in 1942 and began to work full time as an artist. Drawing was his first love and he came to public attention when some of his drawings were published in the wartime literary journal *Horizon*.

Freud first exhibited his work in 1944 and from 1948 to 1958 he taught at the Slade School of Fine Art in London. Major public recognition came when he won a prize at the FESTIVAL OF

BRITAIN for his *Interior at Paddington* (1951, Walker Art Gallery, Liverpool), which placed an archetypal 'Angry Young Man', in dishevelled raincoat, cigarette in one hand, the other fist clenched, close to a huge potted plant in an anonymous interior space. Such closely observed, meticulously finished, unsettling juxtapositions of human and inanimate subjects became characteristic of Freud's work. From the late 1960s his technique was broader, less meticulous, with richer colouring, but still intense and more disturbing than conventional figurative representation. His work included still lifes, interiors and urban scenes, but his specialities were portraits and nudes, often in close-up with close attention to the painting of flesh. He preferred to paint people he knew well. His mother sat for an extensive series in the 1970s (including *The Painter's Mother*, Tate Gallery, London, 1982) and several of his daughters modelled nude. His compositions in the 1980s and 1990s were increasingly ambitious in both scale and complexity. These included a series of monumental male nudes of his friend, the transvestite performance artist, Leigh Bowery. He also painted portraits of more conventional sitters, including Sir Jacob Rothschild, Lord Goodman and Baron Thyssen-Bornemisza. Freud was named a Companion of Honour in 1983 and was awarded the Order of Merit in 1993.

FURTHER READING L. Gowing, *Lucian Freud* (1982).

Friends of the Earth. *See* ENVIRONMENTALISM.

Frink, Elisabeth (1930–93), sculptor and graphic artist. She was born at Thurlow, Suffolk. She studied at Guildford School of Art (1947–9) and Chelsea School of Art in London (1949–53), then went on to teach at both Chelsea (1953–61) and St Martin's School of Art (1954–62). In 1964 she became a visiting teacher at the Royal College of Art in London. While still a student in 1953 she won a prize in the international competition for the Monument to the Unknown Political Prisoner.

This competition, financed by an unknown American, was won by a Briton, Reg Butler (1913–81). It was intended to promote interest in contemporary sculpture and to 'commemorate all those unknown men and women who in our time have been deprived of their lives or their liberty in the cause of human freedom'.

Frink stated, 'I think my sculptures are about what a human being or an animal feels like, not necessarily what they look like. I use anatomy to create the essence of human and animal forms.' Typically, therefore, her figures were of bronze horses and riders or male nudes. Frink had numerous public commissions, the first being the concrete *Wild Boar* (1957) for Harlow NEW TOWN. A characteristic work is the bronze *Horse and Rider* (1975) in Piccadilly, London, at the junction with Dover Street. This was commissioned by Trafalgar House Investments Ltd. Later in her career she created numerous portrait busts of distinguished sitters. In addition to sculpture she produced prints and drawings. She became a Dame of the British Empire in 1982.

Fry, Roger Eliot (1866–1934), critic, painter and designer. Born in London into a distinguished Quaker family, he abandoned Christian belief in adulthood, but his Quaker upbringing instilled in him a respect for truth, industriousness and a sense of social responsibility. His father, Sir Edward Fry, was a judge. He was educated at Clifton College and King's College, Cambridge, where he obtained an excellent degree, a double first in natural sciences. He was elected a member of the Apostles, a Cambridge University secret society that is credited with wielding much influence on British society. At Cambridge J.C. Middleton, the art historian, encouraged his interest in painting and drawing. To his parents' dismay, Fry went on to study painting and art history in Paris and Italy. Returning to London in the 1890s he studied art with Walter SICKERT. He then began to paint with dedication and became a compelling critic, lecturer and writer about art. By 1901 he was the regular art critic for the *Athenaeum*. He lobbied for support of the visual arts and was involved in the foundation of the National Art Collections Fund (1903), which acquired works of fine and decorative arts for public collections in Britain; the *Burlington Magazine*, the pre-eminent periodical of art history, which he edited from 1910 to 1919; and the Contemporary Art Society, founded in 1910.

Between 1905 and 1910 Fry was curator of paintings for the Metropolitan Museum of Art in New York, but this turned out to be an unhappy appointment for him. Soon after accepting the post, he was offered the directorship of the National Gallery in London, but felt morally bound to keep his commitment to the Metropolitan. In 1911 he refused the directorship of the Tate Gallery. From 1906 he associated closely with Vanessa BELL, with whom he had an affair for several years (one of many affairs conducted while his wife, Helen Anrep, was incurably mentally ill and institutionalized), and her husband Clive Bell. He was ambitious to succeed as a painter, but his paintings are not outstanding. However, he made a major contribution to the discipline of art history by mounting two major exhibitions of post-impressionist French painting at the Grafton Galleries in London in 1910 and 1912, featuring Manet, Cézanne, Gauguin and van Gogh. The exhibiting of art many contemporaries regarded as outrageous caused a storm of protest, but the exhibitions brought these works to public attention and the term 'post-impressionism' into use in Britain, easing the acceptance of such work.

In 1913, with Vanessa Bell and others of the BLOOMSBURY GROUP and the artist and writer Wyndham Lewis, Fry founded the Omega Workshops in Bloomsbury, London, in order to create decorated objects for domestic use, such as furniture, textiles and pottery. The aim was to improve standards of design in the applied arts and to give opportunities to young artists. A volume of Fry's lectures and reviews, gathered in a volume named *Vision and Design* (1920) was one of the first Penguin books to be published. These were pioneering, cheap paperback books, designed to bring high culture to a mass audience, and they succeeded. The publication helped to give Fry wide influence on popular taste and he kept up a steady stream of writing and lecturing for the rest of his life. His books include monographs on Cézanne (1927) and Matisse (1932). He was twice rejected for the Slade professorship of fine art at Oxford University (1910, 1927) and for the annually elected Slade professorship at Cambridge University in 1904. He was finally appointed to the Cambridge chair in 1933, one year before his death.

FURTHER READING F. Spalding, *Roger Fry: Art and Life* (1980).

G

Gaitskell, Hugh (Todd Naylor) (1906–63), Labour politician; leader of the LABOUR PARTY (1955–63). Gaitskell was educated at Winchester College and New College, Oxford, where he was taught and influenced by the socialist theorist G.D.H. Cole. He taught briefly in ADULT EDUCATION in the Nottinghamshire coalfield, then from 1928 to 1939 was a lecturer in economics at University College, London. During that time he was part of a small group of economists who were anxious to encourage the Labour Party to take up the economic ideas of J.M. KEYNES. During World War II Gaitskell served as a German-speaking economist in the Ministry of Economic Warfare, and then at the Board of Trade as Hugh DALTON's personal assistant.

Elected to Parliament in 1945 for Leeds South, which he represented until his death, Gaitskell became parliamentary secretary to the Ministry of Fuel and Power (1945–6), then minister until 1950. He played an important part in persuading the party leadership to devalue the pound in 1949. He was minister of state for economic affairs, 1950, and CHANCELLOR OF THE EXCHEQUER (1950–1), making the controversial decision to impose selective charges on users of the NATIONAL HEALTH SERVICE, which led to the resignations of Aneurin BEVAN and Harold WILSON from the government. Antagonism between supporters of Bevan and of Gaitskell was a feature of the Labour Party in the 1950s.

In December 1955 Gaitskell became leader of the party, easily defeating his main rivals Bevan and Herbert MORRISON. Conflicts followed within the party over nuclear disarmament (*see* CAMPAIGN FOR NUCLEAR DISARMAMENT). Gaitskell was a strong supporter of multilateral disarmament and sought international agreements on this, but he strongly opposed unilateralism, vowing at the party conference in 1960 to 'fight and fight again to save the party we love' from adopting this policy. He also sought to build up the COMMONWEALTH as a unique multicultural grouping of nation-states, supported close links with the United States, and favoured developing the role of the UNITED NATIONS. He opposed British membership of the EUROPEAN ECONOMIC COMMUNITY, one issue on which he was united with the bulk of his party at that time. He opposed the invasion of SUEZ in 1956. In domestic affairs he preferred a mixed economy to wholesale NATIONALIZATION and sought in 1959–60 to persuade the party to abandon CLAUSE FOUR. This was clumsily handled, in a party already deeply split, and he was unsuccessful. He died prematurely and unexpectedly, and was succeeded as party leader by Harold Wilson.

FURTHER READING K.O. Morgan, *Labour People* (1987); P. Williams, *Hugh Gaitskell: A Political Biography* (1979).

Gallipoli, peninsula in western Turkey guarding the DARDANELLES and thus the route to the Black Sea from the Mediterranean. During WORLD WAR I the Dardanelles expedition of March 1915, to attack Constantinople (Istanbul), failed when the ships of the ROYAL NAVY could not penetrate the shore defences at the Gallipoli peninsula. It was decided instead to land troops on the peninsula to seize forts guarding the approach to Constantinople. The first landings were on 25 April 1915. The Turks had anticipated the landings and offered strong resistance. The fighting went on until August, when there were further Allied landings, but bitter trench warfare continued. Some 4000 soldiers perished by the time that KITCHENER came to inspect in November. He ordered an evacuation, which took place without further casualties.

This disaster caused Winston CHURCHILL, who had supported the expedition, to lose his predominant role in the war council, and he resigned as first lord of the Admiralty. Most of the troops involved were Australians and New Zealanders (ANZACs) serving in support of Britain. Gallipoli was seen as a great betrayal of these EMPIRE troops by incompetent British leaders, and led to the questioning of British rule. In Australia particularly, the experience was a profoundly formative moment in the growth of national consciousness.

FURTHER READING R.R. James, *Gallipoli* (1965); A. Moorehead, *Gallipoli* (1975); A. Thompson, *Anzac Memories. Living with the Legend* (1994).

Galsworthy, John (1867–1933), novelist and playwright. Galsworthy was born in Surrey, the son of a wealthy, property-owning solicitor. He attended Harrow School and Oxford, without distinction; he was apparently mainly interested in clothes and horse-racing. At his father's insistence he then studied for the law in London, but never practised. Instead he collected rents from his father's slum properties, which aroused his interest in social reform. In an attempt to motivate his son, his father sent him to various parts of the empire. While travelling by sea Galsworthy met Joseph CONRAD, who was working as a seaman. They became lifelong friends, supportive of each other's writing careers. Another influence moving Galsworthy towards writing was Ada Cooper Galsworthy, who was unhappily married to John's cousin. They became lovers in Paris in 1895 and she urged him to do something with his life. He began to write. Ada became the model for Irene Forsyte in *The Forsyte Saga*. Fearing that Galsworthy's father would disinherit his son if she divorced and they married, they waited until his death in 1904, when she divorced. They married in 1905.

Galsworthy's first volume of stories, *From the Four Winds*, appeared in 1897, followed in 1898 by his first novel, *Jocelyn*. He published two other novels and another collection of short stories before achieving fame in 1906 with *A Man of Property*, whose central figure, Soames Forsyte, was based upon Ada's ex-husband, Arthur. Two further Forsyte novels, *In Chancery* (1920) and *To Let* (1921), were collected together with two shorter pieces as *The Forsyte Saga* in 1922. Two further trilogies featuring Forsyte characters followed: *A Modern Comedy* (1929) and *The End of a Chapter* (1934). Other novels, such as *The Island Pharisees* (1904), *Fraternity* (1909) and *The Dark Flower* (1913), explored Galsworthy's interest in the effects on individuals of poverty and of social convention.

Galsworthy persued a parallel career as a playwright. *The Silver Box* was a success in the same year as *A Man of Property*. This was a play about theft, the first of several on social and moral themes. His reputation as a dramatist was established with *Strife* (1909), which examined men and managers in industry, followed by *Justice* (1910) and *Loyalties* (1922). Between the wars he ranked second only to George Bernard SHAW in public esteem, and he was placed on a par with J.M. Barrie, Somerset Maugham and J.B. Priestley. He was awarded the Nobel prize for literature in 1932. Galsworthy's critical reputation diminished after his death, though much of his work, especially *The Forsyte Saga*, retained widespread appeal – a BBC drama serial of *The Forsyte Saga* in 1967 was hugely popular.

FURTHER READING A. Frechet, *John Galsworthy: A Reassessment* (1982).

gambling. Gambling, in its many forms, was one of the most popular pastimes in 20th-century Britain. This was the case despite the fact that, for the early part of the century, it was the subject of much vilification, while certain forms of gambling were illegal. Gambling was identified as a curse of modern society by social investigators in the late 19th century, such as B. Seebohm ROWNTREE, who edited *Betting and Gambling: A National Evil* in 1905. Rowntree's concerns were reflected in the passage of the 1906 Street Betting Act, which banned gambling on horse racing outside race-courses. Illegal gambling continued, with bets being taken by 'runners' to what were known as 'street bookies'. These individuals could be identified within the urban working-class landscape, but laws against gambling affected a broad spectrum of British society. As casinos were also outlawed, middle-class gamblers would arrange 'gambling evenings' in private houses. From the 1920s gambling was increasingly dominated by large companies, exemplified by the establishment of urban greyhound-racing tracks, and more particularly football 'pools' in the 1930s. Seen by many as a way of 'escaping' the Depression (*see* UNEMPLOYMENT), football pools were played by one in three Britons by the 1950s, and introduced the phenomenon of instant wealth creation.

Organized attempts to eradicate gambling from society were centred upon the National Anti-Gambling League, which later became the National League of Education Against Gambling (NLEAG). In 1948 NLEAG sponsored a survey by MASS-OBSERVATION of national attitudes to gambling. The survey discovered – much to the chagrin of its sponsors – that gambling in one form or another was both widespread and not thought of as a deadly sin. Despite growing support for the liberalization of gambling legislation, this did not come about until the Betting and Gaming Act (1960), which legalized betting shops and enabled the establishment of members' casinos and bingo clubs. By the 1970s gambling had become both widely accepted and officially sanctioned. Compulsive gambling was, however, recognized as a problem akin to alcoholism, and Gamblers Anonymous, an organization originating in the USA in the late 1950s, was set up in the UK in 1964 to help those who had become addicted.

A national lottery had to some extent been prefigured by premium bonds, introduced in 1956 (although the government denied that buying premium bonds constituted gambling), but it was not until 1994 that such a lottery was introduced by the government of John MAJOR. The National Lottery created a number of millionaires, and provided its operators with big profits, while a percentage of the takings was donated to 'good causes' and a National Lottery Heritage Fund (*see* NATIONAL HERITAGE). Thus by the 1990s the government had moved beyond condoning gambling to direct involvement in a lottery, and public policy had shifted from opposition to participation.

FURTHER READING R. Munting, *An Economic and Social History of Gambling in Britain and the USA* (1996).

Gandhi, Mohandas Karamchand (1869–1948), Indian nationalist who led the campaign for independence for INDIA. Gandhi was born into a prosperous family at Porbandar, a small princely state in western India. He travelled to London in 1888 to study law, and later practised as a barrister in Bombay. In 1893 he moved to SOUTH AFRICA, where from 1907 to 1914 he conducted passive-resistance campaigns of protest against the Transvaal government's discrimination against its Indian minority population, a discrimination he had not encountered in Britain. In 1915 he returned to India, emerging as leader of the Indian National Congress, the principal movement for independence, and became known for the extreme ascetic simplicity of his life. He organized a boycott of

British goods thereby helping to develop Indian village industries. By preaching passive resistance he limited, but could not eliminate, violence from the movement. He was imprisoned for his activities in 1922, 1930, 1933 and 1942, resorting to hunger strikes as part of his campaign of civil disobedience. In 1931 he attended the abortive round-table conference on the future of India. By 1942 he had come to believe that all-out independence was the only solution for India. He collaborated with the last viceroys, WAVELL and MOUNTBATTEN, in developing plans for the independence and partition of India, which came about in 1947. Many of his Hindu followers regarded him as a saint – the 'Mahatma' or 'great soul'. Others rejected his pacifism and his acceptance of the partition between India and Pakistan. He survived an attempt on his life on 20 January 1948, only to be shot dead by a Hindu fanatic ten days later.
FURTHER READING F. Hutchins, *India's Revolution: Gandhi and the Quit India Movement* (1973).

garden cities. *See* TOWN AND COUNTRY PLANNING.

GATT. *See* GENERAL AGREEMENT ON TARIFFS AND TRADE.

Geddes axe, the, nickname for government cuts in social spending in 1923. With the onset of economic recession and UNEMPLOYMENT in 1921 there were growing demands for cuts in public expenditure. The *Daily Mail* and other newspapers launched a furious campaign against 'wasteful' government expenditure, pillorying 'squandermania'; MPs and the CITY OF LONDON demanded economies. With strong support from the Treasury, government expenditure ceased to grow in most areas. In August 1921 a committee was appointed under Sir Eric Geddes (1875–1937), a businessman who had been minister of transport in LLOYD GEORGE's wartime coalition government, to examine the following year's estimates and to recommend economies. Its first reports were issued in February

1922 and recommended severe cuts in all social expenditure. These were implemented in the following year, becoming known as the 'Geddes axe'. They probably contributed to the loss of votes by the Conservative government in their election defeat of October 1923.

General Agreement on Tariffs and Trade (GATT), originally a treaty signed in 1947 by 23 nations of which Britain was one. The agreement, largely masterminded by KEYNES, was intended to be a temporary arrangement. It was designed to boost world trade and to avoid an economic crisis like that of the interwar years by means of an agreement to keep tariffs to a minimum through regular international negotiations. It spawned a long-lasting agency of the UNITED NATIONS, based in Geneva. It worked smoothly while the world economy was stable, until the OIL SHOCK of the 1970s. Thereafter it was more difficult to control states or groups of states such as the EUROPEAN COMMUNITY, anxious to protect their economies from crisis. It was also vulnerable to criticism that it was a 'rich man's club', inhospitable or antagonistic to developing or very poor economies. In 1995 it was replaced by the rather more inclusive World Trade Organization, which initially had 125 members who signed agreements designed to regulate international trade. GATT had played a role in restraining protectionism and especially in the reduction in protection of industrial goods.

general elections. In UK general elections votes are cast to elect members of the House of COMMONS. The party that wins the largest number of seats normally forms the government, by invitation of the MONARCH, as the unwritten constitution dictates. The party which wins the largest number of seats will not necessarily win the largest number of votes, since voting preferences are unevenly distributed across constituencies (*see* figures below for the elections of January 1910, 1951 and – by a very narrow margin – February 1974). Exceptionally in December 1923 the CON-

SERVATIVE PARTY won the largest number of votes and seats, but these were greatly outnumbered by the combined seats and votes of the LABOUR and LIBERAL parties, who allied against them. Voting is by the 'first-past-the–post' system (*see* PROPORTIONAL REPRESENTATION). The ballot is secret, and election expenses are strictly controlled by law.

From the Septennial Act of 1716 until the Parliament Act of 1911 (*see* LORDS, HOUSE OF) an election was obligatory at least every seven years. In 1911 the interval was reduced to five years. The PRIME MINISTER has acquired the right to decide on the date of election. He or she generally tries to choose a date that will maximize the advantage of his or her party, so parliaments rarely last for a full five years, except when a prime minister feels very pessimistic about the outcome, as in 1997. An exception to the five-year interval occurred during World War I and World War II: there was no election between 1910 and 1918 or between 1935 and 1945, since the parties joined a coalition government for the duration of the war and declared a moratorium on opposing one another at the polls. General elections normally took place on Thursdays from 1935 onwards. Previously they were held on variable days, and before 1914, when communications were more difficult, over several days.

The highest turnout of voters after the electorate became fully democratic in 1928 (*see* EQUAL FRANCHISE ACT) was in 1950 (84%), followed by 1951 (82.5%). There were comparably high turnouts in 1906 and the two elections of 1910, in terms of percentages, but of a much smaller electorate. The lowest turnout of the 20th century was in 1918, when the country was still disrupted by World War I. From 1951 to the end of the century turnouts averaged 75%, the lowest being 1997 with 71.5%, though only 72% had voted in 1970 and 72.7% in 1983. The turnout in the June 2001 general election was 59.4%. In addition, the greater ease of voting by post meant that voting again took place over several days for the first time since 1914.

For changes to the entitlement to vote through the 20th century, *see* REPRESENTATION OF THE PEOPLE ACT (1918); EQUAL FRANCHISE ACT (1928); REPRESENTATION OF THE PEOPLE ACT (1948); REPRESENTATION OF THE PEOPLE, ACT (1969).

General election results 1900–2001

1900

General election	Winning party	Turnout	Total votes		MPs elected	
28 September–24 October	Conservative	74.6%	Conservative	1,797,444*	Conservative	402
			Liberal	1,568,141	Liberal	184
			Labour	63,304	Labour	2
			Irish Party	90,076	Irish Party	82
			Others	544	Others	0

1906

General election	Winning party	Turnout	Total votes		MPs elected	
12 January–7 February	Liberal	82.6%	Conservative	2,451,454	Conservative	157
			Liberal	2,757,883	Liberal	400
			Labour	329,748	Labour	30
			Irish Party	35,031	Irish Party	83
			Others	52,387	Others	0

1910

General Election	Winning Party	Turnout	Total votes		MPs elected	
14 January– 9 February	Liberal**	86.6%	Conservative	3,127,887	Conservative	273
			Liberal	2,880,581	Liberal	275
			Labour	505,657	Labour	40
			Irish Party	124,586	Irish Party	82
			Others	28,693	Others	0

1910

2–19 December	Liberal	81.1%	Conservative	2,420,566	Conservative	272
			Liberal	2,295,888	Liberal	272
			Labour	371,772	Labour	42
			Irish Party	131,375	Irish Party	84
			Others	8,768	Others	0

1918

14 December	Coalition***	58.9%	Coalition	5,121,359	Coalition	478
(results declared			Conservative	370,375	Conservative	23
on 28 December 1918)			Liberal	1,298,808	Liberal	28
			Labour	2,385,472	Labour	63
			Irish Unionist	292,22	Irish Unionist	25
			Irish Nat.	238,472	Irish Nat.	7
			Sinn Féin	486,867	Sinn Féin	73
			Others	72,503	Others	10

1922

15 November	Conservative	71.3%	Conservative	5,500,382	Conservative	345
			Liberal	2,516,287	Liberal	54
			Labour	4,241,383	Labour	142
			Nat. Liberal	1,673,240	Nat. Liberal	62
			Others	462,340	Others	12

1923

6 December	Conservative	70.8%	Conservative	5,538,824	Conservative	258
			Liberal	4,311,147	Liberal	159
			Labour	4,438,508	Labour	191
			Others	260,042	Others	7

1924

29 October	Conservative	76.6%	Conservative	8,039,598	Conservative	419
			Liberal	2,928,747	Liberal	40
			Labour	5,489,077	Labour	151
			Communist	55,614	Communist	1
			Others	126,511	Others	4

1929

30 May	Labour	76.1%	Conservative	8,656,473	Conservative	260
			Liberal	5,308,510	Liberal	59
			Labour	8,389,512	Labour	288
			Communist	50,614	Communist	0
			Others	243,266	Others	8

1931

General election	Winning party	Turnout	Total votes		MPs elected	
27 October	(Nat. Govt.)	76.3%	Nat.Govt.	14,532,519	Nat. Govt.	554
			(Conservative	11,978,745)	(Conservative	473)
			(Nat. Labour	341,370)	(Nat. Labour	13)
			(Liberal	1,403,102)	(Liberal	33)
			(Nat. Liberal	809,302)	(Nat. Liberal	35)
			Labour	6,649,630	Labour	52
			Ind. Liberal	106,106	Ind. Liberal	4
			Communist	74,824	Communist	0
			New Party	36,377	New Party	0
			Others	256,917	Others	5

1935

14 November	Conservative	71.2%	Conservative	11,810,158	Conservative	432
			Liberal	1,422,116	Liberal	20
			Labour	8,325,491	Labour	154
			Ind. Labour	139,577	Ind. Labour	4
			Communist	27,117	Communist	1
			Others	272,595	Others	4

1945

5 July	Labour	72.7%	Conservative	9,988,306	Conservative	212
(results declared			Liberal	2,248,226	Liberal	12
on 26 July 1945)			Labour	11,995,152	Labour	393
			Communist	102,780	Communist	2
			Common Wealth	110,634	Common Wealth	1
			Others	640,880	Others	19

1950

23 February	Labour	84.0%	Conservative	12,502,567	Conservative	298
			Liberal	2,621,548	Liberal	9
			Labour	13,266,592	Labour	315
			Communist	91,746	Communist	0
			Others	290,218	Others	3

1951

25 October	Conservative	82.5%	Conservative	13,717,538	Conservative	321
			Liberal	730,556	Liberal	6
			Labour	13,948,605	Labour	295
			Communist	21,640	Communist	0
			Others	177,329	Others	3

1955

26 May	Conservative	76.7%	Conservative	13,286,569	Conservative	344
			Liberal	722,405	Liberal	6
			Labour	12,404,970	Labour	277
			Communist	33,144	Communist	0
			Others	313,410	Others	3

1959

General election	Winning party	Turnout	Total votes		MPs elected	
8 October	Conservative	78.8%	Conservative	13,749,830	Conservative	365
			Liberal	1,638,571	Liberal	6
			Labour	12,215,238	Labour	258
			Communist	30,897	Communist	0
			Plaid Cymru	77,571	Plaid Cymru	0
			Scot. Nat. Party	21,738	Scot. Nat. Party	0
			Others	12,464	Others	1

1964

15 October	Labour	77.1%	Conservative	12,001,396	Conservative	304
			Liberal	3,092,878	Liberal	9
			Labour	12,205,814	Labour	317
			Communist	45,932	Communist	0
			Plaid Cymru	69,507	Plaid Cymru	0
			Scot. Nat. Party	64,044	Scot. Nat. Party	0
			Others	168,422	Others	0

1966

31 March	Labour	75.8%	Conservative	11,418,433	Conservative	253
			Liberal	2,327,533	Liberal	12
			Labour	13,064,951	Labour	363
			Communist	62,112	Communist	0
			Plaid Cymru	61,071	Plaid Cymru	0
			Scot. Nat. Party	128,474	Scot. Nat. Party	0
			Others	201,302	Others	2

1970

18 January	Conservative	72.0%	Conservative	13,145,123	Conservative	330
			Liberal	2,117,035	Liberal	6
			Labour	12,179,341	Labour	287
			Communist	37,970	Communist	0
			Plaid Cymru	175,016	Plaid Cymru	0
			Scot. Nat. Party	306,802	Scot. Nat. Party	1
			Others	383,511	Others	6

1974

28 February	Conservative	78.7%	Conservative	11,868,906	Conservative	297
			Liberal	6,063,470	Liberal	14
			Labour	11,639,243	Labour	301
			Communist	32,741	Communist	0
			Plaid Cymru	171,364	Plaid Cymru	2
			Scot. Nat. Party	632,032	Scot. Nat. Party	7
			National Front	76,865	National Front	0
			Others (G.B.)	131,059	Others (G.B.)	2
			Others (N.I.)	717,986	Others (N.I.)	12

1974

General election	Winning party	Turnout	Total votes		MPs elected	
10 October	Labour	72.8%	Conservative	10,464,817	Conservative	277
			Liberal	5,346,754	Liberal	13
			Labour	11,457,079	Labour	319
			Communist	17,426	Communist	0
			Plaid Cymru	166,321	Plaid Cymru	3
			Scot. Nat. Party	839,617	Scot. Nat. Party	11
			National Front	113,843	National Front	0
			Others (G.B.)	81,227	Others (G.B.)	0
			Others (N.I.)	702,094	Others (N.I.)	12

1979

3 May	Conservative	76.0%	Conservative	13,697,690	Conservative	339
			Liberal	4,313,811	Liberal	11
			Labour	11,532,148	Labour	269
			Communist	15,938	Communist	0
			Plaid Cymru	132,544	Plaid Cymru	2
			Scot. Nat. Party	504,259	Scot. Nat. Party	2
			National Front	190,747	National Front	0
			Ecology	38,116	Ecology	0
			Workers Rev. Pty	13,535	Workers Rev. Pty	0
			Others (G.B.)	85,338	Others (G.B.)	0
			Others (N.I.)	695,889	Others (N.I.)	12

1983

9 June	Conservative	72.7%	Conservative	13,012,315	Conservative	397
			Liberal	4,210,115	Liberal	17
			Social Dem.	3,570,834	Social Dem.	6
			Labour	8,456,934	Labour	209
			Communist	11,606	Communist	0
			Plaid Cymru	125,309	Plaid Cymru	2
			Scot. Nat. Party	331,975	Scot. Nat. Party	2
			National Front	27,065	National Front	0
			Others (G.B.)	193,383	Others (G.B.)	0
			Others (N.I.)	764,925	Others (N.I.)	17

1987

11 June	Conservative	75.3%	Conservative	13,763,066	Conservative	376
			Liberal	4,173,450	Liberal	17
			Social Dem.	3,168,183	Social Dem.	5
			Labour	10,029,778	Labour	229
			Plaid Cymru	123,599	Plaid Cymru	3
			Scot. Nat. Party	416,473	Scot. Nat. Party	3
			Others (G.B.)	151,519	Others (G.B.)	0
			Others (N.I.)	730,152	Others (N.I.)	17

1992

General election	Winning party	Turnout	Total votes		MPs elected	
8 April	Conservative	77.7%	Conservative	14,048,283	Conservative	376
			Lib. Dem.	5,999,384	Liberal Dem.	20
			Labour	11,559,735	Labour	271
			Plaid Cymru	154,439	Plaid Cymru	4
			Scot. Nat. Party	629,552	Scot. Nat. Party	3
			Others (G.B.)	436,207	Others (G.B.)	0
			Others (N.I.)	740,485	Others (N.I.)	17

1997

General election	Winning party	Turnout	Total votes		MPs elected	
1 May	Labour	71.5%	Conservative	9,600,940	Conservative	165
			Lib. Dem.	5,243,440	Liberal Dem.	46
			Labour	13,517,911	Labour	419
			Plaid Cymru	161,030	Plaid Cymru	4
			Scot. Nat. Party	622,260	Scot. Nat. Party	6
			Referendum	811,827	Referendum	0
			Others (G.B.)	549,874	Others (G.B.)	1
			Others (N.I.)	790,778	Others (N.I.)	18

2001

General election	Winning party	Turnout	Total votes		MPs elected	
7 June	Labour	59.4%	Conservative	8,357,622	Conservative	166
			Lib. Dem.	4,812,833	Liberal Dem.	52
			Labour	10,740,948	Labour	413
			Plaid Cymru	195,892	Plaid Cymru	4
			Scot. Nat. Party	464,305	Scot. Nat. Party	5
			Others (G.B.)	986,824	Others (G.B.)	1
			Others (N.I.)	810,374	Others (N.I.)	18

* For the elections of 1900, 1906 and 1910, the classification 'Conservative' includes both Conservatives and Liberal Unionists (those Liberal MPs opposed to HOME RULE for Ireland).
** Both of the 1910 elections were decided by the return of a majority of MPs (Liberals, Irish Party and Labour) who supported the Parliament Bill (*see* LORDS, HOUSE OF) and Irish HOME RULE.
*** 28 December 1918: the Coalition included Liberals, Labour and Conservatives.

General Strike (4–12 May 1926), short-lived nationwide strike by trade unionists. The strike had its origins in a strike of coal miners against wage cuts and longer working hours, one of a succession of disputes in the interwar COAL MINING industry. Before World War I the miners', dockers' and railwaymen's TRADE UNIONS had formed the Triple Alliance to support one another in industrial disputes. This was not put seriously to the test until 1921 when, on 'Black Friday', 23 April 1921, the transport workers and the railwaymen, themselves in fear of their jobs, refused to support a miners' dispute. The Conservative governments settled this dispute, and another in 1925, heading off conflict by subsidizing the industry.

However, in 1926 the prime minister BALDWIN refused to do so. The TRADES UNION CONGRESS (TUC) had agreed to support an embargo on the movement of coal in the case of another dispute. The government prepared its emergency machinery for a general strike; in contrast, the TUC did not expect a strike to come about and was unprepared. The Miners Federation of Great Britain (the miners' union) and the employers reached stalemate. The government refused to intervene, a miners' strike was called, and the TUC had no choice but to call other workers out in support.

The General Strike began at midnight on 3/4 May. Initially the TUC called out only workers in certain key industries: railways, docks, road transport, iron and steel, metals, chemicals, building, gas, electricity and printing. A second group, including engineers and shipbuilders, was called out on 12 May, just before the strike was called off. The strike was well supported and many strikers were surprised when it suddenly ended, but the TUC did not believe that a prolonged confrontation with the government was in the interests of workers in a period of high UNEMPLOYMENT or that it would be successful. The government had extensive powers under the Emergency Powers Act, 1921, to take over and run essential services. It could make use of the army and received the support of a sizeable number of volunteers. It put its case in broadcasts on the BBC, which was not open to the strikers, and a daily newspaper, the *British Gazette* (edited by Winston CHURCHILL, an enthusiastic opponent of the strike), which had access to more newsprint than the TUC's news sheet, the *British Worker*. The government represented the strike as a potentially revolutionary challenge to constitutional government. In reality it was an industrial dispute and a sympathy strike in support of the miners. The miners remained on strike, but by late November they had been forced to return to work on whatever terms the employers offered, which ensured continuing bitterness in the industry. Some other workers who had joined the strike suffered victimization from employers, despite Baldwin's appeal against this.

In the wake of the General Strike the government introduced the Trades Disputes Act, 1927, which banned general strikes and strikes by local-government workers. It also forbade central and local government workers from joining unions affiliated to the TUC, restricted picketing, and ordained that the per capita political levy paid by unions to the LABOUR PARTY (which had kept aloof from the General Strike and whose leadership disapproved of it) could be paid only with the express permission of each individual member. This immediately cut Labour Party funds by one-third. The legislation was reversed by the Labour government in 1946. Another piece of legislation, the Board of Guardians (Default) Act passed in July 1926, allowed the government to dismiss and replace elected local POOR LAW administrators who allowed poor relief to strikers' families, as some had done.

One result of the strike and its aftermath may have been Labour's success in local and government elections in the following years. Another was that minority left-wing hopes of a general strike to bring down the capitalist system were discredited, and that the persistent industrial conflict of the period since 1910 came to an end. Industrial relations were less stormy for some decades after. **FURTHER READING** H. Armstrong Clegg, *A History of British Trade Unions since 1889, Vol. 2, 1911–1933* (1985); G. Phillips, *The General Strike: The Politics of Industrial Conflict* (1976).

gentrification. *See* HOUSING.

George V (1865–1936), king of Great Britain and Ireland and emperor of INDIA (1910–36). The second son of the prince and princess of WALES (later EDWARD VII and Queen Alexandra), George had not expected to become king, but on the death of his elder brother Prince Albert Victor ('Eddy') in 1892 he became second in line to the throne. He was created duke of York that same year, and was made prince of Wales in 1901 when his father became king. In 1893 he married his elder brother's fiancée, Princess Mary of Teck, who later became Queen Mary. The couple had six children: Prince Edward, known as David (the future EDWARD VIII); Prince Albert (the future GEORGE VI); Prince Henry, duke of Gloucester; Prince George, duke of Kent; Prince John (who died in adolescence); and Princess Mary, the princess royal.

George V was the only reigning British king to visit India as emperor, attending a coronation durbar (state reception) at Delhi in 1911. He continued in the tradition of constitutional MONARCHY established by his father and grandmother (Queen Victoria), presenting a public image of the royal family as representing the nation but being above politics. He did make several notable interventions in politics, however, becoming involved, for example, in the crisis concerning the Parliament Act of 1911 (*see* LORDS, HOUSE OF), the HOME RULE crisis in IRELAND of 1913–14, the selection of Stanley BALDWIN over Lord CURZON as prime minister in 1923, and the formation of the NATIONAL GOVERNMENT in 1931. His reign was overshadowed by the downfall of many ancient European monarchies during and after WORLD WAR I, and by the war itself. It was he who chose to change the family name from Saxe-Coburg-Gotha to Windsor in 1917, in an effort to downplay the family's Germanic origins. Although he lacked the glamour of his father, he became a much-loved king, respected for his seriousness and devotion to his royal duties and his family life. He inaugurated the annual royal Christmas broadcast in 1932, and his silver jubilee in 1935 was an occasion for national celebration. He died in 1936, concerned about the prospects of his flamboyant son and heir David, the prince of Wales, who would become the troubled EDWARD VIII.

FURTHER READING K. Rose, *King George V* (1983).

George VI (1895–1952), king of Great Britain and Northern Ireland (1936–52) and the last emperor of INDIA (1936–47). George was the second son of the duke and duchess of York (later GEORGE V and Queen Mary) and was christened Albert. He was educated at Dartmouth Naval College and Trinity College, Cambridge. Like his father, he had not expected to become king, but was thrust into the position by the abdication of his elder brother David, styled EDWARD VIII, in 1936. Prior to this, Prince Albert had led a relatively quiet life centred around his family. From 1909 to 1917 he served in the Royal Navy and during World War I

was present during the battle of JUTLAND. In 1920 he was created duke of York, and afterwards was noted for his organization of summer camps attended by boys of all social classes. He married Lady Elizabeth Bowes-Lyon (later Queen Elizabeth, the queen mother; 1900–) in 1923. They had two daughters, Princess Elizabeth (later Queen ELIZABETH II) and Princess Margaret Rose.

With the ABDICATION CRISIS of 1936, Prince Albert was forced into the unwelcome position of assuming the mantle of kingship; Princess Elizabeth became heir presumptive to the throne. A somewhat reserved and domestic man, he and his wife, the duchess of York, were distressed by the complete shift in their daily lives that their new position demanded. The duke, in particular, struggled with a stammer that made public speaking an ordeal for him. However, he immediately set to work after his coronation in early 1937 to restore the damage done to the MONARCHY by the abdication, and styled himself George VI to emphasize continuity with his father's reign.

George's influence in politics was more limited than his father's had been. During WORLD WAR II he set a symbolic example to the nation by remaining in London and enduring the privations brought on by the conflict. During the BLITZ he and the queen frequently toured bombed areas in London and other cities, gaining the respect and affection of the crowds; Buckingham Palace was itself bombed in 1940. He also visited the Normandy and Italian battlefields.

By 1947, with the independence of India, the designation head of the COMMONWEALTH had been substituted for emperor of India in the king's long list of titles, and his reign saw the beginnings of the DECOLONIZATION of the EMPIRE, a process that would gather speed during his daughter's reign. By the late 1940s his health had begun to deteriorate, and he was later diagnosed with cancer. He died on 6 February 1952 and was widely mourned by the nation.

FURTHER READING S. Bradford, *King George VI* (1989).

Gibraltar, a small rocky peninsula on the southern coast of Spain, strategically guarding the narrow strait between the Atlantic and the Mediterranean. The British captured Gibraltar from the Spanish in 1704, and the territory became a bone of contention between Britain and Spain until Spain formally renounced all claims in 1783. From the early 19th century Gibraltar became the principal British dockyard and naval base in the western Mediterranean.

Spanish demands for the return of Gibraltar were resumed by General Franco 1939, and the issue was taken up by the UNITED NATIONS in 1963. Gibraltar was no longer of strategic importance to Britain, but in a referendum on 10 September 1967 the people of the crown colony voted by 12,138 votes to 44 to remain British rather than to transfer to Spanish sovereignty. Spain at that time was one of the poorest countries in Western Europe and ruled by a dictatorship. Self-government was introduced into Gibraltar in 1964 and expanded in 1969, whereupon Spain closed the land frontier between Gibraltar and Andalucia. After Franco's death (in 1975) talks were held in 1977 between Britain and Spain about relaxing tensions over the territory. Agreement in 1980 to ease frontier restrictions in 1982 was postponed because of tension following the FALKLANDS War, Spain siding with its former colony Argentina. Free movement across the frontier was restored in 1985. Plans for the withdrawal of British troops from Gibraltar were announced in 1991. Tension developed between the Gibraltar Assembly and both the Spanish and British governments in 1994 over local resentment at attempts by the EUROPEAN UNION (EU) to check drug smuggling and money laundering. In May 1995 the British government threatened to rescind the powers of the Assembly if Gibraltar continued to defy the EU. In 1998 talks between Spanish and Gibraltarian leaders revealed continuing divergence. Spain offered autonomy under Spanish sovereignty, while the Gibraltarians sought a relationship to the United Kingdom similar to that possessed by the CHANNEL ISLANDS.

Gill, (Arthur) Eric (1882–1940), sculptor, typographer, engraver and writer. Born in Brighton, he was the son of a clergyman. He studied at Chichester Art School, then was apprenticed to an architect in London from 1900 to 1903. During this period he also took evening classes in masonry at the Westminster Technical Institute and in lettering at the Central School of Art and Design. He began to earn his living as a letter-carver in 1903. Gill was increasingly attracted to left-wing politics and radical approaches to art and in 1905 he joined both the Art Workers Guild and the FABIAN SOCIETY (which he left in 1908). From 1907 to 1924 he lived at Ditchling, Sussex, running the St Dominic's Press and setting up an artistic community.

He became a major figure in book design and typography. An important influence upon him from 1908 was Dr Ananda Coomaraswamy, a botanist and geologist with an interest in the arts of India and Ceylon. Gill was encouraged, among other things, to infuse eroticism into the religious subjects on which he focused. Thereafter sex and religion became his main subjects. Coomaraswamy also drew Gill's attention to C.R. Ashbee's Guild of Handicraft, which emphasized the importance of cooperation and community, and to the work and ideas of William Morris, which were similar in spirit. Gill collaborated with Jacob EPSTEIN and carved the lettering for Epstein's tomb of Oscar Wilde, but they later quarrelled. He became highly influential as a designer of lettering and typefaces. Like Epstein, Gill was one of the leading figures in the revival of 'direct carving' and his work was impressively simple and accessible in conception. He emphasized the importance of the relationship between the artist and natural materials such as stone and wood.

In 1913 Gill converted to the Roman Catholic Church and was commissioned to make 14 relief carvings of the *Stations of the Cross* for the Catholic Westminster Cathedral in London, his first major public work. He served briefly in World War I in the Royal Air Force Motor Transport Division.

His career as a public sculptor was advanced by the need for war memorials following the war. His major memorial, completed for Leeds University in 1923, was *Christ Driving the Money-Changers from the Temple*. He produced more than 1000 wood engravings and in 1920 he was a founder member of the Society of Wood Engravers. He also became known for his erotic sculpture, such as the head and shoulders of *Tobias and Sara* (1926) and *Odysseus Welcomed from the Sea by Nausicaa,* completed for the Midland Hotel, Morecambe, in 1933. His best-known commission, however, was for the series of stone reliefs placed above the principal doorways of the new headquarters of the BRITISH BROADCASTING CORPORATION, Broadcasting House in London, in 1929. The full-frontal nudity of some of the male figures was judged too explicit and their manhood was attenuated in order not to affront the sensibilities of members of the public. Gill had firm views on the role of the artist in modern society, on which he wrote over 500 articles, some of which were published as *Art-Nonsense and Other Essays* (1929). In the 1930s he received a number of official commissions and honours, despite his consistent criticism of conventional values. In 1935 he was commissioned by the government to carve a large relief of *The Creation* for the LEAGUE OF NATIONS building in Geneva. In 1937 he was elected Associate of the Royal Academy. Gill was never conventional. He disliked wearing trousers and preferred smocks; he had incestuous relations with two of his sisters and two of his daughters.

FURTHER READING F. MacCarthy, *Eric Gill* (1989).

Girl Guides. *See* BADEN-POWELL, ROBERT.

gold standard, an exchange-rate and currency system in which all paper money is convertible into gold on demand at the bank. The system was general in Europe, the British EMPIRE and the United States before 1914, but the gold market could not function freely during World War I and Britain

'went off gold' in 1919. It returned to the gold standard in Winston CHURCHILL's budget of 1925. It was argued that the success of the CITY OF LONDON as an international financial centre, and also Britain's international prestige, depended on maintaining the gold standard. Others, including KEYNES, argued that the return effectively overvalued the pound and hence led to reduced manufacturing exports and increased UNEMPLOYMENT, thus worsening the already serious economic situation in Britain. The international economic crisis of September 1931 (*see* GREAT CRASH) forced the NATIONAL GOVERNMENT of Ramsay MACDONALD to suspend the gold standard, leading to devaluation of the pound by 25%. Britain never again returned to the gold standard.

FURTHER READING D.E. Moggridge, *British Monetary Policy, 1924–1931* (1972).

Good Friday Agreement. *See* NORTHERN IRELAND.

government expenditure. Total government expenditure increased steadily through the 20th century, though it was, of course, especially high during the two world wars and during the periods immediately before and after the wars, owing to the costs of preparation and of demobilization and rehabilitation. The BOER WAR (1899–1902) and the KOREAN WAR (1950–3) had real but less noticeable effects. The GULF WAR (1991) and the FALKLANDS conflict (1982) did not have such noticeable impacts upon the higher levels of government expenditure that prevailed later in the 20th century.

Increased central and local government expenditure was partly due to increased WELFARE STATE expenditure, especially after 1945, though continuing defence expenditure remained high, about one-tenth of total expenditure by the end of the century.

Government spending is limited by its income, primarily from taxation, plus its capacity to borrow. The extent of the cost of debt repayments is shown

Total government expenditure, 1900–95, in 1997 prices (£ billion)

Year	Central government	Local government	Debt interest	Total
1900	7.382	3.541	1.921	13.505
1910	5.001	5.342	2.273	13.526
1915	41.457	4.680	3.223	51.037
1920	6.064	4.619	7.509	24.648
1930	6.203	9.063	12.199	36.700
1935	7.973	10.453	10.568	41.011
1945	88,835	10.212	11.773	29.145
1955	33.489	12.191	11.110	78.880
1965	40.692	22.227	14.340	114.177
1975	62.378	44.233	19.021	191.476
1985	78.823	46.497	29.281	247.845
1995	102.173	55.821	27.271	302.207

Source: A. Dilnot and C. Emmerson, 'The Economic Environment' in A.H. Halsey and J. Webb, *20th Century British Social Trends* (2000), 334.

Total government revenue, by source, 1900–95, in 1997 prices (£ billion)

Year	Income taxes	Expenditure taxes	NI* contributions	Local taxes	Other**	Total
1900	1.200	4.482	0	3.001	1.320	10.203
1910	2.273	5.001	0	4.319	2.273	13.867
1915	3.620	5.563	0.927	3.885	2.385	16.380
1920	13.331	7.311	0.613	3.502	1.554	26.312
1930	10.441	10.614	2.791	5.962	6.375	36.183
1935	10.835	14.230	3.739	7.058	5.570	41.431
1945	45.743	28.510	3.239	5.839	3.948	87.279
1955	33.417	31.371	8.560	6.845	7.536	87.728
1965	42.764	40.033	17.912	13.054	12.990	126.752
1975	77.238	46.357	31.562	18.335	20.810	194.302
1985	85.911	71.643	40.310	22.707	24.244	244.815
1995	95.840	109.340	46.773	9.663	17.212	278.829

*National Insurance (introduced in 1911, *see* WELFARE STATE).

**Includes such items as death duties (which raised £17m in 1900 and £92,866m in 1998) and capital gains tax (introduced 1966, abolished 1993).

Source: A. Dilnot and C. Emmerson, 'The Economic Environment' in A.H. Halsey and J. Webb, *20th Century British Social Trends* (2000), 340.

in the table on p.179. Sources of government income are also shown.

The second table demonstrates the changing composition of government revenue over time. Income tax rates rose in particular during the two world wars, continued to rise until the 1980s and then began to level off as the unpopularity with voters of high levels of personal taxation became evident. It was replaced by growing taxes on consumption, such as value-added tax (VAT), levied on a range of consumer goods at the point of purchase, excise duties and by increased National Insurance contributions. In the 1990s an increasingly imaginative range of taxes on expenditure, for example on air travel, home insurance, tobacco and petrol, were introduced or increased by both Conservative and Labour governments, in order to avoid raising income tax. Over the same period the yield of local taxes also fell (*see* LOCAL GOVERNMENT). This was due partly to the growing scale of central government compared with local government in the later decades of the century. The fiasco of the COMMUNITY CHARGE ('poll tax') of 1989–90 also diminished the capacity of local authorities to raise revenue.

grammar schools. *See* EDUCATION.

Great Crash, the (1929), the lowest point of the Great Depression, sometimes called 'the Slump'. From early 1927 until the late summer of 1929, the American economy experienced an artificial speculative boom. A collapse of confidence in certain business undertakings led to panic selling on the New York Stock Exchange in Wall Street on 24 October 1929, 'Black Thursday'; panic selling continued to the end of the month. Banks failed, businesses went bankrupt and there was rapidly rising unemployment in the United States. The crisis disrupted European markets, partly owing to the extent of European indebtedness to the USA following WORLD WAR I. The crisis spread to Britain and elsewhere through 1930 and 1931. In May 1931 a major Austrian bank, the Credit Anstalt,

was unable to meet its obligations. This led to the bankruptcy of many institutions in Germany and central Europe, which imperilled many British bankers who had invested in Germany. Throughout the summer of 1931 there was a run on the pound, which caused a financial and political crisis in Britain (*see* LABOUR PARTY, MACMILLAN COMMITTEE, MAY COMMITTEE) and the formation of the NATIONAL GOVERNMENT in August 1931. Shortage of capital led to a fall in consumption and production in all the industrialized countries, causing high UNEMPLOYMENT. Few governments in such countries long survived the Crash.

Greater London Council (GLC). *See* LONDON GOVERNMENT.

Greene, (Henry) Graham (1904–91), novelist, essayist, playwright and writer of short stories. He was born in Berkhamsted in Hertfordshire and attended Berkhamsted School, where his father was headmaster, and Balliol College, Oxford. His first book of verse, *Babbling April* (1925), was published while he was still at Oxford. In 1926 he was converted to the ROMAN CATHOLIC church and his faith was strongly to influence his writing. However, he was never an orthodox Roman Catholic. The Vatican censured him and demanded that he revise three of his later novels that dealt explicitly with the faith – *The Power and the Glory* (1940), *The Heart of the Matter* (1948) and *The End of the Affair* (1951) – on the grounds that they dealt indulgently with such matters as fornication, drunkenness and adultery. Greene refused.

In 1927 he married Vivien Dayrell-Browning. From 1926 to 1930 he was employed by *The Times*, leaving in order to devote himself to writing. He published three novels between 1929 and 1931, all of them historical and strongly influenced by the work of Joseph CONRAD. Only the first of these, *The Man Within* (1929), a historical thriller set in 19th-century Sussex, had any success and Greene later disowned the two others. His first real success was *Stamboul Train* (1932) and thereafter his reputation steadily mounted as he produced a stream of novels, short stories, books of reportage and travel, plays and children's books, as well as working as a journalist. He travelled widely and restlessly, often to trouble spots, and these experiences were both reported in journalistic accounts and provided the background for many of his novels and other works. *Journey Without Maps* (1936) is a chronicle of his walk across uncharted Liberia and *Lawless Roads* (1939) is a report on the condition of the church in southern Mexico during the revolution of the 1930s.

Greene reviewed several hundred films during the 1920s and 1930s and was keenly interested in FILM. Later he wrote at least nine film scripts, some of them adaptations of his own novels, including *The Third Man* (1949), *Our Man in Havana* (1959) and *The Comedians* (1967). He appeared in François Truffaut's *La Nuit Americaine* (1973). He went through a crisis in the late 1940s and 1950s, separated from his wife, though he never divorced her, and moved to the south of France where he lived for the rest of his life. He moved into other genres, especially drama, with *The Living Room* (1953) and *The Potting Shed* (1957). His work became rather more detached and contemplative, but still dealt with political struggles throughout the world or with COLD WAR espionage. Greene had worked for MI5 and knew Kim Philby well (*see* CAMBRIDGE SPIES). *The Quiet American* (1955), set in Vietnam, was a warning to the West not to seek to re-establish colonialism in Southeast Asia. *A Burnt-out Case* (1961) was set in a leper colony in the Congo; *The Honorary Consul* (1953) was set in Argentina; and *The Human Factor* (1978) was about espionage. He continued to write in a variety of forms, including autobiography: he published *A Sort of Life* (1971) and *Ways of Escape* (1980).

Greene was recognized as one of the major writers of his generation. He was unusual in appealing both to intellectuals, who appreciated his concern for ideas and fundamental human dilemmas, and to a wider audience because of his accessible style that drew on detective fiction, melodrama and the thriller.

FURTHER READING N. Cherry, *The Life of Graham Greene* (2 vols., 1989–94).

Greenham Common, site of a women-only peace camp set up outside a US cruise-missile base in Berkshire in 1981. It was independent of all organized movements such as the CAMPAIGN FOR NUCLEAR DISARMAMENT. In its early years it attracted much support and publicity for its cause, and also much opposition. The protesters were successful in repeatedly entering what was supposedly the most secure air base in Britain. They were ejected by military police. In later years the camp attracted less attention, but a small camp remained in being until the missiles were removed from the base between 1987 and 1992 following the disarmament treaty between the USSR and the USA. The camp was only formally ended at a party on the eve of the new millennium, 31 December 1999. The common was bought by the local council as a public recreation area in the 1930s, but requisitioned by the Ministry of Defence in 1939. After World War II it was briefly returned to the local council, then requisitioned again at the dawn of the COLD WAR and reluctantly sold by the council, under threat of compulsory purchase. A consortium of the council and local businesses bought it back, for public use, in 2000.

Green Party. *See* ENVIRONMENTALISM.

Greenpeace. *See* ENVIRONMENTALISM.

Grey, Edward (1862–1933), LIBERAL politician; FOREIGN SECRETARY (1905–16). Grey was the son of an army officer, from a distinguished family. One ancestor was Earl Grey, the Whig prime minister who piloted through the Great Reform Act of 1832. Grey was educated at Winchester College and Balliol College, Oxford, where he was an undistinguished student and had to leave in 1884 without gaining a degree. His parish clergyman, the distinguished church historian Mandell Creighton, then inspired him to enter public life. In 1882 he succeeded to his father's baronetcy, becoming Sir Edward Grey. In 1884 he became private secretary to Evelyn Baring, later Lord Cromer, then to the Liberal chancellor of the exchequer, H.C.E. Childers. He was elected as MP for Berwick-on-Tweed in 1885, and was under-secretary at the foreign office, 1892–5. He became a leading Liberal imperialist and supported the Conservative government during the BOER WAR. Unlike many other Liberals he believed in the need to maintain Britain's imperial and international military strength.

From his appointment as foreign secretary in 1905 Grey focused upon the need to seek a balance of power against Germany. He supported the ENTENTE CORDIALE with France, and cemented the anti-German alliance of Britain, France, Russia (the Triple Entente) at the Anglo-Russian Convention of 1907. In consequence he was much criticized by radicals and socialists in Britain. On domestic issues he supported women's suffrage (*see* SUFFRAGISTS; SUFFRAGETTES), HOME RULE for IRELAND and land reform, and was more sympathetic than many of his cabinet colleagues to the TRADE UNIONS during the industrial conflicts of 1910–14. He worked hard to maintain peace before the outbreak of WORLD WAR I. Once war had begun he succeeded in winning Italy to the side of the Allies in 1915 (*see* LONDON, TREATY OF) and kept good relations with the United States. His eyesight was failing and when LLOYD GEORGE succeeded ASQUITH as prime minister in 1916 he entered the House of LORDS as Viscount Grey of Fallodon. He devoted most of his subsequent public activity to the LEAGUE OF NATIONS, though he also remained a leading Liberal and was chancellor of Oxford University, 1928–33.

FURTHER READING K. Robbins, *Sir Edward Grey: A Biography of Lord Grey of Fallodon* (1971).

Grimond, Jo(seph) (1913–93), Liberal politician; leader of the LIBERAL PARTY (1956–67). He was born in St Andrews, Scotland, and educated at Eton and Balliol College, Oxford. He was called to the Bar in 1937, and served in the army during World War II. Having decided to become an MP while at Oxford, Grimond succeeded in becoming MP for Orkney and Shetland in 1950, a seat he held until 1983. He was elected leader of the Liberal Party in 1956, overseeing advances in the Liberal vote in the 1959 and 1964 elections. Despite an overall increase in votes, fewer Liberal MPs were elected in the 1964 election, stifling Grimond's ambition to influence government through a coalition. After support for the party decreased in the 1966 election, Grimond's hopes were further undermined, and he resigned the party leadership in 1967, being succeeded by Jeremy THORPE. Grimond's desire to create a new centre party, bringing the Liberal Party together with moderate Conservative and Labour MPs, remained unfulfilled until the creation of the SOCIAL DEMOCRATIC PARTY in the 1980s. He was given a life peerage in 1983, and sat in the House of LORDS as Baron Grimond of Firth until his death in 1993.

Guardian. *See* MANCHESTER GUARDIAN.

Gulf War (1991), more accurately the Second Gulf War, a conflict between UNITED NATIONS forces and Iraq. Iraq had been mandated to Britain after the collapse of the Ottoman empire at the end of World War I, and was ruled indirectly by Britain through an Arab monarchy installed in 1921. From the late 1960s Iraq was controlled by the Ba'ath Socialist Party, dominated from the late 1970s by Saddam Hussein. Threatened by the successful Islamic revolution in Iran in 1979, Iraq invaded its neighbour in 1980 in pursuit of territorial claims. The Iraqi war effort was supported by neighbouring states, particularly Kuwait. With attacks on oil tankers in the Persian Gulf intensifying during the mid-1980s, the US naval presence in the region was increased. US intervention, and the sharpened military strength of Iraq, led to a UN-brokered ceasefire in August 1988.

The First Gulf War (also known as the Iran–Iraq War) left Iraq with a massive military-industrial complex and major debts, in particular to Kuwait. Continued development of the Iraqi military led to increased tension in the region, particularly in Israel, which was by 1989 within range of Iraqi missiles. Iraq had developed and used chemical weapons during the First Gulf War, and it was feared that nuclear weapons were planned. Public attention in Britain was focused on Iraq in early 1990, when Farzad Bazoft, a journalist with the *Observer* who had been arrested for alleged espionage, was executed. Less than a month later British customs officials seized a consignment of steel tubes bound for Iraq, which were alleged to be part of a planned 'supergun' capable of launching shells over long distances.

Iraq's economic difficulties were exacerbated by a depression in international oil prices following overproduction of oil by Kuwait and the United Arab Emirates. Amid rising tension, in which historical frontier disputes between Iraq and Kuwait resurfaced, negotiations between the two governments broke down. Having deployed troops on its southern border, Iraq invaded Kuwait on 2 August 1990. Following immediate international condemnation and the invocation of sanctions against Iraq by the UN, US and British forces began to arrive in the Gulf to implement operation 'Desert Shield', aimed at dissuading Iraq from invading Saudi Arabia. In addition to a build-up of military forces, a variety of diplomatic initiatives were undertaken to bring an end to the crisis, especially following the detention of foreign nationals, particularly Britons, who had remained in Kuwait. Placed in strategically important locations within Iraq, the use of hostages provoked outrage in the British press and prompted a number of politicians, including former prime minister Edward HEATH, to visit Iraq seeking to negotiate their release. On 29 November 1990, the day after John MAJOR succeeded Margaret THATCHER as prime minister, the UN Security Council passed a resolution authorizing 'all necessary means' to force Iraq's withdrawal from Kuwait, giving Iraq until 15 January 1991 to do so. Despite demonstrations in Britain in January 1991, a majority of Britons supported the use of military force in the Gulf. After an initial six-week air campaign, in which British aircraft took part, international forces (including a British contingent) recaptured Kuwait in four days, and a ceasefire was declared on 28 February 1991.

The Gulf War saw a variety of new developments in the technique of warfare, most notably the use of precisely guided missiles designed to undertake 'surgical strikes' against strategic targets, supposedly minimizing civilian deaths and 'collateral damage'. The use of advanced technology combined with unprecedented control over media coverage of the conflict has provoked a number of debates over the cultural significance of the war. Questions have been raised over military restrictions on reporting the war.

An important effect of the war in Britain (despite its popularity) was to increase disillusionment with the Conservative government, whose support for Iraqi military development during the First Gulf War was seen as contributing to the crisis of 1990–1. The British government, like the US government, subsequently faced pressure to recognize the existence of 'Gulf War syndrome' – medical conditions reported by veterans of the conflict that they claimed were the result of exposure to a variety of chemical agents during the war. Britain supported the continuing UN presence in the Gulf, and the resumption of air attacks on Iraq in 1998, after the Iraqi authorities refused to cooperate with UN weapons inspectors.

FURTHER READING D. Hiro, *Desert Shield to Desert Storm: The Second Gulf War* (1992).

H

Hague, William (Jefferson) (1961–), Conservative politician; leader of the CONSERVATIVE PARTY (1997–2001). Hague was born in Rotherham, Yorkshire, and was educated at Wath-on-Dearne comprehensive school and Magdalen College, Oxford. He won recognition when he spoke at the 1977 Conservative Party conference when only 16 years old. After working as a management consultant for McKinsey & Co. and as a political advisor to the Treasury in the 1980s, Hague was elected as Conservative MP for Richmond, Yorkshire, in 1989. He was parliamentary private secretary to the CHANCELLOR OF THE EXCHEQUER (1990–3), undersecretary for the Department of Social Services (1993–4), minister for social security (1994–5) and secretary of state for WALES (1995–7).

Hague was elected leader of the Conservative Party in 1997 after John MAJOR resigned in the wake of his general-election defeat. Promising to unify his party, Hague committed the Conservatives to oppose further European integration, particularly British acceptance of the single European currency. Although acknowledged as a doughty opponent to Tony BLAIR in the chamber of the House of COMMONS, Hague's attempts to win back public support for his party resulted in increasingly right-wing policies and claims that he was making the Conservatives into an English nationalist party.

He resigned as Conservative leader following the party's defeat in the 2001 general election.
FURTHER READING J-A. Nadler, *William Hague in His Own Right: A Biography* (2000).

Haig, Douglas (1861–1928), commander of the British Expeditionary Force on the Western Front (1915–19). Born in Edinburgh of a prominent whisky-distilling family, Haig was educated at Clifton School and Brasenose College, Oxford. In 1884 he entered Sandhurst, the military officers' training college, graduating at the top of his year. He entered the 7th Hussars, serving in INDIA, the Sudan and the BOER WAR. He was inspector general of cavalry in India (1903–6), and director of military training (1906–7). As director of staff duties at the War Office (1906–9), he helped shape and implement the ARMY reforms of R.B. HALDANE. In 1909 he was appointed chief of general staff in India, seeking unsuccessfully to modernize the Indian army. In 1912 he took over the Aldershot command, which gave him a central role when the army was mobilized in WORLD WAR I.

At the first battle of YPRES (October–November 1914) Haig's leadership contributed to the blocking of the German attempt to reach the Channel ports. He succeeded Sir John FRENCH as commander in chief on the Western Front in December 1915, and was promoted to field marshal the following year. He was much respected by his brother officers and made no more mistakes than other Allied commanders during the confusions and difficulties of working with allies in a war of an unprecedented type. When LLOYD GEORGE became prime minister in 1916 he was highly critical of Haig for wasting lives without adequate results (for example in the SOMME offensive), but Haig resisted moves to demote him and carried on his strategy of attrition, for example at PASSCHENDAELE. He played a notable role in the Allied victories that brought the war to an end.

Haig returned home in 1919 to be commander in chief, home forces. He received the thanks of Parliament and £100,000, and in the same year was created 1st Earl Haig. He retired in 1921. For the remainder of his life he worked for ex-servicemen, inspiring the formation of the veterans' association, the British Legion (*see* ROYAL BRITISH LEGION), and becoming its president. He also instituted the Poppy Day appeal for funds to help disabled ex-servicemen, and for the rest of the century the appeal was mounted annually in the lead-up to Remembrance Day (11 November, the day the 1918 ARMISTICE came into effect).

FURTHER READING G.J. De Groot, *Douglas Haig, 1861–1828* (1988); D. Winter, *Haig's Command: A Reassessment* (1991).

Haldane, J.B.S. *See* SCIENCE.

Haldane, R(ichard) B(urdon) (1856–1928), Liberal and subsequently Labour politician, most notable as a reforming secretary of state for war (1905–12). Born and educated at Edinburgh, Haldane then attended Göttingen University, specializing in German philosophy. He subsequently became a lawyer, and was MP for East Lothian, 1885–1911. Committed to the expansion of higher education, he worked especially for the establishment of provincial UNIVERSITIES; he was a co-founder, with Beatrice and Sidney WEBB, of the London School of Economics in 1895. In 1904 he chaired a committee that resulted in the estab-

lishment of the University Grants Committee, which channelled government funding to universities. In 1909 he was chairman of a royal commission on university education in London.

As war minister from 1905 to 1912, Haldane introduced far-reaching reforms of the British ARMY, creating the general staff (1906), the TERRITORIAL ARMY (1907) and the officers' training corps in public schools and universities. He cut military expenditure, but also speeded up mobilization, established the Expeditionary Force and improved medical and nursing services under the territorial system. In 1912 he was sent by the cabinet to Berlin to try to halt the naval armaments race, without success. Douglas HAIG described him as 'the greatest secretary of state for war England ever had'.

Haldane was created a viscount in 1912 and was lord chancellor from 1912 to 1915. In this role he secured an increase in the number of lords of appeal and raised the judicial committee of the privy council to a position of greater respect in its role as court of appeal in cases from courts around the EMPIRE. He tried to appoint MAGISTRATES and judges on the basis of professional merit rather than party-political criteria. In 1915 he was attacked by the press for his knowledge of, and admiration for, Germans and Germany and forced out of public life.

Thereafter he became estranged from the LIBERAL PARTY, and served as lord chancellor in the LABOUR government of 1924. He led the small number of Labour peers in the House of LORDS from 1925 to 1928. Haldane was made a fellow of the Royal Society in 1906, a fellow of the British Academy in 1914 and was president of Birkbeck College, the adult education college of the University of London, from 1919 to 1928. Haldane's brother J.S. Haldane (1860–1936) was an eminent physiologist, and his nephew J.B.S. Haldane (1892–1964) was a noted geneticist, philosopher and Marxist (*see* SCIENCE).

FURTHER READING S.E. Koss, *Haldane: Scapegoat for Liberalism* (1969).

Halifax, Edward Frederick Lindley Wood, 1st earl of

Halifax, Edward Frederick Lindley Wood, 1st earl of (1881–1959), Conservative politician, who was viceroy of India (1925–31) and FOREIGN SECRETARY (1938–40). Born into the aristocracy, Wood was educated at Eton and Christ Church, Oxford. He was a deeply religious intellectual, committed to the High Church wing of the CHURCH OF ENGLAND, which was close to Roman Catholicism (he later went by the nickname of 'the Holy Fox'). He was CONSERVATIVE MP for Ripon (1910–25); assistant secretary, Ministry of National Service (1917–19); undersecretary, Colonial Office (1921); and president of the Board of EDUCATION (1922–4).

In 1925 Wood was ennobled as Baron Irwin, and was appointed viceroy of INDIA. This was a tense period in relations between Britain and the 'jewel in the crown' of the British EMPIRE, as the Indian nationalist movement became increasingly strong. Irwin was not the obvious choice for the role, in view of his entire lack of experience of the subcontinent. His period of office was marked by growing conflict with which he coped with dignity and fairness, winning respect from all sides. He stated publicly that he believed that India would inevitably gain dominion status (self-government within the empire) and in 1931 he negotiated an agreement with GANDHI that temporarily reduced the conflict.

After his return to Britain in 1931, Irwin was president of the Board of Education again, then briefly secretary of state for war in 1935 before being appointed lord privy seal in November 1935 and given special responsibilities for foreign affairs. He had inherited his father's title of Viscount Halifax in 1934. He was leader of the House of LORDS (1935–8) and again in 1940. In November 1937 he visited Hitler, seeking to assess his intentions on behalf of Neville CHAMBERLAIN.

Halifax was appointed foreign secretary in February 1938. Initially he was a supporter of APPEASEMENT, believing, following his visit to Germany, that Hitler did not want war and personally liking some of the Nazi leaders. He was not present,

however, when Chamberlain met Hitler at Berchtesgaden, Bad Godesberg and MUNICH, and by that time he had come to believe that compromise with Hitler was a 'horrible and wretched business', done out of necessity because of Britain's perceived relative military weakness. Thereafter, from March 1939, he helped to persuade Chamberlain to take a firmer line with the Germans; he pressed for more vigorous rearmament, gave military guarantees to Poland, Romania and France and sought a military alliance with the USSR, although with little enthusiasm since he was strongly anti-communist.

Halifax was considered as a candidate for prime minister by both King GEORGE VI and Chamberlain when Chamberlain resigned in May 1940. At a meeting of Chamberlain, Halifax and CHURCHILL, however, Halifax wisely recognized his unsuitability and refused, opting for Churchill as the new PM; another factor was that the LABOUR PARTY refused to join a coalition headed by Halifax. He continued to serve as foreign secretary for seven months under Churchill's premiership, although his suggestion that Britain sue for peace with Germany after the DUNKIRK evacuation and the fall of France was abhorrent to Churchill.

In December 1940 Churchill invited him to become ambassador to the United States, a post that he held from 1941 to 1946. This was a vital period in Anglo-American relations, when the opponents of Germany seriously needed the financial and military assistance of the initially isolationist and reluctant USA. Halifax was reluctant to take the position and accepted out of a sense of duty. He was, however, successful in the post, getting on well with President Franklin D. Roosevelt and conveying to the American public the case for US support for the Allied war effort. He was awarded the title of earl of Halifax in 1944. He retired in 1946, spending the remainder of his life on his country estate in Yorkshire. He was chancellor of Oxford University from 1933 to 1959.

FURTHER READING A. Roberts, *The Holy Fox: A Life of Lord Halifax* (1991).

Hamilton, Richard (1922–), painter, printmaker, teacher, exhibition organizer and writer; one of the pioneers of British pop art. Born in London, he left school at age 14, and worked in advertising and commercial art while attending evening classes in painting. He studied at the Royal Academy (1938–40 and 1946) – interrupted by service in World War II as an engineering draughtsman – and at the Slade School in London (1948–51). From 1952 to 1956 he was a member of the 'Independent Group', which met informally at the INSTITUTE FOR CONTEMPORARY ARTS in London. Members included Eduard Paolozzi (1924–), the printmaker and sculptor, Reyner Banham (1922–88), the architectural and design historian, and several architects. In 1956 Hamilton and other members of the group organized the groundbreaking *This is Tomorrow* exhibition at the Whitechapel gallery in London. Hamilton's photomontage *Just What Is It That Makes Today's Homes So Different, So Appealing?* (1956) was displayed at the entrance to the exhibition. It is a satire on consumerism, made up of advertising images (including a lollipop bearing the word 'pop') and is sometimes considered the first work of pop art. Thereafter his work engaged with popular culture as well as investigating the borderline between handmade and mechanically made imagery. His aim was to break down the boundaries between elite and popular culture and between industrial and artisan production. He played a significant role as an organizer of exhibitions and had a considerable influence upon younger artists, not least as a teacher at Newcastle University from 1953 to 1966.

FURTHER READING R. Morphet, *Richard Hamilton* (1992).

Hardie, (James) Keir (1856–1915), socialist, trade unionist and Labour leader – the first socialist MP to sit in the House of COMMONS. Hardie was born in Legbrannock, Lanarkshire. He experienced poverty in childhood and was forced to work from the age of eight. At ten he went to work in a coal mine, and his formative political experiences came with his later efforts to organize miners into trade unions. He lost his job in his early twenties because of these efforts, but moved on to study at night school and became a journalist. In 1887 he started a newspaper, *The Miner*, which later became the *Labour Leader*. During this time his interest in socialism grew, and he began to move away from his earlier strong Liberal convictions. He stood as an Independent Labour candidate in an 1888 by-election in Mid-Lanark, which he lost. Nonetheless, he helped form the Scottish Labour Party later that year.

Hardie went on to become more successful in parliamentary politics. He won a seat in West Ham South as an Independent Labour candidate in 1892 and held it until 1895. In 1900 he again became an MP, for Merthyr Tydfil, a seat he held until his death in 1915. In 1893 Hardie was instrumental in the formation of the INDEPENDENT LABOUR PARTY (ILP) and thereafter became a widely known figure in the socialist movement. He also participated in the establishment in 1900 of the LABOUR REPRESENTATION COMMITTEE (LRC).

A pragmatic socialist, a pacifist, an evangelical and a supporter of female suffrage and temperance, Hardie came to be acknowledged as a founding father of the LABOUR PARTY. But perhaps as befits his complexity, Hardie's convictions were sometimes at odds with his practice. When the LRC became the parliamentary Labour Party in 1906, he served as its first chairman for a year and a half, though not without controversy. An individualist and an agitator by nature, who believed that the disadvantaged needed to organize if they were to better their situation, he nonetheless chafed against the limitations that the structure of party politics imposed upon him. Some of his political beliefs were also shaped by liberalism, which sometimes placed him at odds with his passionate advocacy of the rights of the working class.

FURTHER READING C. Benn, *Keir Hardie* (1992); K.O. Morgan, *Keir Hardie, Radical and Socialist* (1975).

Harris, Arthur (Travers) (known as 'Bomber Harris') (1892–1984), commander in chief of Bomber Command during WORLD WAR II. Harris was educated at Gore Court, Sittingbourne, Dorset, and All Hallows, Honiton, Devon. At the age of 17 he went to farm in Rhodesia (now Zimbabwe). In 1914 he joined the 1st Rhodesian Regiment as a bugler and fought in South-West Africa. He returned to England in 1915 and joined the Royal Flying Corps (the predecessor of the ROYAL AIR FORCE), with whom he flew fighters. By 1918 he was commanding No. 44 Squadron, which was training in night-fighting. In 1919 he became a squadron leader in the RAF and served in India, Iran and elsewhere in the Middle East. He was deputy director of planning in the Air Ministry, 1934–7, becoming an air commodore in 1937. He was air officer commanding PALESTINE and Transjordan, 1938–9, and then became an air vice marshal and took command of No. 5 (Bomber) Group. He became deputy chief of air staff under Sir Charles PORTAL in 1940, was head of the RAF delegation to Washington in 1941, then, for the remainder of the war, commander in chief of Bomber Command, organizing the bombing of Germany.

Initially the RAF had difficulty in making daylight attacks on Germany and was highly inaccurate at night. Under Harris it became highly effective at 'area bombing', since 'precision bombing' was, realistically, impossible. The strategy, rather, was to destroy large German towns, bombing civilian as well as military and industrial buildings, and killing and injuring civilians, in order to undermine morale and reduce production. The death rate among bomber crews, especially rear gunners, was also very high. Harris was criticized at the time and for long after for bombing too much, too indiscriminately and for too long after the war was effectively won, especially for the bombing of DRESDEN in 1945. He perhaps bore the brunt of criticisms for decisions (such as that to bomb Dresden) that were not his alone but owed something to politicians, especially CHURCHILL. Bomber Command under Harris's leadership clearly played

an important role in the Allied victory, but Harris ended the war under something of a cloud, though he became a marshal of the RAF in 1946. He was not appointed to a peerage as were others of equivalent status in the services; it was offered and he refused in 1953, though he accepted a baronetcy. He retired, aggrieved, to South Africa. He published *Bomber Offensive* in 1947.

FURTHER READING M. Connelly, *Reaching for the Stars* (2001); R. Neillands, *The Bomber War* (2001).

Healey, Denis (Winston) (1917–), Labour politician; CHANCELLOR OF THE EXCHEQUER (1974–9) and deputy leader of the LABOUR PARTY (1981–3). Healey was born in Broadstairs, Kent, and educated at Bradford Grammar School and Balliol College, Oxford. He served in the army during World War II before becoming secretary of the International Department of the Labour Party between 1945 and 1952. He became MP for Southeast Leeds in a 1952 by-election, and held the seat until his retirement in 1992. A supporter of GAITSKELL in the 1950s, Healey became defence secretary under Harold WILSON (1964–70). In this role he oversaw cuts in defence spending and Britain's withdrawal of military forces from 'east of Suez'.

After 1970, when Labour was back in opposition, Healey served as shadow FOREIGN SECRETARY and then shadow chancellor. Following Labour's return to power in 1974 he became chancellor of the exchequer, a post he held until 1979. During this period Healey struggled with harsh economic conditions and international recession, introducing economic policies such as spending cuts (some of them conditions of a loan from the International Monetary Fund). These policies made him unpopular with the left wing of his party. He was defeated by James CALLAGHAN in the Labour Party leadership election following Wilson's retirement in 1976, and again by Michael FOOT in 1980. Despite his conflict with the party's left, Healey became deputy leader (1981–3) and shadow foreign secretary, and resolutely opposed the MPs who left the party to join the SOCIAL DEMOCRATIC PARTY in the early 1980s. He resigned from the shadow cabinet in 1987 and from the House of Commons in 1992, becoming a life peer as Baron Healey of Riddlesden. Healey was known for his robust turn of phrase, referring to Margaret THATCHER as 'Miss Floggie', 'Rhoda the Rhino', 'the Lady with the Blowlamp' and various other epithets. He described himself as 'the Gromyko of the Labour Party' – like the Soviet foreign minister he spent decades near the top of the party, but never quite managed to obtain the leadership.

FURTHER READING D. Healey, *The Time of My Life* (1989).

health. *See* MEDICINE; NATIONAL HEALTH SERVICE.

Heath, Edward ('Ted') (Richard George)

(1916–), Conservative politician; PRIME MINISTER (1970–4). Heath was the first Conservative leader to come from a lower-middle-class background with no history of political involvement. Educated at Chatham House School, Ramsgate, and Balliol College, Oxford, he became president of the Oxford Union before distinguished army service during World War II. He entered politics in 1950 as MP for Bexley, Kent, which he represented until 1974. He was MP for Sidcup (1974–83), then for Old Bexley and Sidcup (following boundary changes) from 1983. Heath was a party whip (1951–5), and as chief whip (1955–9) he creditably managed party opinion over the SUEZ CRISIS. He supported Harold MACMILLAN'S succession as party leader in 1957, and served as minister of labour (1959–60), lord privy seal (1960–3) and secretary for trade and industry (1963–4). He took charge of the unsuccessful negotiations for British entry into the EUROPEAN ECONOMIC COMMUNITY in 1963. He remained strongly pro-European.

Following the victory of the Labour Party under Harold WILSON in the 1964 election, in 1965 Heath was voted leader of the CONSERVATIVE PARTY, the party's youngest leader for over a hundred years. In opposition to Wilson's interventionist economic policies, Heath advocated TRADE-UNION reform and cuts in taxes and public spending. He instituted a comprehensive review of party policy. Having won the 1970 GENERAL ELECTION, his government was faced by a series of economic crises, principally those associated with the rise in oil prices in 1973. The attempt to impose a strict prices-and-incomes policy, after initially rejecting this course, caused conflict with the trade unions. Forced to intervene to save ailing British companies (such as taking Rolls-Royce into public ownership), Heath's government was attacked for taking 'U-turns' in policy in going to the rescue of such 'lame ducks'. The government also witnessed increasing political violence in NORTHERN IRELAND, and after the events of BLOODY SUNDAY in 1972 direct rule from Westminster was imposed upon the province. Heath's government also introduced some significant changes in Britain, with the DECIMALIZATION of sterling in 1971 and entry into the European Community (*see* EUROPEAN ECONOMIC COMMUNITY) in 1973. Following the disruption of the MINERS' STRIKE in the winter of 1973–4, resulting in power cuts and the restriction of industry to a 'three-day week', Heath called an election in February 1974, campaigning on the theme 'Who governs Britain?' The electorate clearly did not think it was Heath, as they returned the Labour Party under Harold Wilson to power, Heath having failed to form a coalition with the Liberals.

When Labour won a second election in October of 1974 Heath's position as party leader was severely weakened. He was defeated by Margaret THATCHER in a leadership election in early 1975, for which he never forgave her. Heath remained as a sometimes combative backbencher, and his staunchly pro-European stance was at odds with many in his party. At the end of the century he was 'father of the House', the longest-serving member of the House of COMMONS. He retired from the Commons in 2001.

FURTHER READING J. Campbell, *Edward Heath: A Biography* (1993).

Henderson, Arthur (1863–1935), Liberal, then Labour politician; leader of the parliamentary Labour Party (1908–10, 1914–17, 1931–2) and FOREIGN SECRETARY (1929–31). Born in poverty in Glasgow, Henderson was the son of a labourer who died when he was aged nine. He left school shortly afterwards, working first in a photographer's shop. His mother remarried, and after the family moved to Newcastle he resumed his schooling. He finally left school at twelve and was apprenticed as an iron moulder. Around this time he converted to METHODISM, a powerful influence for the remainder his life. After completing his apprenticeship he became active in his TRADE UNION, eventually becoming national organizer for the Friendly Society of Ironfounders (1902–11). He was also a Methodist lay preacher, an active temperance reformer and an active member of the LIBERAL PARTY. He was appointed agent to the Liberal MP for Barnard Castle in 1895, and was elected as a Liberal to Durham County Council in 1897 and to Darlington Town Council in 1898. By 1903 he was a justice of the peace (*see* MAGISTRATES) and mayor of Darlington, the first working man to achieve this position.

Following the failure of the Liberals to select him as a parliamentary candidate, Henderson was selected by the LABOUR REPRESENTATION COMMITTEE (LRC) to contest Barnard Castle in a by-election in 1903, in which he was successful. His political views remained essentially Liberal, but like others he was driven into the emerging LABOUR PARTY by the unwillingness of some Liberals to support a working-class parliamentary candidate. In 1904 he became treasurer of the LRC, then chairman in 1905–6 and again in 1908–10. He played a vital role in organizing the constituencies for the 1905 election. He was leader of the Labour Party in the Commons in 1908–10 and chief whip in 1914. As secretary of the Labour Party from 1911 to 1934 he played a key role in developing it into an effective political organization. When Ramsay MACDONALD resigned the party chairmanship because of his opposition to WORLD WAR I, Henderson again

became leader of the parliamentary party, and worked hard to preserve party unity during the war. In May 1915 he joined the coalition government, becoming the first ever Labour CABINET minister, nominally as president of the Board of Education, effectively as adviser on labour matters. He acted as a conciliator in industrial disputes, joining the five-man war cabinet after LLOYD GEORGE's coup in 1916, but he resigned in August 1917 when the cabinet opposed Labour's participation at an international socialist conference in Stockholm.

This freed Henderson to devote his time to building up the Labour Party. He was the chief architect of the 1918 constitution (*see* LABOUR PARTY). In the election of 1918 he stood in East Ham South, but was beaten. He was elected for Widnes in 1919, but lost there in 1922, being re-elected for Newcastle East in 1923, then for Burnley in 1924, which he lost in 1931. He held Clay Cross (Derbyshire) from 1933 until his death in 1935. Throughout this time he worked indefatigably as party manager, supervising the selection of candidates and setting up a regional organization. He was Labour chief whip (1920–4 and 1925–7), and home secretary in the first Labour government in 1924. He was a member of the British delegation to the 1924 London conference on the Dawes Plan to schedule the payments of reparations by the powers defeated in the war. He was later a delegate to the LEAGUE OF NATIONS, where he was one of the main proponents of the Geneva Protocol to institutionalize the peaceful resolution of disputes. He remained a strong supporter of the League of Nations thereafter.

Henderson was foreign secretary in the second Labour government (1929–31), and in this role he sought to achieve international conciliation and disarmament, as far as possible through the League of Nations. In 1931 his opposition to cuts in UNEMPLOYMENT benefits was crucial to the breach between the party and MacDonald. Henderson became party leader, but lost his seat once more in the 1931 election. He retained his presidency of the ultimately abortive international Disarmament

Conference, which collapsed after Germany's withdrawal. In 1934 he was awarded the Nobel Peace Prize.

FURTHER READING R. McKibbin, *The Evolution of the Labour Party, 1910–1924* (1974); C. Wrigley, *Arthur Henderson* (1990).

Hepworth, Barbara (1903–75), sculptor. Born in Wakefield, Yorkshire, the daughter of a civil engineer, she won scholarships to Leeds School of Art, 1919–21, and the Royal College of Art, London, 1921–4. Henry MOORE was a fellow student at both places and they became life-long friends. In 1924 she came second to John Skeaping in the competition for the Prix de Rome, but she won a travelling scholarship and spent the years 1924 and 1925 in Italy, where she studied carving and married Skeaping. They were divorced in 1933. Her early sculptures were quite naturalistic but by the early 1930s her work had become entirely abstract. At this time she worked wholly in wood or stone and stressed her excitement at the direct contact with nature achieved by working in such natural substances. In 1931 she met Ben Nicholson, lived with him and married him in 1938. They lived close to Moore in Hampstead, London, and in the 1930s the three of them worked closely together and were recognized as the nucleus of the abstract movement in Britain. In 1939 Hepworth and Nicholson moved to St Ives in Cornwall, to protect their children (triplets) and themselves from the effects of World War II on London. After the war St Ives became a centre for avant-garde artists, centred upon the two of them (though they divorced in 1951). Hepworth's sculpture thereafter was influenced by the forms of the Cornish landscape and she lived in Cornwall for the rest of her life.

By the 1950s Hepworth had an international reputation and received many honours, including the main prize at the 1959 São Paulo Biennale, and prestigious public commissions, including the memorial to Dag Hammarskjöld – *Single Form 1963* – at the UNITED NATIONS building in New York. She was now working more in bronze, especially when the pieces were big. Occasionally she diversified into other fields, notably with her sets and costumes for the first production of Sir Michael Tippett's *The Midsummer Marriage* in 1955. She became a Dame of the British Empire in 1965. She died in a fire at her home in St Ives.

FURTHER READING A. Hammacher, *Barbara Hepworth* (1970).

heritage, national. *See* NATIONAL HERITAGE.

Hitchcock, Alfred (1899–1980), film director. Born in London, Hitchcock began working in 1919 for the British branch of Famous Players-Lasky, first designing title cards for their films, then as scriptwriter, set designer, assistant director and director. In 1924 he went to Germany for Michael Balcon's Gainsborough Pictures and made his first two features, *The Pleasure Garden* and *Mountain Eagle* (1926). On returning to England he gained a reputation as the country's leading fiction director in a series of six silent suspense films, including *The Lodger* (1926). He made Britain's first talking picture, *Blackmail* (1929), originally shot as a silent film, then re-shot with sound. He signed a contract to make five films for Gaumont-British Picture Corporation, which included several of the thrillers that made his reputation: *The Man Who Knew Too Much* (1934), *The 39 Steps* (1935), *Secret Agent* (1936) and *Sabotage* (1936).

He made three more films in Britain before moving to work for David O. Selznik in the United States. These included *The Lady Vanishes* (1938) and *Jamaica Inn* (1939). He won two Academy Awards for his first American film *Rebecca* (1940), adapted from Daphne du Maurier's novel of the same name. He returned briefly to Britain in 1944 to make two short films for the Ministry of Information and again in 1949 to make the unsuccessful *Under Capricorn* and *Stage Fright*. For the remainder of his career he was based in Hollywood, and he became a US citizen in 1955, though he used British locations for the remake of *The Man*

Who Knew Too Much (1956) and *Frenzy* (1972). In Hollywood he directed a succession of successful thrillers: *Rear Window* (1954), *To Catch a Thief* (1955), *Vertigo* (1958), *North by Northwest* (1959) and *Psycho* (1960). He was less successful as a filmmaker thereafter, though he hosted a successful television show, screened in the USA and Britain. **SEE ALSO** FILM INDUSTRY.

FURTHER READING D. Spoto, *The Art of Alfred Hitchcock* (2nd edn, 1992).

Hoare, Samuel (John Gurney) (1880–1959), Conservative politician. Educated at Harrow School and Oxford University, he succeeded to his father's baronetcy in 1915. He was MP for Chelsea from 1910 to 1944 and held a number of important government posts in the interwar period: secretary of state for air, 1922–9, 1940; secretary of state for India, 1931–5; FOREIGN SECRETARY, 1935; first lord of the admiralty, 1936–7; home secretary, 1937–9; and lord privy seal, 1939–40.

Hoare's most notable achievement was drafting the Government of India Act, 1935 (*see* INDIA). As foreign secretary under BALDWIN he negotiated the 1935 Anglo-German treaty that fixed German naval strength at 35% of the British level, attempting to hold back German rearmament. Then followed the abortive HOARE–LAVAL PACT (December 1935), which led to Hoare's resignation as foreign secretary. Before WORLD WAR II, as a member of the powerful Committee on Imperial Defence, Hoare was an influential member of Neville CHAMBERLAIN's inner circle of advisers who favoured APPEASEMENT. As home secretary he insisted on more humane conditions in prisons and limited the use of CAPITAL PUNISHMENT. He was a key member of Chamberlain's war cabinet, but when Winston CHURCHILL succeeded to power he was sent as ambassador to Spain, where he remained until 1944 when he was raised to the peerage as Viscount Templewood.

FURTHER READING J.A. Cross, *Sir Samuel Hoare: A Political Biography* (1977).

Hoare–Laval pact (December 1935), secret pact between Pierre Laval, premier and foreign minister of France, and Sir Samuel HOARE, British foreign secretary. The agreement was that Hoare would not reveal French noncompliance with the economic sanctions imposed on Italy by the LEAGUE OF NATIONS following its invasion of Abyssinia (*see* ABYSSINIAN CRISIS). They proposed, instead, to negotiate a compromise with Italy, ceding half of Abyssinia to the Italian government. The aim was to prevent Italy allying with Germany against France and Britain. When the pact was leaked to the newspapers on December there was an outcry and Hoare resigned.

Hockney, David (1937–), painter, printmaker, photographer and designer, active mainly in the USA. Born in Bradford into a working-class family, he studied at Bradford School of Art, 1953–7. His early work, including portraits and views of his surroundings, was in the tradition of the EUSTON ROAD SCHOOL. He was a CONSCIENTIOUS OBJECTOR and worked in hospitals for two years in lieu of National Service after leaving art school. He went to the Royal College of Art in London in 1959 and graduated with the gold medal for his year in 1962. The year before, he had exhibited at the Young Contemporaries exhibition (one of a series arranged in London by younger artists since 1949), which was perceived as heralding British pop art. Hockney disliked the label 'pop' though his work made many references to popular culture. In the 1960s with his flamboyant dress and dyed blonde hair, he became a pop icon himself. He had his first one-man show in London in 1963 and a retrospective at the Whitechapel Gallery in 1970. At this time he was painting in a fairly traditional, representational manner, including portraits of friends. In 1976 he moved permanently to live in California, where he had spent some years in the 1960s. He loved the quality of light and bright colours to be found there and his work began to convey a sense of California as a place, particularly his many paintings featuring swimming pools (such as *A*

Bigger Splash, 1967). In the 1970s he took up stage designing successfully and in the 1980s photography. He is a perceptive commentator on art and published two substantial books on his own work: *David Hockney by David Hockney* (1976) and *That's the Way I See It* (1993).
FURTHER READING P. Webb, *Portrait of David Hockney* (1988).

Hodgkin, Dorothy. *See* SCIENCE.

Home Guard, voluntary home defence force during WORLD WAR II. Following a proposal made by Winston CHURCHILL in 1939, Anthony EDEN recommended to the cabinet in May 1940 the establishment of a Local Defence Volunteers Force to provide a role in the war effort for men too old for armed service or exempt due to their occupation. He announced this on the radio the following day. Within 24 hours 250,000 men had volunteered, and 1.5 million by the end of June. On 23 July the name was changed by Churchill to the Home Guard – or, more popularly, 'Dad's Army' (which some time after the war became the title and theme of a popular television comedy series). A month later Home Guard units were affiliated to county army regiments. They were controlled by the commander in chief, home forces, but selection of leaders was locally based. There had been no advance planning. Initially uniforms, training and weapons (of which they had few) were locally improvised, but gradually the units became more professional. By February 1941 ranks and commissions had been introduced and the age limit lowered to extend the role of the Home Guard to training 17- and 18-year-olds prior to CONSCRIPTION.

In December 1941 conscription was extended to the Home Guard, and those conscripted were compelled to undertake a minimum of 48 hours service each month. By the summer of 1943 there were 1.75 million Home Guards, organized into 1100 battalions. Their average age was just under 30. They worked on civil defence in cities and defence against sea or air invasion: manning anti-

aircraft batteries, coast watching, guarding factories, landing fields and bridges, manning roadblocks and above all freeing military personnel for other tasks. They were disbanded on 31 December 1944, by which time the Allied invasion of continental Europe had made their role unnecessary.
FURTHER READING S.P. MacKenzie, *The Home Guard: A Political and Military History* (1995).

Home of the Hirsel, Alec Douglas-Home, Baron. *See* DOUGLAS-HOME, ALEC.

home rule. This is most commonly defined as the movement aimed at amending the 1801 Act of Union between Great Britain and IRELAND, thus granting the latter its own parliament responsible for its own internal affairs. However, both WALES and SCOTLAND had their own movements for home rule from the late 19th and early 20th centuries.

The central figure associated with the Welsh home rule movement in the 1890s was the Liberal MP Tom Ellis, a cultural nationalist. Also prominent was the nationalist movement Cymru Fydd, which issued calls for the promotion of Welsh language and culture, but dissolved in 1896 over its fractious association with the LIBERAL PARTY. The issue of Welsh home rule was raised again briefly after 1910, and in 1914 a Home Rule Bill for Wales was tabled in the Commons by E.T. John. However, it failed to raise great interest. Welsh nationalism at that time was strongly connected to the disestablishment of the Church of England in Wales (*see* CHURCH IN WALES) and the preservation of Welsh culture and language, and much less with political separation. However, the movement continued in being, and strengthened after World War II, focusing on demands for devolved government. This led to a referendum in 1979 to devolve power from Westminster to a Welsh assembly. This failed, but a similar referendum in 1997 succeeded, albeit by a relatively small margin. Elections for the new Welsh assembly took place in May 1999 and resulted in a minority

Labour government, with the Welsh nationalist party Plaid Cymru placed a respectable second.

Home rule in Scotland has also had a long and complex history. There was a very active movement in the 1920s, promoted by the LABOUR PARTY (which had been committed since its foundation to 'home rule all round') in Scotland. This campaign received a serious blow in 1927 when the Government of Scotland Bill failed at Westminster because it was not allowed enough parliamentary time. Thereafter from the 1930s to the 1950s the home rule movement faltered in Scotland, with Labour eventually abandoning its commitment to devolution. Nationalist sentiment did not disappear; the Scottish National Party (SNP) was founded in its present form in 1934, but it was not until the late 1960s and 1970s that interest in home rule began to grow again as a significant force. Although the 1979 referendum on devolution failed in Scotland as in Wales, the movement continued to gain momentum in the 1980s and 1990s, with the Scottish people reacting against the policies of the THATCHER governments; many also considered the North Sea oil reserves to be a viable basis for an independent Scottish economy. A second referendum on Scottish devolution was held in 1997, but this time was passed with a large margin of support. Elections for the Scottish Parliament, with its seat in Edinburgh, took place in May 1999. Labour took the greatest number of seats, but not enough to form a majority, so the party formed a coalition with the Liberal Democrats in order to avoid the prospect of a minority government with the SNP in opposition.

'While home rule movements certainly have their place in Scottish and Welsh history, the original (and most studied) example of a home rule movement was that in Ireland. There, the Home Government (later Home Rule) Association had been founded by Isaac Butt in 1870; in 1874 its members had been elected to 59 seats at Westminster. Greater progress was made, however, under the leadership of Charles Stewart Parnell in the 1880s. He organized the Irish Parliamentary Party (IPP; *see* IRISH NATIONAL PARTY), with home rule as its main priority. By 1885 Parnell had convinced Gladstone, the Liberal prime minister, to support his cause in return for the IPP's support of the Liberal minority government. The first Home Rule Bill was tabled at Westminster in 1886, but did not pass the Commons as the issue split the Liberal Party. A second bill was tabled in 1892 by William Gladstone, but this time did not pass the Lords.

A third attempt was made after the reform of the House of LORDS in 1910–11. The bill met with fierce resistance from Ulster Protestants, concerned that home rule would result in the creation of a Catholic-dominated nation in which they would become a persecuted minority. By 1914 it was clear that the partition of Ireland was the only way to avert civil war over the issue (*see* CARSON, HENRY; CURRAGH INCIDENT). The bill was passed into law, but its implementation was then postponed because of the outbreak of World War I. The EASTER RISING of 1916 was symptomatic of nationalist frustrations over the issue; by 1918, the IPP had collapsed, and new SINN FÉIN MPs seceded from Westminster to form their own Dublin parliament, the Dáil. Attempts were made to revive home rule in the Government of Ireland Act of 1920–1, but calls for greater independence in the south became insistent in the wake of the Anglo-Irish War of 1919–21. The 1921 Anglo-Irish treaty partitioned the island, creating NORTHERN IRELAND and the Irish Free State. Home rule was granted to Northern Ireland, based at Stormont in Belfast, but the Free State was given dominion status, and became a republic in 1948. The failure of the home rule movement to provide a peaceful resolution to the demands of both nationalists and unionists in the late 19th and early 20th centuries has had serious and sometimes violent repercussions, ongoing throughout the remainder of the century.

FURTHER READING C. Davies, *Welsh Nationalism in the Twentieth Century: The Ethnic Option and the Modern State* (1989); R.J. Finlay and T.M. Devine, *Scotland in the Twentieth Century*

(1996); J. Loughlin, *Ulster Unionism and British National Identity Since 1885* (1995).

homosexuality. *See* SEXUALITY, OFFICIAL REGU-LATION OF.

Hong Kong, former British crown colony on the south coast of China. The colony consisted of the island of Hong Kong, the Kowloon peninsula and the New Territories. The island of Hong Kong was under British control from 1842, when it was ceded by the Chinese in perpetuity under the treaty of Nanking. The Kowloon peninsula was ceded in perpetuity by the Chinese in 1860. The New Territories were leased to Britain for a period of 99 years, from 1 July 1898. It was this lease that determined the return in 1997 of the entire colony to the People's Republic of China, which did not recognize any of the previous leases or treaties.

Under British control, Hong Kong became of vital strategic and commercial importance. It provided a base for Allied military operations in the Pacific during WORLD WAR II until it was overrun by the Japanese, on Christmas Day 1941, after considerable resistance. It was not liberated until August 1945. After the war, both its commercial development and its population expanded rapidly. It became a major centre for manufacturing (particularly of electronics) and international finance.

Many successful Hong Kong business people and financiers were thus particularly alarmed by the THATCHER government's announcement in 1984 that the entire colony of Hong Kong – not just the New Territories – would be returned to the jurisdiction of the People's Republic of China under the terms of the 1898 lease. The handover took place on 1 July 1997, amid great celebration by the Chinese but less enthusiasm on the part of the departing administration, represented by Prince CHARLES and the last governor of Hong Kong, Chris Patten, the former chair of the Conservative Party. While the British sought and obtained assurances from China that Hong Kong's existing civil freedoms and capitalist economy would be maintained for 50 years, there was much anxiety as to whether these assurances were legitimate. However, there was irony in the repeated British demands that the Chinese respect 'democracy' in Hong Kong, when in fact the colony had always been run by white British governors appointed by Britain – despite some belated reforms in the 1990s designed primarily to annoy the government of the People's Republic. For many, the handover of control in Hong Kong, the last of Britain's important colonial possessions, marked the symbolic end of the old EMPIRE.

FURTHER READING F. Welsh, *A History of Hong Kong* (1997).

House of Commons. *See* COMMONS, HOUSE OF.

House of Lords. *See* LORDS, HOUSE OF.

housing. Housing, both private and council-built, has undergone significant changes in the 20th century, mainly on class lines. Apart from changes in styles of ARCHITECTURE, typical middle-class housing has shrunk considerably – in terms of size and number of rooms – since 1914, mainly owing to falling family size and to the disappearance of the live-in domestic servant (*see* DOMESTIC SERVICE). Even more significant is the shift over the same period from the norm that most people, in all classes, rented their homes in the private sector, to a steady growth of owner-occupation for those who could afford it, and of the rise and then decline of council housing for those who could not. Before 1914 approximately 10–20% of occupants in England and Wales owned their own homes. By 1938 the proportion had risen to 32%, by 1996 to 67%. Council housing accounted for about 1% of the housing stock in England and Wales in 1914, 10% in 1938, 32% in 1980 and 18% in 1996. Scotland consistently had lower proportions of owner-occupiers.

Victorian philanthropists had called for improvements to the appalling conditions of much working-class housing, but little practical action was taken by governments before WORLD WAR I. Cessation of building during the war, combined with overcrowding and rent increases in munitions centres, led to RENT STRIKES, followed by statutory rent controls. The Rent and Mortgage Interest (Restrictions) Act, 1915, placed restrictions on rises in rents that were abolished only in the 1980s. The level of public discontent about poor housing led David LLOYD GEORGE to promise in 1918 'to make Britain a fit country for heroes to live in'. Legislation providing public subsidies for both private and local-authority building was introduced in 1919. The subsidies were rapidly curtailed in the public expenditure cuts from 1920 (*see* GEDDES AXE), but extended again by a Conservative government in 1923 and a Labour one in 1924. By 1929, 625,000 council houses had been built. In the 1930s attention shifted to 'slum clearance', with the aim of eliminating unfit housing, though by 1939 many thousands still lived in very poor housing. About the same number of private houses as council houses were built for owner-occupation in England and Wales between the wars, many of them on suburban estates and in the semi-detached style that emerged in this period. Some were well planned in the garden city tradition (*see* TOWN AND COUNTRY PLANNING), but some were of poor quality and unsupported by an adequate infrastructure of transport, shops and other facilities, giving rise to protests by their new owners. Owner-occupation grew because there was a growing 'white-collar' middle class with rising real incomes; in addition, modern materials and technology reduced the costs of house building, while low-cost mortgages became more easily available, arising out of the transformation of financial services, assisted by low interest rates and changes in the taxation system.

In World War II enemy bombing (*see* BLITZ) destroyed about 4% of the housing stock. Combined with the suspension of new house building during the war, this led to a shortage of at least 1.25 million houses by 1945. The Labour government sought to increase housing supply while also giving priority to reconstructing industry. It was also determined that new house building, whether public or private, should be of high quality and with adequate infrastructural support. The government gave priority to publicly owned housing, and supported the development of NEW TOWNS. Around 1.2 million houses were constructed between 1945 and 1951 – a considerable achievement in the economic circumstances – but a serious shortage remained, and housing was a major issue in the GENERAL ELECTIONS of 1950 and 1951. Consequently the Conservative governments of the 1950s enabled the building of 2.45 million new houses, two-thirds by local authorities, though generally of lower standards and at higher densities than those built under the Labour governments. In the later 1950s they also encouraged demolition of older city-centre housing and the displacement of residents to out-of-town housing estates, often to high-rise blocks which, with modern technology, could house large numbers of people at low cost, often with poor infrastructure. Some of these buildings were of such poor quality and were so unpopular with tenants that they were demolished or expensively renovated from the 1980s onwards. The unpopularity of such housing led more immediately to a shift away from such practices towards the renovation rather than destruction of inner-city Victorian housing – a trend that began in London in the 1960s. This older inner-city housing became increasingly fashionable among middle-class owner-occupiers, who gradually, especially in London, 'gentrified' houses that shortly before had been defined as slums. This process was assisted by the CLEAN AIR ACT, 1956, which gradually removed the pollution caused by domestic coal fires and steam engines.

By the late 1970s the housing stock had greatly improved. Whereas in 1951 28% of households lacked a bath and in 1971 this was still true of 16.7%, by 1981 the figure was down to 6.3%. In the 1970s private house-building and renovation took precedence over council housing. Rapidly rising house prices and mortgage tax relief made owner-occupation attractive for all who could afford it. In the 1980s the Conservative government was determined to encourage owner-occupation to the maximum and to minimize public ownership. Restrictions on local-authority expenditure reduced local-authority house building. Existing tenants were encouraged to buy their council houses, often at heavily discounted prices. Even so, some purchasers found they had bought property with virtually no market value. Tenants could also become part of a private housing association rather than having the local authority as landlord. In many places local authorities handed over their entire stock (and housing staff) to housing associations. The numbers of council houses fell. This had the beneficial effects that many people had greater control over their own housing and that the stark social divide between council and private housing, which had grown up in many areas since World War I, was eroded. The bad side was that the remaining council housing was more precisely confined to people in severe need – and by the end of the century was conventionally described as 'social' (or, even more ambiguously, 'affordable') rather than 'council' housing; another result was an increase in homelessness, because too little of such housing remained.

FURTHER READING J. Burnett, *A Social History of Housing, 1815–1985* (2nd edn, 1986); M. Daunton, *A Property Owning Democracy? Housing in Britain* (1987); S. Lowe and D. Hughes (eds.), *A New Century of Social Housing* (1991); M. Swenarton, *Homes Fit for Heroes: The Politics and Architecture of Early State Housing in Britain* (1981).

Howe, (Richard Edward) Geoffrey (1926–),

Conservative politician; CHANCELLOR OF THE EXCHEQUER (1979–83), FOREIGN SECRETARY (1983–9) and deputy prime minister (1989–90). Howe was born in Glamorgan, the son of a solicitor. He was educated at Winchester College and Trinity Hall, Cambridge, where he read law. He became a barrister in 1952, practising with some success (he served as a member of the Bar Council from 1957 to 1961), before becoming Conservative MP for Bebington in 1964. He lost the seat in the 1966 election, but returned to the Commons in 1970 as the member for Reigate (which became Surrey East in 1974).

Howe had been an opposition front-bench spokesperson on labour and social services in the mid-1960s, and was made solicitor general under Edward HEATH in 1970, taking a prominent role in introducing Heath's Industrial Relations Act (*see* TRADE UNIONS) and in the harmonization of British law with the treaty of Rome following Britain's entry into the EUROPEAN ECONOMIC COMMUNITY. Following the election of Margaret THATCHER as party leader, Howe was made shadow chancellor, and became chancellor after the Conservative election victory in 1979. His introduction of strict monetarist policies, cutting income tax in his first budget, established the break from the economic policy of the 1970s.

From 1983 Howe served as foreign secretary, and his pro-European views brought him into direct conflict with the opinions of the prime minister. Along with the chancellor, Nigel Lawson, Howe threatened to resign in 1989 if Margaret Thatcher did not compromise over British entry into the European Exchange Rate Mechanism (ERM). Although they persuaded the prime minister to reassess government policy, she demoted Howe to leader of the House of Commons and the nominal position of deputy prime minister; his disillusionment led to his resignation in November 1990. He used his resignation speech to the Commons to attack Thatcher's position on Europe and her handling of the cabinet, precipitating a chain of events that ended with her downfall later that month. The effect of his speech was particularly devastating as for a decade Howe had appeared as a wholly compliant Thatcher loyalist, earning him the nickname 'Mogadon Man'; Denis HEALEY had described his debating style as 'like being savaged by a dead sheep'. Howe retired from the House of Commons in 1992 and took a seat in the House of LORDS as Lord Howe of Aberavon.

FURTHER READING J. Hillman and P. Clarke, *Geoffrey Howe – A Quiet Revolutionary* (1988).

Huddleston, (Ernest Urban) Trevor (1913–98), archbishop and human-rights campaigner. Born in Bedford, Huddleston was educated at Lancing College and Christ Church College, Oxford. Joining the priesthood in the 1930s, Huddleston became a member of the Anglo-Catholic Community of the Resurrection, based in Mirfield, Yorkshire. He was sent by the Community to SOUTH AFRICA in 1943, where he was established in the Johannesburg suburb of Sophiatown. Working with his Sophiatown parishioners, Huddleston gained deep insight into the conditions of life of ordinary urban Africans. Witnessing the effects of the South African government's racial policies, Huddleston became increasingly outspoken in his opposition to apartheid during the 1950s, until his recall to Mirfield in 1955. Shortly after his return to the UK the following year his book *Naught for Your Comfort* was published, relaying the reality of life under apartheid to a mass audience.

Back in Britain, Huddleston continued to campaign against apartheid, helping to organize the Boycott Movement, the immediate forerunner of the ANTI-APARTHEID MOVEMENT in 1959. In 1960 Huddleston became bishop of Masasi in what is now Tanzania, where he established a close friendship with Julius Nyerere, later president of Tanzania. He returned to the UK again in 1968, to become bishop of Stepney. After ten years in London, continuing to campaign against racism both in South Africa and Britain, Huddleston left for Mauritius, to become archbishop of the Indian Ocean.

Huddleston resigned his post in 1983 to head both the Anti-Apartheid Movement and the International Defence and Aid Fund, working full time towards coordinating international opposition to apartheid. In 1991, following the un-banning of the African National Congress (ANC) and the release of Nelson Mandela, Huddleston returned to South Africa after over thirty years. Despite ill health, Huddleston was able to vote in the 1994 election that brought the ANC into power. After a failed attempt to retire in South Africa, Huddleston returned to Mirfield until his death in April 1998.

FURTHER READING R. Denniston, *Trevor Huddleston – A Life* (1999); D.D. Honoré (ed.), *Trevor Huddleston – Essays on his Life and Work* (1988).

Hume, Basil (George) (1923–99), Roman Catholic archbishop of Westminster. The son of a consultant physician, Hume was educated at Ampleforth College and entered the monastery there in 1942. After studying at St Benet's Hall, Oxford, and in Switzerland, he was ordained a priest in 1950. After a time teaching at Ampleforth College – becoming a housemaster and then head of modern languages – he was elected abbot of Ampleforth in 1963.

When Hume was made archbishop of Westminster and a cardinal in 1976 his appointment was a surprise to many Catholics. His appointment may have been due in part to his ecumenical tendencies, of huge importance in his national role. He was consecrated in March 1976, when only 53 years old. His approach soon marked him out as different from the popular perception of a Catholic bishop, being characterized by his 'simple', non-intellectual faith that appealed to many both inside and outside the English Catholic Church.

While anti-dogmatic, Hume also retained a belief in the ultimate authority of the Vatican. When the Vatican restated its position on homosexuality in 1993 Hume managed to condemn discrimination without appearing to defy Catholic teaching. Thus, despite exhibiting a degree of independence, Hume also retained a strong belief in church tradition. His ability to compromise was perhaps most clearly illustrated by his actions during the CHURCH OF ENGLAND's crisis over the ordination of women priests in the early 1990s, when Hume negotiated the entry of hundreds of Anglican clergy into the Catholic Church, without alienating either Rome or his Anglican counterparts. In April 1999 Hume announced that he was dying of cancer; his death came two months later, on 17 June.

Hume, John (1937–), Northern Ireland politician; leader of the SOCIAL DEMOCRATIC AND LABOUR PARTY (1979–). After attending university, Hume undertook research at Trinity College, Dublin, and at the Centre for International Affairs at Harvard. He was elected to the Northern Ireland Parliament as an independent in 1969. A founder-member (with Gerry FITT) of the Social Democratic and Labour Party (1970), he served as an SDLP member of the Northern Ireland Assembly 1973–4. He became member of the European Parliament for Northern Ireland in 1979, when he also became leader of the SDLP. As well as being a member of various European Community committees, Hume served as SDLP MP for Foyle in the House of COMMONS from 1983. Hume has been given much of the credit for initiating the peace process in NORTHERN IRELAND, and he played a leading role in the successful negotiations resulting in the Good Friday agreement in 1998. He shared the Nobel Peace Prize with the Ulster Unionist leader David TRIMBLE in the same year.

hunger marches, a number of marches on London to protest against mass UNEMPLOYMENT and hardship in the 1920s and 1930s (unemployment figures hit a peak of 3 million in 1933). Most of the marches were backed by the National Unemployed Workers' Movement (NUWM), which received funding through COMMUNIST PARTY sources. The first national hunger march in 1922–3 attracted tens of thousands along its various routes, as participants included iron and steel workers from Scotland, shipyard workers from the Tyne, dockers

and seamen from Liverpool, iron-ore miners from Cumberland, cotton operatives from Lancashire, coal miners from South Wales and engineers and mechanics from the Midlands. Their central demand of government was to be provided with either work or full maintenance at TRADE-UNION rates.

A second march in 1929 saw participants protesting against demeaning features of the Unemployment Insurance Act, 1927, and calls to abandon means testing (*see* DOLE, THE). During this and other marches, marchers were often forced to enter workhouses nightly while en route, for shelter and food. There were bitter complaints about the humiliating way in which they were treated by some workhouse officials, who regarded the marchers as lazy malingerers burdening the public purse. The march was made more trying by the monotony of the workhouse diet; marchers subsisted for weeks on tea, bread, margarine and bully beef.

A third march in 1930 was the smallest, with approximately 350 participants, and was notable for the fact that workhouse and other POOR LAW facilities had to be used all the way to London. There was also for the first time a small contingent of women taking part. The fourth march of 1932 attracted 1500 participants, and for the first time there were violent clashes between marchers and the police. The press portrayed the marchers as lawless yobs and the NUWM's communist backing as inherently dangerous. Some of the leaders of the march were briefly imprisoned.

For the fifth march in 1934 organizers had learned their lesson. There was great emphasis placed on organization and on the discipline of the marchers. As a result there was no major recurrence of violence, and the marchers began to win public sympathy for their plight. A rally in Hyde Park at the end of the march attracted an estimated crowd of 50,000 people. Two years later, in 1936, the last and most successful march took place. One of the many contingents from around the country to march on London was the famous Jarrow

Crusaders from the Tyne. Two hundred strong, they were not affiliated with the NUWM but instead marched to London supported by their local MP, Ellen WILKINSON. In an audience with the prime minister and other ministers, they drew attention to the fact that 73% of insured workers in Jarrow were unemployed. Their march specifically called attention to the town's plight and gained much publicity and public sympathy, if little practical assistance. The Jarrow Crusade has come to symbolize the hunger-march movement as a whole, although it was basically the NUWM that was responsible for much of the organization. The marches may have had some effect in encouraging the government to give assistance to the 'Distressed Areas', as they were called in the 1930s; for example, by 1939 a new steelworks had been built in Jarrow.

FURTHER READING P. Kingsford, *The Hunger Marchers in Britain, 1920–39* (1982); E. Wilkinson, *The Town that was Murdered. The Life Story of Jarrow* (1939).

hydrogen bomb. *See* NUCLEAR WEAPONS.

immigration. The largest immigrant group into England, Wales and Scotland throughout the century came from IRELAND, the majority female. The numbers grew when the United States, previously the emigration destination of choice, imposed immigration quotas in 1921, and again during a period of labour shortage in Britain in the 1940s and 1950s, when the Irish economy was less successful. Net emigration to Britain from the Republic of Ireland in the second half of the 1950s averaged about 40,000 per year. After 1921 citizens of independent Ireland retained the rights they had previously held as British subjects. They continued to do so from 1949 when Ireland left the COMMONWEALTH. Irish migrants worked in a wide variety of occupations. By the end of the century there were strong and long-established Irish communities in London, Birmingham, Liverpool, Manchester and Glasgow. Throughout the 19th and early 20th centuries there were small groups of immigrants from many countries, such as Italy, HONG KONG and Poland.

Throughout the 19th century there was a small flow of mainly German-speaking Jewish immigrants, many of them business people. By about 1880 the Jewish community numbered about 60,000. From the 1880s to 1914 there was a substantial flow of perhaps 100,000 (the exact number is uncertain) Jewish refugees from economic hard-

ship and from 'ethnic cleansing', as such processes were later described, a long series of anti-Semitic 'pogroms' (murderous attacks on Jews) in the Russian empire. They settled especially in east London, and also in Manchester, Leeds and Glasgow. They attracted a certain amount of racist abuse, which led to the restriction of immigration in the Aliens Act, 1905. German Jews in particular faced further hostility after the outbreak of World War I, which led to further restrictions in the British Nationality and Status of Aliens Act, 1914. In the 1930s the BRITISH UNION OF FASCISTS led anti-Semitic protests in east London. Also in the 1930s there were about 50,000 Jewish refugees from Nazism, most of them wealthier and better qualified than the earlier wave. A smaller group of Jews displaced by World War II came to Britain after the war. Since the 1950s Jewish emigration has exceeded immigration, and many Jews have chosen not to identify with the Jewish community, while others have rejected religious observance. However, it is misleading to refer to a single Jewish community, since there are several – including the ultra-orthodox community centred on Stamford Hill in northeast London. Very many have been successful economically and in public life and have dispersed from the city centres.

In the second half of the century the entry of non-white people from the former lands of the

EMPIRE received most attention, combined with efforts by successive governments to restrict their entry. At the beginning of the century everyone who could prove that they had been born within the British empire could claim full nationality rights in Britain and throughout the empire. Some 300 million of the empire's estimated 425 million population were not white, and very few of them lived within the British Isles. In the early part of the century some came to Britain as students or for training in the professions, while others came as merchant seamen and settled, most often in ports such as Liverpool, Cardiff and east London, which, generally peaceably, had multiracial communities throughout the century. During World War I, especially large numbers of seamen were recruited within the empire, many of whom settled in Britain. Hostility to such residents increased in the interwar years with the growth of UNEMPLOYMENT and of welfare benefits, such as unemployment relief, to which everyone of British nationality was entitled. Such hostility – in combination with the growth of race-equality movements and nationalist movements within the empire – led to the creation of new organizations, often based in Britain, such as the League of Coloured Peoples, the major black self-help organization in Britain in the 1930s and 1940s. This was dominated by West Indian students and professionals, with some West African participation. The anticolonialist Pan-African Congress met in Manchester in 1945.

During World War II merchant seamen were again in demand, and munitions workers and other war workers, as well as servicemen, were brought to Britain from INDIA and elsewhere. After the war nationalist anti-colonial movements grew, generally involving elites, while working people increasingly migrated from the colonies, encouraged by the labour shortage in Britain, poor prospects in their home countries and, from 1952, restrictions on migration from the WEST INDIES to the United States. The British Nationality Act of 1948 confirmed the right of entry into Britain for all 'subjects of the British crown' or citizens of the

COMMONWEALTH, as the empire was now called; these terms could now by law be used interchangeably in a concession to the growing movement for DECOLONIZATION. The arrival in London of the Caribbean migrant ship *Empire Windrush* in 1948 is often taken as the start of immigration from the Commonwealth, though it was just part of an ongoing process that speeded up from the later 1940s. Large numbers of migrants came from India, Pakistan and East Africa, though throughout the second half of the 20th century the largest numbers of migrants came from the 'white' Commonwealth, from the United States and, increasingly at the end of the century, from within Europe. Black immigrants were far more likely than white to encounter hostility and discrimination when seeking jobs or homes and in other aspects of life.

By the late 1950s there were approximately 192,000 black immigrants in Britain, constituting less than half of one per cent of Britain's population: approximately 107,000 West Indians, 50,000 Indians and Pakistanis, 5000 Nigerians and 30,000 others. Their presence caused disproportionate alarm when the economy began to flag in the later 1950s. There were attacks on residents in Nottingham and in Notting Hill, London, in 1958. The 1962 Commonwealth Immigrants Act restricted the admission of Commonwealth immigrants to those with vouchers of guaranteed employment or 'special skills'. This prompted a wave of immigrants hoping to beat further restrictions. The act was extended and tightened in 1968 in response to the influx into Britain of Asians with British passports fleeing from discrimination in Kenya. White Commonwealth citizens retained the right of free entry. The Immigration Act of 1971 ended free right of entry for all but those with a parent or grandparent born in Britain.

This steady restriction of immigration was accompanied by a racially charged public debate. A speech by Enoch POWELL in 1968 predicting racial conflict was long remembered with especial bitterness by the black and Asian communities.

Powell's most inflammatory comment, subsequently much misquoted, was: 'As I look ahead, I am filled with foreboding. Like the Roman, I seem to see "the River Tiber foaming with much blood."' (Powell, a classical scholar, was referring to a passage in Virgil's *Aeneid*.) At the same time there were attempts by Labour governments to diminish racial intolerance by the Race Relations Act of 1965, which established the Race Relations Board to receive and investigate complaints of racial discrimination. Racial discrimination was made unlawful in places of public resort, but not in employment or housing. Subsequently Labour introduced the Race Relations Act, 1968, which enlarged the Race Relations Board and extended its scope. It also set up the Community Relations Commission, with a positive brief to work to establish harmonious race relations rather than just preventing or punishing racial discrimination. A further Race Relations Act in 1976 made discrimination unlawful in employment, training, education and in the provision of goods and services, and made it an offence to stir up racial hatred. It extended the definition of discrimination to include indirect discrimination and discrimination by means of victimization. It replaced both the Race Relations Board and the Community Relations Commission with the Commission for Racial Equality, which remained in operation for the remainder of the century.

The Single European Act of the European Parliament, passed in 1987, established that by 1992 the people of member states of the EUROPEAN UNION (EU) would be free to work, study and live (provided, normally, that they could support themselves) in any country of the EU. This was followed by increased flows of migration between Britain and other European countries of the EU.

By the late 20th century immigrant neighbourhoods had formed in most industrial centres, composed of West Indians, Bangladeshis, Pakistanis and Indians, with also substantial numbers of Hong Kong Chinese, Greek and Turkish Cypriots, Africans, and Asians expelled from both KENYA and Uganda after those countries declared independence in the 1960s. There were large Asian populations in Leicester, Bradford and Glasgow, and substantial black and Asian populations in parts of Birmingham, Manchester, Leeds and Bristol. In London, the areas of Brixton, Tottenham and Notting Hill, the site of the annual Notting Hill Carnival, had large West Indian communities. Southall had a large Asian population, but no district of London was exclusive to any one racial group. Especially in large urban areas, and above all in London, Britain became increasingly ethnically diverse and cosmopolitan, particularly during the last 40 years of the century. However, this did not come about effortlessly, as problems of racism often accompanied the immigrants' arrival. At the end of the century the worst fears about racial conflict had proved ill founded, but there was strong evidence of continuing racism in sections of the population at large and in important institutions (*see* LAWRENCE, STEPHEN), and of discrimination in employment against members of ethnic minorities.

SEE ALSO REFUGEES; RELIGIOUS BELIEF AND OBSERVANCE.

FURTHER READING G. Alderman, *Modern British Jewry* (1992); C. Holmes, *John Bull's Island: Immigration and British Society, 1871–1971* (1988); Z. Layton-Henry, *The Politics of Immigration: 'Race' and 'Race Relations' in Postwar Britain* (1992); J. Solomos, *Race and Racism in Contemporary Britain* (2nd edn, 1993).

imperial conferences, series of meetings between the leaders of Britain and the dominions held in London in 1911, 1921, 1923, 1926, 1930 and 1937. Their predecessors, the colonial conferences, had been held in the late 19th century among the prime ministers of the dominions and colonies of white settlement within the EMPIRE, including CANADA, AUSTRALIA, New Zealand and SOUTH AFRICA. The first colonial conference took place in 1887 when the colonial prime ministers came to London for the occasion of Queen Victoria's golden jubilee. Matters of mutual concern were discussed, such as trade and defence. The conferences became a regular occurrence so as to provide a formal structure for discussion and liaison between Britain and its colonies of white settlement. Other colonial conferences were held in London in 1897, 1902 and 1907, during which issues such as IMPERIAL PREFERENCE were discussed. An additional conference had been held in Ottawa in 1894.

By the last colonial conference in 1907 both Australia and New Zealand had joined Canada in assuming the status of dominions, and afterwards the gatherings were renamed imperial conferences. These saw the dominions increasingly putting forth their desire for greater self-determination, particularly in foreign affairs. The 1926 conference laid the groundwork for just such a transfer of control, when it defined the dominions of Canada, Australia, New Zealand, South Africa, the Irish Free State and Newfoundland as 'autonomous communities within the British Empire, equal in status and freely associated as members of the British Commonwealth of Nations'. This definition of autonomy was later recognized in the 1931 Statute of Westminster, which granted legislative independence to the parliaments of the dominions.

The colonial and imperial conferences were the forerunners of the much-expanded COMMONWEALTH conferences (so renamed in 1944) that took place with increasing regularity by the second half of the 20th century. The early Commonwealth conferences began to include the representatives of other colonies and territories besides those of the dominions, and so came to reflect better the Commonwealth as a whole. The 1949 conference recognized INDIA's place in the Commonwealth even though it had become a republic. The increasing influence of the larger Commonwealth nations was seen at the 1961 conference, when, against Britain's wishes, a declaration was made against the policy of apartheid, which drove South Africa out of the Commonwealth. By the late 1990s over 50 nations were entitled to send their representatives to the conferences.

FURTHER READING M. Ollivier, *The Colonial and Imperial Conferences from 1887 to 1937* (1954).

imperial preference, an economic arrangement contemplated by Britain and its colonies in the early 1900s and later implemented in the 1930s. Its earliest champion was Joseph CHAMBERLAIN, who promoted preferences as part of an overall package of TARIFF REFORM in 1903. Encouraged by support for the plan from CANADA, he envisaged Britain and its colonies and dominions becoming a self-contained trading unit, protected from foreign competition by high tariffs. However, Chamberlain failed in his efforts because of strong support for FREE TRADE among both members of the government and leaders of industry.

Some tariffs were erected after World War I, but the impetus to abandon free trade only came with the Depression of the 1930s (*see* GREAT CRASH). In 1931 the NATIONAL GOVERNMENT adopted imperial preference, and this was extended to the dominions by way of the Ottawa Agreement of 1932. The following year a series of bilateral preferences was negotiated with many British colonies. In 1947 the system of preferences was weakened when Britain was compelled to ratify the General Agreement on Tariffs and Trade (GATT) as a condition of its obtaining a vital loan from the US government. In the 1960s the system of imperial preference became a hindrance to Britain's negotiations for membership of the EUROPEAN ECONOMIC COMMUNITY, and when it joined in 1973 it was forced to phase out all imperial trade preferences to make way for agreements with Europe.

FURTHER READING A. Sykes, *Tariff Reform in British Politics, 1903–1913* (1979).

incomes. *See* STANDARDS OF LIVING.

Independent Labour Party (ILP), democratic socialist party founded in 1893, with the labour leader Keir HARDIE as its first chair. Its purpose was to help improve the lot of working-class people in

Britain by placing working-class MPs in Parliament to fight for their rights. The ILP was instrumental in the founding in 1900 of the LABOUR REPRESENTATION COMMITTEE, which became the LABOUR PARTY in 1906, although the ILP itself remained an independent body. Many prominent Labour politicians, including Hardie, Ramsay MACDONALD and Philip SNOWDEN, were early members of the ILP. Its newspaper, the *Labour Leader*, gave it an influential voice. The party's membership, which by 1910 had reached some 28,000, declined somewhat after 1918 when it became possible to join the Labour Party directly without joining an affiliated organization. In the 1920s the ILP was increasingly at odds with the Labour Party leadership, to which it acted as a left-wing ginger group. The Scottish MP James Maxton (1885–1946) chaired the party from 1926 until his death. The ILP had little TRADE-UNION support. In 1932 it dissociated itself from Labour after Labour ministers had decided to participate in the NATIONAL GOVERNMENT. Thereafter it moved firmly to the left and its membership figures plummeted. While it continued to have some public visibility through participation in events like the HUNGER MARCHES of the 1930s, it steadily became more marginal – and more so still owing to its opposition to Britain's participation in WORLD WAR II (traditionally, many ILP members were pacifists). The party's last MP lost his seat in 1959, and the ILP was reabsorbed into the Labour Party in 1975, taking on the name Independent Labour Publications. However, on the occasion of its centenary in 1993 the ILP relaunched itself as a left-wing political pressure group, though it remained a tiny minority voice.

FURTHER READING D. Howell, *British Workers and the Independent Labour Party, 1893–1940* (1983); D. James, T. Jowitt and K. Laybourn (eds.), *The Centennial History of the Independent Labour Party* (1992).

Independent Television Authority. *See* BRITISH BROADCASTING CORPORATION.

India, the richest, most populous and most prized of all of Britain's colonial possessions, feted throughout the 19th century as the 'jewel in the crown'. India was also the first non-'white' colony in the EMPIRE to achieve independence (1947), thus setting the stage for mass DECOLONIZATION in the 1950s and 1960s. The history of India in the 20th century has largely centred on its struggles for independence and its later efforts to maintain itself as the world's largest democracy.

British India was governed from London by the secretary of state for India and the India Office, but control was largely wielded from within India by the viceroy and members of the Indian civil service. By the early 20th century there were already calls from the Indian National Congress (established in 1885) for Indian independence. A number of British officials recognized that India would eventually come to self-rule, but advocated slow and cautious progress towards this end, which antagonized nationalists. The Indian Councils Act of 1909 and the India Act of 1919 went some way towards granting greater Indian participation within government, but such reforms were seen as inadequate by nationalists. They were particularly upset that India's faithful support of the Allied effort during World War I had not garnered rewards in the shape of political reform. The 1919 AMRITSAR MASSACRE of unarmed demonstrators also strengthened nationalist feeling. From the early 1920s Mohandas K. ('Mahatma') GANDHI became the most prominent nationalist leader; he became known for his successful and influential protest policy of nonviolent 'noncooperation' *(satyagraha)* against the British authorities.

Nationalist pressure was such that by 1930 a two-year series of 'round-table' talks and consultations on the political future of the subcontinent was convened in London, with the aim of encouraging Indian participation in the creation of a new constitution for India. The round table was judged by nationalists to be a failure, however, and the early 1930s saw renewed waves of civil disobedience in India. By this point Gandhi had been arrested and imprisoned several times and new figures, such as Jawaharlal Nehru and Subash Chandra Bose, had risen to prominence within the nationalist movement. In 1935 the results of the round-table conference were given substance in a new constitution, embodied in the Government of India Act. The act granted responsible government in domestic matters to provincial assemblies and attempted to create a new federal structure. Although the act would later form the basis for the 1950 constitution of independent India, it did not satisfy many radicals and was also seen as flawed by Muslims, who were granted no special recognition or protection. The Muslim League, headed by Muhammad Ali Jinnah, was soon consolidated and began campaigning against the Indian National Congress. However, Congress was widely successful in the 1937 assembly elections.

WORLD WAR II saw a divided response from India, with Indian troops again fighting for the Allied cause while radicals under the leadership of Bose formed the pro-Japanese Indian National Army among Indian troops taken prisoner by the Japanese (*see also* BURMA). In a desperate attempt to gain the support of Congress, a 1942 British delegation led by Sir Stafford CRIPPS offered, among other benefits, full dominion status for India. However, this offer was derided by Congress as too little, too late. Led by Gandhi, the 'Quit India' movement of civil disobedience ensued, leading to mass arrests of Gandhi and other nationalist leaders.

Britain's perilous economic and diplomatic position at the end of World War II, and the coming to power of the LABOUR government in 1945, meant that the final granting of full independence quickly gained momentum, with several appeals and attempts to promote a united India all failing. The agitation of Hindu nationalists and the Muslim League led both Congress and the last viceroy, Lord MOUNTBATTEN, to approve the plan to partition India, creating the separate Muslim state of Pakistan. Partition was viewed by the British as a disaster, and the antithesis of all they had worked to achieve in India, but they accepted that it was the only available option if civil war was to be averted.

The date of independence was set for midnight on 14 August 1947. It was met with great celebration as well as mass rioting, violence and massacres. Hundreds of thousands were killed and injured in the migrations that took place between India and Pakistan. The victims included Gandhi himself, who was killed by a Hindu fanatic in early 1948. India implemented a new constitution in 1950, under which it became a republic but remained a member of the COMMONWEALTH. Although India has evolved into the world's largest democracy, the legacy of partition – which the British tried so hard to avoid – remains painful. British hopes that partition would be a temporary measure have proven to be in vain, and Indian-Pakistani tensions were still as high at the end of the century as they had been fifty years before.

FURTHER READING J.M. Brown, *Modern India: The Origins of Asian Democracy* (2nd edn, 1994); P. Chatterjee, *The Nation and its Fragments: Colonial and Postcolonial Histories* (1993).

industrial relations. *See* TRADE UNIONS.

infant mortality. *See* POPULATION.

inflation. *See* PRICES AND PURCHASING POWER.

influenza pandemic (1918–19), probably the most severe epidemic to hit Britain during the 20th century. It killed perhaps 200,000 people in Britain (the exact number is uncertain) and about 10,000 British servicemen. Known as 'Spanish flu' or 'the Spanish lady', it swept through much of the world. Its virulence is often attributed to the vulnerability of populations weakened by the privations of WORLD WAR I, and its spread to the dislocation of war, as soldiers and refugees moved around. However, this is unlikely. Neutral countries and those whose economies were not seriously affected by the war suffered mortality rates as high or higher than those involved in the war. The highest mor tality rates were recorded in the United States and India, very different countries and neither of them involved in the war to the same degree as many European countries. Military doctors reported that stronger, more robust men succumbed more rapidly than weaker men and in general death rates among people in the prime of life were greater than among more vulnerable groups such as older people. The pandemic appears to have been *sui generis* rather than a result of the war.

FURTHER READING J.M. Winter, *The Great War and the British People* (1985).

In Place of Strife (1969). *See* TRADE UNIONS.

Institute of Contemporary Arts (ICA). This cultural centre was founded in London in 1947 by Roland Penrose (1900–84), the writer and artist, and Herbert Read, (1893–1968), the poet and critic, to encourage new developments in the arts and cooperation among the different branches of the arts and media. To achieve this, exhibitions, lectures, films, poetry readings and discussions were organized. The ICA aimed to show noncommercial experimental work and to be a commissioning agent, with its own library and archives. It encouraged experimentation in new popular media, such as film and radio. Penrose and Read had been instrumental in the international surrealist exhibition held in London in 1936, which was the inspiration for the new organization Its original home was in Dover Street but it moved in 1968 to the Mall, where it remains. It played a major role in certain developments in the arts, especially British pop art, and in 1969 it was the venue for the first exhibition of conceptual art in Britain, *When Attitudes Become Form*. It continued into the 21st century as a centre for innovation in British cultural life, though its contact with popular culture was more remote than its founders had hoped.

intelligence service. *See* MI5 AND MI6.

International Brigades. *See* SPANISH CIVIL WAR.

internment. For the first time in modern British history, during WORLD WAR I and WORLD WAR II the civilian nationals of enemy states residing or travelling in Britain when war was declared were arrested and interned, for fear they would engage in espionage or sabotage. In 1914 internment was at first very limited, but in October 1914 orders were issued for the arrest of all male aliens of military age from enemy countries. By November 1914 over 10,000 were under arrest and finally removed to a makeshift camp on the Isle of Man. Conditions there were so poor that the internees revolted and five were killed. This led to the release of 2700. But as public hostility towards Germany grew, Prime Minister ASQUITH announced further arrests on 13 May 1915. Altogether about 30,000 German, Austrian and other male nationals of enemy powers were interned for the remainder of the war, often in poor conditions. Women were evidently not expected to act as spies or saboteurs.

At the outbreak of World War II the Home Office summoned enemy aliens for interview by special tribunals. They were then divided into three categories: class C were classified as harmless and freed; class B were considered safe to be at large under observation; class A were considered a security threat and interned. Some 64,200 were placed in class C and only 600 were classified as class A and interned – not surprisingly, since most German nationals in Britain in 1939 were Jews and other anti-Nazi refugees. In 1940 the success of the German thrust through Europe was widely, and wrongly, attributed to the work of traitors in the occupied countries. Fears arose of a 'fifth column' of spies in Britain. Encouraged by Prime Minister Winston CHURCHILL, the scope of internment was extended. By June 1940 over 27,000 men and (this time) women, most of them anti-Nazis, were interned, mainly, once more, in the Isle of Man. Again, internment camps were hastily prepared and inadequate, though the often highly educated and talented internees created a social and cultural life for themselves, which helped them get through. A plan proposed by Churchill to ship enemy aliens to Canada and Australia proved disastrous when the liner *Arandora Star*, carrying internees and prisoners of war to Canada, was sunk by U-boats, with 650 deaths. In consequence in July 1940 shipment overseas and the internment process were halted. As fear of invasion diminished and the fortunes of war reversed, internees were gradually released until by the end of 1942 only class A remained in custody. Most of these were repatriated in exchanges arranged by the International Red Cross in 1943 and 1944.

SEE ALSO   NORTHERN IRELAND.

FURTHER READING   P. Gillman and L. Gillman, *'Collar the Lot!' How Britain Interned and Expelled Its Wartime Refugees* (1980); F. Lafitte (ed.), *The Internment of Aliens* (rev. edn, 1990).

Invergordon mutiny (1931), sailors' mutiny at the ROYAL NAVY dockyard at Invergordon, on the Cromarty Firth, northeast Scotland. It was prompted by pay cuts introduced in the navy (as in other public-sector occupations) in 1931 by the NATIONAL GOVERNMENT as part of a package of measures to deal with the economic crisis (*see* GREAT CRASH). This led sailors of the Atlantic Fleet at Invergordon to refuse to go on duty. The government responded by slightly reducing the cuts. The leaders of the mutiny were discharged from the navy.

IRA. *See* IRISH REPUBLICAN ARMY.

Ireland. The 20th century saw great upheaval in Ireland and a change in the status of most of the island from union with Britain to dominion, and then to republic.

By the end of the 16th century the entire island of Ireland had come under English rule. In 1801 the Act of Union came into force, abolishing the Irish Parliament and joining Ireland and Great Britain. However, by the 1880s there was much dissatisfaction with Westminster and increasingly vociferous demands for land reform (*see* IRISH LAND ACTS) and self-government (*see* HOME RULE and IRISH NATIONAL PARTY). After delays in the 1880s

and 1890s, a Home Rule Act passed into law in 1914, but implementation was postponed owing to the outbreak of WORLD WAR I. The delay aroused the anger of radical nationalists, which boiled over in the EASTER RISING of 1916, an abortive rebellion aimed at proclaiming complete independence for Ireland. The resulting climate of anger and distrust meant that home rule was all but forgotten, and in 1919–21 the Anglo-Irish War erupted between the IRISH REPUBLICAN ARMY (IRA), representing the SINN FÉIN government that had declared Irish independence in 1918 (*see also* MARKIEWICZ, CONSTANCE), and British forces, the most notorious members of which were the BLACK AND TANS.

In December 1921 the Anglo-Irish treaty was signed (*see* COLLINS, MICHAEL), creating the Irish Free State. The treaty gave dominion status to most of Ireland, and separate status to the northeastern region of Ulster (populated mainly by Protestants), which remained part of the United Kingdom. However, Republican nationalists, led by the 'Irregulars' faction of the IRA and Sinn Féin, felt betrayed by the treaty and by supporters of the Free State, and civil war was waged between the two factions in 1922–3. The IRA was eventually driven underground, but the Fianna Fáil party, led by former SINN FÉIN leader Eamon DE VALERA, won an electoral majority in 1932 and began to work peacefully for the complete independence of Ireland. The Free State was gradually dismantled, and a new constitution was ratified in 1937 proclaiming 'Eire' as a sovereign state, encompassing the entire island of Ireland. In 1949 links with the Commonwealth and the British crown were entirely severed and the Republic of Ireland was established.

Ireland's history in the latter half of the 20th century still bears testimony to the friction caused by partition in 1921, which was regarded by leading British politicians of the time as a temporary measure until problems could be resolved. In the 1980s the Irish government took a more active role in talks with the British government over the issue of NORTHERN IRELAND. The 1985 Anglo-Irish agreement signed by prime ministers Margaret THATCHER and Garret Fitzgerald made provision for regular intergovernmental conferences between the two states, to discuss matters such as border security, civil rights and economic issues. It also reiterated the tenet that any changes in Northern Ireland's status had to have the approval of a majority of its people. In recognition of this, a 1998 referendum resulted in 94% of voters in the Republic ratifying the 'Good Friday' peace agreement (*see* NORTHERN IRELAND) by approving constitutional amendments that would dilute the Republic's historic claim to the six counties of Northern Ireland.

Ireland joined the EUROPEAN ECONOMIC COMMUNITY in 1973. Because of its poor economic standing compared to other European member states it began to receive a good deal of funding and other economic incentives from Brussels by the 1980s. As a result, by the late 1990s Ireland became known as the 'Celtic Tiger', with the fastest-growing economy in the European Union. **FURTHER READING** R.F. Foster, *Modern Ireland, 1600–1972* (1988); K.T. Hoppen, *Ireland Since 1800: Conflict and Conformity* (1989); D. Keogh, *20th-Century Ireland: Nation and State* (1994).

Irish in Britain. *See* IMMIGRATION.

Irish Land Acts (1903, 1909, 1923), series of land reforms in IRELAND, aimed at ameliorating long-standing grievances. The concentration of land ownership in Ireland in the hands of large landowners (often Protestant and of English origin) and the relative impoverishment of the mass of the mainly rural population (who had only small, mainly tenant, land-holdings) was a major focus of nationalist protest in the later 19th century. The Land Acts of 1870, 1881 and 1885 had started the process of diminishing landlord rights and facilitating land purchase.

At the beginning of the 20th century an extensive campaign, including the use of boycott and intimidation, was organized by the United Irish League, which was believed to have 100,000 members in almost 1000 branches through most of Ireland in 1901. The League's aim was the buying out of landlords by compulsory purchase and the redistribution of the land to poor farmers. There were arrests, but official coercion was less extensive than in previous episodes of protest.

George Wyndham, the chief secretary for Ireland from November 1900, had family connections with Ireland and a desire to settle the land question peaceably, indeed to maintain the union between Great Britain and Ireland by taking constructive measures to settle Irish grievances. In 1903 he proposed, and Parliament passed, a land act. This built upon the proposals from a conference held in the previous year of representatives of tenants and of a minority of landlords. The act was near-revolutionary in its implications. Landlords were to be encouraged to sell entire estates, not just piecemeal holdings, provided that three-quarters of the tenants on any estate agreed. Land prices would be fixed and the money would be advanced to the purchasers by the state, to be repaid over 68½ years at a rate of 3.25%. The incentive to landlords to sell was a bonus on each sale to be paid out of Irish revenues, which meant that the sales were not disadvantageous to their interests.

Nationalists argued that the purchase price was too high, but could not deny that this was a great advance. The opportunity was seized: between 1903 and 1920 almost 3.6 hectares (9 million acres) changed hands and a further 800,000 hectares (2 million acres) were in the process of being sold in 1920. £83 million had been advanced to purchasers and a further £24 million of sales were pending. An amending act of 1909 allowed for a limited amount of compulsory purchase. However, the Land Acts did not, as Wyndham hoped, usher in a new period of negotiated resolution of tension between Great Britain and Ireland.

In 1923 the recently founded Irish Free State completed the process of land reform with another

Land Act (amended in 1925), under which all land in which landlord and tenant both had an interest passed automatically into the hands of an official Land Commission. Such land was to be granted in due course to the tenants as proprietors, subject to fixed annual payments, and the vendor received from the state a bonus of 10% of the standard price. The Irish government refused to make further repayments to the British state. The annual sum due was £3 million.

The British government endeavoured to collect the money by imposing tariff duties on Free State exports to the UK, and the Free State retaliated with duties on UK imports. The question was settled in April 1938 by an agreement signed in London, under which the Irish government paid £10 million in commutation of the annuities, the special trading duties were amended, and the British government relinquished the rights in the Irish naval ports (such as Cobh and Lough Swilly) that it had been given by the treaty of 1921.

FURTHER READING R.F. Foster, *Modern Ireland, 1600–1972* (1988); F.S.L. Lyons, *Ireland since the Famine* (1973).

Irish National Party, political party, otherwise known as Irish Parliamentary Party, founded in 1870. It became electorally successful after the Parliamentary Reform Act of 1884 greatly expanded the Irish electorate. Its success was led by Charles Stewart Parnell, although it suffered from his fall in 1890–1. In the House of Commons it generally supported the Liberals after Gladstone's adoption of HOME RULE. It gained popular support from its association with the land campaigns (*see* IRISH LAND ACTS), and John REDMOND's leadership from 1900 restored its credibility. It won between 82 and 84 seats in each of the elections from 1900 to 1910. Though there was tension within it about the desirable future for IRELAND, the party supported home rule. The narrow victory of the LIBERAL PARTY in the general elections of 1910 ensured that the Irish Nationalists, along with the LABOUR PARTY, held the balance of power in the House of Commons.

(The Irish Nationalists had the advantage that the number of Irish seats in the Commons had been fixed by the 1800 Act of Union at 103. Since that time the population of Ireland had declined while that of Great Britain had grown, with the result that by 1910 Ireland was relatively over-represented in Parliament.)

This pivotal role increased the Nationalists' influence over the Liberal government (whose support for home rule had probably lost it votes in the 1910 GENERAL ELECTIONS), and in 1912 the government introduced a third Home Rule Bill. This aroused strong opposition in Ulster and from the CONSERVATIVE PARTY, but was passed and became law on 18 September 1914. However, the implementation of home rule was suspended for the duration of World War I, in which the Nationalists supported the Liberal government, despite criticism in Ireland.

The EASTER RISING and its harsh suppression invigorated the movement for outright independence in Ireland, rather than just home rule. In consequence in the general election of 1918, SINN FÉIN, the independence party, won 73 Irish seats, while the Nationalists won only 7, having fielded 58 candidates. The Sinn Féin candidates, including Michael COLLINS and Eamon DE VALERA, refused to take their seats. A single Irish Nationalist MP was returned for an English constituency: T.P. O'Connor, who represented the Scotland division of Liverpool (which was a stronghold of Irish immigrants) from 1885 until his death in 1929.

From 1922, following the partition of Ireland, candidates under the label of the Irish Nationalist Party fought only two or three seats but returned at least one MP to Westminster at every election until 1955. The moderate nationalist tradition that they represented was taken up in NORTHERN IRELAND by the SOCIAL DEMOCRATIC AND LABOUR PARTY from 1970.

FURTHER READING R.F. Foster, *Modern Ireland, 1600–1972* (1988); T. Garvin, *The Evolution of Irish Nationalist Politics* (1981); F.S.L. Lyons, *The Irish Parliamentary Party, 1890–1910* (1951).

Irish Republican Army (IRA), a nationalist, Republican paramilitary organization devoted to the creation of a united IRELAND, free from British rule. The IRA was formally established in 1919 from the Irish Volunteers. Using guerrilla tactics, the IRA fought the Anglo-Irish War of 1919–21 on behalf of the Dáil government. It experienced a schism in late 1921 over the signing of the Anglo-Irish treaty, which gave dominion status to southern Ireland within the British EMPIRE. Elements of the IRA took up arms against the new Irish Free State in the civil war of 1922–3, but were essentially defeated by the time a ceasefire was called. However, its continuing use of terrorist tactics, against both Britain and the Free State, meant that it was outlawed by the Irish prime minister (and former IRA member) Eamon DE VALERA in the 1930s. It then became an underground organization, but waged only occasional campaigns over the coming decades.

The IRA found new life in NORTHERN IRELAND in 1969 in the wake of the Catholic civil-rights movement and the subsequent violence and social upheaval. By 1970 a split had become evident between the Dublin-based 'Official' IRA, which had become more of a Marxist pressure group, and the Belfast-based revolutionary nationalist 'Provisional' IRA, which began waging a high-profile campaign of terrorism in an attempt to force the British out of Northern Ireland. The Provisional IRA gained support throughout the 1970s (notably after BLOODY SUNDAY) and early 1980s, particularly among Irish-Americans in the wake of the 1981 hunger strikes when ten IRA men starved themselves to death in the Maze prison when the British government refused to grant them political status. The IRA's terrorist attacks became progressively more brutal as time passed. The Grand Hotel in Brighton was blown up in 1984 in an attempt to assassinate Margaret THATCHER and her cabinet, staying there during the Conservative Party conference. In 1987 eleven people were killed when a Remembrance Day parade was bombed in Enniskillen, and in 1991 there was a mortar attack on Downing Street. A ceasefire was called in August 1994, leading to hopes for a lasting peace, but these were shattered in January 1996 when the IRA planted a bomb in London's Docklands, causing massive damage and killing two. Later that year a bomb devastated Manchester's city centre. Another ceasefire called in July 1997 was met with scepticism, but was necessary to allow the IRA's political wing, SINN FÉIN, to enter into all-party peace talks at Stormont, which led to the 1998 'Good Friday' peace agreement. In August 1998, a group calling themselves the 'Real' IRA exploded a bomb in OMAGH town centre, killing 29 civilians and exacting the highest death toll of any terrorist attack in Irish and British history. The Provisional IRA distanced itself from the attack, and the Real IRA declared its own ceasefire shortly thereafter. This proved temporary and the attack made clear the continuing extent of terrorist activity in Ireland and the fragility of the peace process.

FURTHER READING T.P. Coogan, *The IRA: A History* (1993); B. O'Brien, *The Long War: The IRA and Sinn Féin, 1985 to Today* (1993).

Iron Curtain, the, metaphor used to describe the physical and ideological barrier which, during the COLD WAR of the late 1940s to 1989, divided the communist regimes of Eastern Europe from democratic Western Europe. The term was made popular by Winston CHURCHILL who, in a speech given in Fulton, Missouri, USA, on 5 March 1946, stated: 'From Stettin in the Baltic to Trieste in the Adriatic, an iron curtain has descended across the continent.' The Iron Curtain was fiercely defended and patrolled from the communist side, as epitomized by the Berlin Wall. It also proved a barrier to the free exchange of ideas and civilian travel between East and West. The Iron Curtain was dramatically shattered when the Berlin Wall came down in 1989, and any residual traces were removed by 1991 after Germany was reunified and the Soviet Union broke up.

FURTHER READING F.J. Harbutt, *The Iron*

Curtain: Churchill, America and the Origins of the Cold War (1986).

Isaacs, Rufus Daniel (Lord Reading) (1860–1935), Liberal politician and lawyer, who was attorney general (1910–13), lord chief justice (1913–21), viceroy of INDIA (1921–6) and briefly FOREIGN SECRETARY (1931).

Isaacs was the son of a successful Jewish fruit merchant in Spitalfields, east London. He was educated in Brussels, at the Anglo-Jewish Academy in London and then at University College School, London. He entered the family business at the age of 15. He was briefly a ship's boy on the *Blair Athole* in 1876–7, then a jobber on the stock exchange, 1880–4. He was called to the Bar in 1887 and established a successful practice, dealing especially with commercial and trade-union law. He became a Queen's Counsel in 1898 and was regarded as one of the country's leading advocates. Among other cases, he achieved the victory of the Taff Vale Railway Company over the railway union in 1902, winning a verdict that crippled the TRADE UNIONS for some years (*see* TAFF VALE JUDGEMENT).

Isaacs was Liberal MP for Reading from 1903 to 1914. He was appointed solicitor general in March 1910, then attorney general in October 1910, when he was also knighted. As attorney general he was promoted to the cabinet in 1912. In 1912–13 he was implicated in the MARCONI SCANDAL. His errors of judgement in handling this affair, combined with his Jewishness, caused him to be fiercely attacked. He resigned his parliamentary seat in 1914 and became a baron, having been appointed lord chief justice, an office he held until 1921. In 1915 he negotiated a loan of $500 million from the United States, which was vital to Britain for the financing of WORLD WAR I. He was high commissioner for finance in the United States and CANADA, September–November 1917, then ambassador to Washington (1918–19). He became a viscount in 1916 and an earl in 1917.

His period as viceroy of India (1921–6) was a sensitive time in which the movement for independence was very active. Isaacs avoided exacerbation of potential conflict, handling tensions tactfully. He became marquess of Reading in 1926, and became director, and later president, of Imperial Chemical Industries. He took a prominent role in the Round Table Conference about the future constitutional status of India in 1930–1. He was foreign secretary in the NATIONAL GOVERNMENT, August–October 1931.

FURTHER READING H. Montgomery Hyde, *Lord Reading. The Life of Rufus Isaacs, First Marquess of Reading* (1967).

Isaacs, Stella (Lady Reading) (1894–1971), founder of the Women's Voluntary Service (later the WOMEN'S ROYAL VOLUNTARY SERVICE). As a child, owing to a spinal ailment, she was educated at home. She became secretary to Lady Reading, wife of Rufus ISAACS, Lord Reading, when he was viceroy of India, and later private secretary to Reading himself, whom she married in 1931, one year after the death of his first wife. She supported her husband until he died in 1935. In 1938 she was invited by the home secretary, Sir Samuel HOARE, to form a voluntary service for women to deal with civil dislocation in time of war. This was the Women's Voluntary Service (*see* WOMEN'S ROYAL VOLUNTARY SERVICE), in which she was active until her death. As Baroness Swanborough she became the first woman life peer in 1958 (*see* LORDS, HOUSE OF).

J

Jarrow marchers. *See* HUNGER MARCHES; UNEMPLOYMENT.

Jenkins, Roy (Harris) (1920–), Labour and then Social Democrat politician; home secretary (1965– 7, 1974–6), CHANCELLOR OF THE EXCHEQUER (1967–70) and leader of the SOCIAL DEMOCRATIC PARTY (1982–3). The son of a Labour MP, Jenkins was educated at Abersychan Grammar School, then at University College, Cardiff, and Balliol College, Oxford. After serving in the army during World War II, Jenkins was elected Labour MP for Central Southwark in 1948. In 1950 he became MP for Stechford, Birmingham, a seat he held until 1976. He became minister of aviation in 1964 then in 1965 home secretary under Harold WILSON, and directed the liberalization of the laws on homosexuality (*see* SEXUALITY, OFFICIAL REGULATION OF), ABORTION and DIVORCE, and the abolition of the CENSORSHIP of the theatre by the lord chamberlain.

Jenkins became chancellor of the exchequer in 1967 after the devaluation of the pound, and succeeded in bringing spending under control before Labour's defeat in the 1970 election. He was elected deputy leader of the LABOUR PARTY, but resigned in 1972 after the party decided to call for a referendum on British membership of the EUROPEAN ECONOMIC COMMUNITY. He returned to the cabinet in 1974 as home secretary, but, increasingly disillusioned with the party's move to the left and by his poor showing in the 1976 leadership election, Jenkins left the Commons to become president of the European Commission, a post he held from 1977 to 1981.

In 1981 Jenkins, calling for a restructuring of British politics, became the first leader of the Social Democratic Party (SDP); he continued as leader of the party until 1983. In 1982 he returned to the Commons as SDP MP for Glasgow Hillhead, holding the seat until the 1987 election, after which he entered the House of LORDS as Lord Jenkins of Hillhead.

A well-respected essayist and biographer, Jenkins was made chancellor of Oxford University in 1987. His major publications include: *Asquith* (1964, reissued 1978, 1986, 1994), *Mr Balfour's Poodle: An Account of the Struggle Between the House of Lords and the Government of Mr Asquith* (1954, 1986), *Truman* (1986), *Baldwin* (1987, 1995), *European Diary, 1977–81* (1989), *A Life at the Centre* (1991, 1994) and *Gladstone* (1995).

Jews in Britain. *See* IMMIGRATION.

John, Augustus (1878–1961), painter and draughtsman. Born in Tenby, in Wales, he was the son of a solicitor and the younger brother of the painter Gwen JOHN. He studied at the Slade School of Fine Art in London, 1894–8, but appeared unremarkable until he injured his head while diving into the sea in Wales in 1897. Thereafter he changed dramatically, becoming the very image of the bohemian artist, complete with beard, though John always denied that the diving accident had been responsible for this change. His painting also changed, becoming more vivid and spontaneous, especially his brilliant drawings. On graduation from the Slade in 1898 he won first prize for the Summer Composition and had an outstanding reputation. He became identified with all that was independent and rebellious in British art and was a well-known figure around London. He travelled energetically, teaching at Liverpool University in 1900–2 and at Chelsea Art School, 1903–7. His domestic life was equally energetic. In 1901 he had married Ida Nettleship, a fellow student at the Slade. She died in 1907, but he had already fathered a child with Dorothy ('Dorelia') McNeill, who became his favourite model and de facto wife, though John, who was perceived as handsome and charismatic, was notoriously promiscuous. At the end of his life he was rumoured to have fathered 100 children. A picture of Dorelia as a Gypsy, *The Smiling Woman* (1909), made his name. From 1911 to 1914 he led a nomadic life, sometimes living in a caravan and camping with Gypsies. He painted romanticized pictures of Gypsy life and colourful small-scale landscapes, as well as some ambitious figure compositions. He also left some ambitious projects unfinished. He was one of a number of official war artists in World War I.

Augustus John is best remembered as a portraitist. After the war he was taken up by London high society and painted a host of society beauties as well as leading literary figures, including Thomas Hardy, T.E. LAWRENCE, James JOYCE and W.B. YEATS, who greatly admired him. His work increasingly became flashy and repetitive and did not develop further. He remained a colourful celebrity, one of the few British artists known to the general public. As he aged his image changed from rebel to Grand Old Man. He was awarded the Order of Merit in 1942, but by the time of his death his reputation as an artist had declined, outlasted by the legend of his personality and exploits.

FURTHER READING M. Holroyd, *Augustus John: A Biography* (2 vols., 1974–5).

John, Gwen (1876–1939), artist. Born in Haverfordwest, Wales, she was the elder sister of Augustus JOHN, but very different both artistically and in her personal style. She studied at the Slade School in London, 1895–8, then took lessons in Paris from Whistler, who much influenced her style of painting. In 1899 she returned to London, but in 1904 settled permanently in France. She lived at first in Paris, earning her living by modelling for other artists, including Rodin, who became her lover. In 1913 she became a Catholic and began to lead a reclusive life, dominated by her art and her religion. Most of her paintings were of single female figures in interiors, including self-portraits, painted with great sensitivity. She had only one exhibition devoted to her work in her lifetime and at the time of her death her work was little known. However, her brother prophesied that she would come to be considered a better artist than he, and from the 1960s this was increasingly so, as she came to be valued as a major artist.

FURTHER READING S. Chitty, *Gwen John* (1981).

Johnson, Amy (1903–41), aviator. Born and educated in Hull, then at Sheffield University, Johnson learned to fly in her free time while working for a firm of London solicitors. She also studied aircraft maintenance, becoming the first woman to hold an Air Ministry ground engineer's certificate. In May 1930 she flew solo from Croydon to Darwin, Australia, in 20 days. In July 1931 she flew from London to Tokyo, via Siberia, in 10 days, a new record. She later flew solo to Cape Town. These achievements made her into a national heroine. On the outbreak of WORLD WAR II she joined the Air Transport Auxiliary, and was killed when her aircraft crashed in the Thames estuary on 5 January 1941.

Joseph, Keith (Sinjohn) (1918–94), Conservative politician. Joseph was educated at Harrow School and Magdalen College, Oxford, then becoming a fellow of All Souls, a sign of intellectual distinction in Oxford. After service in World War II, Joseph passed his Bar exams but never practised. He became MP for Leeds Northeast in 1956 and held various minor posts in the Conservative government under Harold MACMILLAN. After serving as secretary of state for social services under Edward HEATH from 1970 to 1974, Joseph's politics shifted to the right and he became a staunch supporter of the 'free market'. He supported the election of Margaret THATCHER as leader of the CONSERVATIVE PARTY in 1975, and became a leading ideologue of 'Thatcherism', calling for reductions in taxation and public expenditure and greater control of trade unions. He was made secretary of state for industry following the 1979 GENERAL ELECTION, moving to the Department of Education in 1981. Joseph provided many of the ideas in the 1988 Education Reform Act (*see* EDUCATION), for which he faced much opposition from teachers and teaching unions. He inherited his father's baronetcy in 1942, became a life peer in 1987 and died on 10 December 1994.

journalism. *See* NEWSPAPERS.

Joyce, James (Augustine Aloysius) (1882–1941), Irish novelist, a major figure in modernist literature. Joyce was born at Rathgar, Dublin, and educated at two Jesuit schools, Clongowes Wood College and Belvedere College, then at University College, Dublin. He was an excellent linguist and in 1901 wrote a letter of admiration in Dano-Norwegian to Ibsen. He had come to think Irish Catholicism narrow and bigoted and he went to Paris for a year in 1902. There he wrote verse and discovered Édouard Dujardin's novel *Les Lauriers sont coupés* (1888). He regarded this as the source of his own use of interior monologue, which became a distinguishing feature of his creative writing. He returned to Dublin in 1903 for his mother's death, then in 1904 left IRELAND for good, apart from brief visits. He took with him Nora Barnacle, with whom he spent the rest of his life and who became the mother of his two children. They lived for some years in Trieste, where Joyce taught English. In 1915, because of World War I, they moved to Zurich, then settled finally, after the war, in Paris.

Joyce's first published work was a volume of verse, *Chamber Music* (1907). Then came *Dubliners* (1914), a volume of short stories published after much delay. During Joyce's last visit to Ireland, in 1912, the printed version of the work had been destroyed by the prospective publisher for fear of libel, as the stories were highly critical of the stifling effect on Irish society of the Catholic Church, nostalgic politics, close family life, repressed sexuality and ubiquitous alcoholism. Such views were not popular in a country asserting its independence and national identity. When the book appeared it was praised, especially by the poet Ezra Pound, whose support greatly assisted Joyce's reputation. He also attracted the support of Harriet Shaw Weaver, founder of the *Egoist* in 1914, initially a feminist magazine on literature and the arts, later, under the influence of Pound, an outlet for the Imagist poets. Weaver became Joyce's lifelong benefactress.

Joyce's *Portrait of the Artist as a Young Man*, which was largely autobiographical and again highly critical of Irish culture, was published serially in the *Egoist* in 1914–15. His play *Exiles* was similarly controversial. It was staged unsuccessfully in Munich in 1918, first performed in London in 1926, then not revived until 1970. With backing from W.B. YEATS and Pound, Joyce received a grant from the philanthropic Royal Literary Fund in 1915 and, shortly after, a grant from the Civil List. Despite his growing reputation, Joyce and his family continued to struggle against poverty. He was also troubled by eye problems.

Joyce's major novel *Ulysses* was published in Paris in 1922 and was received as a work of genius by writers as varied as T.S. ELIOT, Arnold BENNETT and Ernest Hemingway, though others, including

Virginia WOOLF, were less impressed. Again, it was controversial for its sexual frankness and its unconventional style and form, notably the innovative stream-of-consciousness technique. The first British edition appeared in 1936. A small volume of verse, *Pomes Penyeach*, appeared in 1927. In 1939 Joyce published his last major work, the highly acclaimed and controversial *Finnegans Wake*, in which he took the linguistic experiments and wordplay of *Ulysses* to extremes.

FURTHER READING R. Ellman, *James Joyce* (1959, 2nd edn 1982).

Joyce, William ('Lord Haw-Haw') (1906–45), Nazi propagandist. Born in the United States, the son of a naturalized Irish-American father, Joyce moved to Britain and studied at the London School of Economics. He became an outspoken supporter of Oswald MOSLEY's BRITISH UNION OF FASCISTS. He felt that Mosley did not sufficiently recognize his talents and set up his own pro-Nazi organization, the National Socialist League. His brother Quentin worked at the Air Ministry and shared his pro-Nazi views.

Joyce slipped out of Britain to Germany days before the outbreak of WORLD WAR II, outwitting MI5 who had him under observation. From Germany he made PROPAGANDA broadcasts to Britain, which opened with the phrase 'Germany calling'. This and the exaggerated public-school accent he affected (his own accent being a blend of Irish and Cockney) earned him the nickname 'Lord Haw-Haw' and he became a butt of humour in wartime

Britain. One of his tasks in Germany was to win over British prisoners of war to the German side, but he had little success. After the war he was sentenced to death for treason since, despite his background, he held a British passport.

justices of the peace. *See* MAGISTRATES.

Jutland, battle of (31 May–1 June 1916), the principal naval engagement of WORLD WAR I. There were two distinct actions: the battle-cruiser squadrons of the ROYAL NAVY (commanded by Admiral BEATTY) and the German High Seas Fleet engaged each other on the afternoon of 31 May, and the main fleets (that of Britain commanded by Admiral Jellicoe, 1859–1935) met in the early evening, lost contact in the dark and resumed action the following morning. Tactically, the battle was indecisive. Despite British preponderance in vessels (151–99) and gun power, the Germans were able to return to port. The British lost three battle cruisers and eight destroyers and suffered 6100 casualties; the Germans lost one battleship, one battle cruiser, four cruisers and five destroyers, with 2550 casualties. Strategically the battle was a British victory since it led the German command to keep surface vessels close inshore for the remainder of the war.

SEE ALSO SUBMARINES.

FURTHER READING G. Bennett, *The Battle of Jutland* (1999); G.A.H. Gordon, *The Rules of the Game: Jutland and the British Naval Command* (1996).

K

Kennedy, Charles. *See* LIBERAL PARTY.

Kenya, former British protectorate and colony in East Africa. In 1895 Britain took over the East Africa Protectorate, the territory that would later become Kenya, from the British East Africa Company. The company had administered the region from 1887 but was sliding into bankruptcy. By the turn of the century Britain was encouraging white settlers to develop the agricultural potential of the White Highlands region. By 1906 a legislative council had been established, but was dominated by the white settlers. In 1920 their efforts led to Kenya – as it was then renamed – becoming a crown colony. Groups such as the Central Association, organized by Kenya's most powerful indigenous tribe, the Kikuyu, began to agitate from the 1920s for greater African involvement and, eventually, independence from Britain. Civil war threatened in the 1950s, with the so-called Mau Mau rebellion. The Mau Mau were a secret society that engaged in terrorist activities between 1952 and 1957; the British army was called in to quell the violence. However, the rebellion, when coupled with the general movement towards DECOLONIZATION sweeping the EMPIRE, increased demands by local politicians for greater African control over Kenyan affairs, and eventually for independence. This was achieved in 1963. The following year Kenya became a republic, with Jomo Kenyatta – a suspected Mau Mau leader who had been imprisoned by the colonial authorities throughout much of the 1950s – as its first president. Though a republic, it has remained part of the COMMONWEALTH.

FURTHER READING J. Lonsdale, *Politics in Kenya* (1992); W.R. Ochieng' (ed.), *A Modern History of Kenya, 1895–1980* (1989).

Keynes, John Maynard (1883–1946), one of the most influential economists of the 20th century. At King's College, Cambridge, he gained a first-class degree in mathematics (1905) and was active in political debating and became friends – indeed had homosexual relationships – with some of those who, like himself, became the core of the BLOOMSBURY GROUP. He became an economist under the tutelage of the distinguished Cambridge economist Alfred Marshall, though he always had reservations about economics as a field of study; he never received the title of professor of economics, though he taught it for some years at Cambridge as a fellow of King's College. His early research concerned probability theory. He worked as a civil servant in the INDIA Office, 1906–8, before returning to Cambridge. In 1913 he was applying his academic expertise to practical matters as a member of the Royal Commission on Indian

Finance and Currency. Thereafter he preferred this policy-related role to strictly academic activity.

During WORLD WAR I Keynes entered the Treasury and soon had wide responsibility for the finance of the war, though he did not wholly support it. He attended the Paris peace conference as the representative of the Treasury, but resigned in June 1919 in disagreement with the heavy reparation payments being imposed on Germany. He feared that this could prolong conflict in Europe and prevent the economic recovery of Germany, which would disrupt the world economy. He expressed his views in the widely influential *Economic Consequences of the Peace* (1919).

Keynes retained his fellowship at King's but did not return to full-time academic life after the war. He divided his time between Cambridge and his house in Bloomsbury, became rich through speculation, married the ballerina Lydia Lopokova and became a patron of the arts. In 1942 he became chairman of the COUNCIL FOR THE ENCOURAGEMENT OF MUSIC AND THE ARTS (CEMA) and supervised the expansion of government patronage of the arts and the creation of the ARTS COUNCIL OF GREAT BRITAIN.

Keynes argued against the return to the GOLD STANDARD in 1925, which he believed would cause UNEMPLOYMENT. In the 1920s he became active in the LIBERAL PARTY and worked closely with David LLOYD GEORGE in developing radical policies for the recovery of the economy, in particular recommending that the government should fund essential projects such as road building ('public works') in order to provide work and stimulate consumption. The LABOUR government of 1929–31 did not follow his advice (or the similar advice of Oswald MOSLEY, which Keynes supported), but gave him an opportunity to influence policy by appointing him to the MACMILLAN COMMITTEE on FINANCE AND INDUSTRY and the Economic Advisory Council. Meanwhile he published his academic study *A Treatise on Money* (1930), in which he began to set out his economic theories. In the 1930s he devoted himself more thoroughly to economic theory and less to politics, working with other Cambridge economists. In 1936 he published *The General Theory of Employment, Interest and Money*, which emphasized the centrality of consumption and investment in the workings of the economy, together with the need for economic management. It challenged the classical theoretical belief that economies were self-regulating. The book had little directly to say about policy and had little immediate political impact.

In 1940, during WORLD WAR II, Keynes returned as a top-level adviser at the Treasury. Here he influenced the financing of the war, and also plans for national and international economic reconstruction and full employment after the war. Plans for full employment were embodied in the government's *Employment Policy* white paper of 1944. Keynes was created Baron Keynes of Tilton in 1942. He became increasingly absorbed by planning for the post-war international economy, seeking a replacement for the outdated gold standard. He played a major part in the Bretton Woods conference, 1944, which helped to establish the International Monetary Fund and the World Bank. He advocated liberalization of trade to raise levels of world trade and hence of employment. When the United States abruptly ended the wartime LEND-LEASE agreement with Britain, he negotiated a large loan from the USA and CANADA to help Britain through the transition to a peace-time economy.

Keynes had suffered a major heart attack in 1937 and worked under great pressure through the war. He died suddenly in April 1946. His ideas remained influential among scholars and politicians to the end of the century, although they suffered a period of relative obscurity in the 1970s and 1980s.

FURTHER READING P. Clarke, *The Keynesian Revolution in the Making, 1924–36* (1988); G.C. Peden, *Keynes, The Treasury and British Economic Policy* (1988); R. Skidelsky, *John Maynard Keynes: Hopes Betrayed, 1883–1920* (1983); R. Skidelsky, *John Maynard Keynes: The Economist as Saviour, 1920–1937* (1992).

Kinnock, Neil (Gordon) (1942–), Labour politician; leader of the LABOUR PARTY (1983–92). Born into a working-class family in Tredegar, South WALES, Kinnock was educated at state schools and the University of Wales, Cardiff, where his academic record was undistinguished but his interest in Labour politics developed.

It was at university that he met his future wife, Glenys Parry, who shared his political views. His working life started in the Labour Party, and he was MP for Bedwellty from 1970 to 1994. He was of the left, but not the 'hard left', and remained popular through much of the party. He was elected to the party's National Executive Committee in 1978 and became the party's education spokesman in 1979. He was supported by the patronage of Michael FOOT, whom he succeeded as leader in 1983.

When Kinnock took over the leadership the party was in a poor state. It was split by faction fighting, with a vocal left wing, challenged by the new SOCIAL DEMOCRATIC PARTY and weakened by the decline of manufacturing employment and of the TRADE UNIONS. Kinnock worked, with some success, to reconstruct the party. He attacked the Trotskyite MILITANT group that had influenced sections of the party, started to reform the party organization and to improve its media presentation, and initiated a policy review.

By the time of the 1992 election Labour was committed to a mixed economy and membership of the EUROPEAN UNION (EU), and opposed to unilateral nuclear disarmament (*see* CND). But Labour lost the election. Kinnock could not convince the mass of the electorate that he would lead the country well, and many people were optimistic that John MAJOR would do a better job. Kinnock resigned from the party leadership (being succeeded by John SMITH) and became an EU commissioner.

FURTHER READING R. Harris, *The Making of Neil Kinnock* (1984); C. Hughes and P. Wintour, *Labour Rebuilt: The New Model Party* (1990).

Kitchener, (Horatio) Herbert (1850–1916), commander in the Boer War and war secretary (1914–16) in World War II. Kitchener was born in County Kerry, Ireland, and educated in Switzerland and at the Royal Military Academy, Woolwich. He was, and remained throughout his life, a devout Anglican. In 1870 he was commissioned in the Royal Engineers, served in the MIDDLE EAST and joined the Egyptian army in 1882. He was governor general of Eastern Sudan, 1886–8, then became adjutant general of the Egyptian army and commander in chief in 1892. He reconquered the Sudan after the death of his hero, General Gordon; during the campaign he was shot in the throat and saved his life only by managing to swallow the bullet. The reconquest of the Sudan, culminating in the victory at Omdurman in 1898, made him a national hero, and he was made Baron Kitchener of Khartoum.

In December 1899 Kitchener was sent to SOUTH AFRICA as chief of staff to Lord Roberts in the BOER WAR, taking over as commander in chief in November 1900. He provoked criticism by establishing civilian concentration camps, but his military tactics were successful and he took a conciliatory approach at the peace talks. He boasted that every promotion during the war was given as a reward for active service. He was commander in chief, INDIA, 1902–9, where he introduced important army reforms. In 1909–11 he advised the governments of AUSTRALIA and NEW ZEALAND on defence. In 1911 he became British agent and consul general in Egypt.

Kitchener was in Britain on leave when WORLD WAR I was declared, and reluctantly accepted the post of secretary of state for war. His face became famous when Alfred Leete's drawing of him was reproduced on recruiting posters throughout the British Isles. Like Douglas HAIG he was one of the few to recognize that the war would be long and would require extensive commitment of land forces. He set out immediately to build a large army and raised almost 2.5 million voluntary recruits within 17 months, thus making an important contribution to the ultimate victory. He also achieved increased munitions output, but the indiscriminate military recruitment had removed potential factory workers, and this hindered the capacity of industry to respond to the needs of war. After the loss of 8000 men at the battle of Neuve Chapelle in March 1915 he remarked, chillingly, to LLOYD GEORGE, 'It isn't the men I mind … but I can't replace the shells so easily.' In May 1915 he was widely attacked for the shell shortage (*see also* FRENCH, JOHN). Responsibility for munitions was then transferred to the newly created ministry of munitions, under Lloyd George. Kitchener broadly supported the DARDANELLES and GALLIPOLI campaigns, and his influence waned following these and other setbacks in 1915, though he remained popular in the country. He failed to give a clear lead on CONSCRIPTION when voluntary recruitment fell in 1915. He was uncomfortable in political circles, and devoted his spare time in later life to his porcelain collection and to studying pictures of Italian gardens. He drowned on 5 June 1916 when HMS *Hampshire,* taking him on a mission to Russia, struck a mine off the Orkneys and sank. He never married, and belonged to the Guild of the Holy Standard, whose members pledged themselves to be 'sober, upright and chaste', which, indeed, he was.

FURTHER READING J. Pollock, *Kitchener* (2001); T. Royle, *The Kitchener Enigma* (1985).

Korean War (1950–3), conflict between North Korea and South Korea, in which British units fought with UNITED NATIONS (UN) forces. On 25 June 1950 the Communist People's Democratic Republic of North Korea, backed by the Soviet Union, invaded the separate, non-communist, American-backed state, the Republic of Korea, to the south. The COLD WAR appeared to be heating up dangerously. Seoul, the capital of the Republic of Korea, fell three days later. The Security Council of the UN, boycotted by the USSR, recommended UN states to assist the Republic of Korea to repel the invasion. Eventually 16

nations sent troops to Korea, where they were organized under the command of the US general Douglas MacArthur, the bulk of the forces being American.

The North Koreans had occupied all of the South, except the vital port of Pusan, by the end of August. On 15 September 1950 MacArthur landed American and South Korean marines at Inchon, 320 km (200 miles) behind the North Korean lines, and on the following day launched an offensive from Pusan. The North Koreans hurriedly retreated. In November the People's Republic of China came to the support of North Korea with 180,000 men. The UN troops were forced to retreat and Seoul was captured again in January 1951.

By June 1951 the two sides found themselves in a military stalemate around the 38th parallel, although bitter fighting continued for another two years. Peace talks began in July 1951 and continued for two years at Panmunjom. In 1953 the change of US president from Harry S. Truman to Dwight D. Eisenhower and the death of Stalin led to a relaxation of international tension. An armistice agreement, maintaining a divided Korea, was signed at Panmunjom on 27 July 1953. In the course of the war 142,000 Americans were killed and many more Koreans; about 7000 Commonwealth servicemen died, 749 of them British. The cost of the war to Britain was about £50 million.

FURTHER READING M. Hastings, *The Korean War* (1987); C.A. MacDonald, *Korea: The War before Vietnam* (1986).

Kosovo, region of southern Yugoslavia, mainly inhabited by ethnic Albanians and known by them as Kosova. Its principal town is Pristina. The region contains potentially the richest concentration of minerals in the Balkans. A 1991 Serbian-sponsored census showed that Albanians formed 82% per cent of the population. Under the 1946 constitution of socialist Yugoslavia, Kosovo became an autonomous province within federal Serbia. President

Tito gradually devolved powers to the province, but the revival of Serbian nationalism under Slobodan Milošević from 1987 reversed the process and autonomous rights were rescinded. Serbian refugees from Croatia and Bosnia were settled in the region. The response was a resurgence of Kosovar Albanian nationalism, with the formation of a Kosovo Liberation Army in 1998 and intense fighting against Serb troops. Reports of Serb violence against civilian Kosovans and the failure of attempts to negotiate a settlement led NATO, with the strong support of the British government, to bomb Belgrade and other areas of Serbia for 78 days from April 1999 to force them to withdraw troops from Kosovo.

By the end of the century it was unclear whether this action had been necessary or had had desirable effects, though shortly afterwards Slobodan Milošević was driven from office following an uprising in Serbia. In 2001 he was taken to the Netherlands and indicted before the International War Crimes Tribunal.

FURTHER READING N. Malcolm, *Kosovo: A Short History* (1998).

L

labour exchanges. *See* UNEMPLOYMENT.

labour force. Over the 20th century there was a far-reaching transformation of the nature of work and of the skills of the workforce in Britain. In particular there was a shift from an economy in which manufacturing industry was prominent to one dominated by service industries. Technical change and the growing complexity of work processes were associated with the need for higher levels of skill in the workforce. There was also a major change in the gender composition of the workforce.

The main trends in the first half of the century were that the manufacturing industries expanded and diversified, while COAL MINING and DOMESTIC SERVICE sharply declined. AGRICULTURE had already declined in significance by the beginning of the century, employing only 6.7% of the workforce in 1911. This had declined further to 5% by 1951, while manufacturing grew from 35% of the workforce in 1921 to 38% in 1951. This expansion, however, masked major differences among industries: between 1931 and 1951 employment in chemicals grew by 115% and in metal industries by 104%, while textiles and clothing, the dominant manufacturing industries at the beginning of the century, employing about 40% of the workforce, fell sharply. In the second half of the cen-

tury manufacturing contracted. By 1991 only 21% of the total workforce of Great Britain was employed in manufacturing. The decline was spread fairly evenly over all categories of industry, though coal mining continued to fall particularly sharply. At the same time service industries grew from employing about 50% of employees in 1966 to 67% in 1991. This was partly due to the expansion of the WELFARE STATE: employment in EDUCATION rose by 33% between 1966 and 1991 and in the health sector by 60% (*see* NATIONAL HEALTH SERVICE). But financial and business services saw the fastest rise (136%), followed by leisure services (101%). These trends continued in the last decade of the century. The patterns of change were comparable with those of other European countries.

The changing structure of occupations brought about an increasingly specialized division of labour. In 1881 the census listed 12,000 different occupations; in 1981 the number had risen to 23,000. The broad pattern of change was that in the first half of the century the most striking development was the growth in the number of clerical workers, who comprised 4.5% of employees in 1911 but 10.4% in 1951. The increase was especially marked for women: in 1931 men comprised 56% of clerical workers, but by 1951 their share had fallen to 41%. Professional work also expanded, especially among the 'lower' (i.e. less independent, less well paid and predominantly female) professions, such as nursing and teaching. These occupations as a share of the total workforce rose from 3.1% in 1911 to 4.7% in 1951. The 'higher' (i.e. better paid, more independent and predominantly male) professions, such as accountancy and engineering, rose from 1% to 1.9% over the same period, while the number of managers and administrators grew from 3.6% in 1921 to 5.5% in 1951. Among manual workers (three-quarters of the workforce in 1911 and still two-thirds in 1951) the numbers of skilled and semi-skilled workers remained stable, while the numbers of unskilled workers rose. Over the second half of the century manual employment declined to 38% by 1991. Clerical work continued to grow, but slowly, while the numbers at all levels in professional and managerial employment tripled. By 1991 professional and managerial occupations comprised 33% of the whole workforce. The change has been associated with a rise in the general skill levels of the workforce.

The 20th century witnessed a major shift in the gender composition of the workforce. More women entered paid employment, in a wider range of occupations. There remained throughout the century, however, substantial gender segregation in types of employment. Women were as likely at the end as at the beginning of the century to be working predominantly with women; men became somewhat less likely to be working in a segregated environment. The participation in the paid labour force of males aged 16 or above fell steadily from 93.5% in 1911 to 71.3% in 1998, due, above all, to increasing numbers remaining in education until later ages and to more widespread and earlier retirement. The participation of females in the same age group rose from 35.3% to 53.8%, though they also had increasing access to education and to retirement. The increase was greatest among married women, especially those aged 35–54, 10% of whom were recorded as economically active in 1911, compared with 72% in 1991. This increase moved especially fast in the second half of the century. Over this period the proportion of women in manual occupations fell faster than that of men, while clerical work effectively became feminized. The number of women in the higher professions and in senior management positions rose, but they remained a decided minority in such occupations.

The increased participation of married women in the labour force in the second half of the century was associated with an increase in part-time working: 11% of all female employees worked part time in 1951, 45.6% in 1998, though some had more than one part-time job. The whole of the increase in women's employment over the last three decades of the century can be accounted for by the growth of part-time work. Such occupations were especially concentrated in the service sector (92%, compared with 6% in manufacturing), in everything to hotel and restaurant work to the education and health sectors.

An unexpected change at the end of the century was in the number of self-employed workers: between 1979 and 1998 the numbers rose from 10% of employed men to 16%, and 3.3% of employed women to 7.2%. This had much to do with large institutions of all kinds reducing their core workforce and 'outsourcing' a variety of tasks in order to reduce costs and increase flexibility, but also arose from the capacity of increasing numbers of people with new skills (for example in information technology) to work independently. There was also an increase in the number of workers on short-term contracts.

Although it was widely predicted in the 1960s that technological change would reduce working hours, average hours worked, after declining steadily through the century, stabilized in the 1980s and then tended to rise. It was widely believed at the end of the century that a once predominant pattern of a 'job for life' had been replaced by increased occupational insecurity. Rather, an insecurity once normal for manual workers spread to some (though by no means all) white-collar occupations, the appearance of change being heightened by the increased presence of women, especially as part-time workers, in the labour force.

FURTHER READING D. Gallie, 'The Labour
Force' in A.H. Halsey and J. Webb, *20th
Century British Social Trends* (2000), 281–323;
G. Routh, *Occupations of the People of Great
Britain* (1987).

Labour Party, principal party of the left in Britain.
The Labour Party emerged in 1906, following the
GENERAL ELECTION of that year, when the LABOUR
REPRESENTATION COMMITTEE formally adopted the
name 'Labour Party' and elected Keir HARDIE as
chairman of the parliamentary party. For the first
time Labour had gained a significant number of
seats in the election – 29, shortly to increase to 30,
when a LIB-LAB member joined the parliamentary
party. This success was partly due to the secret pact
(known subsequently as the 'Lib-Lab pact') made
in 1903 between the Labour and LIBERAL parties
before the election that they would not run candidates against one another where there was a
danger that they might split the vote and enable a
Conservative to win. However, the numbers were
still too small for Labour to have a big impact in
Parliament, and Labour remained at a disadvan-
tage while many working men and all women
lacked the vote. All the same, Labour did help to
persuade the Liberal government to introduce
changes in TRADE-UNION and social legislation such
as the Trade Disputes Act, 1906 (*see* TAFF VALE
JUDGEMENT), and OLD-AGE PENSIONS.

In the two general elections of January–
February and December 1910, Labour increased
its representation in the COMMONS to 40 and 42
respectively, owing mainly to a decision of Lib-Lab
MPs (for the most part representatives of coal
miners) to join the Parliamentary Labour Party.
Following the elections Labour, together with the
Irish nationalists (*see* IRISH NATIONAL PARTY), held
the balance of power between the Liberals and the
Conservatives. This enabled Labour to bargain
with the ruling Liberals for legislative concessions.
In particular, Labour agreed to support the National Insurance Bill, 1911 (*see* WELFARE STATE) in
return for legislation that granted salaries to MPs

for the first time (from 1912) and the reversal (in
the Trade Union Act, 1913) of the Osborne judgement, a decision of the law courts in 1909 that
judged trade-union contributions to political parties to be illegal, which seriously threatened the
financial position of the Labour Party.

Hardie was succeeded as party chairman by
Arthur HENDERSON (1908–10), who in turn was
succeeded by George Barnes (1910–11). In 1911
Ramsay MACDONALD took over the chair. The party
was divided over support for WORLD WAR I, and
Macdonald, who opposed the war, resigned in
1914, and was replaced by Henderson. The war
period strengthened the party's national support,
partly because the Liberal Party became divided
after LLOYD GEORGE ousted ASQUITH as prime minister in 1916. A small number of Liberal MPs transferred their allegiance to Labour, though few
retained their seats after the war. Henderson joined
the war CABINET, but left the government in 1917
and turned his energies to building a strong party
organization and drafting its first constitution. The
latter was done in consultation with Sidney WEBB
and the trade unions and was adopted in 1918 (*see*
CLAUSE FOUR). Labour now had a centralized
framework and consisted of members who joined
local, constituency-based branches rather than, as
before, 'affiliated organizations', such as trade
unions, the FABIAN SOCIETY or the INDEPENDENT
LABOUR PARTY. An annual conference voted on
policy and elected the National Executive Committee (NEC). This gave great power to the
unions, whose representatives voted at the conference in proportion to the number of their members, and thus outnumbered the votes of individual
members of constituency parties. In 1918 the party
also adopted a policy statement, *Labour and the
New Social Order*, which was drafted by Sidney
Webb. This laid down the policies the party was
to follow until the 1950s, including the establishment of a national minimum of living standards,
substantial public ownership, educational reform
and redistribution of wealth and income.

In 1918 Labour also benefited from the

extension of the vote to include all adult men and most women over 30. In the general election of 1918 Labour's votes increased by about 2 million. In 1922 it gained a further 2 million votes and won 142 seats. Ramsay MacDonald, who had done much to foster the popular appeal of the party, became party leader. In the election of December 1923 Labour won more seats than the Liberals. When the Conservatives were defeated in the Commons over TARIFF REFORM in January 1924, Labour formed its first government. Since Labour had a minority of seats in the Commons (191, while the Liberals had 159 and the Conservatives 258) it had limited room for manoeuvre, but it did have some achievements, such as a major HOUSING Act. It lost the election of October 1924 after a virulent campaign in which Conservatives and their supporters sought, without justification, to associate Labour with the communism of the Soviet Union (*see* ZINOVIEV LETTER).

In May 1929 Labour returned to government, again with a minority of seats (288, while the Conservatives had 260 and the Liberals 59). It faced a worsening economic crisis to which neither it nor its opponents had a convincing response (*see* GREAT CRASH; UNEMPLOYMENT). The international financial crisis of 1931 put the government under international pressure to cut government spending, including unemployment benefits. MacDonald as prime minister and Philip SNOWDEN as chancellor agreed to the cuts, but were opposed by the bulk of the party. MacDonald, Snowden and a handful of other Labour members formed a NATIONAL GOVERNMENT with the Conservatives and Liberals in August 1931, on the grounds that the scale of the crisis was such that it required a coalition government to deal with it. No government of a major power affected by the 1931 crisis survived for long after it hit.

Labour suffered a serious defeat in the election of 1931. Thereafter it revived, doing well in local elections, working more closely with the unions and increasing its votes and seats (from 52 to 154) in the election of 1935. George LANSBURY

had become leader in 1931, but in 1935, as a pacifist, he disagreed with the majority of the party about rearmament and resigned. He was succeeded by Clement ATTLEE.

Labour made further gains in WORLD WAR II. It joined CHURCHILL's coalition government in May 1940 and was given a disproportionate number of government positions, including the most powerful domestic ministries. The success of Attlee, BEVIN and MORRISON, among others, in the wartime government, together with popular hopes that Labour would bring about better conditions than those of the 1930s (for which the Conservatives were widely held responsible), led to Labour winning a majority of 146 seats over other parties in the election of July 1945. The government prioritized rebuilding the economy, in which it had much success, though this entailed continuing RATIONING and controls, which alienated some voters. It introduced a number of innovative social policies – including the NATIONAL HEALTH SERVICE (NHS) – which were described collectively as a WELFARE STATE. It also carried out a programme of NATIONALIZATION: the BANK OF ENGLAND (1946), civil AVIATION (1946), cable and wireless (1946), COAL MINING (1947), RAILWAYS (1947), electricity (1947), road transport (1947), gas (1948) and iron and STEEL (1949). By 1950 about 20% of the economy was in the public sector. There were significant steps towards DECOLONIZATION: INDIA and Pakistan became independent in 1947, BURMA in 1948. There were a series of economic crises in 1947 worsened by a very severe winter (*see* CRIPPS, STAFFORD; DALTON, HUGH) and high defence costs.

The economy was recovering by the time of the election of 1950, but Labour was returned with a majority of only six seats in an election in which the votes cast were the highest of any election in British history, with a turnout of 84% of the electorate, and in which the votes were very closely divided between Labour and the Conservatives. Labour's leading figures had had ten exhausting years in government. They were ageing and ailing. The party had fulfilled most of the objectives it had set out since its foundation and was somewhat directionless and increasingly divided. Hugh GAITSKELL as chancellor of the exchequer imposed charges on certain NHS services, which provoked the resignation of Aneurin BEVAN, Harold WILSON and John Freeman, a junior minister. In October 1951 Labour called another election at which it polled more votes than the Conservatives in a total poll only slightly lower than in 1950, but it won 26 fewer seats.

Labour was then in opposition for 13 years. For much of this time it was occupied by division and recrimination, initially between a left-wing group around Bevan and a right-wing group around Gaitskell. In the election of May 1955 the Conservatives gained a more decisive victory. In December Attlee retired and was succeeded by Gaitskell, who defeated Bevan and Morrison. Gaitskell and Bevan then made a rapprochement, but the party remained divided, especially over nuclear disarmament (*see* CAMPAIGN FOR NUCLEAR DISARMAMENT) and the extent of nationalization. The Conservatives won the election of October 1959 with a still larger majority. Labour did not appear to be in touch with an increasingly affluent society.

In 1963 Gaitskell died unexpectedly of a rare viral disease and was succeeded by Wilson. The economy was faltering, the Conservatives were divided and in 1963 they acquired an apparently ineffectual new leader in Sir Alec DOUGLAS-HOME. The election of October 1964 gave Labour a majority of four seats. It set out to plan the reconstruction of the economy and to expand the welfare state. Wilson called another election in March 1966 and won a majority of 98 seats. This government faced increasing criticism from the left, much of it unjustified, for failing to be sufficiently radical in its social and economic policies. It faced economic difficulties owing above all to balance-of-payments problems, but had successes in encouraging new technological initiatives. Roy JENKINS as home secretary initiated or supported an impressive series of reforms affecting personal life, from the legal-

ization of ABORTION to the abolition of theatre CENSORSHIP, the abolition of CAPITAL PUNISHMENT and the reform of laws concerning homosexuality (*see* SEXUALITY, OFFICIAL REGULATION OF). There were major reforms and expansion of the education system at all levels (*see* CROSLAND, ANTHONY), housing was expanded and most aspects of the welfare system improved. EQUAL PAY for men and women was introduced in 1970. But Labour lost the election of June 1970. Again there were divisions in opposition, notably over the Britain's entry to the EUROPEAN ECONOMIC COMMUNITY.

Labour returned to power as a minority government in February 1974, then achieved a small majority in October 1974. In the aftermath of the OIL SHOCK it faced, like many other governments of the day, an economic crisis to which it had no clear solution (*see* HEALEY, DENIS). The party was divided between left and right and was at odds with the trade unions. In March 1976 Wilson unexpectedly resigned and was succeeded by James CALLAGHAN. By 1978 the economy appeared to be improving, but the failure of the government to reach an agreement with the unions caused widespread strikes (especially in the public sector) in the 'winter of discontent', as it was labelled by a press increasingly hostile to Labour. At the same time referendums in SCOTLAND and WALES on devolution did not gain enough votes to achieve implementation (*see* HOME RULE). This was a serious blow to the government, which had placed all its support behind the proposals. Labour lost the election of March 1979. Callaghan resigned as leader and was replaced by Michael FOOT.

The party again fell into bitter conflict between left and right (defined mainly by support for or opposition to nationalization). This led in 1981 to a breakaway by prominent right-wingers to form the SOCIAL DEMOCRATIC PARTY. This was successful enough for long enough to split the anti-Conservative vote in the elections of 1983 and 1987, so helping to keep Labour in opposition. After the election of June 1983 Foot resigned and was replaced by Neil KINNOCK, who gradually and often painfully diminished the conflicts by expelling some of the extreme left (*see* MILITANT) and by establishing better relationships with the unions. He also began to improve the party machinery, reformed the internal voting system and undertook a major review of policy. In 1987 and 1992 he ran more effective though unsuccessful election campaigns. The defeat of 1992 was unexpected. Kinnock immediately resigned and John SMITH was elected leader. He had begun to take further the overhaul of policy and organization when he died of a heart attack in 1994. He was succeeded by Tony BLAIR, who led the party to its largest victory ever in 1997. By the end of the century it was too soon to evaluate the effects of the changes introduced by 'New Labour', as Blair sought to name the party he strove to modernize, but he returned to office with a second landslide majority in the election of June 2001 with a clear mandate to improve public services, especially hospitals and schools.

For further details on the Labour Party see entries on its most prominent leaders through the century: Keir HARDIE (1906–8); Arthur HENDERSON (1908–10, 1914–17,1931–2); J. Ramsay MACDONALD (1911–14, 1922–31); George LANSBURY (1932–5); Clement ATTLEE (1935–55); Hugh GAITSKELL (1955–63); Harold WILSON (1963–76); James CALLAGHAN (1976–80); Michael FOOT (1980–3); Neil KINNOCK (1983–92); John SMITH (1992–4); Tony BLAIR (1994–).

SEE ALSO GENERAL ELECTIONS.

FURTHER READING H. Pelling and A. Reid, *A Short History of the Labour Party* (11th edn, 1997); D. Tanner, P. Thane, N. Tiratsoo (eds.), *The Labour Party: The First Hundred Years, 1900–2000* (2000); A. Thorpe, *A History of the British Labour Party* (2nd edn, 2001).

Labour Representation Committee (LRC),

organization formed in February 1900 at a conference in London of TRADE UNIONS, COOPERATIVE societies and socialist groups, including the INDEPENDENT LABOUR PARTY (ILP). The aim of the LRC was to establish a distinct group in Parliament representing the working-class interest, though prepared to cooperate with other parties. Trade-union support was impelled by recent threats to their legal rights. Unions that supported the LRC were initially of the 'new', general and less skilled variety, representing about one-quarter of all trade unionists; they tended to be more radical than the older craft unions. In the following years, however, more unions affiliated to the LRC. The LRC embraced a wide range of views, from the Liberalism of many trade unionists to the socialism of many in the ILP; but the 1900 conference refused to endorse a commitment to class struggle, and in consequence the Social Democratic Federation, which defined itself as Marxist, withdrew. The conference was dominated by the ILP leader Keir HARDIE. He was already a member of Parliament and was re-elected, together with only one other LRC candidate, in the election of 1900. This inauspicious beginning was not surprising given that the election occurred in the middle of the BOER WAR; wartime elections tend to favour governments in power. With limited funds and with many of its potential voters still deprived of the franchise – but with the aid of a secret electoral pact with the Liberals (*see* LABOUR PARTY) – the LRC improved its performance in the election of 1906, gaining 29 seats, whereupon it named itself the Labour Party.

FURTHER READING F. Bealey and H. Pelling, *Labour and Politics, 1900–1906: A History of the Labour Representation Committee* (1958).

Lady Chatterley's Lover case (1960). *See* CENSORSHIP.

Lancaster House agreement. *See* ZIMBABWE.

land question. Resistance to the concentration of land ownership in the hands of a wealthy minority was an important political issue in 19th-century Britain. It continued to be significant in Britain and Ireland (*see* IRISH LAND ACTS) in the early part of the 20th century, but then diminished in importance. In 1919 the Forestry Commission was established as a government department with a brief to promote afforestation and timber production. In the same year the Land Settlement Act and the Land Settlement (Scotland) Act encouraged local authorities to provide land to enable people to take up farming (partly as a means of maximizing employment and also to maintain food production in peacetime) and to provide urban dwellers with allotments (small parcels of land suitable for growing vegetables, for example). It was not obligatory for local authorities to comply with this legislation, though allotments were widely established. In 1926 the Small Holdings and Allotments Act ordered county councils to provide smallholdings for people wanting to settle on the land, with central government approval; this had limited effect. Thereafter, in highly urbanized Britain the land ceased to be an issue of central political importance, though it continued to be an issue in the Scottish Highlands and Islands. There were campaigns also more widely in Britain for public access to private land, primarily by walkers (*see* ENVIRONMENTALISM).

Lansbury, George (1859–1940), Labour politician; party leader (1932–5). Born a working-class Londoner, Lansbury became a manual worker. Before the age of 30 he had six children and was accustomed to poverty, although his wife – whose father owned a small saw mill and veneer works (for which Lansbury worked in the 1880s) – was somewhat more prosperous. He became active in LIBERAL politics in the 1880s, converting to socialism by 1892. He became and remained an active member of the CHURCH OF ENGLAND. He was elected to the POOR LAW board in Poplar, east London, where he lived, and with other socialists he campaigned to humanize the treatment of people who were poor because of UNEMPLOYMENT and other causes, a campaign he continued into the 1920s. In 1921, as mayor of Poplar, he led a campaign for cross-subsidy between richer and poorer London boroughs for support of the poor, which led to him and other councillors being briefly imprisoned before the law was changed.

In 1910 Lansbury became LABOUR member of Parliament for Bow and Bromley in east London. In 1912 he gave up his seat to force a by-election on the issue of women's suffrage (*see* SUFFRAGISTS; SUFFRAGETTES). He sought to force Labour to refuse to support the Liberal government until it gave votes to women, even if this brought the Conservatives – who were even more opposed to women's suffrage – to power. He disregarded the majority belief in the party that this tactic was futile, and lost his seat in the by-election.

In 1911 Lansbury had become editor of the new left-wing newspaper, the *Daily Herald*, which gave him a platform for criticism of the Liberal government and for promoting a libertarian, anti-statist socialism. He was a pacifist in WORLD WAR I. He returned to Parliament in 1922, again for Bow and Bromley, which he represented until his death. He refused a minor position in the 1924 Labour government, but in 1929 he became first commissioner for works. He supported the majority of the party in the crisis of 1931 over the formation of the NATIONAL GOVERNMENT, and was the only member of the previous cabinet to retain his seat for Labour in the election of that year. He then became party leader. He resigned in 1935 after disagreeing with the majority of the party about the need for rearmament in the face of the threat of war; he was succeeded by ATTLEE. Lansbury remained a pacifist and met Hitler and Mussolini in 1937 in a vain attempt to avert war. He welcomed Neville CHAMBERLAIN's apparent settlement with Hitler at MUNICH (*see* APPEASEMENT).
FURTHER READING R. Postgate, *The Life of George Lansbury* (1951); J. Schneer, *George Lansbury* (1990).

Laski, Harold (Joseph) (1893–1950), socialist political theorist. Born in Manchester, Laski was educated at Manchester Grammar School and

New College, Oxford. His earliest major writings, *Studies in the Problem of Sovereignty* (1917) and *Authority in the Modern State* (1919), were written while he was a lecturer at Harvard Law School in the United States. These publications established his reputation as a pluralist critic of the modern state. His support for a police strike in Boston in 1919 ended his career in the USA and he returned to Britain to teach at the London School of Economics, where he was promoted to a professorship at the age of 33.

During the 1920s Laski increasingly came to believe that firm state action was necessary to bring about change, and he became active in the LABOUR PARTY and the FABIAN SOCIETY, though in the 1930s he became pessimistic about the future of parliamentary democracy. He came to combine a form of Marxist analysis of the sources of social inequality with a deep commitment to liberal values and hostility to violence. His views were expressed in *The State in Theory and Practice* (1935), *The Rise of European Liberalism* (1936) and *Parliamentary Government in England* (1938). He believed that socialist reform (i.e. greater social and economic equality, political democracy and pluralism) was essential for the preservation of liberal civilization. In 1936 he was one of the founders of the LEFT BOOK CLUB, which sought to make radical ideas widely accessible. He strongly supported WORLD WAR II and opposed fascism, and during the war he sought to maintain unity with the Soviet Union in order to influence the Soviet government and the British government to bring about essential reform. He was highly influential in the Labour Party during the 1930s and World War II, but his influence waned during the COLD WAR owing to his belief that there was something to be said for and against both sides – a view that was unpopular in powerful circles. He became disillusioned with both the USA and the USSR, and criticized the Labour Party for its pro-Americanism and its attitude to the crisis in PALESTINE and the formation of the state of Israel.

FURTHER READING I. Kramnick and

B. Sheerman, *Harold Laski: A Life on the Left, 1893–1950* (1993).

Law, (Andrew) Bonar (1858–1923), Conservative politician; PRIME MINISTER (1922–3). Law was born in Canada, the son of a Presbyterian minister whose family had come from Ulster. He was educated in Scotland and began his career in the Glasgow iron trade. He was unexpectedly elected to Parliament for Glasgow Blackfriars in the patriotic atmosphere of the 'khaki election' of 1900 during the BOER WAR. He proved to be an effective debater and was appointed parliamentary secretary to the Board of Trade in 1902. In the GENERAL ELECTION of 1906 he switched to the safer seat of Dulwich, south London, which he represented until 1910, in a party disrupted both by its poor performance in the election and by divisions over TARIFF REFORM. In December 1910 he opted to stand for a near-hopeless seat in the FREE TRADE capital, Manchester, and duly lost, but captured the seat of Bootle, on Merseyside, in a by-election in 1911. In 1911 Arthur BALFOUR resigned as party leader, and Law emerged as the compromise successor following a deadlock between Walter Long and Austen CHAMBERLAIN. His career in the next few years was mainly notable for his vehement opposition to HOME RULE for IRELAND and his encouragement of Ulster separatist militancy. This was an opportunity to restore Conservative Party unity but it appeared to condone conflict.

At the outbreak of war in 1914 Law accepted the suspension of partisan politics. In May 1915 he took office as colonial secretary in the new coalition government led by ASQUITH. In 1916 he supported the revolt against Asquith's premiership and, having declined GEORGE V's offer of the premiership, became CHANCELLOR OF THE EXCHEQUER and leader of the House of COMMONS at the invitation of David LLOYD GEORGE. He was lord privy seal and leader of the House of Commons (1919–21). In 1919 he became lord privy seal, while continuing as leader of the House. He resigned from the government and his leadership of the party in March 1921. His wife had died in 1909, two sons were killed in World War I and he was suffering from throat cancer. However, he supported the Conservative Party revolt against Lloyd George in October 1922. He resumed the party leadership and became prime minister, sick and morose though he was. In May 1923 he resigned (being succeeded by Stanley BALDWIN) and died five months later.

FURTHER READING R. Blake, *The Unknown Prime Minister: The Life and Times of Andrew Bonar Law, 1858–1923* (1955); J. Ramsden, *The Age of Balfour and Baldwin 1902–1940* (1978).

Lawrence, D(avid) H(erbert) (1885–1930), novelist, one of the most important figures in English literature in the 20th century. Lawrence was born at Eastwood, Nottinghamshire, one of five children of an ex-schoolteacher mother and a semi-literate father who worked as a coal miner for more than fifty years. Lawrence grew up in considerable poverty and was often in poor health as a child. His parents were unhappily married and Lawrence became particularly attached to his mother, who was determined to keep him out of the mines and encouraged his education. He gained a scholarship to Nottingham High School but had to leave at 15 to take a clerical job owing to family poverty. He then became a pupil-teacher and from 1906, having worked to save the £20 fee, attended Nottingham University College to study for a teacher's certificate. During this time he formed a close friendship with Jessie Chambers, a farmer's daughter, on whom he was to base the character of Miriam in his novel *Sons and Lovers* (1913). She sent four of his poems to the prestigious *English Review* edited by Ford Madox Ford. They were published in 1909, followed by a short story in 1911. He became disillusioned with university life, then wrote the first draft of a novel 'Laetitia', which was published as *The White Peacock* (1911) and was dedicated to his mother who had died of cancer in 1910. In 1908 Lawrence had taken a job

at an elementary school in Croydon, Surrey, where he excelled as an art teacher. He was so upset by his mother's death that he was ill during much of what he called 'the sick year', 1911, and was advised to give up teaching, which he did readily.

Lawrence continued to write and in 1912 he published *The Trespasser*, based on an episode in the life of his friend Helen Corke and her music teacher, who killed himself. In 1913 he completed and published *Sons and Lovers*, a fictionalized autobiographical account of his early years, begun in 1910. He was later to think that he had been unjustly harsh to his father in the novel. Before its publication he broke his engagement to Jessie Chambers. In 1912 he met Frieda Weekly, *née* von Richthofen, the German-born wife of his French professor. They married in 1914, after eloping to Germany, and embarked upon a nomadic, tempestuous and impecunious existence. During the tumultuous period before the marriage Lawrence worked on a novel about three generations of women, which became two novels: *The Rainbow* (1915) and *Women in Love* (published in America in 1920 and in Britain in 1921). *The Rainbow*, published during World War I, aroused hostility due to its frankness about sexual passion and its heroine's opposition to war and nationalism. It was seized by the police and declared obscene, and in consequence the publisher withdrew it.

Lawrence was physically unfit for war service. He and his wife lived in Britain through the war, where they were persecuted as suspected German agents, though he did make literary and intellectual friendships, for example with Aldous Huxley and Katherine Mansfield. In 1917 he published a volume of poetry, *Look! We Have Come Through*. He could publish no novels during the war, though he published four volumes of poetry in all and a travel book, *Twilight in Italy* (1916). He also completed *The Lost Girl* (published in 1920), which received the James Tait Black Memorial Prize, the only public honour he received during his lifetime. He also wrote a novella about lesbianism, *The Fox* (1922).

In 1919, as soon as they could after the war, Lawrence and Frieda left Britain for Italy. Thereafter, for the rest of his life, Lawrence returned to Britain only for brief visits. Publication of *Women in Love* was delayed because of the reaction to *The Rainbow* and even in 1920 it had to survive an unsuccessful prosecution for obscenity in New York. In the early 1920s Lawrence published some nonfiction works: *Movements in European History* (1921), *Psychoanalysis and the Unconscious* (1921) and *Fantasia of the Unconscious* (1922). He also began, and published in 1922, *Aaron's Rod*, the first of three 'leadership' novels, which explore the connection between politics and personal relationships. The others were *Kangaroo* (1923), written in Australia, and *The Plumed Serpent* (1926), which he regarded as his most important novel, written in Mexico. In 1922 he published a volume of short stories, *England, My England*. In 1923 he also published a work of criticism, *Studies in American Literature*, and he continued to produce travel books: *Sea and Sardinia* (1921), *Mornings in Mexico* (1927) and the novella *St Mawr* (1925), which records his response to the American southwest.

Lawrence was struggling with constant anxiety about money, poor health and a fraught marriage. He dreamed of establishing an ideal community in Mexico. However, while in Mexico in 1924 he became seriously ill and was diagnosed as having an advanced case of tuberculosis with only a few years to live. He and Frieda returned to live in Italy, near Florence. There he wrote *Lady Chatterley's Lover*, two earlier versions of which have been published posthumously. This story of a love affair between Lady Chatterley and a gamekeeper was regarded as more infamous even than *The Rainbow*, and was condemned for its sexual frankness and violation of social norms. It was privately printed in Italy in 1928 and only illegal, smuggled copies were available in Britain for thirty years until an unexpurgated version was finally allowed to be published (*see* CENSORSHIP).

Lawrence's remarkable output continued even as he was dying. He produced more short stories and poetry, a travel book, *Etruscan Places* (1932), and *The Man Who Died* (1929), a novella about the sexuality of Jesus, originally called *The Escaped Cock*. Throughout he combined a commitment to frankness about sexuality with a mystical approach to sexual relationships and a stern moralism and belief in social order. He also combined a profound idealism with a dislike of abstraction.

FURTHER READING H.T. Moore, *The Priest of Love: A Life of D.H. Lawrence* (1974).

Lawrence, Stephen (1974–93), black sixth-form student from south London who at the age of 18 was stabbed to death in Eltham, south London, on 22 April 1993, after he and a friend were set upon by a gang of white youths. Although the youths had used racist language during the attack, the POLICE initially denied that the murder was a racist one. Dissatisfied with police conduct of the investigation, and the way in which they were being treated, Lawrence's parents, Doreen and Neville, began to voice their suspicions that racism within the police force was undermining their hopes to see their son's killers brought to justice.

In May 1993 Doreen and Neville Lawrence met Nelson Mandela, who made a public statement of support for their case. A day later a number of arrests were made in connection with the attack. Two of those arrested, Neil Acourt and Luke Knight, were charged with Lawrence's murder, but in July 1993 the Crown Prosecution Service (CPS) dropped the charges. The investigation continued into the next year, and a second police investigation was begun, but no further charges were made. An internal review of the case (subsequently condemned by the MacPherson Inquiry) began in 1993, found no evidence that the police had mishandled the investigation and was particularly critical of the attitude and behaviour of the Lawrence family.

In 1995 the Lawrence family began a private prosecution against Acourt, Knight and a third associate, Gary Dobson. Two others were also charged, but the case against them was dropped (owing to lack of evidence) before it came to trial. The trial began at the Old Bailey in April 1996, but soon collapsed. In the following February the inquest into Stephen Lawrence's death, twice adjourned, returned a verdict of unlawful killing in a racist assault undertaken by a gang of white youths. The following day pictures of the five suspects were published by the *Daily Mail*, under the headline 'Murderers', and the Police Complaints Authority began an investigation into the family's formal complaint about the original police investigation.

In July 1997 the new Labour home secretary, Jack STRAW, announced a public inquiry into the affair, chaired by Sir William MacPherson. The inquiry ran from March until November the following year, and MacPherson's report, published in February 1999, concluded that the 'investigation was marred by a combination of professional incompetence, institutional racism and a failure of leadership by senior officers'. 'Institutional racism' was defined in the report as 'the collective failure of an organization to provide an appropriate and professional service to people because of their colour, culture or ethnic origin'. The report made a number of wide-ranging recommendations for government policy, police and CPS procedure and recruitment as well as more general strategies to reduce 'institutionalized racism' in public services. **FURTHER READING** *The Stephen Lawrence Inquiry – Report of an Inquiry by Sir William MacPherson of Cluny* (1999).

Lawrence, (Arabella) Susan (1871–1947), Labour politician, one of the first female Labour MPs. Lawrence studied mathematics at University College, London, and Newnham College, Cambridge. She was a member of London County Council (Municipal Reform candidate), 1910–12, and then for Labour, 1913–28. She became a Labour member of Poplar Borough Council in 1919, and was Labour MP for East Ham North, 1923–4, 1926–31. She was parliamentary secretary to the

Ministry of Health, 1929–31, and chair of the LABOUR PARTY, 1929–30.

Lawrence, T(homas) E(dward) (1888–1935), soldier, writer and impossibly romantic figure, popularly known as 'Lawrence of Arabia' after his wartime exploits in the MIDDLE EAST. Lawrence was born in North Wales in 1888, the illegitimate son of a Scottish-born governess and an Anglo-Irish baronet. After brief stays in Scotland and the north of France, the family settled in Oxford, where Lawrence attended Oxford High School and later Jesus College, Oxford. Intellectually very bright, it was during his undergraduate years that he began to foster his interest in the Middle East seriously. He made his first trip there in 1909 in order to conduct research for a thesis on Crusader castles, which helped earn him first-class honours in history. Subsequent visits saw him engaged in archaeological work as he received funding to conduct research towards a BLit at Oxford.

While Lawrence was on one of his trips WORLD WAR I broke out. His remarkable knowledge of both the history and the culture of the Middle East led to his being appointed to the officer corps of the British ARMY (he attained the rank of colonel), and he undertook intelligence work with the Arab Bureau in Egypt. In 1916 his talents led his superiors to appoint him British military adviser to Prince Faisal (later the ruler of Iraq), who was leading the Arabs in rebellion against the Turks. Lawrence worked with Faisal in the training of the Arab forces, which most famously captured the port of Aqaba on the Red Sea in 1917. Lawrence's daring desert exploits and the fact that he had 'gone native' (he was often pictured in Arab dress) made him a romantic wartime hero overnight.

After the war Lawrence represented Arab interests at the Paris Peace Conference of 1919 and fought to obtain European pledges for Arab independence. However, he was frustrated by the lack of response to his efforts. In 1921 he worked briefly in the Colonial Office as an adviser on

Middle Eastern affairs. In 1922 he took the unexpected decision to enlist, under a different name, in the ROYAL AIR FORCE as an aircraftsman. He served in the RAF under the name J.H. Ross in 1922, and in the Royal Tank Corps as T.E. Shaw from 1923 to 1925, when he returned to the RAF. It has been suggested that his pseudonymous enlistment stemmed from a desire to escape the fame that now followed him, but the men he served with later reported that they were all well aware of his true identity. Despite his attempts at anonymity, his memoir of his years in Middle East, *The Seven Pillars of Wisdom*, was published in 1926 and went on to become a bestseller. Lawrence was returned by the RAF from India to England in 1929, and thereafter worked with sea planes on the English Channel and North Sea. He was discharged in 1935 and thereafter lived a solitary life in a small cottage at Clouds Hill, Dorset, but met an untimely death shortly afterwards in a motorcycle accident. A British hero in his lifetime, the legend of 'Lawrence of Arabia' later went on to capture the imagination of the world with the release of David Lean's 1962 film starring Peter O'Toole as Lawrence.

FURTHER READING J. Wilson, *Lawrence of Arabia: The Authorized Biography of T.E. Lawrence* (1990).

League of Coloured Peoples. *See* IMMIGRATION.

League of Nations, international organization, a forerunner of the UNITED NATIONS. It was conceived by Woodrow Wilson, the US president, during and after World War I. After extensive talks in 1919, the League officially came into being with 58 member states on 16 January 1920. Its primary purpose was to prevent another world war like the one Europe had just endured, and indeed to mediate in any kind of conflict among its members, through diplomacy and economic pressure.

The League of Nations was crippled from the beginning, however, by two factors. First, it was born as part of the treaty of VERSAILLES, and for that reason was resented by the vanquished nations of World War I. Second, it did not count all the great powers among its members. Initially, the only major powers to join were Britain and France. Germany was excluded until 1926 and then joined half-heartedly; however, Hitler sneered at the League and its association with the treaty of Versailles, and Germany withdrew just nine years later. The Soviet Union was suspicious of the League's domination by countries from the capitalist West and did not join until 1934. Most damaging was the fact that, despite the League being the brainchild of Woodrow Wilson, he could not persuade the US Senate to ratify American membership. The lack of American participation from the beginning alarmed the British government. Some historians have suggested that without US involvement the question of British membership was in doubt for some time. LLOYD GEORGE was known to support the idea of the League publicly but thought little of it privately.

The League did have some modest successes, though these were mainly in social and economic arenas rather than in politics. It established an International Labour Office in Geneva and a Permanent Court of International Justice at the Hague, institutions that still operate in a similar form today. It also undertook action to combat global issues as varied as health, communications and the drugs trade. However, the League's tragic flaw was its lack of any real clout when it came to combating aggression on the part of the major powers. It had no military resources of its own, and so resorted to the imposition of economic sanctions on any member state that violated the terms of its membership. These were very difficult to enforce, however, particularly with so many major powers outside the League. It met, and failed, its first major tests in the 1930s, when it was unable to do anything about the Japanese invasion of Manchuria in 1931 or the Italian invasion of Ethiopia in 1935 (*see* ABYSSINIAN CRISIS). Sanctions and condemnations were issued, but the responses of the aggressors were simply to leave the League. In the case of Italy, the efforts of the League to impose sanctions were nullified by Britain and France's policy of APPEASEMENT. As Europe lurched towards yet another war in 1939, it was obvious to all that in its original aims the League had proven impotent. On 8 April 1946 it handed over its remaining powers to the newly formed United Nations.

FURTHER READING G.W. Egerton, *Great Britain and the Creation of the League of Nations: Strategy, Politics, and International Organization, 1914–1919* (1979); F.S. Northedge, *The League of Nations: Its Life and Times, 1920–1946* (1986).

Leavis, F(rank) R(aymond) (1895–1978), literary critic. Leavis was born in Cambridge, the son of a shopkeeper who sold musical instruments. Educated at the Perse School, Cambridge, he served in World War I with a medical unit on the Western Front. After the war he gained a BA and a PhD in English literature at Downing College, Cambridge. For the remainder of his career Leavis taught at Cambridge, while being a controversial, oppositional figure within it. His work was marked by profound cultural pessimism and a rigidly prescriptive approach to literary appreciation. In this he was supported by his wife, Queenie Roth (1906–81, whom he married in 1929), whose *Fiction and the Reading Public* (1932) shared his perception of the debilitating commercialization of contemporary culture.

From 1932 to 1953 Leavis edited *Scrutiny,* a journal of literary and cultural criticism, which promoted his views of excellence in English literature; these were highly influential, especially in the 1950s. He became reader in English literature at Cambridge in 1959, but always felt marginalized within the university. In 1962 he engaged in a widely publicized controversy with the Cambridge scientist and novelist C.P. Snow about the relative cultural importance of science and the arts. His influence waned in his later years.

FURTHER READING A. Samson, *F.R. Leavis* (1992).

Left Book Club, organization established in 1936 by the publisher Victor Gollancz, with the support of John STRACHEY and Harold LASKI. Its aim was to make cheap editions of books promoting left-wing ideas widely available in order to create a broad anti-fascist 'popular front'. Such a front had developed in France, and at this point the idea was supported by the international communist movement and the COMMUNIST PARTY OF GREAT BRITAIN. The club included communists and socialists of all persuasions and many people of left-wing inclination who appreciated the access to political debate and good writing. The red-bound volumes, issued monthly, included novels and memoirs, some of them of future distinction (for example Vera BRITTAIN's *Testament of Youth,* Ellen WILKINSON's *The Town That Was Murdered* (*see* HUNGER MARCHES) and Christopher ADDISON's *A Policy in British Agriculture*) as well as political commentary. Even the latter covered the whole spectrum of left debate: it included Clement ATTLEE's characteristically moderate *The Labour Party in Perspective* (1937). The club was based on local study groups who subscribed to receive a book and a journal, *Left News,* every month. At its peak in April 1939 it had 57,000 members in 1500 study groups. It was deeply divided by the Nazi–Soviet pact of August 1939, and, although it continued until 1948, it was much weakened.

FURTHER READING P. Laity (ed.), *Left Book Club Anthology* (2001); J. Lewis, *The Left Book Club* (1970).

leisure. Leisure is sometimes equated with time free from paid work, but this would exclude most adult women for most of the 20th century from experiencing leisure, since they were not in paid work. Nor is its full meaning conveyed by defining it as time spent on pleasurable activities. It is perhaps best regarded as time free from externally imposed occupations, time that is at one's own disposal.

Male manual workers experienced an increase in leisure time over the century, owing to the fall in their hours of paid work. The first major reduction came in 1919–20 when the better organized TRADE UNIONS negotiated for their members (most skilled male workers) a reduction in the normal working week from 54 to 48 hours. There was a further substantial reduction after World War II, to 44.6 hours on average by 1950. This followed a substantial increase in working hours during both world wars due to the demands of war production. It was only after 1945 that large numbers of workers had Saturday totally free from work, although the Saturday half-holiday had been established by the beginning of the century. Hours fell further to under 40 per week by the 1980s.

Only a minority of manual workers had holidays with pay at the beginning of the century. By 1945, 10 million workers did so, mostly for two weeks each year. By 1988 99% of full-time manual workers were entitled to four weeks or more of paid holiday, in addition to bank holidays.

For women, leisure time was less clearly demarcated, since even those in paid work normally had responsibility for domestic duties when they returned home. In 1991, women in full-time employment enjoyed 10 hours less free time each week than men.

It is more difficult to ascertain the hours at the personal disposal of people above the social level of the working class, because their working time was not legally regulated. At least until the 1950s, it was common to refer to the ARISTOCRACY and other wealthy people as 'the leisured class'. This was not always justified, but clearly such people had more opportunities for leisure and pleasure than those with less control over their own time, and there were always some who took ample advantage of it. At the end of the century there was a growing culture of very long hours of work among professional and business people (the so-called '24/7 society' – working 24 hours a day, seven days a week), compensated by shorter bouts of intense leisure time, for which a new phrase was invented – 'quality time'. This change to a situation in which long working hours became the

norm for the rich rather than for the poor created talk of a new social division between the 'work-rich' and the 'work-poor', who were generally also rich or poor in terms of wealth and income in the more familiar sense.

Men and women of all classes had more leisure time at some points in the life cycle than others. The early working years for working people, or, for the better off, the period between school and marriage (often including a period of higher education), tended to provide most opportunities for leisure. Marriage and parenthood reduced leisure time, especially for women. The spread of retirement to manual workers after World War II (*see* OLD AGE AND AGEING) gave growing numbers of people increasingly lengthy periods of leisure in later life.

The uses of leisure also varied at different age stages. Participation in or watching SPORT was common to very many people across classes and age groups through the century, as was dancing, in a variety of forms: in the 1930s to the 1950s most working-class married couples first met at a ballroom dance; at the end of the century they were most likely to meet in a less formal nightclub. Annual visits to the cinema (*see* FILM INDUSTRY) peaked at 1.6 billion in 1946. In 1955 the national average number of visits to the cinema was 23; by 1988 the equivalent figure was 1.5; but the percentage of persons aged 7 and over visiting a cinema at least once a year rose from 56% in 1989 to 68% in 1994. Television (*see* BRITISH BROADCASTING CORPORATION), then home video-viewing, took the place of cinema for many people: by 1993, 6.3 million prerecorded VCR tapes were being hired in each week. Drinking in pubs, clubs and other institutions was a popular leisure pursuit throughout the century, while holidays became increasingly so for working-class and middle-class people. In 1983, 18.1 million people travelled abroad for leisure purposes; in 1994 the number was 34.2 million, partly because the numbers holidaying in Britain declined. Radio, reading and listening to various kinds of music occupied the free time of very many people throughout the century. From 1946 the ARTS COUNCIL OF GREAT BRITAIN sought to encourage leisure pursuits associated with 'high culture'. The popular acclaim and high numbers of visitors attending such end of century/new millennium 'high culture' ventures as the Lowry Gallery in Salford, the new gallery of modern art in Walsall and Tate Modern in London suggested that this had some success.

SEE ALSO GAMBLING.

FURTHER READING J. Gershuny and K. Fisher, 'Leisure' in A.H. Halsey and J. Webb (eds.), *Twentieth Century British Social Trends* (2000), 620–49.

Lend-Lease, agreement by which Britain and other Allied nations received defence supplies and equipment from the United States during WORLD WAR II, with repayment to be made when the war ended. In 1939 the US Congress had passed a Neutrality Act, and so could not sell munitions or supplies directly to nations at war. However, the US president, F.D. Roosevelt, soon devised a plan to assist 'any country whose defence the President deem[s] vital to the defence of the United States'. The Lend-Lease Act was passed in March 1941, allowing the USA to 'sell, transfer title to, exchange, lease, lend or otherwise dispose of' any necessary supplies. In December 1941 the USA was itself dragged into the war, but the Lend-Lease plan had stepped up war-related production and helped prepare the US economy for what was to come.

While Lend-Lease was eventually extended to many countries, including the Soviet Union and China, Britain took greatest advantage of the plan. Over the course of the scheme the USA loaned Britain some $27 billion worth of supplies. There was also a reciprocal aid agreement made between the USA and Britain, unoccupied France, AUSTRALIA and NEW ZEALAND, put in place after the USA had entered the war. Under its terms, American forces stationed overseas in these nations received material assistance and supplies. By the end of the war Britain had paid some $667

million in 'reverse Lend-Lease' to the USA.

By 1941 Britain's cash flow had been severely restricted by the war, and it was in desperate need of munitions and supplies for which it could not pay. Lend-Lease enabled Britain to concentrate on doing its part to win the war and not to have to worry about cash problems. Lend-Lease was ended unexpectedly abruptly by Harry S. Truman when he assumed the presidency of the USA in 1945. After negotiations by KEYNES and others the scheme was effectively replaced by the MARSHALL PLAN, and Britain slowly repaid the amount owed over the next two decades. One of the outcomes of Britain's indebtedness to the USA was the loosening and eventual abolition of COMMONWEALTH economic preference (*see* IMPERIAL PREFERENCES).

FURTHER READING L. Martel, *Lend-Lease, Loans, and the Coming of the Cold War: A Study of the Implementation of Foreign Policy* (1979).

Lessing, Doris (May Tayler) (1919–), novelist. Lessing was born in what was then Persia (now Iran) to British parents. When she was 5 the family moved to a farm in what was then Southern Rhodesia (now ZIMBABWE); the farm was subsidized by the British government as part of a scheme to encourage settlement by British people in the colony. Lessing left school at 15 and worked as a nursemaid, then as a typist and telephonist in Salisbury (now Harare). She married, divorced, became involved in radical politics, re-married in 1945, but in 1949 left for England with her youngest child and the manuscript of her first novel to be published, *The Grass is Singing* (1950). This is the story of the complex relationship between a white farmer's wife and her black servant, which ends violently. Thereafter she supported herself and her son by writing.

Lessing's five-volume series *Children of Violence*, published from 1952 to 1969, traces the history of Martha Quest from her childhood in Rhodesia, through post-war Britain to an apocalyptic ending in 2000. The earlier volumes draw on her own experiences, giving a vivid impression of life for a woman in colonial Rhodesia and in post-war London. *The Golden Notebook* (1962) made an impact for its discussion of the state of Britain, its socialist politics and its feminism, at a time when feminism was unfashionable.

Lessing was a member of the COMMUNIST PARTY until 1956 and a supporter of the CAMPAIGN FOR NUCLEAR DISARMAMENT. She then became disillusioned with all political belief, describing it as no better than religious bigotry. Her later work, such as *Briefing for a Descent into Hell* (1971) and *Memoirs of a Survivor* (1975), explored mental breakdown and the breakdown of society. Then in a series of works she broke with traditional realism, inventively describing a mythical universe, interspersed with pessimistic writings about contemporary Britain, such as *The Good Terrorist* (1985). The first volume of her autobiography, *Under my Skin*, was published in 1994, the second, *Waiting in the Shade: 1949–1962*, in 1997.

Liberal Democrats, *see* LIBERAL PARTY; SOCIAL DEMOCRATIC PARTY.

Liberal Party, one of the two dominant British political parties for much of the 19th century. At the beginning of the 20th century it appeared to be losing ground and votes. However, two factors increased support for the Liberals, who were traditionally advocates of FREE TRADE and identified with Nonconformity. The first was the TARIFF REFORM issue, and the second was the Conservative Education Act of 1902 (*see* EDUCATION), which extended RATE (i.e. local-tax) support to Church of England and Roman Catholic schools, so alienating those NONCONFORMISTS who objected to rate subsidies for any denominational school. The Liberals still felt insecure and threatened by the growth of the LABOUR REPRESENTATION COMMITTEE (LRC) since traditionally they had won the votes of TRADE UNIONISTS and other workers.

In 1903 Ramsay MACDONALD (for the LRC) and Herbert Gladstone, the Liberal chief whip, made a secret pact that the LRC and the Liberals

would not compete against each other in any constituency where doing so would split the anti-Conservative vote and assist a Conservative victory (known as the 'Lib-Lab pact'). This pact operated in the election of January 1906, unnecessarily as it turned out from the Liberal point of view, since the party, under Henry CAMPBELL-BANNERMAN, gained 400 out of 670 seats. The pact was more helpful to Labour (*see* LABOUR PARTY). Awareness of the need to hold working-class votes did, however, encourage the Liberals to introduce a string of social reforms that have been seen as laying the foundations of the WELFARE STATE, including the introduction of free school meals in 1906 and OLD-AGE PENSIONS in 1908. The Liberals also introduced the Trade Disputes Act, 1906, to restore and indeed to increase legal privileges that the trade unions had recently lost (*see* TAFF VALE). ASQUITH as CHANCELLOR OF THE EXCHEQUER in 1907 introduced a progressive income tax for the first time. The following year Asquith became party leader and PRIME MINISTER owing to the illness of Campbell-Bannerman, who died shortly afterwards. David LLOYD GEORGE succeeded Asquith as chancellor of the exchequer. In 1911 the House of LORDS lost further powers, having opposed further redistributive taxation proposed in Lloyd George's 'People's Budget' of 1909. In the two GENERAL ELECTIONS in 1910 – which resulted from this crisis with the Lords – the Liberals lost their absolute majority; to remain in office they needed to reach a compromise with the Irish nationalists and with Labour. The latter extracted in return the payment of salaries to MPs and the reversal of the legal judgement in the Osborne case of 1909 that trade unionists must give explicit consent to the payment of a levy by their union to the Labour Party on their behalf. In return, Labour agreed to support the introduction in 1911 of national health insurance (introduced by Lloyd George), and unemployment insurance (introduced by Winston CHURCHILL, then a Liberal). In the years before 1914 the government was shaken by the MARCONI SCANDAL of 1912–13, by industrial conflict, and by the conflict over HOME RULE in IRELAND. Its refusal to grant votes to women (*see* SUFFRAGETTES; SUFFRAGISTS) alienated many women and men. In the same period hostility to war and to public expenditure were both strong in the party and held back rearmament.

Many Liberals only supported Britain's role in WORLD WAR I with reluctance, and opposed CONSCRIPTION until 1915. As the war became more demanding than anticipated the government faced increasing criticism, and in May 1915 Asquith felt forced to form a coalition government, which included the first Labour cabinet minister, Arthur HENDERSON. Criticism of Asquith's leadership continued until in December 1916 Lloyd George resigned from the cabinet, forcing the resignation of the government. Lloyd George then formed a new coalition government, mainly with Conservatives. The Liberal Party never recovered from this schism; about 175 Liberal MPs supported Lloyd George, while the remainder stayed loyal to Asquith. Lloyd George's coalition survived until 1922, the Liberals fighting the election of December 1918 in two camps: Lloyd George's faction was the more successful, gaining 127 seats compared with the Asquithians' 36. Lloyd George was dumped by the Conservatives in 1922 (*see* BALDWIN, STANLEY).

Lloyd George and Asquith agreed an unenthusiastic reconciliation in 1923 to fight Baldwin's protectionism, but the success of Labour in the December 1923 election confirmed that the Liberals were no longer the second major party. Faction fighting among the Liberals continued and they won only 40 seats in the December 1924 election. They were also declining in support in local elections. Lloyd George took over the leadership in 1926, following Asquith's retirement, and sought to improve its fortunes with a new policy to 'conquer' UNEMPLOYMENT, but only 59 Liberals were returned to Parliament at the election of 1929. Lloyd George was seriously ill during the crisis of 1931 and unable to stop his deputy Herbert SAMUEL taking the party into the NATIONAL GOVERNMENT.

The party was even more weak and divided thereafter. Its various factions contributed ministers to the coalitions of the 1930s and 1940s, but the number of official Liberal MPs fell from 33 in 1931 to 6 in 1951, and its share of the overall votes cast fell to 3% in 1951 and 1955.

The Liberal Party had difficulty in devising a political programme sufficiently distinct from those of the other two parties, but successive leaders (Herbert Samuel, 1931–5; Archibald Sinclair, 1935–45; Clement Davies, 1945–56; Jo GRIMOND, 1956–67) determined that it should remain independent. In the second half of the century it tended to revive, mildly, when voters were especially disillusioned with the other parties, as at the beginning of the 1960s, when the Liberal Eric Lubbock won a spectacular by-election victory at Orpington in southeast London in 1962. The party held consistent support only in southwest England, in Devon and Cornwall. In the 1970s Liberals had greater success in local government, often by taking a populist stance on local issues. This enabled the party to rebuild its local branches, and in the 1974 election (another time of voter disillusion with Labour and Conservatives, amid economic crisis) the Liberals, led by Jeremy THORPE from 1967 to 1976, gained 6 million votes – the largest number in their history and close to 20% of the total vote – but only 14 MPs. This increased the party's enthusiasm for PROPORTIONAL REPRESENTATION, which it had long supported. Thorpe refused a coalition offer from the Conservative prime minister Edward HEATH, and Labour returned to power.

David STEEL, Thorpe's successor as leader (1976–88), negotiated a second 'Lib-Lab pact' in 1977 to keep a minority Labour government in office. Steel was keen to avoid an election, partly because he was new to the job and partly because of the scandal surrounding his predecessor, Jeremy Thorpe, who had been forced to resign when it was revealed that he faced charges of conspiracy to murder a male model with whom he was alleged to have had an affair. The main terms of the pact were consultation on economic policy, direct elections to the European Parliament and devolution for SCOTLAND and WALES (*see also* HOME RULE). Criticism from within the Liberal Party forced Steel to abandon the pact in August 1978, but, even then, the ongoing, much-publicized Thorpe case and the Liberals' poor showing in the polls made them reluctant to bring the government down.

In 1981 Steel made an electoral alliance with the SOCIAL DEMOCRATIC PARTY (SDP). The 'Alliance' gained 25% of the vote in 1983 and 23% in 1987, but obtained only 23 and 22 MPs respectively, 17 of them Liberals. In a ballot in March 1988 party members voted 46,376 to 6365 to merge with the SDP to form the Social and Liberal Democrats, whereupon Steel retired and was succeeded by Paddy ASHDOWN. In October 1989, following another membership ballot, the party announced that it was henceforth to be known as the Liberal Democrats, though for legal purposes it retained its full title of Social-Liberal Democrats. The new party performed well for a while in by-elections, again boosted by the unpopularity of Labour and Conservatives, and increased its number of parliamentary seats to 46. However, with the election of a centrist Labour government in 1997 it again became unclear whether the Liberal Democrats had a distinctive role. In 1999 Ashdown resigned and Charles Kennedy (1959–), who had entered politics as a very young member of the SDP, succeeded him. Under Kennedy the party continued the electoral advances begun under Ashdown, winning 52 seats in the 2001 general election, the most seats won by the Liberals or Liberal Democrats since 1929.

FURTHER READING G. Searle, *The Liberal Party: Triumph and Disintegration, 1886–1929* (1992); D. Steel, *Against Goliath: David Steel's Story* (1991).

Lib-Lab pact (1903). *See* LABOUR PARTY; LIBERAL PARTY.

Lib-Lab pact (1977–8). *See* CALLAGHAN, JAMES; LIBERAL PARTY.

Lib-Labs, a group of working-class MPs – mostly trade unionists and mostly also coal miners – who sat in the House of COMMONS as representatives of working people, but who were Gladstonian LIBERALS in their politics. The first to be elected were Thomas Burt and Alexander MacDonald. Burt was a mining trade-union leader from Northumberland who sat in Parliament from 1874 to 1918, whereas MacDonald, a Scottish miner, sat only from 1874 until 1881. The number of Lib-Lab MPs increased following the extension of the franchise in 1884; at the 1885 election 12 Lib-Labs were successful. Between 1874 and 1906 a total of 24 MPs accepted the 'Lib-Lab' label, which was then in common use, having been invented (as a term of abuse) by their socialist opponents. The Lib-Labs were recognized as an independent grouping in the Commons, though they sat on the Liberal benches and took the Liberal WHIP.

The Lib-Labs retained their independence after the formation of the LABOUR REPRESENTATION COMMITTEE (LRC) in 1900, though most of them cooperated with it. Their numbers shrank after the GENERAL ELECTION of 1906 and diminished further in 1909 when the Miners Federation of Great Britain affiliated to the LABOUR PARTY. By this time the Lib-Labs were an anachronism. The three remaining MPs who refused to join the Labour Party – Burt, and his fellow miners Charles Fenwick and John Wilson – were now in reality conventional Liberal MPs.

FURTHER READING J. Shepherd, 'Labour and Parliament: the Lib-Labs as the first working-class MPs, 1885–1906' in E.F. Biagini and A.J. Reid, *Currents of Radicalism: Popular Radicalism, Organized Labour and Party Politics in Britain, 1850–1914* (1991), 187–213.

life peers. *See* LORDS, HOUSE OF.

Limehouse Declaration. *See* SOCIAL DEMOCRATIC PARTY.

literature. *See* NOVELS; POETRY; DRAMA.

Livingstone, Ken. *See* LONDON GOVERNMENT.

Lloyd George, David (1863–1945), Liberal politician; PRIME MINISTER (1916–22). Lloyd George was born in Manchester of Welsh parents and brought up to be bilingual. His father, William George, was a teacher, and died in 1864, whereupon he went with his mother to live with Richard Lloyd, his mother's brother, a master shoemaker and Baptist lay preacher in Llanystumdwy, Caernarfonshire. 'Uncle Lloyd' raised him as a son and David always used the double surname. The family circumstances were relatively comfortable, notwithstanding Lloyd George's later claims to have grown up in poverty. Richard Lloyd's family, including David's mother, sister and younger brother, moved to Criccieth, North Wales, in 1880. David attended an Anglican elementary school, then was apprenticed to a law firm in Portmadoc. He became active in the LIBERAL PARTY and was licensed as a solicitor. In 1888 he married the wealthy Margaret Owen, of Criccieth. In 1890 he was elected Liberal MP for Caernarvon Boroughs, which he held for 57 years. His wife disliked London and raised her family in Criccieth and the pair spent much time apart, a situation that freed Lloyd George to indulge his notorious taste for infidelity. Nevertheless, the marriage lasted until Margaret's death in 1941. Two of their five children, Gwilym and Megan Lloyd George, also became politicians, albeit of no great distinction.

Lloyd George quickly became known as a flamboyant politician, speaking out opportunistically on a range of issues. However, he opposed the BOER WAR – an unpopular position. He began to be taken seriously by the Liberal leadership when he played a leading role in the opposition to the 1902 Education Act (*see* EDUCATION), which subsidized denominational, mainly CHURCH OF ENGLAND and ROMAN CATHOLIC, schools – a measure that was deeply unpopular in NONCONFORMIST Wales. He entered the cabinet formed by Sir Henry CAMPBELL-BANNERMAN late in 1905 as president of the Board of Trade.

When ASQUITH succeeded Campbell-Bannerman in 1908 Lloyd George was appointed CHANCELLOR OF THE EXCHEQUER, a post he retained until 1915. He guided the first OLD-AGE PENSIONS Act through the Commons in 1908, but the gratitude that he received for this measure really belonged to his predecessor Asquith. His 1909 'People's Budget' introduced a small tax on land values, higher-rate taxes on higher incomes and a development fund to create employment by improving roads, forestry and agriculture. Resistance to the budget by the House of LORDS led to two GENERAL ELECTIONS in 1910 and the restriction of the Lords' powers in the 1911 Parliament Act. In 1911 Lloyd George, working closely with Winston CHURCHILL (then a Liberal cabinet minister), introduced national insurance (*see* WELFARE STATE), an innovative approach to social-welfare payments for health and UNEMPLOYMENT. During the AGADIR CRISIS of 1911 he was the cabinet's spokesman in warning Germany of the risk of war. He was increasingly concerned about the danger of war, and, while urging attempts to maintain peace with Germany, he at the same time advocated defence preparedness. The MARCONI SCANDAL of 1912–13 – when he was accused of corruption and made to apologize publicly – almost ended his career.

During WORLD WAR I Lloyd George was critical of the government's management of the war, and played an important role in its replacement by a coalition in May 1915. He became an effective minister of munitions, meeting the demands of TRADE UNIONS in order to maximize war production. He and others continued to criticize the handling of the war until in December 1916 he joined with other Liberals, Conservatives and powerful newspaper owners to remove Asquith from power. This split the Liberal Party irredeemably. Lloyd George became prime minister in a coalition government that was predominantly Conservative. He made changes in the machinery of government and also in the military management of the war, though it is doubtful that this alone brought about victory. He skilfully managed public and parliamentary opinion, making promises for improved social conditions in peacetime. As a successful war leader he led the coalition government to a large victory in the 1918 election.

At the Paris Peace Conference in 1919 (*see* VERSAILLES, TREATY OF) Lloyd George sought to restore pre-war international economic normalcy, to minimize Germany's war reparations and to avoid the destruction of its economy – arguing against the vengeful urgings of the French, although he was less moderate than the US president, Woodrow Wilson. Lloyd George was also anxious to prevent the spread of communism following the Russian Revolution of 1917 and to avoid Soviet Russia becoming isolated from the influence of other powers. He re-established Anglo-Russian trade, but he could not restore normal relations between Germany, Soviet Russia and other major powers. His government achieved the Anglo-Irish treaty of 1921, which, after two years of war, gave independence to much of IRELAND, a development that alienated many Conservatives. Lloyd George also attracted criticism for giving peerages and other honours in return for donations to his National Liberal Party (the official Liberal Party continued under the leadership of Asquith). Lloyd George had hoped to sustain the coalition as the spearhead of a new progressive party, but there was increasing opposition to him in the CONSERVATIVE PARTY, in particular to his plans to increase public expenditure in order to improve HOUSING and provide other social services, and to allay the economic slump. In October 1922 he was ousted as premier by a revolt of junior ministers and backbenchers (*see* BALDWIN, STANLEY).

A half-hearted reconciliation with Asquith in 1923 failed to revive the Liberal Party; nor did Lloyd George's succession to the leadership of the official Liberal Party in 1926. Equally ineffective in reviving Liberal fortunes was Lloyd George's development, with advice from KEYNES, of a policy designed to reduce unemployment (published in 1929 as *We Can Conquer Unemployment*). He gave

up the party leadership owing to serious illness in 1931, and opposed the involvement of Liberals in the NATIONAL GOVERNMENT. In the 1930s he wrote his memoirs, managed a farm in Surrey, and argued in the press for rearmament, cooperation with the Soviet Union and support for the Republicans in the SPANISH CIVIL WAR, and against APPEASEMENT. When World War II began he viewed Britain as inadequately prepared and proposed a negotiated peace with Germany; in 1940 he declined an offer from Churchill of a position in the war cabinet. In 1943 he married Frances Stevenson, his longtime secretary and mistress. In 1945 he was created Earl Lloyd-George of Dwyfor, shortly before he died of cancer.

FURTHER READING J. Grigg, *Lloyd George* (1997); A.J.P. Taylor (ed.), *Lloyd George: 12 Essays* (1994); C. Wrigley, *Lloyd George* (1992).

local government. At the beginning of the century, local government consisted of a number of different, overlapping, separately elected authorities. School boards administered primary and secondary EDUCATION, and boards of guardians administered the POOR LAW. Borough councils were responsible for most others areas of local responsibility (such as public health and policing) in larger urban areas. The remainder of the country was governed by county councils, which had authority over – and delegated powers (e.g. for public health and the maintenance of highways) to – the smaller non-county boroughs, urban district councils and rural district councils (in SCOTLAND called large burghs, small burghs and districts, respectively). London was governed by the London County Council, beneath which London was divided into metropolitan boroughs (*see* LONDON GOVERNMENT).

All male ratepayers (i.e. those who paid local taxes; *see* RATES) qualified for the vote for all of these authorities and had the right to stand for election, provided that they were on the electoral register. The situation of women was more complicated. Independent female ratepayers (mainly widows and single women who headed their own households) qualified for the vote in all of these elections, but could stand for election only for school boards, boards of guardians, and rural and urban district councils. In 1900 270 women were members of school boards and 1147 were members of boards of guardians. The Education Act, 1902, abolished the separate school boards and education became the responsibility of borough and county councils. In 1907 women were enabled to stand for election in county and borough elections; 48 successfully did so by 1914. In 1918 the local vote was extended to all men at age 21 after six months residence in an area and to all women at age 30 in the place where she, or her husband, had resided for six months. In 1928 women obtained the local vote on the same terms as men. In 1929 boards of Poor Law guardians were abolished and their powers of public assistance transferred to borough and county councils. Otherwise the structure of local government remained unchanged until 1972.

At the beginning of the century local authorities had a high degree of independence of central government, both as to how they raised their income and as to the extent and direction of expenditure. The powers and expenditure of local authorities grew as central government took on more responsibilities and delegated many of them – e.g. for HOUSING and education – to local authorities. In consequence local authority expenditure grew. It was £100,862,000 in 1900, £289,353,000 in 1920, £578,798,000 in 1940, £1.8 billion by 1960, £5.4 billion by 1970, £17.1 billion in 1985 and by 1995 £48 billion. As its range of activities grew, so did its dependence upon subsidy from central government; this was accompanied by increasing control of local government by central government. The process of tightening central control began in the interwar years. By the end of the century local government autonomy had all but disappeared.

Throughout the century local elections were characterized by low turnouts, rarely above 50%, more often about 40% or below, and falling later in the century. Increasingly over the century the political parties tightened their grip on local councils and voting often expressed views about national rather than local matters.

London government was reorganized in 1963. In 1972 the existing structure throughout England and Wales was abolished and replaced by a top tier of metropolitan counties in six conurbations (for example, Merseyside, which straddled what had been the boundaries of Lancashire and Cheshire) and 47 non-metropolitan counties in the rest of the country. This entailed the abolition as administrative units of some ancient counties, such as tiny Rutland, which caused local resentment. A new second tier consisted of 36 metropolitan districts, within the areas of the metropolitan counties, and 333 districts in the rest of the country. In 1975 Scottish government was also rearranged into regional and district councils. Then the Local Government Act, 1985, led to the abolition in 1986 of the Greater London Council and the six metropolitan councils in England and Wales and distributed their responsibilities and powers among their component boroughs plus some newly invented joint authorities. In 1994 the regional and district councils in Scotland were replaced by 29 unitary authorities, and in Wales 22 unitary authorities took over from the previous 12 counties and 37 districts.

FURTHER READING T. Byrne, *Local Government* (5th edn, 1990); P. Hollis, *Ladies Elect. Women in English Local Government, 1865–1914* (1987); J. Redlich and F. Hirst (ed. B. Keith-Lucas), *The History of Local Government in England* (1958); K. Young and N. Rao, *Local Government since 1945* (1997).

Locarno pact (1925), series of agreements among Britain, France, Germany, Italy and Belgium designed to ease international tension. The agreements were reached at a conference held at Locarno, Switzerland, on 5–16 October 1925, and were all signed on 1 December. The most important of the treaties confirmed the inviolability of the Franco-German and Belgian-German frontiers and the demilitarized zone of the Rhineland. This treaty was signed by France, Belgium and Germany and guaranteed by Britain and Italy. The Germans also concluded arbitration treaties with France, Belgium, Poland and Czechoslovakia. France signed treaties of mutual guarantee with Poland and Czechoslovakia. The architects of the agreements were Aristide Briand of France, Gustav Streseman of Germany and Austen CHAMBERLAIN. The principal treaty was violated by Hitler in March 1936 when he sent troops into the Rhineland; the other signatories were preoccupied with the ABYSSINIAN CRISIS and made only formal protests.

London County Council (LCC). *See* LONDON GOVERNMENT.

London government. London in 1900 was the world's largest city, accounting for one-fifth of the population and one-third of the income-tax receipts of England and Wales. The London Government Act, 1900, established a two-tier system : the London County Council (LCC), created in 1888, handled city-wide matters, while 29 metropolitan boroughs exercised local powers. An exception was the wealthy, powerful and long-established financial district, the CITY OF LONDON, whose Corporation, chaired by a lord mayor selected by the Corporation, exercised authority, including control of POLICE, within the square mile of London's medieval boundary. There were other anomalies. The boundaries of the LCC were the boundaries of the administrative county of London first defined in 1855, but by 1901 more than 30% of Londoners lived outside this area. The Metropolitan Police had been controlled by central government since its creation in 1829.

The LCC at the turn of the century was controlled by the Progressive Party (mostly radical LIBERALS, with some LABOUR support). They promoted London's first large-scale publicly owned HOUSING schemes and bought and operated its tramway system. They were defeated by opponents of the expenditure that resulted, and between 1907 and 1934 the LCC was controlled by Conservatives, or 'Municipal Reformers' as they were known in London. In the period 1934–63 the LCC was Labour-controlled.

By the 1930s the LCC was responsible for the education of 750,000 children, having taken over control of state education in 1904, following the 1902 Education Act (*see* EDUCATION). By 1939 it controlled almost 100,000 housing units, following the interwar housing drive. With the reform of the POOR LAW in 1929 it became responsible for public assistance, 140 hospitals and the London ambulance service. It controlled tramways until 1933 when the publicly owned corporation, the London Passenger Transport Board, took over all London public transport, included the underground railway system. During WORLD WAR II the LCC supervised evacuation, civil defence and the Rescue Service, which was especially important during the BLITZ. After the war its powers contracted. As central government provided more funding for local-government activity, it demanded more control. In 1948 the LCC's health services passed to the NATIONAL HEALTH SERVICE. In the 1950s there was political friction between the Conservative government and the Labour-controlled LCC. In consequence, in 1957 a royal commission on metropolitan government was established, which led to legislation in 1963 replacing the LCC with a larger Greater London Council (GLC). The GLC governed almost the entire built-up metropolitan area and included more Conservative-inclined outer suburbs. At the same time the second tier was reshaped by creating 32 enlarged London boroughs, which were envisaged as the primary authorities. The new system was introduced in 1965. The GLC was assigned a 'strategic' London-wide role, which was in fact vague and minimal, and given control of London Transport. Education was controlled by a new Inner London Education Authority in the old LCC area and by the boroughs in the outer areas. In the

1980s the Labour-controlled GLC, led by Ken Livingstone (1945–), clashed with Margaret THATCHER's Conservative government over the GLC's proposals for economic regeneration, cheap public transport and aid to voluntary groups, including those representing ethnic minorities in an increasingly multicultural city. In consequence the council was abolished in 1986.

Many of the GLC's powers passed to central government, others to the boroughs and the City Corporation and others again to new agencies such as the London Regional Transport Authority and the London Fire and Civil Defence Authority. The Labour Party, which also regarded Livingstone and the GLC as too leftist, and so harmful to the party as a whole, had made little effort to defend the GLC. But the Labour government elected in 1997 proposed to revive a city-wide elected authority and to introduce an innovation: a separately elected mayor of London. The election campaign in 2000 was fraught with controversy. Ken Livingstone, having been rejected as the official Labour candidate by the Labour Party leadership, stood as an independent, and won the election in May 2000.
FURTHER READING J. Davis, *Reforming London: The London Government Problem, 1835–1900* (1988); K. Young and P. Garside, *Metropolitan London* (1982).

London, treaty of (26 April 1915), secret agreement signed by Britain, France and Russia on the one hand, and Italy on the other. It guaranteed Italy generous territorial gains provided that it entered WORLD WAR I on the side of the Allies within one month. The territory promised was: the Austrian provinces of the Trentino, South Tirol, Istria, Gorizia, Gradisca and Trieste; a large stretch of the Dalmatian coast and its islands; a segment of Albanian territory around Valona; full sovereignty over the formerly Turkish Dodecanese islands; and the Turkish province of Adalia in Asia Minor. In addition Italy was promised colonial gains in Africa and a share in any war indemnity. This generous offer of territory belonging to their opponents was made because the Allies believed that Italian intervention would rapidly destroy the Austro-Hungarian challenge and thus 'open the back door to Germany'.

Italy entered the war on 24 May 1915, but without the hoped-for results. When, following the October Revolution, the Bolsheviks withdrew from the war and repudiated all the international obligations of tsarist Russia early in 1918, they revealed the terms of the secret treaty. President Wilson of the United States was furious and made it clear that America would not regard its terms as binding. At the Paris Peace Conference Britain and France also refused to honour all their promises to Italy. The resulting resentment in Italy contributed to the rise of Mussolini.

Lord Haw-Haw. *See* JOYCE, WILLIAM.

Lords, House of, the upper house of the Westminster Parliament. In 1900 the House of Lords was a legislative body of just under 600 members, all holding hereditary titles, apart from 26 CHURCH OF ENGLAND bishops and 6 judges, who conducted the House's role as supreme court of appeal in judicial matters without reference to lay members of the House. It was dominated by the landowning elite, though increasing numbers of businessmen and financiers were appointed from the 1880s. Its political role gradually diminished in the later 19th century. The Conservative Lord SALISBURY was the last PRIME MINISTER to sit in the Lords (1900–2).

The constitutional convention survived that the Lords did not intervene in the financial decisions of the COMMONS. When a LIBERAL government with a large majority was elected in January 1906, it faced a Lords with a large Conservative majority that blocked some of its social-reforming legislation. The confrontation intensified when the Lords rejected David LLOYD GEORGE's redistributive 'People's Budget' of 1909; the proposed land taxes and higher income-tax rate were abhorred by the wealthy land-owning class who dominated the Lords. ASQUITH's Liberal government forced two elections in 1910 on the issue and threatened (with the reluctant agreement of King GEORGE V) to flood the Lords with new Liberal peers. This persuaded the majority of Conservative peers to back down and allow the passage of the Parliament Act, 1911. This act allowed the Lords to delay but not ultimately to reject any decision of the Commons and removed all their powers over finance bills. The 1909 budget was finally passed. Lloyd George got his revenge by creating over 100 peers during his premiership (1916–22), some of whom were thought to have bought their peerages by donations to Lloyd George's political campaigns.

Throughout the interwar years there were proposals for reform of the Lords, for example, the Bryce Report of 1918 (set up by Lloyd George) proposed an elected house. No action was taken on this or similar later proposals. The Labour government elected in 1945 changed the role of the Lords (in which they had few supporters) less than some expected: the 1949 Parliament Act reduced the period for which the Lords could delay Commons decisions to one year. From 1946 the government also allowed regular attenders at the Lords to claim travelling expenses. Members of the Lords were unpaid, which created problems for some peers who were appointed by Labour to boost their numbers. The Conservative governments of Harold MACMILLAN made more fundamental changes. In 1957 peers were allowed to claim a maximum of three guineas a day for expenses when they attended the Lords. In 1958 life peerages were introduced, which could not be passed to heirs. They were open to men and women, admitting women to the Lords for the first time. Led by the prominent feminist Lady Rhondda, who inherited her father's peerage, women had been campaigning since the 1920s for the minority of women who inherited peerages to be admitted to the Lords. This demand was again rejected.

In 1963, under pressure from a Labour MP, Anthony Wedgwood BENN, who wished to stay in the Commons following the death of his father,

Lord Stansgate, the Peerage Act allowed people to renounce hereditary titles and also admitted female holders of hereditary peerages to the Lords. In consequence Benn stayed in the Commons and Lords Home (*see* DOUGLAS-HOME, ALEC) and Hailsham left the Lords in order to contest the Conservative leadership following MACMILLAN's resignation. The Labour government in 1964 increased the maximum daily expenses payable for attendance at the Lords. In 1967 it announced its intention to reform the Lords, with no outcome. Similar resolutions and promises followed into the 1990s. Only six hereditary titles were created after 1964, three for members of the royal family, the remainder for Conservative politicians. Membership of the Lords rose to about 1150 in the 1990s, about one-third of whom were life peers.

In 1999 the Labour government, with the official support of the Conservative leadership, made the Lords reduce to 92 the number of hereditary peers allowed to participate in the work of the Lords; these were elected by their fellow hereditaries. This was announced as a first step towards a reconstitution of the Lords, though the final steps were unclear at the end of the century. At the end of March 2000 there were almost 700 members of the Lords, 202 Labour supporters, 236 Conservatives, 63 Liberal-Democrats, 161 without party affiliation ('cross-benchers') plus 26 archbishops and bishops, and 27 law lords. The House of Lords retained its judicial role. Both before and after the reform the Lords frequently rejected or revised legislation of both Conservative and Labour governments, forcing revisions despite their apparently weak constitutional position.

FURTHER READING D. Cannadine, *The Rise and Fall of the British Aristocracy* (1990); D. Shell, *The House of Lords* (1991).

Lowry, L(aurence), S(tephen) (1887–1976),

artist. He lived all his life in or near Manchester, working as a rent collector and clerk for a property company, rising to become chief cashier by the time of his retirement in 1952. His painting was done in the evenings and weekends. He studied intermittently at art schools between 1905 and 1925. He led a somewhat solitary life and said, 'Had I not been lonely I would not have seen what I did.' His paintings observed the urban landscapes of his home environment, often depicting crowds or groups of people, represented in his characteristic stick-like style, against industrial backgrounds. He helped to fix in the popular imagination a particular image of the industrial north of England of his lifetime. His first one-man exhibition, in London in 1939, established his reputation outside his home area and thereafter it steadily grew. Later in life he diversified into painting land- and seascapes and, occasionally, portraits. He continued to lead an austere life, turning down a knighthood and other honours, though he accepted honorary degrees from three universities. Professional critical opinion of his work was split between those who thought him a major artist with an original vision and those who regarded him as a minor artistic talent but an interesting social commentator. But unlike many artists who achieved more unanimous critical acclaim he had wide popular appeal. The first comprehensive retrospective exhibition of his work, at the Royal Academy in 1976, shortly after his death, broke attendance records.

M

Maastricht, treaty of (February 1992), the common name for the Treaty of European Union, signed at Maastricht in the Netherlands but not ratified by all the member nations until the following year, when the EUROPEAN UNION came into being. A revision of both the treaty of Rome (1957) and the Single European Act (1986), the treaty of Maastricht aligned the member states of the European Community (EC; *see* EUROPEAN ECONOMIC COMMUNITY) towards greater union in other matters besides the economic. It laid out plans for a degree of political union, a timetable for European monetary union and the establishment of a European central bank (which came into effect in 1999). There were also provisions made on common foreign and defence policies and on policing, and the endorsement of a European Charter on Social Rights (the 'Social Chapter').

The passing of the treaty began a fresh page in the history of European integration, but also provoked plenty of opposition. Its movement into social and political areas that had formerly been the exclusive preserve of individual member states alarmed many, and in Britain gave a boost to the 'Eurosceptic' faction of the CONSERVATIVE PARTY during the premiership of John MAJOR. Major himself had signed the treaty, but had secured opt-out clauses for Britain on both the single currency and the Social Chapter – a strategy that satisfied nei-ther the pro-Europe faction nor the Eurosceptics.
FURTHER READING M.J. Baun, *An Imperfect Union: The Maastricht Treaty and the New Politics of European Integration* (1996); A.M. Blair, *Britain and the Maastricht Treaty: Negotiations on Common Foreign and Security Policy* (1997); R. Corbett, *The Treaty of Maastricht from Conception to Ratification: A Comprehensive Reference Guide* (1993).

MacDonald, (James) Ramsay (1866–1937), Labour politician; PRIME MINISTER of the first two Labour governments (1924, 1929–31), and of the NATIONAL GOVERNMENT (1931–5). MacDonald was born in Lossiemouth, Scotland, the illegitimate son of Anne Ramsay, a domestic servant, and, possibly, John MacDonald, a farmworker; he was brought up by his mother and grandmother. He did well at local schools and became a pupil teacher. In 1885 he took an administrative post in Bristol, where he joined the Social Democratic Federation, which regarded itself as Marxist. He then took a series of clerical jobs in London until 1888 when he became private secretary to Thomas Lough, a radical Liberal politician.

In 1892 MacDonald left his position to pursue a career in politics and journalism. Throughout the 1890s he moved in Liberal, radical and socialist circles. He was selected as Liberal candidate for

Dover shortly after the 1892 election, making it clear that he was a 'LIB-LAB' representative, associated with the Labour Electoral Association. (The LEA was a forerunner of the LABOUR REPRESENTATION COMMITTEE (LRC), and was formed in 1886; it aimed to work with the Liberals in the interests of the working class.) There was no hope of success in Conservative Dover and in the 1895 election he ran as INDEPENDENT LABOUR PARTY (ILP) candidate in Southampton, having failed to gain selection by the Liberals as a Lib-Lab. He came bottom of the poll with 867 votes. In the early 1890s he joined the FABIAN SOCIETY, touring as a Fabian lecturer. In 1896 and 1897 he was also a member of the progressive intellectual Liberal Rainbow Circle, which hoped, briefly, to form a new centre party. In 1896 he married Margaret Gladstone, whose income provided them with security, though not wealth, and helped him to pursue a political career. Their home, 3 Lincoln's Inn Fields in central London, was to be the base for the Labour Representation Committee. Margaret died in 1911, partly worn out by combining the rearing of six children (for which she refused to have more than minimal domestic help) with political activism for the labour movement and women's suffrage (*see* SUFFRAGISTS; SUFFRAGETTES). MacDonald never recovered from her loss. He remained close to his children.

MacDonald had become a leading figure in the ILP and secretary of the LRC, then of the Labour Party after its foundation in 1906. He was heavily defeated in Leicester as LRC candidate in the 1900 election. He negotiated the secret electoral pact with the Liberals in 1903 (*see* LIBERAL PARTY) because he believed that this was the only way for Labour to gain seats quickly. In the 1906 election the LRC put up 50 candidates, of whom 29 were successful, only five having faced Liberal opposition. MacDonald was elected for Leicester. He had played a major part in building the organization of the party and holding together its disparate supporters. He defined Labour's socialism ('British socialism' as he called it, in distinction

from Marxism) and conveyed it to a wide audience in a number of publications, including *Socialism and Society* (1905), *Socialism and Government* (1909) and *The Socialist Movement* (1911). In 1911 he became leader of the parliamentary Labour Party. He opposed WORLD WAR I and in consequence withdrew from party office, since the party supported the war. He was not a pacifist but believed that this was an unjust and unnecessary war that drove working people to their deaths for reasons that amounted to no more than the diplomatic manoeuvres of politicians. He supported the Union of Democratic Control, which shared these sentiments. Largely owing to his opposition to the war he lost his seat in Leicester in 1918, and concentrated on building up the party machine with Arthur HENDERSON. In 1922 he was elected for Aberavon and again became leader of the parliamentary Labour Party. After the Conservatives failed to achieve a majority in the election of December 1923, he was asked to form a minority Labour government in January 1924. His government lasted less than ten months.

After Labour's defeat in the October 1924 election and his resignation as prime minister on 4 November, MacDonald became increasingly absorbed in foreign affairs and DECOLONIZATION, to which he had long been committed. In 1929 he was elected for the safer seat of Seaham and again led a minority Labour government. This was destroyed by the economic crisis of 1931 (*see* GREAT CRASH). The majority in the cabinet opposed the proposal to cut UNEMPLOYMENT benefits. MacDonald offered his resignation to King GEORGE V, but was persuaded to remain as leader of a coalition NATIONAL GOVERNMENT with the Conservatives and Liberals (August 1931). The new cabinet contained only three other 'National Labour' members, one of whom was Philip SNOWDEN. The great majority of the Labour Party opposed the coalition.

MacDonald has since been reviled as a traitor to the Labour Party, but there is every reason to believe that he was convinced that he was acting in the interests of the nation and of the party, because the scale of the crisis necessitated a coalition, as in wartime. In addition, he did not believe the economy to be the only issue of political importance. In particular he was anxious to achieve peace in Europe and to see through the negotiations about the future constitutional position of INDIA, in which he was deeply involved and which he did not wish to abandon to Conservative control. He was genuinely surprised at the hatred shown towards him in the party, which suggests that he had lost touch with it. The damage inflicted on the Labour Party was severe but short-lived.

MacDonald remained as prime minister of the National Government, which won a large majority in the 1931 election. The government was increasingly dominated by Conservatives. MacDonald involved himself in foreign affairs, especially the Geneva Disarmament Conference and the Lausanne Conference on German reparations, both in 1932. Thereafter he went into decline and resigned as prime minister in favour of Stanley BALDWIN in 1935. He lost his seat at Seaham in 1935. He then sat for the Scottish Universities and was lord president of the council, but scarcely active until his death in 1937.

SEE ALSO LABOUR PARTY.

FURTHER READING D. Marquand, *Ramsay MacDonald* (1977).

Mackintosh, Charles Rennie (1868–1928), Scottish architect, one of the leading exponents of the Art Nouveau style. Mackintosh studied art and architecture in Glasgow. He won the competition for designing the new Glasgow School of Art (1894–1908), probably his best work, which established him as a leader of a distinctive style of Art Nouveau. He designed a number of houses and other buildings (including a school) in and around Glasgow and, with his wife, Margaret Mackintosh, designed furniture and interiors, for example for the Willow Tea Rooms in Glasgow (1897–1909). His work was highly influential elsewhere in Europe but much less so in Britain, outside Scot-

land. Exhibitions of his work were held in Venice, Munich, Dresden, Budapest and Moscow. He moved to London in 1923, seeking to establish himself as an architect and designer there, but his practice soon folded and he retired to the south of France and devoted himself, successfully, to painting watercolours.

FURTHER READING J. McKean, *Charles Rennie Mackintosh: Architect, Artist, Icon* (2000); R. Tarnes, *Charles Rennie Mackintosh* (2000).

Maclean, Donald. *See* CAMBRIDGE SPIES.

Macleod, Iain (Norman) (1913–70), Conservative politician. Macleod was born in Skipton, Yorkshire, where his father, a Liberal, was a medical practitioner. He was educated at Fettes School, Edinburgh, and Cambridge University, where he read history. He had a strong interest in the game of bridge, on which he wrote extensively. He showed no sign of interest in politics until in 1945 he unsuccessfully contested the Western Isles for the Conservatives. He had served in the army in World War II, then worked for the CONSERVATIVE PARTY Research Department, where his mentor was R.A. BUTLER.

In 1950 he became MP for Enfield, in the London suburbs, which he held until his death. He became minister of health, 1952–5, then minister of labour, 1955–9. As colonial secretary, 1959–61, he encouraged the speedy DECOLONIZATION of Africa, convinced that the alternative was bloodshed. He gained a reputation – damaging in the Conservative Party – for intelligence; Lord Salisbury's description of him as 'too clever by half' stuck. He also gained a reputation for radicalism on social questions. An unsuccessful party chairman and leader of the House, 1961–3, he retired from office in 1963, disagreeing with the choice of Alec DOUGLAS-HOME as leader, and became editor of the *Spectator*. He returned to government under Edward HEATH in June 1970 as CHANCELLOR OF THE EXCHEQUER, but died suddenly a month later.

FURTHER READING N. Fisher, *Iain Macleod* (1973).

Macmillan Committee on Finance and Industry

Industry (1929–31), committee of inquiry into the banking system, established in September 1929, when the international financial crisis was becoming increasingly serious and the GOLD STANDARD appeared to be threatened (*see* GREAT CRASH). The BANK OF ENGLAND had raised the bank rate to 6.5%, the highest level since 1921, and Philip SNOWDEN, the Labour CHANCELLOR OF THE EXCHEQUER, decided to fulfil Labour's promise to inquire into the banking system by appointing this committee.

The committee was chaired by Hugh Pattison Macmillan (1873–1952), a distinguished Scottish lawyer, who became a lord of appeal and a life peer in 1930 and minister of information in 1939–40. The members included the economists T.E. Gregory and John Maynard KEYNES, who was now distancing himself from the Liberals and seeking to influence Labour; the trade unionist Ernest BEVIN; Lord Bradbury (1872–1950), the former joint permanent secretary at the Treasury and a major influence on the restoration of the gold standard in 1925; Cecil Lubbock, representing the Bank of England; the City banker R.H. Brand; W.E.D. Allen of the COOPERATIVE MOVEMENT; some industrialists; and Reginald McKenna, the former Liberal chancellor, now chairman of the Midland Bank and, unusual in banking circles, a critic of the Bank of England.

The committee was charged with discovering whether the arrangements for banking, finance and credit, internal and international, were helping or handicapping trade and industrial employment. This followed many years in which the banks, and the CITY OF LONDON in general, had been blamed for Britain's assumed relative economic decline, because of their preference for lending overseas rather than at home. At the hearings in 1930 (at which 57 witnesses were interviewed) Keynes and Bevin scored a triumph by forcing

Montagu NORMAN, governor of the Bank of England, to admit that Britain had returned to the gold standard at too high a rate in relation to the dollar, for the sake of the City's international financial connections, and that this had led to UNEMPLOYMENT and wage reductions in Britain. The report was largely written by Keynes and provided a detailed and invaluable account of British banking, credit and investment practices. Keynes had worked hard to convince the committee that the problem to be considered was not just that of finance for industry, as Snowden assumed, but about monetary and economic fundamentals, in particular the problem of the overvalued pound. The report concluded that the overvaluation of sterling had given Britain a substantial 'competitive handicap'.

But the committee's recommendations were more cautious than Keynes wished. Following pressure from the Bank of England, it reported in favour of retaining the gold standard at its current level. Keynes, whose views were always tempered by his political acuteness, accepted this on grounds of expediency, recognizing the need to preserve financial confidence and to ensure that Britain retained the prestige to supply international leadership. But, as a long-term reform, a larger, more flexible issue of currency was proposed to increase insulation from world fluctuations. The report declared that the banks were, contrary to much criticism, providing adequate credit for industry (apart from financing sales abroad) but that relations between the City and industry could be closer.

Though the tone of the report was reassuring, its documentation of Britain's position in the world economy – in particular the lack of balance between demand and supply, the fall in prices and the decline of British exports – made the crisis seem even more hopeless. In one addendum to the report a group of committee members, including Bevin, McKenna, Allen and Keynes, recommended more flexible use of low interest rates to stimulate borrowing and employment, and the use of TARIFFS (*see* TARIFF REFORM) and bounties to encourage exports. Bevin and Allen added the reservation that serious consideration should be given to devaluation of the pound, and that state planning and NATIONALIZATION, including nationalization of the Bank of England, should come before tariffs. In another reservation Bradbury alone defended the existing operation of the gold standard. Lubbock wrote yet another dissenting memorandum, arguing that the chief sources of the problems were non-monetary. This was one of a number of other dissenting comments. The range of views expressed revealed that the committee represented, more than anything, the great differences of opinion among influential figures responsible for the British economy. By the time the report appeared, in July 1931, it had largely been bypassed by events and it had little effect, not too surprisingly, given the acute differences in opinion that it embodied.

FURTHER READING P. Williamson, *National Crisis and National Government: British Politics, the Economy and Empire, 1926–1932* (1992).

Macmillan, (Maurice) Harold (1894–1986), Conservative politician; PRIME MINISTER (1957–63). Son of a publisher of Scottish ancestry and an American mother, Macmillan retained a lifelong interest in the Macmillan publishing firm. Educated at Eton and Balliol College, Oxford, he obtained a first-class degree in classics in 1919. Before university he served in World War I and was wounded three times, once severely. In 1919–20 he was aide-de-camp to the duke of Devonshire, governor general of Canada, and in 1920 married his daughter, Lady Dorothy Cavendish (d.1966). The marriage was unhappy and for most of his public career Macmillan was extremely lonely, while his wife had a long and close relationship with Robert Boothby, a Conservative MP.

Macmillan became MP for Stockton in northeast England in 1924, was defeated in 1929, reelected in 1931 and defeated again in 1945. It was an area of high UNEMPLOYMENT and focused his attention on social problems; this in turn prompted

him to write extensively, and his publications included *The Middle Way* (1937), which advocated economic planning. For a while in the mid-1930s he renounced the party whip, opposed Stanley BALDWIN's and Neville CHAMBERLAIN's foreign policies (APPEASEMENT in particular) and favoured CHURCHILL as party leader. He was seen at this time as too left-wing to have a glittering future in the party. He held junior appointments as parliamentary private secretary to the Ministry of Supply, 1940–2, and undersecretary at the Colonial Office, 1942. He became minister resident at Allied HQ in northwest Africa, 1942–5, which made him responsible for the whole Mediterranean theatre at an important stage of the war. This established his reputation, and he returned to Britain to serve as secretary for air, 1945. After losing his Stockton seat in the 1945 election, he won the safe seat of Bromley, Kent, in a by-election later in the year and held it until his retirement.

Macmillan took an active part in the opposition, and was appointed minister of housing and local government when the Conservatives returned to government in 1951. The failure of the Labour government to end the serious HOUSING shortage had been an important election issue. The Conservatives had promised to build 300,000 houses a year, a seemingly impossible target. Macmillan achieved it, partly by reducing the quality of council housing and the infrastructure of housing developments. He was minister of defence, 1954–5, FOREIGN SECRETARY under Anthony EDEN for eight months in 1955, then CHANCELLOR OF THE EXCHEQUER for 13 months. He supported the SUEZ venture, then insisted upon stopping it when it became clear that the value of the pound was about to collapse because of American opposition to the war.

Macmillan was the obvious successor as party leader and prime minister when Eden resigned in January 1957. He had gained an aloof, patrician, but also flamboyant image – expressed from 1958 in the cartoon image of him as 'Supermac' – although the image was rather at odds with the reality. He also displayed a taste for sound bites, such as his (accurate enough) assertion in 1957 that 'most of our people have never had it so good'. He reunited a divided party, leading it to a resounding victory in the 1959 general election, and built a good relationship with the USA, culminating in the 1962 Nassau agreement by which Britain obtained US Polaris missiles. With the support of his colonial secretary Iain MACLEOD he carried through DECOLONIZATION in Africa, declaiming in another famous comment that 'a wind of change' was blowing through Africa. He abolished CONSCRIPTION, announced the Nuclear Test Ban treaty in 1963 and persuaded his party to agree to Britain's application to join the EUROPEAN ECONOMIC COMMUNITY in 1961. But in January 1963 General de Gaulle vetoed British entry. The economy was in difficulties, not least because Macmillan and his party had encouraged personal consumption at the expense of saving and investment. UNEMPLOYMENT was rising. Macmillan made a desperate attempt at recovery by dismissing seven cabinet ministers, including the chancellor of the exchequer, Selwyn Lloyd, in the so-called 'night of the long knives', 13 July 1962, bringing in others, and by inflating the economy in preparation for an election in 1964. Then in 1963 the PROFUMO AFFAIR discredited the government further. Macmillan then became ill and resigned in October 1963, playing a large and controversial role from his sickbed in the selection of his successor, Alec DOUGLAS-HOME.

Thereafter Macmillan played a quiet role in politics, living a frugal and often lonely life. He enjoyed his role as chancellor of the University of Oxford, and in his later years was very critical of the governments of Margaret THATCHER, famously in the House of Lords (which he entered as earl of Stockton in 1984), where he criticized privatization of publicly owned utilities as 'selling off the family silver'.

FURTHER READING A. Horne, *Macmillan: The Official Biography* (2 vols., 1988–9); H. Macmillan, *Memoirs* (6 vols., 1966–73); J. Turner, *Macmillan* (1994).

McMillan, Margaret (1860–1931), early member of the labour movement and a pioneer in early childhood EDUCATION. She conducted most of her work to improve the lives of children in the slums of Deptford, in southeast London. She was born in New York of Scottish parents, and her father died when she was five years old. Shortly thereafter she returned to Scotland with her mother and beloved elder sister, Rachel McMillan, who herself became a philanthropist and reformer. Margaret was educated at Inverness High School and the Royal Academy, Inverness, and in 1879 took her first job as a governess in Edinburgh. From 1881 to 1889 she studied and taught English in Switzerland, then returned to Britain and took up several other positions as a governess.

By 1889 Margaret and Rachel were living together in Bloomsbury in central London, and Margaret's life might well have continued in the same direction as thousands of other educated young women forced to work for their living. But her interest in the theory of education as well as the labour movement had begun to grow. She began doing voluntary work for labour organizations, and in 1893, after the sisters had moved to Bradford, Margaret became one of the founder members of the INDEPENDENT LABOUR PARTY (ILP). For a time the sisters did voluntary work for the socialist movement in Bradford, but in 1894 Rachel left to train as a sanitary inspector and afterwards worked for Kent County Council.

The same year Margaret was elected as an ILP representative on the Bradford school board. This experience led to her increasing concern for working-class children. In 1899 she organized the first ever medical inspection of schoolchildren in England. In 1901 she published her first work on education, *Early Childhood*, and the next year left Bradford and moved to Bromley in Kent to live with Rachel. In 1904, she began working for London County Council as a manager of schools; she also published her second work, *Education Through the Imagination*. In 1907 she was elected a member of the National Administrative

Council of the ILP, and published *Labour and Childhood*.

Starting in 1910, McMillan began what many consider her most important work, in Deptford. There she opened health clinics, treatment centres, overnight camps and play areas for deprived children, while campaigning for better provision for children everywhere. She became particularly interested in improving and extending nursery-school education for very young children. She also wished to see more rigorous standards and training for their teachers, not subscribing to the common contemporary view that women were fit to teach very young children solely by nature of their gender. 1917 proved to be a bittersweet year for Margaret; she was invested with the CBE in recognition of her work on behalf of children, but she was devastated by the death of Rachel, her sister and best friend with whom she had shared most of her life. In 1923 she was made president of the Nursery School Association, now the British Association for Early Childhood Education, a post she held until 1929. The following year, as a tribute to her sister, she founded the Rachel McMillan Training College for Teachers. She died in 1931.

Margaret McMillan lived to see many of the things she campaigned for – such as free school meals and school clinics for deprived children – become a reality. However, it took many decades for her ideas about nursery-school provision to become accepted practice. Her calls for free nursery-school places to be provided for all children only began to be implemented in the mid-1990s, over sixty years after her death.

FURTHER READING E. Bradburn, *Margaret McMillan: Portrait of a Pioneer* (1989); C. Steedman, *Childhood, Culture and Class in Britain: Margaret McMillan, 1860–1931* (1990).

MacPherson Report. *See* LAWRENCE, STEPHEN.

magistrates. The office of magistrate in England and Wales dates from at least the 14th century and is normally a part-time, unpaid crown appointment. Magistrates are usually also called 'justices of the peace' (JPs). This system of lay justice is probably unique throughout the world. Stipendiary (paid) magistrates (most recently called 'district judges') date from *c.*1780. In the late 20th century they numbered about 100, normally recruited and trained from among solicitors, barristers and justices' clerks and found usually in London or the larger cities, where pressure on the justice system is greatest. Unlike lay magistrates, they sit alone (with a clerk) and usually take on difficult cases such as those that last several days and cannot easily be heard by lay justices, or are brought in when pressure of work in the magistrates' courts is especially high.

The lord chancellor appoints magistrates in England and WALES, except in Lancashire where historically they have been appointed by the chancellor of the Duchy of Lancaster. In SCOTLAND they are appointed by the secretary of state for Scotland. Appointments of magistrates have always been based upon local recommendations. At the beginning of the century, and for long before, the magistracy was drawn narrowly from men of property, usually landed gentry rather than the ARISTOCRACY. There was a property qualification, which maintained this social exclusivity. There was a distinction between the county bench (rural areas) and the borough bench (towns), which was held to be socially inferior. The property qualification was abolished in the boroughs in the 19th century, and in the counties by the LIBERAL government in 1906. The Liberals also introduced a system whereby appointments were based on the recommendations of local advisory committees, usually composed of existing magistrates. At this time there was widespread criticism that the bench was overwhelmingly CONSERVATIVE, which the Liberals were under pressure to remedy. However, the mainly Conservative and aristocratic lord lieutenants continued to control selection in the counties, so the social composition of the magistracy was not transformed. In the boroughs, the politicians in LOCAL GOVERNMENT controlled appointments. Local mayors qualified automatically as JPs, unless they were female. The system of selection was part of the patronage system used by politicians to reward local people and influence municipal elections. Advisory committees often met infrequently compared with later in the century. New magistrates might be appointed infrequently, courts met less frequently and some were rarely called upon to serve.

The social and political composition of the magistracy was contentious in the 20th century as never before. Women were excluded from the bench until the Sex Disqualification Removal Act of 1919. The first women to be appointed were in Lancashire, under the jurisdiction of the Duchy of Lancaster, where Ada Summers, the mayor of Stalybridge, Cheshire, became the first woman magistrate in 1919. The lord chancellor Lord Birkenhead (F.E. SMITH) set up a special committee of women to advise on the appointment of women as magistrates; its members, all of whom were magistrates themselves, included Beatrice WEBB. Over 200 women were appointed nationwide in 1919–20, out of several thousand magistrates in total. There was considerable resistance to the appointment of women over most of the country, and after World War II the Royal Commission on the Selection of Justices found women to be severely under-represented. Of 16,800 JPs in 1947, only 3700 were women. Women were similarly under-represented in the legal profession. The first woman stipendiary magistrate was Sybil Campbell in London in 1945. By 1990, 16,090 magistrates were male, 12,587 female.

It was at least as difficult to include in the magistracy working-class people, or indeed anyone in a demanding or inflexible occupation, as the demands on JPs became greater over the century. By the end of the century they were required to sit in court for a minimum of 26 working days each year. In practice 35–40 sittings was normal, and they were expected to devote increasing amounts of time to formal training, which was not a requirement at the beginning of the century. Undoubt-

edly, however, the social composition of the magistracy broadened over the century.

Magistrates were recruited from their local communities, with which they were expected to be familiar. For centuries they were the main arms of local government, administering a range of functions, from maintaining the highways to licensing and regulating markets and fairs. In the 19th century many of these functions were taken over by elected local authorities. At the beginning of the 20th century magistrates could still summon troops to control episodes of public protest, and did so in major industrial disputes up to World War I. The last reading by a magistrate in public of the 18th-century Riot Act (which required crowds to disperse within an hour) was at Stockport in 1919. In the later 20th century the magistrates' administrative function remained only in the power to control local liquor and betting and gaming licensing.

Normally three magistrates heard cases. Each court had a legally trained clerk, normally a solicitor or barrister, to advise on points of law. The main function of magistrates concerned the administration of criminal justice. About 97% of crime cases brought before the courts were dealt with in the magistrates' courts, the more serious of them then being committed to higher courts. The bulk of cases concerned accusations of drunk and disorderly behaviour, theft, a host of infringements of motoring laws, drugs, deception and fraud cases and various kinds of assault and public-order offences. After 1945 the advent of the motor car probably had the greatest impact on magistrates' courts in the 20th century, bringing more middle-class/professional defendants into court. Magistrates who were themselves found guilty of a drink-and-drive offence were expected to resign immediately, though judges were not. Magistrates also dealt with civil matters, such as domestic cases in the family proceedings courts. Moreover, magistrates could be contacted at home, for example by social workers to sign an urgent order to take an abused child into care.

At the end of the century it was increasingly suggested that the ancient lay magistracy should be replaced by legal professionals, but the future of this large, unpaid body remained undecided.
FURTHER READING Sir T. Skyrme, *The Changing Image of the Magistracy* (1983); Sir T. Skyrme, *History of the Justices of the Peace* (1994 edn).

Major, John (1941–), Conservative politician; PRIME MINISTER (1990–7). Coming from a modest background in south London, Major left school at 16 and went to work in a bank. He served as leader of Lambeth local authority in the 1960s, and became MP for Huntington in 1979. After a time as a party whip, Major entered the CABINET as chief secretary to the Treasury in 1987, before replacing Geoffrey HOWE as FOREIGN SECRETARY in 1989. He was uncomfortable in this post, and after only a few months he became CHANCELLOR OF THE EXCHEQUER, bringing Britain into the European Exchange Rate Mechanism (ERM) in September 1990 (*see* EUROPEAN MONETARY SYSTEM). Major supported Margaret THATCHER in the November 1990 party leadership election. Following her resignation after the first vote, Major went on to win the election (with Thatcher's support), and became prime minister on 28 November.

Much of Major's term as prime minister was taken up with dealing with divisions in the CONSERVATIVE PARTY over Europe, but he did manage to build a good relationship with US president George Bush senior during the GULF WAR. Perhaps his most important achievement was in his negotiations over the MAASTRICHT treaty, where he was able to extract a compromise that avoided a catastrophic split in cabinet. Criticisms of his leadership were increasingly heard from the Conservative right, who unfavourably compared his quiet and pragmatic style with the radical drive of his predecessor.

Major managed to lead the party to victory in the GENERAL ELECTION of April 1992, against the predictions of opinion polls, but with a reduced majority. He suffered a blow to his popularity later that year when he was forced to withdraw from the ERM; on 'Black Wednesday' (16 September 1992), Norman Lamont, chancellor of the exchequer, failed in a desperate attempt to protect the pound from the pressure of speculative selling. Recovery from the economic recession of the early 1990s was postponed. With his parliamentary majority further eroded by by-election losses, the Eurosceptic wing of the Conservative Party appeared to have won control of his government. Increasingly irritated by the opposition within his own party, Major threw down the gauntlet to his critics by resigning the party leadership in 1995, successfully defeating John Redwood in the subsequent leadership election.

By 1997 the economy was clearly beginning to recover, with inflation and interest rates at low levels. In addition, Major had played an important role in encouraging initiatives for a negotiated peace in NORTHERN IRELAND, which had resulted in the 1993 'Downing Street Declaration'. Yet, after 18 years in office, the Conservative Party suffered its worst defeat of the century in May 1997, and Major resigned the leadership. He was succeeded by William HAGUE.

Malaya/Malaysia. At the beginning of the 20th century the geographical area that would later become Malaysia was a complex patchwork of territories. The British held the Straits Settlements, which consisted of SINGAPORE, Penang and Malacca. The British-controlled area of the Malay Peninsula, immediately south of Thailand, was known as the Federated and Unfederated Malay States. The Federated States (formed in 1895) included Perak, Selangor, Negri Sembilan and Pahang. The Unfederated States included Johore, Brunei, Perlis, Kedah, Kelantan and Trengganu. The British were also in control of the regions of North Borneo and Sarawak (which was ruled by its 'rajahs', the Brooke family, for over a century). All these 'native states' were presided over by a British high commissioner, who was also the governor of the Straits Settlements.

The Malay States, Sarawak, North Borneo and Singapore all fell to the Japanese in 1942, and remained under Japanese control until the end of WORLD WAR II. With the resumption of British control in 1945 came calls for greater self-determination, and the Federation of Malaya was founded in 1948. It included the Straits Settlements of Penang and Malacca and all the Federated and Unfederated Malay States except Brunei. Kuala Lumpur was made the capital city of the new federation. However, from the beginning there were disputes based on ethnic lines about the structure of government and the economy. By the 1940s the population of the Malay States was only 50% ethnic Malay. The remaining population was made up mainly of Chinese (37%) and Indian (12%) immigrants whom the British had recruited to work in the lucrative tin and rubber industries. The immigrant community regarded the British as the rulers of the Malay States and the ethnic Malays as their fellow subjects. They therefore did not take kindly to the Malays assuming control of the new federation. Added to the problem of ethnic tension was the emergence of communist-backed rebel guerrilla forces, who took advantage of British colonial weakness in the late 1940s and engaged in conflict with the authorities between 1948 and 1960. This period is often referred to as the 'Malayan Emergency'. In late 1951 the British high commissioner in Malaya, Sir Henry Gurney, was assassinated by the rebels. British forces launched an offensive and over the next few years successfully neutralized the rebel movement, though the state of emergency did not officially end until 1960.

In 1957, once the situation was under control, Britain bowed to Malayan pressure and granted the federation its independence, as part of a wider movement towards the inevitable DECOLONIZATION of the EMPIRE. In 1961 the first prime minister of Malaya, Tunku Abdul Rahman, proposed a new political federation, to include Malaya, Singapore, Sarawak, Brunei and Sabah (formerly North Borneo). This new nation, the Federation of Malaysia, came into being in 1963, but did not include Brunei, and two years later Singapore left to become an independent state of its own. The British maintained a military presence in Malaysia until 1971. It remains a member of the COMMONWEALTH.

FURTHER READING B.W. Andaya and L.Y. Andaya, *A History of Malaysia* (1982); J.G. Butcher, *The British in Malaya, 1880–1941: The Social History of a European Community in Colonial Southeast Asia* (1979).

Malta, small island group in the Mediterranean, 100 km (60 miles) south of Sicily, consisting of Malta, Gozo and a number of smaller islets. Malta was one of Britain's spoils from the Napoleonic Wars; it was occupied from 1802 and was formally annexed to the British EMPIRE in 1814. Malta was of strategic importance to the British as, after the completion of the SUEZ Canal, it lay directly on the supply route to INDIA, and the harbour in the capital city of Valletta provided for many years the base for the British fleet in the Mediterranean.

There was tension between Britain and the Maltese during the interwar years, when persistent calls by the Nationalist Party for union with Italy resulted in the suspension of the Maltese legislature (which had been established in 1921) and the reimposition of direct rule from Britain in 1936. Anti-British feeling began to evaporate during WORLD WAR II, however, when Malta was subject to constant bombing by the Axis powers after 1940 because of its strategic importance to the Allies. King GEORGE VI awarded the George Cross to the people of Malta in 1943 for their bravery during the assaults.

After the war, however, political agitation again grew, with the Nationalist Party advocating independence and the Maltese Labour Party promoting the direct integration of Malta into the United Kingdom. A referendum was held in 1956 in which three-quarters of voters approved the plan for integration, but the low voter turnout and the bitter past experience of Irish integration made

Westminster hesitate. Opposition to the British presence arose yet again. The Nationalist Party won the 1962 elections and began negotiations for independence which Britain, in the throes of the general DECOLONIZATION of the old empire, was in no position to deny. Independence and COMMONWEALTH membership were granted in 1964, and Britain maintained a naval and RAF presence on the island for a few years afterwards. In 1974 Malta became a republic, though it remains a member of the Commonwealth.

FURTHER READING D. Austin, *Malta and the End of Empire* (1971).

Manchester Guardian, newspaper that has normally taken a liberal position, independent of political parties. It was founded as a regional newspaper in 1821. The paper became nationally prominent under its best-known editor, C.P. Scott, who retired in 1929. To this day the newspaper is owned by the Scott Trust, a body created in 1936 to maintain Scott's journalistic and commercial principles. Scott came out firmly against the BOER WAR, leading to threats of violence against him and the newspaper's offices. Scott was pro-Zionist and a strong supporter of the BALFOUR DECLARATION in favour of a Jewish national home in PALESTINE. He was also highly critical of British policy in IRELAND in the period 1916–21 and of Allied treatment of Germany after WORLD WAR I (*see* VERSAILLES, TREATY OF). The newspaper was warning against Nazi anti-Semitism from 1932 and was always wary of Hitler. It strongly supported CHURCHILL during WORLD WAR II. After the war it became increasingly national in orientation: in 1959 'Manchester' was removed from its title, and in 1960 it began to be published from London. It supported the Conservative Party in the elections of the 1950s, but opposed the SUEZ episode and, in 1982, the FALKLANDS War. It was strongly critical of the THATCHER governments at a time when the majority of the British press was pro-Thatcher, and it was seen as pro-Labour. During John MAJOR'S premiership it uncovered some of the 'sleaze' in which the government was increasingly mired, notably by starting the process that led to the conviction and imprisonment of the Conservative MP Jonathan Aitken for perjury in his responses to accusations of corruption. The Labour government of Tony BLAIR elected in 1997 also quickly came to regard it as a critic. The paper maintained broad news and cultural coverage and successful sales to the end of the century.

FURTHER READING D. Ayerst, *Guardian: Biography of a Newspaper* (1971).

Marconi scandal (1912–13), financial scandal involving prominent members of the Liberal government. In March 1912 the Post Office agreed a tender with the British Marconi Wireless Telegraphy Company for the construction of an imperial wireless network. It was rumoured that Marconi had benefited from connections with the LIBERAL government and that ministers had profited from inside knowledge of the deal. Those accused included the postmaster general, Herbert SAMUEL, and the attorney general, Sir Rufus ISAACS, whose brother Godfrey was a director of both the British and US Marconi companies. The US company had no holdings in the British company, but stood to gain from its success. The Isaacs brothers and Samuel were Jewish and became targets of anti-Semitic attacks. Also implicated were David LLOYD GEORGE, chancellor of the exchequer, and the Liberal chief whip and patronage secretary to the treasury, the master of Elibank. For the Conservatives it was an opportunity to attack the Liberals. Godfrey Isaacs successfully sued a journalist who alleged that a Jewish radical conspiracy lay behind the scandal. Those involved were cleared of wrong-doing by select committees of both Houses of Parliament, although it emerged that Rufus Isaacs, Lloyd George and Elibank had bought shares in the American Marconi Company (offered to them by Godfrey Isaacs) but not in the British company. They apologized to Parliament for their indiscretion.

FURTHER READING G. Searle, *Corruption in British Politics, 1895–1930* (1987).

Markiewicz, Constance, Countess (1868–1927), Irish nationalist. She was born into the Anglo-Irish ascendancy, as a Gore-Booth of County Sligo, then married a Polish count of modest means. Beautiful and dynamic, she became active in politics initially because she was interested in women's rights and was equally concerned about poverty. She saw Irish nationalism as the best way forward in IRELAND on both issues and joined SINN FÉIN. However, she was unenthusiastic about some of its male leaders and poured most of her energy into Maud Gonne's women's organization, Inghinidhe na h Eireann, and into a youth movement for boys, the Fianna, which she created in 1909 to train boys to participate in a war of liberation.

Markiewicz worked hard to support the families of workers involved in the Dublin lock-out of 1913 and sheltered first James Larkin and then James Connolly (the leaders of the Irish National Transport and General Workers' Union) in her Dublin home. She was a founder-member of the Irish Citizen Army, which was formed under Connolly's command during the lock-out. She was active at the centre of the EASTER RISING, and was the only woman tried by court martial following the rising, with 170 men; with 169 of the men she was convicted. She was initially sentenced to death, but this was commuted to penal servitude for life because of her sex (to her great indignation). The sentence was reduced, and she spent a year in Aylesbury jail. A second term of imprisonment (from May 1918) did not prevent her being a candidate, like other Sinn Féiners, in the GENERAL ELECTION of 1918 and, like 72 others, she was elected. She was the only woman among them and indeed the first woman to be elected to the House of COMMONS, to which women had only just been admitted (*see* REPRESENTATION OF THE PEOPLE ACT, 1918), but she did not take her seat. However, while she was still in prison she was appointed minister of labour in the unofficial government formed by Sinn Féin in 1919. After the establishment of the Irish Free State in 1921 she fought with DE VALERA and the anti-treaty Republicans in the civil war that followed. She went on to lead a revitalized and strongly Republican women's movement, the Cumann na m Bann, in a new state that she believed had done disappointingly little to promote gender equality.

FURTHER READING F.S.L. Lyons, *Ireland since the Famine* (1973).

Marne, battles of the (1914 and 1918), two key battles of WORLD WAR I. The river Marne, a tributary of the Seine to the east of Paris, was the point of furthest penetration into France of the German army during war. The first battle, 5–11 September 1914, was a series of interrelated actions by British and French forces designed to force the Germans to retreat from their advance on Paris. This was successful, but also marked the beginning of the long trench-based war of attrition. The second battle, 15–20 July 1918, was a last offensive thrust enabling the Germans to cross the river, but they were pushed back by a vigorous French counter-offensive. This began the Franco-British-American advance that forced the Germans to sue for peace 15 weeks later.

FURTHER READING Sir E. Spears, *Liaison 1914: A Narrative of a Great Retreat* (1930, 1969, 1999).

marriage. *See* DIVORCE; POPULATION.

Marshall Plan, name commonly given to the European Recovery Programme, which was publicly proposed by the US secretary of state George Marshall (1880–1959) in 1947. The Marshall Plan involved the granting of economic aid by the USA to some 16 European nations, most of whom had been devastated by WORLD WAR II. The plan was designed to help Europe recover economically and politically, and to avoid the kind of problems it had encountered in the 1920s and 1930s in the wake of WORLD WAR I. The USA had other motives in promoting the Marshall Plan. Initially, aid was offered to all European states, including the Soviet Union and what would become its satellites in Eastern Europe. However, the Soviets were suspicious of US motives and rejected the Marshall Plan, calling it an instrument of American imperialism. Other nations that had initially expressed interest in the Plan, such as Poland, Yugoslavia and Czechoslovakia, followed suit. As a result of communist non-participation, the Marshall Plan was soon being promoted in America as a way to rebuild and strengthen the democratic states of Western Europe and enable them to resist any possible attempts at communist expansion (*see also* COLD WAR).

The Marshall Plan came into effect in April 1948. It was administered by the newly formed Organization for European Economic Cooperation (OEEC), along with the US Economic Cooperation Administration. Sixteen countries were involved: Britain, Ireland, Switzerland, Austria, France, Belgium, the Netherlands, Luxembourg, Italy, Portugal, Greece, Turkey, Sweden, Denmark, Norway and Iceland. Though not receiving direct Marshall Plan aid, West Germany was given some assistance in rebuilding its economy so that it would not be tempted by communism, and with an eye to preventing it becoming a military threat again. Over the four years of the programme Britain received some $2.7 billion in aid. The Plan as a whole disbursed some $13.3 billion. By 1952 all the participating countries had regained or even surpassed their pre-war standards of living. Industrial production rose some 35% over pre-war levels. By enabling Britain and other European nations to rebuild their economies more quickly and to work together while doing so, the Marshall Plan is widely regarded as having helped to bring political stability to Western Europe after 1945.

FURTHER READING A.W. Dulles (edited with an introduction by M. Wala), *The Marshall Plan* (1993); H. Pelling, *Britain and the Marshall Plan* (1988).

Mass-Observation (MO), social-survey organization founded in 1937 by Tom Harrisson, an anthropologist; Charles Madge, a journalist (later a sociologist); and Humphrey Jennings, a documentary filmmaker. They aimed to establish a 'democratic social science' that would reveal the real feelings and activities of ordinary British people, as distinct from what they believed were the distortions promoted by politicians and the media. In this way they hoped to encourage an authentic sense of national identity and momentum for change. Harrisson's interest in bird-watching and natural history influenced the approach: volunteer observers were encouraged to watch people and to record their actions and words without their knowledge.

The first observation of everyday life in 'Worktown' (Bolton), Lancashire, was carried out by a group led by Harrisson from 1937 to 1940. They recorded conversations and behaviour in such places as pubs and churches. At the same time, Madge and Jennings recruited a national panel of volunteers to keep diaries of their everyday observations and to carry out observations on specified topics, including the coronation day of King GEORGE VI, ARMISTICE Day and the MUNICH crisis. In the first year 500 volunteers participated; they were from a variety of backgrounds, though the women proved the most assiduous. About 2847 individuals replied to at least one directive in the period 1937–45. From January 1939 to 1949 MO sent out regular short questionnaires to panel members on a variety of topics. It also conducted sample surveys in which people were interviewed about such topical matters as the birth rate and their choice of family size.

With the outbreak of WORLD WAR II, Tom Harrisson took sole charge of MO. He persuaded the home intelligence department of the Ministry of Information that MO was ideally placed to monitor civilian morale, and the department paid for regular research reports from early 1940 until late 1941. MO was also contracted by other government departments in the course of the war for specific investigations, for example to monitor reactions to the BEVERIDGE Report in 1942. MO also continued its own investigations of everyday life during the war, receiving panel reports on such matters as RATIONING, EVACUATION, CONSCRIPTION, air raids (*see* BLITZ), war work and political aspirations after the war. In 1942 Harrisson joined the army and became a member of the Special Operations Executive (SOE) in Borneo. H.D. (Bob) Willcock took over.

Over 20 books were based on MO material between 1937 and 1950, such as *The Pub and the People*, *Britain by Mass Observation* and *War Factory*. These books, together with newspaper articles and radio broadcasts, made the organization well known and helped to fund the work. In 1949 MO became a consumer research organization directed by Len England and Mollie Tarrant, who had been Mass-Observers during the war. On a brief return to Britain in 1959 Harrisson took a team of former Mass-Observers back to Bolton to assess changes since 1937.The results were published as *Britain Revisited* (1961). The pre-1949 records of MO investigations remained the property of Tom Harrisson, and in 1970 they were deposited on trust at the University of Sussex, where they remain. Harrisson died in 1976. From 1981 MO revived, recruiting a new panel of observers to respond to directives sent to them at least three times a year, again on a variety of topics, including the attitudes to the FALKLANDS War, the death of DIANA, PRINCESS OF WALES, OLD AGE AND AGEING, and the European Community (*see* EUROPEAN ECONOMIC COMMUNITY). Into the 21st century MO provided a unique research archive, under the direction of Dorothy Sheridan.

FURTHER READING A.Calder, 'Mass-Observation, 1937–1947' in M. Bulmer (ed.), *Essays on the History of British Sociological Research* (1987), 121–36; D. Sheridan, 'Mass Observation in the 1980s and 1990s' in *Social History* (1992).

May Committee on National Expenditure

(1931), committee of inquiry into government expenditure. By February 1931 the international financial crisis (*see* GREAT CRASH) had made the position of the Labour government precarious. The Conservatives moved a vote of censure on what they defined as the government's wasteful expenditure and borrowing, especially for the

UNEMPLOYMENT insurance fund. The Liberals called for the appointment of a special committee to review government expenditure and to recommend economies. This amendment was accepted by the government and supported by Philip SNOWDEN, the chancellor of the exchequer, who recognized the gravity of the situation. In consequence a committee on national expenditure was appointed, chaired by Sir George May, previously the secretary of the Prudential Assurance Company. There were six other members, including two representatives of the labour movement, an accountant, Lord Plender, and the remaining two representing business.

The committee reported in July 1931. The majority report predicted a budget deficit of £120 million. This alarming (and alarmist) prediction was a product of accounting conventions: it assumed, unrealistically, that all unemployment expenditure should be met from current income, rather than from borrowing. The majority of businessmen on the committee treated the situation as a business rescue rather than as the international political crisis that it was. They spoke for views widespread in the business and financial communities, placing all the blame upon politicians. They recommended taxation increases of £24 million and cuts in public expenditure of £96 million: cuts were to be made in health and education; public servants (such as teachers) were to have their salaries cut by up to 20%; and unemployment benefit was also to be cut by 20%. The committee assumed that if 'the nation did without [a service] a few years ago … it cannot be essential'. Effectively it recommended reversing many of the post-war social and economic improvements, assuming that the economy had been burdened by unnecessary and wasteful expenditure upon improving the living conditions of the mass of the population.

The two Labour members, representing the TUC and the Automobile Trades Association, issued a less pessimistic dissenting report. This treated the crisis as resulting less from public expenditure than from the effects of the return to the

GOLD STANDARD, aggravated by the fall in world prices. They argued that social expenditure was essential investment in improving industrial efficiency and that sacrifices should be common to all sections of society, in view of the level of wasteful luxury spending by the rich. They also pointed out that the greatest proportionate increase in expenditure was actually payments not on unemployment benefits and other social expenditure, but on the national debt, largely resulting from World War I. This minority report was almost wholly ignored in the public debate. The majority report seriously lowered public confidence even further, and served to intensify the crisis. The failure of the Labour government to agree on the cuts proposed led to its downfall in August 1931 (*see* LABOUR PARTY).

FURTHER READING P. Williamson, *National Crisis and National Government: British Politics, the Economy and Empire, 1926–32* (1992).

means test, a test of qualification for UNEMPLOYMENT assistance introduced in 1931 when the NATIONAL GOVERNMENT, following the economic crisis of 1931, tightened up the system of payments of benefit to the unemployed. Those who had exhausted their entitlement to unemployment insurance no longer qualified for an agreed schedule of payments but received payments assessed according to need. Need was assessed by taking account of the whole income of the household, including that of working children, and of the value of household possessions, if they were deemed luxuries, such as pianos or 'excess' chairs. Unemployed people were expected to sell such goods and apply for relief only when they owned little more than basic necessities. At the worst point of the recession almost 1 million people were subject to means-tested benefit. Similar tests had always been applied to applicants for POOR LAW relief, but many unemployed people had been 'respectable' workers, used to avoiding pauperism, and they felt degraded by this prying into their personal affairs. Means tests were more stringently carried out in some places than in others. The changes led to riots in 1934, which in turn led to administrative improvements, although the principle of the household means test remained unchanged.

FURTHER READING W.R. Garside, *British Unemployment, 1919–1939: A Study in Public Policy* (1990).

medicine. The capacity of medicine to cure sickness expanded massively over the 20th century, as did understanding of the causes and progress of disease. In the first half of the century the main victories were against infectious diseases, especially those affecting children, leading to a substantial decline in child mortality (*see* POPULATION). Tuberculosis, diphtheria, measles, whooping cough, scarlet fever and infantile diarrhoea declined, in some cases (e.g. diphtheria) to vanishing point. At the beginning of the century almost 1500 people in every million in the population died each year from respiratory tuberculosis; in 1971, 13 people in every million died from this cause. These changes were partly, perhaps largely, an outcome of improved STANDARDS OF LIVING, especially as they led to better diets and HOUSING. Diseases caused primarily by malnutrition, such as rickets, almost disappeared, though they showed signs of resurgence in the high UNEMPLOYMENT period of the 1980s. Inoculation has been important (e.g. against diphtheria, whooping cough, measles), as have antibiotics (e.g. against pneumonia and tuberculosis), but in general the downward curve in the incidence of the relevant diseases began before these procedures were introduced on a large scale.

Medicine has been more indisputably effective in delaying death by curing or palliating non-infectious conditions, such as the advances in surgery for various forms of heart disease later in the century. Successful procedures were also introduced that greatly improved the quality of life for people with crippling but non-fatal diseases, such as the development from the 1970s of joint replacement surgery and from the 1980s of laser treatment for the removal of cataracts, which otherwise cause blindness. Procedures such as these have differentially benefited older people (*see* OLD AGE AND AGEING). Similarly beneficial has been the increased use from the 1940s of paramedical skills, such as the use of physiotherapy to assist stroke victims.

The use of various forms of drug therapy expanded greatly, especially from the 1930s, when penicillin, the first of the antibiotics, dramatically improved the capacity to cure pneumonia and puerperal fever – the latter had been a major cause of death among women following childbirth (*see* FLEMING, ALEXANDER). Later in the century, however, there were concerns that the overuse of antibiotics was itself leading to the emergence of drug-resistant strains of bacteria. There were similar concerns about the over prescription of a range of other drugs, and fears that this was encouraged by large and powerful drug companies.

Improved understanding of the immune system, due to the work of Sir Peter Medawar and others from the 1950s, enabled the development of drugs that facilitated the transplant of organs (such as heart, lungs and liver), which had become almost routine by the end of the century. Advances in surgical techniques, supported by technological change, assisted these and other developments. The introduction of 'keyhole surgery', for example, performed using only a small incision, meant some forms of major surgery could be much less invasive.

Investment in medical research expanded especially rapidly in the second half of the century. Government investment began during WORLD WAR I with the foundation of the Medical Research Council with an annual grant of £50,000 a year. This increased to £195,000 in 1937–8, then grew with increasing speed after WORLD WAR II to £97 million in 1981–2 and £146 million in 1988–9. Charitable funding was also important, whether from single-disease organizations such as the Imperial Cancer Research Fund (established 1902) or the Asthma Research Council (1928), or from the Wellcome Foundation, which was founded in 1936 with profits from the Wellcome drug company and which by the end of the century was a major source of funding for medical research. Funding from such charitable foundations totalled £128 million in 1987–8. Both the government and charity contributions were outweighed by spending on research and development by the pharmaceutical industry in Britain, which came to £871 million in 1989.

SEE ALSO NATIONAL HEALTH SERVICE.

FURTHER READING W. Bynum and R. Porter (eds.), *Companion Encyclopaedia to the History of Medicine* (2 vols., 1993).

Methodism, religious movement that originated in the 18th century within the CHURCH OF ENGLAND, which Methodists believed to be complacent and sometimes corrupt, and which they wished to reform. Methodism was critical of the hierarchy of bishops and archbishops and emphasized the teaching of the scriptures and personal conversion. It separated from the Church of England and by 1900 was the largest NONCONFORMIST church in Britain. During the 19th century it developed a number of strands, but these gradually reunited in the early 20th century, unity being completed in 1932 when the Methodist Church was formed. At the beginning of the century the various strands of Methodism had about 800,000 adherents in total in the UK. By the time of unification the figure was about 860,000. After World War II Methodists worked hard to win converts, but membership fell steadily to 531,000 in 1980 and to 468,000 by 1990. Its long-established identification with temperance and hostility to gambling alienated many, although it also became openly committed to improvements in race relations, world development and peace. From the 1960s there were protracted but inconclusive discussions with the Church of England about closer relations between them, which failed largely because of lack of enthusiasm among Anglicans. In 1974 the first woman was ordained to the Methodist ministry. The Methodist annual conference in 1939 had declared that there were no theological objections to such a move, but there had long been fears that ordaining women would delay union with the Church of England.

MI5 and MI6, abbreviations for branches of British 'military intelligence'. MI5 is the internal intelligence and counter-intelligence service, while MI6 – the Secret Intelligence Service (SIS) – is concerned with overseas espionage. The abbreviationns represent institutions that have guarded the secrecy of their operations with such intensity – encompassing vigorous dissemination of misinformation – that it is only possible to provide an outline account of them as institutions, and not possible to give any trustworthy information on their operations.

In the 19th century Britain had a minimal secret service. Such activities were thought to be immoral and counterproductive. They appear to have grown persistently through the 20th century, accelerated by the world wars and, still more, by the COLD WAR. The expansion began with the formation of the Special Branch of the (London) Metropolitan Police in 1881–7 to pursue anarchists who were believed, surprisingly with hindsight, to be a threat to the British state. MI5 and MI6 originated in 1909 with the formation of the Secret Service Bureau in response to rising international tension, especially between Britain and Germany. Their activities expanded greatly during WORLD WAR I. In 1916 the internal arm, known as MO5, was reorganized and became known as MI5. The SIS was given the designation MI1(c) in 1916, but by the 1920s had become known as MI6.

Between the wars MI5 provided reports, on whose reliability views are mixed, on a variety of groups and individuals known or believed to be subversive. It is thought that the left – such as TRADE UNIONS and the National Unemployed Workers Movement (*see* HUNGER MARCHES; UNEMPLOYMENT) – was targeted more than the right. The true dimensions of the activities of both MI5 and MI6 in this period, as in others, are unknown and unavailable to researchers since the relevant public records are closed or destroyed. However, it

is now clear that MI6 played a central role in the destabilization and defeat of the first LABOUR government in 1924 by possibly originating and certainly widely circulating the ZINOVIEV LETTER. Public records that might reveal details of these activities were destroyed.

Both MI5 and MI6 certainly made an important contribution to the Allied victory in WORLD WAR II, although, again, details remain secret. They were greatly admired by Hitler, who credited their skills at lying and deception to the education of the overwhelming majority of their agents in English public schools. After the war their record, so far as it reached the public eye, was mixed. In the 1950s and 1960s they were at their most active, while being seriously undermined by 'moles' (secret British agents of the USSR) in their ranks (*see* CAMBRIDGE SPIES). In this period MI6, which had very close relations with the US Central Intelligence Agency (CIA), explicitly believed that it was the true arbiter of the national interest and it appears to have operated largely independently of politicians. As its then deputy chief, George Young, put it: 'It is the spy who has been called upon to remedy the situation created by deficiencies of ministers, diplomats, generals and priests', but it was the 'spies' themselves who diagnosed and defined these 'deficiencies', not necessarily objectively. Among other operations, it is believed that joint MI6/CIA operations failed to destabilize communist governments in Eastern Europe, such as Albania, but were occasionally successful against popular nationalist movements, as when the popular and moderate prime minister of Iran, Mohammed Mossadeq, was ousted in 1953. MI5 was active in NORTHERN IRELAND throughout the 'Troubles' from the 1960s to the end of the century.

Increasingly, by the end of the century, both institutions were accused of serious right-wing bias and gross incompetence. This was revealed, among other scandals, by the unsuccessful attempts to prevent the publication of the memoirs of a former agent, Peter Wright (published in 1986), which accused MI5 of, among other things, plots to undermine the Labour governments of Harold WILSON. Partly in consequence, in 1989 MI5 was put on a statutory footing for the first time by the Security Service Act. In 1994 the Intelligence Services Act put MI6 in a similar position. This statute established a joint committee of both houses of Parliament to bring the intelligence services under parliamentary scrutiny. This was greeted without enthusiasm by the services. The century ended with a number of former agents making public allegations of bizarre plots and routine incompetence against both departments. There were vigorous attempts to silence them, which led to increasing public questioning of the activities of the intelligence services and growing demands for more open, external scrutiny of their activities.

FURTHER READING C. Andrew, *Her Majesty's Secret Service: The Making of the British Intelligence Community* (1985); S. Dorril, *MI6: Fifty Years of Special Operations* (1999); B. Porter, *Plots and Paranoia: A History of Political Espionage in Britain, 1790–1988* (1989).

Middle East. British influence in the Middle East expanded militarily, politically and economically throughout the 19th century and in the early decades of the 20th century. Defence of sea and land to INDIA led Britain to subsidize rulers and deploy troops in the area so that by 1900 Britain controlled the Suez Canal and had occupied CYPRUS, EGYPT and the Sudan. By 1914 Britain had effective control of the Persian Gulf, including the Anglo-Persian Oil Company, and shared influence in the Ottoman empire with other European powers.

By the end of WORLD WAR I British forces had taken large areas of the Middle East from the Ottoman Turks, including Sinai, PALESTINE, Trans-Jordan, Syria and Iraq. Immediately after the war there were Arab nationalist revolts against British control in Egypt, Syria, Iraq and Palestine, which were crushed. At the Paris Peace Conference Britain was mandated by the LEAGUE OF NATIONS to administer Palestine, Trans-Jordan and Iraq,

while mandates over Syria and Lebanon were given to France (*see* VERSAILLES, TREATY OF).

In 1922 Britain recognized Egypt's sovereign independence, but kept a substantial military force there until 1936 when, following persistent opposition, they were gradually withdrawn except from the canal zone. In 1930 a treaty with Iraq gave it full independence in return for a 25-year military alliance with Britain; British influence remained considerable. In the 1930s the influx of Jewish immigrants into Palestine led to an Arab revolt in the late 1930s, and in 1939 Britain restricted further Jewish immigration. During WORLD WAR II Britain maintained a large military presence in the Middle East. It removed pro-Axis leaders in Iran, Iraq and Palestine, expelled Axis armies from Libya, fought alongside American forces in North Africa (*see* EL ALAMEIN) and the Mediterranean and coordinated the region's economy by means of the British-run Middle East Supply Centre.

From 1947 to 1967 Britain was in retreat in the region. Palestine was given up to the new state of Israel in 1948 and Britain gradually lost its formal and informal power elsewhere. The SUEZ CRISIS in 1956 made Britain's weakness clear. British troops were withdrawn from ADEN in 1967. Between 1970 and 1975 British officers and SAS units were involved in suppressing a communist rebellion in Oman, and British troops were based in the British-administered Trucial States of the Persian Gulf until 1971, when the states federated as the United Arab Emirates. The United States, having been opposed to British power in the region in the 1950s, thereafter allied itself with Britain in order to prevent the spread of communism while building up its own power there as another move in the COLD WAR.

FURTHER READING E. Monroe, *Britain's Moment in the Middle East, 1914–1971* (2nd edn, 1981).

Militant, the most prominent of a number of political groups describing themselves as Trotskyite that were active on the fringes of British politics, especially after the discrediting of the COMMUNIST

PARTY from 1956. Leon Trotsky (1879–1940) was an attractive figurehead for those who regarded themselves as revolutionary socialists and who were disillusioned with the Soviet Union – particularly in view of Trotsky's disagreements with Lenin and even more vehement disagreements with Stalin, one of whose agents assassinated him. However, the political views and strategy of these groups were, at best, a crude reduction of Trotsky's own.

The most prominent Trotskyite groups from the late 1950s were the International Socialists (later the Socialist Workers' Party), the Workers' Revolutionary Party and the Revolutionary Socialist League, founded in 1955, which later became Militant, adopting the name of its national newspaper, which was founded in 1964. Membership numbers are uncertain, but were certainly unstable. They especially attracted younger, idealistic, often highly intelligent intellectuals, at least for a while. With varying degrees of energy and effectiveness all of these organizations sought to influence the LABOUR PARTY by secretly infiltrating it, since this seemed to be the only possible way to promote revolution in Britain, remote though such a prospect was.

This tactic began to have some impact only in the 1980s, when the Labour Party was in serious disarray and the membership of local branches fell so low that a small number of 'entryists' in a few branches could have a disproportionate impact, especially on the annual party conference. Militant was the most successful of these groups, mainly in Liverpool, where Labour had always been weak, while the Conservative and Liberal parties had slumped in a region that suffered exceptionally from the economic depression and UNEMPLOYMENT of the 1980s. At its peak in the mid-1980s Militant had about 8000 members and achieved prominence by leading Liverpool City Council's opposition to Conservative spending controls. Two Militant members were elected as Labour MPs in 1982 and a third in 1983. Neil KINNOCK, as leader of the Labour Party, was determined to purge the party of the 'Trotskyite' influence, which was

proving divisive and alienating to voters, and he ensured that Militant's leaders and many activists were expelled from the party.

In 1992 Militant abandoned the policy of entryism, itself expelled leading members who had supported it, and sought to work as an independent body called initially Militant Labour, then, from 1997, the Socialist Party, under which name it fielded 19 unsuccessful candidates in the general election of 1997. Its leader, Tommy Sheridan, was elected to the Scottish Parliament in 1999, fighting under the name Scottish Socialist Party.

Milner, Alfred (1854–1925), imperialist, politician and colonial administrator. Milner was born in Germany of Anglo-German parents. He was educated at Tübingen, King's College, London, and Balliol College, Oxford. As a young man he first tried his hand at a career in journalism, working on the *Pall Mall Gazette*, but became more interested in public service. In 1884 he began working as secretary to G.J. (later Viscount) Goschen, a Liberal, and cooperated with Goschen in forming the Liberal Unionist Association in 1886. It was Goschen who recommended him in 1889 for a position in the civil service in Egypt, where Milner became undersecretary in the Egyptian Ministry of Finance, 1890–2. He returned to Britain and was chairman of the Board of Inland Revenue, 1892–7, in which role he played a large part in introducing a new system of death duties. He was knighted in 1895.

In 1897 Milner was appointed as high commissioner for SOUTH AFRICA, a position he held until 1905. He also served as governor of the Cape Colony from 1897 to 1901 and then as governor of the Transvaal and Orange River Colony from 1901 to 1905. During his years in South Africa he sought to bring about a peaceable settlement of the grievances of the Uitlanders (British immigrants in the Boer republic of the Transvaal) by proposing a unified South Africa but he failed to prevent war. His administration of South Africa during the BOER WAR and his efforts at reconstruction when it was over won him high praise in Britain. In recognition of his work during and after the Boer War he was elevated to the peerage in 1901. He became the 1st Viscount Milner in 1902.

During his South African years and after, Milner established what became known as his 'kindergarten', a group of young men from Oxford whom he mentored, many of whom went on to careers in imperial and Commonwealth service. On his return from South Africa in 1905 he discovered a Britain that was past the era of high imperialism, and a government that was less than enthusiastic about his ideas. For the next few years Milner stayed largely out of the political limelight, taking lucrative work in the CITY OF LONDON. He supported movements for national service and TARIFF REFORM, and opposed LLOYD GEORGE's budget of 1909, the Parliament Bill of 1911 (restricting the powers of the House of LORDS), and HOME RULE for Ireland. He was called back into government in 1916 to serve in Lloyd George's war cabinet. Milner became secretary of state for war in April 1918, where he established the army education branch. In the following year became colonial secretary. He retired from public life in 1921 and married Lady Violet Cecil, a widow, in the same year. He died in 1925, having developed sleeping sickness after returning to Britain from a trip to South Africa.

At a time when the cost and value of the British EMPIRE were beginning to be questioned by many, Milner was a vociferous advocate of imperial unity. His conception of unity, however, was largely shaped by his racial views. He conceived of a two-tiered empire, consisting of Britain and the 'white' dominions at the top and the so-called 'dependent' colonies at the bottom. He believed that if Britain was to compete in the new world order alongside the United States, Russia and Germany, then unity with the dominions, which to this period had been well populated by British migrants, was essential. Although he acknowledged that the 'dependent' colonies (among which he included INDIA) would one day be self-governing, and that

this eventuality had to be prepared for, he did not believe they were capable or deserving of dominion status. Milner's thought had a strong influence on the policies of empire in the early 20th century, and he was – alongside CURZON – among the last of the great imperialist statesmen.

FURTHER READING J. Marlowe, *Milner: Apostle of Empire* (1976).

miners' strikes (1972, 1973–4, 1984–5). The miners' strikes of the 1970s and 1980s were an outcome of the rapid rundown of COAL MINING in the later 20th century, and the consequent loss of jobs. This decline was due to increasing competition from other sources of power, primarily oil and gas.

The strike in 1972 was the first since the strike of 1926, which had precipitated the GENERAL STRIKE. The strike, over pay demands, was short-lived and successful, since the National Union of Mineworkers was better prepared than the government or the National Coal Board (NCB). In particular, a militant member of the Yorkshire miners, Arthur Scargill (1938–), flamboyantly led the strikers in a new tactic: secondary picketing. This meant that organized groups of miners from a number of pits formed 'flying pickets' to prevent movement of coal from centres at which they did not themselves work. This caused a shortage of coal and the closure of power stations. The government declared a state of emergency, parts of industry were placed on a three-day week and homes and businesses experienced power cuts. Nevertheless there was considerable public sympathy for the miners. Edward HEATH's Conservative government capitulated and conceded pay rises.

Then in 1973 Heath's government faced further demands from the miners for higher pay. This was part of wider demands by workers in the face of rapid inflation, but the government was most fearful of the miners, whose bargaining power was greatly increased by the effects of the OIL SHOCK of the same year: rocketing oil prices made coal a cost-effective form of fuel once more, at least temporarily. Again, industry was put on a three-day week, but Heath helped to precipitate the crisis by bungling his negotiations with the miners and the TUC. Public sympathy was again stronger for the miners than for the government and the strike played a major role in the defeat of the Conservatives in the election of February 1974.

The memory of these events increased the determination of Margaret THATCHER's Conservative government, elected in 1979, to reduce the size of the industry and the power of the National Union of Mineworkers (NUM), as indeed it sought to reduce the power of all TRADE UNIONS. Thatcher appointed as chair of the National Coal Board (NCB) Ian McGregor, who had little liking for public ownership or trade unions and had just spent three years cutting the size of the nationalized British Steel Corporation. McGregor introduced a programme of rapid pit closures. This led Arthur Scargill, now the leader of the NUM, to call a strike. Scargill did not, as was legally necessary, call for a national ballot and so could not call a national strike, relying instead on each district of the NUM to make it effective. This lost the strike its possible legitimacy and potential support from other unions, as did Scargill's unpopularity with many in the trade-union movement, who regarded him as a left-wing maverick. Scargill feared, possibly rightly, that a ballot would be unsuccessful, but justified the strike in terms of his belief that a wider class struggle was in progress. He also claimed – rightly – that the government intended to close many more pits than had been stated. The miners who went on strike did not necessarily share his political views; they were fighting for their jobs. Not all did strike. The miners of Nottinghamshire, where proposed pit closures were few, went on working and formed a breakaway union, the Democratic Union of Mineworkers, which was influential only for a short time. The government was well prepared for the strike, having learned the lessons of the crises experienced by the Heath government. Coal stocks were high, alternative energy sources readily available and changes in the law

under the Conservatives prevented secondary picketing. The miners were in a weaker position than in the previous strikes and mass picketing had limited effects in stopping coal moving, especially in the face of unusually heavy policing. There were violent incidents between pickets and police, for which both sides bore responsibility. But McGregor showed little skill in public relations, and the government little sympathy for the genuine desperation of many of the miners and their families; in consequence there was, again, considerable public support for the miners, if not for Scargill. Scargill was not disposed to negotiate, and nor were Thatcher or McGregor (though the government, not he, was in charge). The strike lasted a year. More days were lost than in any dispute since 1926. Privation drove increasing numbers of miners back to work at the beginning of 1985 and the strike petered out. Pit closures continued; more miners lost their jobs; Scargill remained unrepentant.

FURTHER READING G. Goodman, *The Miners' Strike* (1985).

minimum wage. From the beginning of the 20th century the FABIAN SOCIETY, broadly supported by the LABOUR PARTY, proposed a 'national minimum' of civilized life, to include a minimum wage for those in work and a minimum level of welfare benefits for the workless. The Trade Boards Act – introduced by Winston CHURCHILL for the LIBERALS in 1909 following a campaign by the Fabian Women's Group – introduced minimum wages in a number of the lowest-paid occupations that were also nonunionized, and so lacked procedures to negotiate wages. A trade board was established for each occupation, consisting of representatives of employers and workers, to negotiate a minimum wage. The occupations concerned employed mainly females, who were relatively poorly paid throughout the century (*see also* EQUAL PAY), and included tailoring, lace-making and chain-making. The system was poorly resourced and difficult to regulate. In 1912 the Mines (Minimum Wage) Act, which followed a national strike, gave miners a low minimum wage, which varied from district to district. Surveys consistently found low pay a more serious cause of POVERTY than unemployment.

During WORLD WAR I a minimum wage was established for munitions workers (1916) and for agricultural workers (1917). Trade boards were also extended to a wider range of industries. By 1921 they covered 63 industries and 3 million workers. Thereafter the Treasury discouraged their further expansion, regarding them as excessively intrusive on the free market and especially harmful in a period of gathering recession. In addition, following a 1917 recommendation of a government subcommittee under the MP J.H. Whitley, 'Whitley councils' were established in certain industries to represent both employers and trade unionists and to discuss not only wages and conditions but also participation, job security, technical education and management issues. They were greeted without enthusiasm by TRADE UNIONS but were valuable to the nonunionized, and by 1921 they covered 3.5 million workers; they were most successful among white-collar and municipal employees.

The post-war LLOYD GEORGE cabinet and some employers considered a general minimum wage, but rejected it for reasons that continued to be repeated by opponents almost to the end of the century: it would be inflationary; it might increase unemployment as employers sought to compensate for the increased wages bill; it might lead to pay demands from higher-paid workers anxious to preserve pay differentials, and hence fail to solve the problem of relatively low pay rates. All of these objections were speculative, but influential. Most important, however, was the fact that the Ministry of Labour preferred pay scales to be locally rather than nationally negotiated, given local variations in conditions, and thought that trade boards and Whitley councils were the way forward.

In the interwar years women's organizations and various individuals, including William BEVERIDGE and later J.M. KEYNES, advocated FAMILY ALLOWANCES as an alternative means to secure a minimum family income. By the early 1940s the Labour Party had come to the same view, and family allowances were introduced in 1945. Unemployment and poverty in the interwar years brought forward other proposals. B.S. ROWNTREE advocated a statutory minimum wage following his second poverty survey of York in 1936 (*see* POVERTY). So also did Harold MACMILLAN in *The Middle Way* (1937), which advocated a planned economy as the way out of the depression.

The demand for a minimum wage was relatively muted during the period of full employment that followed World War II. It was rarely seriously advocated by Labour Party or trade-union leaders. It revived with the growth of UNEMPLOYMENT in the 1970s, as did the old arguments against, especially the spectre of inflation. During the vogue for deregulation under the THATCHER governments in the 1980s there was no hope for the minimum wage. Soon after the victory of the BLAIR government in 1997 an independent committee was appointed to consider a minimum wage. In consequence a national minimum wage was introduced in 1999, at the cautiously low level of £3.60 per hour for workers aged 22 and above, raised to £3.70 in 2000. Workers aged 18–21 received £3.00 per hour, raised to £3.20 in 2000. The law did not apply to workers below the age of 18. Fears that unemployment and other long-predicted harmful consequences would result were unfounded, and even the Conservative shadow chancellor Michael PORTILLO withdrew his party's objections. The main beneficiaries were workers in service industries, such as fast-food restaurants, women and members of ethnic minority groups.

modernism, the comprehensive term for an international tendency in POETRY, NOVELS, DRAMA, MUSIC, art and ARCHITECTURE that emerged at the end of the 19th century and influenced these fields in the 20th century. The tendency is often believed to have reached its peak in the interwar years and there is some question as to when, if ever, it came to an end. In the late 20th century some promoted a new style that they called post-modernist, which was a self-conscious reaction against the formalism of modernism, but this was by no means a universal tendency. Modernism contained a number of smaller movements characterized by reaction again the naturalistic, representational aspects of 19th-century artistic production: for example, abstraction in painting, free verse in poetry, spare undecorated functionalism using modern materials in architecture, atonalism in music, and rejection of conventional linear narrative in literary fiction.

monarchy. The British monarchy has undergone considerable change in the 20th century, and appeared far less stable as an institution in the 1990s than it had in the 1900s. Historically, as the monarch's effective powers to rule and influence government were steadily stripped away up to the 19th century, the monarchy itself became a largely symbolic institution. In the 20th century it became clear that ultimately it would only survive if it changed with the times and continued to appear relevant to the British people. Perhaps the most remarkable feature of monarchy in the 20th century was its increasing exposure to and use of the media to achieve these aims.

Queen Victoria, who died in 1901, weathered a good deal of turmoil during her own reign, including a serious movement towards republicanism that gathered steam in the 1860s after the death of Prince Albert and her own subsequent lengthy withdrawal from public life. By the end of the 19th century, however, Victoria had become an immensely popular monarch, she and her family being seen as supra-political figureheads of the nation, and as essential to the fabric of the EMPIRE. King EDWARD VII, Victoria's son and heir, inherited this position of respect and stability in 1901 and continued its reinforcement, placating those who feared that his hedonistic nature would not make him a good king. Edward's more notable achievement, however, was to realize that the popularity of the monarchy as an institution was tied both to its visibility and to its extraordinary nature.

He revived various historic ceremonies and trappings for the court and for official state events – and invented others. He understood that part of the attraction of the royal family lay in its mystery – in the fact that they were not like any ordinary British family. He made sure that the public were exposed to seemingly ancient royal ceremonies and eccentric customs, and that they were regularly able to view royal personages in jewels and furs riding in gilt carriages to open Parliament or to greet visiting heads of state. The result of Edward's interpretation of his role was the creation of a glamorous and formal monarchy characterized by much pomp, pageantry and, most importantly, publicity. This was something that Victoria had never enjoyed, and it set the tone for the rest of the century.

GEORGE V, Edward's successor, largely followed in his father's footsteps, though he was never as glamorous as his father. That role was to be filled again by George's son, the ill-fated EDWARD VIII, whose brief reign in 1936 was overshadowed by the spectre of Mrs Simpson and the ABDICATION CRISIS. Though Edward had been immensely popular as prince of Wales, cutting a dashing playboy figure, his decision to reject his duty in order to seek personal fulfilment was a bitter pill for some (including the royal family) to swallow. Considerable damage was done to the monarchy by Edward's abdication. It made it increasingly difficult for future generations to present the monarchy as an institution in which its members justified their wealth and social position by working in the service of the nation. In hindsight the abdication illustrated just how tenuous and uncertain the monarchy's position could become, should its members fail to do their duty.

However, Edward's successor, GEORGE VI, worked hard and successfully to re-establish respect for the monarchy. His image was that of a quiet and dedicated family man with a great sense of seriousness and duty. Both his wife, Queen Elizabeth, and his daughters, Princess Elizabeth (the future Queen ELIZABETH II) and Princess Margaret, were almost universally popular, especially during the war years.

Elizabeth II's reign, which began in 1952, witnessed the beginnings of an explosion of media coverage of the royal family, in which audiences beyond London or those sites where royal tours took place were increasingly exposed to the royals. George V had initiated the annual Christmas radio broadcasts of the monarch to the nation and empire in 1932. The medium of television was to prove even more popular. Elizabeth's coronation was the first to be broadcast to a mass audience on TV and was an immense success, allowing ordinary people the chance to peep in on a seemingly ancient and most prestigious ceremony. The BBC estimated that over 20 million Britons watched it on television and a further 11.7 million listened to it on the radio. The coronation whetted the public appetite for more exposure, and events such as the state opening of Parliament and royal weddings were soon being broadcast live on television as a matter of course.

By the 1980s and 1990s, however, it appeared that the public was getting too much of a good thing. Edward VII's belief that the monarchy's survival as a relevant institution depended on cracks being opened up and a little light shone on the mystery of the royal family itself had been carried to the extreme, with the doors flung open and the family's dirty laundry being aired almost daily on the front pages of British tabloid newspapers. The marital problems of the queen's children, especially Prince CHARLES and later Prince Andrew, became subjects of speculation and ridicule. There was oppressive and salacious media coverage of the family's every move, particularly of the royal in-laws Sarah, duchess of York, and DIANA, PRINCESS OF WALES. Pleas from members of the royal family to be left alone were often scorned by the press who claimed that members of the royal family, particularly Diana, courted the media.

The media circus surrounding the monarchy came to a head in August 1997 when Diana was killed in a car crash in Paris. The wave of grief that swept Britain and the world in the following days was followed by a backlash of ill feeling towards the royal family who, it was claimed, were cold and unfeeling, had never respected the modern, compassionate and vivacious Diana, and were irrelevant and out of touch with the nation. Surveys showed that approval ratings for the queen, Prince Charles and the institution of the monarchy itself had plunged to all-time lows. Approval of the queen recovered somewhat, and the queen mother continued to be widely regarded with affection as she celebrated her 100th birthday in 2000. In the wake of Diana's death, the queen publicly committed herself and her family to a programme of reform in order to ensure its survival, but it remains to be seen whether her efforts will carry the monarchy far into the new millennium.

FURTHER READING J.A. Cannon, *The Modern British Monarchy: A Study in Adaptation* (1987); T. Nairn, *The Enchanted Glass: Britain and its Monarchy* (1994).

monetarism, economic theory that states that inflation is caused by the government's allowing the money supply (the notes and coins in circulation) to grow too fast. It sees the causes of UNEMPLOYMENT as located in the labour market itself and unemployment as unresponsive to government attempts to stimulate demand in the economy (as J.M.KEYNES had recommended).

As unemployment and inflation rose in the mid-1970s Keynesian policies were thought by many to be ineffective, and monetarism – promoted most vigorously by the American economist Milton Friedman (1912–) – influenced both LABOUR and CONSERVATIVE governments, but was most influential in the THATCHER years. Monetarists argued that inflation could be controlled by limiting the domestic money supply, and that unemployment occurred because of rigidities in the labour market – such as the legal protection allowed to workers (e.g. against unfair dismissal or rights to maternity leave) and to TRADE UNIONS (e.g. the right to strike) – and because 'overgenerous' unemployment benefits provided a disincentive to work. The consequence of adhering to monetarist theory in the 1980s was extensive deregulation of business and the cutting back of welfare payments to workers. However, it proved extremely difficult to control or even to measure the money supply, not least because transactions increasingly occurred in the form of credit rather than in cash. Furthermore, unemployment did not fall significantly following deregulation. In consequence monetarism fell out of fashion in the 1990s in Britain and elsewhere.

FURTHER READING P. Minford, *Unemployment: Cause and Cure* (1985).

Monte Cassino, hill-top monastery dominating the small town of Cassino in the mountains of southeastern Lazio in Italy. It was the sight of fierce fighting during WORLD WAR II. In November 1943 Field Marshal Kesselring ordered the construction of extensive fortifications around the town as part of the German defence against the Allied advance up the Italian peninsula towards Rome. In February and March 1944 the Germans withstood attacks by Allied forces. On 15 February General ALEXANDER ordered the destruction of the monastery by bombing, wrongly believing it to be occupied by Germans. Subsequently the Germans set up strong defensive positions in the ruins. After bitter fighting Monte Cassino was taken by Polish and British troops on 18 May 1944, opening the way to Rome, which was taken 17 days later.

SEE ALSO ANZIO.

FURTHER READING F. Majdalany, *Cassino: Portrait of a Battle* (1981).

Montgomery, Bernard (Law) (1887–1976), one of Britain's most prominent generals in WORLD WAR II. Son of an Anglican bishop, Montgomery attended Sandhurst, after which he was commissioned and served in France in World War I. He became known after the war for professional excellence but as a difficult personality. He married Mrs Betty Carver, happily, in 1927, but her death in 1937 left him lonely and unhappy. In World War II he served with distinction in France, then in August 1942 went to lead the 8th Army against Erwin Rommel's Axis forces in North Africa. The victory at EL ALAMEIN in October–November 1942 made him a national hero. After campaigns in Italy he commanded Allied ground forces during the invasion of Normandy in June–July 1944 (*see* D-DAY). The US supreme commander, Dwight D. Eisenhower, superseded him when he felt that Montgomery was proceeding too slowly, which caused Montgomery to feel resentment and led to continuing conflict between the two. In 1946 he became chief of the imperial general staff, then from 1948 to 1951 he was chairman of the commanders-in-chief committee of the Brussels Treaty Powers, and from 1951 to 1958 he was deputy supreme commander of NATO. He retired in 1958. He was knighted in 1942, and in 1946 became a knight of the garter and Viscount Montgomery of Alamein.

FURTHER READING N. Hamilton, *Monty* (3 vols., 1981–6).

Moore, Henry (1898–1986), sculptor, draughtsman and printmaker. He is regarded as one of the greatest sculptors of the 20th century and from the 1940s to his death was the most celebrated British artist of his time. Born in Castleford, Yorkshire, the son of a miner, he began a career as an elementary schoolteacher at the insistence of his father, despite an early desire to be a sculptor. From 1917 to 1918 he served in the army during WORLD WAR I and was gassed at the battle of Cambrai. After the war, he returned briefly to teaching, then went to Leeds College of Art, 1919–21, on an ex-serviceman's grant. In 1921 Moore won a scholarship to the Royal College of Art and after completing his training in 1924 he taught there until 1931. His first one-man exhibition was at the Warren Gallery in 1928 and his first public commission was a stone relief, *West Wind,* for the new headquarters of the London Underground, to which Jacob EPSTEIN also contributed. They faced severe public criticism: 'Grotesque caricatures' according to a letter to *The Times*. In 1932 Moore became the first head of sculpture at Chelsea School of Art, where he remained until the outbreak of World War II in 1939, when the school was evacuated to Northampton. During the 1930s he lived in Hampstead, north London, close to Barbara HEPWORTH and Ben NICHOLSON and other prominent figures in the art world. In 1940, after the bombing of his studio, he moved to Hertfordshire, where he lived for the rest if his life.

Most of Moore's early work was carved, rejecting the academic tradition of modelling in favour of truth to materials, the doctrine popular among British artists of this period, which laid down that the nature of the stone or wood was part of the conception of the work. Moore was much influenced by ancient sculpture and found in it a force and vigour that he preferred to classical conceptions of beauty. Although he produced some purely abstract pieces, his sculpture was mostly based on forms in the natural world: the human figure, bones, pebbles and shells. The reclining female figure and the mother and child were frequent themes in his work. By the later 1930s he had a secure reputation in artistic circles. He established wider fame in his role as official war artist in World War II, especially his drawings of Londoners sheltering in Underground stations from the BLITZ in 1940–2. After the war his reputation grew rapidly and his commissioned works stood in prominent places around the world; for example outside the Lincoln Center in New York. Increasingly he worked in bronze rather than stone, often on a very large scale. His output was immense: about 6000 pieces are known.

FURTHER READING R. Berthoud, *The Life of Henry Moore* (1987); H. Moore and J. Hedgecoe, *Henry Moore* (1986).

Morrison, Herbert (Stanley) (1888–1965),

Labour politician. Born in London into a working-class family, Morrison was educated in state elementary schools, then worked as a shop assistant. He joined the Social Democratic Federation in 1907. In 1910 he moved to the Brixton (south London) branch of the INDEPENDENT LABOUR PARTY (ILP). By the end of 1910 he was its chair, and also secretary of the southwest London federation of the ILP. In 1912 he stood unsuccessfully as an ILP candidate for the London County Council (LCC). He chaired the Brixton branch of the National Union of Clerks, 1910–13. He supported public works to tackle UNEMPLOYMENT, and also women's suffrage. He opposed World War I.

During the war Morrison became secretary of the London LABOUR PARTY and a part-time agent of the National Labour Press. He received conscription papers in 1916; although his blind right eye exempted him from military service he agreed to do war service on the land. In 1920 he was elected to Hackney Borough Council in London and was mayor of Hackney in 1920 and 1921. He went on to become a member of the LCC (1922–45), becoming leader in 1939. One of his most important contributions to Labour was in building a successful London Labour Party. He was the architect of the process by which London transport was brought into public ownership in 1933, under the London Passenger Transport Board. This took the form of a public corporation, as set out in his book *Socialization and Transport* (1933), and this was to be the form of NATIONALIZATION adopted by the post-war Labour government.

Morrison was elected to the national executive of the Labour Party in 1920, and was MP for South Hackney in 1923–4, 1929–31 and 1935–45, for East Lewisham in 1945–50 and for South Lewisham in 1950–9. He was minister of transport 1929–31 and minister of supply briefly in 1940 before becoming a highly effective wartime home secretary and minister for home security (1940–5), where he was especially responsible for air-raid precautions and victims, becoming a member of the war cabinet in 1942. He was lord president of the council and deputy prime minister, 1945–51, and FOREIGN SECRETARY in 1951. He was largely responsible for the nationalization programme and was the chief promoter of the

FESTIVAL OF BRITAIN in 1951. He continued in opposition as deputy leader of the party from 1951 to 1955, when he was defeated by GAITSKELL in the attempt to succeed ATTLEE as leader.

Morrison was a great party organizer. He recognized that Labour had lost steam by 1950 and encouraged younger thinkers, such as Gaitskell, CROSLAND and R.H.S. CROSSMAN. He retired from the Commons in 1959 and was created Lord Morrison of Lambeth. He was president of the British Board of Film Censors from 1960 to 1965.

FURTHER READING B. Donoughue and G.W. Jones, *Herbert Morrison: Portrait of a Politician* (1973).

Mosley, Oswald (Ernald) (1896–1980), Conservative, then Labour politician, who ended up as a fascist. Mosley was born into the landed aristocracy (he subsequently inherited a baronetcy) and was educated at Winchester and Sandhurst. He served with distinction in the Royal Flying Corps during WORLD WAR I, and was honourably discharged in 1916 after a plane crash. In 1918 he was elected Conservative MP for Harrow and became the youngest MP serving in the Commons. Later he married Lady Cynthia ('Cimmie') Curzon, daughter of the Conservative foreign secretary Lord CURZON.

Mosley's restlessness and desire for change was representative of the generation of youth who had survived the war, and were impatient with the old men continuing to run government in old-fashioned ways. This contributed to his fleeting allegiances in party politics. In 1922, disillusioned with Conservative policy, he was re-elected MP for Harrow as an independent. In 1924, however, he crossed the floor and joined the LABOUR PARTY, and was elected as MP for Smethwick that year. Again, however, he became dissatisfied with Labour's policies, and was embittered by the party's rejection of his policy suggestions concerning UNEMPLOYMENT in 1929, when he was a junior minister in the second Labour government.

In 1930 Mosley left the government, and in 1931 he left the Labour Party. That year he formed the 'New Party', but its poor performance in the 1931 elections led him in 1932 to found the BRITISH UNION OF FASCISTS (BUF). Believing that in fascism he had at last found a political system capable of regenerating Britain, he laid out his beliefs in *The Greater Britain* (1932). Though he met Mussolini and Hitler and shared their outlook, he considered himself a patriot and sought to promote British interests. His second wife, Diana Guinness (*née* Mitford), was a great admirer of Nazism, and they were married in 1936 at the propaganda minister Joseph Goebbels's house in Berlin. Charismatic, attractive and a brilliant orator, Mosley organized mass rallies that often turned violent. The BUF recruited thugs, known as the Blackshirts, to act as Mosley's 'bodyguards'. The BUF's later promotion of anti-Semitism provoked an outraged response from both the Jewish community (whose neighbourhood in the East End of London the BUF attempted to march through) and the wider British public. BUF demonstrations led the government to pass the Public Order Act in 1936, forbidding the wearing of political uniforms in public and giving the home secretary the right to ban BUF marches.

Despite the attention it gained for itself, the BUF never managed to win a seat in parliamentary elections. In 1940 Mosley and his wife were both interned under wartime regulations, and the BUF itself was proscribed. Mosley was released in 1943. After WORLD WAR II he attempted to re-enter politics and founded the Union Movement in 1948. Campaigning for greater British participation in and eventual leadership of the burgeoning EUROPEAN ECONOMIC COMMUNITY, as well as the restriction of non-white IMMIGRATION from the COMMONWEALTH, Mosley failed to gain any widespread support, as the public were wary of his fascist past. However, overtones of his movement were later to be found in such groups as the NATIONAL FRONT.

FURTHER READING O. Mosley, *My Life* (1968); R. Skidelsky, *Oswald Mosley* (1990).

motor industry. The first commercial motorcar manufacturer in Britain was the Daimler Company, founded in Coventry in 1896. Thereafter the motor industry profoundly affected the British economy and British society. By the late 1930s it employed 1 million people and there were 2 million motor vehicles on the roads.

In 1896 the industry was still at an experimental stage, with the initial technical breakthroughs coming from continental Europe. Daimler derived its early designs from the German patents of Gottfried Daimler. The Red Flag Act, which required a person to walk in front of any motorized vehicle to warn pedestrians, had recently been repealed and the official speed limit had been raised to 14 miles (22.4 km) per hour. By 1910, led by Ford, the technical lead had shifted to the United States; in 1911 Ford began manufacturing in Manchester. Ford brought with it practices perfected in Detroit: hostility to TRADE UNIONS, routinized assembly-line techniques suitable for less skilled workers, and relatively high pay. By 1914 Ford was the largest producer of vehicles in Britain.

British producers – such as Rover, Sunbeam and Morris – diversified from bicycle production, adopted American methods and dislodged American dominance of the British market. The British industry successfully produced luxury vehicles (such as those produced by Daimler and Rolls-Royce), and also moderately priced cars. Morris, which produced its first car, the Morris Cowley, in Oxford in 1915, and Austin, which introduced the Austin Seven in 1922, successfully challenged Ford and other American manufacturers in the more popular market. The British designs were better suited to the roads, scale of travel and relatively high fuel costs of Britain than the larger, fuel-inefficient American designs; British cars were also protected by the McKenna duties on imported luxury goods introduced in 1915. British firms were more tolerant of trade unions, especially after World War II when labour shortages increased the bargaining power of workers, and made greater use of skilled workers who, supported by their unions, retained greater control over their systems of working than their counterparts in American firms.

The British industry reached a peak in the 1950s, when its European competitors had been temporarily destroyed in World War II and American producers were occupied with satisfying their large and growing domestic market. The industry was encouraged especially by the Labour government of 1945–51, which was keen to build up export industries, and by the Conservative governments of the 1950s, which also wished to encourage domestic consumption. But by the late 1950s the British industry was facing competition from the revival of European manufacturers and the cost-effectiveness of American production methods. British firms suffered from their small size, relatively poor management and troubled industrial relations. They were further hit by the gradual elimination of protective tariffs between 1963 and 1977. A series of mergers, followed in the late 1960s and early 1970s by effective government takeover in an attempt to save the industry, had little effect. By the end of the 1970s over 50% of new British car purchases were imports. Over the next two decades British-owned motor manufacturing was displaced first by American, then by Japanese and German manufacturers. Meanwhile new car registrations rose from 2 million in 1950 to almost 20 million in 1994, and total passenger miles travelled by all forms of motor transport rose from 122,400,000 (195,840,000 km) in 1952 to 410,100,000 (656,160,000 km) in 1990, with profound effects on personal mobility, road building and the environment.

FURTHER READING T. Barker and D. Gerhold, *The Rise and Rise of Road Transport, 1700–1990* (1993); R. Church, *The Rise and Decline of the British Motor Industry* (1994).

motorways, multiple-carriageway roads confined to the use of long-distance motor transport. Motorways were first proposed in Britain by the early motor enthusiast Lord Montagu of Beaulieu in 1906, and were proposed in Parliament by a private member's bill in 1924. The first motorways were built in Mussolini's Italy and Hitler's Germany, primarily for military use. A parliamentary delegation evaluated the German scheme in 1937 and a toll-financed road from London to Birmingham was surveyed in 1938, but rearmament was thought to be a more immediate financial priority. Reservation of publicly funded roads for specified users broke the ancient principle of open access to the king's highway. It was made lawful by permissive legislation in the Special Roads Act, 1949, a feature of the integrated transport policy of ATTLEE's Labour government, though this government had neither the time nor the funds to implement the policy fully.

The first motorway built on these principles was the Preston bypass (now part of the M6), completed in 1958, precursor to the opening in 1959 of the first part of the first acknowledged motorway, the M1, which was much trumpeted by Macmillan's Conservative government. The motorway network grew slowly: by 1963 310 km (194 miles) were open, by 1973, 1531 km (957 miles), by 1984, 2770 km (1731 miles), by 1994, 3150 km (1969 miles). Motorways cut journey times, halving that of the bus journey from Birmingham to London once the M1 was opened. Fatal accidents were half those on other roads. Motorways extended the commuting zone, especially around London, and they encouraged the movement, and hence the increase, of traffic. Their building caused protests from the 1970s to the end of the century. Their space requirements were high, as were their costs – about £1.24 million per km (£2 million per mile) even in 1970, and mounting thereafter. Motorways, like other aspects of transport, were increasingly controversial by the end of the century.

Mountbatten, Louis (1900–75), relative of the British royal family; his notable public career included service as the supreme commander of Allied forces in Southeast Asia (1943–5) during WORLD WAR II and as INDIA's last viceroy (1947).

He was born in Germany on 24 June 1900 as Prince Louis of Battenberg (but was known throughout his life as 'Dickie'). He was the son of Prince Louis Alexander of Battenberg and Princess Victoria of Hesse-Darmstadt. His mother was a granddaughter of Queen Victoria; he counted the royal families of Germany, Britain and Russia (among others) as his relatives. Members of his family living in Britain dropped the surname Battenberg in favour of the anglicized Mountbatten in 1917, following the British royal family's lead in expunging their own family's German surname (*see* GEORGE V). Mountbatten's personal influence and connections to the British royal family were strengthened further when his nephew Lieutenant Philip Mountbatten married the future Queen ELIZABETH II in 1947. Later, Mountbatten enjoyed a close relationship with the young Prince CHARLES.

Mountbatten was educated in England at Locker's Park School, at the naval colleges of Osborne, Dartmouth and Devonport, and for a brief spell at Cambridge. He married the heiress Edwina Ashley in 1921 and had two children, Patricia (born in 1924) and Pamela (born in 1929). Mountbatten's naval career began in 1916 soon after he graduated from naval college. His work as a signals officer in the interwar period earned him a good deal of respect within the ROYAL NAVY. In 1941 the destroyer he was commanding, the *Kelly,* was sunk and he narrowly escaped death. By 1942 he had been promoted and assigned to the Chiefs of Staff Committee, though his work at this stage in the war effort was not universally appreciated. He was involved with and partly responsible for the disastrous landing of Allied troops at Dieppe in August 1942. By the following year he had been promoted to admiral and from 1943 to 1945 he served as supreme commander of the Allied forces in Southeast Asia, playing a prominent part in the retaking of BURMA. In 1947 he was created viscount, then Earl Mountbatten of Burma.

Mountbatten's liberal political leanings and his experience of Asia endeared him to the LABOUR government of the post-war period, who chose him to serve as the last viceroy of India and to oversee the transfer of power there. He arrived in India in March 1947, but he did not foresee the partition of India and Pakistan and the associated bloodshed. After independence, he stayed on in the capacity of governor general until June 1948.

After his service in India, Mountbatten returned to the navy and was promoted to second sea lord and commander of the NATO fleet in the Mediterranean in 1953. The following year he realized a lifelong ambition by becoming first sea lord, a position his father had held until 1914 when he was forced to resign because of anti-German pressure. In 1956 he was made admiral of the fleet and in 1959 chief of the defence staff. He served in the navy until his retirement in 1965, but still maintained a fairly active role in public life thereafter. The prominence that his distinguished record and his connections with the royal family afforded him no doubt led to his being made a target by the IRA, and he was assassinated in 1979 while on a fishing trip in Ireland. His state funeral was held in Westminster Abbey. Though he saw himself primarily as a naval officer, Mountbatten wielded influence in British politics, most notably through his royal connections and his particular experience and understanding of Britain's former empire in Asia.

FURTHER READING P. Ziegler, *Mountbatten: The Official Biography* (1985).

Munich agreement (29 September 1938). Generally regarded as the culmination of the policy of APPEASEMENT, the Munich agreement was the result of talks between the British prime minister Neville CHAMBERLAIN, the French premier Edouard Daladier and the dictators Hitler and Mussolini, ostensibly aimed at avoiding war in Europe. Specifically, Germany sought to annex the Sudetenland region of Czechoslovakia, populated mainly by ethnic Germans. The Sudeten Germans were agitating for autonomy, and Hitler threatened immediate military intervention in Czechoslovakia to protect their rights. Alarmed by the

prospect of another European war that Britain neither wanted nor was prepared for, and anxious to work out a diplomatic settlement, Chamberlain chose to appease Hitler rather than challenge him and convinced Daladier that this was the best course of action. The Czechoslovaks were neither consulted nor present.

The agreement was signed on 29 September 1938, granting Germany the Sudetenland as well as some other strategic Czech territory, and thus ostensibly placated Hitler. In the text of the agreement, Hitler and Chamberlain expressed 'the desire of our two peoples never to go to war with one another again'. The agreement was received with relief by the British public and Chamberlain was praised for his efforts on his return to Britain. He famously declared that the agreement had ensured 'peace with honour … peace in our time'. Chamberlain genuinely believed the assurances of the dictators that their expansionist aims in Europe were limited. However, by March 1939, when Hitler broke his word and invaded the rest of Czechoslovakia, it became clear that the agreement was worthless (*see* WORLD WAR II). The Munich agreement, along with the policy of appeasement generally, has since become identified with betrayal, shame and weakness on the part of the British government, and Chamberlain in particular.

FURTHER READING J. Charmley, *Chamberlain and the Lost Peace* (1989).

municipal socialism. *See* FABIAN SOCIETY.

music. Edward ELGAR (1857–1934) was predominant at the beginning of the century, developing the Victorian oratorio and establishing the British 20th-century symphonic tradition. He was active and prominent in the world of music until World War I, but composed little thereafter.

Elgar's contemporary Frederick Delius (1862–1934), who lived mainly in France, was strongly influenced by Richard Wagner and Edvard Grieg, and he produced a number of orchestral works (such as *North Country Sketches*, 1914), concertos and sonatas later in his career. From around 1920 he was in failing health and produced little. Ralph Vaughan Williams (1872–1958) succeeded Elgar as the leading English composer. He produced nine highly individual symphonies, large-scale choral and orchestral works, operas, songs and song cycles, concertos and some chamber music. Key influences on his work were folk-song (as in his *Norfolk Rhapsody*, 1906), English music of the 16th century (most famously in his *Fantasia on a Theme by Thomas Tallis,* 1910) and, to a lesser degree, the music of continental modernists such as Debussy and Ravel. He remained highly influential throughout his life. William Walton (1902–83) was more inclined towards occasional modernist experiments, although at heart his works are in the Elgarian tradition. *Façade*, his work for recitation and chamber ensemble, was written before he was 20 and first performed in 1923; it was unique in English music at the time. His greatest work was produced before World War II, when, like Vaughan Williams, he began to write film scores (including the music for Olivier's film of Shakespeare's *Henry V*, 1944), though after the war he produced some fine work, such as the cello concerto of 1956. His contemporary Lennox Berkeley (1903–89) made a more sustained commitment to modernism, but was at heart another traditionalist.

The dominant figures after the war were Benjamin BRITTEN (1913–76) and Michael Tippett (1905–98). The first performance of Britten's opera *Peter Grimes* (1945) marked the revival of British opera; eleven more operas followed. Britten preferred to write for the voice, and his works include 13 song cycles, about half of which were written for his lifelong companion, the tenor Peter Pears. He believed strongly in making music widely accessible, as in his children's opera *Noye's Fludde* (first performed 1958), and he created an annual music festival at Aldeburgh, Suffolk. In 1947 he was among those who formed the English Opera Group, which was subsequently responsible for the direction of the Aldeburgh Festival. He also wrote music for film and theatre. He continued to be active and influential until close to his death.

Michael Tippett began to compose just before World War II. He developed a highly individual style, drawing on English Renaissance music, Stravinsky, Beethoven and jazz, especially the blues. From the 1940s he produced a succession of operas (such as *The Midsummer Marriage*, 1952), oratorios (for example *A Child of Our Time*, written 1939–41 and first performed 1944), symphonies and other orchestral and instrumental works.

For younger composers traditionalism was also less dominant after World War II. For example there was the atonal style of Peter Racine Fricker (1920–90), then the avant-garde music of the 'Manchester School': Alexander Goehr (1932–), Peter Maxwell Davies (1934–) and Harrison Birtwhistle (1934–). More conservatively, Richard Rodney Bennett (1936–) wrote film music, jazz and several operas. The range of styles a composer could adopt became ever more eclectic, producing experimental work, such as that of Cornelius Cardew (1936–81), and the mystical individualism of John Tavener (1943–). Meanwhile, towards the end of the century, many players and audiences became attracted to the revival of medieval and other 'early' music and to the discovery or rediscovery of female composers in a surprisingly male-dominated field, including Ethel Smyth (1858–1944), who was jailed in 1911 for suffragette activities, Elizabeth Lutyens (1906–83) and Thea Musgrave (1928–).

FURTHER READING M.J. Trend, *The Music Makers* (1985).

N

national assistance. *See* POOR LAW.

national debt. *See* MAY COMMITTEE ON NATIONAL EXPENDITURE.

National Economic Development Council (NEDC or **'Neddy'),** organization established by the Conservative government in 1961 to help deal with signs of weakness in British industry, especially slow growth and poor export performance, which had resulted in repeated balance-of-payments crises. It was a forum in which management, TRADE UNIONS, government and some independent institutions and individuals could meet. Although its exact functions and powers were never clear, it was valued by its participants.

The first task of the NEDC was to consider obstacles to growth and efficiency. In 1964 specialist Economic Development Committees ('Little Neddies') were set up in individual industries and services. These engaged in economic forecasting, studying the effects of DECIMALIZATION, of changes in taxation, and of devaluation; they also disseminated and exchanged information of value to business. The NEDC lacked executive powers and the LABOUR government elected in 1964 established a new department, the Department of Economic Affairs (DEA) headed by George BROWN, to engage in long-term economic planning. The DEA only lasted until October 1969, having been outmanoeuvred by the Treasury, which was determined not to be supplanted. The NEDC, however, remained a useful forum for discussion among the major players in the economy, until it was abolished by the Conservative government in 1991.

National Farmers' Union. *See* AGRICULTURE.

National Front (NF), right-wing political party that was formed in 1967 when a number of small racist, neo-Nazi and neo-fascist groups merged. The party was in the tradition of Sir Oswald MOSLEY'S BRITISH UNION OF FASCISTS. The party's central aims included the ending of non-white IMMIGRATION into Britain and the repatriation of all non-white people who had been admitted since the 1940s; it also campaigned against Britain's membership of the EUROPEAN ECONOMIC COMMUNITY, believing it to be a threat to British sovereignty. The NF fielded candidates in a number of national and local elections in the 1970s, but never came close to winning a seat. Although it claimed support among some young working-class men in urban areas, the NF was more successful in earning publicity than in gaining concrete political support. Its extremist views meant that it both attracted and condoned violence, and emerged a vociferous opponent, the Anti-Nazi League.

The National Front came into being in the 1960s in response to a climate of uneasiness created by mass non-white immigration into Britain. This fear was also exploited at the time by mainstream politicians such as Enoch POWELL. By the late 1970s, however, the NF began losing popularity as anti-fascist feeling began to grow, while at the same time the Conservative government elected in 1979 began further restricting immigration. The NF finally split in 1982 when its leader, John Tyndall, left to lead his own organization, the British National Party.

FURTHER READING N. Fielding, *The National Front* (1981); S. Taylor, *The National Front in English Politics* (1982).

National Government, the name given to the coalition government that held office in Britain from 1931 to 1940. It was formed specifically to cope with the nation's severe economic problems during the Depression of the 1930s (*see* GREAT CRASH; UNEMPLOYMENT), the participants believing that solving the nation's economic crisis should come before party loyalties. The first National Government was formed by the Labour leader Ramsay MACDONALD after the collapse of the second Labour minority government in 1931. This came about because the majority of the Labour government refused to bow to international pressure to cut government spending, unemployment benefits in particular. The majority of the LABOUR PARTY viewed the National Government as a traitorous collaboration with the Conservatives and Liberals, and most of its parliamentary members promptly went into opposition. The Labour Party expelled those members, including MacDonald and the former chancellor Philip SNOWDEN, who did not join them. The remaining rump in government, under MacDonald's leadership, became known as the National Labour Party. In the election of October 1931 the National Government won a landslide victory of 554 seats (473 Conservative, 13 National Labour and 68 Liberal).

The LIBERAL PARTY also experienced a schism over the government's formation. In 1932 disgruntled Liberals under Herbert SAMUEL (who ironically had been one of the earliest supporters of the idea of national government) went into opposition. As time went on the suspicions of the Labour Party proved valid as the National Government became increasingly dominated by the CONSERVATIVE PARTY. Although Labour did better in the 1935 GENERAL ELECTION, the National Government was returned to power, and MacDonald was succeeded as PRIME MINISTER by the Conservative Stanley BALDWIN. He in turn was replaced two years later by Neville CHAMBERLAIN. The National Government lasted until 1940 when Winston CHURCHILL's wartime coalition took office.

Many critics of the National Government have suggested that its overall performance and effectiveness was mediocre. Its efforts to stimulate the economy lacked vision; its main policy was the abolition of FREE TRADE and the establishment of tariffs (*see* TARIFF REFORM) in the form of IMPERIAL PREFERENCES. However, this had little appreciable effect in solving Britain's economic problems, and unemployment continued to plague the nation and fire discontent, particularly among working-class men in the north of England, Scotland and Wales. Their plight was publicized in the HUNGER MARCHES of the 1930s. The government did seek to improve social conditions through such measures as slum clearance and house-building, and to stimulate the economy by investment in public works such as road-building. However, the economy did not substantially improve until the later 1930s, and this was mainly due to non-governmental factors, with some stimulus from rearmament. By the end of the 1930s Neville Chamberlain's pursuit of APPEASEMENT in foreign policy also proved unpopular in retrospect.

FURTHER READING G.R. Searle, *Country Before Party: Coalition and the Idea of 'National Government' in Modern Britain, 1885–1987* (1995); P. Williamson, *National Crisis and National Government: British Politics, the Economy, and Empire, 1926–1932* (1992).

National Health Service (NHS), one of the central features of the WELFARE STATE. The NHS came into being in 1948 primarily owing to the efforts of Aneurin BEVAN, the Labour minister for health. The National Health Service Act had been passed in 1946, based on the recommendations made by William BEVERIDGE in his report of 1942 following growing demands in the 1930s. The NHS promised free medical care for all Britons. It covered a full range of medical services from general practitioners and consultants (though the latter were also allowed to retain some private practice), as well as free prescriptions and free hospital, dental and optical care. Bevan had great difficulty persuading doctors to support the service, especially the elite of consultants who dominated the British Medical Association, and in the end succeeded only, as he put it, because he 'stuffed their mouths with gold': in other words he gave in to their demands to allow private practice to continue and for general practitioners to be paid on a basis of fees per head of patients rather than as salaried employees of the state, even though these concessions were contrary to official LABOUR PARTY policy. Over 90% of doctors enrolled voluntarily in the NHS in 1948. The majority of existing hospitals, whether voluntary (and therefore not publicly funded) or controlled by local authorities, were also enrolled in the service.

The NHS was to be funded partly through national-insurance contributions, but mainly through taxation. The high cost, Bevan believed, would lessen with time as the nation's health gradually improved. He could not take into account, however, the enormous but unforeseeable backlog of pre-existing health problems that strained the system from the beginning, nor the growing cost of new medical technologies. In relation to the NHS, as in other respects, the Labour government was cautious about spending. No new hospital was completed until the early 1960s, under a Conservative government. The first compromise of NHS provision came in 1951, when Hugh GAITSKELL, the Labour chancellor of the exchequer,

introduced charges for dentures and spectacles. These changes provoked Bevan's indignation, and, soon after, his resignation along with that of Harold WILSON and another junior minister, John Freeman. The Conservatives introduced charges for prescriptions in the following year.

The health of the nation was unquestionably improved as a direct result of the introduction of the NHS. This particularly applied to working-class women and children, as previously they had had very restricted access to free health care, and poor families had tended to reserve any money set aside for medical bills for the principal breadwinner, in order to keep him working and earning. However, the coming decades saw further cuts and continual struggles to provide high-quality care with diminished funds. The 1980s saw some of the biggest changes in NHS policy. Despite Margaret THATCHER'S 1982 promise on behalf of the Conservative Party that the NHS was 'safe in our hands', her governments scrutinized the service to find ways to make it more cost-effective and in the process made successive cuts and changes. Greater emphasis was also laid on encouraging people to purchase private health insurance, though with limited success. But increased running costs coupled with decreased funding meant that the NHS was in crisis as it approached its 50th anniversary, with differences in standards of care from region to region and lengthy waiting lists. Tony BLAIR'S Labour government was beset at the end of the century by serious criticisms of the efficiency of the NHS compared with health-care systems elsewhere in Europe, and by the problems of tackling the costs of improving the British system.

SEE ALSO MEDICINE.

FURTHER READING C. Webster, *The National Health Service: A Political History* (1998).

national heritage. A desire to protect historical buildings and monuments had motivated the establishment of various organizations, such as the NATIONAL TRUST, since the 19th century. In the latter part of the 20th century the protection of 'national heritage', including buildings, ancient monuments, landmarks and natural habitats, came under the control of a variety of official bodies. English Heritage (formerly the Historic Buildings and Monuments Commission for England) was set up in 1984 to identify historic sites, fund their protection and advise the government on the historic environment. A similar body was set up in Scotland. In the same year the government ratified the UNESCO World Heritage Convention, which up to the end of the century had identified 17 'world heritage sites' (including Stonehenge, Hadrian's Wall, the islands of St Kilda, the Cairngorms Mountains and the Tower of London) in the UK. In 1999 English Heritage merged with the Royal Commission on the Historical Monuments of England. Funds for the protection of heritage were also provided by the National Lottery Heritage Fund (*see* GAMBLING). 'Heritage' came to be understood as comprising a wide range of activities associated with the protection and promotion of the national past as a resource, and increasingly as an important element of tourism. The heritage 'industry' has also been subject to much criticism as the 'commodification' of the past and the reduction of 'serious' history to the level of entertainment.

FURTHER READING R. Samuel, *Theatres of Memory. Vol. 1: Past and Present in Contemporary Culture* (1994); P. Wright, *On Living in an Old Country: The National Past in Contemporary Britain* (1985).

nationalization, the bringing of industries, land and services into state ownership. The LABOUR PARTY was committed from its foundation to the public ownership of land and key sectors of the economy, though since the 1870s local authorities (notably Birmingham on the initiative of Joseph CHAMBERLAIN as mayor) had bought up public utilities, such as water and gas supplies, in order to run them for public benefit and profit.

Successive governments took over enterprises when it suited their interests. In 1914 the LIBERAL government subscribed £2 million, over half the equity, to the Anglo-Persian Oil Company (later British Petroleum) in order to secure supplies of fuel for the ROYAL NAVY. In the interwar years a number of enterprises were taken over because control by the market was either unsuccessful or (as in the case of the BRITISH BROADCASTING CORPORATION) thought inappropriate. Such enterprises were established as publicly owned corporations, independent of government, and so free from day-to-day political control. This became the model for future nationalization. The first corporations included the Central Electricity Generating Board (established in 1924), the London Passenger Transport Board (established in 1933), the BBC, and the British Overseas Airways Corporation (established 1939).

The Labour government that was elected in 1945 implemented the extensive nationalization programme that it had always promised, adopting the public corporation model. The programme principally involved the BANK OF ENGLAND (1946), civil AVIATION (1946), cable and wireless (1946), COAL MINING (1947), RAILWAYS (1947), electricity (1947), road transport (1947), gas (1948) and iron and steel (1949). There was little opposition to most of these changes, even from the CONSERVATIVE PARTY leadership. It was widely acknowledged that most of these enterprises were vital to the economy and had performed badly under private ownership before the war. More questionable and controversial was the decision to nationalize iron and steel. In consequence Conservative governments in the 1950s denationalized only iron and steel (1953) and, partially, the road-haulage sector of transport.

There were some extensions of state ownership by the Labour governments of 1964–70, for example the formation of the British Steel Corporation in 1967 (*see* STEEL INDUSTRY). A new wave of nationalization came in the 1970s, impelled by the decay of British industry rather than by socialist ideology. The Conservative government of 1970–4 nationalized the Rolls-Royce aero-engine business after the firm went bankrupt. In 1975 British Leyland, the last British-owned volume producer in the MOTOR INDUSTRY, was nationalized following a long decline in its share of the market, culminating in financial crisis. In 1977 the shipbuilding and ship-repairing industry, which had also long been in decline, was nationalized, as, in the same year, was the British aircraft-manufacturing industry, which formed British Aerospace. By 1979 almost 2 million people were employed by nationalized industries, which accounted for 10% of British output.

The performance of the nationalized industries is difficult to judge fairly because most were suffering from severe problems when they were nationalized, and some later faced further problems that were beyond their control. The coal industry, for example, had been notoriously poorly run by private owners. It performed well, by West European standards, after nationalization, but faced a contracting market. The performance of nationalized industries was, in fact, variable, but not consistently inferior to that of the private sector. In the 1960s the public sector led the private sector in introducing improved techniques of management. Its greatest problem, however, was often government uncertainty about the role of nationalized industries and excessive government interference in investment, pricing and employment strategies. In addition, the nationalization of failed companies in the 1970s associated the sector with failure.

The Conservative governments led by Margaret THATCHER became increasingly militant about reducing the public sector and improving the efficiency of what remained of it. Privatization began in 1981 with the sale of Cable and Wireless and part of British Aerospace. Between 1984 and 1990 British Airways, British Gas, British Leyland, British Shipbuilders, British Steel, British Telecom, the National Bus Company and the electricity and (especially controversially) water industries were privatized. The sectors that remained in public ownership, including coal, railways and nuclear power, were especially unattractive to buyers,

though in the early 1990s the railway tracks and most of the network were sold, as were most of the remnants of the coal mines. The government used income from the sales to cut taxes. The government also increasingly sought to encourage wider share ownership, often by underpricing assets to encourage the buying of shares by more people. This aroused criticism, even in the Conservative Party. Famously Harold MACMILLAN (by then Lord Stockton), who had supported nationalization as a Conservative front-bencher in the 1940s, criticized the Thatcher government in the House of LORDS for 'selling off the family silver'. It was not obvious that privatization led to greater efficiency in these industries, partly because many of them were effectively monopolies, either nationally (for example, British Telecom; *see* COMMUNICATIONS) or regionally (many railway, gas, water and electricity companies), though in the later 1990s competition increased.

FURTHER READING D.N. Chester, *Nationalization of British Industry* (1975); J. Kay, C. Mayer, D. Thompson (eds.), *Privatization and Regulation: The UK Experience* (1986); R. Pryke, *The Nationalized Industries: Policies and Performance since 1968* (1981).

National Lottery. *See* GAMBLING.

National Service. *See* CONSCRIPTION.

National Theatre, theatre company created in 1963, and renamed the Royal National Theatre in 1998. The idea of a national theatre had been proposed at various times from the 18th century. Foundation stones were laid, on different sites, in 1938 and 1951 (at the time of the FESTIVAL OF BRITAIN). When the National Theatre company was formed it moved into the Old Vic Theatre as a temporary home while a permanent theatre was built, on yet another site, nearby on the South Bank of the Thames. The first directorial team, under the actor-manager Laurence Olivier, was largely recruited from the innovative Royal Court

Theatre, together with the prominent critic Kenneth Tynan. As well as performing Shakespeare and other classics, the company encouraged ambitious new works, such as Peter Shaffer's *The Royal Hunt of the Sun* (1964), and unknown writers such as Tom Stoppard, whose *Rosencrantz and Guildenstern are Dead* (1967) it premiered. It also developed younger acting talent, such as that of Maggie Smith. In 1973 Peter Hall took over the directorship. In 1976 the company moved into its new theatre, designed by Denys Lasdun, with three stages: the conventional, proscenium-arched Lyttelton, the open-stage Olivier and the small, flexible Cottesloe. The company continued to attract innovative, controversial new writers, such as Howard Brenton and David Hare, as well as staging a variety of revivals, including the musical *Guys and Dolls*. In 1986 Richard Eyre replaced Hall and in 1997 Trevor Nunn became director. Government subsidies were smaller and the company tended to become more conservative and to aim for more popular productions, while seat prices rose, but it retained to the end of the century a strain of innovation and encouraged performances and productions of high quality.

SEE ALSO DRAMA.

FURTHER READING J. Elsom and N. Tomalin, *The History of the National Theatre* (1978).

National Trust, conservation organization founded as a charity in 1895 by the social reformer Octavia Hill, the 1st duke of Westminster (the wealthiest landowner of his day), Sir Robert Hunter, a lawyer with a long-standing interest in the preservation of open spaces, and Canon H.D. Rawnsley, a clergyman committed to preserving public access to the Lake District. The National Trust covers England and Wales, while a separate, smaller National Trust for Scotland was established in 1931.

The main concern of the National Trust's founders was to preserve access to the countryside for urban dwellers in order to counter what many contemporaries saw as their physical and spiritual 'degeneration'. The organization was strictly non-political and highly respectable, and it quickly obtained substantial bequests of land and money. By the 1920s it controlled over 100 properties, especially in the Lake District and in parts of Surrey that were threatened by the expansion of London. Initially the Trust was mainly concerned with the acquisition of land in the countryside, but its founding charter also enabled it to acquire buildings. In its early years it mainly took over medieval relics recommended by the Society for the Protection of Ancient Buildings, which was closely associated with the Trust. In the 1930s aristocratic members of the Trust, led by Lords Esher, Zetland and Lothian, became increasingly influential and began to look to the Trust to take over many of the great COUNTRY HOUSES that were threatened by the decline of AGRICULTURE between the wars. Parliamentary legislation in 1937 and 1939 facilitated these acquisitions, especially after World War II, when owners were under financial pressure. Many of these houses were secured by James Lees-Milne, the scheme's secretary until 1951. Throughout its history the Trust benefited from tax exemptions and statutory powers bestowed by Parliament.

After the war the Trust sought to be a model landlord in managing the agricultural land under its control. It also increasingly became a mass-membership organization as country-house tourism took off in the 1950s; membership included free admission. The Trust also took on a wider variety of properties. In the 1960s it launched a successful appeal to fund the purchase of areas of coastline threatened by development. There were growing tensions arising from the Trust's diverse commitments to tourism, conservation and agriculture, and also conflicting pressures from different sections of the membership, for example over whether deer- and fox-hunting should be allowed on its land. The Trust was increasingly professionalized and commercialized from the late 1960s. Partly in consequence membership grew from 100,000 in 1960 and 250,000 in 1971 to over 2 million by the end of the century. Still larger numbers visited its properties, but conflicts about its role continued.

FURTHER READING J. Gaze, *Figures in a Landscape: A History of the National Trust* (1988); R. Hewison, *The Heritage Industry: Britain in a Climate of Decline* (1987); J. Lees-Milne, *Diaries 1942–1945* (1995); J. Lees-Milne, *Diaries 1946–1949* (1996); J. Lees-Milne, *The National Trust: A Reward of Fifty Years' Achievement* (1945); P. Mandler, *The Fall and Rise of the English Country House* (1998).

National Union of Societies for Equal Citizenship (NUSEC). *See* SUFFRAGISTS; WOMEN'S MOVEMENT.

NATO, the North Atlantic Treaty Organization, a defence alliance founded in 1949 and including the USA, CANADA, Britain, France, Belgium, Denmark, Iceland, Italy, Luxembourg, the Netherlands, Norway and Portugal among its earliest members. Greece and Turkey were admitted in 1952, West Germany in 1955, Spain in 1982 and Poland, the Czech Republic and Hungary in 1999. The USA is the driving force behind NATO, but the organization maintains its headquarters in Brussels. The North Atlantic Council governs the organization, and is composed of delegates from all the member nations led by a secretary general. At the end of the century, this post was held by a Briton, George Robertson, who had been defence secretary in the Labour government that came to power in 1997.

NATO was brought into existence in the wake of WORLD WAR II in order to provide collective security for its members with the advent of the COLD WAR. Fear and uncertainty about the future of Germany and, more immediately, the Soviet threat lead Britain and France to pledge mutual defence assistance in the Dunkirk treaty of 1947. The following year a wider Brussels treaty was signed by many Western European countries. The descent of the IRON CURTAIN and fears of communist aggression and expansion into Western Europe led the USA and Canada to enter into negotiations with Western European nations, which eventually resulted in the signing of the North Atlantic treaty in 1949. In response, a similar collective defence treaty, the Warsaw Pact, was signed by the Soviet Union and its Eastern European satellites in 1955.

After the end of the Cold War in 1991 NATO was faced with adapting to a new global power structure, in which the collective defence issues on which it was founded suddenly became much less urgent. In 1991 it set up the North Atlantic Cooperation Council to facilitate communication between NATO, the former Soviet Union and the nations of Eastern Europe. In the 1990s it also began working more closely with the UNITED NATIONS, most notably stepping in to implement the Dayton Accord in Bosnia-Herzegovina from 1995. More controversially, and without the sanction of the UN, NATO intervened militarily in the 1999 KOSOVO crisis, with the USA and Britain spearheading the organization's activity there.

FURTHER READING W. Park, *Defending the West: A History of NATO* (1986).

navy. *See* ROYAL NAVY.

New Party. *See* MOSLEY, OSWALD.

newspapers. The readership of national daily newspapers rose rapidly in the first half of the century, faster than the rate of POPULATION growth, then fell.

National daily newspaper readership, UK

1910	4,365,000	1965	15,399,000
1939	10,534,000	1980	15,012,000
1951	16,921,000	1998	12,534,000

The growth in readership can be attributed to rising incomes and levels of education. The growing readership of national newspapers may have been partially at the expense of the local press, which flourished at the beginning of the century. Readership of the local press, however, appears to have broadly risen and declined on a similar trajectory to the national daily press, though certain papers continued to play a significant role in the constituent nations of the United Kingdom to the end of the century, in Scotland (in particular the *Scotsman*, founded in Edinburgh in 1871, and the Glasgow-based *Daily Record* and *Herald*), Wales (the *Western Mail*, founded 1869) and Northern Ireland (*Irish News* and *Belfast Morning News*). National Sunday newspapers experienced a similar pattern of change.

The popular press, aimed at a working-class audience, grew fastest in readership up to the mid-1960s. The leading popular papers were the *Daily Express* (founded 1900), the *Daily Mirror* (founded 1903, initially with the 'new' emancipated woman as its target audience), the *Daily Mail* (founded 1896, increasingly in the second half of the century targeting women who were not especially emancipated) and the *Daily Herald* (founded 1912 as a radical Labour Party newspaper, edited by George LANSBURY). The *Daily Herald* changed its name to the *Sun* to greet the dawn of a new Labour government in 1964, then changed its ownership and its politics in 1969. All these papers also had Sunday equivalents. These popular papers were collectively described later in the century as 'tabloids', from their relatively small, almost square shape, and at the end of the century as 'redtops', from the red banner headings of their front pages.

From the mid-1960s the more elite section of the press (at the end of the century described colloquially as the 'quality' press or the 'broadsheets' from the larger size of their pages compared with the popular papers) increased their relative share of the market, though this remained smaller than that of the tabloids. This gain was accompanied by a fierce battle for circulation among the broadsheets. The Conservative-supporting *Daily Telegraph* was the leader at the end of the century, with 1 million readers, followed by *The* TIMES with 760,000 and the left/liberal *Guardian* (the MANCHESTER GUARDIAN until 1959, when it recognized the hegemony of a London-based press and moved from the Manchester base that it had occupied since 1821 to a London headquarters) with

393,000. The *Independent* was founded in 1986, in a bid to replace *The Times* as the respected, pre-eminent national newspaper of reliable record. *The Times* had previously taken this role, until its takeover by the Australian media magnate Rupert Murdoch. Murdoch's determination to cut costs and break the strong print TRADE UNIONS led to a long strike at *The Times*. The strike failed, the power of the unions was broken and *The Times* returned, but it never regained its previous trusted status; indeed by the end of the century its approach was more down-market than that of its fellow broadsheets. It had been replaced as the (justly) trusted newspaper of the financial and business elite by the *Financial Times* (founded 1888). This had the smallest circulation, and the highest price, of all the daily newspapers, and differed from all except one horse-racing paper in being printed on pink paper, but it was the most influential internationally, later in the century printing in New York and Frankfurt as well as London.

The changing pattern of newspaper readership from the 1960s owed much to the growth of television, which increasingly met a large share of the demand for information and leisure once dominated by newspapers. By the end of the century both television and the press were competing with the Internet, as well as seeking to capitalize upon its growth by providing their own Internet services to complement their accustomed product. Newspapers could not compete with television, radio or the Internet in the speed with which they could convey news. In consequence, they increasingly devoted space to leisure and 'lifestyle' features in place of hard news.

The role of the press in British politics was always controversial. Most newspapers had a clear political stance and editors and proprietors sought to influence politics, some more vigorously and/or effectively than others. There was always a Conservative majority among the press though this was least visible during the 2001 election campaign. The *Daily Mirror* consistently supported Labour through the second half of the century, whereas the *Sun* shifted towards Conservatism, and more strident populism, after its change of ownership in 1969, though it opted to support Tony BLAIR in 1997, following his wooing of its proprietor, Rupert Murdoch.

The *Guardian* had a long Liberal tradition, but inclined towards Labour as the Liberal Party declined, though often sitting on the fence between them and supporting the SOCIAL DEMOCRATIC PARTY and the Liberal/Social Democratic Alliance. The *Financial Times* also inclined towards Labour at the end of the century, although it had traditionally supported Conservatism. Whether the newspapers led or followed the political opinions of their readers was never clear, nor indeed how many readers read newspapers for political advice, rather than for news of sports or gossip about the royal family; though the *Sun* famously, and characteristically, boasted 'IT WAS THE SUN WOT WON IT' in its headline following John Major's victory in 1992.

Until the 1960s, a succession of powerful proprietors, such as Lords BEAVERBROOK, NORTH-CLIFFE and Rothermere, were close associates of politically influential people and actively sought to influence politics, as did editors with close political connections, such as Geoffrey Dawson at *The Times* between 1923 and 1941. The extent of their influence remains debatable. Thereafter, the press came increasingly to be concentrated in the hands of fewer owners, as part of global media empires. By the end of the century, for example, Murdoch owned *The Times*, the *Sun*, the *Sunday Times* and the *News of the World*, as well as having interests in TV companies, newspapers, book publishers and film companies in Britain and other parts of the world. There were, however, anti-monopolistic legal constraints preventing too great a concentration of press ownership.

Professional standards, in particular concerning newspaper intrusion into personal life, were policed by the General Council of the Press, in 1963 renamed the Press Council, becoming in 1991 the Press Complaints Commission, which was estab-

lished by the newspaper industry itself as a self-protective device. Newspapers were, however, prevented by government from publishing items deemed harmful to Britain's security interests, by means of official 'D-Notices' covering prohibited information (*see* CENSORSHIP). At the end as at the beginning of the century newspapers played a central and often controversial role in British culture.

FURTHER READING G. Boyce, J. Curran and P. Wingate (eds.), *Newspaper History from the Seventeenth Century to the Present Day* (1978); S. Koss, *The Rise and Fall of the Political Press in Britain* (2 vols., 1981–4); C. Seymour-Ure, *The British Press and Broadcasting since 1945* (1991).

new towns, planned urban developments created from 1946 by the LABOUR government and its successors. The idea of new towns originated in the garden-cities movement of the late 19th century, which aimed to stop the unplanned sprawl of cities and replace it with low-density HOUSING and workplaces in urban units of manageable size (*see also* TOWN AND COUNTRY PLANNING). This aspiration was reinforced by government white papers during World War II proposing the planned development of town and country.

The first minister of town and country planning, the Conservative W. Morrison, was appointed in 1942. The first Labour minister was Lewis Silkin, who held the post from 1945 to 1950. Under the New Towns Act, 1946, nine new towns were designated within three and a half years to take surplus population ('overspill' as it was called) from London, and three more to provide new employment in South Wales and County Durham. In 1947–8 two Scottish new towns were designated to take overspill from Glasgow and to provide new employment.

The new towns, especially those close to London, were established in rural areas where the inhabitants often resented the transformation of their environment, and there was strong if ultimately ineffective opposition to some of the new towns at public inquiries and in the courts. As building began, the towns acquired a reputation as bleak, lonely places, especially for women at home, who were alleged to suffer 'new town blues' in unfamiliar environments, away from family and friends; but as the towns grew and matured such criticism diminished. The towns were developed and initially controlled by publicly owned corporations – similar to those established to run the nationalized industries (*see* NATIONALIZATION) – with powers of acquisition, planning and development. The 1946 act laid down that when development was complete the assets of each new town corporation would pass to the local authority. However, in 1961 the Conservative government created the New Towns Commission to take over the assets of all completed new towns, including ownership of the houses, which were rented or leased. The first of the new towns to be completed were Crawley and Hemel Hempstead, in 1962.

In the early 1960s the Conservatives designated a second generation of new towns: two for Merseyside, two for Birmingham, one designed to revive the economy of Tyneside and Wearside, and Livingstone, designed to serve a similar purpose in Scotland. In 1965 the Labour government consolidated new-towns legislation and initiated a third generation of new towns. These were mainly expansions of existing towns: Peterborough, Northampton, Warrington and Preston. The showpiece, Milton Keynes, was a new development but it incorporated existing towns, such as Bletchley. The 1967 Leasehold Reform Act allowed all tenants of leasehold housing, including those in the new towns, the right to buy the freehold. In 1976 the remaining housing owned by the New Towns Commission was transferred to local authorities. In the 1970s Labour shifted its policy from the creation of new towns to the renewal of old ones and no further new towns were created by public authorities for the remainder of the century. The THATCHER governments ordered the Commission to sell its industrial and commercial property and local authorities to give their tenants the right to buy their houses.

FURTHER READING J.B. Cullingworth, *Environmental Planning, 1939–69. Vol. 3: New Towns Policy* (1980).

New Zealand. New Zealand became a British colony following the treaty of Waitangi (1840) with the Maori people – one of the few cases in which British control of a territory was formally agreed with the indigenous population. New Zealand was granted a constitution in 1852 and was a self-governing colony until it gained dominion status in 1907. It was the first country in the world to introduce women's suffrage, in 1893. At this time it had a highly prosperous agricultural economy, trading mainly with Britain. It was dominated by migrants, for the most part of Anglo-Scottish descent; but the Maori were more fully integrated than was the case with indigenous peoples in other dominions, such as AUSTRALIA and CANADA. New Zealand troops fought for Britain in the BOER WAR, and they fought with distinction in WORLD WAR I, suffering especially at GALLIPOLI; they experienced a higher casualty rate than any Allied nation other than Russia.

In 1935 New Zealand elected its first Labour government, which introduced progressive social legislation, building on the reforms of the late 19th century, such as old-age pensions. The country increasingly sought a role independent of Britain: although it supported Britain and the Allies in WORLD WAR II, it increasingly looked to the United States as the major power in the Pacific. In 1947 it ratified the Statute of Westminster (1931; *see* IMPERIAL CONFERENCES), which gave it and the other dominions independent status within the COMMONWEALTH. In 1951 it entered an alliance without Britain for the first time; this was ANZUS, consisting of Australia, New Zealand and the USA. In 1954 it joined the South East Asian Treaty Organization (SEATO). Britain remained New Zealand's main export market until Britain joined the European Community (*see* EUROPEAN ECONOMIC COMMUNITY) in 1973. Thereafter New Zealand had to seek markets elsewhere. Britain took 80% of New Zealand's, still mainly, exports in 1935, but only 9% by 1985. In the 1980s New Zealand rejected nuclear weapons, so alienating the USA and destroying ANZUS. It determinedly asserted its independence of US, Australian and British domination, while remaining a member of the Commonwealth and showing no strong republican tendency to reject the British crown.

FURTHER READING K. Sinclair, *A Destiny Apart: New Zealand's Search for National Identity* (1986); K. Sinclair (ed.), *The Oxford Illustrated History of New Zealand* (1990).

Nicholson, Ben (1894–1982), artist. He was born at Denham, Buckinghamshire, of parents who were both artists. From 1910 to 1911 he studied at the Slade School in London and then spent some years abroad to help the asthma from which he suffered. Nicholson did not devote himself seriously to art until 1920 when he married the artist Winifred Dacre, the first of his three wives. His work at this stage consisted mainly of still lifes and landscapes, though he was influenced by cubism after a visit to Paris in 1921. From the early 1930s Nicholson turned to abstraction, partly under the influence of Barbara HEPWORTH, with whom he shared a studio from 1932 and whom he married in 1938, and partly because of several visits to Paris. He was especially impressed by the work of the Dutch abstract artist Piet Mondrian. Soon he was producing the most uncompromisingly abstract art in Britain at this time (e.g. *White Relief* 1935). In 1939 he and Barbara Hepworth moved to St Ives in Cornwall, where Nicholson remained until 1958, when he settled in Switzerland with his third wife, the Swiss photographer Felicitas Vogler. His international reputation grew in the 1950s and he won many prizes. In 1968 he was awarded the Order of Merit. In the same year he had a major retrospective at the Tate Gallery in London. He returned to England in 1971 and died in London.

FURTHER READING S.-J. Checkland, *Ben Nicholson* (2000).

1922 Committee, the committee of CONSERVATIVE PARTY backbenchers in the House of COMMONS. Created by a group of MPs who first entered Parliament at the GENERAL ELECTION of November 1922 and named for this reason, it was formed in April 1923 as a support group for these new MPs. In December 1925 it was opened to all Conservative backbenchers. In general it was loyal to the leadership, providing a useful sounding board of backbench opinion. Since elections for the leadership of the party were introduced in 1965 the committee has acquired the role of administering these elections.

FURTHER READING P. Goodhart, *The 1922* (1973).

Nonconformists, Protestant Christians who rejected the established churches (*see* CHURCH OF ENGLAND and ROMAN CATHOLIC CHURCH), generally minimizing hierarchy and ceremony and emphasizing a personal relationship between the worshipper and the deity rather than the intermediary role of the clergy.

The main groups in Britain were the METHODISTS, Baptists and Congregationalists. The membership of the Baptist Union in the British Isles was 366,000 in 1900, 406,000 in 1930, then declined to 202,000 in 1998. Membership of the Congregational Union in the United Kingdom was 436,000 in 1900, 490,000 in 1930, then declined to 165,000 in 1971. In 1972 it merged with the Presbyterian Church in England to form the United Reformed Church. This had 192,000 members in 1973 and 97,000 in 1997. All of these remained larger and politically and culturally more influential in NORTHERN IRELAND than elsewhere.

There were a number of other, smaller Nonconformist denominations of uneven influence. Among long-established dissenting groups in Britain, there were 18,072 Quakers in 1992 and 7000 Unitarians in 1998. The Salvation Army, founded in the late 19th century, numbered 65,168 members in 1998. Migrants, especially from the Caribbean, introduced new forms of worship from the 1950s. Of these, there were 75,000 adherents of the Assemblies of God in 1998, and 68,000 members of the Elim Pentecostal Church. The Mormon Church (180,000 members in 1998) and Scientologists (80,000 in 1992) were imported from the United States.

SEE ALSO CHURCH OF SCOTLAND; RELIGIOUS BELIEF AND OBSERVANCE.

FURTHER READING D. Bebbington, *Evangelicalism in Modern Britain: A History from the 1730s to the 1980s* (1989); A. Hastings, *A History of English Christianity, 1920–1990* (1991).

Norman, Montagu (Collet) (1871–1950), governor of the BANK OF ENGLAND (1920–44); the most influential figure in interwar British finance. Norman worked first for his grandfather's investment-banking firm, Brown, Shipley and Co., then joined the Bank of England in 1915, becoming deputy governor in 1918 and governor in 1920. The bank remained a private institution but worked closely with the government, especially in raising loans (particularly from the United States) to finance World War I. After the war Norman worked with the governors of the Federal Reserve Bank of New York and the German Reichsbank to enhance the financial control of a central bank in each major economy, to stabilize currencies and to return to the GOLD STANDARD. In 1925 he persuaded Winston CHURCHILL to return Britain to the gold standard, only to see it abandoned again after the crisis of 1931. Thereafter Norman turned to developing and nurturing the sterling area (the area, consisting mainly of the British EMPIRE, in which the pound sterling was the normal currency) as a substitute. However, his influence was much weakened after 1931 and the Treasury exerted greater control over international financial transactions.

SEE ALSO MACMILLAN COMMITTEE.

FURTHER READING A. Boyle, *Montagu Norman: A Biography* (1967).

North Atlantic Treaty Organization. *See* NATO.

Northcliffe, Alfred Charles William Harmsworth, 1st Viscount (1865–1922), NEWSPAPER proprietor. Born in Dublin but raised in England, Northcliffe was the son of an unsuccessful barrister who died prematurely, forcing him to leave school to seek work in 1880. He worked as a journalist, then for a Coventry publisher, then in 1888 launched the successful weekly journal *Answers to Correspondents*. This was followed by other successful weeklies, such as *Comic Cuts*. They were the first attempts both to entertain and inform a mass audience, consisting mainly of schoolchildren and men and women from the lower middle and upper working class. Northcliffe's younger brother Harold Harmsworth (1868–1940), later Lord Rothermere, joined him. The success of these ventures enabled them to enter the market for daily papers, and they founded the *Evening News* in 1894 and the highly successful *Daily Mail* in 1896. The latter was inexpensive and attractive in style. Its circulation soared during the BOER WAR. It was followed by the *Daily Mirror*, launched as a paper for the 'New Woman' in 1903; after a shaky start it reached a circulation of 1 million by 1914.

In 1905 Northcliffe bought the Sunday *Observer*, entering the world of 'quality' journalism; then in 1908 took over the daily newspaper of the elite, *The TIMES*, without changing its character as the reasonably moderate and reliable 'newspaper of record'. Northcliffe was a supporter of the CONSERVATIVE PARTY and an imperialist, though his papers did not serve the Conservatives uncritically. He stood once, unsuccessfully, as a Conservative candidate for Portsmouth in 1895. He opposed TARIFF REFORM and his newspapers gave the accused Liberal ministers the benefit of the doubt during the MARCONI SCANDAL. During World War I his papers attacked the alleged incompetence of Lord KITCHENER and campaigned for a coalition government of national defence. Northcliffe cooperated with David LLOYD GEORGE when he became prime minister in December 1916. He served as minister plenipotentiary in charge of the British war mission to the United States in 1917 and as director of propaganda in enemy countries in 1918. However, he quarrelled with Lloyd George over the composition of the post-war government and fell from favour. He worked to promote the settlement in IRELAND in 1921, dying shortly afterwards. He became a baronet in 1903, a baron in 1905 and a viscount in 1917.

FURTHER READING S. Koss, *The Rise and Fall of the Political Press in Britain* (2 vols., 1981–4).

Northern Ireland, province of the United Kingdom, comprising six of the nine counties of the ancient Irish province of Ulster. The current political boundaries of Northern Ireland were drawn in 1920 by the Government of Ireland Act, and confirmed by the 1921 Anglo-Irish treaty and the 1925 Boundary Commission. Partition was seen by the British government as an unavoidable, but, they hoped, temporary measure necessary to prevent civil war in IRELAND. Ulster Unionists had fiercely opposed moves towards HOME RULE in the late 19th and early 20th centuries, convinced that their Protestant faith and culture would be oppressed in a Catholic Irish state. Partition infuriated many nationalists in the south and Catholics in the north, but was welcomed by Protestant Unionists wishing to remain part of the United Kingdom, and who now formed the majority in the north.

Home rule was granted to Northern Ireland by 1921, with a Parliament established at Stormont in Belfast. The ULSTER UNIONIST PARTY (UUP) always held a majority and controlled the government until 1972. However, there were growing incursions on Catholic civil rights: proportional representation in government was suspended to ensure a Protestant majority, and constituency boundaries were manipulated to the same end; and discrimination was practised in matters of employment and housing. The Northern Ireland prime minister Terence O'NEILL, a liberal Unionist, made some attempts at reform after his election in 1963, but continued Catholic frustrations led to the foundation of the Northern Ireland Civil

Rights Association (NICRA) in 1967. Modelled on the American civil-rights movement, it called for equal opportunities for Catholics in education, housing, employment and electoral representation. NICRA marches in 1968 led to clashes with Protestant mobs, resulting in riots. In 1969 the British ARMY was called in to restore order, and soon came under attack from the re-emergent IRISH REPUBLICAN ARMY (IRA). The conflict, now involving the British army, continued, leading to the internment, from August 1971, of people suspected of membership of the IRA or of giving aid to it. The situation deteriorated further early in 1972, culminating in BLOODY SUNDAY (30 January). Weeks after the events of Bloody Sunday the Northern Ireland Parliament was dissolved and direct rule was reimposed from Westminster.

Serious violence became endemic throughout the 1970s and 1980s, with various attempts made to set up representative bodies. A Northern Ireland Assembly was elected on 28 June 1973, but collapsed on 29 May 1974 owing to Protestant intransigence. A constitutional convention that met from 3 February to 5 March 1976 was no more successful. Direct rule continued, as did outrages committed by both the IRA and Protestant paramilitaries (*see* ULSTER VOLUNTEER FORCE), despite the efforts of the predominantly female Ulster Peace Movement, who demonstrated and prayed for peace. Two of its leaders, Maire Corrigan and Betty Williams, were awarded the Nobel Peace Prize in 1976 in recognition of their efforts. From 1976 closer collaboration was established between the British government and the government of the Republic of Ireland. This culminated in the 1985 Anglo-Irish agreement, which laid the foundation for redoubled efforts on the part of the British and Irish governments to work for a solution to the 'Troubles', although the agreement was initially scorned by Unionists. In 1993 the 'Downing Street declaration' signed by the British prime minister John MAJOR and the Irish prime minister Albert Reynolds spelled out conditions for peace negotiations. It stated that any changes to

Northern Ireland's status had to be approved by a majority both in Northern Ireland itself and in the Republic. It also stated that any party could join peace talks if it renounced violence.

The declaration led to ceasefires being announced in 1994 by both Loyalist paramilitaries and the IRA. Although the IRA ended its ceasefire and there was another flare-up of violence, elections to all-party peace talks were held in the summer of 1996 and negotiations began. These were notable for the fact that in the end all the major parties were represented for the first time, the IRA having declared another ceasefire in July 1997, so allowing the participation of its political wing, SINN FÉIN, led by Gerry ADAMS. This followed a visit to the province by Tony Blair and Mo Mowlam (the secretary of state for Northern Ireland) shortly after Labour's election victory; Blair announced that British government officials were willing to talk with Sinn Féin.

The negotiations resulted in the hard-won 'Good Friday' peace agreement of 10 April 1998, which called, among other issues, for a new 108-seat assembly to be established, as well as various cross-border bodies. The agreement was ratified in referendums in both Northern Ireland and the Republic. It was supported by 71% of voters in Northern Ireland, indicating that it was supported by a majority of both Protestants and Catholics; the referendum day saw a remarkable turnout of over 80% of the population. Elections in June 1998 for the assembly established Ulster Unionist leader David TRIMBLE as first minister, and Seamus Mallon of the nationalist SOCIAL DEMOCRATIC AND LABOUR PARTY (SDLP) as deputy first minister.

The hope that was inspired by the new agreement and its potential for change were both recognized in the autumn of 1998 when the Nobel Peace prize was awarded jointly to the two biggest players in the peace negotiations, David Trimble and SDLP leader John HUME. However, the fragility of the peace process had already been demonstrated by the bombing of OMAGH city centre in August 1998 by the anti-agreement 'Real' IRA,

killing 29. Thereafter the history of peace negotiations in Northern Ireland was marred by setbacks. The peace process continued to be bedevilled by the issue of decommissioning of terrorist (particularly IRA) weapons. The general election of 2001 revealed an apparent hardening of attitudes, with significant electoral gains made by SINN FÉIN and the Democratic Unionists over their more moderate rivals in the SDLP and UUP. It remained uncertain whether the Good Friday agreement could be put into practice, making lasting peace a reality.

FURTHER READING M. Elliott, *The Catholics of Ulster* (2000); S. Wichert, *Northern Ireland Since 1945* (1991); T. Wilson, *Ulster: Conflict and Consent* (1989).

North Sea oil. Following the OIL SHOCK of 1973–4 there was a search by oil-consuming countries for alternative oilfields. Oil and natural gas had been found in the North Sea, off SCOTLAND, in 1971, and by 1975 it was on stream. By 1981 North sea oil production exceeded home demand. There were further findings in the North and Irish seas, ensuring a constant supply of oil and gas to the end of the century. Much of the production was fuelled by American investment and technology. The British government was criticized for failing to establish public control of the industry and its large profits, while Scottish nationalists claimed that the revenues should have been directed north of the border.

novels. Fiction writing in Britain in the 20th century, as at other times, was highly varied in content and quality. From the period before World War II the novels that sustained critical acclaim into the 21st century were generally defined as MODERNIST, in that they broke with much that was defined as conventional in the form and content of previous literary production, for example, linear storytelling and fully developed 'lifelike' characters. The solid, social world of the 19th-century realist novel, with its moral certainties, was abandoned by modernist writers such as James JOYCE and Virginia WOOLF, who instead explored the subjective experience of individuals, sometimes only tenuously connected to the outside world. These new perspectives were realized through stylistic innovations and experiments in nonlinear narrative technique, that sought to jolt the reader into new forms of awareness. Outstanding examples are Joyce's *Ulysses* (1922) and Woolf's *The Waves* (1931).

Popular novelists of an older generation, such as Arnold BENNETT and John GALSWORTHY, were criticized by Woolf for their old-fashioned, uncritical realism and conservatism. In fact, Bennett's *Clayhanger* series (1910–18) portrayed social change and discontinuity, and Galsworthy's portrayal of a domestic tyrant and rapist in *A Man of Property* (1906), for example, did not unquestioningly support conventional norms. Such works as *Nostromo* (1904) by Joseph CONRAD sought to use realistic narrative to break with romantic representations of the present, whereas E.M. FORSTER used conventional narrative forms to challenge social convention. Forster's *Howards End* (1910), for example, calls in question accepted social and gender differences, as the two female heroines espouse feminism and challenge male dominance; one of them unashamedly becomes the unmarried mother of the child of a working-class father. Forster's *A Passage to India* again challenges sexual convention, and also imperialist assumptions about the superiority of European over Asian culture.

More overtly political and visionary was H.G. WELLS. In *The New Machiavelli* (1910) he sought a new theory of politics in a world where there was growing democratic representation, but also ever stronger nation-states and increasing international interdependency and conflict. Wells suggested that the political way forward could not be dissociated from the need to rethink both sex and gender relations. Like others at the time, he questioned the conventions of monogamous marriage and of gender inequality and felt that both were

obstacles to a peaceful international order. Conventional gender roles and heterosexual norms were questioned also by Virginia Woolf in such novels as *Orlando* (1928) and in her feminist and pacifist polemic *Three Guineas* (1938), and by writers such as Ronald Firbank (1886–1926) and Sylvia Townsend Warner (1893–1978). Heterosexual pleasure was celebrated by D.H. LAWRENCE and Joyce, who both also explored the multiple cultural constraints upon its expression at that time. Sometimes exploration of inner life and enjoyment of private pleasure appeared to be the only accessible response to a changing, puzzling and often threatening world, as expressed in *Parade's End* (1924–8) by Ford Madox Ford (1873–1939).

At the time, World War I inspired few novels that achieved literary acclaim, compared with the POETRY produced during the war, though there were many minor, popular novels (often less critical of the war than the canonized poetry) that were welcomed by a growing novel-reading public.

Realistic depiction of everyday domestic life with all its ambiguities characterized the work of such writers as Ivy Compton-Burnett (1905–73) – for example *Parents and Children* (1941) – and Elizabeth BOWEN. In the latter case, such depictions are more explicitly related to world events of the time, as in *The Heat of the Day* (1949), in which the lives of two women are caught up in World War II. Henry Green (1905–73) explored modern urban life, social change and the conflicts that often resulted. He used a variety of modes, from realism (*Living*, 1929) to fantasy (*Concluding*, 1948). Thus fiction writing in the first half of the century was characterized by varying degrees of challenge to the conventions of society and literature.

The numbers and the variety of novels written, published, bought and read (often borrowed from public libraries) grew throughout the century, though novel-reading appeared to remain more predominantly a female than a male pleasure.

The military experience of World War II, like the Great War before it, did not produce distinguished fiction, though the civilian experience was more fruitful, giving birth to such work as Bowen's *The Heat of the Day*. The restless experiment with form that characterized the interwar years receded, but the variety of output of high quality defies easy summary. Concern with social change continued, though it was as often regretful and nostalgic as critical – as, for example, in Evelyn WAUGH's *Brideshead Revisited* (1945). The immediate post-war period was dominated by such writers as Waugh who had emerged in the 1930s somewhat in reaction to the leading conventions of the time, though not uninfluenced by them. Waugh satirized the ruling elite, but affectionately and increasingly nostalgically. Both he and Graham GREENE sought to reinsert a religious (in both cases Roman Catholic) sensibility into British fiction.

The COLD WAR inspired more influential fiction than the hot war that preceded it, above all George ORWELL's warnings of the continuing dangers of totalitarianism, *Animal Farm* (1945) and *Nineteen Eighty-Four* (1949), and the protest by Aldous Huxley (1894–1963) against the atomic age, *Ape and Essence* (1948).

In the 1950s there emerged a new vein of criticism of the continuing inequalities and social prejudices in society, and many younger writers expressed disappointment at the limited transformation in class relations visible in post-war Britain. This strain was most evident in the early work of the 'Angry Young Men': Kingsley Amis (1922–95) in *Lucky Jim* (1954), John Braine (1922–86) in *Room at the Top*, (1957), John Wain (1925–94) in *Hurry On Down* (1953), Alan Sillitoe (1928–) in *Saturday Night and Sunday Morning* (1958), and the dramatist John Osborne (1929–94; *see* DRAMA). Many of these works, marked by uncompromising social realism, were successfully adapted by a reviving British FILM INDUSTRY. A strain of less realistic pessimism is found in the fable-like early work of William Golding (1911–93), such as *Lord of the Flies* (1954) and *Pincher Martin* (1956), which examine the human condition *in extremis*.

From the 1960s British literary fiction became less critical of society and more absorbed in exploring contemporary personal life and, increasingly from the 1980s, British history. As a result, it was criticized by some for its narrowness of vision and lack of imaginative scope, and some even proclaimed the death of the novel in Britain. However, others perceived a continuing vitality and variety of voices; and there was certainly no sign of a decline in the market for new literary fiction.

Margaret Drabble (1939–), in a succession of novels from the mid-1960s, expressed the problems of ambitious young women trapped in conventional domesticity, before moving to more expansive themes, while others such as Nell Dunn (1936–) described the ambiguous experience of those who rebelled against convention. Doris LESSING's autobiographical fiction, culminating in *The Golden Notebook* (1962), similarly expressed a female restlessness that presaged the revival of feminism in the later 1960s, while also representing the experience of left-wing political engagement at the time.

Muriel SPARK's successful novel *The Prime of Miss Jean Brodie* (1961) drew on her very different experiences of growing up in Edinburgh. Her succession of sharply observant, tautly written novels to the end of the century defied simple categorization, as did those of the Dublin-born Iris Murdoch (1919–99), from *A Severed Head* (1961) to *The Message to the Planet* (1989). Murdoch's often allegorical fiction expressed dilemmas familiar in her own vocation as an academic philosopher. Her ethical preoccupations include the nature of love, goodness and individual freedom; these are explored within the framework of labyrinthine plots that describe sexual entanglements of bewildering complexity. Jean Rhys (1890–1979), who similarly fitted into no neat pattern of literary 'schools' and trends, was rediscovered after a long silence with the publication of *Wide Sargasso Sea* (1966).

Meanwhile, the successive volumes of *A Dance to the Music of Time* (1951–75) by Anthony Powell (1905–2000) described, with only gentle satire, changes in the social and political elite since before the war, though Anthony Burgess (1917–94) in *A Clockwork Orange* (1962) provided an early warning that post-war society was becoming more divided and more violent, at all levels, than many had hoped. Gentler satire characterized the series of amusing novels about academic life in provincial universities written by David Lodge (1935–), beginning with *The British Museum is Falling Down* (1965). These were altogether less agonized and conspiratorial, though no more or less realistic, than the tales of C.P. Snow (1905–80) of scientists and other academics at Cambridge, published between 1940 and 1970.

Work that was experimental in form continued, such as that of B.S. Johnson (1935–73), whose *Albert Angelo* (1964) was much admired by some critics, but ignored by a wider audience. The anarchic, highly individual works of Alasdair Gray (1934–), such as *Lanark: A Life in Four Books* (1981) and *1982, Janine* (1984), were more widely engaging and heralded a new outpouring of literary and artistic talent from Scotland. Martin Amis (1949–) and Julian Barnes (1946–) won praise for excursions into experimentation, which they interspersed with fairly conventional writing.

An important strand in the fiction of the 1980s and 1990s was the work of authors wholly or partly of COMMONWEALTH origins, writing in English from a variety of perspectives, often about the post-colonial experience in Britain and abroad. Such writers included V.S. Naipaul (1932–), Michael Ondaatje (1943–), Timothy Mo (1950–), Salman Rushdie (1947–), J.M. Coetzee (1940–), Hanif Kureishi (1954–) and Zadie Smith (1975–); others of overseas origins included Kazuo Ishiguro (1954–). Also important were those who examined the lesbian and gay experience, such as Alan Hollingshurst (1954–) and Jeanette Winterson (1959–), and those who explored aspects of the British past, such as Peter Ackroyd (1949–) in *Hawksmoor* (1985) and later works, and A.S. Byatt (1936–) in *Possession* (1990), and the successful evocations of World War I by Pat Barker (1943–) and Sebastian Faulks (1953–). Others,

such as Anita Brookner (1928–) and Ian McEwan (1948–), continued to focus upon personal life in the present. The British novel perhaps grew more introspective over the century, but it certainly did not die.

FURTHER READING M. Drabble (ed.), *The Oxford Companion to English Literature* (2000); M. Green, *The English Novel in the 20th Century* (1984).

nuclear weapons. British scientists had contributed to the development of the atom bomb during WORLD WAR II, and in the aftermath of the war in 1947 a British nuclear-weapons programme was set in motion. The project was started by the ATTLEE government, fearful of the potential duopoly of nuclear power in the hands of the USA and the USSR. A research centre was established at Harwell and a reprocessing plant and reactor at Windscale (now Sellafield) on the Cumbrian coast. The decision to build a 'British bomb' was made in the utmost secrecy, without consulting Parliament, but when the first test explosion took place off the coast of Australia in October 1952 it became impossible to argue that Britain had no nuclear-weapons programme. Weapons testing continued to take place in Australia until 1958; additional tests took place on Christmas Island in the late 1950s, and from the 1960s to the 1990s at the US underground test site in Nevada.

By the late 1950s the UK and the USA were beginning to work together in the field of nuclear arms, illustrated by the 1958 UK–US Mutual Defence agreement, which secured supplies of enriched uranium for Britain in exchange for weapons and civil-grade plutonium. Britain also successfully tested a hydrogen bomb. By this time popular disapproval of British nuclear weapons began to be heard, and the CAMPAIGN FOR NUCLEAR DISARMAMENT was established in 1958. With public fears over nuclear weapons focused by the Cuban Missile Crisis of 1962, the world's first nuclear treaty, the Partial Test Ban treaty, was signed by Britain, the USA and the USSR in 1963.

Initially, British nuclear weapons were to be delivered by the RAF's V-Bombers (Vulcan, Valiant and Victor). By the mid-1950s it was decided that a ballistic-missile system was more suitable, and work got underway in 1954 on a medium-range missile, Blue Streak. The project was cancelled in early 1960, a shock to those involved, but a symptom of Britain's post-war inability to continue to keep pace with the superpowers in terms of military technology. The government turned instead to US technology to support an 'independent' British nuclear force. From the late 1960s Britain's nuclear capability relied upon submarine-launched US Polaris missiles (whose acquisition was the subject of the Nassau agreement in 1962). In 1980 the government announced its intention to replace Polaris with another US system, Trident, which was introduced in 1994. In addition to buying US technology for the remainder of the century, Britain also provided bases for US missiles, which by the 1980s became a focus for antinuclear protest, notably at GREENHAM COMMON.

FURTHER READING M. Gowing, *The Atomic Bomb* (1979).

O

Official Secrets Act, legislation restricting disclosure of government information. The first Official Secrets Act was passed in 1889 and was largely ineffective in convicting even known spies. Its successor in 1911 was passed in a panic, during an anti-German spy scare when few MPs were in the House of COMMONS to vote. Section 1 dealt with the legal measures required to convict an individual of espionage. Section II outlawed the unauthorized revelation of any government information, however unthreatening to national security. All civil servants were required on appointment to swear to obey the act. In 1985 Clive Ponting, a civil servant, was acquitted of a charge made under the act, despite having revealed that, in one of the most shocking and controversial incidents of the FALKLANDS War, the Argentinian battleship *General Belgrano* had been sunk with serious loss of life despite the fact that it was sailing away from engagement with British forces at the time. The jury judged that he had acted in the public interest in revealing this information to his member of Parliament. This led to a third Official Secrets Act in 1989, which narrowed the range of information covered but made it impossible to plead 'public interest' as a defence.
FURTHER READING C. Ponting, *The Right to Know: The Inside Story of the Belgrano Affair* (1985); R. Thomas, *The British Official Secrets Act and the Ponting Case* (1986).

oil shock, the big rise in oil prices decided on by the Organization of Petroleum-Exporting Countries (OPEC) following the 1973 Arab-Israeli war. OPEC was formed in 1960 by representatives of oil-producing countries, initially Iran, Iraq, Kuwait, Qatar, Saudi Arabia and Venezuela. Later Abu Dhabi, Indonesia, Libya and Nigeria, then Egypt, Syria and Algeria joined. At this time these were weak countries in terms of international influence. The original purpose of the organization was to protect these countries from overdevelopment by Western-owned oil companies and to maintain steady prices. As world dependence upon oil as a major source of fuel grew, they became aware of the power conferred on them by the possession of oil.

Hostility to Israel on the part of some of the Arab oil-producing countries led them to cut supplies of oil to Western countries in protest against the West's perceived support of Israel during the 1973 Arab–Israeli war. Other OPEC members criticized this action. Prices – which had remained stable between 1950 and 1973 at £7–8 per ton – rose fourfold in November–December 1973 and to over £60 per ton by 1979. This caused oil shortages, general price rises and severe economic difficulties in the oil-consuming countries, including Britain. It also led to the search for locally available oil (*see* NORTH SEA OIL).

old age and ageing. During the 20th century, for the first time in history, living into and beyond one's 60s became a normal expectation in most countries of the world, including Britain. This was because of reduced rates of mortality in younger age groups. Old people were not rarities in earlier periods; in the 350 years before 1900 the proportion of persons over age 60 in England and Wales fluctuated between 6% and 10% of the population, but many people below that age were prematurely aged by poverty and hard work. Another change in the 20th century was that more people remained fit and active to later ages. Average life expectancy for women at the end of the century was 81, for men 77. Age was, as it had long been, predominantly a female condition, because more women than men survived into old age. The reason why old age was popularly associated with poverty was that old women were more likely to be poor than old men, throughout the century, owing to their lesser opportunity to acquire assets earlier in life, and the very old were more likely to be poor than were younger people. However, for most of the century most old people were not poor: some of the richest people in Britain were past retirement age, as were a high proportion of middle-income earners.

It is not helpful to compare average life expectancy at birth over the whole century, because earlier in the century very high infant mortality rates had a dramatic effect on the averages. Those who survived the hazardous years of infancy and childhood had a good chance of living at least well into middle age. Here comparisons are useful: a woman who was aged 50 in 1901 could expect to live to about 72, and a 50-year-old man to 66; in 1931 the respective life expectancies were 74 and 71; in 1961, 77 and 73. The numbers living to very old age were rising significantly at the end of the century. In 1981 there were 400,000 women and 100,000 men aged 85 or over, in 1991 600,000 and 200,000. Before World War I an average of 74 people a year reached the age of 100 in England and Wales; in 1997 3000 people did so. In the total population of England and Wales those aged 60 and above were 7.6% in 1900, 11.7% in 1931, 17% in 1962 and 20.7% in 1991. The rising percentages were largely attributable to the falling birth rate over most of the century: the falling number of younger people in the population, combined with the longer survival of older people, increased the proportion of older people in the population as a whole.

Life expectancy was affected by living standards as well as by gender, and class differences in life expectancy narrowed only slightly over the century. Cultural imagery of older people tended to be negative and undifferentiated, despite the fact that differences of income, health and fitness among the large section of the population over age 60 are greater than among any other age group, in addition to the obvious differences of gender, ethnicity and class. Both in the 1930s–1950s and again at the end of the century there was panic-ridden public discussion about the ill effects upon society of the ageing of the population. But such stereotypes were increasingly being challenged at the end of the century as evidence revealed the increasing fitness of older people, showing that even most of those who survived into their 80s and 90s did not suffer a long period of ill health and dependency before death – though a minority did suffer from debilitating diseases for which there was no cure, such as Alzheimer's disease. Research also showed that most people could continue efficiently at their accustomed tasks, both mental and physical, at least into their 70s and could acquire new skills (such as use of information technology) in their 80s and beyond.

By the end of the century more older people had private or occupational pensions in addition to state OLD-AGE PENSIONS, and more also owned their homes, which could be converted into additional income, and so were better off. Retirement from work while still fit and active, almost unknown for manual workers before the 20th century, became the norm in the 1940s and 1950s, when a retirement age of 60 or 65 became common. From the 1980s increasing numbers of people were retired, often involuntarily, in their 50s. This was encouraged by Conservative governments as a means to cut UNEMPLOYMENT, and some employers found that they could cut costs by dismissing older workers and employing younger people. However, by the end of the century some employers were regretting the loss of experienced workers as a result. The Labour government elected in 1997 sought to encourage later retirement ages in order to cut pension costs and to maximize the value to the economy and society of the skills of older people. Retirement combined with greater prosperity meant that more people enjoyed a period of leisure in later life.

Increasing numbers of older people lived alone at the end of the century. This was sometimes interpreted as a sign of their loneliness and neglect by their families. However, researchers pointed out that living alone was a growing characteristic of all age groups, and that most old people who lived alone were in close contact with family and friends but chose to live independently rather than with relatives – with increasing prosperity, more could afford to do so. Contrary to popular belief, older people at the end of the century were more likely to have surviving children than at the beginning of the century, and to have more rather than less contact with their families.

SEE ALSO POPULATION.

FURTHER READING P. Thane, *Old Age in English History: Past Experiences, Present Issues* (2000).

old-age pensions. The first state old-age pensions were introduced in 1908. This followed 30 years of pressure from the labour movement and from social reformers such as Charles Booth and politicians such as Joseph CHAMBERLAIN. The state had long provided pensions for its own employees in the civil service and the armed services. Old-age pensions were intended to provide for the very poor, whose poverty was deemed not to be their own fault and who did not deserve the punitive treatment handed out under the POOR LAW. The

demand for pensions grew out of the contemporary critique of the Poor Law.

The first pensions legislation was devised and introduced by ASQUITH as chancellor of the exchequer in 1907, but it was guided through Parliament in 1908 by LLOYD GEORGE, who by then had taken over as chancellor and who received, undeservedly, most of the credit for it. It provided minimally for those who were very old, very poor and very 'respectable'. The pension age was fixed at 70, which most supporters of the scheme thought at least five years too late, but the Treasury insisted on this age, since it cut the cost of the scheme – many people died between the ages of 65 and 70. It provided a maximum of 5 shillings a week, which was recognized by the government to be too little to live on, but was intended to encourage saving or help from other sources. It was rigorously means-tested, and character tests were also introduced: the pension could be refused to anyone who had been convicted of a crime, including drunkenness, within ten years of their claim, or whom the pension authorities judged to have been guilty of 'habitual failure to work according to his ability, opportunity or need, for his own maintenance and that of his legal relatives'. Also excluded were aliens or those married to aliens, i.e. residents of Britain who had not taken British nationality, the largest number of whom were Jews (*see* IMMIGRATION).

However, the old-age pension was the first cash payment made by the British state outside the Poor Law, and was administered in a less stigmatizing manner. It was also popular. Old people came forward to claim it who were in a state of serious destitution but who had not applied for poor relief. The great majority of them were women, who lived longer than men and who were generally poorer, owing to their lesser opportunities to work and to accumulate assets. The pensions were paid directly from taxation, rather than funded partly from workers' contributions (like the national insurance system introduced in 1911; *see* WELFARE STATE). A major reason for this was that it was recognized that the neediest old people were women, who were too low paid when in work – if they were in paid work at all – to afford contributions.

The pension was doubled during World War I owing to inflation. In 1925 the pensionable age was reduced to 65 and the scheme was integrated into national insurance, though those people (mainly women) who were not covered by national insurance could still qualify for a pension at 70. In 1940 the pension age for women was reduced to 60, partly in response to a campaign by unmarried women workers who argued that women were forced into retirement at earlier ages than men. This remained unchanged until 1990, when protests from British men led to a ruling by the European Court of Justice that gender differences in pension ages was discriminatory. The British government committed itself to equalizing the pension age at 65 by 2010.

Wartime surveys revealed extensive poverty among pensioners, and supplementary pensions were introduced. The BEVERIDGE Report of 1942 recommended that pensions should be extended to the whole population – to avoid what Beveridge saw as the evil of MEANS-TESTING – and that they should be wholly integrated into the national-insurance system. Beveridge argued that state pensions should provide only for subsistence; above that level people should save for themselves, preferably through non-profit institutions.

Broadly the Beveridge proposals were implemented by the LABOUR government in 1948. However, the pension still did not provide enough to live on, and for the remainder of the century the poorest older people had to supplement it with means-tested benefits. Initially (from 1948) these benefits were called national assistance, but they subsequently went through a succession of name changes. The CONSERVATIVE governments that followed retained this structure, and encouraged people to supplement the state pension with private and occupational pensions. In the 1950s high levels of poverty were found among poorer pen-

sioners. Labour governments in the 1960s and 1970s raised the flat-rate state pension and in 1975 introduced an earnings-related supplement to it. However, Conservative governments in the 1980s, under Margaret THATCHER, were hostile to state welfare and they and the Treasury were concerned about the growing costs of pensions arising from the ageing of the population (*see* OLD AGE AND AGEING). In consequence the real value of the pension was eroded until it reached the lowest level of any developed country, with surprisingly little protest. The government encouraged private saving for old age.

The Labour government elected in 1997 sought to avoid raising the universal state pension, despite strong pressure from its supporters (notably Barbara CASTLE) to do so, because it too was concerned about the cost and the number of pensioners, not all of them poor. It preferred to improve payments to the poorest pensioners through the means-tested income-support system while encouraging others to save for additional pensions through private or occupational schemes; these were more carefully regulated than during the period of Conservative government, when they had given rise to some serious scandals involving the mis-selling and mismanagement of pensions.
FURTHER READING P. Thane, *Old Age in English History. Past Experiences, Present Issues* (2000).

Omagh bomb, terrorist attack undertaken by dissident Irish Republicans in August 1998. Following the 'Good Friday' agreement in 1998, SINN FÉIN, along with other parties in NORTHERN IRELAND, had signed up to the 'Mitchell principles' on nonviolence and eventual decommissioning of terrorist weapons. Divisions emerged in October 1998 during a summit of the Provisional IRA (*see* IRISH REPUBLICAN ARMY), but dissident Republicans opposed to the peace process were defeated. The following month 20 leading members of the IRA resigned in protest. A number of dissidents supported a new organization, the 'Real IRA'.

Over the next few months terrorist activity by Republican dissidents increased. On 15 August, in the middle of a busy Saturday afternoon, the media received a telephone call warning of a bomb at the courthouse in Omagh County Tyrone. Police began evacuating the area, but a huge car bomb exploded at the opposite end of the High Street from the courthouse, killing 29 people and injuring over 200. The attack received immediate condemnation from all parties in Northern Ireland and the mainland, including Sinn Féin, who had never previously condemned any Republican terrorist attacks. Three days after the attack the 'Real IRA' issued an apology, and then announced a ceasefire. The attack highlighted the fragility of the peace process in Northern Ireland, but it underlined the extent to which terrorist groups had become marginalized by the same process.

ombudsman, the popular name for an officer of state formally known as the parliamentary commissioner for administration. The word 'ombudsman' is the formal term in Sweden, where the office was first introduced. The office exists to uphold the rights of citizens against governmental action. In principle, it enables a citizen who feels that she or he has been the victim of maladministration by a government department to make a complaint. This system was introduced in Britain by the LABOUR government in 1967.

Complaints by members of the public who claim to have experienced injustice as a result of maladministration must be referred to the commissioner by a member of the House of COMMONS. The commissioner is required to report the results of each investigation to the MP who referred the complaint to him, and to make an annual report to both houses of Parliament. The commissioner may also make other reports to Parliament on specific issues if he (as all seven commissioners were to the end of the century) thinks it necessary. The commissioner may be removed from office only with the assent of both houses of Parliament.

The number of cases referred to the commissioner varied considerably from year to year, from 245 in 1990 to 1305 in 1978, though it tended to rise in the 1990s: it stood at between 1100 and 1700 in each year in the period 1994–8. However, the overwhelming majority of cases were ruled to be outside the commissioner's jurisdiction. The largest numbers investigated were in 1968, when 374 were investigated out of 1181 referred, and in 1997, when 376 out of 1679 were investigated. Since 1972 there have been separate health commissioners for England, Scotland and Wales. There is a separate parliamentary commissioner for administration for Northern Ireland.

O'Neill, Terence (1914–90), ULSTER UNIONIST politician, prime minister of NORTHERN IRELAND (1963–9). As prime minister O'Neill, who saw himself as a modernizer, was keen to promote economic development in the province and to diminish hostility between Unionists and Nationalists. He welcomed Sean Lemass, the taoiseach (prime minister) of the Republic of IRELAND, to Belfast in 1965, the first such official visit since partition. However, his actions alienated hard-line Loyalists, and he offered too little to alienated Ulster Catholics, who became increasingly militant. The formation of the Northern Ireland Civil Rights Association in January 1967 increased pressure on O'Neill to bring about change, but, despite conceding some reforms, he failed to satisfy either group (which would indeed have been difficult, if not impossible) and on 28 April 1969 he resigned amid deepening divisions within Unionism. Thereafter conflict in Northern Ireland intensified.

Open University, higher-education institution established in 1969 to provide distance learning for mature students. Funded by the Labour government, on the initiative of Harold WILSON, the Open University was an international pioneer in the use of new broadcasting technology to provide access to higher education for adults previously deprived of it. Initially it was called the

University of the Air. It was part of the Wilson government's larger policy of widening access to EDUCATION (*see also* UNIVERSITIES). It devised new approaches to higher education, with imaginative curricula suited to the needs of adults who had limited prior qualifications and could not attend a college regularly. Courses were broadcast by the BBC on radio and television, supported by tutorials at local study centres and annual one-week summer schools on the campuses of conventional universities. It was highly successful in giving a second chance for thousands of people, a majority of them women, to obtain a degree, though it could not meet the needs of the very poorly educated. It also functioned as a conventional university at postgraduate level. In the late 1980s it reluctantly admitted 18-year-olds for the first time, under pressure not only from the Conservative government as part of its policy of widening access to university as cheaply as possible, but also from young people who could no longer afford conventional universities owing to the abolition of grants or who did not wish to attend one. At the end of the century the Open University remained highly successful, and had been widely imitated in other countries.

FURTHER READING W. Perry, *The Open University* (1977).

opinion polls. The first public opinion-poll organization to be established in Britain, following American precedent established in the 1930s, was the British Institute of Public Opinion (BIPO) founded in 1937. Its aim was to use the then rather primitive social-science research techniques to assess public opinion on any matters that institutions were prepared to fund. Polls of voting intentions came to be best known because they were widely publicized in the press and the broadcast media. In 1952 BIPO's name was changed to Social Surveys (Gallup Poll) Ltd and in 1995 to the Gallup Organization. Its findings were published regularly in the *News Chronicle* until this was closed in 1960. Thereafter they were published in the *Daily Telegraph* and the *Sunday Telegraph*. Polls often had close links with newspapers.

National Opinion Polls (NOP) was established in 1957 as an affiliate of Associated Newspapers Ltd, and its findings were published in the *Daily Mail*, which was owned by that group, until NOP was sold in 1979. It then found a wider range of media outlets, including the BBC. Marplan was founded in 1959 and was closely linked with the *Guardian* newspaper (*see* MANCHESTER GUARDIAN). In 1989 its principal researchers left to form ICM Research. From its formation in 1964 the Opinion Research Centre conducted private polls for the Conservative Party. In 1983 it merged with Louis Harris Research Ltd to form the Harris Research Centre. Louis Harris had been established by the American polling expert Louis Harris in 1969, in collaboration with the *Daily Express*, which, until that time, had run an independent poll since the 1940s. Harris marketed its polls widely in the media, one of its customers being London Weekend Television. Market and Opinion Research International (MORI), under the chairmanship of Robert Worcester, conducted extensive political surveys from 1969, including private studies for the Labour Party, as well as publishing in a range of newspapers and with the BBC. Since 1984 Social and Community Planning Research (SCPR) has published annual, wide-ranging and widely respected surveys of social attitudes to taxation, social welfare, crime and much else. In the 1990s there were three regularly published monthly series of poll findings on voting intentions: Gallup in the *Daily Telegraph*, ICM in the *Guardian* and MORI in *The TIMES*.

Polls had at their disposal the whole range of social-science survey techniques, which became more refined over the second half of the century. However, the polls publicized in the press rarely used the most accurate techniques because these were expensive and could not provide results as quickly as was often required. A typical opinion poll had a sample of between 800 and 1200 voters, selected by a system known as 'quota sampling', which seeks a representative sample of the population primarily in terms of class (as defined by the registrar general; *see* SOCIAL CLASS), age and gender. With this method, interviewers are sent to perhaps 50 locations, usually parliamentary constituencies chosen by a method known as 'random sampling' (in which, say, 1 in every 15 in a list of constituencies is chosen). Any outcome from a sample of 1000 is liable to a margin of error of plus or minus 3%. A high proportion of differences in poll results lie within this margin.

Over the second half of the century politicians paid increasing attention to the findings of public and private polls. Questions were raised as to the possible distorting effects of polls upon political decision-making, and upon voting, especially since they were not invariably accurate. They could vary considerably in their findings. For example, on the morning of the Common Market referendum on 5 June 1975, which yielded a 67.2% 'yes' vote, the opinion-poll 'yes' forecasts were: Gallup 68%, ORC 73.7%, Louis Harris 72% and Marplan 58%. The polling organizations' general-election forecasts were generally within 3% of accuracy, though all polls were at some point embarrassingly inaccurate, and, although such a margin of error would be acceptable in many statistical calculations, in very close-run elections, such as those of 1950, 1951 and 1964, it was unhelpful. The polls were most seriously inaccurate in the general election of 1992, when they all underestimated the Conservative vote by around 4% and overestimated the Labour vote by between 6.8% (NOP) and 2.8% (Gallup and Marplan). The margin of the resulting Conservative victory was a general surprise. The reasons for the error have never been fully explained, though it was suspected that an increasingly educated and sophisticated electorate was not necessarily inclined to tell pollsters the truth. Surveys taken after elections regularly find more people claiming to have voted for whichever party won the election than could have been the case; there is no reason why pre-election polls should be more trustworthy. On balance, polls have a fairly good record of predicting which proportion of the total vote is likely to go to each party. They are less good at predicting the effects of regional variations or the vagaries of voting systems on the outcome.

FURTHER READING R. Worcester, *British Public Opinion* (1991).

opposition, the, in Parliament, the second largest party in the House of COMMONS. The leader and since 1965 some WHIPS of the largest opposition party are given formal recognition by the granting of publicly funded salaries. The opposition also has the right to reply to major government statements both in Parliament and in the press and broadcast media.

Orange Order, Irish Protestant organization dedicated to the preservation of the Protestant constitution and the 'glorious and immortal memory' of William of Orange (King William III), who defeated the Catholic James II at the battle of the Boyne (1690). The order was founded in County Armagh in 1795. It became so discredited, owing to the violence of its activities, that it went into voluntary dissolution in the mid-19th century. However, it revived later in the century, becoming one of the foundations of popular Unionism in the 1880s. From 1905 it was formally associated with the ULSTER UNIONIST PARTY. It continued to attract a large Ulster Protestant membership to the end of the 20th century, when its membership was perhaps 80,000–100,000. Orange lodges were also active in Scotland.

The order remained the primary focus for the Loyalism of very many Protestants in NORTHERN IRELAND, but by the end of the century was increasingly identified with intransigent opposition to a peace settlement with the Nationalists, and its relationship with the Ulster Unionist Party became increasingly tense. Throughout the 20th century it organized triumphalist marches, ostensibly following routes taken by the forces of William of Orange. Later in the century these often passed through Catholic districts, where they met increasing resistance. This reached a peak in 1996–8. In July 1998 an attempt by hardline Orange marchers to continue a march, against Catholic, Republican resistance, was defeated by heavily armed British troops and the Royal Ulster Constabulary with the support of the leadership of the Ulster Unionist Party.

Orpington by-election. *See* LIBERAL PARTY.

Orwell, George (pseudonym of Eric Arthur Blair) (1903–50), novelist and essayist. Orwell was born in India, where his father was a civil servant. With his mother and older sister he returned to England in 1907. He characterized himself as a member of the 'lower-upper-middle class': his parents were from well-established, comfortably off families but his own family, while being extremely comfortable compared with the great majority of the population at the time, was not among the seriously rich or influential. Like most boys of his class he was sent to a boarding preparatory school, St Cyprian's, Eastbourne, at the age of eight, which, like very many boys of his class, he hated. There he shared the popular patriotism of the period of World War I. He moved on to the most prestigious school in the country, Eton, where, as a king's scholar, he was among the intellectual elite, but he carried on his lifelong sense of being on the margins of society. After Eton, unusually for one of his ability, he did not go to university but, like his father, entered the colonial service, becoming a police officer in BURMA. When he returned to England on leave in 1927 he decided to abandon this career in order to become a writer.

Unusually for his class, Orwell had little inherited income. This, combined with his initial lack of success as a writer, gave him an experience of relative poverty, on which he capitalized in his first book, *Down and Out in Paris and London* (1933). He wrote under an assumed name, partly in order not to embarrass his family, partly to distance himself from his social background. He chose the name Orwell from a river in Suffolk near where his parents were now living. He developed a distinctive style of plain, straightforward writing, and during the 1930s became a fairly well-known novelist and essayist. His first novel, *Burmese Days* (1934), drew upon his police experience and, like some of his other writings, was anti-imperialist in an unsentimental, unrhetorical way. His next novels, *A Clergyman's Daughter* (1935) and *Keep the Aspidistra Flying* (1936), dealt with the relative poverty of some of the middle class. He was not very successful financially, though he was assisted by earnings from increasing amounts of journalism. At this stage he was commissioned to write an account of poverty in England for the LEFT BOOK CLUB. The outcome was *The Road to Wigan Pier* (1937), an influential account of the effects of UNEMPLOYMENT, which embodied a somewhat romantic depiction of the lives of working-class people and an indictment of the inability of middle-class socialists to understand them.

Orwell went to Spain as a journalist shortly after the outbreak of the Spanish Civil War. In Barcelona he thought that he had found a new socialist world that he must fight to defend. He joined the POUM, a dissident, semi-Trotskyite militia. He was seriously injured at the front and on his return to Barcelona he observed the communists' betrayal of their Trotskyite allies. His experience in Spain made him a socialist and an anti-communist, an unfashionable combination at the time. This stance did little for his reputation, or for the success of his account of his Spanish experience, *Homage to Catalonia* (1938). The book did not become well known until its reissue after his death, in the very different political climate of 1952.

On his return to England Orwell published a further novel, *Coming Up for Air* (1939), which contrasted the values of English society at the time, which Orwell considered false, with what he considered the more genuine values prevalent before World War I. His essays and journalism, embodying his conception of straightforward Englishness, had greater popular resonance during World War II. His communitarian notion of England as 'a family … but with the wrong members [i.e. the aristocrats and plutocrats] in control' was expressed in *The Lion and the Unicorn* (1941). He wished to serve in the war, but owing to his age and poor health, he was acceptable only to the HOME GUARD. He worked for the BBC and wrote regular columns for the socialist weekly *Tribune*.

Orwell's hostility to dictatorship was profound, and he directed it against the Soviet Union as well as against the fascists, even during the war, when the USSR was an ally of Britain and these sentiments were unpopular. His critique of the Soviet Union was embodied in the fable *Animal Farm* (1945), which he had difficulty in getting published during the war. However, it became celebrated during the COLD WAR, whose sentiments it better suited, and in consequence Orwell acquired an international reputation. This was consolidated by the publication of *Nineteen Eighty-Four* (1949), another indictment of totalitarianism, which was widely, if not quite accurately, read as an attack on communism alone. Orwell was dying of tuberculosis as he wrote it. He died in 1950, at the beginning of his greatest fame, which grew after his death. Many of his essays were only published posthumously.

FURTHER READING B. Crick, *George Orwell* (1980).

Osborne judgement (1909). *See* LABOUR PARTY; TRADE UNIONS.

Ottawa Conference (21 July–20 August 1932), imperial economic conference convened on the initiative of the Canadian Conservative prime minister R.B. Bennett. Bennett hoped to achieve the guaranteeing of wheat prices, which had fallen like other commodity prices owing to the world Depression (*see* GREAT CRASH). The conference agreed to introduce a partial IMPERIAL PREFERENCE following the British introduction of protective tariffs (*see* TARIFF REFORM) earlier in the year. The agreement was seen as an affirmation of mutual agreement within the EMPIRE.

FURTHER READING B. Porter, *The Lion's Share: A Short History of British Imperialism* (3rd edn, 1996).

Owen, David (1938–), Labour, then Social Democratic Party politician. Born in Plympton, Devon, Owen attended Bradfield College and Sidney Sussex College, Cambridge, where he studied medicine. After practising medicine, he entered politics in 1966 when he became Labour MP for Plymouth Sutton (Plymouth Devonport from 1974). Having resigned from the shadow cabinet in 1972 over party policy on the EUROPEAN ECONOMIC COMMUNITY, Owen was made foreign secretary in 1977 following the death of Tony CROSLAND.

Despite being seen as a potential party leader, Owen was increasingly unhappy with the leftward movement of the party, its hostility to Europe and its defence policy. In 1981 he resigned from the LABOUR PARTY as one of the leading movers in the establishment of the SOCIAL DEMOCRATIC PARTY (SDP), of which he was elected deputy leader. After the resignation of Roy JENKINS in 1983, Owen became party leader. He took charge of negotiations for an alliance between the SDP and the LIBERAL PARTY in the mid-1980s, but was unable to work cooperatively with the Liberal leader David STEEL. When the SDP voted to enter merger negotiations with the Liberals after the 1987 election, Owen resigned. After the merger went ahead in March 1988 he was re-elected leader of the remnant of the SDP, which gradually faded away. He was made a life peer in 1992, and was co-chair of the International Conference on the Former Yugoslavia between 1992 and 1995.

P

Paisley, Ian (Richard Kyle) (1926–), NORTH-ERN IRELAND politician; leader of the Democratic Unionist Party (*see* ULSTER UNIONIST PARTY). Born in Armagh, the son of a Baptist pastor, Paisley was educated at the Ballymena Model School and Ballymena Technical High School. He was ordained a minister in the Free Presbyterian Church in 1946, an organization vehemently opposed to Roman Catholicism. He served as the Protestant Unionist MP for Bannside in the Northern Ireland Parliament, 1970–2. He co-founded the Democratic Unionist Party in 1972, and served as the Democratic Unionist member of the Northern Ireland Assembly from 1973 to 1975. The party, representing extreme Loyalist views, has relentlessly opposed any political contact between the UK government and the Republic of IRELAND over Northern Irish affairs. Paisley's political style has resulted in a temporary suspension from the House of COMMONS and eviction from 10 Downing Street. He has been Democratic Unionist MP at Westminster for North Antrim since 1974, and a member of the European Parliament since 1979, notorious for haranguing the pope in the Parliament chamber. Unsurprisingly, he was a vociferous opponent of the 'Good Friday' agreement, refusing to participate in the negotiations leading to the establishment of the devolved Northern Ireland Assembly in 1999.

Palestine. British administration in Palestine began in December 1917 when General Sir Edmund Allenby entered Jerusalem after defeating the Ottoman Turks (who had ruled Palestine since 1517) in southern Palestine. Britain occupied the remainder of the country in autumn 1918, and until June 1920 it was ruled by British military administrators under martial law. The future of Palestine, in particular the competing claims of Zionists and Arabs, had been contentious for some years. In 1917 the British government had promised in the BALFOUR DECLARATION to facilitate the establishment of a Jewish national home in Palestine, but it also hoped to satisfy the Arabs. In 1920 Britain was granted a mandate, on behalf of the LEAGUE OF NATIONS, to rule Palestine until it was judged ready for independence. Zionists secured in the terms of the mandate guarantees in international law for the establishment of a Jewish national home in Palestine. Before the mandate was finalized there were anti-Jewish riots in Jerusalem, which led the British government to replace the military government with a civil administration.

In June 1920 the former Liberal minister Sir Herbert SAMUEL, who was Jewish, was appointed first high commissioner. Further anti-Jewish riots in 1921 led him to issue in 1922 a white paper reformulating British policy. This sought to balance support for a Jewish national home with safeguards for the Arab majority. Samuel tried to establish an elected legislative council, but it was boycotted by Arabs. Subsequent attempts to set up an unelected council also failed. Effectively Britain ruled Palestine autocratically until the end of the mandate in 1948.

Samuel and, after 1925, his non-Jewish successor, sought to balance Jewish and Arab interests, for a while with success. The rioting revived in 1929, causing 200 deaths in Jerusalem. A reason for this was Arab alarm at the doubling of the Jewish population of Palestine in the previous ten years. The riots were sparked by controversy between Arabs and Jews over religious rights on the Temple Mount and at the Western ('Wailing') Wall in Jerusalem. Jewish immigration reached higher levels in the 1930s, due mainly to Nazi persecution in Europe. The numbers of immigrants rose from 4075 in 1931 to 61,854 in 1935, when Jews constituted 27% of the population of Palestine. Arabs feared that they would shortly become a minority in their own country. In 1936 an Arab general strike in protest against Jewish immigration developed into a revolt against British rule and against the Jewish national home. When conciliation failed, British military force was deployed, eventually amounting to 40% of the field strength of the British army. Over 100 Arabs were hanged before the revolt temporarily collapsed in early 1939.

In 1937 a royal commission, headed by Earl Peel, recommended partition of Palestine into Jewish and Arab states with a residual British mandatory area. This was opposed by Arabs and open warfare followed. A conference in London early in 1939 failed to achieve agreement. The British government wished to reduce its military commitment in Palestine, in view of the dangerous international situation. It announced in May 1939 that Jewish immigration would be limited to a total of 75,000 over the next five years, and that land transfers from Arabs to Jews would be restricted. This policy was maintained throughout

the war, the British authorities using force to prevent Jewish refugees from Europe landing in Palestine. Arabs, nevertheless, complained that the authorities were lax about preventing unauthorized landings; and Jewish resentment against the British led to the rise of terrorist organizations, such as Irgun Zvai Leumi, headed by Menachem Begin (who in 1977–83 was to be prime minister of Israel, representing the right-wing Likud party) and the Stern Gang. In 1944 members of the Stern gang assassinated the British minister in the Middle East, Lord Moyne, in Cairo. Thereafter there was continuous warfare between the Jewish terrorists and the British army.

The LABOUR government in Britain from 1945 did not change British policy in Palestine, despite a history of sympathy for Zionism. It was caught, like its predecessors, between conflicting Arab and Jewish claims. If it gave way to Zionist claims it feared endangering its position elsewhere in the MIDDLE EAST, including control of the Suez Canal and the oil fields of Iraq. On the other hand, Zionists were successfully lobbying the United States government, on whose financial aid Britain was dependent. In the autumn of 1945 the British and American governments agreed to appoint a joint Anglo-American committee of inquiry into the issue. In April 1946 it recommended admitting 100,000 Jewish refugees to Palestine. The British government refused, Prime Minister ATTLEE announcing that an essential precondition for acceptance would be the disarming of all illegal forces in Palestine. The Zionists refused and conflict escalated, again involving large numbers of British troops. Terrorist incidents, in particular the huge explosion in 1946 at the King David Hotel in Jerusalem, which killed 90 British, Jewish and Arab victims, led to a partial breakdown of morale in the British forces; it also led to counter-terrorism against Jews, and anti-Semitic incidents in Britain. At the same time Arab-Jewish violence increased. In 1947 the British government announced that it would withdraw, handing over the mandate to the UNITED NATIONS (UN).

In November 1947 the UN General Assembly voted in favour of the partition of Palestine into separate Arab and Jewish states. The British mandate was officially to continue until 14 May 1948, but the Palestinian Arabs refused to recognize the new state of Israel or the enlargement of Jordan, which it was proposed would take over the Arab part of Palestine. British authority collapsed. By April 1948 there was full-scale civil war between Jews and Arabs, the latter supported by the surrounding Arab states. There was a massive flight of Palestinian Arabs from the area designated as the state of Israel; in some areas they were directly forced to leave by Zionists, while in other areas they fled in anticipation of force. On 14 May 1948 the Zionist leader David Ben-Gurion declared the establishment of the state of Israel. The last British high commissioner left. War between Arabs and Jews continued into 1949 before subsiding into an uneasy truce, followed by recurrent conflict to the end of the century.

SEE ALSO SUEZ CRISIS.

FURTHER READING C. Sykes, *Crossroads to Israel: Palestine from Balfour to Bevin* (1965).

Pankhurst, Christabel (Harriette) (1880–

1958), militant SUFFRAGETTE and co-founder of the Women's Social and Political Union (WSPU) along with her mother, Emmeline PANKHURST. Born in Manchester in 1880, Christabel spent much of her childhood in London and later attended the Manchester High School for Girls with her sister Sylvia PANKHURST. She studied to become a solicitor at Manchester University and gained an LL.B., but was barred from the profession because of her gender. Receiving her political and social education from her parents, she was roused to activism at an early age. Annoyed by the lack of attention paid to the issue of women's suffrage by the INDEPENDENT LABOUR PARTY (of which her parents were among the earliest members), she urged her mother to form the WSPU, which they did together in October 1903.

Over the next few years the WSPU remained largely unknown. Then in 1905 the group gained instant publicity when Christabel and a friend, Annie Kenney, heckled the speaker at a LIBERAL PARTY meeting with questions about female suffrage; afterwards there was a scuffle and they were arrested for assaulting the POLICE. Refusing to pay the fines imposed, Christabel was sent to prison for seven days and Annie for three. The sensational attention they gained in the press convinced the WSPU that militant protest was the best route to take, and the Pankhursts – Emmeline, Christabel and Sylvia – moved the organization to London in 1906 and increased its activity. As the WSPU began to blossom and attract more support, Christabel was soon named as chief organizer and was dubbed the 'Maiden Warrior' of the cause of female suffrage. Her face soon adorned WSPU posters and badges. She became the editor of *The Suffragette*, the WSPU newspaper, devised the organization's 'Moral Crusade' (whose slogan was 'votes for women, chastity for men') and continued to be arrested and imprisoned for her militant activities. These were scaled down with the outbreak of war, when the WSPU supported the Allied effort, and in 1918 came a partial victory when limited female suffrage was granted. Votes for all women later followed in 1928, shortly after the death of her mother.

After 1918, with her life's mission having been largely accomplished, Christabel faded from public view in Britain, and concentrated mainly on writing and lecturing in the United States and Canada, where she was rapturously received as a heroine by female audiences. Her aim to become the first woman to sit in the House of COMMONS in 1919 was thwarted – to Christabel's bitterness – by Nancy ASTOR. She became an evangelical Christian in the 1920s, and religion became her new passion. In 1936 she was made a dame commander of the Order of the British Empire in recognition of her role in the suffrage campaign, which pleased her immensely. In 1939 she moved to the United States, eventually settling in California, where she died in 1958. Since her death, and especially with the rebirth of the women's movement in the 1970s, her efforts as the 'Maiden Warrior' have gained her legendary status and great posthumous fame.

FURTHER READING D. Mitchell, *Queen Christabel: A Biography of Christabel Pankhurst* (1977).

Pankhurst, Emmeline (1858–1928), militant SUFFRAGETTE and co-founder of the Women's Social and Political Union (WSPU) along with her daughter Christabel PANKHURST. Born Emmeline Goulden in 1858, she was the daughter of a Manchester cotton manufacturer. Educated at private schools in Manchester and Paris, Emmeline married Richard Marsden Pankhurst in 1879. He was a barrister and a supporter of socialism and women's rights, having helped to draft the Married Women's Property Acts of 1870 and 1882. Initially supporters of the LIBERAL PARTY, the Pankhursts abandoned it in frustration over its lack of interest in the issue of female suffrage. They then went on to support the FABIAN SOCIETY and were among the earliest members of the INDEPENDENT LABOUR PARTY (ILP). Emmeline was elected a POOR LAW guardian in 1894 and a schoolboard member in 1900. She had two daughters in addition to Christabel, Sylvia PANKHURST and Adela, and two sons, one of whom died in childhood whereas the other, Harry, died as a young man. Her husband died in 1898.

Despite her varied political interests, Emmeline's main passion always remained votes for women. She had been one of the founders of the Women's Franchise League. But she was impatient with the overall slow rate of change, the refusal of the ILP to prioritize the issue, and the seeming lack of progress made by peaceful movements such as Millicent Garrett FAWCETT's National Union of Women's Suffrage Societies (NUWSS). At the urging of Christabel, also an ardent supporter of votes for women, mother and daughter founded the WSPU in 1903. Sylvia soon came to work for the WSPU as well. The organization advocated militant tactics and its followers were known as the suffragettes, to distinguish them from nonmilitant SUFFRAGISTS such as those of the NUWSS. The WSPU first gained notoriety in 1905 when Christabel and a friend were arrested after heckling the speaker at a LIBERAL PARTY meeting. Emmeline, believing that there was no such thing as bad publicity, soon moved the WSPU to London in order to attract more attention and support.

Emmeline placed herself on the front line of the campaign, never shying away from putting herself in danger or at risk of arrest. She was arrested for the first time in 1908 after breaking into the lobby of the House of COMMONS and urging other supporters to follow her example. She was sentenced to three months in prison. After her release, the WSPU stepped up its campaign of violence against property, with members breaking windows and setting fire to the contents of pillar boxes. They conducted unruly demonstrations and chained themselves to public buildings. Most famously, Emily Wilding Davison became a martyr to the cause when she threw herself beneath the king's horse at the 1913 Derby.

In 1912 Emmeline was arrested again on a charge of conspiracy to commit damage after a window-smashing spree. She was given a ninemonth sentence and, like other suffragettes, promptly went on hunger strike while in prison. The following year, not long after she had been released, she was convicted of bombing LLOYD GEORGE's house and was again sentenced, this time to three years. By this point the government had passed the 'CAT AND MOUSE' ACT, so when Emmeline began her hunger strikes again she found herself being released and then re-arrested after her health improved. Over the course of the year she was re-arrested twelve times under the act, but eventually served only about thirty days of her sentence.

With the outbreak of WORLD WAR I the WSPU agreed to suspend its campaign and aid the war effort, which redeemed it somewhat in the eyes of its critics. All suffragettes were released from prison. At the war's end in 1918 the WSPU gained a partial victory when married women and university graduates over the age of 30 were finally given the right to vote in parliamentary elections. But after the success of 1918, Emmeline and Christabel retreated from public life in Britain. Bitterly disappointed by the failure of Christabel to become the first woman MP, Emmeline spent much of the early 1920s lecturing in Canada and the United States. She returned to Britain in 1926 and later was set to run as the Conservative candidate for Whitechapel, but died before she could begin the campaign. Just a month after her death, Parliament passed the EQUAL FRANCHISE ACT (1928), which granted the franchise to all British women over the age of 21. Although some historians consider that the militancy of the suffragette movement may have hindered the eventual granting of the vote to women, it is Emmeline Pankhurst, her daughters and the WSPU who are best remembered today and who have come to symbolize the fight for female suffrage in Britain.

FURTHER READING E. Pankhurst, *My Own Story* (1979); T. Vicary, *Mrs Pankhurst* (1993).

Pankhurst, (Estelle) Sylvia (1882–1960), SUFFRAGETTE, communist and anti-fascist activist. Born in Manchester in 1882, Sylvia Pankhurst was the second-eldest daughter of Emmeline PANKHURST and the younger sister of Christabel PANKHURST, the founders of the Women's Social and Political Union (WSPU). Sylvia's role as a militant suffragette was less visible than that of her more famous mother and sister. However, she did demonstrate and take part in the WSPU's campaign of violence against property; she was arrested several times and was subject to force-feeding while in prison. Her artistic talents and training were put to use in the movement, and she designed many posters and other materials for the WSPU in the suffragette colours of purple, green and white.

Sylvia parted ways with her family at the outbreak of WORLD WAR I in 1914. Unlike her mother and sister, who suspended WSPU activity in order to support the war effort, Sylvia was a committed pacifist (*see also* HARDIE, (JAMES) KEIR). During and after the war she engaged in philanthropic work with poor women and children in the East End of London. She also became very interested in global political issues. She passionately supported the Russian Revolution and met Lenin during a trip to the Soviet Union. She was a founder member of the COMMUNIST PARTY OF GREAT BRITAIN. Her refusal to marry Silvio Cori, the father of her son Richard (born 1927), completed her estrangement from her mother. She was an early, active anti-fascist. From 1936 she took up the cause of Abyssinian independence (*see* ABYSSINIAN CRISIS) and opposed Mussolini's regime. She died in Addis Ababa in 1960.

FURTHER READING S. Pankhurst, *The Suffragette Movement* (1931, 1977); P.W.E. Romero, *Sylvia Pankhurst: Portrait of a Radical* (1987); B. Winslow, *Sylvia Pankhurst: Sexual Politics and Political Activism* (1998).

Parliament. *See* COMMONS, HOUSE OF; LORDS, HOUSE OF.

Parliament Act (1911). *See* LORDS, HOUSE OF.

party system. British politics throughout the 20th century was dominated by parties: at the beginning of the century by the CONSERVATIVE and LIBERAL parties, and from the end of WORLD WAR I by the Conservative and LABOUR parties. Smaller parties had passing influence, such as the IRISH NATIONALIST PARTY up to World War I and the SOCIAL DEMOCRATS in the 1980s, and it was the withdrawal of support by Scottish Nationalists from CALLAGHAN's Labour government in early 1979 that precipitated its fall. Such influences were usually more apparent when the government had a slender majority and needed the support of smaller parties. A very few independent members were elected to Parliament and rather more to local councils. But overwhelmingly in the 20th century,

GENERAL ELECTIONS, parliamentary politics and, increasingly, LOCAL GOVERNMENT were dominated by the policies set by the leaders of the dominant parties, and elected representatives were under pressure – which grew over the century – to conform to these imperatives. In Parliament, such pressure was exerted by the party WHIPS.

SEE ALSO COMMONS, HOUSE OF.

Pasmore, Victor (1908–98), artist. Born in Chelsham, Surrey, he worked as a clerk for the LONDON COUNTY COUNCIL from 1927 to 1937 while attending evening classes at the Central School of Arts and Crafts. His early work was figurative but he experimented with abstraction, though he returned to naturalistic painting in the 1930s and joined with William Coldstream and Claude Rogers in founding the EUSTON ROAD SCHOOL. The patronage of Sir Kenneth CLARK enabled him to concentrate full time on his art. In 1948 he switched dramatically to pure abstraction and by the early 1950s he had developed a personal style of geometrical abstraction. Pasmore was an influential teacher and was concerned to bring abstract art to the general public. He taught at Camberwell School of Art, 1943–9, the Central School of Art and Design, 1949–53 and Newcastle University, 1954–61. From 1966 he divided his time between Malta and London. He was recognized as one of the leading British painters of the 20th century.

FURTHER READING N. Lynton, *Victor Pasmore, Nature into Art* (1990).

Passchendaele, a village on a ridge 13 km (8 miles) east of Ypres in Belgium, the furthest point reached by British and Empire troops during the third battle of YPRES (31 July to 10 November 1917), during WORLD WAR I. Capturing the ridge was one of the first objectives in HAIG's plan for a breakthrough into Belgium, but, partly due to constant rain, it was impossible to launch an attack on Passchendaele itself until 12 October, and the ruins of the village were finally taken by Canadian soldiers only on 10 November, when the weather was too bad to carry on the assault with weary and demoralized troops. The Germans used mustard gas for the first time in defending Passchendaele, and the attackers had had to advance in appallingly muddy conditions. Allied troops lost 300,000 casualties while trying to hold this dangerously exposed salient. The Allied offensive cost some 300,000 casualties, and extended the Ypres salient by just a few kilometres, placing the Allied front line in a dangerously exposed position. It was speedily evacuated five months later when the Germans launched their spring offensive. The offensive was one of the most futile of the war, and one of the most terrible experiences for the participants.

FURTHER READING L. Macdonald, *They Called It Passchendaele* (1978).

Peace Ballot (1935), poll of British public opinion devised by the National Declaration Committee set up in 1934 by the LEAGUE OF NATIONS Union, led by Lord Robert Cecil and the eminent classical scholar Gilbert Murray. The National Declaration Committee was organized to gather support for the League, and the poll was to test support for British membership of the League, arms reduction, abolition of military aircraft by international agreement and the end to the private manufacture of arms. It also asked a fifth question: 'Do you consider that, if a nation insists on attacking another, the other nations should combine to compel it to stop by (a) economic and non-military measures? (b) if necessary, military measures?' The poll elicited 11.5 million replies, 90% of them agreeing with all of the propositions, except 5(b), which only 20% accepted. When the results were announced on 27 June 1935, Prime Minister Stanley BALDWIN was persuaded to reverse his hostility to collective efforts to achieve peace and to proclaim the League of Nations 'the sheet anchor of British policy'. However, there was strong opposition to economic sanctions imposed by the League from CONSERVATIVES, pacifists and people on the left. Other polls were conducted to counter the Peace Ballot, but they attracted little attention. Britain took a lead in mustering support for League sanctions against Italy in October 1935, following the invasion of Ethiopia (*see* ABYSSINIAN CRISIS), but they were incompletely applied and ineffective. Peace Ballot supporters believed that an opportunity to make collective security work had been lost. The Axis powers interpreted the result as an indication of British unwillingness to go to war on behalf of other countries.

FURTHER READING D.S. Birn, *The League of Nations Union* (1981).

Peace Pledge Union, pacifist organization established in 1936. In October 1934, alarmed by the deteriorating international situation, the Reverend Dick Sheppard, a well-known pacifist Anglican clergyman, sent a letter to several newspapers requesting readers to send him a postcard stating their support for the following proposition: 'We renounce war and never again, directly or indirectly, will we support or sanction another.' By December 1935 he had received 100,000 postcards. In May 1936 he organized this body of support into a new organization, the Peace Pledge Union (PPU), open only to men. It produced a weekly paper, *Peace News*, formed over 1100 groups, issued pamphlets and held demonstrations. Sheppard died suddenly in October 1937, but the PPU continued to grow, opening up to women. It peaked at 136,000 members in early 1940, including such prominent figures as Bertrand RUSSELL, George LANSBURY, Siegfried SASSOON and Vera BRITTAIN. When WORLD WAR II was declared the PPU did not oppose it, but worked to support pacifists, including conscientious objectors (*see* CONSCIENTIOUS OBJECTION), engaged in relief work and encouraged initiatives to secure a negotiated peace. It went into rapid decline after the war, though it continued in tenuous existence until the end of the century. *Peace News* also continued in existence, but severed its connection with the PPU, becoming the organ of the CAMPAIGN FOR NUCLEAR DISARMAMENT.

FURTHER READING M. Ceadel, *Pacifism in Britain, 1914–1945: The Defining of a Faith* (1980).

pensions. *See* OLD-AGE PENSIONS.

People Party. *See* ENVIRONMENTALISM.

People's Budget (1909). *See* LLOYD GEORGE, DAVID.

permissive society. A new, more 'permissive' society emerged in Britain during the 1960s. There are many indications that a substantial proportion of the population was involved and that there was a change of substance as well as style, of behaviour as well as attitude, taking place. Actions that had been construed as self-indulgent and that had been highly stigmatized in the 1950s had become acceptable to much of the community by the 1970s.

In the 1950s there was still considerable political and social support for restrictive social values. For example, the 1955 Morton Commission on Divorce was profoundly conservative, supporting the belief that DIVORCE was the result of a self-indulgent failure to face up to the realities of married life. However, change was taking place, both privately and publicly. Self-imposed censorship by the media was loosening. For example, in 1955 the Family Planning Association began for the first time to be mentioned in the national media, although no actual methods of BIRTH CONTROL were discussed in the press and broadcast media.

The Obscene Publications Act of 1959 and the *Lady Chatterley's Lover* case of 1960 (*see* CENSORSHIP) were early signs of change. In the early 1960s there was a new director general of the BRITISH BROADCASTING CORPORATION, Hugh Greene, who brought it into the forefront of change. In 1962 Professor G.M. Carstairs, a psychiatrist and academic, gave the prominent annual BBC Reith Lectures. He suggested that 'premarital sexual licence has been found to be quite compatible with stable married life'. The press relayed what were then very controversial statements to a wider audience. They also showed greater willingness than in the past to report fully on sexual scandals involving prominent people, such as the PROFUMO AFFAIR in 1963. By the mid-1960s there was a widely perceived erosion of moral authority, not just that of the Christian churches, but also that of society as a whole, which had hitherto upheld a consensus as to what constituted 'correct' behaviour.

Meanwhile private sexual behaviour was changing. The incidence of premarital sex appeared to be rising, and the proportion of all births that were 'illegitimate' (as births to single mothers were described at the time) rose sharply in the 1960s. Having an 'illegitimate' baby was still highly stigmatized in the 1960s. There was little assistance available for single mothers, and many gave their babies up for ADOPTION, often with much grief. Illegal ABORTION rates seem to have been rising, but the operation was often dangerous and expensive. Information on birth control could be difficult for women to obtain, and the only easily accessible methods (condoms and withdrawal) were male-controlled. In the early 1960s the birth-control pill was introduced, and by the mid-1960s sales of the pill were rising rapidly. In 1967 the abortion law was reformed to try to end illegal abortions. Sexual behaviour was more widely discussed and written about, for example in Alex Comfort's *Sex in Society* (1963), which excited much media discussion.

By the early 1970s many aspects of sexual and social mores had changed substantially. Following legislation in 1969 there was a sharp rise in divorce rates, and the homosexual law reform of 1967 (*see* SEXUALITY, OFFICIAL REGULATION OF) was followed by a growing visibility of gay men and women. Sex became more visible in a variety of ways. By 1970 naked actors were simulating sex on stage in *Oh! Calcutta!*, an erotic review by the theatre critic Kenneth Tynan. The vast majority of the population did not see either pornographic magazines or theatre shows, but they were reported extensively by the press; and the sexual content of films,

television and popular music also increased greatly. The rise in sexually explicit printed matter available was evident from seizures by customs-and-excise authorities, who impounded only 5600 books and magazines in 1960, but about 1.5 million in 1968. In the 1970s there were growing fears that sexual liberation was going too far, and there were calls for restraint from some quarters; however, a substantial long-term shift away from lifelong monogamous marriage and nuclear families, and greater tolerance of sexual diversity, had begun in the 1960s (*see* POPULATION).

FURTHER READING S. Bruley, *Women in Britain since 1900*, (1999); C.H. Rolph, *The Trial of Lady Chatterley: Regina v. Penguin Books Limited* (1961); J. Weeks, *Sex, Politics and Society: The Regulation of Sexuality since 1800* (1981).

Perutz, Max. *See* SCIENCE.

Philby, Kim. *See* CAMBRIDGE SPIES.

Phoney War, name first coined by American journalists, and then popularly given in Britain to the period of World War II between the declaration of war on Germany on 3 September 1939 and May 1940. In the intervening period, the attention of the German leadership was fixed upon eastern rather than western Europe, and Britain and France were reluctant to fight until attacked. This period came to an end with the successful German invasion of Denmark and Norway in April–May 1940, followed by that of the Netherlands, Belgium, Luxembourg and then France in May.

SEE ALSO WORLD WAR II: MILITARY.

Piper, John (1903-92), painter, designer and writer. He was born in Epsom, Surrey. His father was a solicitor and after leaving school he reluctantly joined his father's firm. After his father's death in 1926, Piper studied at Richmond College of Art and then at the Royal College of Art, 1926–8. From 1928 to 1933 he wrote art criticism for the weekly journals the *Listener* and the *Nation* and was among the first to recognize the talent of contemporaries such as William Coldstream and Victor PASMORE. Piper was meanwhile building a reputation as one of the leading British abstract artists, but at the end of the 1930s he became disillusioned with nonrepresentational art and reverted to figurative painting. Piper concentrated on paintings of landscape and architecture, notably during World War II with his paintings of bomb-damaged buildings. However, he was not appointed an official war artist until 1944. He also made a number of paintings of country houses at this time, either on commission or on his own initiative. In the 1950s his work diversified, when he was recognized as not only one of the most versatile British artists of his generation, but also one of the more popular. His work included designs for stained glass for Coventry Cathedral as well as stage sets, including some for Benjamin BRITTEN operas. He also produced book illustrations and designed pottery and textiles.

FURTHER READING Tate Gallery, *John Piper* (1984).

Plaid Cymru. *See* WALES.

planning. *See* TOWN AND COUNTRY PLANNING.

poetry. Poetry in Britain exhibited little inspiration in the first decade of the century. A fresh spirit emerged with the five anthologies of new poetry edited by Edward Marsh (1872–1953) and Harold Monro (1879–1932) between 1912 and 1922. This new poetry came to be known as 'Georgian', emerging as it did in the reign of King GEORGE V. Poets represented included Rupert Brooke (1887–1915), Lascelles Abercrombie (1881–1938), Walter de la Mare (1873–1956), Robert Graves (1895–1985), D.H. LAWRENCE, Edward Thomas (1878–1917) and Wilfred Owen (1893–1918). The anthologies included poets with different techniques and sensibilities – some of them traditionalist, others rather less so – but their work had certain characteristics in common, in particular

a preoccupation with the sounds of English speech and song and a love of the English countryside. It is decidedly English, rather than British, poetry.

More self-consciously experimental, modernist and intellectual were the Imagists, who included T.E. Hulme (1883–1917), F.S. Flint (1885–1960) and the American Ezra Pound, who arrived in London in 1909. They believed that the late-Romantic poets had lost touch with living speech, and sought to turn from the clichés and wordiness of late Romanticism to sharper perceptions of reality rendered via pure visual imagery, concisely expressed. Between 1914 and 1917 the group published annual anthologies, which included poems from James JOYCE, Ford Madox Ford (1873–1939) and D.H. Lawrence.

The poetry arising directly from the all-too-real experiences of WORLD WAR I made a wider and longer-lived impact. Poetry expressed the shifting realities of the war. In 1914 and 1915 the most popular poetry was nationalistic and militaristic. The first war poetry by a participant to make an impact was Rupert Brooke's five idealistic war sonnets published after his death from blood-poisoning in 1915. These stressed homesickness, fear of death and hope of personal redemption. Then came the poetry of the men who endured the prolonged trench warfare and revealed its horrors: Wilfred Owen (who died shortly before the end of the war), Siegfried Sassoon (1886–1967) and Isaac Rosenberg (1890– 1918). Their poems embodied realistic descriptions of the war, intended to eliminate any romantic illusions. Less noticed has been the body of poetry by women, expressing their emotions on the home front: Charlotte Mew (1869–1928), Alice Meynell (1846–1922), Frances Cornford (1886–1960) and Sylvia Townsend Warner (1893–1978).

The interwar years were a period of conflict between modernist and traditional modes, the latter represented by Thomas Hardy (1840–1928), de la Mare and Robert Bridges (1844–1930) and perhaps the Irish nationalist William Butler YEATS, but he was too individual a poet to fit easily in any school. These were the leading poets of the post-war period for most readers and critics. But the sense that a new and more 'modern' world had dawned created a different poetry, as found in the work of T.S. ELIOT, Pound, D.H. Lawrence, increasingly Yeats, and Edith Sitwell (1887–1964), whose *Façade* was published in 1922. MODERNISM was to dominate English and American poetry from the 1920s to the 1950s, incorporating free verse, realistic speech, jazz syncopations, Freudian images, wide-ranging cultural allusions and explicit criticism of the dominant contemporary culture.

In the 1930s a new modernist generation emerged. This included the Scottish nationalist, communist and key figure in the Scottish cultural renaissance of the period, Hugh MacDiarmid (Christopher Murray Grieve; 1892–1978), Basil Bunting (1900–85) and William Empson (1906–84). Another important development of the interwar years was the emergence of the 'Auden group' at Oxford: W.H. AUDEN, Stephen Spender (1909–95), Louis MacNeice (1907–63) and Cecil Day Lewis (1907–72). Their poetry was conventional in form but unconventional in ideas. Politically they regarded themselves as of the left (whereas Eliot and Pound were more conservative), and they combined a Georgian celebration of England with a modernist internationalism. Like the modernists they described urban and technological subjects, but juxtaposed them with the English landscape. Auden combined references to modern culture (e.g. to Freud) with references to cricket and to traffic jams, using such forms as those of popular song.

WORLD WAR II did not give rise to a war poetry as the previous war had done. Eliot portrayed bombing raids in *Four Quartets*; Day Lewis wrote contemplatively about England; Sitwell used Christian symbolism to write about Hiroshima. Eliot and Auden dominated the 1940s, but during that decade there began a 'neo-romantic' reaction against modernism, represented by Dylan Thomas (1914–53) and, among others, Kathleen Raine

(1908–) and Lawrence Durrell (1912–90). Robert Graves continued to write in an independent traditionalist style. Different again, and widely popular, was John Betjeman (1906–84), writing accessible, unintellectual social satire. Also satirical, independent-minded and popular, especially in the 1950s, was Stevie Smith (Florence Margaret Smith, 1902–71).

In the 1950s a group of sceptical, realist, anti-romantic poets came together in what came to be called 'the Movement', though in reality their styles and preoccupations differed greatly. They were, chiefly, Philip Larkin (1922–85), Kingsley Amis (1922–1995), Donald Davie (1922–), Elizabeth Jennings (1926–), D.J. Enright (1920–), Robert Conquest (1917–), Thom Gunn (1929–) and John Wain (1925–94). Gunn later shifted to a preoccupation with popular culture, increasingly that of the West Coast of the United States.

The predominant poets at the end of the century were Ted Hughes (1930–99), whose wife Sylvia Plath (1932–63) was also a striking independent poetic voice before her suicide, and Seamus Heaney (1939–). Hughes was a tough-minded realist with romantic inclinations. He confronted the brutality of life in poems that are often rooted in the natural world, written in a blunt style suited to his themes. Heaney is a Roman Catholic from NORTHERN IRELAND, although he subsequently took up residence and citizenship in the Republic of IRELAND. His strong Irish identity is clearly expressed in his poetry. He was awarded the Nobel prize for literature in 1995.

FURTHER READING N. Corcoran, *English Poetry since 1940* (1993); M. Drabble (ed.), *The Oxford Companion to English Literature* (2000).

police. In 1900 policing was a function of LOCAL GOVERNMENT, largely funded from local RATES (taxes) with minimal central direction. Only the London ('Metropolitan') police were controlled by central government, through the Home Office. There were 200 local forces, with little or no cooperation among them and no common standards of pay or pension. WORLD WAR I, industrial unrest during and just after the war and fears of wider civil unrest led to greater coordination. Closer links developed between senior police officers and the Home Office, mainly through the Central Conference of Chief Constables.

Women carried out police functions during the war for the first time, initially in voluntary groups because they believed that police forces provided insufficient protection for women, who were often living, travelling and working alone due to war conditions; they also believed that they should act to uphold public morals generally. From 1920 local authorities were allowed to appoint women to permanent police posts, but there was strong resistance in many forces and by 1939 only 43 out of 183 authorities did so. There was active pressure from women's organizations, who argued that many cases, especially those involving assault on women and children, were not being reported to male police officers, or were not necessarily best handled by them. Policewomen numbered 174 out of a total police strength of 65,000 in England and Wales in 1939. By the mid-1990s they made up 10% of the 135,000 police officers in England, Wales and Scotland. At the end of the century a number of policewomen alleged harassment and discrimination on the part of their male colleagues, and several won compensation through the legal system.

Working conditions in the police force continued to be poor during and after World War I, provoking the formation of the National Union of Police and Prison Officers and the outbreak of two police strikes. This led to the appointment of the Desborough Committee and the passing of the 1919 Police Act, which introduced improved and uniform pay scales, a centrally guided, federal structure of local police forces, banned the police from striking or forming trade unions and provided instead the officially approved Police Federation as a representative body.

In the interwar years, the GENERAL STRIKE of 1926 and demonstrations of the unemployed fur-

ther prompted government direction of policing and increasing central control over local forces, though chief constables retained a high degree of operational independence. This process continued after World War II, with central direction coming most overtly to the fore during episodes of civil unrest, such as the urban riots of 1981 and strikes such as the MINERS' STRIKE of 1984–5.

Throughout their history, British police have been unarmed, except with a truncheon, though the use of firearms was increasingly sanctioned later in the century in response to the growing numbers of criminals who carried and used such weapons. Most police officers carried out their duties responsibly and respectably, though in the later decades of the century a number of cases were detected of corruption, fabrication of evidence and forced admissions of guilt from innocent people. In the 1990s, following the Stephen LAWRENCE case, it became obvious that racism was all too prevalent in at least some forces, and measures were introduced to try to eliminate it.

The number of recorded indictable offences rose steadily through the century, especially from the 1960s, but the proportion of crimes solved declined. For example, the clear-up rate for burglary fell from 40% in 1951 to 28% in 1984.

FURTHER READING C. Emsley, *The English Police: A Political and Social History* (1991); R. Reiner, *The Politics of the Police* (1985).

poll tax. *See* COMMUNITY CHARGE.

Ponting, Clive. *See* OFFICIAL SECRETS ACT.

Poor Law, the only source of state assistance for impoverished people at the beginning of the 20th century. The Poor Law had been in existence since the late 16th century and had been extensively revised in 1834. It was intended to be minimal in its provision, and also stigmatizing. The state had a legal obligation to prevent anyone from dying of starvation, but no more; it provided only for the destitute. It did so in two forms: minimal cash handouts (known as 'outdoor relief') to those living in their own homes, whose poverty was deemed not to be their own fault; and admission to an institution, the workhouse, for those who were held to blame for their poverty (by not seeking work, for example) or who, in addition to being destitute, were too old or physically or mentally sick to care for themselves and had no relatives or friends to help them. In principle, those whose poverty was deemed to be their own fault (the 'undeserving poor') were to be treated more strictly than the other workhouse inmates ('the deserving poor').

In reality poor relief varied considerably from place to place, both in respect of workhouse conditions and the amount of outdoor relief granted. Some places, mainly large urban areas, provided adequate hospital and OLD-AGE accommodation for those in need. In other areas workhouses could be grim and punitive for all inmates. The Poor Law was administered locally, in local-government units known as 'unions', by elected boards known as 'guardians'. It was financed by a separate local RATE (tax). This tended to mean that districts with high levels of poverty could least provide for their poor because they had low rate income. In London this was resolved by a system whereby richer unions subsidized poorer unions – but the capital was unique in this respect.

By the beginning of the century the system was facing strong criticism from, among others, the growing LABOUR movement. The experience of working-class activists was that there was a great deal of poverty that was not the fault of the poor, due for example to UNEMPLOYMENT, and among the large numbers of widowed single mothers, who merited more generous treatment. This was borne out by major POVERTY surveys, such as that carried out by Charles Booth in London in the 1890s and by B. Seebohm ROWNTREE in York and published in 1901. These found that poverty was diminishing but was still at very high levels: about 30% per cent of the population of both places. The Poor Law, by contrast, never provided for more

than about 5% of the population at any one time. There was strong evidence that many people preferred starvation to the shame of applying for poor relief.

Criticism of the system led BALFOUR's Conservative government in 1905 to establish a Royal Commission on the Poor Laws and Relief of Distress. Members of the commission included Beatrice WEBB, George LANSBURY (who was a Poor Law guardian in Poplar, east London, and an advocate of reform) and Charles Booth. The commission made exhaustive inquiries and reported in 1909. There were two reports, a majority and a minority report, the latter drafted by the Webbs. The reports in fact had much in common. Both supported fundamental reform of the welfare system, abolition of the Poor Law and its replacement with a range of social services and benefits related to the different categories of need: old age, sickness and so on. The difference between them was that the majority would have kept a large role for the voluntary sector in the administration of the system, whereas the minority preferred to entrust it to paid administrators.

The LIBERAL government that was in office in 1909 took no direct notice of the reports – despite an active three-year campaign by the Webbs to 'break up' the Poor Law – though it did recommend to guardians that they take a less punitive approach, especially to the deserving poor. Indirectly, however, such measures as OLD-AGE PENSIONS (introduced in 1908), national health and unemployment insurance (1911) and the Children Act (1908) (*see* WELFARE STATE) removed the most vulnerable groups from the scope of the Poor Law. For example, substantial numbers of impoverished old people, who had somehow survived without poor relief, came forward for the pension. The numbers of paupers fell further during WORLD WAR I largely because of rising family incomes.

After the war, the role of the Poor Law was to act as a safety net for those of the unemployed who did not qualify for national insurance benefit, often owing to the length of their unemployment. It also supported widows and their children (until the introduction of widows' and orphans' pensions in 1925), and provided institutional care for older people, the mentally and physically disabled and the chronically sick. Increasing numbers of boards of guardians came under Labour control and gave outdoor relief to the unemployed at higher levels than was officially sanctioned, and sometimes also to strikers (for example during and after the GENERAL STRIKE of 1926), which was not sanctioned at all. In consequence Neville CHAMBERLAIN, as minister of health from 1924 to 1929, tightened control over the guardians. He laid down strict limits to the amount of relief that could be paid, and to whom, and threatened to dismiss and replace guardians who paid out too much or paid anything to strikers; in a few cases this threat was carried out.

These controls were preparatory to Chamberlain's complete overhaul of the Poor Law in the Local Government Act, 1929. This abolished the separately elected guardians and the poor rate, subsuming Poor Law administration into that of the county and borough authorities. Outdoor relief was renamed 'public assistance', and local authorities took over the running of the institutions. The public-assistance system changed little from the old system until WORLD WAR II, when the discovery of continuing levels of severe poverty, especially among old people, led to the introduction of improved supplementary benefits. Many institutions were improved in the 1930s and 1940s. The Poor Law was formally abolished only in 1948 when the National Assistance Act replaced public assistance with the new means-tested benefit, national assistance. The name was changed several more times before the end of the century: it was known successively as supplementary benefit, social security benefit and income support.

SEE ALSO LOCAL GOVERNMENT; WELFARE STATE.
FURTHER READING M.A. Crowther, *The Workhouse System, 1834–1929* (1981); P. Thane, *The Foundations of the Welfare State* (2nd edn, 1996).

Poppy Day. *See* HAIG, DOUGLAS.

Popular Front, coalition of parties of the left and centre, advocated by the COMMUNIST PARTY OF GREAT BRITAIN (CPGB) in 1935, in line with Soviet foreign policy, to unite all political forces opposed to fascism and to APPEASEMENT. The inspiration came from similar movements in France and Spain, in both of which Popular Front governments were elected in 1936. The outbreak of the SPANISH CIVIL WAR in July 1936 brought further support for the idea in Britain. Still more support for it followed Hitler's annexation of Austria in 1938. The idea was endorsed by leading LIBERALS but regarded by LABOUR leaders with great suspicion, as they did all things associated with the CPGB; however, it gathered support among Labour left-wingers such as Stafford CRIPPS and Aneurin BEVAN, both of whom were expelled from the Labour Party in 1938 in consequence. Denied Labour support, the movement fizzled out, and the Nazi–Soviet pact of August 1939 discredited it.

FURTHER READING D. Blaazer, *The Popular Front and the Progressive Tradition: Socialists, Liberals and the Quest for Unity, 1884–1939* (1992).

popular protest. For most of the 20th century political culture in Britain could be characterized by a consensus over the validity and usefulness of 'normal' political activity. Before the late 1950s what could be described as 'popular protest' usually comprised various types of industrial action, most notably the 1926 GENERAL STRIKE. Strikes and industrial action continued throughout the 20th century, although the ability of TRADE UNIONS to exert pressure through such actions was much curtailed under the government of Margaret THATCHER. Campaigns such as the MINERS' STRIKE of 1984–5 did, however, extend beyond straightforward workforce discontent into something more akin to a conflict between the state and communities that saw themselves as defending a way of life.

Unconventional forms of political protest against government policy or social conditions did, however, occur throughout the century. As well as the highly public protests undertaken by the SUFFRAGETTES before World War I, the interwar period saw a series of HUNGER MARCHES publicizing the problem of UNEMPLOYMENT in Britain. Race and IMMIGRATION have also been the catalysts for protests: since World War II urban Britain has seen a number of 'race riots', such as those in Notting Hill during the 1950s or, most notoriously, those in a number of major British cities in 1981 and in London in 1985. Perhaps the most successful popular anti-government protest was the campaign calling for the abolition of the poll tax (COMMUNITY CHARGE) in the late 1980s and early 1990s. Bringing together a broad spectrum of British society, the protest involved large numbers of people who refused to pay and willingly made themselves liable to court appearances. A mass rally organized by the campaign in 1990 led to a major riot in central London. It was the campaign in general, rather than the riots, that prompted the Conservative government to climb down over the tax, which it restructured into the council tax under John MAJOR.

Observers have noted that new forms of political activity have emerged since the 1960s. It has been argued that the post-war generation, coming of age in a relatively prosperous society, exhibited greater concerns about issues such as 'personal development' and humanitarian ideals than the material ambition that had previously driven popular movements. The 'new social movements' of the 1960s onwards have been characterized by such ideals, as well as by loose, informal organization, a desire to encourage fundamental social change rather than to affect specific policies, and by an interest in combining personal with social change. The late 1960s saw a wave of protests, mainly carried out by young people, and particularly directed against the Vietnam War. But these protests – many conducted by students on university campuses – also expressed a more general opposition to the materialism of society.

Many more conventional forms of protest, such as the 1984–5 miners' strike or the ANTI-APARTHEID MOVEMENT, shared the features of social movements, but it is the more broadly ambitious movements such as the CAMPAIGN FOR NUCLEAR DISARMAMENT (CND), the WOMEN'S MOVEMENT and the environmental movement (*see* ENVIRONMENTALISM) that are most often associated with this new form of political campaign. Popular protests such as the CND Aldermaston marches of the late 1950s and 1960s, the GREENHAM COMMON protest of the 1980s (combining both feminist and anti-nuclear protest), the anti-road-building protests at Twyford Down and Newbury and the highly public protests of organizations such as Greenpeace have been seen as examples of a 'new politics' emerging in the latter part of the 20th century.

Popular protest underwent significant change over the course of the century. By the 1990s much protest was, in comparison with the early part of the century, a far more middle-class phenomenon. This was illustrated most clearly in the emergence of the Countryside Alliance in the 1990s, which mobilized the tactics of the new social movements in support of a more traditionalist agenda associated with the political right, focusing upon the defence of fox-hunting, among other things.

FURTHER READING P. Byrne, *Social Movements in Britain* (1997).

population. The population of Great Britain rose from 36,999,946 in 1901 (the year of the first decennial CENSUS of the century) to 57,807,900 in 1991. Within that overall rise there was a pattern of decline in both birth and death rates. Throughout the century there were gains and losses to total population due to IMMIGRATION and EMIGRATION, though these were modest. In 1901–11 there was a net loss of 50,000 people from the UK due to the combined effects of immigration and emigration. In 1921–31 the loss was 17,000. In 1951–61 there was a gain of 47,000, and by 1981–91 a net loss of 5000. In 1996–7 there was a net gain of 110,000. Throughout the century there were more females in the population than males: in 1901, 19,097,000 females to 17,903,000 males; in 1931, 23,336,000 and 21,459,000 respectively (the gender gap was somewhat wider following the slaughter of young men in World War I, but the effect was less dramatic than is sometimes thought). By 1961 the gender balance was somewhat more even at 26,496,000 and 24,792,000, but the superiority in female numbers persisted to the end of the century, mainly owing to the longer life expectancy of females (*see* OLD AGE AND AGEING).

The birth rate began to fall steadily from the 1870s, at all social levels, though with regional differences that affected all social groups; these differences are hard to explain. In 1901–5 there was an average of 28.2 live births per 1000 population in England and WALES, and 29.2 in SCOTLAND; by 1936–40 the birth rate had fallen to 14.7 in England and Wales, and 17.6 in Scotland. This decline caused great concern that Britain would be weakened economically and politically by falling numbers, leading to the appointment in 1943 of a Royal Commission on Population, which thoroughly investigated the issue. But by the time it reported in 1949 the birth rate had recovered in World War II and the post-war period to 18 in 1946–50 in England and Wales, and 20 in Scotland (the so-called 'baby boom'). After a fall to 15.3/17.9 in 1951–5 the birth rate rose again until the later 1960s, followed by a steady decline to an average of about 13.5 in England and Wales (higher in Scotland) between the mid-1970s and the end of the century. The reasons for these changes are not easy to explain. They cannot be attributed simply to the easier availability of modern BIRTH CONTROL devices, since the birth rate had fallen fast earlier in the century, when such devices were difficult for most of the population to obtain.

The fall in death rates can be more easily explained by, above all, improved STANDARDS OF LIVING and of MEDICINE and health care (*see* NATIONAL HEALTH SERVICE). Infant and childhood mortality fell especially dramatically from about 18 per 1000 of the population at the beginning of the century until it averaged around 6.2 in the 1990s. Death rates at later ages have declined more slowly but equally steadily. In consequence life expectancy at birth rose from 55 years for women and 51 years for men at the beginning of the century to 81 and 77 respectively at the end. The effect of the combination of falling birth rates and falling death rates was that the proportion of older people in the population rose throughout the century.

As a consequence of the falling birth rate average family size fell, and there were fewer very large families as the century went on. Mothers gave birth to an average of 3.5 children in the first decade of the century, but the figure had fallen to 2.2 by the 1930s. By the 1990s it was 1.8 and tending to fall further. Also by the 1930s, very large families, of 10 or even 15, were becoming rare, and mothers were concentrating births into a shorter time period. They also started their families at later ages, in their mid-20s on average. Over the same period a higher proportion of the population had children, though marriage rates remained broadly stable, with some fluctuations, at least until the 1980s, when there was a trend towards cohabitation without marriage. As a result, in the 1990s approximately one-third of children were born to parents who were not formally married, though they were highly likely to live together. This increase in the previously low numbers of so-called 'illegitimate' births in turn brought about a change in the social status of children whose parents were not married.

But more striking than the relatively small decline in marriage rates was the rise in DIVORCE rates, especially due to the legal changes following World War II, from around 7000 each year before the war to about 150,000 annually at the end of the century. A high proportion of divorced people remarried.

FURTHER READING M. Anderson, 'The Social Implications of Demographic Change' in F.M.L.

Thompson (ed.), *The Cambridge Social History of Britain, 1950–1950. Vol. 2* (1990), 1–70; D. Coleman and J. Salt, *The British Population* (1992); A.H. Halsey with J. Webb, *Twentieth-Century British Social Trends* (2000).

Portal, Charles (Frederick Algernon) (1893–1971), chief of air staff during WORLD WAR II. Portal came from a Berkshire gentry family, of Huguenot extraction. Educated at Winchester and Christ Church, Oxford, he was called to the Bar, then joined the army at the outbreak of WORLD WAR I. In 1915 he transferred to the Royal Flying Corps and flew more than 900 sorties before 1918, with distinction. He joined the ROYAL AIR FORCE in 1919 and was chief flying instructor at the RAF cadet college, Cranwell, 1919–22. He returned to active service and commanded British forces in Aden in 1934–5, then was air vice marshal and director of organization at the Air Ministry, 1937–9, responsible for dealing with the problems of expansion of the RAF, making extensive improvements to air-training schemes. He was appointed to Bomber Command in 1940 and supervised air attacks on the enemy in Norway and France. Later in 1940 Portal was appointed chief of air staff and was promoted to acting chief air marshal. He was highly regarded by CHURCHILL, who commented that he 'had everything'. He cooperated skilfully with the other service chiefs and with the American allies: Eisenhower thought him the finest of the war leaders, 'greater than Churchill'. Portal strongly advocated strategic bombing of German targets, working, with difficulty, with 'Bomber' HARRIS.

Portal was made a baron in 1945, and became Viscount Portal of Hungerford in 1946. He retired from the RAF in 1945, becoming controller of production in the Atomic Energy Directorate of the Ministry of Supply, 1946–50, then controller of the Atomic Energy Establishment at Harwell, 1950–1. He was chairman of the British Aircraft Corporation, 1960–8, and director of a number of companies.

FURTHER READING D. Richards, *Portal of Hungerford* (1977).

Portillo, Michael (Denzil Xavier) (1953–), Conservative politician. Portillo was educated at Harrow County Boys' School and Peterhouse, Cambridge. After serving as a special adviser to the secretaries of state for energy and trade and industry and the chancellor of the exchequer, he was elected MP for Enfield Southgate in 1984. He joined Margaret THATCHER's government in 1986, and later became a member of John MAJOR's CABINET, serving in the latter as chief secretary to the Treasury, secretary of state for employment and secretary of state for defence. His defeat in the 1997 election, standing in what was normally considered a safe Conservative seat, was seen as the primary symbol of the rout suffered by his party. After a period as a writer and broadcaster, he returned to Westminster as MP for Kensington and Chelsea following the death of the maverick Alan Clark in 1999, and was appointed shadow chancellor by William HAGUE soon afterwards. His political future became uncertain, however, when he was unexpectedly eliminated in the parliamentary phase of the voting for a successor to Hague following the massive Conservative defeat in the June 2001 GENERAL ELECTION.

poverty. The first systematic, large-scale attempts to define and quantify poverty in Britain were Charles Booth's surveys between 1886 and 1902 of, firstly, poverty in east London, then in London as a whole. Booth (1840–1916) was a philanthropic businessman with a passion for statistics. He did not conduct a house-to-house survey, nor did he obtain comprehensive information on household income or construct a clearly defined 'poverty line'. He collected information obtained in the course of their work by school-board visitors, whose job was to investigate why children failed to attend school and who consequently were in frequent touch with poor families. This was not an unreasonable procedure at a time when poverty was starkly evident in the clothing people wore, their household goods, or lack of them, and their undernourished bodies. Booth cross-checked this information with other local people, such as clergymen, and with the observations of his own investigators, who were sent to live for a while in poor communities. One of these investigators was Beatrice WEBB, then Miss Potter, his cousin by marriage. Booth claimed only that he collected 'a statistical record of impressions of degree of poverty'.

Booth's conclusions were published in 1902 in the 17 volumes of his *Life and Labour of the People of London*. He found that 30% of the inhabitants of London were living 'in poverty or want'. He defined poverty as 'having no surplus', i.e. having the bare essentials for survival most of the time, but with nothing to spare for the type of crisis that frequently afflicted poor people, such as sickness or unemployment. He concluded that 8.4% lived in the worst condition of being 'at all times more or less in want', 'ill-nourished and poorly clad'. In east London, where poverty was most heavily concentrated, the figures were 35% 'in poverty or in want' and 13.3% 'at all times more or less in want'.

Booth believed that these figures represented an improvement upon previous times. It might also be thought that such high levels of poverty were peculiar to London, which contemporaries believed was a magnet for the poor. B. Seebohm ROWNTREE, another philanthropic businessman with a taste for social investigation, set out to establish the level of poverty in his home town of York, which was supposedly a more typical urban centre than London. The investigations were carried out in 1899–1900, a time, Rowntree believed, of 'average prosperity'. Unlike Booth, he set investigators to survey the income and expenditure of every working-class household in York (11,560 in all) and to record also their impressions of living conditions. The results were published in 1901 as *Poverty: A Study of Town Life*. Rowntree perceived poverty not simply as lack of means for subsistence, but as a lack of sufficient means to live a 'decent,

independent life', in other words he defined poverty as a relative and not just an absolute concept. However, he felt the need to define a level of absolute poverty, i.e. the minimum income on which survival in a state of 'physical efficiency' was possible. He found that 3.6% of the whole population of York lived with incomes below this level. These he described as living in 'primary poverty'. He recognized that this was a stringent definition, allowing only for the essential minimum of food, clothing, shelter and fuel; as he put it: 'no expenditure of any kind is allowed for beyond that which is absolutely necessary for the maintenance of purely physical efficiency.' He also recognized that such efficient economy could rarely be achieved and, even if it was, hardly allowed for a 'decent existence' and that many, even with earnings above the minimum, might be 'obviously in a state of poverty'. Such people Rowntree defined as living in 'secondary poverty' and estimated that they made up almost 18% of the population of York. Hence he found levels of poverty in York scarcely lower than in London.

The main causes of poverty in York were similar to those found by Booth in London: above all low pay, and to a lesser extent OLD AGE and single motherhood, the latter due mostly to widowhood. Rowntree also pointed out that the risk of poverty was greatest at certain points in the life cycle: for children and parents in large, young families, and in old age. He later undertook, with May Kendall, a more impressionistic study of poverty in the English countryside, which was published as *How the Labourer Lives* in 1913, and also described serious poverty. There were a number of other localized surveys of poverty carried out by various investigators before 1914, with similar results.

Techniques of measuring poverty were further developed by A.L. Bowley (1869–1957), an academic statistician. He introduced the sample survey, and sought to gather measurable facts rather than impressions. In 1912–14 he surveyed five representative English towns, applying Rowntree's stringent definition of primary poverty. The findings were published (co-authored by A. Bur-nett-Hurst) as *Livelihood and Poverty* in 1915. This claimed that 12.6% of people in the towns surveyed were in primary poverty, due above all to low pay, often exacerbated by large family size. Such findings fuelled the growing campaign for FAMILY ALLOWANCES. A further study carried out by Bowley during WORLD WAR I (published in 1920 as *Prices and Wages in the UK, 1914–20*) concluded that poverty levels had fallen owing to more regular work and higher wage-rates, especially for less skilled workers. Because of rising prices, however, the poorest – who did not benefit from these changes – were relatively poorer. In 1924, after the onset of mass UNEMPLOYMENT, Bowley repeated his pre-war five-towns survey adopting the same stringent poverty line. Published as *Has Poverty Diminished?* (1925), it found 6.5% to be in severe poverty, a high proportion of them children.

A succession of surveys in the 1920s and 1930s focused upon the areas of heaviest unemployment, reinforcing the view of continuing poverty. In 1929–30 the recently retired chief government economic adviser Sir Hubert Llewellyn Smith (1864–1945) directed a partial repeat of Booth's survey, *The New Survey of London Life and Labour*, published in 1934. This found that around 14% of the population of east London (9.6% of the county of London population) were 'subject to conditions of privation which, if long continued, would deny them all but the barest necessities and cut them off from access to many of the incidental and cultural benefits of modern progress'.

In 1936 Rowntree repeated his survey of York, using a slightly more generous definition of poverty, which allowed for a higher level of food expenditure and a small margin above bare necessity for such items as newspapers. He found that 20% of the population lived below this standard, while 3.9% lived below the old stringent standard (*Poverty and Progress*, 1941). Rowntree's new definition was the basis on which benefit rates were fixed when the social-security system was revised after WORLD WAR II (*see* WELFARE STATE). Wartime

surveys again showed a general diminution in poverty, except among those excluded from gains in the labour market, older people in particular.

After World War II it was widely believed that poverty had been more or less eradicated owing to full employment and the welfare state. This view was reinforced by Rowntree's final survey of York, in 1950, with G.R. Lavers (*Poverty and the Welfare State*, 1951). This time it was a sample survey using the 1936 poverty line, uprated in line with current prices, but it was a slighter piece of work. It showed only 0.41% living in primary poverty, 4.23 % in secondary poverty. Old age was now the major cause of poverty, followed by sickness; low wages, unemployment and large family size had shrunk to insignificance.

However, between 1953/4 and 1960, a team based at the London School of Economics conducted another poverty survey, analysing national (rather than local) survey data and using as a poverty line the means-test limit applied by the National Assistance Board (*see* POOR LAW) for payments to those judged to have inadequate incomes. This study (Brian Abel-Smith and Peter Townsend, *The Poor and the Poorest*, 1965) revealed that about 3.8% of the population were living below the National Assistance minimum. An important cause of poverty was low incomes and large family size. This revelation that the young as well as the old were still at severe risk of poverty gave rise to the Child Poverty Action Group and a new campaign. These findings were reinforced by a larger national survey carried out by Townsend in 1968–9, but not published until 1979 (*Poverty in the United Kingdom*). Absolute starvation-level poverty of the type discernible at the beginning of the century was now very rare, though not absent. Poverty was now defined in relative terms, to include those able to survive, but seriously excluded from activities other than those essential for basic survival.

Surveys of poverty were out of fashion in the 1980s, but in 1995 the independent Joseph Rowntree Foundation published an *Inquiry into Income and Wealth.* This showed that the living standards of the poorest had improved since the 1960s, but that their numbers and, more strikingly, the gap between their incomes and those of the rest of British society had grown. Still the poorest were older people, the low paid and those in large families, though unemployment had again become a significant factor.

The numbers suffering from absolute destitution had greatly decreased over the century though they had not disappeared, but the gap between rich and poor and the relative deprivation of large numbers of poorer people, despite the great increase in national wealth, remained serious problems at the end of the century.

Powell, (John) Enoch (1912–98), Conservative and Ulster Unionist politician. Powell was born in Birmingham and studied classics at Trinity College, Cambridge. His first career was as an academic; he was professor of Greek at the University of Sydney in Australia from 1937 to 1939. He returned to serve in the British army in World War II, rising from private to brigadier. He was elected Conservative MP for Wolverhampton South-West in 1950, and held the seat until 1974. In 1957–8 he served as financial secretary to the Treasury, and from 1960 to 1963 he was minister of health. He resigned the post because he refused to serve under the new prime minister, Alec DOUGLAS-HOME. He attempted to win the leadership of the CONSERVATIVE PARTY in 1965, but was defeated by Edward HEATH.

Powell was associated with right-wing economic policy, foreshadowing that of Margaret THATCHER, and was vehemently opposed to British membership of the EUROPEAN ECONOMIC COMMUNITY (EEC). This brought him into conflict with his colleagues, and he resigned from the Conservative Party in 1974, advising his supporters to vote for anti-EEC Labour candidates. He re-emerged as an ULSTER UNIONIST and was re-elected that year as MP for South Down. He held the seat until his resignation from politics in 1987.

Powell became notorious for his vociferous opposition to non-white IMMIGRATION into Britain. In 1968 Heath sacked him from the shadow cabinet after a particularly inflammatory speech on the subject, in which he prophesied: 'I seem to see the "River Tiber foaming with much blood".' Claiming that unchecked immigration would lead to social disintegration and perhaps even to civil war, Powell also urged that non-white immigrants already in Britain be repatriated. Despite his punishment by the Conservatives, the party went on to embody Powell's views in law when the Heath government passed the Immigration Act, 1971.
FURTHER READING S. Heffer, *Like the Roman: The Life of Enoch Powell* (1998); R. Shepherd, *Enoch Powell* (1997).

press. *See* NEWSPAPERS.

prices and purchasing power. Changes in prices and the effects of inflation are best conveyed by means of a table of indices, which provide a stable basis for comparison over the century.

Table of indices

Year	Retail price index (1963 = 100)	Purchasing power of £ (1900 = £1)
1900	19	20s
1910	20	18s 1d
1917	37	9s 1d
1920	52	7s
1930	33	11s
1939	34	10s 10d
1945	49	6s 10d
1950	61	5s 5d
1960	91	3s 11d
1970	135	2s 8d
1980	488	3.5p
1990	921	2p
1997	1149	1.5p

Source: D. and G. Butler, *20th Century British Political Facts* (2000), 410–12.

Prices are the payments made by consumers for goods and services. They are determined by the cost of producing the goods and services (wages, rent, interest, profit), and by market conditions of supply and demand. If demand rises or falls, without a commensurate adjustment in supply, prices will also tend to rise or fall, if other factors are unchanged. Prices of goods imported from abroad will also be influenced by changing currency values. A general rise in prices across all commodities is known as inflation; a fall in prices in known as deflation.

The table on p.323 shows, for example, the sharp rise in prices during WORLD WAR I due to high demand for a limited supply of goods. Prices then slumped during the Depression of the interwar years because of UNEMPLOYMENT and falling worldwide demand. Prices rose again during WORLD WAR II, though less sharply than in the previous war, owing to government price controls. They continued to rise steadily after the war, though slowly under the Labour governments of 1945–51 because of continuing price controls. They jumped sharply in the 1970s following the OIL SHOCK and the consequent rise in fuel prices. The period of most rapid inflation – at 10% and more – was in the early 1980s. The rate of inflation eased towards the end of the century.

prime minister, the leader of the governing political party, normally the largest party in the House of COMMONS. The exceptions were: David LLOYD GEORGE, who was prime minister of a coalition government, 1916–22; Ramsay MACDONALD, who similarly headed a coalition NATIONAL GOVERNMENT, 1931–5; and Winston CHURCHILL from May 1940 when he was appointed prime minister a few months before becoming leader of the Conservative Party.

In the 18th and 19th centuries the prime minister became accepted as the channel for the communication of advice from the CABINET and the houses of Parliament to the monarch, who was the formal head of government. It was not until 1937 that the Ministers of the Crown Act recognized the title of prime minister in law. Previously the official title of the leader of the governing party was first lord of the Treasury, a title that prime ministers continued to hold.

The powers of the prime minister are not clearly defined but they are extensive. He or she appoints all other ministers (and can transfer or dismiss them), chairs cabinet meetings, determines their regularity and appoints ministers to the numerous cabinet committees. The prime minister has no CIVIL SERVICE department of his/her own and consequently for most of the century had a weaker policy apparatus than comparable political leaders in most other countries. However, he or she controls the CABINET OFFICE, which came into being in 1938 to service the cabinet and its many committees, and can appoint personal policy advisers. Some prime ministers (notably Lloyd George and Tony BLAIR) have surrounded themselves with larger numbers of personal advisers than others. Honours such as knighthoods and peerages are awarded on the recommendation of the prime minister. As leader of the government he/she exercises a general authority over policy, which some prime ministers have exercised more effectively than others.

In theory, the prime minister is first among equals, able to wield power only with the acquiescence of members of the cabinet, who officially have 'collective responsibility' for all government decision-making. The reality throughout the 20th century was highly variable, depending upon circumstance and the personality of each prime minister. There was not a clear trajectory over time towards more personalized rule by the prime minister. The increasing workload of governments over the 20th century and the urgency of some decision-making may have created a tendency in this direction. But we should not underestimate how autocratic were some 19th-century prime ministers, or the extent to which most in the 20th century at some time acted without the assent of their cabinet colleagues, some more than others.

In 1903 A.J. BALFOUR, not conventionally regarded as a 'strong' prime minister, abruptly sacked all the FREE TRADE ministers in his government. Most of the Liberal cabinet in 1914 were unaware of the extent of planning for a possible war with Germany. David LLOYD GEORGE was notoriously independent of his cabinet, and Neville CHAMBERLAIN consulted his cabinet on major issues only fitfully. The important decision in 1947 to develop NUCLEAR WEAPONS in Britain was taken by the Labour prime minister Clement ATTLEE with the knowledge of only a small number of cabinet members.

Arguably Britain's diminished world role made the prime ministers at the end of the century weaker in terms of the significance of decisions to be made than their predecessors. Both Margaret THATCHER and Tony Blair were believed to rely too much upon personal advisers and too little upon their cabinets. In February 1997, 8 special advisors worked in the prime minister's office at 10 Downing Street; in July 1999 there were 22. Thatcher's sudden fall from power in 1990 demonstrated the danger for a prime minister of losing touch with cabinet colleagues.

FURTHER READING P. Hennessy, *The Prime Minister: The Office and its Holders since 1945* (2000); P. Weller, *First Among Equals* (1985).

privatization. *See* NATIONALIZATION.

Profumo affair, political scandal involving the Conservative secretary of state for war John Profumo (1915–), whose affair with Christine Keeler in 1961 came to light in the national press early in 1963. At the time of her relationship with Profumo, Keeler was also involved with Commander Yevgeny Ivanov, the assistant Soviet naval attaché in London. Profumo, after initially denying to Parliament the existence of a relationship, resigned as secretary of state in June 1963. Keeler had met Profumo through her association with the osteopath Stephen Ward, who was tried and found guilty of living off immoral earnings in July

1963 and committed suicide as the trial ended. The scandal weakened Harold MACMILLAN'S government and the prime minister personally, particularly after the issue was debated in Parliament and Lord Denning's report into the affair was published in September 1963. Exploited by increasingly confident political satirists, the Profumo affair represented the first of a series of high-profile political scandals that would characterize the popular image of politics during the final decades of the 20th century.

FURTHER READING P. Knightley, *An Affair of State: The Profumo case and the framing of Stephen Ward* (1987).

propaganda. The systematic, centrally directed use of propaganda by the British government began during WORLD WAR I. Members of the government soon became aware of the importance, and the possibility, of maintaining morale in Britain and of undermining that of the enemy by this means. Initially, uncoordinated agencies were established to deal with CENSORSHIP, news management, recruitment, the subversion of enemy morale, and appeals to Allies, neutrals and the EMPIRE. In 1916 these activities were coordinated under the Ministry of Information. Varied channels of communication were used: mass rallies and posters encouraged recruitment, and there were also postcards, stamps and pamphlets, while strategically displayed news items were placed in home and foreign newspapers (the latter often with the assistance of Reuters news agency). Newsreels and feature films were increasingly used as the war went on. Newspapers, pamphlets and leaflets were circulated in enemy countries.

Planning for a propaganda campaign in WORLD WAR II began in the 1930s. A secret propaganda planning committee was established in 1936 to prepare for a new Ministry of Information (MOI) should war come. In 1937 the Foreign Office organized broadcasts in retaliation against Italian anti-British broadcasts aimed at the Middle East. In September 1939 the MOI was established.

Propaganda channels were similar to those used during World War I, but more extensive. The aims were similar. Film and broadcasting were more extensive and air power was used to drop leaflets in enemy territory. The press was severely censored and the public were exhorted by posters that 'careless talk costs lives' and informed about RATIONING and air-raid protection.

FURTHER READING I. McLaine, *Ministry of Morale: Home Front Morale and the Ministry of Information in World War II* (1979); P.M. Taylor, *British Propaganda in the 20th Century* (2000).

proportional representation (PR), electoral system by which parties are represented in a legislature according to the overall percentage of votes gained. From the early 19th century there were those in Britain who argued for an electoral system that produced elected assemblies, at any level, that reflected the wide range of views among the electorate, those of minorities as well as majorities. This debate continued through the century and into the early years of the 20th century, generating a variety of proposals for alternative electoral systems to the established one of 'first past the post', whereby the party that gained a majority of constituency seats gained total control.

A Speaker's Conference was established during World War I to examine the entire system of parliamentary representation, including votes for women. It recommended in favour of proportional representation, but the House of COMMONS, after prolonged discussion, voted against this. After debate, the single transferable vote (one of the several PR systems under discussion) was accepted for university seats only: university graduates, in addition to voting in the constituency in which they were resident, might vote for candidates for one of the university seats. MPs were returned thereafter representing graduates of Oxford, Cambridge and London universities (three separate seats); the combined English universities, the Welsh universities, the Scottish universities and Belfast (each with one seat); until 1920, there were also three

Dublin representatives. PR was regarded as the only way of preventing the university seats becoming safe seats for the Conservatives.

In the 1920s many who had previously opposed PR came to consider it the solution to the difficulty of obtaining legitimacy for governments without clear majorities following the split in the LIBERAL PARTY and the emergence of the LABOUR PARTY, but they had difficulty in agreeing on a scheme. The Proportional Representation Society, founded in the 19th century, lobbied vigorously. In 1919, 1920 and 1921 bills giving local authorities the option of being elected by PR passed the house of LORDS. The government expressed sympathy but did not give the bills parliamentary time in the Commons, although PR was incorporated in the Government of IRELAND Act, 1920. In the 1920s a succession of bills for the introduction of various forms of PR in national and local elections were put before Parliament; they were unsuccessful, but gained significant numbers of votes. After Labour became, for the second time, a minority government in 1929, it established another inquiry into the voting system. The inquiry members failed to agree, as did the cabinet, and the discussion continued through the lifetime of the government. Between 1931 and World War II the NATIONAL GOVERNMENT had clear majorities and the issue was little discussed. In 1948 the Labour government, favouring 'one person, one vote', abolished the university seats, and with them the only trace of PR in the British voting system; 116,647 votes had been cast for university members in 1945.

At this time only the Liberal Party advocated PR, as it was to continue to do for the remainder of the century; its influence was small. PR became a significant issue again in the 1980s when the formation of the SOCIAL DEMOCRATIC PARTY again led to the election of Conservative governments on a minority of votes cast. The subsequent alliance between the Social Democrats and Liberals made them a more important political force. The Labour government elected in 1997 showed some sympathy for PR, and introduced one of its variants for the elections for the devolved assemblies in WALES and SCOTLAND in 1999. In Scotland 56 (of 129) members, and in Wales 20 (of 60) members, were elected by the 'additional member' system. Under this system additional elected members were chosen from party lists in proportion to votes cast for each party by the electorate as a whole. The outcome in Scotland was a sharing of power between Labour and the Liberal Democrats. In NORTHERN IRELAND, under the Good Friday agreement, the new Northern Ireland Assembly was elected in 1998 under the 'single transferable vote' system of PR, which is also in use in the Republic of Ireland. In multi-member constituencies, preference votes are allocated according to a pre-set quota. This system is designed to ensure representation of minority parties. The mayor of London (*see* LONDON GOVERNMENT) was elected in 2000 by the method of the single transferable vote.

FURTHER READING D. Butler, *The Electoral System in Britain since 1918* (1963); J. Hart, *Proportional Representation: Critics of the British Electoral System, 1820–1945* (1992).

prostitution. *See* SEXUALITY, OFFICIAL REGULATION OF.

protectionism. *See* FREE TRADE; IMPERIAL PREFERENCE; TARIFF REFORM.

public assistance. *See* POOR LAW.

punk. *See* YOUTH CULTURE.

R

race relations. *See* IMMIGRATION.

Race Relations Acts. *See* IMMIGRATION.

Race Relations Board. *See* IMMIGRATION.

radar, acronym for *ra*dio *d*etection *a*nd *r*anging. It refers to the method of detecting and locating distant objects by by means of radio waves. Researchers in several countries were investigating its uses in the 1930s, and Britain decided to develop radar for defence purposes in 1935. A trial by Robert Watson-Watt (1892–1973) in February 1935 plotted the progress of a bomber as it flew through the beam of a short-wave radio transmitter by detecting the small amounts of radio waves reflected back from it. This prompted the decision to equip Britain with an early-warning system against aerial attack, and a highly secret development programme was urgently set up.

By 1939 a chain of radar stations was established on the eastern coast of Britain; by 1941 they covered most of the coastline. They were highly conspicuous, the antennas being supported by 90-metre (300-foot) towers. Radar played an essential role in the success of the ROYAL AIR FORCE in the battle of BRITAIN. As the battle of the ATLANTIC got under way, smaller, more mobile radar systems were established and fitted to aircraft and ships. More accurate and sensitive systems were developed, playing an important role in limiting losses of merchant ships by 1942 and finally driving German SUBMARINES from the North Atlantic. Improved radar also enabled bombers and night fighters to increase accuracy and improved the direction of anti-aircraft guns. After the war radar was adapted for use by air-traffic controls and shipping worldwide.

SEE ALSO SCIENCE.

radio. *See* BRITISH BROADCASTING CORPORATION.

RAF. *See* ROYAL AIR FORCE.

railways. At the beginning of the century railways provided Britain's primary means of transport for passengers and freight. The railway network that had developed during the 19th century covered the entire country and was run by about 150 private companies, many of them with regional or local monopolies, though companies competed on main lines. The main companies included the Great Western, running west from Paddington station, London, to the west coast of England and south Wales; the London and North Western, running north from Euston station through Lancashire to Scotland; and the Great Northern, running north from London's King's Cross to Yorkshire and connecting with Edinburgh and the east coast of Scotland. Main-line passenger services were frequent. Travel was stratified into first, second and third classes, with seats affordable by all but the poorest, including cheap daily return tickets for working people.

During WORLD WAR I the government took temporary control of the railways. The Railways Act, 1921, enforced consolidation of companies, mainly on a regional basis. For example, most railways south of London were grouped into the new Southern Railway; and the London, Midland and Scottish was created from the former London and North Western, Midland, Lancashire and Yorkshire, Caledonian and other smaller companies. The Great Western took over lines in south Wales. The reason was the growing competition from motor transport (*see* MOTOR INDUSTRY), which was enforcing the closure of some rural lines. Railways became less profitable and companies in most instances did not respond by innovating. The exceptions were the Southern Railway, which undertook extensive electrification of its London commuter lines, thus speeding up journeys; and the London and North Eastern invested in express locomotives for a nonstop London–Edinburgh service.

In WORLD WAR II railways were again temporarily nationalized, and freight and passenger traffic increased by 50% and 68% respectively. Permanent NATIONALIZATION came in the Transport Act, 1947, which, theoretically, created a unified national transport system, including air, canal and road services. In 1962 the theory was abandoned and British Railways was created to manage the railways, divided into six semi-autonomous regions: southern, western, eastern, London Midland, northeastern and Scottish. Modernization was slow and the railways were unprofitable in the face of ever-expanding competition from road transport. They relied upon government subsidy. In 1963 the British Railways chairman Richard Beeching (1913–85) produced a report (the Beeching

Report) that resulted in closures of 8000 km (5000 miles) of line and about one-third of all stations, mainly in rural areas that were expected to be served by buses. The savings that resulted allowed for investment in electrification and the abandonment of steam power.

By the beginning of the 1990s the railway network consisted of 16,507 km (10,307 miles) of track, with a staff of about 130,000. Passenger service dominated, freight having been largely lost to the roads. But less than 7% of passenger miles took place by rail, much the same as long-distance bus mileage, whereas 84% of passenger mileage was by private car. Margaret THATCHER's Conservative governments took this as proof of the irrelevance of railways in the modern world (Thatcher herself famously refused to travel by train unless it was quite unavoidable) and were unwilling to invest, for example, in a high-speed link to the CHANNEL TUNNEL, which was under construction and opened in 1994.

John MAJOR's governments privatized the railway system, leasing the entire track and stations to a single firm, Railtrack, and franchising rail operations to a number of companies, often with local monopolies. The service and safety record of many of these companies was criticized to the end of the century and beyond, especially following some serious crashes. They were more strictly regulated by the LABOUR government elected in 1997, although it showed no inclination to renationalize. Where rail travel was efficient it continued to be popular, as with the Eurostar route to Paris and Brussels, opened in 1994, which for the first time enabled passengers to travel entirely by rail to and from mainland Europe.

FURTHER READING M. Freeman and D.H. Aldcroft, *The Atlas of British Railway History* (1985).

rates, a centuries-old term for taxes levied on property by and for LOCAL GOVERNMENT. Rates were abolished by the enactment of the COMMUNITY CHARGE from 1988.

Rathbone, Eleanor (Florence) (1872–1946), social reformer, independent politician and feminist. Rathbone was born in Liverpool in 1872, into a family with a long history of reforming and philanthropic endeavour. She attended Kensington High School in London and Somerville College, Oxford. Returning to Liverpool after finishing her studies, she soon followed her family's tradition and began philanthropic work.

An examination into the situation of working-class women and children living under the provision of the POOR LAW was the genesis of her eventual campaign for FAMILY ALLOWANCES. Her experience of administering a WORLD WAR I scheme that paid allowances to women whose husbands were fighting the war convinced her of the value of paying family allowances directly to mothers. She published two books on the subject: *The Disinherited Family* (1924) and *The Case for Family Allowances* (1940). When family allowances were finally brought into being and began to be paid in 1945, she considered this her greatest achievement.

However, Rathbone had many other interests and concerns. An ardent supporter of the campaign for female suffrage, she took over the presidency of the National Union of Women's Suffrage Societies (NUWSS) in 1919 after the retirement of Millicent Garrett FAWCETT. During her presidency, which lasted until 1929, the society's name was changed to the National Union of Societies for Equal Citizenship (NUSEC). Rathbone was also very concerned about the position of women in other countries, especially INDIA. In 1929, expressing the belief that her reform activities could be given greater impetus if she held public office, she stood for election and became an independent MP for the combined English universities. She remained unaffiliated to any party throughout her political career, and believed non-partisanship to be especially important in her own particular constituency. Throughout the 1930s she strenuously opposed the foreign policy pursued by the NATIONAL GOVERNMENT, in particular Neville CHAMBERLAIN's policy of APPEASEMENT. In the last years of her life she became sympathetic to the plight of REFUGEES, as well as very interested in the problems of PALESTINE. She was also very supportive of the BEVERIDGE Report, and urged that its provisions be applied particularly to women and children. She died suddenly in 1946, having continued to work tirelessly for the issues that concerned her until the end.

FURTHER READING Johanna Alberti, *Eleanor Rathbone* (1996).

rationing, system of controlling the distribution of food and other essential items, introduced in Britain during both world wars. By 1914 Britain had become a net importer of food and so was vulnerable to German blockades during WORLD WAR I, despite a great increase in home food production during the war. The full-scale rationing of foodstuffs did not come into effect until late in the war, in 1918, though sugar had been rationed from 1916. However, rationing was not strictly regulated and was mainly left to the discretion of retailers, with the result that the well-to-do generally ignored the regulations, creating shortages and a market for profiteering.

With the outbreak of WORLD WAR II the government, having learned its lesson, almost immediately implemented a much stricter rationing scheme in order to ensure fair distribution of limited supplies. From January 1940, bacon, butter and sugar were rationed weekly, followed later by sweets, tea, eggs, cheese and red meat. Rations of other foodstuffs were somewhat more flexible. With the seas around Britain a battleground (*see* ATLANTIC, BATTLE OF THE), the supply of fish was interrupted. In June 1941 clothing and shoes began to be rationed, as imports of cloth, leather and rubber were restricted. Adults were given an annual ration of 66 clothing coupons per year. The UTILITY SCHEME was soon introduced for clothing and footwear design, as well as furniture. Petrol was also rationed throughout the war, being deemed necessary for 'essential journeys' only.

Rationing was felt to be one of the greatest privations on the home front, although in nutritional terms it improved the diet of many. The government quickly began producing instructional material showing housewives how they could best 'make do and mend' for the war effort. Cookery classes were organized showing women how to substitute popular ingredients with alternatives such as artificial flavourings, powdered eggs and offal (which was not rationed). The ubiquitous ration book of coupons had to be carried by housewives everywhere when they did their shopping

Although rationing was accepted by the populace during wartime as unpleasant but necessary, and the scheme operated remarkably well in its aim of ensuring fair distribution of adequate supplies for everyone, it was much resented after the war ended. ATTLEE'S Labour government continued the scheme for some years as part of its austerity measures, but because of to improving conditions and public protest it was gradually phased out after 1950. Sweets were the last item to be rationed, and this ended in 1953. Petrol was briefly rationed again during the SUEZ CRISIS of 1956.

FURTHER READING F. Reynoldson, *Rationing* (1993); I. Zweiniger-Bargielowska, *Austerity in Britain: Rationing, Controls and Consumption 1939–1955* (2000).

Reading, Lord. *See* ISAACS, RUFUS DANIEL.

Redmond, John (Edward) (1876–1918), Irish nationalist leader. Redmond was born in County Wexford and educated at Clongowes and Trinity College, Dublin. He became a clerk in the House of COMMONS in 1880, then an MP for the IRISH NATIONAL PARTY (the Irish Parliamentary Party) for New Ross, Wexford, from 1881. He was a strong supporter of Charles Stewart Parnell and led the Parnellite wing of the party when it split into contending factions after Parnell's death in 1891. Redmond successfully sought to reconcile these factions and led a united Irish Party from 1900.

Redmond supported Wyndham's IRISH LAND ACT of 1903, but he and his party lost support in Ireland because of their support for the Liberal government's devolution scheme, and because of the party's appearance of general dependence upon the Liberal alliance. Redmond recovered somewhat, but seemed weak and vacillating during the growing crisis in IRELAND, underrating the depth of resistance in Ulster to Irish HOME RULE.

On the outbreak of WORLD WAR I Redmond did his best to promote recruitment in Ireland, which did not help his party, though he opposed CONSCRIPTION in Ireland. He was surprised and horrified by the EASTER RISING in 1916 and did not strongly oppose the British government's vengeful response. Thereafter he lost the leadership of Irish nationalism to SINN FÉIN. He died before the GENERAL ELECTION of 1918, at which his party was trounced in the Irish polls by Sinn Féin.

FURTHER READING P. Ben, *John Redmond* (1996).

refugees. In the 19th century immigrants fleeing from persecution were allowed relatively freely into Britain, although growing prejudice, especially against Jewish immigrants, led to restrictive legislation in 1905, 1914 and 1919 (*see* IMMIGRATION), allowing the government tight control over the entry, movement and deportation of aliens. In the interwar years there was a small flow of refugees from Bolshevik Russia and then from Mussolini's Italy. The numbers increased as Hitler imposed his control on parts of Europe. Jewish refugees to Britain were not encouraged and they encountered anti-Semitism, but between 1933 and 1939 about 56,000 refugees from the German Reich – the vast majority of them Jewish – entered Britain. The government required that they should not be a charge on public funds, and the Jewish community and other donors had to provide guarantees of this. Some Jewish refugees found it hard to find employment in Britain despite being highly qualified. The 1930s also saw other groups of refugees flee to Britain from the SPANISH CIVIL WAR.

After WORLD WAR II came successive, though generally small, waves of refugees from a series of crisis-torn parts of the world: Poles fleeing from communism, Hungarians following the failed uprising in 1956, Czechs in similar circumstances in 1968, Asians from Kenya and Uganda, Chileans after the coup against Allende in 1973, Vietnamese after the war from mid-1970s. In the 1990s crises multiplied, most acutely in the Balkans and parts of Africa; and Gypsies (Roma) began to flee to western Europe from discrimination and persecution in parts of post-communist central and eastern Europe. Britain did not receive disproportionate numbers of refugees relative to other western European countries, but by the end of the century there was mounting hostility to refugees in some of the popular press and in some sections of the population. The CONSERVATIVE and the LABOUR governments responded to this by tightening controls, in the face of criticism from other strands of British opinion.

FURTHER READING C. Holmes, *John Bull's Island: Immigration and British Society, 1871–1971* (1988); J. Torpey, *The Invention of the Passport. Surveillance, Citizenship and the State* (2001).

Reith, John (Charles Walsham) (1889–1971), first general manager, then director general of the BRITISH BROADCASTING CORPORATION (BBC). Born in Scotland, Reith was the seventh and youngest child of Ada and George Reith, a minister in the Free CHURCH OF SCOTLAND. Educated at Glasgow Academy and Gresham's School, Norfolk, Reith left school at the age of 17, and was apprenticed as an engineer to the North British Locomotive Company, while also studying at the Royal Technical College, Glasgow. He remained in engineering from 1906 to 1914, working in Glasgow and London. He then served in WORLD WAR I until he was wounded in 1915, suffering permanent facial scars, and he was excluded from further armed service; instead he was sent to the United States to help to organize the manufacture and supply of rifles for the British army. After the war he was employed by William Beardmore and Co. as general manager. In 1921 he married Muriel Odham, the daughter of a wealthy publisher.

In 1922 Reith was offered the post of general manager of the new British Broadcasting Corporation, the future of which was quite uncertain. He shaped British broadcasting from its beginning in conscious opposition to what he saw as the commercialism of American radio, developing a vision of public service for the new medium. He demanded and received monopoly powers from the government in 1923, and on the renewal of the BBC's corporate charter in 1926 and 1936 he emphasized the importance of making high culture accessible to a wide audience. BBC programmes emphasized classical music, educational features and religious programmes on Sundays.

In 1938 Reith resigned from the BBC to become head of another new enterprise, Imperial Airways, a move that he regretted. In 1940 he was elected National MP for Southampton, immediately becoming minister of transport, then minister of works and 1st Baron Reith. Planning was added to his ministry in 1942, but shortly afterwards Winston CHURCHILL dismissed him, which permanently soured their relationship. Reith joined the Royal Naval Volunteer Reserve and became director of Combined Operations Material Department, 1943–4. He was awarded the CB (Military) in 1945. After the war he chaired a number of organizations: the Commonwealth Telecommunications Board, 1946–50, the NEW TOWNS Commission, 1945–6, Hemel Hempstead Development Corporation, 1947–50, the National Film Finance Corporation, 1949–50, and the Colonial Development Corporation, 1949–50. Nevertheless, despite all these achievements, and having left an indelible impression on the BBC, he felt an enduring sense of failure.

FURTHER READING A. Boyle, *Only the Wind Will Listen: Reith of the BBC* (1972); I. McIntyre,

The Expense of Glory: A Life of John Reith (1994); J.C.W. Reith, *The Reith Diaries* (1975).

religion, non-Christian. Non-Christian religions were of growing importance in 20th-century Britain, mainly as a result of IMMIGRATION. Membership of the religious Jewish community grew from 160,000 in 1900 to 450,000 in 1950–70, then declined to 285,000 in 1998, above all because of secularization among Jewish-born people. The number of Buddhists rose from 6000 in 1970 to 28,000 in 1990, mainly owing to immigration. There were an estimated 300,000 Hindus in the United Kingdom in 1970, and 500,000 in 2000; 300,000 Muslims in 1970, and 1.4 million in 2000; 75,000 Sikhs in 1970, and 600,000 in 1990.

SEE ALSO RELIGIOUS BELIEF AND OBSERVANCE.

FURTHER READING G. Davie, *Religion in Britain since 1945* (1994).

religious belief and observance. The practice of religion has undergone considerable change in Britain during the course of the 20th century. In 1900 Britain could accurately be termed a Christian country. Although census and other figures show that church attendance for all the Christian denominations was far from high, there was general acceptance that Britain was a Protestant nation, and that its culture was shaped and informed by Protestant Christian precepts. There was a widespread belief that Britain's global dominance and the growing EMPIRE were proof of God's favour, and British missionaries went by the thousands to convert the heathen of the globe and thus bear the heavy burden of responsibility the Lord had laid upon them in granting them world power.

In very general terms, the CHURCH OF ENGLAND claimed a majority of English people as its members, although NONCONFORMIST denominations such as METHODISM were also prominent. WALES had established a solid tradition of chapel-going Nonconformity, and the Presbyterian Church of Scotland – the 'Kirk' – was the established church in SCOTLAND. IRELAND was largely Roman Catholic, but had a prominent and vociferous Presbyterian minority in the north. A century on, however, the religious complexion of Britain had changed dramatically. Membership of all the Protestant denominations, already in decline by 1900, had diminished still further. The ROMAN CATHOLIC CHURCH in Britain bucked this trend, actually gaining members in the 20th century, largely because of an influx of Irish immigrants. In the last decades of the century, however, it too experienced a decline in membership. In England by the end of the century the Church of England was no longer the national church in terms of attendance figures: in 1996 it claimed about 1.3 million members, while the Catholic Church drew approximately 1.9 million to its services. In Wales, the tradition of Nonconformity deflated, with more active participants at the end of the century in the Anglican and Catholic churches. While the Kirk in Scotland continued to influence national life, it too lost ground to the Catholics, who claimed slightly more regular attenders.

Overall, active Christian church membership in Britain declined from about 30% of the adult population in 1900 to only 12% in 1990. Figures for regular attendance at services were even lower. The only area in which Christianity continued to enjoy widespread support was in NORTHERN IRELAND, which was galvanized by the 'Troubles' and their religious (and therefore cultural) overtones.

Yet at the end of the century the Christian churches were still a visible part of British national life, and the majority of Britons, when asked to define themselves, reported that they were at least nominally Christian. While they continued in large numbers to ask for the services of their particular denominations during rites of passage (baptisms, weddings and funerals), this was done more for reasons of tradition and culture than of actual belief.

At the end of the 20th century Britain could no longer claim to be a solely Christian nation. It had become a nation of many faiths. This was mainly a result of the great increase in IMMIGRATION after World War II, although an obvious exception to this was the Jewish community, which numbered about 450,000 and which had maintained a presence in Britain for centuries. While Judaism, like the Christian churches, experienced a decline in its membership, other religions brought to Britain by immigrants grew as their members clung to them as a badge of their cultural identity. The most important of these religions included Islam, Hinduism and Sikhism. (*see* RELIGION, NON-CHRISTIAN). The black British population, which numbered about 900,000 and whose forebears emigrated mainly from the Caribbean, largely counted themselves as Christian, but relatively few belonged to the mainstream denominations and instead most attended their own black-led churches such as the Pentecostal Church.

Clearly many white Britons turned away from the mainstream Christian denominations. However, an interesting new feature in the spiritual landscape began to emerge in the 1980s with greater awareness of so-called 'New Age' beliefs. 'New Ageism' attracted the suspicion of many, but in the late 1990s its growing popularity was increasingly reflected in the media and in popular culture. The vast scope of New Age belief included areas as diverse as UFOs, dream therapy, crystals, 'earth mysteries', paganism/Wicca/nature religions/goddess worship, herbalism, feng shui, meditation, aromatherapy, shamanism, chakras, Daoism and the Kabbalah. Although New Ageism was dismissed by traditional church leaders because of its lack of unified vision, dogma or doctrine, it is often suggested that its appeal stems from the spiritual yearnings of individuals disillusioned by mainstream religion, who are attracted to its generally benign, holistic outlook and its 'pick-and-mix' nature.

FURTHER READING P. Badham (ed.) *Religion, State and Society in Modern Britain* (1989); S. Bruce, *Religion in Modern Britain* (1995).

Remembrance Day. *See* ARMISTICE; HAIG, DOUGLAS.

rent controls. *See* RENT STRIKES.

rent strikes. During WORLD WAR I there were significant increases in rents in working-class areas. These were brought about by a number of factors: increased demand for housing in munitions centres, where work was plentiful, on top of the inadequate quantity and quality of working-class HOUSING existing before the war; and the restrictions on new building and repairs during the war. This led to rent strikes by tenants in 1915, starting in a lower-middle-class area of Glasgow and spreading to the London suburbs, Coventry and elsewhere. David LLOYD GEORGE visited Glasgow to pacify the strikers, and the strikes led directly to the Rent and Mortgage Interest (Rent Restriction) Act, 1915, which placed statutory restrictions upon rent and mortgage interest rises. Rent controls in some form remained in place until effectively removed by the THATCHER governments in the 1980s.

FURTHER READING J. Melling, *Rent Strikes* (1983).

reparations, payments made by Germany in compensation for damage caused during WORLD WAR I. The question of how much Germany should pay continued to be an international issue for several years after the end of the war. Discussions began at the Paris Peace Conference in 1919 (*see* VERSAILLES, TREATY OF), and in May 1921 the Allied reparations commission announced that the amount to be paid was 132 million gold marks. Germany was hostile to and resentful of these demands, and claimed inability to pay.

The British government, led by David LLOYD GEORGE, influenced by John Maynard KEYNES's views as expressed in his *Economic Consequences of the Peace* (1919), recognized that such severe demands on Germany would have serious effects on the international economy in view of Germany's important role in manufacturing and international trade before the war. The French took a different view, and in January 1923 occupied the Ruhr in retaliation for Germany's default on reparations payments. The German economy suffered hyper-inflation and ruin. In 1924 the British and US governments constructed the Dawes Plan, which tied reparations payments to the success of the German economy, planning for a gradual resumption of payments until in 1928 the original target would be met. This was combined with substantial private US loans to Germany, designed to revive its economy. Initially the scaled-down repayment plan was met, but by 1929, when full payments were to resume, the German government protested that they could not be met. Ramsay MACDONALD's Labour government would have preferred to reduce the German war debt, but the USA and France would not agree. A new reduced-payment agreement, the Young Plan, was agreed in 1929, but the effects of the world financial crisis of 1929–31 (*see* GREAT CRASH) led to the agreement at the Lausanne Conference of April 1932 that, in order to revive European trade, reparations would be cancelled.

FURTHER READING B. Kent, *The Spoils of War: the Politics, Economics and Diplomacy of Reparations, 1918–32* (1989).

Representation of the People Act (1918), legislation that granted the vote to all men at age 21, for the first time, and to men under 21 who had served in World War I. It also granted the vote for the first time to women aged 30 or above who were independent householders, wives of householders or university graduates (*see* SUFFRAGISTS; SUFFRAGETTES). The act reduced the residence qualification for voter registration to six months. The electorate grew in size from 6,730,935 in 1900 to 21,392,322 in 1918.

SEE ALSO EQUAL FRANCHISE ACT (1928); REPRESENTATION OF THE PEOPLE ACT (1948, 1969).

Representation of the People Act (1948), legislation that abolished plural voting by abolishing the business vote (the additional vote held by owners of businesses in the constituency in which their business was located) and the university-graduate vote (*see* PROPORTIONAL REPRESENTATION). The act also abolished the six-month residence qualification for voter registration (*see* REPRESENTATION OF THE PEOPLE ACT, 1918).

Representation of the People Act (1969), legislation that lowered the voting age from 21 to 18. The electorate grew from 35,964,684 in 1966 to 39,342,013 in 1970.

Rhodesia. *See* ZIMBABWE.

Riley, Bridget (1931–), British artist and designer. She was born in London and studied there at Goldsmiths' College, 1949–52, and at the Royal College of Art, 1952–5. She became one of the most celebrated exponents of op art in the world. (Optical art is a type of abstract art in which patterns create the impression that the image is flickering.) Her interest in optical effects partly came about through her study of the neo-impressionist technique of pointillism. She took up op art in the 1960s, working initially in black and white, but turning to colour in 1966. Her work attracted widespread interest, culminating in her winning the International Painting Prize at the Venice Biennale in 1968. Thereafter she continued to be a celebrated artist in the same mode.

FURTHER READING R. Rudielka, *Bridget Riley* (1978).

Roman Catholic Church. There were about 2.5 million Roman Catholics in Great Britain at the beginning of the 20th century. A minority of Catholics were mostly upper-class descendants of pre-Reformation Catholics and later English converts, whose recognized leaders were the hereditary dukes of Norfolk. The majority of Catholics, however, were immigrants from IRELAND and their descendants, clustering particularly in Glasgow, Liverpool, Manchester, Birmingham and parts of

London. In 1915, 58% of the Catholic population of England and Wales lived in Liverpool and 26.2% in London. By 1951 there were about 4 million Catholics: 38% now lived in Liverpool, 51% in London. In 1990 there were an estimated 5.6 million Catholics in Great Britain, not all of them necessarily active communicants. Throughout the century Catholicism played a larger part in the lives and politics of the people of NORTHERN IRELAND than of the remainder of the United Kingdom.

In 1900 there was a single Roman Catholic archdiocese for England and Wales. In 1911 it was divided into three archdioceses: Birmingham, Liverpool and Westminster. A fourth English archdiocese, Southwark, was added in 1965, reflecting the population shift of Catholics towards London. In SCOTLAND, which had a substantial population of Irish origin, there were two: St Andrews-Edinburgh and Glasgow. In 1916 the archdiocese of Cardiff was created. The Archbishop of Westminster was pre-eminent. Throughout the century the church successfully retained state funding for a network of Roman Catholic schools, both primary and secondary, though their survival and character was threatened by the declining numbers of men and women entering the religious orders that even in the middle of the century provided the bulk of their teaching staff.

SEE ALSO HUME, BASIL.

FURTHER READING G.A. Beck (ed.), *The English Catholics, 1850–1950* (1950); M.P. Hornsby-Smith, *Roman Catholics in England: Studies in Social Structure since World War II* (1987).

Rowntree, Benjamin Seebohm (1871–1954), businessman and philanthropist. Rowntree was born into the Liberal chocolate-manufacturing Quaker family based in York. He was educated at the Quaker Bootham School in York and Owens College, Manchester, then joined the family firm of H.I. Rowntree & Co. in 1889, becoming a director in 1897 and chairman, 1923–41.

Rowntree's family background disposed him towards concern about the POVERTY that was endemic in Britain in the late 19th and early 20th century. He was inspired by Charles Booth's pioneering study of poverty in London in the 1890s (which found that about 30% of the population lived in poverty) to investigate poverty in his supposedly more typical home town of York. He found that poverty levels in York were as high as in London, in a study published as *Poverty: A Study of Town Life* in 1901. With May Kendall he undertook a more impressionistic study of poverty in the English countryside, published in 1913 as *How the Labourer Lives*, which also described serious privation. He made two further studies, tracing the decline of poverty in York over the first half of the 20th century. One was carried out in 1936 and published as *Poverty and Progress* in 1941. Finally *Poverty and the Welfare State*, published in 1951, was written with G.R. Lavers, with whom he also wrote *English Life and Leisure* (1951), a study of post-war life.

Rowntree was also a leader in the field of scientific management and industrial welfare. He was industrial welfare director in the welfare department of the Ministry of Munitions, 1915–18, and published *The Human Needs of Labour* (1918) and *The Human Factor in Business* (1921). He also collaborated with Lord Astor on studies of British agriculture, publishing *The Agricultural Dilemma* in 1935.

FURTHER READING A. Briggs, *Social Thought and Social Action: A Study of the Work of Seebohm Rowntree, 1871–1954* (1961).

Royal Air Force (RAF). The RAF was established in April 1918. It was preceded by the Royal Flying Corps (RFC), founded in 1912, which included military and naval wings. At the beginning of WORLD WAR I the naval wing became separate as the Royal Naval Air Service (RNAS). Air power did not play an important role in the war; it was regarded as an adjunct to military and naval operations. Perceptions of its potential changed in 1917 when German Gotha aircraft bombed London, killing almost 500 people; previously there had only been occasional ZEPPELIN raids, causing little damage. In response a cabinet committee was formed under General Jan Christian Smuts (*see* SOUTH AFRICA) to examine air defence, and it recommended the creation of a third independent service. This led to the creation of the RAF, absorbing the RFC and the RNAS, and of an air ministry.

Nevertheless, after the war there was strong pressure, especially from the ARMY and ROYAL NAVY, to disband the new service and return air operations to the control of the older services. The chief of air staff Sir Hugh Trenchard (1873–1976) fought hard and effectively for the survival of the RAF. He realized that he could not increase its size in peacetime, but he could increase levels of training and effectiveness. He ensured the establishment of boy entrants and apprenticeship schemes, the RAF College at Cranwell for officer cadets, and the RAF Staff College. Trenchard also established university and public-school air squadrons, reserves, auxiliary squadrons and short-service commissions, both to increase popular awareness of the service and to create a reserve of skilled men to be drawn upon in an emergency.

The problem was finding a role for the RAF in peacetime. One was found by Winston CHURCHILL as air minister in 1919. He realized that the RAF could police remote areas of the EMPIRE more effectively and cheaply than could the army. This 'air control' role was established from 1921 and proved a useful means of quelling endemic rebellion in such places as ADEN, Somaliland and remote parts of INDIA. The RNAS was revived in 1924 as the Fleet Air Arm, which was under joint control of the RAF and Royal Navy until 1937, when it came completely under naval control.

In the later 1930s recognition of the danger of a major war led to the expansion of the RAF, although this was sluggish until 1939, when Hurricane and Spitfire fighter planes were ordered. In the period 1920–35 the RAF rarely numbered above 30,000 men, but by 1939 there were over 100,000 and by 1943 over 1 million. Early in WORLD WAR II it faced the test of the battle of BRITAIN, which established the indispensability of RAF Fighter Command commanded by Sir Hugh Dowding (1882–1970), while Bomber Command and Coastal Command attacked the German invasion fleet in the French ports. For the remainder of the war the RAF, assisted by RADAR, played a major role in all the major campaigns, not least the strategic bombing offensive against Germany (*see* HARRIS, ARTHUR; DRESDEN).

After the war the RAF played a role in the occupation of Germany and then in the wars of DECOLONIZATION, including a series of crises in the MIDDLE EAST, in MALAYA and in the FALKLANDS War, 1982. The RAF was also involved in the GULF WAR (1991) and in the NATO bombing of Serbia in 1999 (*see* KOSOVO). Early in the COLD WAR the RAF handled Britain's NUCLEAR WEAPONS until the ROYAL NAVY took over this role with Polaris submarines.

From the 1970s women were gradually, often reluctantly, admitted to operational activities in the RAF. Previously they had been confined to auxiliary, land-based and largely non-technical roles in the separate Women's Royal Air Force (WRAF), formed in April 1918, later renamed the Women's Auxiliary Air Force (WAAF). Their role had been to free men for combatant duties. By the end of the century the RAF numbered about 65,000 men and women having, like the other armed services, experienced a succession of cut-backs by both Conservative and Labour governments. From 1964 the three services were directed by a single ministry of defence.

FURTHER READING M. Dean, *The Royal Air Force and Two World Wars* (1979); J. Trevenen, *The Royal Air Force: The Past Thirty Years* (1976).

Royal British Legion, association of veterans of the armed forces. The Legion evolved out of Britain's first veterans' associations, chiefly the National Federation of Discharged and Demobilized Sailors and Soldiers, which were formed in 1916 and 1917 by servicemen discharged from the armed forces on account of war-related disabilities. These organizations were closely related to the LABOUR movement and came into being to express the men's dissatisfaction with government policies on HOUSING, war pensions and job training for the disabled. Fearing their radicalism, in 1917 a group of senior military officers founded a more moderate rival body, the Comrades of the Great War. After the war the two groups ran mutual-aid societies and social clubs and sponsored Remembrance Day ceremonies. In July 1921 they merged with two smaller groups to form the British Legion.

Thereafter the organization devoted itself to charitable work and social activities, supplementing state assistance for veterans with its own voluntary fund, raised chiefly from the proceeds of Poppy Day sales each Remembrance Day (*see* HAIG, DOUGLAS). An affiliated, but separate, women's section acted as fund-raisers, propagandists and volunteer workers. The British Legion gained a royal charter in 1925. It was unusual, compared with veterans' organizations in most other major combatant countries, in not playing the role of a political pressure group. It tended towards the right, but was prevented by its constitution from political partisanship.

However, as WORLD WAR II approached, the Legion made contacts with German veterans and argued for the need to prevent another war, supporting APPEASEMENT. During the MUNICH crisis of September 1938 it sent a volunteer force of 10,000 to Czechoslovakia to police the transfer of the Sudetenland into German hands, though this force was recalled before it reached France. Only when Hitler seized Czechoslovakia did the Legion cease trying for peace. During World War II legionaries contributed to home defence as air-raid wardens and in the HOME GUARD.

After World War II to the end of the century the Legion continued its activities: raising funds from the sale of poppies every year; assisting needy veterans; acting as advocate for war-pensions claimants; organizing pilgrimages to overseas war graves; operating business enterprises employing disabled veterans; and running Legion clubs.

FURTHER READING G. Wootton, *The Official History of the British Legion* (1956); G. Wootton, *The Politics of Influence: British Ex-Servicemen, Cabinet Decisions and Cultural Change, 1917–57* (1963).

Royal Flying Corps. *See* ROYAL AIR FORCE.

Royal Naval Air Service. *See* ROYAL AIR FORCE.

Royal Navy, the front line of the defence of the British Isles for centuries, and hence known as the 'senior service'. The navy also provided security for British trade and the British EMPIRE. At the beginning of the 20th century it was overseen by the Board of the Admiralty, which was responsible for the fleets, supporting bases and dockyards throughout the world. The years before WORLD WAR I saw improvements in the design and range of fighting ships, with the development of the DREADNOUGHT and then of submarines. However, World War I was the first major war in which the ARMY was at least as important as the navy, in terms of Britain's contribution to the Allied victory.

At the end of 1917 the Women's Royal Naval Reserve (eventually the Women's Royal Naval Service, popularly known as the 'Wrens') had been established, to free men for combat by transferring land-based support tasks to women. It also played an important role in WORLD WAR II and remained in existence thereafter. Only in the 1990s were women fully absorbed into the navy, after much opposition, and allowed to perform combatant roles.

In the 1920s pay, conditions and morale among sailors deteriorated, leading to a mutiny on battleships at INVERGORDON, Scotland, in 1931. Conditions improved thereafter. Except during the periods of general CONSCRIPTION the navy was recruited from volunteers. During the interwar years it became clear that the ROYAL AIR FORCE, which had been formed out of the Royal Naval Air Service and the Royal Flying Corps in 1918, would play an essential role in any future war. However, the navy re-established control over the Fleet Air Arm in 1937, and carrier-based aircraft were to prove crucial in the forthcoming conflict. In World War II the Royal Navy played an important part in defeating the Italian navy in the Mediterranean (*see* CUNNINGHAM, ANDREW) and against German commerce raiders and SUBMARINES in the battle of the ATLANTIC.

After the war DECOLONIZATION and the decline in Britain's world role further diminished the importance of the navy for Britain's interests, although the FALKLANDS War in 1982 briefly gave the navy a major role again. In 1964 the armed forces were unified under the Ministry of Defence, with Earl MOUNTBATTEN, first sea lord after World War II, as the first unified chief of staff. From 1968 the navy was closely linked to other NORTH ATLANTIC TREATY ORGANIZATION (NATO) and less independent. Its decreasing size was largely tailored to carry out the COLD WAR tasks allocated to it, principally tracking Soviet submarines in the North Atlantic. The navy also carried out fishery-protection duties, as in the COD WAR of the 1970s. Despite this diminution of importance, from the late 1960s Britain's independent NUCLEAR WEAPONS delivery capability was based on submarine-launched missiles.

SEE ALSO   BEATTY, DAVID; FISHER, JOHN; JUTLAND, BATTLE OF.

FURTHER READING   P.M. Kennedy, *The Rise and Fall of British Naval Mastery* (4th edn, 1991).

Royal Shakespeare Company (RSC), with the

NATIONAL THEATRE, one of the two major state-subsidized theatre companies in Britain. The company was founded in 1932 with the building of the Shakespeare Memorial Theatre in Stratford-upon-Avon, Shakespeare's birthplace. This followed the destruction in a fire in 1926 of the playhouse built there in 1879. Until the 1950s short summer seasons of Shakespeare's plays were presented there by companies assembled annually.

In 1961 Peter Hall was appointed artistic director. He formed a permanent Royal Shakespeare Company and acquired a London base also, initially the Aldwych Theatre, then, after its completion in 1982, at the Barbican Centre. The company's range was extended to include other classical and modern drama. In 1968 Peter Hall was replaced by his protégé, Trevor Nunn. In 1986 a second, smaller theatre, the Swan, was built at Stratford. The company also undertook, to the end of the century, regular tours around Britain.

Russell, Bertrand (Arthur William) (1872– 1970),

mathematician, philosopher, peace campaigner and Nobel laureate. Russell was born in 1872, the grandson of the former prime minister Lord John Russell. He was educated at Trinity College, Cambridge, and was made a fellow of the college in 1895, soon after his graduation. He was fascinated by logic and its mathematical and philosophical applications, and his remarkable intellectual gifts and grasp of contemporary continental European thought meant his work soon appeared in print.

Russell's early work, such as *An Essay on the Foundations of Geometry* (1897), remained within the confines of the neo-Hegalianism that then dominated philosophy. However, together with the other influential British philosophers, G.E. Moore and A.N. Whitehead, Russell undermined that dominance with a dazzling series of papers and books.

His major work, *Principia Mathematica*, which he co-wrote with A.N. Whitehead, appeared in three volumes between 1910 and 1913. Thereafter, he largely abandoned the endeavour to make original contributions to philosphy and he was determined to devote himself to the reform of society and to pacificism.

Russell always possessed a strong social conscience, and his pacifism and socialism got him into trouble during the early years of WORLD WAR I.

His condemnation of war and support of CONSCI-ENTIOUS OBJECTORS meant he was stripped of his fellowship at Trinity College, Cambridge, in 1915. Later, in 1918, he was fined and imprisoned for his 'seditious' anti-war writings. He was reinstated at Trinity in 1919, but resigned in 1921.

In 1931 he succeeded to his brother's title, becoming the 3rd Earl Russell. He also travelled, spending a number of years teaching and lecturing in China and the United States. Returning to Britain from the USA in 1944, he supported the Allied effort during WORLD WAR II, but was passionately opposed to the use of the newly created NUCLEAR WEAPONS. Later he was to become one of the founders of the CAMPAIGN FOR NUCLEAR DISARMAMENT, and in 1958 was made its first president. In 1961, at the age of 89, he was briefly imprisoned for his role during an anti-nuclear demonstration. In 1945 he published *A History of Western Philosophy*, perhaps his most famous work, which sold well. This, combined with several other accessible works of popular philosophy, earned him the Order of Merit in 1949 and the Nobel prize for literature in 1950. Russell died in 1970 at the age of 98.

In his personal life, Russell was a serial womanizer who married four times, conducted innumerable affairs, and believed monogamy to be unnatural. He also had radical ideas about the education of children and had difficult relationships with his own children. However, to the public he was known and appreciated for his love of humanity and peace, and was viewed as a moral leader.

FURTHER READING R. Monk, *Bertrand Russell: The Spirit of Solitude* (1996); R. Monk, *Bertrand Russell, 1921–70: The Ghost of Madness* (2000); B. Russell, *The Autobiography of Bertrand Russell* (3 vols., 1967–9).

Rutherford, Ernest. *See* SCIENCE.

S

Salisbury, Robert (Arthur Talbot) Gascoyne-Cecil, 3rd marquess of (1830–1903), Conservative politician, PRIME MINISTER (1885–6, 1886–92 and 1895–1902). A younger son of a long-established Tory aristocratic family, Salisbury was educated at Eton and Oxford. His elder brother died in 1865, and he inherited his father's title and estates in 1868. Salisbury was intellectual, devoted to the high-church tendency in the CHURCH OF ENGLAND, somewhat rigid by temperament and anti-democratic by instinct. He became increasingly committed to FREE TRADE over time. He became MP for Stamford in 1853 and had a long political career: as secretary for INDIA, 1866 and 1874–8; FOREIGN SECRETARY, 1878–80; leader of the opposition in the Lords, 1881–5; leader of the CONSERVATIVE PARTY, 1885–1902; prime minister and foreign secretary, 1885–6; prime minister, 1886–7; prime minister and foreign secretary, 1887–92 and 1895–1900; prime minister and lord privy seal, 1900–2.

Salisbury was a skilful diplomat but made relatively little impact on domestic politics, not least because his governments depended upon the support of LIBERAL unionists. His ministries were notorious for nepotism and he promoted the career of his nephew, and successor as Conservative Party leader, Arthur BALFOUR. By 1900 Salisbury's health was failing and his policies and attitudes were look-ing dated to younger politicians. It was Joseph CHAMBERLAIN, the colonial secretary, not he, who conducted the policy that drew Britain into the BOER WAR. He resigned in 1902.

FURTHER READING A. Roberts, *Salisbury, Victorian Titan* (1999).

Samuel, Herbert (1870–1963), Liberal politician. Born in Liverpool, the son of a wealthy banker, Samuel lived mainly in London. He was educated at University College School, London, and Balliol College, Oxford, gaining a first-class degree in modern history, and was an active member of the LIBERAL PARTY even as a student. His book *Liberalism* (1902) foreshadowed many of the social reforms enacted by the Liberal governments after 1905. Samuel was a voluntary social worker in the East End of London until elected in 1902 as Liberal MP for Cleveland, which he represented until 1918. He was notably critical of oppressive aspects of imperialism as conducted by Britain and other powers (*see* EMPIRE). As undersecretary of state at the Home Office, 1905–9, he helped to devise and draft such important pieces of social legislation as the Probation Act, 1907, which established a national probation service, and the Children Act, 1908, which extended state responsibility for child welfare (*see* WELFARE STATE). When he was appointed chancellor of the duchy of Lancaster in 1909 he became the first practising Jew to become a CABINET minister. He was postmaster general from 1910 to 1914 (during which time he was involved in the MARCONI SCANDAL) and again from May 1915 to January 1916. He was president of the local government board (February 1914–May 1915) and home secretary (January–December 1916), in which role he was in charge of affairs in IRELAND at the time of the EASTER RISING.

When David LLOYD GEORGE formed his coalition government in December 1916, Samuel supported ASQUITH and refused a government post. His chief preoccupation now was Zionism. In early 1915 he was the first to propose to the cabinet a British-sponsored Jewish national home in PALESTINE, and he played a crucial role in the discussions that led to the BALFOUR DECLARATION in 1917. He lost his COMMONS seat in the 1918 election, and became the first British high commissioner in Palestine, 1920–5. On his return to Britain he chaired the Royal Commission on the COAL MINING industry, 1925–6, which failed to avert the GENERAL STRIKE, but acting as an unofficial mediator Samuel helped to persuade the TRADES UNION CONGRESS to call off the strike.

In the run-up to the 1929 election he tried, with little success, to reinvigorate the Liberal Party machine. He was elected for Darwen (Lancashire), which he represented until 1935. In 1931, deputizing for the ailing Lloyd George, he led the Liberals into the NATIONAL GOVERNMENT, in which he became home secretary, 1931–2. In 1933 he withdrew from the government over the abandonment of FREE TRADE, taking 30 other Liberals with him to the opposition benches in the House of Commons He was defeated in the 1935 election. Samuel was made a viscount in 1937 and became leader of the Liberals in the House of LORDS. He approved of the MUNICH AGREEMENT of 1938. Thereafter he retired from politics and devoted himself to travel and the study of philosophy, appearing regularly on the BBC 'Brains Trust' programmes.

FURTHER READING B. Wasserstein, *Herbert Samuel: A Political Life* (1992).

Sanger, Frederick. *See* SCIENCE.

Sankey Commission, body established in February 1919 to deal with a crisis in the COAL MINING industry. During WORLD WAR I the industry had been under state control and conditions for miners had generally improved.

After the war the miners' union, the Miners' Federation of Great Britain, sought further improvements: a 30% wage increase, reduction of the working day from eight hours to six, and NATIONALIZATION. The LLOYD GEORGE government was anxious to avoid industrial conflict. It offered a pay rise of one shilling a day and a committee of inquiry. The miners rejected this and a strike ballot supported a strike by almost six to one. Lloyd George offered a royal commission on which the miners would participate.

The commission consisted of three miners' officials, three intellectuals sympathetic to the miners (including Sidney WEBB and R.H. TAWNEY), three coal owners and three other industrialists. The chair was the lawyer Sir John Sankey, a former CONSERVATIVE. Following investigations, the commission proposed a pay increase of two shillings per shift and the reduction of the working day to seven hours, with a further cut to six hours in 1921 if the economic situation in the industry justified it. This offer was strongly endorsed by a miners' ballot on 5 April 1919. The commission then considered nationalization, which in June 1919 it endorsed by seven votes to six, Sankey voting for it. In August Lloyd George rejected the recommendation. The Miners' Federation could not mobilize support for a strike on the issue, the miners having achieved their other aims. Industrial conflict in the industry was, however, to continue (*see* MINERS' STRIKES).

FURTHER READING B. Supple, *The History of the British Coal Industry, 1913–46: The Political Economy of Decline* (1987).

Sassoon, Siegfried (1886–1967), writer and soldier best known for his poetry critical of WORLD WAR I. He served with distinction in the Royal Welch Fusiliers, being awarded the Military Cross for valour. In July 1917, while still in the army, he published a statement of support for pacifists and CONSCIENTIOUS OBJECTORS. Rather than court-martialling him, the army had him examined by a medical board, which declared him unfit for active service and sent him to Craiglockhart, the hospital for shell-shocked servicemen near Edinburgh. He became a national symbol of disillusionment with the war, along with other war poets (*see* POETRY) including Wilfred Owen (whom he met at Craiglockhart) and Robert Graves. After the war he showed no clear sense of direction, flirting with socialism and later converting to Roman Catholicism. His best-known post-war work was his partly fictionalized memoirs: *Memoirs of a Fox-Hunting Man* (1928), *Memoirs of an Infantry Officer* (1930), *Sherston's Progress* (1936), *The Old Century* (1938), *The Weald of Youth* (1942) and *Siegfried's Journey* (1945).

FURTHER READING P. Fussell, *The Great War and Modern Memory* (1975).

Scargill, Arthur. *See* MINERS' STRIKES.

science. Throughout the century chemistry and physics developed along separate but often closely related tracks. Important fields of research in Britain, such as radioactivity and the structure of atoms, did not belong clearly in either domain. In the second half of the century much outstanding work in both physics and chemistry was closely associated with the biological sciences and with research in MEDICINE.

In 1900 several chairs of chemistry existed in British UNIVERSITIES, but British chemistry was less well regarded than chemistry elsewhere in Europe, especially in Germany. Most leading British chemists were educated in universities abroad. Physics in Britain was at least equal in status to and as well endowed as in Germany and France.

Throughout the century the Royal Institution of Great Britain (founded 1799) in London played an important role as a centre both of high-quality research and of the diffusion of scientific knowledge to the public. Its small size meant that research followed the interests of its director. From the beginning of the century until 1923 this post was held by the chemist James Dewar (1842–1923).

Two areas to which scientists based at British universities made significant contributions in the first half of the century were radioactivity and the structure of atoms. William Ramsay (1852–1916), professor of chemistry at University College, London, received the Nobel prize for his discovery of the inert gases in 1904, the same year that Lord Rayleigh (1842–1919) received the Nobel prize for physics. Between 1904 and 1919 Frederick Soddy (1877–1956), first at the University of Glasgow, then at Aberdeen, was acknowledged as the world expert in radio-chemical research. He helped to elucidate the nature of isotopes, for which he received the Nobel prize for chemistry in 1921. In 1913 at the University of Manchester H.C.G. Moseley (1887–1915; he died at GALLIPOLI) used the frequency of x-rays emitted by different elements to determine the positive charge of the atomic nucleus of each element, and hence its atomic number; this revealed gaps in the periodic table, which in turn led to the discovery of new elements. In 1908 Ernest Rutherford (1871–1937; a New Zealander who trained in research at Cambridge and was to become Britain's most distinguished physicist) received the Nobel prize for chemistry for showing that radioactivity involved the change of an atom of one chemical element into an atom of another. He had collaborated with Soddy on this work while both were working at McGill University, Montreal. In 1911, now working at the University of Manchester, where he built a successful research school, Rutherford proposed that atoms had a central core, or nucleus, and in 1919 he reported that he had artificially disintegrated the nucleus of a nitrogen atom. At Manchester he collaborated with H.C.G. Moseley, the

German Hans Geiger (1882–1945) and the Dane Niels Bohr (1885–1962) among others. Bohr extended Rutherford's ideas and succeeded in accounting for the properties of simple atoms, such as hydrogen. The Rutherford–Bohr model of the atom became one of the foundations of quantum mechanics, the modern theory of atomic behaviour. While the main development of quantum mechanics took place elsewhere in Europe, also at Cambridge in the late 1920s Paul Dirac (1902–84) made fundamental mathematical contributions to the field. He predicted the existence of antimatter and provided a quantum theory of radiation. He shared the 1933 Nobel prize for physics.

During WORLD WAR I, Rutherford and others, on behalf of the Admiralty Board of Invention and Research, used sonar to detect submarines. They and other scientists greatly assisted the war effort, for example in the development of aircraft. However, the disadvantages of Britain's weakness in chemistry became evident during the war, leading the government to promote research into basic chemicals used, for example, in explosives. This led to the setting-up of the Department of Scientific and Industrial Research (DSIR) in 1917, the forerunner of the Science and Engineering Research Council (SERC), which channelled government funding to research at the end of the century.

In 1919 Rutherford became Cavendish professor of physics at Cambridge. The CAVENDISH LABORATORY was the main centre for research in physics in Britain from the beginning of the century to World War II. It was here that Rutherford assembled a group of researchers, including P.M.S. Blackett (1897–1974) and John Cockcroft (1897–1967), who together profoundly influenced the course of nuclear research. Other members of the team included F.W. Aston (1877–1945), who made advances in understanding atomic structure and was awarded the Nobel prize for physics in 1922. Here also C.T.R. Wilson (1869–1959) had, in 1911, developed the cloud chamber, which was used to detect ionizing radiation and to study other nuclear phenomena. He shared the Nobel prize

for physics in 1927. In 1932 James Chadwick (1891–1974) discovered the neutron, a component of the nucleus long predicted by Rutherford. In the early 1930s N.F. Mott (1905–) moved from Cambridge to Bristol University, where he brought into being one of the first groups to study the problems of steady-state physics. From 1954 to 1971 he was Cavendish professor at Cambridge, and in 1977 shared the Nobel prize for physics for his work on semiconductors.

Molecular biology was pioneered in Britain in the mid-20th century and was a major force in scientific development in the second half of the century. Its origins lay in the field of x-ray crystallography, which was devised by W.H. Bragg (1862–1942) at University College, London. He investigated the structure of chemical crystals by means of x-rays and later by use of electrons, for which he shared the Nobel prize for physics in 1915 with his son Lawrence Bragg (1890–1971), a unique family triumph. In 1923 Bragg senior became director of the Royal Institution and built up a formidable team of researchers in x-ray crystallography, including his son and other scientists who were later to achieve great distinction, notably J.D. Bernal (1901–71) and Kathleen Lonsdale (1903– 71). Lawrence Bragg was also to become director from 1953 to 1966. He did much to expand the Royal Institution's already well-established series of public lectures, in particular by introducing lectures for schoolchildren. In 1927 Bernal moved to Cambridge, where he worked on structural crystallography. He collaborated with others on investigating the structures of sex hormones, water and protein crystals. At Cambridge he pioneered the analysis of amino acids.

In biology the leading figure early in the century was J.B.S. Haldane (1892–1964). After serving in World War I, he worked in genetics and physiology at Oxford before moving to Cambridge in 1922. In a series of papers published from 1924 to 1932 (when they were collected as *The Causes of Evolution*) he made a major contribution to uniting Darwinian evolutionary theory and Mendelian genetics. His initial training was in mathematics and much of his work involved the application of mathematics to biological problems, mainly concerning genetics and evolution. He was also active in popularizing science, and he published a number of books designed to reach a wide public and to raise questions about the public role and responsibilities of science. He transferred in 1933 to University College, London, where he remained until he moved to research in INDIA in 1957. He became an Indian citizen in 1961. He joined the COMMUNIST PARTY in the 1930s and fought in the Spanish Civil War, where he gained experience for his book *A.R.P.* (1938), a quantitative study of the likely bomb damage in the anticipated world war. He also undertook physiological experiments. In 1939 he investigated the causes of casualties following the sinking of submarines by observing the effects on himself and three others of being enclosed in a sealed chamber simulating submarine conditions. Later in the war he undertook similar work for the Admiralty on the physiological effects of gases at high pressure.

Haldane was only one of many academic scientists who made an important contribution through their research in WORLD WAR II. P.M.S. Blackett became a scientific civil servant at the Air Ministry's Royal Aircraft Establishment, applying his skills to the practical needs of warfare by working on the design of bombsights, then on the statistical analysis of the use of equipment in action, first studying anti-aircraft defences, then anti-submarine warfare. J.D. Bernal, a Marxist all his adult life, conducted research for the Ministry of Home Security on the effects of air raids of different levels of intensity. Thereafter he worked for Lord MOUNTBATTEN on preparations for the invasion of Europe, including studying ways of measuring the Normandy beaches and the construction of artificial harbours. After the war he worked for the remainder of his career at Birkbeck College, London, continuing his study of the structure of biological and inorganic materials and inspiring outstanding work in crystallography.

The sciences had expanded as academic subjects in the interwar years, with increased provision of university facilities, while research based in industry and in government establishments (e.g. those related to defence) also increased. The British chemicals industry was strengthened somewhat by mergers, in particular the formation of Imperial Chemical Industries (ICI) in 1926, and its development was dependent upon high-quality research. In 1927 ICI established a research council to link research in the universities with the chemical industry. British scientists made notable contributions to organic chemistry. Chemists in the 1930s and 1940s produced several significant synthetic medical compounds, including the first effective sulphonamide drugs (which were highly effective against severe infection) and Paludrine, which was effective against malaria. They also established the formula for penicillin (*see* FLEMING, ALEXANDER).

But in the 1930s American scientists were overtaking those of Europe and the second half of the century was to see a strong drift of outstanding British scientists across the Atlantic. The American lead was greatly increased during World War II with the development in particular of RADAR (first developed in Britain in the 1930s) and of atomic weapons, which owed much to physicists based in the United States, though not necessarily born there. Nevertheless, the development in 1940 of the cavity magnetron by J.T. Randall (1905–84) and H.A.H. Boot (1917–83) at Birmingham University made an important contribution to the development of radar. Also in 1940, following the discovery of nuclear fission, Otto Frisch (1904–79) and R.E. Peierls (1907–), both refugees in Britain from Nazism, recognized that by using one rare isotope of uranium, it might be practicable to build a weapon using the energy released in the process of nuclear fission. It became clear, however, that in wartime conditions further progress on an atomic bomb was possible only through collaboration with the American Manhattan Project.

In Britain at the beginning of the war there were five times as many people (mainly men; there were few female chemists) working in pure or industrial chemistry (about 6000) as in 1914. The chemical industry expanded faster under the pressure of war needs, employing half a million people at its wartime peak. After the war it expanded at almost twice the rate of other manufacturing industries, mainly in the field of petrochemicals, due to the refining in Britain of crude oil from the MIDDLE EAST. With such expansion came a growing need for research, and increasing numbers of research scientists were employed by industry.

From 1945 there was more generous government funding for British science. The decision in 1947 to build NUCLEAR WEAPONS in Britain led to the foundation of new government laboratories at Harwell and Aldermaston, where nuclear reactors were designed, initially for the production of plutonium for nuclear weapons, later for the production of electricity. The number of science places in universities was increased, as was funding for research, though the teaching of the sciences in state and many independent schools remained limited and underfunded for the remainder of the century.

High-quality university research continued. Blackett had moved from Cambridge and developed two of the largest university physics departments in the country, first as professor at Manchester (1937–53), then at Imperial College, London (1953–65). He won the Nobel prize for physics in 1948 for his work on cosmic rays. A lifelong socialist, Blackett was committed to the efficient and humane use of science and technology. He had opposed the strategic bombing campaign during the war, believing that more effective use could be made of the bombers in the anti-submarine campaign. He was not directly involved with the development of the atomic bomb during the war and opposed its further development in peacetime; he was thereafter excluded from official consultations on the military uses of science. In the early 1960s he turned his attention to technology and Britain's lagging industrial performance, becoming a leading adviser to the Labour Party during Harold WILSON's premiership.

After the war there was an influx of physicists into the biological sciences, which were largely government-funded through the Medical Research Council (MRC, founded in 1920). In 1946 the MRC established a Biophysics Unit at King's College, London, directed by John Randall, then a year later a unit at Cambridge, initially attached to the Cavendish and directed by Max Perutz (1914–). This became the centre of the new molecular biology. From 1962 it became a separate unit known as the Laboratory of Molecular Biology (LMB). In 1962 Perutz and John Kendrew (1917–) shared the Nobel prize for chemistry for identifying the structure of the respiratory proteins, haemoglobin and myoglobin.

From the same laboratory, Francis Crick (1916–), the American James Watson (1928–) and Maurice Wilkins (1916–) of the King's College unit shared the 1962 Nobel prize for physiology or medicine for identifying the molecular structure of DNA. This is the famous 'double helix', which revealed the way in which the genetic materials that influence heredity are replicated. The fourth member of the team, Rosalind Franklin (1920–58), who worked with Wilkins on the x-ray crystallography that contributed to Crick and Watson's discovery, was deprived by her early death from cancer from sharing the prize. Crick himself was initially a physicist who entered biology after working on naval research during the war. The discovery of the structure of DNA launched a decade of international activity in which the relationship between DNA structure and protein structure was worked out, on a theoretical basis largely formulated by Crick. By the mid-1960s the genetic code had been broken and Crick moved on to have a major influence upon further developments in the biological sciences. From 1976 he worked in California. The study of genes was to power major advances in science in Britain, the United States and elsewhere for the remainder of the century, though as knowledge advanced about their structure, understanding of the precise functions of genes did not grow commensurately, despite much assertion and counter-assertion.

A dominant figure in molecular biology was Frederick Sanger (1918–), the only person to have been awarded the Nobel prize for chemistry twice. As head of the Cambridge LMB, he was awarded the prize in 1958 for work on the structure of insulin; then he shared it in 1980 for devising a technique for sequencing DNA. From the 1960s the LMB pioneered the molecular study of cellular sciences and was awarded two further Nobel prizes: Aaron Klug (1926–) in 1982 for chemistry, for his work on the structure of chromosomes; and in 1984 Cesar Milstein (1927–) shared the prize for physiology or medicine. The Imperial Cancer Research Fund, in London, also became an important centre of research in molecular biology.

In 1964 Dorothy Hodgkin (1910–99), who had previously worked with Bernal before moving to Oxford, received the Nobel prize for chemistry for her work on the structure of penicillin and vitamin B12. The new specialism of molecular biology was somewhat more open to women than older-established scientific fields, though even in this field distinguished women such as Hodgkin and Kathleen Lonsdale were not appointed to influential professorships. The appointment in 1999 of Susan Greenfield (1950–), a biochemist who researched on the structure and functions of the brain (an important research field at this time) and a professor at Oxford, as the first female director of the Royal Institution was perhaps a sign of a reversal of the long-term failure of science in Britain to draw upon the talents of women. This was frequently commented upon in official and unofficial surveys of relative British weakness in science and technology in the second half of the century.

Later in the century there was increasing international collaboration in important areas of research, for example British high-energy physicists contributed to CERN (the European Laboratory for Nuclear Research) based near Geneva, though in the 1980s and early 1990s they faced British government reluctance to contribute sufficiently to the funding of CERN. From the late 1980s research on nuclear fusion was undertaken by British scientists as part of a European project, the Joint European Torus (JET).

At the end of the century the public perception of science was marred by growing awareness of the environmental ill effects of the increased use of chemicals over the century. This view was sometimes distorted owing to the all too frequent inadequacy of scientific education at school level. However, there was also wide appreciation of the benefits and achievements of scientific research in Britain and elsewhere over the century.

FURTHER READING W.H. Brock, *The Fontana History of Chemistry* (1992); J.G. Crowther, *The Cavendish Laboratory, 1874–1974* (1974); K.R. Dronamaju (ed.), *Haldane and Modern Biology* (1968); M. Gowing, *Britain and Atomic Energy, 1939–45* (1964); J.D. Watson (ed. G.S. Stent), *The Double Helix: A Personal Account of the Structure of the Discovery of DNA* (1981).

Scotland, an independent kingdom with its own Parliament until the Act of Union of 1707, after which it retained a separate and distinctive legal system and a distinct, Presbyterian, established church (*see* CHURCH OF SCOTLAND), and in many respects remained culturally different from England or Wales.

In 1926, when the secretaryship for Scotland (established 1885) became a full secretaryship of state, the Edinburgh-based departments responsible for aspects of Scottish affairs were reorganized. Further reorganizations followed. From 1928 Scotland had a Board of Agriculture and a Board of Health, both statutorily defined as independent, but in reality responsible to the secretary of state. The Reorganization of Offices (Scotland) Act, 1939, brought into being four departments of the Scottish Office: Agriculture, Education, Health and Home Affairs. These changes were largely a response for demands for Scottish self-government that emerged from the late 19th century. Before 1914 this was a feature of the wider constitutional debate about HOME RULE. However, the question of IRELAND took precedence, and proposals for varying degrees of Scottish self-government got nowhere. However, a Scottish Grand Committee, comprising MPs for Scottish constituencies, was established on an experimental basis in 1894–5 to deal with legislation specific to Scotland. It had a permanent existence from 1907.

The National Party for Scotland (NPS) was formed in 1928 to promote self-government. It absorbed the more separatist Scottish National League, founded in 1920, which promoted Gaelic culture. The new party included a wide spectrum of views as to the degree of desirable separation from the rest of Britain. In 1934 it merged with the moderate Scottish Party (a Conservative breakaway group established in 1932) to form the Scottish National Party (SNP). The SNP promoted a policy of self-government within the empire: Scots had played a large role in the development of the empire and there was strong imperialist sentiment in the party. The SNP split during World War II and a secessionist campaign for home rule was dominant, though not very influential, after the war.

The SNP gradually reasserted control of the nationalist movement. However, it was not strong, the SNP gaining fewer than 22,000 votes in the 1959 election. The party finally gained its first Westminster seat in November 1967, when Winifred Ewing won a by-election at Hamilton. Eleven Scottish nationalists were elected to the House of COMMONS in 1974, and the SNP polled over 839,000 votes. The change came about as a result of growing UNEMPLOYMENT in Scotland, about which London was thought to be insufficiently concerned, and to the discovery of NORTH SEA OIL off the Scottish coast. Although North Sea oil brought prosperity to some parts of Scotland, such as Aberdeen, some thought the oil should be claimed by Scotland, while others were concerned about the environmental effects of development.

The rising fortunes of the SNP meant that Scottish nationalism now had to be taken seriously. In November 1973 the Kilbrandon Report recommended a Scottish assembly. Devolution measures were intermittently discussed in Parliament in 1976–8, and a bill providing for an elected assembly received the royal assent in July 1978. Devolution was to be dependent on support from at least 40% of the Scottish electorate. In a referendum held on 1 March 1979 a majority of voters favoured devolution, but they formed only 32.85% of the total electorate and devolution did not go ahead. This failure on an issue to which it was committed contributed to the downfall of the Labour government of James CALLAGHAN shortly afterwards.

Thereafter the SNP suffered a period of electoral decline and internal conflict. The 1980s, however, saw increased political divergence between England and Scotland, the latter moving especially strongly against the CONSERVATIVES (*see* COMMUNITY CHARGE). Scottish cultural nationalism flowered in literature, painting, film and popular music. Membership of the EUROPEAN UNION encouraged hopes for independence within Europe. The Labour government elected in 1997 was committed to devolution for Scotland and Wales. Referendums held in 1997 this time supported devolution. A Scottish Parliament was elected by PROPORTIONAL REPRESENTATION in 1999. Although there was a strong SNP presence in the new Parliament, the first Scottish Executive (devolved government) was a Labour–Liberal Democrat coalition.

FURTHER READING T. Devine, *The Scottish Nation 1700–2000* (2000); T. Gallagher (ed.), *Nationalism in the Nineties* (1991); C. Harvie, *Scotland and Nationalism* (1977).

Scott, Robert Falcon (1868–1912), naval officer and Antarctic explorer. Scott was born near Plymouth and entered the navy as a boy in 1880, and by 1897 was a lieutenant and torpedo officer. He was appointed leader of the Royal Geographical Society and Royal Society Antarctic expedition of 1901–4. He proved a capable captain of the

Discovery, the ship employed for the expedition, and a good leader of the members of the expedition, who carried out scientific and exploratory work in the Ross Sea and Victoria Land region. In 1902 Scott and SHACKLETON made a sledge journey to beyond 82 degrees south, which was the highest latitude yet reached in the Antarctic.

As a result of this success, Scott (who had been promoted to captain in 1906) was chosen to lead another expedition in 1910 in the *Terra Nova*. The expedition was scientific in its aims, and also aimed to reach the South Pole. Scott and four others reached the pole on 18 January 1912. They then discovered that a Norwegian expedition, led by Roald Amundsen, had preceded them by over a month. All five members of the British expedition died on the return journey. The three last survivors, including Scott, died less than 18 km (11 miles) from a depot, probably in late March, owing to lack of food and bad weather conditions. Scott's journal of the expedition ended: 'We shall stick it out to the end … It seems a pity but I do not think I can write any more.' Their bodies, together with Scott's diaries, were discovered about eight months later. The trip was not, however, a total failure. The explorers had, among other scientific discoveries, found the first evidence for continental drift in fossilized plant and animal remains, which they were bringing back.

The events of the expedition were popularly represented as epic tragedy. There was national mourning, Scott was posthumously awarded a knighthood and a Scott Polar Institute was founded at Cambridge. The expedition was almost certainly doomed by the mistake (not Scott's decision) to use man-hauled sledges to carry the heavy scientific equipment and others items that accompanied them; Amundsen's sledges were hauled by dogs.

FURTHER READING M. De-la-Noy, *Scott of the Antarctic* (1997); R. Huntford, *Scott and Amundsen* (1993).

Scottish National Party. *See* SCOTLAND.

Scouts. *See* BADEN-POWELL, ROBERT.

SDLP. *See* SOCIAL DEMOCRATIC AND LABOUR PARTY.

secondary modern schools. *See* EDUCATION.

Second World War. *See* WORLD WAR II: HOME FRONT and WORLD WAR II: MILITARY.

security service. *See* MI5 AND MI6.

servants. *See* DOMESTIC SERVICE.

settlement houses. *See* TOYNBEE HALL.

Sex Discrimination Act (1975). *See* EQUAL PAY.

sexuality, official regulation of. The regulation of sexuality during the first half of the 20th century was shaped by the social-purity campaigners of the 1880s, who sought to control both prostitution and male homosexuality. The 1881 Industrial Schools Amendment Act decreed that the children of prostitutes could be taken away from their mothers and committed to industrial schools. The 1885 Criminal Law Amendment Act defined brothels more narrowly, created more stringent penalties for those identified as brothel keepers, and raised the female age of consent to 16. The Labouchere amendment to the Criminal Law Amendment Act, 1885, made acts of gross indecency between men punishable by up to two years hard labour. The 1898 Vagrancy Act tightened up the law against importuning for 'immoral purposes' by both men and women. Legislation on incest in 1908 was intended to restrict the exploitation of young girls and women by adult men.

Support for such campaigns was widespread. During WORLD WAR I the Public Morality Council succeeded in closing a number of music halls and in driving prostitutes from many of their customary haunts on licensed premises. After the war there is strong evidence of a decline in prostitution; certainly it attracted less attention from the authorities and seems to have become less blatant. There was considerable regional variation in POLICE activity, but in 1900 there were 66 brothel keepers in Holloway prison; during the late 1920s the prosecution of prostitution offences plummeted in London and by 1930 there were only 14 prosecutions. During the same period the overall number of women in prison for prostitution offences fell from 546 in 1900 to 85 in 1930. Voluntary CENSORSHIP by the newspapers and legislative prohibitions also became more severe. For example, advertisements intended to combat venereal diseases were so edited that they were unable to provide any useful information, while a statute preventing salacious reporting of divorce cases was passed in 1926. Close control was exerted over the content and action of plays and performances in the theatre; book censorship was maintained by legal pressure on publishers and distributors rather than authors (*see* CENSORSHIP).

An average of 500 men a year were arrested for consensual homosexual offences through the 1930s, but after World War II numbers rose to 2504 in 1955. There was a series of high-profile court cases during the 1950s in which upper-middle-class or prominent men were charged with importuning other men for immoral purposes. The number of women working as prostitutes grew following the war. In response, in 1954, the Conservative government set up an interdepartmental committee on homosexual offences and prostitution. The 1957 report of the WOLFENDEN Committee recommended that behaviour that took place in private between consenting adults, including consensual sex between adult males, should be decriminalized, but that the legal penalties for public displays of sexual behaviour, such as street soliciting, should be strengthened.

The home secretary R.A. BUTLER rushed through the Street Offences Act of 1959, which made illegal open soliciting on the street but imposed no penalties on clients of prostitutes. The law on homosexuality was reformed in 1967. Homosexual acts in private between consenting adults over the age of 21 were made legal, but the

conditions were so restrictive that convictions rose for some years. In the 1960s and 1970s there was a broad retreat of government from control over individual sexual activity, beginning with the Obscene Publications Act of 1959. The homosexual age of consent was lowered to 18 in 1994. Demands that it should be equalized with the age of consent for heterosexuals (16) continued to the end of the century.

SEE ALSO BIRTH CONTROL; PERMISSIVE SOCIETY; SEXUALLY TRANSMITTED DISEASES.

FURTHER READING J. Weeks, *Sex, Politics and Society: The Regulation of Sexuality since 1800* (1981); J. Weeks, *Coming Out: Homosexual Politics in Britain, from the Nineteenth Century to the Present* (1977).

sexually transmitted diseases. Sexual mores in the 20th century have been greatly affected by three major diseases : syphilis, gonorrhoea and AIDS. Sexually transmitted diseases (or venereal diseases, as they were known for much of the century) were considered by many to be 'misconduct diseases', a deserved penalty for the sin of fornication; however, there were also 'innocent victims', such as infected wives, and syphilis could also be passed from mothers to their unborn children. Syphilis goes through three stages over several decades, the last of which can include insanity, blindness and death. Although incidence of the disease was falling, in 1924 it caused more deaths than either cancer or tuberculosis. Gonorrhoea can cause infertility in women and genital discharge and pain in men.

In the early 20th century medical knowledge of venereal-disease prevention and cure was improving. A 1913 royal commission on venereal disease rejected compulsory notification and isolation of sufferers, and instead recommended government-funded health education and centres offering free treatment. By 1917, 68 such clinics were open, but it was difficult to publicize means of prevention owing to the opposition of social-purity campaigners, who still saw fear of disease as a weapon in the fight to drive people away from vice into a life of virtue. The result was the 1917 Venereal Disease Act, which suppressed publications about such diseases (*see* CENSORSHIP).

However, during WORLD WAR II men in the armed forces were provided with condoms and information, and by the 1950s drugs that could cure venereal diseases were widely available. The removal of the threat of disease, along with improved contraception, substantially undermined the belief that sexual expression was bad or wrong, and contributed to the sexual revolution of the 1960s (*see* PERMISSIVE SOCIETY; SIXTIES, THE).

The first hint that sexually transmitted diseases had not been conquered came at the end of the 1970s with a surge in cases of genital herpes, which, though not serious, is incurable. In the early 1980s a much more sinister disease began to appear: acquired immune deficiency syndrome (AIDS), which destroys the body's ability to fight off infections so that the sufferer becomes susceptible to opportunistic infections. The HIV virus, which causes AIDS, can only be transmitted when a carrier's infected body fluids such as blood or semen come into contact with another's body fluids. Awareness of AIDS in the UK gay male community slowly grew from 1981 to 1983, and the formation of voluntary organizations to provide support for those infected began. As broader public awareness grew, conservative Christians and tabloid newspapers expressed fear and loathing of homosexuals, who were felt to have brought the disease on themselves. Another major group of AIDS victims were intravenous drug-users, who also aroused little public sympathy. In contrast haemophiliacs, who were not infected sexually, were seen as 'innocent victims'.

Initially the political response to AIDS was fearful and threatening of civil liberties. However, it became increasingly obvious that there were growing numbers of 'innocent' AIDS sufferers, for example, female partners of HIV-positive men, and babies of HIV-positive mothers. Another factor was that previous campaigns against infectious dis-

eases had taught that compulsory notification and similar measures would deter sufferers from coming forward and worsen the epidemic. Civil servants and politicians accepted this, and substantial amounts of money were put into research and into improving treatment and services. By the end of the century, as the epidemic in the UK waned, the greater visibility of homosexuals resulting from the epidemic appeared to have contributed to a more open and tolerant sexual environment.

FURTHER READING V. Berridge, *AIDS in the UK: The Making of Policy, 1981–1994* (1996); R. Davenport-Hines, *Sex, Death and Punishment* (1991); M. Spongberg, *Feminizing Venereal Disease: The Body of the Prostitute in 19th-Century Medical Discourse* (1997).

Shackleton, Ernest (Henry) (1874–1922), Antarctic explorer. Shackleton was apprenticed in the merchant navy in 1890 and served in the White Star, Shire and Union Castle lines. He successfully applied to join SCOTT's Antarctic expedition of 1901–4. In 1902 he and Scott reached 82 degrees south by sledge. After the expedition Shackleton gave up marine service and planned his own Antarctic expedition. He led an expedition in 1907–8, on which he discovered and named the Beardmore Glacier, recognizing it as the route onto the 3000 m (10,000 foot) high plateau at the centre of the continent. He himself reached 88 degrees south, only 155 km (97 miles) from the South Pole. He became a national hero (being knighted in 1909) and was encouraged to lead another expedition to cross the continent. This went ahead despite the onset of World War I. His ship *Endurance* was lost when it was crushed by ice in November 1915. With small boats and sledges he led his men to Elephant Island by the following April, sailed 1300 km (800 miles) in an open boat to South Georgia and crossed an unmapped glaciated mountain range to the whaling station on the island. After several attempts he eventually managed to return to Elephant Island to rescue his men, all of whom survived.

Shackleton organized the winter equipment of the North Russian Expeditionary Force, 1918–19, in which he participated. He carried out some diplomatic service in South America, then set out on a third Antarctic expedition in 1921, but died suddenly after reaching South Georgia.
FURTHER READING R. Huntford, *Shackleton* (1985, 1996).

Shaw, George Bernard (1856–1950), playwright, drama and music critic and Nobel laureate. He was also a socialist, a pacifist and a supporter of women's rights. Shaw was born in Dublin into what he later termed a Protestant 'shabbygenteel' family. He was schooled in Dublin and worked briefly for an estate agent. He then decided to move to London in 1876, following his mother and sisters who had left the year before to escape Shaw's alcoholic father. In London Shaw spent several years writing and dabbling in various studies at the British Museum library. His interest in Marxism and later in a wider range of socialist ideas also started at this time, as he began reading and attending lectures. He joined the FABIAN SOCIETY in 1884 and became a committed member; he edited *Fabian Essays in Socialism* in 1889. In the 1890s he began working as a drama and music critic and writing plays in earnest, though widespread success and acclaim eluded him until 1904, when he wrote *John Bull's Other Island*. Some of his best-known plays are *Man and Superman* (1903), *Major Barbara* (1905), *Pygmalion* (1912) – his most popular play – and *Saint Joan* (1923), which has been critically acclaimed as his masterpiece. Shaw was long considered to be the most important English-language playwright of his time (*see* DRAMA), and was awarded the Nobel prize for literature in 1925. From the 1960s his reputation as a playwright declined, but he continued to be regarded as a significant intellectual force. He went on writing until his death in 1950, including many works on social and political issues. However, he became increasingly disillusioned with politics, and felt unable to support either the Labour or the Communist Party, despite a brief attraction to Soviet Russia.
FURTHER READING A. Ganz, *George Bernard Shaw* (1983); M. Holroyd, *Bernard Shaw: The One-Volume Definitive Edition* (1997).

shell scandal (1915). *See* FRENCH, JOHN.

Sickert, Walter Richard (1860–1942), painter, printmaker, teacher and critic, and one of the most important figures of his time in British art. He was born in Munich of a Danish-German father and an Anglo-Irish mother and he remained highly cosmopolitan. His family settled in London in 1868. Both his father and grandfather were painters but Sickert initially trained for a career on the stage, but in 1881 he abandoned it and became a student at the Slade School of Fine Art in London. In the following year he became a pupil of James Whistler, then worked in Paris with Edgar Degas. Between 1885 and 1905 he spent much of his time in France. He returned to England in 1905 and became the main channel for the influence of avant-garde French painting on younger British artists, in particular the CAMDEN TOWN GROUP, although his influence was rather overtaken by that of the post-impressionist exhibitions of 1910–12 mounted by Roger FRY. Sickert lived in France again from 1918 to 1922, but thereafter settled in Britain. His favourite subjects were urban scenes and figure compositions. From the 1920s Sickert received many honours, though the quality of his work was judged to have declined.
FURTHER READING W. Baron, *Sickert* (1963).

Simon, John Allsebrook (1873–1954), Liberal and National Liberal politician. Born of Welsh parents in Manchester, Simon was educated at Fettes College, Edinburgh, and Wadham College, Oxford, gaining a first-class degree in classics and becoming a fellow of All Souls. He was called to the Bar, becoming a king's counsel after only nine years; he soon became one of the most successful barristers in London. Elected Liberal MP for

Walthamstow in 1906, he was appointed solicitor general and knighted in 1910. In 1912 he became a privy councillor and in 1913 entered the cabinet as attorney general.

Simon considered resignation over Britain's participation in WORLD WAR I but refrained. When ASQUITH formed his coalition government in May 1915 Simon refused the lord chancellorship and became home secretary. In January 1916 he resigned over the introduction of CONSCRIPTION, and served for the remainder of the war with the Royal Flying Corps in France. He opposed the LLOYD GEORGE coalition and was defeated in the 1918 election.

Re-elected for Spen Valley in 1922, Simon headed a commission into the government of INDIA in 1927–30, proposing moderate reforms. He returned to office as foreign secretary in the NATIONAL GOVERNMENT, 1931–5; unlike Herbert SAMUEL and other Liberals who left the National Government in 1933, he supported the Conservative view on the need for protective tariffs (*see* FREE TRADE), and led the 'National Liberals' through the 1930s. Committed to disarmament and non-intervention, he did nothing to oppose fascism and can be considered one of the architects of APPEASEMENT. Stanley BALDWIN appointed him home secretary and deputy leader of the House of COMMONS, 1935–7. In 1937 Neville CHAMBERLAIN made him CHANCELLOR OF THE EXCHEQUER; he had Chamberlain's full confidence and was a member of the small inner cabinet. However, when Hitler attacked Poland in 1939, Simon recognized the need for resistance and led a delegation of ministers to Chamberlain demanding a declaration of war. In May 1940 Winston CHURCHILL appointed him lord chancellor, with the title Viscount Simon of Stackpole Elidor. He retired from office in 1945.

FURTHER READING D. Dutton, *Simon: A Political Biography of Sir John Simon* (1992).

Simpson, Mrs Wallis. *See* ABDICATION CRISIS; EDWARD VIII.

Singapore, island republic, south of the Malay peninsula. The island was acquired for the East India Company by Sir Stamford Raffles (1781–1826) in 1819, remaining under the authority of British India until 1867. It then formed part of the Straits Settlements, the main British colony in MALAYA, until 1946, when Singapore became a separate colony with internal self-government.

Singapore was a ROYAL NAVY base of great strategic importance, and a major dockyard was completed there in 1938. During WORLD WAR II Singapore was captured by the Japanese in February 1942 with the surrender of over 70,000 British and Commonwealth servicemen in what was seen as a major humiliation for Britain. The British had made the mistake of expecting the Japanese to attack from the sea and fortified the island on the seaward side, but instead the Japanese invaded from the opposite direction, from Malaya. British troops reoccupied Singapore in September 1945.

Singapore became independent in 1959. In September 1963 it joined the Federation of Malaysia, but seceded within two years on the grounds that the Federation discriminated against people of Chinese origin, who made up three-quarters of the population of Singapore. It became an independent republic within the COMMONWEALTH in 1965, maintaining close commercial and defence links with Malaysia. It grew prosperous as the fourth largest port in the world, and from its development of trade, banking and industry.

Sinn Féin (Gaelic, 'ourselves alone'), currently the political wing of the Provisional IRA (*see* IRISH REPUBLICAN ARMY). Sinn Féin was founded in 1905 by a journalist, Arthur Griffith, as an Irish nationalist organization; over time it became a Republican political party. In the 1918 general election Sinn Féin won an overwhelming majority of the parliamentary seats in Ireland: 73 out of 105 (*see also* IRISH NATIONAL PARTY). However, the new MPs refused to take their seats at Westminster, seceding instead to form a new Irish Parliament, the Dáil, and declaring independence for

Ireland in 1919. In the ensuing Anglo-Irish War (*see* IRELAND), the Sinn Féin government was represented militarily by the IRA. Under the leadership of Eamon DE VALERA, Sinn Féin experienced a schism over the 1921 Anglo-Irish treaty, de Valera and his followers supporting the Republican, anti-treaty side in the civil war of 1922–3. In 1926 the party split again over the issue of support for the Free State Dáil: the minority retained the name Sinn Féin and refused to participate in the government of the Free State, which was still not a republic and which had accepted the partition of Ireland; the majority, under de Valera, formed a new party, Fianna Fáil .

Persistent refusal to participate in government, whether at Westminster or the Dáil, and its continued close links with the IRA, meant that Sinn Féin's fortunes dwindled over the next few decades. However, they revived in 1969 when the Troubles flared in NORTHERN IRELAND. Following the IRA, Sinn Féin also split (in December 1969) into two factions, Official and Provisional. Official Sinn Féin became increasingly left-leaning and abandoned its policy of abstention from the Dáil after the 1981 IRA hunger strikes; it changed its name to the Workers' Party in 1982 and later became known as the Democratic Left. It remains a minor political party in the Republic. Provisional Sinn Féin, however, enjoyed growing support among the Catholic working class in Northern Ireland.

Since the 1970s it has consistently won seats in both local and GENERAL ELECTIONS at Westminster and in Ulster, although Sinn Féin MPs such as president Gerry ADAMS still refuse to sit at Westminster. Its continued strong links with the IRA have meant that sanctions have been issued against it in the past. For example, the voices of Sinn Féin politicians were banned from British broadcast media for much of the 1980s and into the 1990s. However, the election of Sinn Féin members to all-party peace negotiation committees in the late 1990s gave it an increased public profile, and the party played a prominent and vital role in hammering out the 'Good Friday' peace

agreement of 1998 (*see* NORTHERN IRELAND) and subsequently took up seats on the new Northern Ireland executive. In the GENERAL ELECTION of 2001 Sinn Féin outpolled their nationalist rivals in the SOCIAL DEMOCRATIC AND LABOUR PARTY (SDLP) for the first time, winning 4 seats to the SDLP's 3.

FURTHER READING M. Elliot, *The Catholics of Ulster* (2000); B. O'Brien, *The Long War: The IRA and Sinn Féin, 1985 to Today* (1993); M. Ryan, *War and Peace in Ireland: Britain and the IRA in the New World Order* (1994).

sixties, the. In the early 1970s many people across the political spectrum believed that British society was in the throes of major change (*see* PERMISSIVE SOCIETY). The LABOUR governments of 1964–6 and 1966–70 passed a stream of legislation that helped create the perception of a society in which class barriers were being broken down and social mores transformed (*see* ABORTION; BIRTH CONTROL; CENSORSHIP; DIVORCE; SEXUALITY, OFFICIAL REGULATION OF). In 1971 a leader in *The* TIMES stated that there had 'undoubtedly been a revolution in sexual attitudes'. At the same time there was a transformation in popular culture, in which Britain, especially 'swinging London', was perceived as shaking off the drabness of the 1950s and to be taking a new international lead, especially in popular music (*see* BEATLES), FASHION and YOUTH CULTURE.

There was also a growth of political radicalism from the late 1960s, outside and often in opposition to the established political parties: a new WOMEN'S MOVEMENT, opposition to racial intolerance (as expressed, for example, by the ANTI-APARTHEID MOVEMENT), a squatting movement in protest against homelessness, 'claimants' rights' campaigns for improved social-security benefits, and various other forms of POPULAR PROTEST. Growing egalitarianism and rising expectations of participation within the existing social structures were also occurring and were of equal importance. There was an erosion of deference. The major change taking place in the 1960s was the breaking down of a rule-bound social consensus. Much of this change was in areas of personal life and personal behaviour that were not traditionally seen as political.

FURTHER READING A. Marwick, *The Sixties: Cultural Revolution in Britain, France, Italy, and the United States, c.1958–c.1974* (1998).

Slim, William (Joseph) (1891–1970), commander of the Burmese campaign during WORLD WAR II. Slim grew up in Birmingham and was educated at King Edward's School, Birmingham, a middle-class, fee-paying day school, and Birmingham University. He became an officer in the Royal Warwickshire Regiment in 1914, at the beginning of WORLD WAR I, and served mainly in the Middle East, where he was twice wounded and emerged with the rank of major. He spent most of the interwar years with the army in INDIA, for part of the time commanding the Gurkhas.

In World War II, in 1940, he was despatched to command an Indian brigade in Eritrea, against the Italians, then commanded Indian forces in Iraq and Syria. In 1942 he was given a command in BURMA, and in 1943 he took command of the 14th Army in Burma. In 1944 he successfully repelled a major Japanese offensive at Imphal and was able to launch a counter-attack that achieved the recovery of Burma. He was then promoted to full general and appointed commander in chief of Allied land forces in Southeast Asia. After the war, from 1948, he served as chief of the imperial general staff, then as governor general of Australia, 1953–60. He was knighted in 1944 and became a viscount in 1960. MOUNTBATTEN described him as 'the finest general the Second World War produced'.

FURTHER READING R. Lewin, *Slim: The Standard-bearer* (1999).

Smith, F(rederick) E(dwin) (1872–1930), Conservative politician. Educated at Birkenhead School and Oxford University, Smith gained a first-class degree in law. He became a successful barrister in Liverpool, where he was elected MP for the Walton division in 1906. He became noted for his rhetorical onslaughts on the LIBERAL government, opposing LLOYD GEORGE's budget of 1909, the Parliament Bill of 1911 (*see* LORDS, HOUSE OF), HOME RULE for IRELAND and the disestablishment of the CHURCH IN WALES. His extravagance and fondness for enjoyment made some underestimate him. In 1911 he joined the opposition front bench while carrying on a successful and well-respected legal practice. In 1914 he became head of the government press bureau.

In 1915, in ASQUITH's wartime coalition government, Smith was appointed solicitor general, before succeeding his friend Edward CARSON as attorney general; in this role he prosecuted the Irish nationalist Roger CASEMENT (1916). In 1919 he was made lord chancellor as Baron Birkenhead. He supported Ulster's right to opt out of home rule and played a key role in negotiating the Anglo-Irish treaty of 1921, which secured independence for most of the island of Ireland, but led to a falling-out with Carson and other staunch unionists in the Conservative Party. As lord chancellor he devoted much time to law reform, being responsible for the Law of Property Act, 1922. He became Viscount Birkenhead in 1921 and earl of Birkenhead and Viscount Furneaux in 1922. He was secretary of state for INDIA, 1924–8.

Smith, Ian. *See* ZIMBABWE.

Smith, John (1938–94), Labour politician; leader of the LABOUR PARTY (1992–4). Educated at Dunoon Academy and Edinburgh University, Smith was an advocate before being elected MP for Lanarkshire in 1970, a seat he held until 1983. He then represented Monklands East until his death. Despite defying the party whip to vote for the Heath government's application to join the European Community (*see* EUROPEAN ECONOMIC COMMUNITY) in 1971, Smith was given a junior post in the Department of Energy after Labour returned to power in 1974. He became secretary of state for trade in 1978, holding the post for the short time before the election of 1979. After the 1979 election Smith was in the shadow cabinet as spokesperson, successively, for trade, energy, employment, and trade and industry. From 1987 until 1992 he was shadow chancellor. In the early 1990s Smith became the likely successor to Neil KINNOCK as leader of the Labour Party; he was duly elected after the 1992 general election, despite facing criticism for the 'tax and spend' nature of his pre-election 'shadow budget'. As leader he began to implement reform in party structures, introducing 'one member, one vote' in the 1993 party elections, and encouraging a larger role for women in the party and Parliament, although he remained committed to the principle of CLAUSE FOUR of the party's constitution. He died of a heart attack in 1994, and was succeeded as leader by Tony BLAIR in July of that year.

FURTHER READING G. Brown and J. Naughtie, *John Smith: Life and Soul of the Party* (1994); C. Bryant (ed.), *John Smith: An Appreciation* (1994); A. McSmith, *John Smith* (1994).

Snowden, Philip (1864–1937), Labour politician. Snowden was born in the Pennine textile village of Cowling near Keighley, in the West Riding of Yorkshire. Nonconformity, especially Wesleyan METHODISM, was a strong influence in the community and on Snowden's life. Educated at elementary school, he hoped to become a schoolmaster, but family circumstances forced him to leave school early and become a clerk and then a civil servant. He was unemployed because of illness in the early 1890s and while recuperating became involved in LIBERAL politics, then joined the INDEPENDENT LABOUR PARTY (ILP) in January 1895. He remained strongly attached to radical Liberal views: opposition to war, support for FREE TRADE, and economical government. He was elected to Cowling School Board in 1895, was editor of the *Keighley Labour Journal*, 1898–1902, and was elected to both the Keighley School Board

and Keighley Town Council in 1899. He joined the National Administrative Council of the ILP in 1898, becoming its chair, 1903–6 and 1917–20, and treasurer, 1920–1. He was also involved in the Labour Church movement, gaining a reputation as a speaker on ethical socialism. In 1905 he married Ethel Annakin, an active member of the ILP, who encouraged him to support women's suffrage (*see* SUFFRAGETTES; SUFFRAGISTS). He stood unsuccessfully in parliamentary elections in Blackburn in 1900 and Wakefield in 1902 before being elected for Blackburn in 1906, which he represented until he was defeated in 1918 owing to his opposition to WORLD WAR I. During the war he attacked the treatment of CONSCIENTIOUS OBJECTORS and from 1917 led the ILP's peace campaign. In 1922 he was re-elected to Parliament for Colne Valley, which he represented until his defeat in 1931, leaving the ILP as it moved leftwards in the early 1920s.

Snowden was CHANCELLOR OF THE EXCHEQUER in the LABOUR governments of 1924 and 1929–31, giving priority to balancing the budget and reducing the national debt while cautiously funding social reform. He played an active role in the Hague conference on German REPARATIONS in 1929. He was unwilling to shift from his cautious policies in the financial crisis of 1931 and strongly influenced the prime minister Ramsay MACDONALD, who was less interested in economic than in international affairs and delegated such matters to the chancellor. Snowden joined MacDonald in the NATIONAL GOVERNMENT in 1931 and in consequence has, like MacDonald, been much vilified in accounts of the episode. He had, however, always been, and continued to be, a critic of MacDonald. After his defeat in the 1931 election he was elevated to the House of LORDS as Viscount Snowden, serving as lord privy seal in the National Government until his resignation in September 1932. He died after a long illness in 1937.

FURTHER READING C. Cross, *Philip Snowden* (1966).

Social and Liberal Democrats. *See* LIBERAL PARTY; SOCIAL DEMOCRATIC PARTY.

social class. Britain in the 20th century, and before, was often described as being exceptionally socially divided compared with other industrialized countries. This was not so, but it was the case that British social divisions were almost universally defined in terms of 'class', rather in terms of wealth or income, race or inherited social position, as in other societies.

Class is a protean concept, well suited to the complexities and shifts over time and place in its uses in British language and culture. There has been a considerable amount of theoretical writing on class since the early 19th century, in which the theories of Karl Marx and Max Weber and their commentators and critics have been prominent. However, the impact of these writings on 20th-century Britain was confined to small groups of intellectuals, although crude notions of class conflict – attributed, not always convincingly, to Marx – were expressed by various left-wing groups throughout the century.

More influential was the official definition of class devised by the registrar general in 1911. This arose from a concern to analyse the fall in the birth-rate at that time (*see* POPULATION) and to assess how justified were contemporary fears that it was falling fastest at the higher social levels. A linear social class model was devised for analysis of the pattern of shifts in the birth rate. This remained in use by government statisticians (for example in interpreting the decennial CENSUS) and by other researchers (e.g. in market research and OPINION POLLS) throughout the century, long outliving its original purpose. It underwent some refinement over time as occupations shifted in their perceived social status and hence in their placing in the classification. The model grouped occupations into five classes. At the time of the census of 1951 the model included the following:

Class 1: professional and similar occupations, e.g. higher civil servants, secretaries and registrars of companies, ministers of religion, lawyers, doctors, professional engineers.

Class 2: 'intermediate' occupations, e.g. farmers, retailers, local-authority officers, pharmacists, teachers.

Class 3: skilled occupations, e.g. coal miners, most factory workers, shop assistants, most clerical workers, actors.

Class 4: semi-skilled occupations, e.g. plumbers' labourers, locomotive firemen, bus conductors, domestic servants, window cleaners.

Class 5: unskilled occupations, e.g. dock labourers, costermongers, watchmen and most labourers.

There was a certain arbitrary quality to some of the classification, for example, that of actors. High levels of UNEMPLOYMENT in the 1920 and 1930s, and again in the 1980s and 1990s (in the later period afflicting highly skilled people, including professionals, as well as the unskilled), suggested the limitations of this approach. Another serious problem was the fact that the registrar general classified British society by household, and hence according to the occupations of heads of household, who were predominantly male (although this predominance diminished towards the end of the century). This classification became increasingly problematic, and was increasingly criticized, in the second half of the century as more married women were in paid work and more daughters living with their parents acquired different qualifications and occupations from theirs. If husband and wife can be assigned different class positions on the basis of their individual occupations, the class position of the household is not clear-cut. Similarly, the lifestyle of families with two wage-earners, and the life chances of their children, may differ significantly from those officially in the same class with only one wage-earner. This is especially true if the one earner is female, since women generally experience lesser returns than men on their formal qualifications, and worse chances of career progression and thus of upward social mobility. Hence the most widely used means of describing British class structure during the century disguised important features of that structure and provided at best a somewhat loose guide to understanding it.

There are no signs that there was significant mobility of individuals between classes through the century. The numbers employed in manual working-class occupations declined as manufacturing industry declined, but this was replaced by a growth of low-paid service occupations (for instance in fast-food restaurants) and by unemployment. More people acquired educational qualifications, including UNIVERSITY degrees, from the late 1980s, but it remains unclear whether this led to upward social mobility.

Distinct from the attempts of government statisticians and academics to devise objective measurements of class structure is the loose, vernacular sense in which 'class' was used in everyday discourse to refer to perceived social differences. This is most evident from the fact that manual workers declined from about 80% of the population on the eve of World War I to about 45% in the 1980s, yet social surveys showed that about two-thirds of the population consistently described themselves as 'working class' throughout the 1980s. Everyday language divided society either into three classes – working, middle and upper – or, more antagonistically, though not militantly so, into two – 'us' and 'them'. These perceptions could be embraced by the same individuals in different contexts, without awareness of inconsistency. Arguably such perceptions were more important in 20th-century British culture than the statistical measurements of class in that they influenced and expressed the ways in which different social groups and individuals behaved towards one another. The use of the term 'class' in relation to these interactions may well have declined at the end of the century, while awareness of social difference did not. When footballers, pop stars and media 'celebrities' were among the wealthiest people in the country and excited popular interest just as the ARISTOCRACY once had, the old terminology of difference seemed

inappropriate. Deference to an old elite, which was in decline from the time of World War I, was replaced by a (perhaps less antagonistic) deference to a new elite.

In fact, we are far from understanding the shifting meanings of class in 20th-century culture, despite much scholarly effort, precisely because they are complex and slippery. The problems are illustrated by examining the relationships of the principal political parties to class. The LABOUR PARTY is often characterized (by some of its own supporters, and by others) as having represented the working class throughout the century. Yet its leaders, especially the five who became prime ministers, consistently represented it as a cross-class party speaking for the nation, while giving closer attention to working-class interests than other parties. The leaders were especially anxious to distance the party from notions of class conflict. This was expressed in the party's first constitution, which equally embraced 'workers by hand or by brain'. The revised constitution of 1995 was even more inclusive, stressing the 'common endeavour' of the entire national 'community' (*see* CLAUSE FOUR). Certainly Labour never won a secure majority without attracting significant numbers of middle-class votes. By the end of the century the decline of manufacturing industry meant that its most dependable core voters were white-collar public-sector workers.

Similarly the CONSERVATIVE PARTY was seen as, and in many respects was, the party of the middle and upper classes, but it assiduously (with some lapses) represented itself as a 'one-nation' party, and was always dependent upon working-class voters for a majority, since they were a majority of the population. Its leaders in the later part of the century strove to emphasize the disappearance of class. The sociological analysis of voting ('psephology') in the 1960s and 1970s made much of class as the primary indicator of voting preferences, but it became increasingly clear that it was not. In the 1980s only 52% of the electorate voted as might be expected from their class position (i.e. middle-class people voting Conservative); 56% did so in 1992, fewer than 50% in 1997.

Whether or not the difference is defined as one of class, one thing that is clear in this complex area of social difference is that throughout the century socio-economic position decisively influenced such essential aspects of life as standards of health, education and employment, and life expectancy itself. The average years of post-16 education received by the children of professional fathers was 3 in 1974, 2.2 in 1990; the children of unskilled fathers received 0.3 at both dates. In 1974 long-standing illness was reported by 8% of professional men and 9% of professional women; unskilled men and women both reported 23%. In 1994 the equivalent percentages were 11% and 15% for professional men and women respectively; 23% and 31% for unskilled men and women. There were equivalent social gulfs in life expectancy (*see* OLD AGE AND AGEING), similarly stable over time. They were, if anything, greater earlier in the century.

FURTHER READING D. Cannadine, *Class in Britain* (1998); R. McKibbin, *Classes and Cultures: England 1918–1951* (1998); W.G. Runciman, *A Treatise on Social Theory*, Vol. 3 (1997).

social contract (1973–6). *See* TRADE UNIONS.

Social Democratic and Labour Party (SDLP),

NORTHERN IRELAND political party founded in 1970 to provide an effective constitutional voice for the Roman Catholic minority for the first time since the partition of IRELAND in 1922. It emerged from the civil-rights movement of the 1960s and was a coalition of old IRISH NATIONAL PARTY members, Republican socialists and civil-rights campaigners, above all representing the growing Catholic middle class. Its first leader was Gerry FITT, who had a strong association with the Belfast labour movement, and was an SDLP MP at Westminster, 1970–9. The SDLP accepted the role of main opposition party to the Unionists at Stormont (the Northern Ireland parliament) until

1971, when they boycotted Stormont over the issue of internment. They joined the power-sharing executive of 1973–4 but suffered from its rapid collapse. In 1979 John HUME was elected leader. He was an SDLP MP at Westminster from 1983 to the end of the century. He developed good contacts with politicians in Dublin, Brussels, elsewhere in Europe and in the USA. The party's claim to represent Catholics in Ulster was challenged always by SINN FÉIN, but the SDLP provided an alternative, mediating, voice that was valuable throughout the attempts to seek a settlement in Northern Ireland, not least in negotiating the Good Friday Agreement of 1998 and the establishment of the Northern Ireland Assembly in 1999. Seamus Mallon, Hume's deputy and a Westminster MP since 1986, became deputy first minister in the new power-sharing executive.

Social Democratic Party (SDP), centre-left political party founded in 1981 largely as a breakaway from the Labour Party. The SDP's founders felt that Labour had become too strongly influenced by the left, which had formed an unprecedentedly close alliance with the TRADE UNIONS.

The SDP's first leader was Roy JENKINS. Jenkins had long been on the liberal, revisionist wing of the Labour Party, and had been an ally of Anthony CROSLAND and a supporter of Hugh GAITSKELL, although – unlike Gaitskell and much of the left of the party – Jenkins was a strong supporter of Britain's entry into the EUROPEAN ECONOMIC COMMUNITY. Since 1976 he had been remote from British politics, serving as president of the European Commission. In 1979 he gave an influential Dimbleby Lecture on BBC television arguing that the Labour Party no longer offered a relevant vehicle for reformist politics in Britain. At the time there was little influential support for a break with the Labour Party.

However, following Labour's defeat in the 1979 general election three Labour MPs – William Rodgers (who had been a devoted supporter of Gaitskell and then of Jenkins), Shirley Williams (a former cabinet minister) and David OWEN (foreign secretary 1978–9) – agreed to work together to oppose the left, becoming known as the 'gang of four' once joined by Jenkins. Led by Williams, they campaigned with a stridency that matched their leading opponent on the left of the parliamentary party, Tony BENN. A crucial issue was the role of the trade-union 'block vote' (*see* LABOUR PARTY) in party-conference decision making. The 'gang of four' sought unsuccessfully to replace the block vote with 'one member, one vote'. A special party conference at Wembley in January 1981 granted the unions the major say in a new system of electing the parliamentary party leadership.

This led Williams, Rodgers and Owen to make the 'Limehouse declaration' (from Owen's home in Limehouse, London), signalling support for Jenkins. Initially they envisaged only a campaign for social democracy within the Labour Party, but within a few weeks they set up the new party. They were widely described as 'breaking the mould' of British politics, though the origin of the phrase is uncertain. There was a certain rivalry for leadership between Williams and Jenkins. Jenkins emerged as the leader and consolidated his position by standing in the next by-election, in Warrington in northwest England in July 1981, which he came close to winning the seat from Labour. Jenkins then negotiated an alliance with the LIBERAL PARTY. The alliance was shown in opinion polls to have more support than either the Labour or CONSERVATIVE parties, and reached its peak in November 1981 when Williams achieved a sensational by-election victory over the Conservatives at Crosby in Lancashire. In the House of COMMONS she joined 26 MPs who had defected from Labour and one defector from the Conservatives, together with eleven Liberals.

In the 1983 general election (dominated by the FALKLANDS War) the alliance polled 25.4% of the vote, substantially weakening the Labour vote, but gained only 23 MPs, only six of them members of the SDP. It gained, and was to gain, notably little support in SCOTLAND. Jenkins resigned as

leader and was replaced by Owen, who was more distant from the Liberals and determined to maintain a distinctive profile for the SDP. Increasingly he appeared to lean to the right, especially on defence issues (he took a hard line in favour of Britain's independent NUCLEAR deterrent), while the Liberal leader David STEEL inclined to the left. In the 1987 election the alliance polled 22.6% and 22 MPs were elected, again making inroads into Labour's vote. Steel proposed a full merger of the two parties but was rejected by Owen. Williams supported a merger. A proposal to negotiate with the Liberals was narrowly accepted in a ballot of members in August 1987. Owen resigned the leadership and Robert Maclennan (one of only two SDP MPs to vote in support of the merger) was elected leader unopposed. Owen and his supporters refused to accept proposals for a merged party. In 1988 the party was again balloted and supported the merger. On 3 March 1988 the SDP was formally subsumed into the new Social and Liberal Democrats. Owen led a rump, still calling itself the SDP, for a few years. In its short life the SDP helped to shock the Labour Party into a process of reform (*see* KINNOCK, NEIL) and to keep Margaret THATCHER's Conservatives in power with secure majorities through the 1980s.

FURTHER READING H. Stephenson, *Claret and Chips: The Rise of the SDP* (1982).

socialism in Britain. *See* COMMUNIST PARTY OF GREAT BRITAIN; FABIAN SOCIETY; INDEPENDENT LABOUR PARTY; LABOUR PARTY.

social security. *See* OLD-AGE PENSIONS; POOR LAW; UNEMPLOYMENT; WELFARE STATE.

Somme, battle of the (1 July–18 November 1916), major Allied offensive on the Western Front in WORLD WAR I. After a week's intensive bombardment the British 4th Army and the French 6th Army launched the first of a series of attacks on German positions along a 32-km (20-mile) front north of the river Somme between the towns of

Albert and Peronne. The intention was to relieve pressure on the French at Verdun. There were nearly 60,000 British casualties (including 20,000 killed) on the first day of battle (1 July). In the following 20 weeks the Allies advanced about 16 km (10 miles) in rain and mud and lost about 600,000 casualties. TANKS were used for the first time by the British on 15 September, but with no great success in muddy, marshy ground. It was not obvious that any advantage over the Germans was gained, although German military historians later argued that the Somme and Verdun fatally weakened their fighting forces. The Somme may have been the turning point of the war in France, but at the time it was seen as a failure. It further weakened ASQUITH's government and helped to bring about the succession of David LLOYD GEORGE in December 1916.

FURTHER READING M. Brown, *The Imperial War Museum Book of the Somme* (1997).

South Africa. In 1910, just under a decade after the conclusion of the BOER WAR, the four colonies of South Africa – the Cape Colony, Natal, the Orange River Colony and Transvaal – were amalgamated into the Union of South Africa following the British Parliament's passage of the South Africa Act in 1909. The act incorporated constitutional proposals drawn up by a convention composed of white representatives of the colonies and dominated by Alfred MILNER and the Boer leaders Jan Smuts (1870–1950) and Louis Botha. The act sought to appease Afrikaner interests while maintaining British imperial control, making both English and Afrikaans the country's official languages. While it incorporated protection of the existing non-racially based franchise in the Cape, a colour bar was established for membership of the new South African parliament – despite pleas to the British Parliament from a delegation of prominent black South Africans.

As a self-governing dominion, South Africa was drawn into WORLD WAR I following the British declaration of war. On behalf of the British, a South African army under Jan Smuts took control of the German territory of South West Africa and fought in Tanganyika. While this alienated a section of South Africa's Afrikaner population and prompted a minor armed rebellion, Smuts's wartime career brought him into the international sphere of politics and involvement with the creation of the LEAGUE OF NATIONS at the Paris Peace Conference. Smuts was prime minister of South Africa from 1919 to 1924.

The interwar period saw the gradual establishment of a system of racial segregation in South Africa, maintaining white dominance by restricting African land ownership and freedom of movement, and by eroding existing voting rights. At the same time British influence over South African affairs was weakened by the increasing independence allowed to the dominions, made concrete by the Statute of Westminster in 1931 (*see* IMPERIAL CONFERENCES). The 1930s saw the increasing popularity of Afrikaner nationalism, which manifested itself in the establishment of Afrikaner cultural organizations and strict opposition to racial unity.

South African involvement in WORLD WAR II further heightened tension with Afrikaner nationalists, some of whom gave their support to the Axis powers (even establishing a small militant organization, the 'Oxwagon Sentinel'). But many Afrikaners chose to join the South African forces (over 50% of the South African forces during the war were Afrikaners); they fought in East Africa, North Africa and Italy. South Africa was also a significant source of minerals, manufactured goods and foodstuffs for the Allied cause; and, with Axis control of the Mediterranean, the Cape of Good Hope became strategically important. Smuts, who became premier for a second time in 1939, was again prominent on the world stage during and immediately after the war, playing an important role in the establishment of the UNITED NATIONS in 1945. He was subject to criticism from nationalist circles in South Africa, and lost power when the National Party under D.F. Malan won the 1948 election.

Following the 1948 election legislation began to be passed that put in place the system of racial segregation known as apartheid, which envisaged the completely 'separate development' for the different races of South Africa. Much of this legislation was passed during the 1950s, which also saw the consolidation of Afrikaner nationalist power. The same decade also saw the emergence of mass opposition to white dominance, led by the African National Congress (ANC). By the end of the 1950s the South African government was responding to opposition in increasingly coercive and authoritarian ways. Political opponents began to leave the country, many of whom found themselves in Britain, where they helped to establish the beginnings of British opposition to apartheid.

In February 1960 prime minister Harold MAC-MILLAN, while touring Africa, spoke in Cape Town of a 'wind of change' sweeping across the continent, a speech seen as a landmark in the course of DECOLONIZATION. When South African police shot and killed 67 protesters at Sharpeville the following month, South Africa received worldwide condemnation. In Britain the ANTI-APARTHEID MOVEMENT coordinated campaigns against the purchase of South African goods and cultural contacts (*see also* HUDDLESTON, TREVOR). Sporting events became a focus for protest, particularly cricket and rugby. In 1960 a referendum voted in favour of South Africa becoming a republic; when the government put the case to the 1961 Commonwealth Conference for South Africa staying in the Commonwealth as a republic, other members attacked the country's racial policies and South Africa withdrew from the organization. Despite voicing opposition to apartheid, successive British governments in the 1960s and 1970s did little to put pressure on the South African government, and Britain remained one of the most important investors in the country (although the USA had become South Africa's largest trading partner, Britain still provided 40% of all foreign investment in 1978). The most vocal opponent of economic sanctions against South Africa was Margaret THATCHER, who fought hard during the 1980s against attempts by the Commonwealth to take joint action against South Africa. Nevertheless, economic sanctions imposed by various countries, notably the USA, combined with the withdrawal of many multinational corporations from South Africa, did play an important part in bringing about constitutional change.

In the 1990s the dismantling of apartheid, the creation of a new multiracial constitution and the fully democratic election of an ANC government with Nelson Mandela as president (1994) saw South Africa return to membership of the international organizations it had left, or been expelled from, in the previous decades. Sporting links were re-established and economic relations began to be normalized (although British trade was now regulated through agreements between South Africa and the EUROPEAN UNION). Within South Africa efforts were made to begin reconstructing the country. As part of the process, the South African government set up a Truth and Reconciliation Commission, which aimed to allow South Africa to come to terms with its recent past.

FURTHER READING W. Beinart, *Twentieth Century South Africa* (1994); S. Dubow, *The African National Congress* (2000); L. Thompson, *A History of South Africa* (1995).

Spanish Civil War (1936–9), conflict between the centre-left Republican government of Spain and right-wing Nationalist rebels, largely consisting of fascists, monarchists and Catholic conservatives.

Political instability had been endemic in Spain for decades. During much of the 1920s Spain was ruled by a military dictatorship, which was eventually dismissed by King Alfonso XIII in 1930. Following the elections of 1931 the Republican Party came to power, the king went into exile and a republic was proclaimed. Over the next few years the centre-right government was dogged by political violence from both right (monarchists and Falangists – Spanish fascists) and left (communists and anarchists). In the elections of May 1936 a centre-left POPULAR FRONT government came to power, consisting of Republicans, socialists, syndicalists, anarchists, Marxists and communists. Ten weeks later army revolts broke out in several garrisons, starting in Spanish Morocco, and a civil war broke out in which General Francisco Franco emerged as leader of the Nationalist rebels. The Nationalists were supported by 'volunteers' from Nazi Germany and fascist Italy, who gained useful experience for the coming international war; the Republicans received much more modest support from the Soviet Union.

The attitudes of Britain and other countries to events in Spain were conditioned by the international situation. The NATIONAL GOVERNMENT, supported by most Conservatives, was opposed to the Spanish government, which they regarded as too left wing, but it feared escalation into an international war. However, Winston CHURCHILL and a few others who were hostile to APPEASEMENT believed that a pro-Axis Spain would threaten British interests in the Mediterranean and should be opposed. In August 1936 a non-intervention agreement (NIA) was signed by 27 countries and a non-intervention committee (NIC) was established, based in London, to monitor outside interference in Spain. However, it was powerless to prevent intervention by Germany and Italy in support of the Nationalists and of the Soviet Union in support of the Republicans.

Many on the British left, initially mostly intellectuals, supported the Republicans against Franco; this support became increasingly passionate as the war went on. The LABOUR PARTY and the TRADE UNIONS were at first cautious, fearing that support for the Republicans would strengthen the credibility of the COMMUNIST PARTY OF GREAT BRITAIN (CPGB), which followed the Soviet line. But as it became obvious that non-intervention was in reality assisting the Nationalists, in the autumn of 1937 both the TRADES UNION CONGRESS and the Labour Party, though still opposing direct intervention in Spain, pressured the British government to lift its embargo on arms to the Republican forces, without success. Eye-witness reports by George ORWELL

and other writers and politicians, and horror at the destructive bombing by German bombers of the Condor Legion of the Basque capital of Guernica in April 1937, moved many to action. Sections of the labour movement provided humanitarian aid such as food, clothing and medical relief. Mineworkers contributed over £55,000 for orphaned children of Asturian miners. An adoption scheme funded from a public appeal brought over 4000 Basque orphans to Britain by the end of the war.

The CPGB obeyed the Comintern's call to form an international contingent to fight with the Republicans. Owing to their efforts about 2000 British men and women fought in the International Brigades in Spain between 1936 and 1939, most of them young and idealistic, from a variety of backgrounds. Some served as ambulance and truck drivers, though most were engaged in active combat, despite limited military training. Of approximately 2000 British combatants, over 500 were killed and 1200 wounded. But increasingly events in Spain were overshadowed by those elsewhere. By the winter of 1938 the Republicans were all but defeated, and in February 1939 the British and French governments recognized Franco and his government as rulers of Spain. The civil war was formally ended on 1 April 1939.

FURTHER READING T. Buchanan, *The Spanish Civil War and the British Labour Movement* (1991); J. Edwards, *The British Government and the Spanish Civil War, 1936–39* (1979); H. Thomas, *The Spanish Civil War* (1971).

Spark, Muriel (Sarah) (1918–), novelist. Born Muriel Camberg in Edinburgh of Jewish-Scottish parents, she was educated at James Gillespie's High School for Girls in Edinburgh, which inspired the setting for her best-known novel, *The Prime of Miss Jean Brodie* (1961), a rather chilling account of the influence of a schoolmistress over a group of favoured pupils. She was married briefly to Sydney Spark, with whom she travelled to Southern Rhodesia (now ZIMBABWE), which became the setting for a number of her short stories. She returned to Britain and during World War II worked for the intelligence service. She then became an editor and biographer, editing *Poetry Review* for the Poetry Society, 1947–9. The problems of writing biography and autobiography form the theme of *Loitering with Intent* (1981). In 1951 she won the *Observer* short-story competition. In 1954 she became a Roman Catholic.

Spark's first published novel, *The Comforters* (1957), was rapidly followed by *Memento Mori* (1959), a comic and characteristically macabre story of old age; *The Ballad of Peckham Rye* (1960), a strange tale of the underworld; *The Prime of Miss Jean Brodie* (1961); *The Girls of Slender Means* (1963), a tragi-comedy set in a Kensington hostel in 1945; and *The Mandelbaum Gate* (1965), a long and unsatirical novel about Palestine, which was awarded the James Tait Black Memorial Prize. Her novels after this were more of a type: short, crisply written, sharply observant, wholly unromantic about everyday existence and often unsettling in their bizarre twists. They included: *The Public Image* (1968); *The Driver's Seat* (1970), about a woman consumed by a death wish; *The Abbess of Crewe* (1974), a satirical fantasy about ecclesiastical and other forms of politics; and *The Take Over* (1976), set in Italy, where she then lived and remained thereafter. Her *Collected Poems* and *Collected Plays* were published in 1967. A further volume of poems appeared in 1982. Her later novels included *A Far Cry from Kensington* (1988) and *Symposium* (1990). A volume of autobiography, *Curriculum Vitae*, appeared in 1992.

FURTHER READING A. Bold, *Muriel Spark* (1986).

Spencer, Stanley (1891–1959), artist. Spencer was born in Cookham, Berkshire, where he lived for most of his life. The village played a large part in his paintings. He studied at the Slade School of Fine Art in London from 1908 to 1912, winning a prize for composition in his final year. In World War I he served in the army. He was appointed an official war artist in 1918, but his experiences during the war found their most memorable expression a decade later in a series of murals he painted for the Sandham Memorial Chapel at Burghclere in Hampshire (1927–32), built to commemorate a soldier who had died of illness during the war. The mural concentrated realistically on the everyday life of the soldier during the war rather than in battle. By this time Spencer was increasingly well known, above all thanks to the exhibition in 1927 of his *The Resurrection: Cookham* (Tate Gallery, 1924–6), which was hugely celebrated. His somewhat visionary realism made him more popularly accessible than many of his contemporaries, though the eroticism of some of his paintings alienated sections of public opinion and incurred the official disapproval of the Royal Academy.

His personal life underwent some turmoil in the 1930s. He divorced his first wife Hilda Carlin (a highly talented artist), and married Patricia Preece. This marriage was a disaster and Hilda continued to play a large part in his life. He also painted a number of self-portraits at this time and later. He was again an official war artist in World War II when he again concentrated on life away from battle. His series of canvases showing shipbuilding on the Clyde, around Glasgow, captured an important dimension of the war effort and were a popular success. After the war he was acknowledged as Britain's senior artist and he was knighted in 1958.

FURTHER READING D. Robinson, *Stanley Spencer* (1990).

sport. Many different sports played an important role in the LEISURE activities of British people throughout the century, whether as participants or spectators, or both. The relative popularity of different sports remained fairly stable through the century, with angling (almost wholly a participation sport) the most popular. Also consistently attracting large followings were: swimming (mainly from participants), athletics (mainly from spectators), association football ('soccer' – attracting both participants and spectators), rugby football (both rugby union, which had a mainly middle- and upper-class following, except in Wales where the appeal was more comprehensive; and working-class, mainly northern English, rugby league), cricket, boxing, horse-racing, cricket, bowls, golf, tennis, rowing, badminton, squash, netball (wholly female), basketball, hockey and snooker.

There were significant regional, social and gender differences in the appeal of different sports. Shooting remained largely the preserve of the possessors of old and new wealth. Cricket was always more popular in England than elsewhere in Britain, and with men rather than women. It appealed to all classes, but for much of the century the classes were not equally treated within it. There was a strict distinction between 'gentlemen', who could afford to play without pay, and paid professionals, called 'players'. 'Players' tended to perform the sweaty, unglamorous work of bowling, while most 'gentlemen' were batsmen; 'gentlemen' were addressed as 'Mr', 'players' by their surnames. The two groups often had separate dressing rooms, the 'players'' accommodation being inferior. Only 'gentlemen' could captain teams, until the deleterious effect of this became obvious. A professional (Len Hutton) first captained the England side in 1952, and the categories of gentlemen and players and the more obvious forms of discrimination that accompanied them were abolished only in 1962.

Boxing also had amateur and professional divisions and separate championships, but many amateurs were young working-class men often trained in clubs funded by middle- and upper-class patrons, and they sometimes later moved into the parallel professional strand of the sport. However, black boxers were excluded from fighting for any British title until 1948. Randolph Turpin, who was black, became British middleweight champion in 1951. A succession of successful black British fighters followed, to the end of the century. Throughout the century there were concerns voiced about the physical dangers of the sport to the participants.

Horse-racing, throughout the century, similarly brought together wealthy and plebeian participants, spectators and gamblers. Other sports were seen as essentially the preserve of 'gentlemen' for much of the century and payment for participation was forbidden and despised. Amateurism (playing for the love of sport alone) was valued until it became clear that many 'amateurs' (or 'shamateurs' as they were called) were accepting illicit payments. As the standards of international sport became more demanding, often driven by nations that did not observe such social conventions, few first-class sports people could afford the time to train and to play at the highest level without pay. In 1968 the Wimbledon tennis championship became open to professionals for the first time, though in Britain tennis remained a primarily middle-class sport and one in which the country went on being notably unsuccessful in international competition, despite hosting one of the premier international championships at Wimbledon. The pressure to open Wimbledon to professional players came primarily from abroad; it was feared that outstanding players would not attend the championship if they could not compete for substantial prize money.

The Football Association amateur cup was competed for in 1974 for the last time (having started in 1894). Soccer attracted a large working-class following from its earliest days, initially mainly in the north. Towards the end of the century there was increasing commercialization of the sport, leading to increasing ticket prices for spectators (and improved conditions in the previously primitive grounds) and huge salaries for star players. At the same time the game came into vogue among people who regarded themselves as fashionable. In 1982 track and field athletes were allowed to accept fees, and in 1992 even the most militantly amateur sport, rugby union, allowed payment of players. With professionalization came increasing commercialization of all sports. This was stimulated by the mass audience for sport, and hence for advertising, shown on television. Business firms believed that associating their names with popular sports was an effective form of promotion. Commercial sponsorship of sport was worth £2.5 million in 1971, and more than £200 million in 1992.

There were national and regional and well as social differences within and between sports. Golf in England was a middle-class sport, associated with social exclusiveness and even racism: still at the end of the century some clubs excluded Jews and black and Asian people and did not allow female members equal access to facilities with males. In contrast, in Scotland it was a socially inclusive, popular sport. In both countries it was an unpaid leisure pursuit for most participants, though at international level it became, like other sports, highly professionalized and highly paid.

Association football was played throughout Britain, but England, Scotland, Wales and NORTH-ERN IRELAND fielded separate teams in international competitions. Matches between them became opportunities, especially later in the century, to express mutual hostility, especially of the smaller nations towards England, while international matches were an opportunity for some followers of the England team to exhibit aggression towards most other nations. English clubs were banned from European competition between 1986 and 1990, following the 1985 European Cup final in Brussels when English fans became involved in fighting that led to 39, mostly Italian, spectators being crushed to death.

Cricket played a different role, initially cementing ties within the EMPIRE (it was not seriously played outside the area of the British diaspora), then providing a field for the playing out of tensions: the superiority of the West Indian team over England for a long period until its decline at the end of the century gave West Indian immigrants to Britain opportunities to express cultural pride in an often hostile environment. Sport became more and more political as the century went on. It was the fascist governments in Germany and Italy in the 1930s that first promoted the idea

that sport was the business of the state and deliberately sought the prestige and promotion of their ideologies that success in international sport could bring.

In Britain sport was seen as an individual, voluntary activity, but the state increasingly became involved. From 1907 local authorities were allowed to spend their income on providing sporting facilities in public parks. At the beginning of the century physical exercise was also encouraged in state schools; it had always played a big role in the activities of private schools. Anxiety about the physical condition of the nation during the UNEMPLOYMENT of the inter-war years led to the Physical Training Act, 1937, which funded the training of coaches in athletics. The 1944 Education Act (*see* EDUCATION) for the first time made it compulsory for state schools to include sport in the curriculum, but the British performance in international sport was dismal in the post-war years. In 1965 the Labour government set up the Sports Council, with government funding, to encourage participation in sport and to improve British performance. As a result the 27 sports centres in existence in 1972 became 770 by 1981. They did not revolutionize British sporting performance, though levels of popular interest and of participation in sporting activity remained high.

FURTHER READING T. Mason, *Sport in Britain: A Social History* (1989).

standards of living. Sustained economic growth in Britain through most of the 20th century led to a great increase in average real incomes. This enabled people to buy more and better food, and resulted in access to better HOUSING, EDUCATION, LEISURE and health (*see* MEDICINE), which constituted a significant overall rise in living standards. As a result diseases associated with severe poverty and malnutrition – such as rickets, which was common at the beginning of the century – almost disappeared. But there remained great differences between the richest and poorest households.

It is difficult to measure changes in living

standards precisely over time because expectations, and also the goods available, change – for example, goods that were commonplace at the end of the century, such as televisions and washing machines, were not available at the beginning. One way to measure changes in the standard of living is to compare the monetary value of national income per head of population, adjusted for changes in prices over time. Using constant 1990 prices, national income per head rose from about £2000 in 1900, to £2500 in 1930, £4000 in 1960 and £9000 in 1990. By this measure the average Briton was over four times better off at the end of the century than at the beginning. This does not mean that the spending power available to all individuals has increased at the same rate. The average weekly earnings of an adult male manual worker in 1900 were £1.8s (£1.40), which equals £63 in 1990 prices, whereas the average male manual worker in 1990 actually earned £214 per week. Women's earnings averaged between half to two-thirds of the male average throughout the century. Until 1940, however, manual workers paid no direct (i.e. income) tax, but thereafter almost all earners had to pay tax on their incomes, which reduced their spending power. The post-tax income of an average male manual worker in 1990 was about £160, two and a half times greater than in 1900. However, some of that taxation went to fund a growing range of services (e.g. for health, education, housing and improved roads and transport) that contributed to improved general living standards, including those of the poorest who paid little or no tax. A significant indicator of the real improvement in living standards over the century was the great increase in life expectancy (*see* OLD AGE AND AGEING and POPULATION).

But higher personal and government incomes are not the only influences upon living standards. Falling family size made an important contribution to increasing the disposable incomes of households, in view of the fact that Rowntree's POVERTY survey in 1900 found that large family size was the second greatest cause of poverty. Smaller family size also enabled more women to engage in paid work and to contribute to family income. But not everyone shared equally in the improvement in living standards, and large differences in economic resources and living standards continued. WELFARE STATE provision prevented the old, the sick and the unemployed from becoming relatively even poorer, but it did not make them rich or even provide for much more than basic subsistence.

The poorer half of the population in 1949 received about one-quarter of total after-tax income. At the end of the century the proportion they received was almost exactly the same. To take a different form of measurement: in 1992, 1% of the UK population owned 18% of all marketable wealth, while 10% owned 49% of wealth; this was an improvement from 1923, when 10% of the population of England and Wales owned 89% of marketable wealth. Even where it can be shown unambiguously that living standards rose in terms of material possessions and health, it does not necessarily follow that they rose in terms of greater personal feelings of well-being, which is still more elusive to measure than material conditions.

FURTHER READING J. Burnett, *Plenty and Want* (3rd edn, 1989); G. Routh, *Occupation and Pay in Great Britain, 1906–79* (2nd edn, 1980).

Statute of Westminster (1931). *See* IMPERIAL CONFERENCES.

Steel, David (1938–), Liberal politician; leader of the LIBERAL PARTY (1976–88). The son of a clergyman, Steel was educated in Scotland and Kenya before attending Edinburgh University. He entered Parliament as MP for Roxburgh, Selkirk and Peebles in 1965, becoming the youngest MP at that time. After 1983 he became MP for Tweeddale, Ettrick and Lauderdale. As a private member he sponsored the ABORTION Act (1967), which legalized abortion up to the 28th week of pregnancy. After a period as chief whip to the Liberal Party, Steel became party leader in 1976 following the resignation of Jeremy THORPE. As leader he negotiated the 'Lib-Lab pact', giving parliamentary support to the minority Labour government of James CALLAGHAN in 1977–8.

During the 1980s Steel helped to engineer the electoral alliance with the SOCIAL DEMOCRATIC PARTY, but his uneasy relationship with the SDP leader David OWEN contributed to the collapse of the alliance after the 1987 election. The parties merged in 1988 to form the Social and Liberal Democrat Party, but Steel decided not to stand as leader; the post went to Paddy ASHDOWN. Steel left the House of COMMONS in 1997 when he became a life peer, Baron Steel of Aikwood. In 1999 he was elected as a Liberal Democrat member of the newly created Scottish Parliament.

Outside Parliament, Steel spent a number of years working as a broadcaster and journalist, while he held a number of important posts in extra-parliamentary pressure groups, being president of the ANTI-APARTHEID MOVEMENT from 1966 to 1969 and a leading member of the countryside movement from 1995.

FURTHER READING D. Steel, *Against Goliath: David Steel's Story* (1991).

steel industry. In 1900 Britain ranked third among the world's steel producers, having been first two decades earlier. The USA produced 36% of the world's tonnage, Germany 23% and Britain 18%. By 1990 Britain ranked tenth. The industry had played a major role in British industrialization in the 19th century. It was specialized by region, and business units were often small. Pressure of international competition, exacerbated by falling world demand in the interwar years, led to the abandonment of FREE TRADE in the industry in 1932 and the introduction of a 33.3% TARIFF on imports, by value. In return the industry committed itself to rationalization within the framework of a new central organization of firms, the British Iron and Steel Federation (BISF). Mergers, concentration of production, plant closures and much new construction were carried through before the outbreak of WORLD WAR II. But not all firms cooperated and

many older, unreconstructed companies survived. During the war plans were made for more far-reaching reconstruction after the war. A series of development plans were implemented between 1945 and the mid-1960s, though reconstruction was less thorough than might have been desirable since in this period international demand rose, the British industry gained from the absence of German and Japanese competition, and production rose even where there had been little change. British output grew, but production was less efficient than that of competitors.

The industry was nationalized in 1951 (following the Iron and Steel Act, 1949; *see* NATIONALIZATION), then denationalized in 1953 by the incoming CONSERVATIVE government, though leaving 'an adequate measure of public supervision' to the Iron and Steel Board. At the end of the 1950s trade recession and revived competition checked increasing output. By 1964 the industry was producing 26.6 million tonnes, twice as much as in any pre-war year and over five times the output of 1900, but its annual growth rate of 2.5% in 1950–69 compared with 6.4% in the EUROPEAN ECONOMIC COMMUNITY and 34% in Japan. In 1967 the 14 major companies (those producing over 500,000 tonnes annually) were renationalized under the title of the British Steel Corporation (BSC). The remaining firms, producing over 2 million tonnes a year but generally in small works, remained in private ownership. Over the next few years the private sector grew more rapidly than the public sector, with which it had some collaboration. It was planned that BSC would progress towards fewer, bigger, better located works. Instead production shrank. By 1980 for the first time Britain was a net importer of steel. The workforce fell from 257,000 in 1967 to 47,000 by 1990; production fell from 23.3 to 17 million tonnes per year in the same period. BSC was privatized in 1988. For a while it made large profits, but it fell into deficit in the early 1990s. The industry was struggling at the end of the century.

FURTHER READING D.L. Burn, *The Economic*

History of Steel Making, 1867–1939 (1961);
D.L. Burn, *The Steel Industry, 1939–59* (1961);
J. Vaizey, *The History of British Steel* (1974).

Stopes, Marie (Charlotte Carmichael) (1880–1958), sex reformer and advocate of BIRTH CONTROL. Stopes became notorious following the publication of her book *Married Love* (1918), in which she argued that respectable married women could and would enjoy sexual pleasure provided that the husband 'wooed' his wife with soft words and gentle caresses each and every time sexual congress took place.

Stopes's own mother had been a feminist, and a Shakespeare scholar. She had supported the feminist rejection of 'conjugal rights', that is the legally supported right of the husband to have sexual intercourse with his wife; and, like many women of the late Victorian period, she herself did not enjoy sex, and appears to have rejected her husband's advances except for the purposes of reproduction.

Her daughter Marie inspired the generation that followed World War I by incorporating the rejection of conjugal rights into an argument that women could feel sexual pleasure. She claimed that women's sexual desire followed a monthly cycle, thus giving a scientific stamp to women's desire for sex at times determined by themselves.

Stopes's writing drew heavily on her own experience. In 1911 she married Reginald Ruggles Gates, but in 1914 she filed a nullity petition, alleging that her marriage had not been consummated. She claimed that her sexual ignorance had been so absolute that she had not realized anything was amiss until she failed to become pregnant. Historians have argued as to whether this was true or an elaborate tale designed to obtain a divorce on the only grounds available to her. Whatever the answer to this question, the thousands of letters people sent to Stopes asking for advice and reassurance revealed that basic sexual ignorance was not unusual. Stopes was socially conservative, supporting EUGENICS and rejecting ABORTION or support for unmarried mothers. However, her success was in part due to this very conservatism, which enabled her to reach a 'respectable' mass audience, which was unable to cope with the ideas of more radical sex reformers.

Birth control made this relaxation of women's sexual attitudes possible, and *Wise Parenthood*, Stopes's first slim volume on birth control, came out only a few months after *Married Love* in 1918. She had married again that same year and in 1921, following her second husband's suggestion, she set up a birth-control clinic intended to help working-class women prevent unwanted pregnancies. From then on she worked tirelessly to promote birth control. Although Stopes probably contributed more than any single individual to this cause, her Achilles heel was her inability to work with other birth-control supporters on an equal basis: as provision of birth control became more accepted, her belief in her own importance led her to fall out with others in the emerging organizations, and historians have found it almost as hard to accept her emotional and messianic personality as did those who tried to work with her. Yet it was because she was an extraordinarily forceful, contradictory and intense woman that she contributed so substantially to changing sexual mores and extending women's access to birth control.

FURTHER READING R. Hall, *Marie Stopes: A Biography* (1977); R. Hall, *Dear Dr Stopes: Sex in the 1920s* (1978); J. Rose, *Marie Stopes and the Sexual Revolution* (1992).

stop-go, label given to the economic policy regime of the period 1951–67. First Conservative, then Labour governments responded to economic problems (typically relating to BALANCE OF PAYMENTS) by taking action designed either to expand or to contract the economy, using both fiscal and monetary measures to 'fine tune' it.

Fiscal policies typically entailed changes in the rates of both income and expenditure taxes and in levels of government expenditure, with the purpose of either increasing effective demand in the economy (thus initiating a 'go' phase) or of reducing effective demand (initiating a 'stop' phase). Fiscal policies were supported by a range of monetary policies: in order to contract the economy, the government could raise interest rates; increase the amount of money that clearing banks had to keep in reserve, thus reducing their ability to lend; restrict new capital issues or building-society lending; or introduce new hire-purchase controls. This last measure was attractive to the Treasury and to the chancellors of the exchequer at this time, because hire purchase was popular in the expanding consumer economy; controlling hire purchase directly controlled consumption without damaging the economy in the long-term, especially since so many consumer items purchased in this way were imports.

Some economists have argued that 'stop-go' was harmful to the British economy because it created an unstable environment that was detrimental to the long-term growth of the economy. Politicians appeared to be manipulating the economy, especially in the run-up to GENERAL ELECTIONS, and placing short-term political considerations above the long-term good of the economy. This argument was put forward by Harold WILSON in the 1964 election campaign, though his Labour government was unable to restrain the 'stop-go' cycle until 1967, not least owing to its anxiety to win the election of 1966 and to escape from the small majority achieved in 1964. Labour criticisms were later supported by some economists and economic historians, who believed that the long-term structural problems of the economy, in particular the over-reliance on imports, were overlooked. It was argued that the alternation of expansion and contraction undermined the confidence of businessmen and made them wary of long-term investment, planning and innovation. The truth of this is uncertain. Others have argued that, in contrast to earlier periods, 'stop-go' took place within a stable policy environment in which it was clear that governments were committed to full employment, a stable exchange rate and economic growth. Busi-

ness investment was high compared with the period before 1930. However, it is impossible to know whether investment would have been even higher in the absence of 'stop-go'. Other West European economies at this time suffered even greater fluctuations than the British, but also achieved higher growth rates over the long-run. Hence, whatever the short-term ill-effects of 'stop-go', it is unlikely that it was a major cause of Britain's relative economic decline in this period. The explanation must be found elsewhere.

FURTHER READING S. Pollard, *The Development of the British Economy* (3rd edn, 1983); M. Surrey, 'United Kingdom' in A. Boltho (ed.), *The European Economy: Growth and Crisis* (1982).

Stormont. *See* NORTHERN IRELAND.

Strachey, (Evelyn) John (St Loe) (1901–63), socialist writer and Labour politician. Educated at Eton and Oxford, Strachey was the son of the owner and editor of the weekly political journal the *Spectator*, for which he worked after graduating. He joined the LABOUR PARTY in 1923 and contested Birmingham, Aston, unsuccessfully in 1924, but became its MP from 1929 to 1931. Meanwhile he collaborated with Oswald MOSLEY in devising a policy designed to revive the economy, having become very concerned about unemployment. His book *Revolution by Reason* (1925) provided a theoretical rationale for these proposals. In 1926 he became editor of the INDEPENDENT LABOUR PARTY's *Socialist Review* and of the *Miner*. In 1929 he became parliamentary private secretary to Mosley, resigning with him from the party in May 1930, when the cabinet rejected Mosley's proposals. He joined Mosley's New Party but left it in July 1931, recognizing Mosley's sympathy for fascism. Strachey had become increasingly attracted to Marxism, but his application to join the COMMUNIST PARTY OF GREAT BRITAIN was rejected because he was regarded as an unreliable intellectual. Nevertheless in the 1930s he was a leading pro-communist propagandist and theorist, the most widely read Marxist writing in English, mainly because he was an outstanding writer. His first influential text of this period was *The Coming Struggle for Power* (1932). In 1936 he joined Victor Gollancz and Harold LASKI in forming the LEFT BOOK CLUB, becoming its most popular author. *The Theory and Practice of Socialism* (1936) was the most influential book published by the club, and *Why You Should be a Socialist* (1938) sold more than 250,000 copies within two months. By this time Strachey was influenced by the economic theories of KEYNES and was coming to believe that capitalism could be reformed. He expressed these views in *A Programme for Progress* (1940). His disillusion with communism was completed by the Nazi–Soviet pact of 1939.

During WORLD WAR II Strachey joined the RAF and was transferred to the air ministry to work in PROPAGANDA, making successful broadcasts for the BBC on matters of concern to the ministry. He rejoined the Labour Party, becoming MP for Dundee from 1945 to 1950 and for West Dundee, 1950–63. As minister for food, 1946–50, he was involved in the abortive ground-nut scheme in Tanganyika in 1949, and was responsible for postwar food RATIONING. He was secretary of state for war, 1950–1, and supported Hugh GAITSKELL as successor to ATTLEE in 1955. He returned to writing after the CONSERVATIVE victory in 1951. His *Contemporary Capitalism* (1956) was a major work of democratic socialist theory, and *The End of Empire* (1959) was a timely critique of imperialism. He supported Anglo-American NUCLEAR WEAPONS policy and bitterly opposed the CAMPAIGN FOR NUCLEAR DISARMAMENT. His final book, *On the Prevention of War* (1962), expressed these views.

FURTHER READING H. Thomas, *John Strachey* (1973); N. Thompson, *John Strachey: An Intellectual Biography* (1993).

Straw, Jack (John Whitaker Shaw) (1946–), Labour politician. Straw was educated at Brent-wood School, Essex, and the University of Leeds. He served as president of the National Union of Students (NUS) from 1969 to 1971. After university and the NUS Straw became a lawyer, being called to the Bar in 1972. He was a member of Islington Borough Council and deputy leader of the Inner London Education Authority in the early 1970s. After unsuccessfully contesting Tonbridge and Malling for LABOUR in 1974, Straw served as a political adviser on social services and the environment between 1974 and 1977. He was elected MP for Blackburn in 1979, and served as opposition spokesman in a variety of areas, including the Treasury, environment, education and home affairs, between 1980 and 1997. A member of the shadow cabinet from 1987, Straw was appointed home secretary following the Labour party election victory in 1997. As home secretary Straw had to deal with a number of controversial issues, including organizing the public inquiry into the death of Stephen LAWRENCE and the arrest and subsequent release of the former Chilean dictator General Pinochet. He was subject to criticism for imposing restrictions upon the introduction of a Freedom of Information Act; for changing the definition of terrorism in a way that that broadened the types of groups and activities that could be described as terrorist; and for introducing an Asylum Act that tightened the rules on claims for asylum in the UK (*see* REFUGEES). In the cabinet reshuffle that followed Labour's 2001 election victory, he became FOREIGN SECRETARY, replacing Robin Cook.

strikes. *See* GENERAL STRIKE; MINERS' STRIKES; TRADE UNIONS.

submarines. The first effective submarine was invented by John Holland in 1898, and the world's navies experimented with them until 1914. In WORLD WAR I the German navy moved fastest to develop their use: in the first months of the war German submarines, known as U-boats, sank several ROYAL NAVY warships and were highly effective against British merchant ships. The sinking of civilian passenger vessels such as the *Lusitania* (1915) outraged neutral, especially US, opinion. Early in 1917, convinced by the outcome of the battle of JUTLAND (1916) that they could not defeat the Royal Navy in conventional warfare, the Gemans opened unrestricted submarine warfare, threatening to sink any vessel approaching European waters. This threat helped to bring the United States into the war. Thereafter the contribution of US naval resources, together with the adoption of a convoy strategy supported by aircraft, helped to protect merchant shipping, and submarine attack became less effective.

Between the wars the Germans paid more attention to the development of submarine warfare than the British. At the opening of WORLD WAR II the German U-boat commander Karl Dönitz sent groups of submarines into the Atlantic to blockade Britain with the aim of cutting off essential supplies. Until 1942 this was successful, but then increased escort resources for convoys of merchant vessels provided by the USA on its entry to the war, use of RADAR and the successful decoding of German naval communications (*see* BLETCHLEY PARK) allowed the Allies to defeat the U-boats by 1943 (*see also* ATLANTIC, BATTLE OF THE). Allied submarines played an important part in cutting supply lines to German forces in North Africa and in the American blockade of Japan.

During the COLD WAR submarines became vehicles for NUCLEAR WEAPONS. The first British nuclear-powered submarine was HMS *Dreadnought*, commissioned in 1963, and the first British submarine to carry Polaris nuclear missiles was HMS *Renown*, completed in 1968. A submarine, HMS *Conqueror*, was responsible for the controversial sinking of the Argentine cruiser *General Belgrano* during the FALKLANDS War (*see* OFFICIAL SECRETS ACT).

FURTHER READING E.J. Grove, *Vanguard to Trident: British Naval Policy since World War II* (1987); W.S. Roskill, *The War at Sea* (3 vols., 1954–61).

Suez crisis (1956), international and domestic crisis following Anglo-French military intervention in Egypt. Constructed between 1859 and 1869 by a French engineer, Ferdinand de Lesseps, the Suez Canal links the Mediterranean to the Red Sea and was of immense strategic importance to Britain in providing a faster sea route to INDIA. The Suez Canal Company itself was largely controlled by the British government, which was the biggest single shareholder, with 40% of the shares; the French held most of the remaining shares. According to the Suez Canal Convention signed in 1888, the Canal Company was to have concessionary rights in the use of the canal until 1968.

However, in July 1956 President Nasser of Egypt nationalized the Canal Company. The decision is widely believed to have been precipitated by the earlier refusal of Britain and America – because of an arms deal Egypt had made with the Soviet Union – to provide financial backing for the Aswan High Dam project. Nasser claimed he had nationalized the canal in order to charge dues from passing ships, and thus raise money for the building of the dam.

Incensed by Nasser's actions, and the possibility that in future the Egyptians might deny passage of British oil tankers through the canal, the British cabinet (under the premiership of Anthony EDEN) resolved secretly to bring down the Egyptian government by force and to restore Britain's control of the Canal Company. However, both the British and the French were obliged by American and other international pressure to take part in diplomatic negotiations with Egypt, which ultimately proved fruitless. By October 1956 the British, French and Israeli governments had hatched a secret plan to regain control of the canal zone. Israel would attack Egypt, and an Anglo-French force would then be sent in to mediate the conflict and thus regain control of the canal. The Israeli invasion took place on 29 October and the subsequent landing of the Anglo-French force on 5 November. They proceeded to bomb Egyptian air bases and began taking control of the canal zone.

By 6 November an international uproar had become apparent. The LABOUR PARTY was vociferously opposed to the action, as were a few dissident Conservatives and many COMMONWEALTH governments. The UNITED NATIONS cast a vote of condemnation. But most significantly the United States was determined that the operation be stopped immediately. Heavy diplomatic and economic pressure was deployed, the value of sterling collapsed and Britain was denied relief from the International Monetary Fund. By midnight on 6 November the British and French were forced to halt their operation. They then had to accept an unconditional withdrawal on 30 November and to allow a multinational UN peacekeeping force into the region.

The Suez crisis was a humiliation for the nation, the government and Eden himself. It proved the death of his premiership; in January 1957 Eden resigned, on grounds of ill health, but not before lying to the House of Commons about Britain's awareness in advance of the Israeli invasion. He was succeeded by Harold MACMILLAN. More far-reaching, however, was the effect the crisis had in forcing Britain finally to accept, in a very public manner, that it could no longer undertake independent action in foreign affairs without the consent and approval of the United States. The United States and the Soviet Union were the superpowers in the post-war world, and Britain had been relegated to a distinctly second-power status. The debacle of Suez shaped and informed British foreign policy from that time on, and led directly to more DECOLONIZATION.

FURTHER READING D. Carlton, *Britain and the Suez Crisis* (1988).

suffragettes, label frequently applied to all women who campaigned for the vote in the early years of the 20th century, although the suffragettes are more accurately defined as the members of the Women's Social and Political Union (WSPU), founded in 1903, in contrast to the more moderate SUFFRAGISTS. Led by the PANKHURSTS, the suffragettes supported the use of militant tactics to force the government into granting female suffrage.

At the height of their campaign, from 1908 to 1913, the suffragettes of the WSPU held noisy mass demonstrations and pickets, and embarked on a campaign of violence towards property. They smashed windows and set fire to pillar boxes in order to draw attention to their cause. Frequently arrested, many suffragettes embarked upon hunger strikes when imprisoned. At first the government responded to this by force-feeding them, but when public opinion opposed this practice, the 'CAT AND MOUSE' ACT was passed in 1913, releasing suffragettes from prison as soon as they became ill but re-arresting them after they had recovered. The movement gained its first martyr that year when Emily Wilding Davison threw herself under the king's horse at the Derby.

The WSPU agreed to halt its militant campaign when World War I broke out. In 1918 it scored a partial victory when, by the REPRESENTATION OF THE PEOPLE ACT, the vote was granted to women over the age of 30, who were independent householders, wives of householders or university graduates. Historians are divided in their assessment of the role the suffragettes played in this achievement. Some argue that it was their militant tactics that finally brought action after almost fifty years of governments stalling on the issue. Others argue that the change might have come about sooner had the suffragettes not alienated the government and some potential female supporters with their campaign of militancy. Politicians in LLOYD GEORGE's government at the time liked to give the impression that the vote was a reward for women's war effort. At least as important was their desire to counterbalance the enfranchisement of large numbers of working-class men in 1918 – who they feared would vote for the growing LABOUR PARTY – with older, better-off, better-educated women who, they believed, would not.

FURTHER READING D. Atkinson, *The*

Suffragettes (1993); P. Bartley, *Votes for Women, 1860–1928* (1998); M. Pugh, *Women and the Women's Movement in Britain, 1914–99* (2nd edn, 2000).

suffragists, the name used to distinguish those who campaigned peacefully for female suffrage from the militant SUFFRAGETTES of the Women's Social and Political Union (WSPU), led by the PANKHURSTS. The first formal suffragist organization was the London Society for Women's Suffrage, founded in 1867. It later spread to other areas of the country. The more famous National Union of Women's Suffrage Societies (NUWSS) was founded by Millicent Garrett FAWCETT in 1897.

Early suffragists gained prominent support from Liberal figures such as John Stuart Mill, and gained small successes in the later 19th century when women householders were allowed to vote in county-borough and county-council elections and for POOR LAW guardianships and school-board memberships. However, a succession of bills tabled in the 1900s in Parliament to grant women the vote in parliamentary elections failed. Impatient with the apparent inadequacy of peaceful protest, by 1908 the suffragettes launched their campaign of violence, which the NUWSS deplored. The NUWSS continued to lobby and campaign peaceably, winning much support. Arguably they were close to victory when World War I broke out, though they were intransigently opposed by prime minister ASQUITH. They suspended action for the first two years of the war, but by 1916 Garrett Fawcett decided that they should resume because the government was believed to be considering franchise reform to extend the vote to all men, and she feared that women might be overlooked. The NUWSS continued to campaign until the REPRESENTATION OF THE PEOPLE ACT of 1918 gave the vote to most women over the age of 30. The NUWSS then changed its name to the National Union of Societies for Equal Citizenship (NUSEC) and encouraged women to use their vote and become politically active, and campaigned for a range of women's causes, especially for equal voting rights for women and men. This was achieved in the EQUAL FRANCHISE ACT of 1928. NUSEC continued thereafter as a campaigning organization.

FURTHER READING S.S. Holton, *Feminism and Democracy: Women's Suffrage and Reform Politics in Britain, 1910–18* (1986); C. Law, *Suffrage and Power: The Women's Movement, 1918–28* (1997); M. Pugh, *Women and the Women's Movement in Britain, 1914–56* (1992).

Summerskill, Edith (Clara) (1901–80), Labour politician, physician and feminist. Summerskill was born in London in 1901, the younger daughter of a liberal-minded physician. She attended Eltham Hill Grammar School, King's College, London, and Charing Cross Hospital, where she qualified as a doctor in 1924. In 1925 she married Jeffrey Samuel, a fellow physician, and they worked together in general practice for many years. They had two children.

After experiences of working in the field of maternal and child welfare, Summerskill became very interested in socialized medicine. She joined the Socialist Medical Association and began volunteer work for the LABOUR PARTY in her area. She made her first foray into local politics in 1934 when she won a by-election for Middlesex County Council, but lost in her bid to become Labour MP for Bury in 1935. She was successful in gaining a seat in Parliament in 1938, when she became MP for West Fulham.

During WORLD WAR II Summerskill organized Women's Home Defence and undertook rifle practice. She was concerned about the health of the nation in wartime and in 1945 was made parliamentary undersecretary to the Ministry of Food. She worked on an information campaign aimed at preventing the spread of tuberculosis, and referred to her role in helping to pass legislation requiring all milk to be pasteurized as her 'finest hour'. In 1950–1 she served a very brief term as minister of national insurance and industrial injuries before the Conservatives were returned to office. Her personal interests in health and medical issues and women's rights did not marginalize her within the Labour Party. She became a member of the National Executive Committee in 1944 and served as its chair in 1954–5. She was admitted to the privy council in 1949. In 1955 Summerskill's constituency underwent boundary changes and she transferred to become MP for Warrington. In 1961, after 17 years in the House of COMMONS, she was made a life peer as Baroness Summerskill and went to the House of LORDS, where she continued her work on, and interest in, medical and women's issues.

supplementary benefit. *See* POOR LAW.

Sutherland, Graham (1903–1980), painter and designer. He was born in London, where his father was a high-ranking civil servant. Sutherland abandoned a career as a railway engineer to study engraving and etching at Goldsmiths' College, London, 1921–6. Up to 1930 he worked as a printmaker, specializing in landscape etchings in the 19th-century Romantic tradition. From 1926 to 1935 he taught engraving at Chelsea College of Art and from 1935 to 1940 he taught composition and book illustration there. In the early 1930s, following a decline in the market for prints, Sutherland began experimenting with oils and turned to painting as his main activity. Again he concentrated upon landscapes, though of a haunting, semi-abstract kind showing the influence of surrealism. During the 1930s he also designed bold and imaginative posters and these brought him to the attention of Kenneth CLARK, who became a patron and friend. In World War II, as one of the official war artists recruited by Clark from 1940 to 1945, he mainly recorded the effects of the BLITZ. His pictures of shattered buildings provided some of the most famous images of the home front.

After the war he took up religious painting and portraiture, the two fields in which he made his mark in later years. His most famous portrait was of the author Somerset Maugham (1949), which was commissioned by Maugham himself. Another famous portrait, of Winston CHURCHILL (1954), commissioned by Parliament, was so hated by the sitter, who though it made him look 'half-witted', that Lady Churchill had it secretly destroyed. Like all of Sutherland's best portraits it expressed the psychological strain in the face of the sitter. Sutherland's most celebrated work, however, became widely popular. This was his immense tapestry *Christ in Glory* (completed 1962) in Coventry Cathedral, rebuilt after the wartime bombing. Sutherland was one of the most celebrated British artists of the 20th century and received many honours, notably the Order of Merit in 1960. He also had a high reputation outside Britain. In 1952 he had retrospectives at the Venice Biennale and the Musée Nationale d'Art Moderne in Paris. Indeed, in his later career Sutherland was more admired abroad than in Britain, where his work was thought rather old-fashioned.

FURTHER READING R. Berthoud, *Graham Sutherland* (1982).

T

Taff Vale judgement (1901), legal decision that was a formative episode in the early history of the LABOUR PARTY. It arose from a railway strike in South Wales in August 1900. This began as an unofficial action by workers on the Taff Vale Railway to gain recognition of their right to join a TRADE UNION. It was then made an official dispute by the Amalgamated Society of Railway Servants (ASRS). After settlement of the strike, the company sought damages from the union for losses due to the strike. This case was successful in a lower court, but was overturned by the Court of Appeal. This decision was then reversed by the appeal judges in the House of LORDS in July 1901. By December 1902 the ASRS had incurred a total of £42,000 in settlement with the company and in legal costs. This set a precedent that in practice severely restricted the right to strike.

The CONSERVATIVE government of the day showed no inclination to introduce legislation to overturn the judgement, nor did the LIBERAL PARTY show any enthusiasm for supporting such a move. This convinced many trade unionists of the need for an independent political party to support the interests of labour. In the year following the judgement the number of trade unionists affiliating to the LABOUR REPRESENTATION COMMITTEE (LRC) doubled. The Liberals reversed the judgement in the Trades Disputes Act, 1906, which gave trade unions exceptional immunities from prosecution. This was a condition of the 'Lib-Lab pact' made before the 1906 election.

FURTHER READING H.A. Clegg, A. Fox and A.P. Thompson, *A History of Trade Unions since 1889, Vol. 1, 1889–1910* (1964).

tank warfare. The tank – a heavily armoured military vehicle with moving 'caterpillar' tracks instead of wheels – was a major influence upon the course of warfare during the 20th century. The British ARMY first employed tanks during WORLD WAR I: initial attempts to use the tank (for example at the battle of the SOMME) were hampered by mechanical failures, but in November 1917 at Cambrai 400 tanks successfully broke through the heavily defended Hindenburg Line on the Western Front. During the interwar period, two forms of tank emerged: a smaller, lighter mobile tank (designed to play a role similar to that previously played by cavalry) and a larger, more heavily armoured tank (designed to provide support for the infantry). At the start of WORLD WAR II, however, British tanks were far less developed than those of Germany and the Soviet Union. The effectiveness of the tank was underlined by the successful mobilization of massed tank divisions by the German army in its advance across Europe in 1939–41. During the war the British army's Churchill and Crusader tanks were found to be under-armed in comparison to the German Panzers, and by 1944 armoured divisions were equipped with US Sherman tanks, purchased under the LEND-LEASE agreement.

The Centurion tank, developed in 1943 but which did not come into service until after the war, remained the main British battle tank until the early 1960s, when it was replaced by the Chieftain. From the 1960s British tanks saw military service around the world in various armies. By the end of the century such tanks as the Challenger (brought into service in the British army from 1982 to 1991) were protected by new types of armour.

FURTHER READING T. Donnelly, *Clash of Chariots: The Great Tank Battles* (1996); P. Wright, *Tank: The Progress of a Monstrous War Machine* (2001).

Taranto raid. *See* CUNNINGHAM, ANDREW.

tariff reform. The first proposal by a leading politician for tariff reform was that made in May 1903 by Joseph CHAMBERLAIN, Liberal Unionist colonial secretary in the Conservative government. He suggested the reversal of the policy of moving towards FREE TRADE in favour of levying tariffs where necessary to protect British industry and agriculture. Fearing that the Conservatives were alienating working-class voters by their failure to improve living conditions, Chamberlain saw tariff reform as a means to increase employment and hence improve living standards, and also as an opportunity to raise revenue to fund necessary social reforms, such as OLD-AGE PENSIONS and improved HOUSING. Chamberlain also proposed that by giving preferential remission of tariffs to the colonies the scheme would help to bind the EMPIRE together at a time when, following the BOER WAR, it seemed vulnerable.

The proposals aroused the opposition of many in the Conservative Party, including that of the prime minister Arthur BALFOUR, in particular because tariffs were likely to raise the price of agri-

cultural imports and hence of food, which would be electorally unpopular, especially with working people. Balfour feared that the proposal would split the party. It came close. A number of prominent free-traders, including Winston CHURCHILL in 1904, defected to the LIBERALS, while others retired from politics. This division contributed to the Conservatives' crushing defeat in the election of 1906.

Tariff reform continued to be attractive to Conservatives, in particular because it provided a means to increase government income other than by increased, direct, redistributive taxation of the kind introduced by the Liberals between 1906 and 1914 (*see* LLOYD GEORGE, DAVID). However, Conservative leaders judged it wise not to give tariff reform great prominence – and the party remained bitterly split on it – until the interwar economic crisis brought it into the Conservative election programme of 1923. But it was only in 1932 after the GREAT CRASH that the Conservative-dominated NATIONAL GOVERNMENT committed itself to a policy of tariffs (*see* IMPERIAL PREFERENCE).

FURTHER READING E.H.H. Green, *The Crisis of Conservatism, 1880–1914* (1994); A. Marrison, *British Business and Protection, 1903–32* (1996).

Tawney, R(ichard) H(enry) (1880–1962), economic historian, social thinker and Labour politician. Born in India, Tawney was educated at Rugby School and Balliol College, Oxford, where there was a particularly strong ethic of social service. This, combined with Tawney's own deep and enduring Anglicanism, was to shape his future. He spent a period in residence in the TOYNBEE HALL settlement in London's East End, where he engaged in voluntary social work, then ran a charity providing country holidays for poor city children. He became committed to the provision of adult education for working people, joining the executive committee of the Workers' Education Association (WEA) in 1905 (*see* ADULT EDUCATION). The following year he joined the FABIAN SOCIETY (becoming a member of its executive, 1921–33). In 1909 he joined the INDEPENDENT LABOUR PARTY (ILP). He taught political economy at Glasgow University, 1906–8, then, until 1914, WEA classes in Rochdale, Manchester and the Staffordshire Potteries on a scheme jointly organized by the WEA and Oxford University. During this time he published the book that established him as an economic historian of note, *The Agrarian Problem in the Sixteenth Century* (1912); he followed this in 1926 with another major work on economic history, *Religion and the Rise of Capitalism.*

In World War I Tawney enlisted as a private and was seriously, almost fatally, wounded on the SOMME. From 1917 he taught economic history at the London School of Economics, becoming professor there in 1931. He was a member of the SANKEY COMMISSION on the COAL MINING industry in 1919. He also became increasingly committed to LABOUR PARTY politics and to public service, standing unsuccessfully as a Labour candidate in the elections of 1918, 1922 and 1924. He played a large role in drafting the party's election statement in 1928–9, *Labour and the Nation.*

Tawney wrote widely on EDUCATION issues, for the *MANCHESTER GUARDIAN* and other publications. As a member of the consultative committee of the Board of Education, 1912–31, he urged free secondary education for all in order to widen access. His policy document for the Labour Party, *Secondary Education for All* (1922), shaped the party's education policy. Tawney's book *The Acquisitive Society* (1921) attacked the selfish individualism of modern society and supported a communal sense of collective responsibility. A decade later he published an influential assault on the inequality in British society, *Equality* (1931), in which he advanced a high-minded philosophy that promoted equal worth rather than material equality. Tawney remained an influential social thinker from the interwar years through to the 1950s. He was a member of the University Grants Committee, 1943–8, and vice president of the WEA, 1944–8, while continuing to research and write in economic history.

FURTHER READING R. Terrill, *R.H. Tawney and His Times* (1973).

Taylor, A(lan) J(ohn) P(ercivale) (1906–90), historian. Born in Lancashire into a family of well-to-do cotton manufacturers, Taylor was educated at Quaker schools and Oriel College, Oxford, where he gained a first-class degree in history and joined the COMMUNIST PARTY OF GREAT BRITAIN. He then researched in diplomatic history in Vienna and in 1930 became a lecturer in history at the University of Manchester. In the 1930s he published his first works of history and became a reviewer and editorial writer for the *MANCHESTER GUARDIAN.* During this period he left the Communist Party and became an independent radical. In 1938 he was appointed a fellow of Magdalen College, Oxford, and became an outspoken opponent of APPEASEMENT. He remained at Oxford throughout World War II, also broadcasting frequently for the BBC and being employed to lecture by the Ministry of Information (MOI; *see* PROPAGANDA). However, his talks criticized government policy, especially in the Mediterranean; this aroused disapproval in Parliament, and he ceased to be employed by MOI.

Taylor's historical work was especially directed towards analysing the origins of the international conflict: *The Habsburg Monarchy, 1815–1918* (1941), *The Course of German History* (1946), which was widely interpreted as anti-German, and his outstanding work, *The Struggle for Mastery in Europe, 1848–1918* (1954). He was an outspoken opponent of the SUEZ adventure in 1956, then became a prominent supporter of the CAMPAIGN FOR NUCLEAR DISARMAMENT. He never forgave Oxford for his failure to gain appointment as regius professor of modern history in 1956, although he remained there until his retirement in 1976, becoming highly influential among a generation of younger historians. From 1956 he wrote extensively for the *Daily Express* and *Sunday Express*, usually on aspects of British politics and social issues, forming a close relationship with the papers' proprietor Lord BEAVERBROOK. In 1961 he published *The Origins of World War II*, in which he argued that there were wider causes of the war than the wickedness of Hitler; for this he was much criticized. In 1965 he published his idiosyncratic *English History, 1914–1945*. In 1967 he became director of the Beaverbrook Library and began his biography *Beaverbrook*, which was judged too uncritical of its hero when published in 1972. In his later years, until his decline due to Parkinson's disease, he was best known for a series of BBC TV lectures on historical topics, delivered straight to camera and without notes. The lectures – often idiosyncratic in their interpretations, but readily accessible to an audience with no historical training or knowledge – became hugely popular.

FURTHER READING K. Burk, *Troublemaker: The Life and History of A.J.P. Taylor* (2000); A. Sisman, *A.J.P. Taylor: A Biography* (1994).

television. *See* BAIRD, JOHN LOGIE; BRITISH BROADCASTING CORPORATION.

Temple, William (1881–1944), archbishop of Canterbury (1942–4). Temple was the son of Frederick Temple, then bishop of Exeter but later archbishop of Canterbury (1897–1902). He was educated at Rugby School, where his father had been headmaster, and Balliol College, Oxford, gaining a first-class degree in classics and becoming president of the Oxford Union and a socialist. Together with his Anglicanism, this shaped his future commitments. He was a close friend of R.H. TAWNEY, with whom he had much in common. In 1904 he joined, and from 1908 to 1924 was president of, the Workers' Educational Association (WEA; *see* ADULT EDUCATION); he was also a member of the LABOUR PARTY from 1918 to 1925.

Temple was ordained a clergyman in 1909, and also followed a career in education, as a fellow of Queen's College, Oxford (1904–10), then as headmaster of Repton School (1910–14). He maintained close links with the Student Christian Movement in universities. In 1914 he became

rector of St James's, Piccadilly, London, and in 1915 honorary chaplain to King GEORGE V. In 1917 he became full-time chair of the Life and Liberty Movement, which aimed at reform of the CHURCH OF ENGLAND and led to the creation of the Church Assembly. He was a canon of Westminster Abbey (1919–21), then bishop of Manchester (1921–9). During this time he chaired the Conference on Christian Politics, Economics and Citizenship (1924), sought to mediate in the GENERAL STRIKE of 1926 and played a leading role at the 1927 Lausanne World Conference on Faith and Order. He supported Randall Davidson, the radical archbishop of Canterbury, in an unsuccessful attempt to modernize the Book of Common Prayer in 1928–9.

In 1929 Temple was appointed archbishop of York, where he remained until 1942. He chaired the committee of church unity of the 1930 Lambeth Conference and in 1938 chaired a committee that laid the basis for the World Council of Churches. He was devoted to the ecumenical movement and in 1942 inaugurated the British Council of Churches. He chaired the influential Pilgrim Trust investigation into UNEMPLOYMENT, published as *Men Without Work* (1938). He gave frequent talks on BBC radio, disseminating the Christian social gospel, and published *Christianity and Social Order* on the same theme in 1942. He was archbishop of Canterbury until his sudden and much-mourned death in 1944. He did much to promote social reconstruction during World War II, in particular chairing the Malvern conference on reconstruction in 1940 and supporting the 1944 Education Act, because he believed in wide access to free EDUCATION. He also helped to ensure that the one compulsory element in the curriculum embodied in the act was religious instruction.

FURTHER READING J. Kent, *William Temple* (1992).

Territorial Army, force of volunteer soldiers formed in 1908. Following the embarrassments of the BOER WAR there was extensive reorganization of the ARMY by R.B. HALDANE, the Liberal secretary for war. Largely on his own initiative, the Territorial Army (known as the Territorial Force until 1921) came into being in 1908 following the Territorial and Reserve Force Act, 1907. It was intended as a trained, volunteer, home defence force that would be mobilized in time of war. It replaced the long-established militia and volunteers, who were absorbed into the new structure. The proposal was strongly opposed in Parliament, notably by Liberals, and the resulting force was much smaller than Haldane hoped.

On the eve of WORLD WAR I the Territorials numbered 268,777; by December 1914 almost 70,000 of them were serving abroad, and by mid-1917 more than 500,000. In 1918 the Voluntary Aid Detachments (VADs) were established as a female reserve of the Territorial Force Medical Service to provide nursing and medical care for war wounded in Britain, freeing men to serve abroad, and to be available in case of invasion.

Between the wars the Territorial Army was reduced to below its pre-1914 strength. At the beginning of 1939 Neville CHAMBERLAIN suddenly announced an immediate increase, without consulting the chiefs of staff. The Territorials had been called up for training in May 1938, and merged with the regular army at the beginning of WORLD WAR II. Also in 1938 an Auxiliary Territorial Service (ATS) was established for women; this was merged with the regular army in 1941.

At the end of the war the Territorials were given responsibility for anti-aircraft defence until 1955, when a series of cuts began. However, two divisions were charged with supporting NATO troops in any European conflict. In the 1960s the Territorials suffered from recruiting difficulties, since it was not clear that they now had a role. The Reserve Forces Act, 1966, merged them with the Army Emergency Reserve in a Territorial Auxiliary and Volunteer Reserve, to support the regular army in small conflicts.

FURTHER READING J. Strawson, *Gentlemen in Khaki: The British Army, 1890–1990* (1989).

textiles. The woollen textile industry was the first great industry that fuelled English prosperity in the later Middle Ages. Cotton textiles led British industrial expansion from the late 18th century. Both prospered until the late 19th century, but declined through the 20th, especially from the 1920s.

The woollen industry was concentrated in Yorkshire and southwest England, together with strong tweed and hosiery production in the Scottish Borders; the latter proved to have greater powers of survival than the English industry, thanks to the distinctiveness of its products, and remained successful at least until the 1970s. At the end of the 19th century the woollen industry in England began to face the effects of overseas competition. It was not assisted by the fragmented structure of the industry, divided as it mostly was into small family firms. The Depression following World War I hit the industry hard owing to the further contraction of overseas markets. TARIFF protection, followed by expansion of the home market, brought about a revival. However, from the 1950s it was hard-hit by the introduction of manmade fibres, especially in carpet manufacture, and the decline of the industry thereafter was rapid.

The cotton industry grew to a much greater size than the woollen industry in the 19th century. The main centres of production were Lancashire in England and the west of Scotland. The cotton industry also came under much greater international competitive pressure from the late 19th century, but Britain was still dominant in the world cotton market in 1914. The Depression of the interwar years revealed structural weaknesses in the industry which had been hidden when British cotton had easy access to large markets: slowness to adapt to new technology, excessive specialization, and poor industrial relations, often due to poor management. The industry also suffered from protective tariffs introduced by some overseas competitors, and the emergence of new high-volume competitors with lower costs, producing cheaper goods, notably in India. Another blow was the introduction of the first artificial fibres, beginning with rayon. Much, though not all, of the industry was slow to adapt to the potential of these new fibres. The industry recovered somewhat in the 1930s, following state-guided reorganization and merger of small firms, and the formation in 1939 of a cartel under the Cotton Board. After World War II the industry benefited for a while from the fact that some of its competitors had been disabled by the war, but from the early 1950s decline was swift, despite high levels of protection and import quotas. The British industry could not resist the progress of an ever-widening range of artificial fibres and an increasing volume of cheap imports. By 1990 only large, integrated multinational textile firms remained in Britain, working mainly with artificial fibres.

The decline of the industries can be illustrated by the declining numbers employed. In 1921, 521,000 workers were employed in textiles as a whole, the majority female. In 1932 the number had fallen to 492,000. It remained stable through the 1930s, then fell during World War II, since textiles were not regarded as essential war industries. In 1947 the total workforce numbered 340,000. By 1951 it had risen to 566,700 (359,100 females and 197,600 males), but by 1961 had slumped back to 390,000 (245,000 females and 144,600 males). By 1975 the workforce had fallen by half and it continued to decline through the remainder of the century.

Thatcher, Margaret (Hilda) (1925–), Conservative politician; PRIME MINISTER (1979–90). She grew up in Grantham, Lincolnshire; her father, Alfred Roberts, was an ex-Liberal, METHODIST lay preacher, grocer and mayor of Grantham. She was educated at Grantham Girls' School and Somerville College, Oxford, where she studied chemistry. She was a research chemist from 1947 to 1951, when she married the wealthy businessman Denis Thatcher. Their twin son and daughter were born in 1954. She then trained as a barrister and in 1959 was elected MP for Finchley, north London, which

she represented until her retirement from the House of COMMONS in 1992.

Thatcher was parliamentary secretary to the Ministry of Pensions and National Insurance, 1961–4, then while the CONSERVATIVES were out of office she spoke for the party on, successively, housing, energy, transport, education and environment, entering the shadow cabinet in 1967. When she was appointed to Edward HEATH's cabinet as EDUCATION minister in 1970 she was little known to the public. In this role she supported increased public spending on education and the expansion of comprehensive schools, but she first made a widespread impact when her abolition of free milk for primary-school children earned her the label 'Margaret Thatcher, milk-snatcher'.

In the party leadership election in 1975 Thatcher was effectively the candidate of back-benchers disaffected with the leadership of Edward Heath. She was not expected to win. She won by 130 votes of the parliamentary party to 119, gaining only one supporter in the shadow cabinet. She had no clearly expressed policies, and the extent of her following in the parliamentary party was uncertain. The Conservative victory in the election of 1979 was achieved mainly because of the unpopularity of LABOUR and the divided opposition. The Conservative share of the votes was the lowest of any winning party since 1922 and polls showed Thatcher to be less popular than her Labour opponent, James CALLAGHAN.

At the time of the election the economy was in poor shape and Conservative economic policy was unclear, though it was certain that Thatcher was strongly opposed to TRADE UNIONS and to devolution for SCOTLAND. Over the next two years she and Geoffrey HOWE, the chancellor of the exchequer, moved towards MONETARISM as the guiding theory of their economic policy in an atmosphere of worsening economic crisis with UNEMPLOYMENT rising to 3 million. The 1981 budget, contrary to the 'KEYNESIANISM' of the preceding decades (though on a trajectory already piloted by the preceding Labour government), raised taxes in a recession, while the money supply was eased. This was denounced by 364 economists in a letter to *The Times*. The outcome was a sharp fall in inflation (from 21.8% in April 1980 to 3.7% in June 1983) and a mild economic recovery, though unemployment remained high. At the same time in 1980–1 there were serious inner-city riots, in Bristol in April 1980 and in the spring and summer of 1981 in Brixton (south London), Toxteth (Liverpool) and Moss Side (Manchester). These were all areas with large black populations and the riots were probably best explained as expressions of anger by young black people against unemployment and discrimination, exacerbated by the paramilitary tactics employed by the police at this time (and subsequently modified following extensive criticism). Also in March–April 1981 hunger strikes by IRA prisoners brought a new dimension to the problems in NORTHERN IRELAND. More positively, Peter CARRINGTON, the foreign secretary, achieved a resolution of the crisis in Rhodesia (*see* ZIMBABWE).

As she gained more confidence, Thatcher gradually dismissed cabinet members who disagreed with her. She profited politically from the FALKLANDS War, to which she was committed from the beginning and from which she extracted maximum opportunity to gain popular support. The 'Falklands factor' played a significant role in the large majority won by the Conservatives in the June 1983 election, as did the new SOCIAL DEMOCRATIC PARTY (SDP), which, in alliance with the LIBERAL PARTY, helped to split the anti-Conservative vote. The Conservatives won only 13 million votes from a potential electorate of 42 million. The Falklands War further worsened Thatcher's poor relationship with her exact contemporary Queen ELIZABETH II, who made no secret of her dislike of Thatcher's triumphalism about the outcome. Among other differences between them, the queen was a strong supporter of the COMMONWEALTH, for which Thatcher had no time.

At the beginning of her second Parliament Thatcher still had no discernible legislative pro-

gramme, despite the belief of sections of the left that there was such a thing as 'Thatcherism', but dislike of public ownership led her to embark on a process of privatization (*see* NATIONALIZATION) of publicly owned enterprises, mostly at knock-down prices, to the short-term advantage of the government revenue. This was popular, as was the sale of council houses (*see* HOUSING) to tenants at low prices, though it was criticised even in her own party. Dominating all else, however, at this time were two dramas: the coal MINERS' STRIKE (10 March 1984–5 March 1985) and the Westland affair. The miners had much public sympathy, but the industry clearly had little future (*see* COAL MINING) and the strike was disastrously handled by Arthur Scargill, the miners' leader. Had the miners been more shrewdly led, Thatcher might have been forced into a compromise. Instead she was able to claim a victory in her emerging campaign against the trade unions. In the midst of the strike, on 10 October 1984, an IRA bomb exploded at the Grand Hotel, Brighton, during the Conservative Party conference, killing 5 people and injuring 32, which won the party some public sympathy. On 9 January 1986 the defence secretary, Michael Heseltine, resigned following a dispute with Leon Brittan, secretary of state for trade and industry, over the future of the Westland helicopter firm. Thatcher had allowed the dispute to fester for far too long; the battle over the handling of the affair was temporarily damaging to the government and exposed Thatcher's weak control of it.

Nevertheless, following further cuts in income tax and benefiting again from the split in the opposition vote between Labour and the Liberal–SDP alliance, the Conservatives won the election of 1987 with almost the same share of the vote as in 1982. The election exposed serious social divisions: the Conservatives held almost no seats in major cities and Labour almost none in the south of England, other than in inner London (*see* GENERAL ELECTIONS). However, in 1987–8 the economy appeared to be flourishing, surviving the crash in share prices on 'Black Monday' (19 October

1987). Thatcher, however, made a succession of mistakes. The COMMUNITY CHARGE (poll tax) – to which she was strongly committed personally, and which she insisted be implemented rapidly – was hugely unpopular, being widely perceived as unjust. It also proved uncollectable from a substantial section of the population. Thatcher passionately resisted closer links with the European Community (*see* EUROPEAN ECONOMIC COMMUNITY), most clearly in her Bruges speech (20 September 1988), in which she declared her resistance to any diminution of UK sovereignty – in opposition to the views of many people in her party and in business. She faced increasing criticism from a range of influential sectors of opinion, including the churches, the armed services (which she cut), the University of Oxford, whose senior members voted against a proposal to grant her an honorary degree, and one of her predecessors as party leader, Harold MACMILLAN (then Lord Stockton), who in a speech in the House of Lords attacked her policy of bargain-basement sales of public assets. The enmity between her and Edward Heath was legendary.

In her third Parliament, however, Thatcher achieved a certain coherence and consistency in her policies, going beyond narrow economic policies, although disagreements about them led to the resignation of her chancellor, Nigel Lawson, in 1989. There was much rhetoric about 'rolling back the state', which amounted to further privatization, attempts to cut public expenditure and reduce regulation of the private sector. This third Thatcher government was the period of aggressive privatisation, deregulation (e.g. of financial services, with some disastrous results, in particular the mis-selling of private pensions) and encouragement of individual accumulation (for example by a wider social spread of share ownership) for which she is most vividly remembered. The WELFARE STATE was less thoroughly demolished than some of her supporters wished, because of electoral opposition, but the quality of state education and health care undoubtedly fell and the value of

the old-age pension was severely eroded. Reduced control of the economy and cuts to welfare services were accompanied by sharply increased control of those institutions that remained under public control, such as education and local government. Such actions stimulated opposition to Thatcher, as did the worsening economic situation in 1989–90, marked by recession, inflation, high interest rates and continuing high unemployment (which was beginning to affect Conservative supporters among the middle classes). There was also passionate resistance to the poll tax, expressed in the riots of March 1990. Hostility to Thatcher was most dramatically expressed in the resignation speech in the House of Commons by the deputy prime minister Geoffrey HOWE, who had often, humiliatingly, been portrayed as subservient to her, and certainly as unremittingly loyal. This sealed her downfall.

Under Conservative Party rules the leadership could be challenged annually. Michael Heseltine, Thatcher's opponent over Europe and much else, stood against her. He lost by 204 votes to 152, but she was 4 votes short of the majority required for victory in the first round. Under strong party pressure she agreed to resign and was succeeded by John MAJOR. In 1992 she took a life peerage as Baroness Thatcher of Kesteven; thereafter she made periodic appearances in the House of LORDS and spent much time earning high fees on the United States lecture circuit.

Margaret Thatcher's period in government was not glorious or even particularly successful by any obvious criterion. She was guided by a broad commitment to markets and personal freedom and mistrust of government as an instrument of economic planning or social engineering, but these very general principles proved difficult to translate into a set of coherent and effective policies. She did not succeed, for example, in cutting government expenditure, in part because of the high costs imposed by unemployment. Though she cut the taxes of the better off, this was balanced by increases in indirect taxes, which disproportionately burdened the less well-off. She certainly did not leave the British economy in sound shape.

FURTHER READING P. Riddell, *The Thatcher Decade: How Britain has Changed During the 1980s* (1989); H. Young, *One of Us: A Biography of Margaret Thatcher* (1989).

Thorpe, (John) Jeremy (1929–), Liberal politician; leader of the LIBERAL PARTY (1967–76). Born into a political family, Thorpe was educated in the USA and at Eton and Trinity College, Oxford. At university he was president of the Oxford Union; he then went on to become a barrister in 1954. He was elected MP for Devon North in 1959. He succeeded Jo GRIMOND as leader of the Liberal Party in 1967, and although he was not viewed as a serious political figure he successfully managed the party's February 1974 election campaign, which resulted in the party's best post-war results to that time. Edward HEATH offered him a cabinet seat in a coalition with the CONSERVATIVE PARTY, but Thorpe refused, and Labour formed a government instead. The Liberals failed to build upon the potential for influence after 1974, and Thorpe came under increasing criticism.

Following allegations from a male model, Thorpe was forced to stand down as party leader in 1976 and was succeeded by David STEEL. Two years later he was charged with conspiracy to murder, but was acquitted in the summer of 1979. The allegations were, however, enough to prompt Thorpe's defeat in the 1979 election. Thereafter Thorpe built up a firm of Third World development consultants, and was president of his local branch of the Liberal Democrat Party from 1987.

FURTHER READING S. Freeman, *Rinkagate: The Rise and Fall of Jeremy Thorpe* (1997); J. Thorpe, *In My Own Time: Reminiscences of a Liberal Leader* (1999).

Times, The, Britain's oldest surviving daily newspaper, founded in 1785. In the 19th century it established itself as comprehensive, accurate and independent in its presentation of news and opinion. It became known as Britain's 'newspaper of record'. This reputation survived into the 20th century, through the takeovers in 1908 by Lord NORTHCLIFFE and in 1922 by J.J. Astor, whose family owned it until 1966. However, in the inter-war years, under the editorship of Geoffrey Dawson (1912–19 and 1922–41), *The Times* tended to be too close to government, most obviously in Dawson's close collusion with Neville CHAMBERLAIN in promoting the policy of APPEASEMENT. The newspaper came to be seen as the mouthpiece of government until the British military intervention in the 1956 SUEZ CRISIS, which the editor, Sir William Haley, refused to support. In the 1960s the costs of producing the paper, which had always had a relatively small, if influential, readership, grew, and in 1966 the Astor family sold it to Lord Thomson, who combined it in a group with the previously separate *Sunday Times*. In 1981 it was sold to Rupert Murdoch's News International company. Murdoch sought to widen its readership, and it lost its distinctive quality, independence, reliability and prestige.

FURTHER READING H. Evans, *Good Times, Bad Times* (1984); *The Official History of The Times* (6 vols., 1935–93); J.E. Wrench, *Geoffrey Dawson and Our Times* (1955).

Titanic, ocean liner built for the White Star Line by Harland and Wolff of Belfast for the highly competitive cross-Atlantic route in the early years of the century. The *Titanic* was one of the largest liners then in existence, and its system of watertight compartments in the hull was supposed to make it unsinkable. It started from Southampton on its maiden voyage in April 1912 with over 2200 passengers and crew. Four days later, on 14 April, about 625 km (390 miles) east of Newfoundland, it struck an iceberg and sank in two and a half hours, with the loss of more than 1500 lives. The total would have been higher if the liner *Carpathia* had not arrived on the scene 1 hour and 20 minutes after the Titanic went down. Those who were saved included 63% of the first-class passengers, 41% of second class, 38% of third class and 24% of the crew; only 20% per cent of male passengers were saved, along with 74% of females and 52% of children. The ship's speed appears to have been excessive in the icy conditions, and there were far too few lifeboats (there were only 1178 boat spaces for the 2224 people on board). There were also problems with the design of the ship: five of its 'watertight' compartments were ruptured, which accounted for the rapid sinking.

Inquiries were set up in both Britain and America following the disaster. It was suggested that the number of deaths would have been reduced if the radio operator on board the nearby liner *Californian* had been on duty. Subsequently the first International Convention for Safety of Life at Sea was held in London in 1913. It drew up a number of safety rules: every ship was to have a lifeboat space for every person on board; lifeboat drills became compulsory; and all ships had to man their radios round the clock. An International Ice Patrol was also set up to monitor icebergs in the shipping lanes of the North Atlantic. The tragedy has had a recurring fascination for makers of documentary, feature film, literary and other accounts.
FURTHER READING R.D. Ballard, *The Discovery of the Titanic* (1987); W.C. Wade, *The Titanic: End of a Dream* (1992).

Tonypandy riots (November 1910), outbreak of civil unrest at Tonypandy, a mining village in the Rhondda valleys of South Wales, during a coal strike. This was part of a wave of strikes at this time in COAL MINING and other industries (*see* TRADE UNIONS). A request from the chief constable of Glamorgan for the despatch of troops to the region was refused by the home secretary, Winston CHURCHILL, who feared that this might lead to bloodshed. He agreed to send 300 extra police from London to the Rhondda, with military units kept in reserve at a distance. The police kept the peace in the valleys, sometimes with use of their truncheons.

After the strike was over troops camped a few miles from Tonypandy. Churchill was long after accused of having sent the troops against the miners at Tonypandy, but in reality he did not. Nine months later he did mobilize troops to safeguard key routes during the war scare caused by the AGADIR crisis. They opened fire on strikers attacking a train at Llanelli in South Wales, killing four men. Subsequently the two events appear to have become confused in the minds of some of Churchill's critics in the labour movement.

town and country planning. Concern about the unplanned density and sprawl of urban areas grew during the 19th century. This concern was especially voiced by the garden-cities movement at the end of the century, which aimed to build low-density housing and workplaces in urban units of manageable size. The Housing and Town Planning Act, 1909, was the first serious attempt to guide local authorities to regulate land use, density and sanitary provision when drawing up or sanctioning plans for new urban development. But this was not compulsory, and before World War I local-authority planning lagged far behind that of privately planned model developments such as William Lever's Port Sunlight on Merseyside and the Cadburys' Bourneville near Birmingham. Other private ventures included Letchworth, a planned garden city begun in 1903, and Hampstead Garden Suburb in London, started in 1907.

Between the wars there was greater emphasis in public policy on the building of new HOUSING than on planning, though Letchworth and Hampstead Garden Suburb were completed, as was Welwyn Garden City. Nevertheless, the Housing and Town Planning Act, 1919, made compulsory the development plans permitted by the 1909 act. The 1932 Town and Country Planning Act extended these plans to rural as well as urban local authorities, but controls were slight. The London County Council (LCC; *see* LONDON GOVERNMENT) achieved a certain degree of coordinated development, but in general the substantial residential and industrial building of the interwar years, especially in the Midlands and south of England, was sprawling and unplanned.

Demands for planning of all kinds increased during the 1930s, and received official sanction during WORLD WAR II in a series of reconstruction documents: the Barlow Commission on the distribution of the urban population (1940); the Scott Committee on land utilization in rural areas (1942), which urged the establishment of a planning system embracing the countryside as well as the town, and also recommended the setting-up of national parks; and the Uthwatt Committee on compensation and betterment (1942). The outcome of these reports was the Town and Country Planning Act, 1947, and legislation for the creation of NEW TOWNS and national parks. Planning powers were concentrated in the larger authorities (counties and county boroughs), coordinated by the Ministry of Town and Country Planning (established in 1942). The latter's role was taken over by the Ministry of Housing and Local Government from 1951, and the Department of the Environment from 1970. Development rights were essentially nationalized, since local authorities had the power to control land use without paying large compensation to private owners. Historic buildings were protected, cities were prevented from sprawling by a 'green belt' of undeveloped land, and the development of roads and industry were centrally controlled. Broadly these controls remained in place for the remainder of the century, although they were enforced with relative laxity, particularly by Conservative governments, and especially from the 1970s: ministers, to whom appeals might be made against local-authority planning decisions, could, and often did, reverse such decisions.

FURTHER READING W. Ashworth, *The Genesis of Modern British Town Planning* (1965); G.E. Cherry, *Cities and Plans: The Shaping of Urban Britain in the 19th and 20th Centuries* (1988).

Toynbee Hall, the first and best known of a number of 'settlement houses' that were established from the 1880s, initially in east London and then, by 1914, in poorer districts of most other major cities, in an attempt to bring rich and poor closer together. Most were inspired by Christians from a variety of denominations. Toynbee Hall was established in 1884 by Canon Samuel Barnett and his wife Henrietta, both active social reformers, and was named after the social reformer Arnold Toynbee (1852–83). Settlements were communities of men, and later women – initially mainly young graduates of Oxford and Cambridge – who lived for a while in a settlement house in a poor neighbourhood, engaging in voluntary social work and/or providing ADULT EDUCATION classes, often while establishing themselves in a career. Clement ATTLEE, William BEVERIDGE, R.H. TAWNEY and Eleanor RATHBONE were all active for a period in settlements. John PROFUMO, following his disgrace, rehabilitated himself by working at Toynbee Hall. After World War II Toynbee and other settlements ceased to be primarily residential, but they remained important and often innovative centres of voluntary action, offering, for example. free legal advice or literacy training.

FURTHER READING A. Briggs and A. Macartney, *Toynbee Hall: The First Hundred Years* (1984); M. Vicinus, *Independent Women: Work and Community for Single Women, 1985–1920* (1985).

trade boards. *See* MINIMUM WAGE.

Trade Disputes Act (1906). *See* TAFF VALE JUDGEMENT; TRADE UNIONS.

Trade Disputes Act (1927). *See* GENERAL STRIKE; TRADE UNIONS.

Trade Disputes Act (1948). *See* TRADE UNIONS.

Trades Union Congress (TUC), organization established in 1868 as a national forum for trade unions and a pressure group on government. From the beginning the TUC represented most unions but could not control their actions. However, it could give a lead, as in 1899 when its annual congress proposed a conference that would ensure more Labour members of Parliament. The outcome was the foundation of the LABOUR REPRESENTATION COMMITTEE and later the LABOUR PARTY. During World War I the TUC played a leading role in agreeing an industrial truce with government for the duration of the war (*see* TRADE UNIONS). After the war, it increasingly played a quasi-corporate role, representing trade-union interests in negotiations with government, which became a regular occurrence in a way that would have been unthinkable at the beginning of the century. In consequence the TUC grew in size and importance. In 1921 it established a General Council as its policy-making body. This was elected on a representative basis, taking account of sectors of industry and union size, so that it could effectively speak for the trade-union movement.

In 1924 the members gave the General Council powers to intervene to try to settle industrial disputes and, where such attempts failed, to mobilize the whole movement to support the union involved. In 1926 such mediation in a dispute in the COAL MINING industry failed, leading to the GENERAL STRIKE. This had not been sought by the TUC and they were less prepared than the government. They called off the strike after nine days. Thereafter the TUC – led by Walter Citrine, the first nationally powerful general secretary (1926–45) – was willing to work with moderate employers and with government.

The TUC continued to cooperate with government until Labour produced proposals for the reform of industrial-relations law in the white paper *In Place of Strife* in 1969. The TUC opposed these proposals, and even more fiercely opposed the HEATH government's Industrial Relations Act, 1971. It cooperated with the Labour government elected in February 1974, but cooperation broke down in the wave of strikes of 1978–9. Under the THATCHER governments the TUC was sidelined in

national policy-making, though it continued to play a part in the deliberations of the NATIONAL ECONOMIC DEVELOPMENT COUNCIL until its abolition in 1991. It continued to have a low profile after the election of a Labour government in 1997.

FURTHER READING R.M. Martin, *TUC: The Growth of a Pressure Group, 1868–1976* (1980); K. Middlemas, *Politics in Industrial Society* (1979).

trade unions. Trade-union activity was gradually legalized in the 19th century, and the TRADES UNION CONGRESS (TUC) was established in 1868. However, at the end of the century a series of decisions in the law courts eroded trade-union rights, culminating in the TAFF VALE JUDGEMENT in 1901. There were approximately 2 million members of trade unions in Great Britain in 1900, 12.6% of the known workforce; members were overwhelmingly men. The Taff Vale judgement, which made trade unions liable for commercial losses arising out of industrial activity, inhibited trade-union action and growth. However, the judgement was reversed by the liberal government – which was anxious to hold working-class votes – in the Trade Disputes Act, 1906. The prime minister, Sir Henry CAMPBELL-BANNERMAN, under pressure from the LABOUR PARTY, went further than many of his cabinet colleagues wished in this legislation in giving unlimited legal immunity to trade unions for damages incurred during trade disputes.

The 1906 act was followed by an immediate increase in trade-union membership, to 2.5 million in 1907. There were also a growing number of industrial disputes, especially from 1911, impelled by the rising cost of living, relatively full employment (which increased workers' bargaining power) and demands by increasing numbers of workers to join unions. Since the later 19th century many employers had come to recognize the value of unions for ensuring peaceable industrial relations: unions provided clear channels of communication between employers and workers through which disputes could be resolved. Some employers, however, continued to resist unions. Nevertheless by

1914 there were over 4 million trade-union members, fewer than 500,000 of them female.

In 1913 the Liberals, again under pressure from Labour, reversed another legal decision, the Osborne judgement of 1910 (arising from a case brought by a Conservative trade unionist against a railway union). This banned trade unions from funding political activity, and potentially removed the Labour Party's main source of funding. The Trade Union Act, 1913, permitted unions to use their funds for political purposes provided that the majority of members agreed and that those who wished could contract out by withholding part of their subscription.

The rise in trade-union activity was not primarily political in intent and did not pose a major threat to social order, but the Liberals judged it wise to introduce a mechanism for independent conciliation in labour disputes. This operated through the labour department of the Board of Trade, with some success – although more aggressive action by police and the army against strikers ordered by Winston CHURCHILL at the Home Office caused lasting resentment rather than conciliation (*see* TONYPANDY RIOTS).

Union membership rose during WORLD WAR I, especially among semi- and unskilled workers, who had previously been relatively nonunionized. Membership reached 6.5 million in 1918, and rose faster still in 1918–20. Female membership rose proportionately with that of men: in 1920 total membership was 8.3 million (45.2% of the workforce) of whom 1.3 million were women. The wartime rise occurred despite, or, more accurately, because of agreements between trade unions and government to restrain industrial action and limit labour mobility in the interests of the war effort. The most important measure was the Munitions of War Act, 1915, by which arbitration in disputes became compulsory. The DEFENCE OF THE REALM ACT (DORA) also gave the government extensive powers. Nevertheless strikes did continue during the war, in slightly lower numbers than before and of considerably shorter duration. Workers, espe-cially in war-related occupations such as ship-building, had unprecedented bargaining power in view of full employment and the essential contribution of their work to the war effort. In consequence workers were able, often with government support (especially during the prime ministership of David LLOYD GEORGE), to gain real improvements in pay and working conditions.

The unexpected continuation of high levels of employment in the two years after the war, when the wartime constraints on industrial action were removed, led to the largest wave of strikes in British history, in terms both of numbers of disputes and working days lost. Among the strikers were the police, who had never gone on strike before, and many of these disputes were long and bitter as employers put up strong resistance. Their chief effect, however, was to bring about much needed improvements in wages, working hours and conditions. Lloyd George's government was sufficiently alarmed to introduce the Emergency Powers Act, 1920, which gave the government virtually unlimited powers should it declare a national emergency. It remained on the statute book until the end of the century, being used, for example, by the government of Edward HEATH (1970–4) when it introduced the three-day week in parts of industry during the coal MINERS' STRIKE of 1972.

The onset of high UNEMPLOYMENT late in 1920, lasting until 1940, weakened the bargaining power of unions, but it also increased industrial conflict as employers sought to reduce wages and to lay off workers, notably in COAL MINING, culminating in the GENERAL STRIKE and the long miners' strike in 1926. Thereafter the Trade Disputes and Trade Unions Act, 1927, banned general strikes and strikes by local government workers (including police), made picketing more difficult, forbade central and local government employees from joining unions affiliated to the TUC and required trade unionists explicitly to agree that their union funds should support the Labour Party. This cut the Labour Party's income from trade-union sources by one-third. (The legislation was repealed by Labour in the Trade Disputes and Trade-Unions Act, 1946.) Trade-union membership fell from 5.5 million in 1925 to 4.5 million in 1934, 26% of a growing workforce (737,000 of them female); thereafter membership rose again. The number and duration of disputes fell more dramatically during the particularly heavy unemployment of the 1930s, before reviving towards the end of the decade. The revival came with the revival of the economy and of demand for labour; the latter again peaked in WORLD WAR II.

In World War II the government again took exceptional powers: full control over civilian manpower; a ban on strikes and lockouts; and the establishment of a National Arbitration Tribunal. However, the controls were administered by the Ministry of Labour, headed by the prominent trade unionist Ernest BEVIN, who had the confidence of the trade-union movement. As in World War I, pay and working conditions improved during the war. The number of strikes was above pre-war levels, since in practice it was impossible to prevent unofficial strikes and the government was reluctant to risk unpopularity by punishing strikers. The wartime strikes included a significant number by women workers demanding EQUAL PAY, notably in engineering. Trade-union membership rose during the war to 8 million in 1945, over 40% of the workforce.

Strike action remained at somewhat higher levels than before the war during the period of ATTLEE's Labour government (1945–51), and trade-union membership continued to rise, though workers agreed to pay restraint in return for price controls, full employment and WELFARE measures. Quiescence continued into the 1950s. But from the mid-1950s disputes rose as prices climbed and demand faltered. Growing concern about the state of the economy, on all sides, led to further disputes in the 1960s and increased government concern about them, including fears that trade-union practices were lowering productivity and contributing to the faltering of the economy. The Rookes vs. Barnard case in 1964 once more threw doubt on the legal immunity of trade-union officials. The Labour government elected in 1964 appointed a Royal Commission on Trade Unions and Employers' Associations (1965–8) under Lord Donovan to investigate industrial relations. The commission came out against new legislative controls on industrial relations. However, there was growing demand from the Conservative Party, the media and sections of the public for controls on the number of strikes. In response prime minister Harold WILSON and Barbara CASTLE, the employment secretary, produced the white paper *In Place of Strife* in 1969. This proposed that the employment secretary should have the power to impose a 28-day cooling-off period before a strike occurred, to settle inter-union disputes and to order strike ballots. This was strongly resisted by unions, many of whom had come to believe intransigently in their right to unfettered collective bargaining. The government was humiliated into withdrawing an industrial-relations bill based on the white paper by a revolt of Labour backbenchers; this contributed to Labour's defeat in the 1970 election.

Edward HEATH's Conservative government came to power pledged to introduce industrial-relations legislation. The Industrial Relations Act, 1971, went beyond *In Place of Strife*. It established a National Industrial Relations Court with powers to order cooling-off periods, to require strike ballots, to fine unions for 'unfair industrial practices', to award compensation to workers unfairly sacked and to require employers to recognize unions. It banned the 'closed shop' (whereby workers in a particular workplace were required to belong to a particular union), giving workers the right to choose whether or not to belong to a union, and made collective agreements legally binding. A Registrar of Trade Unions and Employee Associations was appointed with some powers of regulation over registered unions. The legislation was greeted with immense hostility by the unions and the Labour Party. The number of union members rose to almost 12 million in 1974, 49.6% of the workforce, the highest level in history. The number of strikes rose, employing more creative tactics: sympathy strikes and boycotts, flying pickets and factory occupations (notably at Upper Clyde Shipbuilders). Five dockers were jailed for disobeying the law, providing martyrs for the cause. The legislation proved inoperable. The Heath government worked instead to secure union cooperation for its prices-and-incomes policy, but the policy was destroyed by the MINERS' STRIKE of 1973–4.

The crisis had brought the Labour Party and the unions closer together and in 1973 they agreed on a 'social contract', the terms of which were vague but which was believed to commit both sides to working together for the good of the economy, living standards and social order. The Labour government that came to power in February 1974 kept its side of the bargain by repealing the Heath legislation in the Trade Union Act, 1974, and the Labour Relations Act, 1976. This kept what trade unionists regarded as the more positive aspects of the Heath legislation, notably on unfair dismissal. Working people were granted further safeguards in the Health and Safety at Work Act, 1974, and the Employment Protection Acts, 1975 and 1978.

But the effects of the OIL SHOCK on the economy, bringing unemployment and inflation, created major difficulties. Labour was able to use its influence with union leaders to moderate wage claims, and in return, with the support of the TUC, the government imposed a freeze on prices, profits and rents as well as on wage increases. This agreement held until the autumn of 1978 when a wave of strikes, including action by public-sector workers, was dubbed in the media the 'winter of discontent'. There were more disputes than in any year on record. This destroyed the social contract and helped to bring down the government.

Margaret THATCHER came into government in 1979 with control of industrial relations as one of her few clear commitments. She introduced legislation step by step and so avoided antagonizing the unions as comprehensively as Heath had done. Growing unemployment, especially in manufacturing industry, was also weakening the unions.

The Employment Acts of 1980, 1982, 1988, 1989 and 1990, the Trade Union Act of 1984 and the Trade Union and Labour Relations (Consolidation) Act of 1992 removed most of the rights the unions had gained since the beginning of the century. Unions were again liable for damages arising from industrial action: they lost their immunity from legal action if they called strikes without holding a secret ballot or if sympathy action was taken by workers not directly involved in a dispute. Picketing was allowed only for workers directly involved in a dispute and only at their own workplace. The 'closed shop' was banned, except where sanctioned by 85% agreement in a workplace ballot. Unions could not discipline members who crossed picket lines or refused to strike, even if the strike had been agreed by ballot. Advice and funds were provided for workers taking legal action against their union and for union ballots. There had to be ballots for the election of union officials and executive-committee members and, every ten years, for unions to maintain political funds.

Union membership declined to under 10 million (34.3% of the workforce) by 1991. There were some dramatic but unsuccessful strikes, notably that of the miners' strike of 1984–5, but these dwindled by the early 1990s. The decline of manufacturing changed the shape of trade unionism. For most of the century the bulk of trade unionists were industrial workers. By the 1990s, however, most trade unionists were service workers, many of them in the public sector and many of them female. There was also a major shift in the economy and employment in the 1980s and 1990s away from heavy manufacturing industry, which was traditionally unionized, to new nonunionized manufacturing industries such as electronics, and service industries, many of which were also nonunionized (for example, burger bars, call centres and privatized cleaning services). These new sectors predominantly employed women, young people and members of ethnic minorities.

The Labour government elected in 1997 avoided too close a public association with the unions, but gradually modified employment and industrial-relations law. A MINIMUM WAGE was introduced, and greater protection was afforded against unfair dismissal, for example, and to part-time workers and those on short-term contracts. Other reforms came from the EUROPEAN UNION, for example, the 48-hour maximum working week. These changes reversed the most severe changes of the Thatcher years.

FURTHER READING H.A. Clegg, A. Fox and A.P. Thompson, *A History of British Trade Unionism, Vol. 1, 1889–1910* (1964); H.A. Clegg, *A History of British Trade Unions since 1899, Vol. 2, 1911–1933* (1985); W. McCarthy (ed.), *Legal Intervention in Industrial Relations* (1992).

Treasury. *See* CHANCELLOR OF THE EXCHEQUER.

treaty of Versailles (1919). *See* VERSAILLES, TREATY OF.

Trenchard, Hugh. *See* ROYAL AIR FORCE.

Trimble, (William) David (1944–), Ulster Unionist politician; leader of the ULSTER UNIONIST PARTY (1990–). Trimble was educated at Bangor Grammar School and Queen's University, Belfast. After being called to the Bar of Northern Ireland in 1969, Trimble worked as a lecturer in law at Queen's University. He served as a member of the Northern Irish Constitutional Convention in 1975–6. He became Ulster Unionist MP for Upper Bann in 1990, and was made party leader in 1995. As leader of the Ulster Unionists, he brought his party into the negotiations that lead to the 'Good Friday' agreement of 1998 (*see* NORTHERN IRELAND). He managed to keep his party together and within the peace process despite strong opposition from a significant section of the party. His role in producing the agreement was rewarded with a Nobel Peace Prize (shared with the Social Democratic and Labour Party leader John HUME) in the same year. He became first minister of the Northern Ireland Assembly in 1998 (this was a 'shadow' role until the formation of the Northern Ireland Executive), and struggled to maintain the momentum of the Good Friday agreement in the face of lack of progress in the decommissioning of paramilitary weapons and opposition from within the Ulster Unionist Party.

Triple Alliance. *See* GENERAL STRIKE.

Triple Entente. *See* ENTENTE CORDIALE.

Trotskyites. *See* MILITANT.

Troubles, the. *See* NORTHERN IRELAND.

U

Ulster Unionist Party, NORTHERN IRELAND political party formed in 1904–5 as the Ulster Unionist Council to resist the threat of all-IRELAND devolution (*see* HOME RULE). It consisted of representatives of local Unionist institutions, the Presbyterian church, the ORANGE ORDER and loyalist MPs. It brought Protestant landowners, businessmen and working people together to oppose the third Home Rule Bill of 1912–14. It was led by Sir Edward CARSON from 1910 to 1921, then by Sir James Craig, previously a key organizer of the Ulster Unionist movement and the first prime minister of Northern Ireland, 1921–40. The Ulster Unionists controlled the Northern Ireland Parliament and government from 1921 until direct rule from Westminster was imposed in 1972, resisting integration of the Roman Catholic minority. It represented highly conservative social and economic views and was frequently accused of the rigging of electoral boundaries and of elections to ensure Protestant dominance. The Catholic, nationalist resistance to this situation from 1967 created a succession of splits between moderate (*see* O'NEILL, TERENCE) and hard-line Unionists, and resulted in the creation of the hard-line Democratic Unionist Party by Ian PAISLEY in 1971.

The Ulster Unionist Party remained the majority representative of Northern Ireland Unionist opinion, supporting the successive attempts at reconciliation in the province up to the end of the century, under the leadership of David TRIMBLE from 1995, despite continuing tensions within the party and with Unionists outside it. The party lost seats to the Democratic Unionist Party in the general election of 2001.

Ulster Volunteer Force (UVF), (1) organization formed by Sir Edward CARSON in 1913 as the military backup to Ulster Loyalist resistance to the third HOME RULE Bill. It was led by former British army officers, and claimed to have a membership of 100,000. Its existence ceased with the declaration of WORLD WAR I, but its members became the basis of the Ulster Special Constabulary, formed in 1920–1. This became an auxiliary armed police force for the new government of NORTHERN IRELAND, funded by the British Treasury. In 1922 it consisted of three sections: 'A' full-time, 'B' part-time and 'C' reserve, with 5500, 19,000 and 7500 members respectively. It was dominated by old UVF and ORANGE ORDER members and was seen as a ruthless sectarian force by the Roman Catholic minority. Gradually the 'A's and 'C's were disbanded, while the 'B Specials' became a major target of criticism for their aggressive, sectarian policing of the civil-rights marches of the late 1960s. Following a report into their conduct in 1969 (the Hunt Report) they were replaced by a new, part-time security force, the Ulster Defence Regiment (UDR). This was supposedly nonsectarian, but attracted very few Catholics and became as controversial as the 'B Specials'. The UDR was amalgamated with the Royal Irish Rangers in 1992 to create the Royal Irish Regiment.

(2) The name Ulster Volunteer Force was revived in the mid-1960s for a secret Protestant paramilitary force. It was outlawed in the 1970s but retained a secret existence. Along with other Loyalist paramilitary organizations, such as the Ulster Freedom Fighters (the cover name of the Ulster Defence Association), the UVF was responsible for many sectarian assassinations of Catholics during the Troubles. Both the UVF and UDA called a ceasefire in October 1994.

Ultra. *See* BLETCHLEY PARK.

unemployment. Throughout modern history there have been people unable to find work, but the term 'unemployment' came into use only at the end of the 19th century. The term emerged from the growth of economics as a field of study: economists increasingly recognized that lack of work was not just a result of human failing or human inability to seek out work, but due to operations of the economy that were beyond the control of those individuals in need of work.

The first influential analysis of the 20th century was *Unemployment: A Problem of Industry* (1909) by William BEVERIDGE. Studies such as this made it clear that unemployment took a number of forms: 'frictional unemployment', the temporary unemployment of those moving between jobs; 'seasonal unemployment', which affects outdoor workers or is caused by regular seasonal fluctuations in demand; and 'structural unemployment', which is due to longer-term changes in demand or in technology, making certain skills redundant or less needed.

Until the 1940s it was generally believed that government policy could do little to affect levels of unemployment. Governments could do no more

than alleviate the difficulties of the unemployed – and this government increasingly did, as they came to recognize that unemployment was not the fault of individuals, and also that large-scale unemployment might lead to threats to public order. The first such measures were the introduction of labour exchanges in 1909, to assist the unemployed to find work, and a limited scheme of unemployment insurance in 1911 to provide benefits for unemployed people. Both were introduced into Parliament (with the advice of William Beveridge) by Winston CHURCHILL, who was president of the Board of Trade in a LIBERAL government at the time. It was only with the introduction of these schemes that the government began to collect regular statistics of unemployment, and only as the schemes became comprehensive after WORLD WAR I did unemployment statistics become comprehensive and approximately reliable.

Government unemployment schemes were extended in the 1920s and 1930s, a period when unemployment reached high levels and changed its character. Before World War I irregular employment due to fluctuations in demand for seasonal or other reasons had been commonplace; but between 1920 and 1940 more people – especially in certain industries and regions – suffered long-term total unemployment. In 1921, 12.2% of all workers were unemployed; in 1925, 8.6%; in 1930, 12.3%; in 1932, 17%; and in 1938, 10%. At the worst point, in 1932, 37.4% of all insured workers in Wales were unemployed, while in the UK as a whole, 34.5 % of coal miners and 62% of workers in shipbuilding were out of work (*see also* DOLE, THE; MEANS TEST; POOR LAW). At the same time, it was increasingly believed that governments *could* act to control unemployment. John Maynard KEYNES in particular argued that government could control the level of demand in the economy by altering taxes and government expenditure: if taxes were reduced people would spend more, and this would create demand for more goods that would create the need for more jobs; similarly, government expenditure on such work as road-building would create employment. To achieve this, government would have to work closely with employers and unions.

These views became influential during WORLD WAR II. They were embodied in the government's 1944 white paper on employment policy, and were broadly followed by governments between 1945 and the early 1970s. Owing partly to these policies, but more to high levels of demand in the world economy, unemployment was low throughout this period, averaging only 1.7% between 1945 and 1966, though it remained higher in pockets such as Merseyside and Clydeside.

From the mid-1970s unemployment began to rise again in Britain and elsewhere, reaching levels comparable with the 1930s, though its occupational and geographical characteristics were quite different. Official statistics for this, or any, period do not provide a consistent or reliable measure of the full extent of unemployment because governments regularly changed the basis on which numbers of the unemployed were counted; they did this in order to minimize the figures, since governments were now held to be responsible for employment and held to blame when unemployment levels rose. Official statistics, however, indicate the magnitude of the change: the percentage of male workers registered as unemployed was 2.9% in 1974, 5.9% in 1976, 11.4% in 1981, 14.9% in 1985. Throughout that period increasing numbers were unemployed long-term, and very many who became unemployed in their forties or fifties were effectively retired, unable to find work again. As in the period between the wars, unemployed people were provided by government agencies with advice (of varying degrees of effectiveness) on finding employment, and also with cash benefits. However, because of the higher LIVING STANDARDS of the remainder of the population, the living standards of the unemployed probably fell further behind those of the employed than in the 1920s and 1930s.

The reasons for the rise in unemployment in the 1970s led to a questioning of the policies that had been dominant since the 1940s, since unemployment appeared to be driven by factors outside government control. The reasons included a rapid rise in the international prices of oil (*see* OIL SHOCK) and other commodities, which drove up prices generally, combined with underlying weaknesses in the British economy to which successive governments had failed to find remedies (*see* STOP-GO). Government policy in the Conservative administrations of Margaret THATCHER and John MAJOR came to be dominated by the concept of MONETARISM (derived from the work of the US economist Milton Friedman), and reverted to the view that government could do little to control unemployment. Unemployment was now said to be due not to insufficient demand in the economy, but to the disincentives to work provided by unemployment and other WELFARE benefits, and to the power of TRADE UNIONS to maintain high and rigid pay levels. Monetarists argued that governments should seek to control spending and wage rises – and thus inflation – by controlling the money supply (the notes and coins in circulation). It was recognized that this was likely to increase unemployment further, but only in the short run. In the longer run the market, freed from government and trade-union controls, would provide jobs, if at lower wages than before.

The Thatcher and Major governments did not apply this approach with its full rigour, for fear of the political effects of too sweeping a withdrawal of welfare benefits from workers and the unemployed. As levels of unemployment continued to be high into the 1990s, governments, especially the Labour government elected in 1997, increased efforts to assist people into work, for example by providing more effective training and guidance about work opportunities. To influence levels of savings, investment and consumer demand – all factors affecting employment – governments also adjusted taxes and interest rates (although from 1997 interest rates were controlled not by government but by the BANK OF ENGLAND with the advice of a committee of economists). At the end of the century unemployment was again declining, though to what extent this could be attributed to government policy was again uncertain.

SEE ALSO MINIMUM WAGE.

FURTHER READING J. Harris, *Unemployment and Politics: A Study in English Social Policy, 1886–1914* (1972); W.R. Garside, *British Unemployment, 1919–1939* (1990); I. Gazeley and P. Thane, 'Patterns of Visibility: Unemployment in Britain during the 19th and 20th Centuries' in G. Lewis (ed.), *Forming Nation, Framing Welfare* (1998), 181–226.

unemployment insurance. *See* UNEMPLOYMENT.

Unionists, Ulster. *See* CARSON, EDWARD; IRELAND; NORTHERN IRELAND; O'NEILL, TERENCE; PAISLEY, IAN; TRIMBLE, DAVID; ULSTER UNIONIST PARTY.

United Irish League. *See* IRISH LAND ACTS.

United Nations (UN), international organization founded on 24 October 1945 with the aim of ensuring world peace and security. It replaced the LEAGUE OF NATIONS, an organization with similar aims, but which had ultimately proved unable to prevent WORLD WAR II. The concept of the UN had its origins in the ATLANTIC CHARTER of 1941, signed by the US president F.D. Roosevelt and Winston CHURCHILL. The principles of the Atlantic Charter were later represented in the Declaration of United Nations, signed in January 1942 by 26 Allied nations. Negotiations to establish the UN began at a 1943 conference in Moscow attended by Britain, the USA, the USSR and China, and were continued the following year at a conference at Dumbarton Oaks, Washington DC. At Dumbarton Oaks the first tentative UN Charter was drawn up. Finally, representatives of the original 50 UN member states met in San Francisco from April to June 1945 to draw up the official UN Charter. It was signed in June and came into effect in October 1945 after it had been ratified by a majority of the member states. Its international

headquarters are located in New York, and by 2000 some 200 nations were members.

Every member state of the UN is entitled to representation in the UN General Assembly. In addition, China, the USA, the USSR (now Russia), France and Britain are permanent members of the Security Council, and each has veto powers. The permanent membership of the Security Council reflected the global power structure at the end of World War II. The great decline in world power and status of both Britain and France since that time has led some to question whether they still deserve their positions on the Security Council.

The UN has at times aided Britain in international matters. It helped Britain release itself from its troubled mandate in PALESTINE in 1948. Although the UN condemned Britain's role in the 1956 SUEZ CRISIS, it sent peacekeepers into the canal zone and at least allowed Britain to withdraw with some semblance of dignity. Britain has also long supplied the UN with peacekeepers, notably in CYPRUS in the 1960s and Bosnia in the 1990s. Britain also supplied forces for the UN in the KOREAN WAR.

FURTHER READING E. Luard, *A History of the United Nations, Vol. 1, The Years of Western Domination, 1945–1955* (1982); E. Luard, *A History of the United Nations, Vol. 2, The Age of Decolonization, 1955–1965* (1989); D. Reynolds, *One World Divisible: A Global History since 1945* (2000).

universities. After the growth in the number of universities in Britain in the 19th century, the early 20th century saw little expansion in higher education in Britain. While some universities were accepting women as students, higher education remained an elite, largely male and minority activity. An element of central planning was introduced into British higher education with the establishment of the University Grants Committee (UGC) in 1919, and increasing numbers of scholarships became available during the interwar period.

It was following World War II, however, that a greater demand for university places prompted major expansion, prefigured by the establishment of Keele University in 1949. Plans for 'new universities' in the late 1950s led to the establishment of the universities of Sussex, Essex, York, East Anglia, Lancaster, Kent and Warwick between 1961 and 1965, and Stirling in 1967. The report of the Robbins Committee on Higher Education (1963) argued for a rapid increase in university places to cope with the 'bulge' in post-war birth rates and the presumed trend of continued increases in the numbers achieving academic qualifications for university places. The report also recommended the conversion of a number of colleges of advanced technology into universities, including Aston, Bath, Loughborough, Heriot-Watt and Strathclyde.

The introduction of mandatory student grants in 1962 and the establishment of a unified admissions system put into place structures that could potentially encourage greater equality of access to universities. Changes in the way higher education was provided, notably with the establishment of the OPEN UNIVERSITY in 1966, also went some way towards allowing greater participation. A further major enlargement of higher education in Britain took place in the wake of the 1992 Education Act, which abolished the distinction between polytechnics and universities, and replaced the UGC with the Higher Education Funding Councils. Funding for universities and students became one of the central issues surrounding higher education in the 1990s, with the replacement of student grants by loans, and the introduction of tuition fees for undergraduates. These changes were accompanied by reduced government funding for universities relative to student numbers, increased central surveillance of teaching methods and research output, and a fall in the salaries of university teachers relative to other professions.

Numbers of university students in Great Britain rose from 20,000 in 1900–1 to 42,000 in 1924–5, 82,000 in 1954–5, 118,000 in 1962–3, 235,000 in 1970–1, 370,000 in 1990–1 and 1.2 million in 1996–7.

FURTHER READING R.D. Anderson, *Universities and Elites in Britain* (1992); A.H. Halsey, 'Further and Higher Education' in *Twentieth-Century British Social Trends* (2000), 221–53.

Utility Scheme, programme set up by the British government in the early years of WORLD WAR II. The Utility Scheme was designed to make best use of various raw materials that were in short supply because of the war, as well as to release more workers for the war effort. The RATIONING of food had begun early in 1940, the government having learned its lesson from WORLD WAR I when food was not widely rationed until 1918 and serious problems had resulted. By 1940 the government began planning how to make best use of all the resources necessary to the daily life of Britons, in order to enable them to fight the war on the home front.

While food was the government's first concern, it soon became apparent that a host of other items would have to be rationed as well. Many raw materials Britain needed, such as timber, cloth, leather and rubber, were in very short supply. The Utility Scheme was designed in response to the problems experienced in World War I, when shortages had resulted in unfair distribution of products and profiteering. The government wanted to make sure that the public were not cheated into buying cheap shoddy goods, or was unable to buy at all because the small amount of quality goods being produced was too expensive. The most important items produced under the Utility Scheme were clothing, footwear and furniture, as well as household textiles and bedding. Other items included cigarette lighters and pencils. All bore the Utility mark, CC41, which was patented in 1941.

The rationing of clothing had been introduced in June 1941, with adults being issued with a set number of coupons per year that could be exchanged for various items. Utility cloth and clothing began to be produced in late 1941 and early 1942, and included hosiery, gloves and braces. Soon afterwards Utility shoes and boots were introduced; in later years the severe shortage of rubber meant that footwear began to be made with wooden soles. The main feature of Utility FASHION was its strict avoidance of any superfluous use of fabric. Women's skirts were no longer than knee length, and jackets for men and women were trim and well tailored. Shirts and undergarments were plain and functional.

The idea of Utility furniture was first conceived in 1942, when Hugh DALTON announced the creation of an advisory committee for furniture. Nine prominent designers were approached later that year for plans, and a catalogue was produced containing just 20 items of basic furniture. An exact set of design specifications was issued to a small number of firms granted licences to continue production. All other production of furniture was made illegal. Unlike Utility clothing, which was made available to everyone, Utility furniture was originally intended as 'standard emergency furniture', and availability was basically restricted to people who had had their homes destroyed by bombing.

Like rationing itself, the production of Utility goods did not end with the war. The scheme was gradually phased out, and ended in early 1953. But while it was in place it was remarkably successful, and Utility style in both clothing and furniture went on to become a landmark in the history of 20th-century British design.

FURTHER READING H. Dover, *Home Front Furniture: British Utility Design 1941–1951* (1991); C. Sladen, *The Conscription of Fashion: Utility Cloth, Clothing and Footwear 1941–1952* (1995).

V

Vaughan Williams, Ralph. *See* MUSIC.

V-1s and V-2s, secret weapons deployed by the Germans against Britain in 1944–5. V stood for *Vergeltungswaffe* (reprisal weapon), and they were intended to wreak havoc in British cities. The V-1s, also known as flying bombs, buzz bombs or doodlebugs, were pilotless planes that carried a 1-tonne warhead. They were used from June 1944 and killed over 6000 people in daytime raids.

The V-2s were liquid-fuel rockets, also carrying a 1-tonne warhead. They were used from September 1944 and killed more than 2500, far fewer than Hitler had hoped. Scientifically they were a breakthrough, the precursor of the rocket (designed by the same scientists) that first took men to the moon in 1969. Anti-aircraft defences were soon able to detect and destroy V-1s, but V-2s were much faster and more elusive.

venereal disease. *See* SEXUALLY TRANSMITTED DISEASES.

Vereeniging, treaty of. *See* BOER WAR.

Versailles, treaty of (1919), the peace treaty between Germany and the Allies at the end of WORLD WAR I. It was signed on 28 June 1919 in the Hall of Mirrors of the palace of Versailles, where the German empire had been proclaimed in 1871. Thus the French gained some revenge for their defeat in 1871. The Allies attempted to combine the British and French desire for revenge and for security against Germany with that of the United States to base international relations on new moral principles.

Under the terms of the treaty Germany had to surrender Alsace and Lorraine to France and considerable territory to a reconstituted Poland. Germany lost all of its colonies, those in Africa becoming mandates under the control of Britain or France (France received part of Togoland and part of the Cameroons, while Southwest Africa went to SOUTH AFRICA); Britain also took over some areas of the Middle East, including PALESTINE, which had previously lain within the Ottoman Empire. The British EMPIRE reached the maximum extent in its history following the treaty. The Rhineland was to be occupied for 15 years. Germany was not allowed to re-arm, the navy was to be limited in size and large REPARATIONS payments were demanded in reimbursement of the war damage suffered by the Allies. The payment was fixed in 1921 at £6600 million plus interest. Germany was also to accept a clause in the treaty acknowledging guilt in causing the war, and the Kaiser and other war leaders were to be placed on trial. The LEAGUE OF NATIONS was also established by the treaty. Germany especially resented the reparations payments and signed the treaty under for example protest. The US Congress refused to ratify it and it was widely feared in the Allied countries (by John Maynard KEYNES) that the punishment of Germany had been too severe and might have dangerous consequences. Others, however, thought it too lenient. The German Kaiser was not placed on trial. Germany rapidly paid a first instalment of £50 million in reparations but further payments were delayed because of the German inflation of 1922, resumed with help from the United States, then stopped altogether after the GREAT CRASH of 1929.

visual arts. The visual arts were vibrant in Britain throughout the 20th century. They were also very, and increasingly, varied in form and in their underlying theories and often aroused controversy both among practitioners and between them and critics and the general public. The very definition of what was and was not artistic representation was repeatedly called in question, perhaps most actively so at the end of the century when performance art was fashionable (practised for example by Gilbert and George and by Tracey Emin; *see* BRITART) which in theory could embrace stylized presentations of almost any aspect of human activity. The tradition of performance art could be traced back to the Dadaists, surrealists and futurists early in the century, but these were less significant in Britain than elsewhere in Europe, whereas British artists

were at the forefront of innovation in art at the end of the century. Closely related and with a similar genealogy was installation art, usually a large-scale permanent assemblage of objects, often filling a room, such as *20:50* (1987) by Richard Wilson (1953–), which consists of a room half-filled with used sump oil. Critics were divided as to whether such activities were indeed 'art'.

So varied were the activities which can be grouped under the label 'visual arts' through the century that they defy straightforward summary and the attempt to summarize risks imposing a spurious unity on what was in fact a very varied, divided, complex set of activities. The history of the visual arts in 20th century Britain is best understood through accounts of the work of practitioners. One thing that was clear, however, was that, in the face of the cultural pessimism of many contemporary commentators, the visual arts, from the outrageous to the traditional, had never been so popular in Britain as in the late 20th century, as evidenced by rising attendance at galleries and exhibitions, in particular the huge success of the new Tate Modern gallery of contemporary art which opened in central London early in 2000.

votes for women. *See* SUFFRAGETTES; SUFFRAGISTS.

voting, qualifications for. *See* EQUAL FRANCHISE ACT; REPRESENTATION OF THE PEOPLE ACTS; SUFFRAGETTES; SUFFRAGISTS.

W

WAAC. *See* ARMY.

WAAF. *See* ROYAL AIR FORCE.

Wales. Mostly annexed by England from 1301 and entirely from 1536, Wales retained some independent judicial institutions into the 19th century, and for much longer a sense of itself as a separate principality within the United Kingdom, with a separate language and distinctive cultural features. The Welsh language was spoken by 44% of the population of Wales in 1911, and nationalist sentiment had strengthened in the later 19th century as English control grew as an integral part of the increasing power of central government. Nationalist sentiment expressed itself through increasingly radical Welsh Liberalism (the Conservative Party was weak in Wales throughout the 20th century) and widespread NONCONFORMITY in religion. The latter led to the disestablishment of the CHURCH OF ENGLAND as the official CHURCH IN WALES by an act of 1914, which came into effect in 1920, having been delayed by World War I. In the 1890s politicians, including David LLOYD GEORGE, were advocating HOME RULE for Wales, and Cymru Fydd, a nationalist Young Wales movement, was founded in 1886 within the Liberal Party. Out of this nationalist movement came new institutions, notably the foundation of the federal University of Wales. After WORLD WAR I nationalistic Liberalism was overtaken by socialism, and after 1922 the LABOUR PARTY became the dominant political force in Wales. It gave some support for a degree of devolution for Wales, but desire for devolution was eclipsed by the effects of the economic crisis, especially in the COAL MINING industry. Welsh nationalism revived after World War II. The Welsh National Party, founded in 1925 and later known as Plaid Cymru ('party of Wales'), had little success until the 1950s. It put up candidates in every election from 1959, gaining its first seat for its leader, Gwynfor Evans, in the Carmarthen by-election in 1966. It performed well in further by-elections and won its first seats in a GENERAL ELECTION in February 1974, when it gained two; it held a handful of seats in every Parliament for the remainder of the century. Pressure for devolved government resulted in the Labour government in 1964 establishing the Welsh Office, based in Cardiff, with the new secretary of state for Wales having a seat in the UK CABINET. In 1963 the Welsh Language Society (Cymdeithas yr Iaith Gymraeg) was founded to campaign for equal status for the Welsh language. The Welsh Language Act, 1967, granted equal status to Welsh in certain circumstances (for example, in official documents and on road signs). In 1981 Welsh was spoken by about 19% of the Welsh population, about 500,000 people. By the 1980s it was increasingly taught in schools, and there were signs that the language was reviving.

In the later 1960s the nationalist movement developed a violent fringe. This was responsible for bombing holiday cottages, which were seen as depriving Welsh people of affordable homes. But the nationalists also won wider support. In 1979 the Labour government carried out a referendum in Wales on devolution (*see also* SCOTLAND), which produced a substantial vote against the idea. Welsh nationalist feeling was highly regionalized, and was especially fervent in the strongly Welsh-speaking rural west of Wales. It did not decline, and the Labour government elected in 1997 established another devolution referendum in the same year, which narrowly agreed to devolution. A Welsh Assembly, based in Cardiff, was elected in 1999 by PROPORTIONAL REPRESENTATION. Labour gained the largest number of representatives, followed by the Welsh nationalists.

FURTHER READING K.O. Morgan, *Rebirth of a Nation: Wales, 1880–1980* (1981).

war poets. *See* POETRY.

Waugh, Evelyn (Arthur St John) (1903–66), novelist. Waugh was born in Hampstead, London; his father was a publisher. He was educated at Lancing College and Oxford University, where he led a life he described as 'idle, dissolute and extravagant' and left with a third-class degree, though he had strengthened his literary and artistic interests and made lifelong friends. He worked for some years, unhappily, as an assistant schoolmaster at obscure and educationally dubious fee-paying schools, an experience that provided material for his first, immensely successful, novel *Decline and Fall* (1928). In 1926 he published a short study of the Pre-Raphaelites. In 1928 he married Evelyn Gardner, who left him a year later. Shocked by this, in 1930 he was received into the Roman Catholic Church.

In the same year he published *Vile Bodies*, another satirical novel, set in London's Mayfair. He then embarked on a series of travels. In 1930 he went as correspondent for *The* TIMES to the coronation of Emperor Haile Selassie in Abyssinia, out of which came a travel book, *Remote People* (1931), and a novel about cultural conflict set in Africa, *Black Mischief* (1932). *A Handful of Dust* (1934) was another novel that captured with acute observation the frivolity of a section of London society in the interwar years, while giving a farcical account of a divorce such as he had recently experienced. He covered the ABYSSINIAN CRISIS for the *Daily Mail* in 1935 and wrote another travel book, *Waugh in Abyssinia* (1936), and *Scoop* (1938), a satire of the newspaper world, largely set in a war-torn African country. He was now a highly successful writer. In 1936 the church annulled his first marriage, enabling him to marry a Catholic, Laura Herbert, in 1937. Thereafter he lived mainly in the country, cultivating the style of a country squire and eventually fathering six children.

His country life was interrupted by WORLD WAR II. Waugh was commissioned in the Royal Marines, joining the Commandos and receiving parachute training. He served in Crete and Yugoslavia without distinction, but the experience contributed to a string of entertaining novels: *Put Out More Flags* (1942) and the *Sword of Honour* trilogy: *Men at Arms* (1952), *Officers and Gentlemen* (1955) and *Unconditional Surrender* (1961). Another novel, *Brideshead Revisited* (1945), marked the end of the war and his nostalgia for a hierarchical social order, underpinned by Christian faith, which he feared was coming to an end. *Brideshead Revisited* was highly successful and established his reputation in the United States. His macabre comedy about Californian funeral practices, *The Loved One* (1948), based on a trip to Hollywood to prepare a film script for *Brideshead Revisited* (the film was not made), similarly suggested civilization in decline. He was a highly conservative figure for the remainder of his life. In 1957 he published *The Ordeal of Gilbert Pinfold*, a bizarre self-caricature about a famous 50-year-old Roman Catholic novelist, overweight, a heavy drinker, insomniac, out of tune with modern life, who sets off on a cruise but is beset by the conviction that he is being attacked as homosexual, Jewish, fascist, alcoholic, a social climber and other characteristics – not all of them inaccurate accusations as far as Waugh himself was concerned. But he was a fine writer and an acute observer of the world in which he moved. **FURTHER READING** C. Sykes, *Evelyn Waugh* (1975); E. Waugh (ed. M.Davie), *Diaries* (1976).

Wavell, Archibald (Percival) (1883–1950), WORLD WAR II general who commanded British forces in North Africa, then in the Far East, before becoming viceroy of INDIA (1943–7). Wavell was born in Winchester and educated at Winchester College, then at Sandhurst. He was commissioned in the Black Watch in 1901, fought in the BOER WAR, then served in India, 1903–11, and with the Russian army, 1911–12. In WORLD WAR I he fought in France, 1914–16, was liaison officer with Grand Duke Nicolas's army in Turkey, 1916, then served on ALLENBY's staff in Palestine, 1917–20. After a variety of posts between the wars, he returned to command British forces in PALESTINE in 1937, then was appointed commander in chief, MIDDLE EAST, in July 1939.

Wavell successfully defended Egypt in 1940, driving the Italians out of Cyrenaica in the first North African campaign and assisting in the conquest of Ethiopia and Italian East Africa. In 1941, against his better judgement, he had to fight in Greece and Crete, and send forces to Iraq and Syria, as well as fighting in North Africa. His resources were overstretched and Greece, Crete and Cyrenaica were lost to the Germans. He was replaced by AUCHINLECK in July 1941 and transferred to take command in India in 1941. He was supreme commander, Southwest Pacific, 1941–3, fighting the war in BURMA with minimal help from home. He was unable to stem the Japanese advance in 1942, and was replaced in June 1943. He became a field marshal, then a viscount and was appointed viceroy of India, where he helped both to relieve famine and to maintain order at a time when India faced invasion. He worked hard to reach a settlement of the Indian dispute with Britain over independence, releasing Congress leaders to take part in discussions. He retired in 1947 and was created 1st Earl Wavell. **FURTHER READING** H.M. Close, *Attlee, Wavell, Mountbatten and the Transfer of Power* (1997).

wealth and income distribution. *See* STANDARDS OF LIVING.

Webb, Beatrice (1858–1943) and **Sidney** (1859–1947), influential socialist thinkers, prominent in the early development of the LABOUR PARTY.

Beatrice Webb (*née* Potter) was one of nine daughters of a wealthy family. Her father engaged in various business enterprises, ultimately mainly in railways. She was beautiful, well educated (at home) and well connected with the intellectual and philanthropic elite of late-Victorian England. Initially a LIBERAL, she was influenced by the philosopher Herbert Spencer and fell in love with Joseph CHAMBERLAIN, but he failed to ask her to marry him. She became a social worker for the Charity Organization Society and later undertook research on Charles Booth's great survey of POVERTY in London. Contact with the social conditions of the 1880s converted her to socialism.

Sidney was born into a lower-middle-class family in London. His father was a hairdresser, later an accountant; he was also a Liberal, who had done some work alongside John Stuart Mill. Sidney spent part of his education in Germany and Switzerland, then at Birkbeck Institute, London, and City of London College. He entered the civil service and was called to the Bar in 1885. He was an early member of the FABIAN SOCIETY (*see also* WELLS, H.G.). In 1892 he was elected to the London County Council (LCC; *see* LONDON GOVERNMENT) as a 'LIB-LAB' member of the Progressive Alliance, and was especially influential on its technical education board. In the same year he married Beatrice. She found him less attractive than

Chamberlain and thought their relationship incongruous, but they formed a strong and lasting friendship and intellectual partnership.

The Webbs collaborated in monumental and lasting works of historical research, principally *The History of Trade Unionism* (1894), *Industrial Democracy* (1897) and the multi-volume history of *English Local Government* (1906–29). They also collaborated in social research, in the work of the Fabian Society and later of the LABOUR PARTY, and in the foundation in the late 1890s of the London School of Economics and Imperial College, London, to promote higher education in the social and natural sciences respectively. Beatrice tended to work behind the scenes, and came to public prominence only through her membership of the Royal Commission on the POOR LAW, 1905–9, and the subsequent, unsuccessful, campaign to 'break up' the Poor Law, in which she was joined by Sidney. They founded the *New Statesman* in 1913 as a left-wing, intellectual weekly journal. Sidney became increasingly active in the Labour Party. He helped to draft CLAUSE FOUR of the party's new constitution in 1918 and its 1918 policy statement *Labour and the New Social Order*, and was also a member of the party's National Executive Committee, 1915–25. He was a member of the SANKEY COMMISSION on the COAL-MINING industry in 1919. He was elected Labour MP for the Seaham division of Durham, 1922–9, and was president of the Board of Trade and became a privy councillor in 1924. In 1929 he was created Baron Passfield, and was secretary for dominions and colonies from 1929 to 1931.

Both the Webbs felt disillusioned with the Labour Party after the crisis of 1931 (*see* NATIONAL GOVERNMENT) and became entranced with the Soviet Union as a model of planned socialism, despite their previous deep scepticism about communism. They visited the Soviet Union in 1932 and were especially impressed by the health, educational and social services they were shown and the ideals of those involved in them. They then published *Soviet Communism: A New Civiliza-*

tion? (1935). Thereafter their health declined, but they remained engaged with politics until their deaths.

FURTHER READING B. Caine, *Destined to be Wives: The Sisters of Beatrice Webb* (1988); R.J. Harrison, *The Life and Times of Sidney and Beatrice Webb, 1858–1905* (2000); J. and N. MacKenzie (eds.), *The Diary of Beatrice Webb* (4 vols., 1982–5).

welfare state, a nation-state that defines as an essential part of its role the prevention of absolute poverty and, more contentiously, the maintenance of an adequate STANDARD OF LIVING for all its citizens. The term entered everyday British discourse after WORLD WAR II, and was a conscious challenge to the 'warfare state'.

The goals of the welfare state may be achieved by a variety of means, including the provision of cash benefits and/or services and the regulation of the fiscal system or the labour market in order to maximize incomes. Over the 20th century such activities have grown in size, range, cost and complexity. Central plus local government expenditure on social welfare services in the UK was 4% of gross national product (GNP) in 1913, 10% in 1921, 11% in 1938, 17.5% in 1951, 23% in 1967 and 22.5% in 1987. This growth has not simply been the result of an increasingly benevolent, or more socialistic, state choosing to levy higher taxes in order to promote social equality. Nor has it been a process of the state displacing other providers of welfare: the family, the labour market, employers, churches and other voluntary organizations. All of these continued to play an essential role in supporting people in need throughout the century, and have been complementary to state welfare.

At the end of the 19th century both central and local government were responsible for a wide range of welfare activities: apart from the growing state responsibility for EDUCATION, the POOR LAW provided benefits and services for the destitute. However, various pressure groups increasingly pointed out the extent of involuntary need that was not provided for. This was perceived as harmful not only to poor people themselves but to the nation as a whole as, at the turn of the century, it was more and more recognized that mass poverty was associated with high death rates and low levels of physical efficiency in much of the population; these in turn lowered productivity in the workforce, military effectiveness (highlighted in the failures of the British army during the BOER WAR), increased infant mortality (owing to the poor health of mothers) and lowered the birth rate. Since market mechanisms were failing to improve these problems it seemed increasingly clear in the early part of the century that only the state had the power to intervene. The emerging LABOUR movement urged such intervention, but few people, even in the Labour movement, favoured the state's taking complete responsibility for welfare. Similarly the WOMEN'S MOVEMENT played an important role in demanding improved provision, especially for the health and welfare of women and children. Most believed that voluntary action and private saving should be encouraged, where possible, and that at least as important a role for the state as the provision of welfare was to ensure full employment and adequate wages, which would enable individuals and families to look after themselves.

The LIBERAL governments in the period 1906–14 were the first to make a substantial response to these pressures, partly owing to pressure from the Labour Party and the fear of losing working-class votes to Labour. The Liberals introduced a series of measures that were not notably costly or redistributive, but which established principles of state action that were to be influential for the remainder of the century. Free school meals for needy children were introduced in 1906, and medical inspection in schools in 1907. These innovations were followed by the Children Act in 1908. This removed those below the age of 16 from the adult criminal justice system, including prisons, establishing a separate system of courts and institutions. Local authorities also gained increased powers to

protect neglected and abused children. All of these measures were designed to improve the physical state of the nation by improving conditions for children, the coming generation. OLD-AGE PENSIONS were also introduced in 1908. The Trade Boards Act, 1909, was the first step in the long progression towards a MINIMUM WAGE. Similarly, the Housing and Town Planning Act, 1909 (*see* TOWN AND COUNTRY PLANNING), was a step towards serious attempts to prevent urban overcrowding and pollution. National-health and unemployment insurance, introduced in 1911, provided for two major causes of need. The scheme chiefly assisted regularly employed male manual workers. They and their employers were obliged to make weekly contributions, in return for which workers received cash benefits when sick or unemployed, free treatment by a General Practitioner and a limited range of other health-care services, such as free treatment for TB. The health insurance scheme covered most regularly employed workers earning £160 per year or less (roughly the upper limit of manual earnings). It did not cover partners or children. Unemployment insurance was restricted to selected industries with relatively low incidences of unemployment. Collectively these measures were a significant leap forward in the state's responsibility, but there was no conscious intention by the Liberals to establish the state as a permanent provider of welfare. Rather the measures were intended in the short run to support self-help and voluntary action, which it was hoped would be the major sources of provision for need in the longer run.

Shortly afterwards, WORLD WAR I led to the extension both of the responsibilities of the state and of popular expectations. Living standards improved as a result of civilian full employment. Fear of public disorder should these expectations be undermined after the war led the LLOYD GEORGE government to plan improvements in UNEMPLOYMENT benefits, HOUSING and state education after the war. From 1920 economic depression and unemployment led to the wielding of the 'GEDDES

AXE', which cut public expenditure. Nevertheless, in the longer run, the interwar years saw expanded welfare services and state expenditure, and a higher degree of redistribution, especially on unemployment benefits, council housing and education (*see* GOVERNMENT EXPENDITURE).

Demands for more state action and planning grew in the 1930s, and grew further during World War II. During the war the state was aware of the need to maintain public morale, and acted to improve health and welfare services and support for impoverished old people. It also initiated a number of plans for post-war improvements, including the BEVERIDGE Plan of 1942. The post-war Labour government was committed to introducing full employment and extending the welfare state. Using modified KEYNESian techniques, assisted by high levels of world demand, it raised employment levels, and this did more to improve living standards than did welfare measures. However, the introduction of universal pensions, health and unemployment insurance and of the NATIONAL HEALTH SERVICE in 1948 was an essential complement to the benefits of full employment, especially for those outside the labour force such as old people, children and many women. There were improvements also in housing, education and community social services. The middle classes as well as the poor benefited from these changes – intentionally, since the Labour government recognized that many such people could not provide for all of their families' needs and was anxious to keep their support (*see*, for example, FAMILY ALLOWANCES). The outcome was a great improvement in welfare provision, but it was constrained by Labour's determination to put reconstruction and development of the economy first. It has been argued that the post-war welfare state was built at the expense of reconstruction of the economy, but this is mistaken. Labour explicitly held back welfare expenditure, lest it divert resources from industrial investment. In consequence the welfare state that was in place by 1950 was a good beginning, albeit hesitant, incomplete and rather ramshackle. There

was notably little spending on capital projects such as schools and hospitals. The CONSERVATIVE governments in the 1950s did not cut back on these projects, despite a certain pressure in the party to do so, but nor did they expand them, apart from a burst of hospital planning from the late 1950s and an increase in the building of council housing (though this was of poor quality). The Conservatives also encouraged private and business-based welfare, such as occupational pensions.

The most extensive growth of public expenditure on welfare, especially on schools, hospitals and housing, came, as it did elsewhere in Europe, in the 1960s and early 1970s under both Conservative and (especially) Labour governments. However, the international economic recession following the OIL SHOCK of the early 1970s led to attempts to cut public expenditure in Britain and elsewhere. Conservative governments in the 1980s and early 1990s sought to cut state services or to privatize them, and to encourage private insurance and private care (for example, there was an extensive transfer of residential care for older people from local authorities to private agencies). Legislative protection of lower-paid workers, a high proportion of them female, was eroded. However, in a period of high unemployment, unemployment benefits were less severely cut, except for the young, because governments feared the political consequences of unemployment. Further cuts to welfare provision were constrained by the electorate, which especially resisted privatization of the National Health Service, and by the EUROPEAN UNION, which set standards of welfare provision for its members that were generally higher than those prevailing in Britain. In consequence, despite the government's efforts, public expenditure on welfare in Britain did not fall as a percentage of GNP in the 1980s, although a higher proportion than before was spent on the unemployed, and there were cuts in housing, education, health and social services. The safety net that since the 1940s had prevented the poorest falling too far behind the mass of the population was rolled back in the

1980s, and the gap between richer and poorer grew. But the structures of state welfare that had been in place for most of the century remained, and the Labour government elected in 1997 began to reverse the process of erosion while encouraging those who could afford to provide for their own pensions and other needs to do so.

FURTHER READING M.A. Crowther, *British Social Policy, 1914–39* (1988); H. Glennerster, *British Social Policy since 1945* (1996); P. Thane, *The Foundations of the Welfare State* (2nd edn, 1996); P. Thane, 'Labour and Welfare' in D. Tanner, P. Thane, N. Tiratsoo (eds.), *Labour's First Century* (2000), 80–118.

Wells, H(erbert) G(eorge) (1866–1946), novelist and writer on social and political issues. Wells was born in Bromley, Kent. His father was an unsuccessful small tradesman and professional cricketer. Wells was apprenticed as a draper, an experience that informed several of his novels. He then became a pupil teacher at Midhurst Grammar School, studying by night and in 1884 winning a scholarship to the Normal School of Science in South Kensington. There he came under the lasting influence of T.H. Huxley, from whom he absorbed Darwinian theory and a certain pessimism about the evolutionary process. He feared that humans might regress to the state of their animal forebears, becoming such creatures as the ape-like Morlocks in his novel *The Time Machine* (1895) or the beast-men of *The Island of Dr Moreau* (1896). He also read Plato and attended socialist gatherings at William Morris's Kelmscott House. From these combined influences he developed a passionate belief in the need for a scientifically planned society if human beings were not to regress into horror. He struggled for some years as a teacher, in poor health, studying and writing articles in his spare time. His marriage in 1891 to his cousin Isabel Wells (1866–1931) proved unhappy and he eloped with his student Amy Catherine ('Jane') Robbins (1872–1927), whom he married in 1895, though this did not prevent his embarking on further relationships and continuing to criticize conventional marriage.

Wells's early novels were pessimistic. The first, *The Time Machine* (1895), made his reputation. A social allegory set in the year 802701, it describes a world in which the upper and working classes have evolved into two distinct species, the former weak, effete and decadent, dependent upon a brutalized class of subterranean workers, which ultimately descends into decay. This was followed, at impressive speed, by *The Wonderful Visit* (1895), *The Island of Dr Moreau* (1896), *The Invisible Man* (1897) and *The War of the Worlds* (1898), a powerful vision of a Martian invasion of Earth. Wells admitted that it expressed his desire to see Victorian society with its inequities and repressions blasted apart by Martian heat-rays. Its success suggested that this desire resonated with others. Then came *When the Sleeper Wakes* (1899) and *The First Men in the Moon* (1901), which conveyed similar sentiments.

Wells's mood became less negative with *Anticipations* (1901), which embodied his forecast for the 20th century. He now placed his hope in the leadership of technocrats, who would establish universal peace and plenty through central planning. This was an attractive vision for George Bernard SHAW and Beatrice and Sidney WEBB who, in 1903, brought Wells into the FABIAN SOCIETY. Wells, however, was too much of an individualist to fit easily into any political organization and his talents belonged elsewhere. He later attacked both Shaw and the Webbs, whom he ridiculed in his novel *The New Machiavelli* (1911). He also produced a series of novels that criticized contemporary society by evoking the lower-middle-class world of his youth. *Love and Mr Lewisham* (1900) told the story of a struggling teacher; *Kipps* (1905) that of an aspiring draper's assistant; *The History of Mr Polly* (1910) that of an unsuccessful shopkeeper who escapes by burning down his shop and finding freedom as man-of-all-work at an inn.

In a different register, *In the Days of the Comet* (1906) and *Ann Veronica* (1909) advocated sexual liberation (which he practised in his affairs with, among others, the writer Rebecca West, who bore him a son) and criticized the morality of the day. *Ann Veronica* was an explicitly feminist novel about a girl inspired by contemporary feminist ideas who defies her father and conventional morality to run off with the man she loves. *Tono-Bungay* (1909), one of Wells's most successful works, is a picture of English society in decay and of the advent of a new rich class, embodied in Uncle Ponderevo, an entrepreneur peddling a worthless patent medicine. Also, in this extraordinary succession of publications, *The War in the Air* (1908) foresaw strategic bombing, and *The World Set Free* (1914) predicted nuclear weapons. In a remarkable way, Wells foresaw not just the mechanics but the impact of future technology. He predicted how tanks, bombers and nuclear science would transform warfare. Leo Szilard, who worked on the Manhattan Project, which created the first atom bomb during World War II, claimed that *The World Set Free* led him to the idea of an atomic chain reaction.

Wells was less far-sighted about World War I, which he proclaimed as 'The War That Will End War'. He was convinced that it would bring about the revolution of technocratic planning he dreamed off, leading ultimately to a world state. These views were expressed in *The Research Magnificent* (1915), *Mr Britling Sees it Through* (1916) and *God the Invisible King* (1917). However, all of these, in terms of the quality of writing, suggested a decline or exhaustion of his talent.

Wells was an early supporter of the LEAGUE OF NATIONS as the precursor of a planned world, but he was quickly disillusioned. His most successful post-war books were nonfictional expressions of his grand visions. *The Outline of History* (1920), which synthesized his world-view, sold in millions and made him rich, followed by the equally successful *A Short History of the World* (1922). Together with his son George ('Gip') and Julian Huxley he produced a survey of biology, *The Science of Life* (1930), which was similarly a bestseller, followed by *The Shape of Things to Come* (1933).

He aimed successfully for an audience of intelligent but undereducated people, such as he had once been, who existed in all too large numbers in interwar Britain. His *Experiment in Autobiography* (1934) was a striking portrait of himself and his contemporaries, including Arnold BENNETT and the Fabians. In the 1930s he looked for hope to the United States and Roosevelt's New Deal, and to Stalin's Russia, but saw little in either. He became increasingly cranky and disillusioned. He was unappreciated by the younger generations of writers, who thought him either not modernist or not Marxist enough; they judged him, probably accurately, as a vivid but not an outstanding writer. Nevertheless, he made a popular impact and had an extraordinary vision that many of them did not. **FURTHER READING** N. and J. MacKenzie, *H.G. Wells* (1973).

Welsh nationalism. *See* WALES.

Welsh National Party. *See* WALES.

Western European Union (WEU), international security and defence organization that grew out of the Brussels treaty, signed by the UK, France, the Netherlands, Belgium and Luxembourg on 17 March 1948. The 50-year treaty committed the signatories to collaboration in economic, cultural and social affairs and to collective self-defence. The defence functions were formally transferred to NATO on 20 December 1950. In 1954 Italy and West Germany were invited to join, and the WEU was formally inaugurated on 6 May 1955. Its social and cultural functions were transferred to the Council of Europe on 1 July 1960, but the WEU continued to hold regular meetings to the end of the century.

West Indies, name applied to the islands of the Caribbean in general, as well as to those that were formerly British colonies. The islands that were part of the EMPIRE were particularly valuable in the 18th and 19th centuries, as producers of foodstuffs such as sugar and coffee. However, declining sugar prices in the 20th century meant that the West Indies suffered economically, and many of its people migrated to Britain after World War II to help alleviate Britain's labour shortage (*see* IMMIGRATION). In 1958, after over ten years of negotiations and in the midst of movements towards the DECOLONIZATION of the empire, the British established the West Indies (or British Caribbean) Federation in an attempt to establish political and economic links among the colonies of Antigua, Barbados, Dominica, Grenada, Montserrat, Jamaica, St Kitts-Nevis-Anguilla, St Lucia, St Vincent and Trinidad and Tobago. This effort to bring unity was, however, unsuccessful. Some of the islands were richer than others, and the economic implications of the Federation caused resentment. Jamaica disliked the fact that the Federation's capital had been placed in Trinidad and voted to secede. Further tensions became evident, and the West Indies Federation was dissolved in 1962 after only four years of existence.

In 1967 a looser federation called the West Indies Associated States was created, including the smaller islands of Antigua, St Kitts-Nevis-Anguilla, Dominica, Grenada, St Lucia and St Vincent. Both Jamaica and Trinidad and Tobago had become independent in 1962. Other islands followed suit – Barbados in 1966, Grenada in 1974, Dominica in 1978, St Lucia and St Vincent in 1979, Antigua and Barbuda in 1981 and St Kitts and Nevis in 1983. At the end of the 20th century only Anguilla, Montserrat and the British Virgin Islands remained colonies of Britain.

SEE ALSO SPORT.

FURTHER READING C. Hamshere, *The British in the Caribbean* (1972).

Westland affair. *See* THATCHER, MARGARET.

whips, parliamentary, members of Parliament in all parties whose role is to police members of their own parliamentary party, for example by ensuring that they turn up to vote when required

and do not behave in ways deemed disadvantageous to the party (*see* COMMONS, HOUSE OF). Two late-20th-century Conservative prime ministers, Edward HEATH and John MAJOR, rose to prominence through the whips' office.

Whitley Councils. *See* MINIMUM WAGE.

widows' and orphans' pension (1925). *See* POOR LAW.

Wilkins, Maurice. *See* SCIENCE.

Wilkinson, Ellen (1891–1947), Labour politician and feminist. Born in Manchester into an upper-working-class family, she grew up as a METHODIST. Educated at elementary schools, she trained as a teacher, then won a scholarship to study history at Manchester University in 1910, conditional on her teaching thereafter. She did so, but found that she deeply disliked conditions in state schools, which made her vow to improve them. At university she became a socialist and a feminist, joining the FABIAN SOCIETY and the university socialist federation. She joined the INDEPENDENT LABOUR PARTY (ILP) in 1912. After leaving teaching she worked for the NATIONAL UNION OF WOMEN'S SUFFRAGE SOCIETIES (NUWSS). She opposed World War I, becoming active in the Women's International League for Peace and Freedom (WIL). In 1915 she became the national women's organizer for the Union of Shop, Distributive and Allied Workers (USDAW). She was a member of the COMMUNIST PARTY OF GREAT BRITAIN, from its foundation in 1920 until 1924, leaving when membership was forbidden to LABOUR PARTY members.

Wilkinson was elected to Manchester City Council for Labour in 1923, but played little part in council affairs as she quickly became involved in national politics. She stood unsuccessfully as a parliamentary candidate for Ashton-under-Lyne (Lancashire) in 1923, but in the following year was returned for Middlesbrough East (which she represented until 1931), becoming one of only four women in the House of COMMONS. She was an outspoken supporter of equal rights for women from her first speech in the Commons, and in the second Labour government (1929–31) became parliamentary private secretary to Susan LAWRENCE. While out of Parliament she headed the India League delegation to INDIA in 1932, supporting self-rule. She also worked as a journalist (one of the first to warn of the dangers of Hitler, while writing from Germany in 1933) and wrote fiction, including a detective story. She returned to Parliament in 1935 as MP for the shipbuilding town of Jarrow in the northeast of England, one of the worst centres of UNEMPLOYMENT. She became a passionate advocate of the plight of the 'distressed areas', as districts of high unemployment were known, giving strong support to the march of the unemployed from Jarrow in 1936 (*see* HUNGER MARCHES). She wrote a memorable book about Jarrow for the LEFT BOOK CLUB, *The Town That Was Murdered* (1939). She was opposed with equal passion to non-intervention in the SPANISH CIVIL WAR. In 1938 she carried the Hire Purchase Bill through Parliament, because she felt that working people were being seriously overcharged by this new, unregulated form of payment.

In the coalition government of WORLD WAR II Wilkinson was parliamentary secretary to the minister of pensions (May–October 1940), then to the minister of home security at the Home Office until 1945, working with people bombed out in the BLITZ. In this capacity she worked with her close companion the home secretary Herbert MORRISON, to whom she was devoted; they did not marry because he could not leave the wife to whom he had been long married. Wilkinson overworked grossly, despite increasing ill health. In 1945 she became minister of education in the Labour government and strove to improve secondary EDUCATION and to raise the school-leaving age to 16. She died in office of a probably accidental overdose of prescribed drugs.

FURTHER READING B.D. Vernon, *Ellen Wilkinson* (1982).

Wilson, (James) Harold (1916–95), Labour politician; leader of the LABOUR PARTY (1963–76) and PRIME MINISTER (1964–70, 1974–6). Born in Yorkshire, the son of an industrial chemist, Wilson was educated at Wirral Grammar School and Oxford University. He was a fellow of University College, Oxford, before becoming director of economics and statistics at the Ministry of Fuel and Power, 1943–4. He was MP for Ormskirk, 1945–50, then for Huyton, also on Merseyside, 1950–83. In the post-war Labour government he was parliamentary secretary, Ministry of Works, 1945–7, secretary for overseas trade, 1947, and president of the Board of Trade, 1947–51. In 1951 he resigned from the cabinet along with Nye BEVAN in protest against GAITSKELL's budget plans to introduce NATIONAL HEALTH SERVICE charges.

Wilson became leader of the Labour Party following the death of Gaitskell in 1963, and led the party to a narrow GENERAL ELECTION victory in 1964. After Labour's more convincing election victory in 1966, Wilson's government resolved to maintain the value of the pound against the dollar, but was forced to devalue sterling in 1967. This led to the resignation of the chancellor, Jim CALLAGHAN, and Wilson's often quoted and unconvincing plea to the British public that devaluation 'does not mean, of course, that the pound here in Britain in your pocket or purse or in your bank has been devalued'.

Wilson's government was also preoccupied with difficult international issues, such as the unilateral declaration of independence announced by Ian Smith's Rhodesian government in 1965 (*see* ZIMBABWE). There were also difficulties regarding Britain's relationship with the USA; Wilson's support for US military involvement in Vietnam disillusioned the left in Britain and provided a focus for widespread student protest during the late 1960s. By 1970 the Wilson government's record on the economy was less than glowing, and social and political discontent had increased. Yet between 1964 and 1970 a number of important changes had taken place: a major expansion of

UNIVERSITY education (including the OPEN UNIVERSITY), the ending of CAPITAL PUNISHMENT, and the legalization of ABORTION and homosexuality (*see* SEXUALITY, OFFICIAL REGULATION OF; JENKINS, ROY). Despite discontent, a Labour victory in the 1970 election seemed likely, yet the Conservative Party under Edward HEATH forced Wilson into opposition.

As opposition leader Wilson was forced to make compromises over policy in order to avoid splits in the party, particularly regarding the question of Europe. Labour's election victories of 1974, producing a minority government in February and a small majority in October, brought Wilson back to power in an economic climate somewhat different from that of four years earlier. With the legacy of the Heath government and international recession following the OIL SHOCK, Wilson's government was unable to reduce inflation, and relied upon an informal 'social contract' with the TRADES UNION CONGRESS (TUC) in the hope of controlling wage increases (*see* TRADE UNIONS). Disagreements within the Labour Party continued, with Wilson avoiding a split in the party by holding a referendum on the European Community (*see* EUROPEAN ECONOMIC COMMUNITY) in 1975, which supported continued British membership. In March 1976 Wilson retired unexpectedly, with foreign secretary James CALLAGHAN replacing him as party leader and prime minister.

Wilson remained a Labour MP until 1983, when he was made a life peer as Baron Wilson of Rievaulx. His health deteriorated seriously after his resignation, and he spent much of his remaining life on the Isles of Scilly.

FURTHER READING A. Morgan, *Harold Wilson* (1992); B. Pimlott, *Harold Wilson* (1994).

Windsor, house of, the name of the British royal family since 1917. The royal family at the beginning of the century were German by ancestry and closely related to the German Kaiser. When WORLD WAR I broke out this was embarrassing. Reluctantly King GEORGE V ordered the banners of the Kaiser and his family to be removed from St George's Chapel, Windsor. In 1917 he declared that all German titles and honours would be renounced and that the family name (hitherto Saxe-Coburg-Gotha, from Queen Victoria's husband Prince Albert) would now be Windsor. Their cousins, the Battenbergs, became Mountbattens (*see* MOUNTBATTEN, LOUIS).

SEE ALSO EDWARD VIII; ELIZABETH II; GEORGE VI; MONARCHY.

winter of discontent (1978–9). *See* TRADE UNIONS.

wireless. *See* BRITISH BROADCASTING CORPORATION.

Wolfenden Report (1957), result of an inquiry by a committee chaired by John Wolfenden (1906–85), vice chancellor of the University of Reading, into the laws relating to homosexuality and prostitution (*see* SEXUALITY, OFFICIAL REGULATION OF). The committee was appointed in 1954 by the Conservative government, following several trials of public figures for sexual offences. The committee reported in 1957, recommending stricter control of public solicitation by prostitutes, and that homosexual acts between consenting male adults (over the age of 21) in private should be decriminalized; at the same time it suggested the need for stricter controls over public manifestations of homosexuality. (Female same-sex sexual activity has never been subject to legal control.) The recommendations on prostitution were embodied in the Street Offences Act, 1959, but there was greater reluctance to change the law on homosexual acts. In consequence the Homosexual Law Reform Society was formed to campaign for reform. In 1967, under a Labour government, homosexual acts between consenting adults in private were decriminalized in the Sexual Offences Act.

FURTHER READING J. Wolfenden, *Turning Points: The Memoirs of Lord Wolfenden* (1976).

Women's Auxiliary Air Force (WAAF). *See* ROYAL AIR FORCE.

Women's Auxiliary Army Corps. *See* ARMY.

Women's Cooperative Guild. *See* COOPERATIVE MOVEMENT.

Women's Institutes. The Women's Institute (WI) movement originated in Canada in 1897. It grew in Britain from 1915, starting during WORLD WAR I. Its main objective was to empower rural women, especially less privileged rural women, and in particular to assist them to bring about improvements in their often grim lives (*see* AGRICULTURE).

Initially the movement was seen as part of the war effort, encouraging the economical use of food and the development by women of gardens and smallholdings for vegetables, poultry, pigs and rabbits (*see also* WOMENS LAND ARMY). By 1918 WIs had 50,000 members and it proved to be an enduring organization that met many needs of countrywomen. Many of the early leaders of the movement in Britain had been SUFFRAGISTS. They saw the WIs as one of many desirable ways to assist and educate women in using the vote after the franchise was extended to include women in 1918 and 1928. The locally based WI branches were notable for their democratic organization, which gave equal voting rights to all members; this could be something of a challenge to the hierarchical traditions of rural communities, where the lady of the manor and the clergyman's wife often assumed an automatic right to precedence.

From the beginning the WIs were resolutely non-sectarian in religious affairs and non-party in politics, but this did not mean that they were irreligious or apolitical. This stance attracted some criticism, but it enabled the organization to be as inclusive as possible. One of the objectives was to educate women in political issues and methods of political organization in order to achieve improvements. Another objective was to nurture the skills and handicrafts of countrywomen, and to encourage women – and society more broadly – to value these skills and prevent their dying out. A third, equally important objective was to provide opportunities for women (who often led isolated lives) to socialize.

In the interwar years WIs led a number of campaigns at local-government level, or participated with other women's organizations in such campaigns. These were aimed at achieving, among other things, better health care and other services in rural areas, replacement of often appalling rural housing, and improvements in water and electricity supplies, public transport, telephones, libraries and ADULT EDUCATION facilities, all of which were lacking in many areas up to WORLD WAR II and often beyond. By 1937 there were 300,000 members. It was widely believed that the WIs had increased the interest of many countrywomen in politics and encouraged them to use their votes.

During World War II the National Federation of Women's Institutes (NFWI), to which local branches were affiliated from 1918, declared that it could not as an institution take part in the war effort, in view of its non-partisan principles. This stance attracted criticism, but NFWI did not prevent large numbers of its members playing an active part in the Women's Land Army, the WOMEN'S ROYAL VOLUNTARY SERVICE and Civil Defence, or contributing substantially to the EVACUATION OF CHILDREN and other forms of war service. Membership fell somewhat, to 288,000 in 1943, but rose to 446,000 in 1951.

Over the second half of the century the size of the permanent rural population fell. The needs of rural women were different from those of the pre-war years, and often less distinct from those of urban women, though by the end of the century they were again having to campaign about inadequate rural services, for example transport and post offices. WIs continued to provide supportive and educational facilities, especially for women at home caring for children. They also continued to campaign on issues important to women: for example, in 1993 they carried out a survey of carers for older, disabled and sick people and their often difficult living and financial conditions, the findings of which were publicized at a conference. At the end of the century there were still 300,000 members. Women of the WI were often derided in the late 20th century as socially and politically conservative, devoted to little more than making jam. Little in their history justified such jibes.

FURTHER READING M. Andrews, *The Accceptable Face of Feminism: The Women's Institute as a Social Movement* (1997); M. Pugh, *Women and the Women's Movement in Britain* (2nd edn, 2000).

Women's Land Army (WLA), established in 1917 with the aim of mobilizing women as workers on the land to maximize food production to meet the needs of the population when food imports were restricted by the German blockade during WORLD WAR I. By the end of the war 23,000 women were working as tractor drivers, field workers, carters, plough workers, thatchers, shepherds and in other forms of agricultural work. It was disbanded at the end of the war, but relaunched in June 1939 as WORLD WAR II approached. Lady Gertrude Denman, chair of the National Federation of WOMEN'S INSTITUTES, who had been involved in organizing the WLA in the previous war, was appointed director. One-third of recruits were from London or other large towns. After training, they carried out similar work to their predecessors in World War I. By 1943 there were 43,000 'Land Girls', plus 4900 in the Women's Timber Corps, a section of the WLA that specialized in cutting trees and caring for forests. The writer Vita Sackville-West was a WLA district representative for a large area of Kent and wrote the official history of WLA, *The Land Army* (1944). The WLA was disbanded in 1950.

women's liberation. *See* WOMEN'S MOVEMENT.

women's movement. A sustained series of organizations of women devoted to the achievement of gender equality in various forms came into being in the mid-19th century. They were well estab-

lished by the beginning of the 20th century. A variety of organizations sometimes worked separately, sometimes together. Their chief goals were: improvement in EDUCATION and employment opportunities for women; reform of the marriage and DIVORCE laws; reform of sexual and moral standards, in particular to protect women and children from physical and sexual abuse; and votes for women, which many saw as the key to all other changes. The campaign for women's suffrage was the most public face of the movement in the years before WORLD WAR I (*see* SUFFRAGISTS; SUFFRA-GETTES). The public campaign for the vote came to an end with the war in 1914: some of its supporters were actively pro-war, others were pacifists. But in 1916 the peaceable campaign for the vote revived, led by Millicent Garrett FAWCETT, and in 1918 most women aged over 30 gained the vote.

It is often thought that thereafter the women's movement split into a variety of conflicting organizations and became ineffectual, but the number of women's organizations was a sign of strength and of the variety of issues on which women were campaigning. More women were actively involved in such bodies than before World War I. Women campaigners did not expect to achieve all their goals immediately, and they were well aware of the antagonism of many men. They worked together on matters of common interest – such as the extension of the vote to women at the age of 21, and EQUAL PAY and employment rights – though there were also conflicts over strategy and priorities.

Women increasingly took a more prominent public role, and also promoted women's rights through a number of different channels: the political parties; feminist organizations whose main purpose was gender equality (such as the National Union of Societies for Equal Citizenship (NUSEC), which had previously been the suffragist NUWSS led by Millicent Garrett Fawcett); and in single-issue organizations (such as women's TRADE UNIONS or the campaign for women POLICE or for FAMILY ALLOWANCES). Women obtained the vote on the same terms as men, at the age of 21, in 1928. A number of other legislative changes in the 1920s, including equalization of divorce and custody rights and the introduction of widows' pensions in 1925, were also the objects of campaigns by women's groups.

The women's movement remained active in this form through the 1930s, although it was perhaps slightly weaker – in part because many women became absorbed in the peace movement as another war loomed. WORLD WAR II temporarily extended public opportunities for women, but, apart from demands for equal pay, campaigns for gender equality were muted. Most women's organizations were absorbed into the Women's Voluntary Service (WVS; later the WOMEN'S ROYAL VOLUNTARY SERVICE), founded in 1938 to mobilize women to support the war effort, for example by managing the EVACUATION OF CHILDREN from the cities and helping victims of the BLITZ. The WVS did not have gender equality among its goals. After the war more women were in the paid workforce than before (*see* LABOUR FORCE), though generally not in highly paid or high-status jobs. The women's movement was more muted than at any point in the century, though it had not disappeared; there was, for example, a successful campaign for equal pay in the public sector, which was achieved in 1954.

The women's movement began to revive in the early 1960s, in the trade unions and the LABOUR PARTY, in the activities of groups such as the Fawcett Society that had survived from the interwar years, and in more diffused activities that led, among other things, to the legalization of ABORTION in 1967 and the Equal Pay Act, 1970. At the end of the 1960s a new 'women's liberation' movement began to emerge, not out of these older groupings and campaign issues, but out of the peace, anti-Vietnam and student movements, inspired by the movement for civil rights for black people in the United States. Women's liberation was less concerned with changing the law by conventional political means than with sexual freedom

and opposition to sexism in personal as well as in public life. In particular it brought the issue of violence against women into a public prominence it retained for the remainder of the century. By the end of the 1970s the more flamboyant and counter-cultural aspects of women's liberation were much less evident; but the new movement, together with the more traditional women's organizations, had put issues of equal opportunities for women and men onto the public agenda again, where, despite setbacks, they remained to the end of the century.

FURTHER READING C. Law, *Suffrage and Power: The Women's Movement, 1918–1928* (1997); M. Pugh, *Women and the Women's Movement in Britain, 1914–1999* (2nd edn, 2000); H.L. Smith (ed.), *British Feminism in the 20th Century* (1990).

Women's Royal Air Force (WRAF). *See* ROYAL AIR FORCE.

Women's Royal Army Corps (WRAC). *See* ARMY.

Women's Royal Naval Service (Wrens). *See* ROYAL NAVY.

Women's Royal Voluntary Service (WRVS), organization founded as the Women's Voluntary Service (WVS) in 1938 by Lady Reading to mobilize women's contributions on the home front in WORLD WAR II. Eventually it coordinated the activities of most existing women's organizations, following a period of resistance by many of them – partly because gender equality was not among the WVS's aspirations. The WVS worked closely with the Home Office and made an especially important contribution to managing the EVACUATION OF CHILDREN and supporting people who suffered in the BLITZ. It continued in existence, though reduced in size, after the war, especially working to develop local social services, such as meals-on-wheels for the elderly and disabled. In 1966 it became the Women's Royal Voluntary Service. It remained an important voluntary organization to the end of the century.

Women's Social and Political Union. *See* PANKHURST, CHRISTABEL; PANKHURST, EMMELINE; SUFFRAGETTES.

Women's Voluntary Service (WVS). *See* WOMEN'S ROYAL VOLUNTARY SERVICE.

Wood, Edward Frederick Lindley. *See* HALIFAX, 1ST EARL OF.

Woolf, Virginia (1882–1941), novelist. Born into an intellectual family, Virginia Woolf was the daughter of Sir Leslie Stephen, the editor of the *Dictionary of National Biography*. She was sensitive and nervous from a young age, and was traumatized in her early years by the death (when Virginia was 13) of her mother and the sexual abuse she suffered at the hands of her two half-brothers. Educated at home, she began writing and working as a critic in London. By around 1910, the famous artistic and literary BLOOMSBURY GROUP had begun to coalesce around her and her family. Its members included her sister Vanessa, Vanessa's husband Clive Bell, her brother Thoby Stephen, Lytton Strachey, John Maynard KEYNES and Leonard Woolf. Virginia was engaged at one time to Strachey, but married Woolf in 1912. Though by most accounts it was a contented and companionate marriage, Virginia was in fact bisexual. She later engaged in a lengthy affair with Vita Sackville-West, who inspired her 1928 historical fantasy novel *Orlando*.

In 1917 Virginia and Leonard founded the Hogarth Press, and in the 1920s her novels began attracting attention. Works such as *Mrs Dalloway* (1925) and *To the Lighthouse* (1927) solidly established her as a leading MODERNIST writer, who eschewed the traditional linear narrative method of storytelling in favour of a new style that came to be known as 'stream of consciousness'. In 1929 she wrote *A Room of One's Own*, a landmark of feminist literature that reflected her frustrations over the restrictions placed on women. While her NOVELS gained her the most attention, she has also been acclaimed as a critic, and the collected essays of her *Common Readers* of 1925 and 1932 earned praise. Despite her successes, Virginia was prone throughout her life to nervous breakdowns and bouts of depression. It was during one of the latter that she took her own life in 1941 by drowning herself in the river Ouse in East Sussex.

FURTHER READING Q. Bell, *Virginia Woolf* (1972); H. Lee, *Virginia Woolf: A Biography* (1996).

Workers' Education Association. *See* ADULT EDUCATION.

working families, tax credit. *See* FAMILY ALLOWANCES.

working hours. *See* LEISURE.

World War I: home front. World War I (1914–18) has been described as the first 'total' war because it involved a much higher proportion of the British population (civilian as well as military) and far more resources than previous wars. It also brought about an unprecedented extension of government control over the economy, the labour force and society as a whole.

From August 1914 the DEFENCE OF THE REALM ACT (DORA) and its subsequent amendments and extensions gave the government wide powers of regulation, first over the flow of information, communications and transport (it took control of the railways and of merchant shipping), then over food distribution, rents and prices, air-raid precautions, propaganda and CENSORSHIP; it also intensified POLICE surveillance of the behaviour of young people in public and covert surveillance of suspected subversives (*see* MI5 AND MI6). Direct taxation was increased to unprecedented levels to help to fund the war, and never returned to pre-war rates. AGRICULTURE was boosted and food supplies maintained, despite pre-war fears that Britain, as a net importer of food, would be starved into surrender.

Initially, the armed services were expanded by calls for volunteers, and men found themselves under strong social pressure to volunteer. Many were eager to do so, partly to escape UNEMPLOY-MENT, which recurred early in 1914. It became apparent, however, that uncontrolled recruitment was denuding some essential industries of skilled workers and controls on recruitment were introduced in 1915. CONSCRIPTION of men who were not in essential occupations was introduced in 1916. A substantial number of men who volunteered or were called for conscription were found to be medically unfit for military service: in 1917–18, for example, 1,007,139 of the 2,425,184 examined by national service medical boards were deemed unfit. This was an eloquent indicator of levels of pre-war POVERTY, though these cursory medical examinations almost certainly *underestimated* the unfitness of males. These findings led to pressure for improved medical care for the population and the formation of the Ministry of Health in 1919.

The state took unprecedented control of labour, industry, the conditions of work and the provision of essential industrial supplies. Britain was the major supplier of weapons and munitions to its allies as well as to its own forces. During the war British industry produced 250,000 machine guns, 52,000 aircraft, almost 3000 tanks, 25,000 pieces of artillery and 170 million artillery shells. In order to maximize output, in March 1915 government representatives met TRADE-UNION leaders, principally from the Amalgamated Society of Engineers, and drew up the Treasury Agreement, in which the unions agreed to the 'dilution' of the skilled work force (meaning the substitution of skilled by semi- or unskilled workers, which sometimes involved women taking over jobs usually reserved for men) for the duration of the war, on the understanding of a return to pre-war norms

after the war. In June 1915, following the 'shell scandal' (*see* FRENCH, JOHN), the Ministry of Munitions was established, with David LLOYD GEORGE as its first minister. It oversaw an unprecedented collaboration among government, employers and unions, which was to outlast the war. The unions agreed to the Munitions of War Act of July 1915, which restricted the movement of workers in key industries and outlawed strikes and lockouts. In reality unions could not prevent unofficial, spontaneous strikes and the government preferred to give in to workers' demands rather than to risk halting war production. In consequence workers were able to improve their wages and conditions. Overall, after a slow start, the British government proved highly successful at managing the war on the home front, maintaining living standards and morale far more successfully than the Germans, despite the latter's stronger tradition of government intervention.

The onset of war disrupted the labour market, causing increased unemployment, but from mid-1915 there was almost full employment. In consequence civilian living standards improved, despite rising rents and increases in the prices of food and other commodities. Standards of diet and health improved and death rates fell (*see* POPULATION) despite the absence of a high proportion of doctors at the front and the clearing of hospitals to give priority to war casualties. Women had access to a somewhat wider range of occupations than before, though the belief that they took over male jobs on a large scale is unfounded. They eagerly deserted DOMESTIC SERVICE, primarily to enter jobs newly created to meet the needs of war, in particular in munitions. Unmarried middle-class women also took up employment in much larger numbers than before the war, as government and other white-collar employment underwent an expansion that was not significantly reversed after the war (*see* LABOUR FORCE). Many young women in consequence experienced unprecedented independence, though for those in manual occupations this did not always outlast the war, once men returned to

reclaim their previous jobs and munitions manufacture contracted.

Hundreds of civilians were killed or wounded
by bombs dropped by ZEPPELINS and other aircraft, or they lost their lives in industrial accidents,
in particular explosions in munitions factories such
as that in Silvertown, east London, in January
1917, which destroyed the factory and the neighbourhood around it.

The war period also saw a fundamental shift
in British politics, as the LIBERAL PARTY split irrev-
ocably and the LABOUR PARTY emerged as a major
political force. The war fundamentally changed
British society, as those who tried after the war to
turn back the clock soon discovered.

FURTHER READING A. Marwick, *The Deluge:
British Society and the First World War* (1965);
J. Turner, *British Politics and the Great War:
Coalition and Conflict, 1915–18* (1992);
J.M. Winter, *The Great War and the British
People* (1985).

World War I: military. The public reason for
Britain's declaration of war against Germany on 4
August 1914 was Germany's unprovoked invasion
of Belgium, whose integrity Britain was bound by
treaty to uphold. However, Britain had long feared
the growth of German power in Europe and its
potential threat to the British EMPIRE. The war was
preceded by a long period of tension and competition for world power among the leading European nations.

The international war began on 28 July 1914
when Austria-Hungary declared war on Serbia.
The pretext was the failure of Serbia to make abject
enough amends for the assassination of the Austrian archduke Francis Ferdinand and his wife at
Sarajevo by a Serbian nationalist, but Austria had
long wished to curb Serb nationalism and expansionism, which threatened the Austro-Hungarian
empire. Russian forces mobilized in defence of
Serbia, whereupon Germany, Austria's ally, declared
war upon Russia, and Russia's ally, France, declared
war on Germany. Germany then invaded Belgium

as part of its plan of attack upon France. Britain,
which had avoided formal alliances before the war,
but which had long been a guarantor of Belgian
neutrality, then allied with France and Russia
against Germany, while being equally determined
to contain the European and imperial ambitions
of both of these powers (*see also* ENTENTE COR-
DIALE). Before the war, the British high command
appeared to be planning for a rerun of the Napoleonic Wars, in which Britain played only a minor
role in the land war and the ROYAL NAVY held the
seas and protected supplies. In 1914 British commanders expected the land war to be short and
highly mobile, with cavalry playing a key role.

Soon after the outbreak of war, it became clear,
at least to some, that this would be a different war,
not least because some of the Allied armies were
too fragile and the opposition too menacing. The
British government set about raising a mass army,
initially of volunteers, and from 1916 by CON-
SCRIPTION. These men took time to train and to
equip. Meanwhile 5 divisions of the small regular
ARMY (7 divisions in total) made up the British
Expeditionary Force (BEF), which fought in
France and Flanders alongside the 70 divisions of
the French army. From August to December 1914
the BEF confronted the Germans at Mons in Belgium, retreated with the French to the MARNE,
where they stopped the German advance on Paris,
and withstood German attacks at YPRES. They held
out by digging into the trench warfare that came to
characterize the war in France. Both sides constructed defensive positions so that lines of trenches
extended from Nieuport on the Belgian coast
through Ypres, Arras, Soissons and Rheims to
Verdun – from the Channel coast to the Swiss frontier. For three and a half years neither side advanced
more than a few kilometres along this line. The
war was also characterized by the use by both sides
of a succession of new, devastating weapons such as
rapid-firing artillery, mortars, high-explosive and
shrapnel shells, machine-guns, poison gas, barbed
wire and tanks.

The small British army had also to be stretched

to defend the empire. A force was despatched to Mesopotamia (then in the hands of Germany's ally Turkey) to safeguard oil supplies in Persia and, unwisely and unsuccessfully, to seek to take control of Mesopotamia. Also unsuccessfully, late in 1915 a French and British force landed in Salonika, in neutral Greece, to try to rescue Serbia. More disastrously, in 1915 the Royal Navy aimed to penetrate the DARDANELLES (with outdated ships) and bombard Constantinople in support of Russia in order to force Turkey to surrender. This was defeated by the shore defences on the GALLIPOLI peninsula. Equally unsuccessful was the attempt to open up the Dardanelles by landing troops (mainly Australians and New Zealanders) on the peninsula. There were also protracted campaigns against German colonies in Africa.

There were small naval actions in the Pacific and south Atlantic against German surface vessels and against the Austro-Hungarian fleet in the Adriatic, but the main British-German naval engagement was off JUTLAND in 1916. This was an unsuccessful attempt by the German navy to end the British blockade of German ports. The British navy suffered more deaths (about 6000 to the Germans 2550) and losses of ships, but the German navy did not venture out again for the remainder of the war. However, German submarines ('U-boats') caused heavy losses of British merchant ships early in 1917, until they were countered by the use of convoys guarded by armed ships and by the development of new weapons such as the depth charge.

From 1916 British military efforts were focused on the Western Front. By that time the expanded British army was trained and equipped and apparently ready to play its full part in land fighting. It also had a new commander in chief on the Western Front: in December 1915 Douglas HAIG had replaced Sir John FRENCH. A major test came at the long battle of the SOMME (1 July–18 November 1916). Despite a huge Allied death rate, this may have been a turning point in the war. However, this was not clear at the time and the losses on the Somme helped to bring down

ASQUITH's government. His replacement LLOYD GEORGE preferred the French to take the leadership in the land battle. The French were not, however, notably successful in the early months of 1917. In July Haig attempted a breakthrough into Belgium, apparently with the agreement of the British political leadership. The outcome was the third battle of YPRES, or PASSCHENDAELE, which lasted from 31 July until 12 November, achieving nothing at great cost in loss of life. Some territory was gained in the battle of Cambrai (20 November–7 December), in which the British used TANKS effectively, but the Germans recovered most of the ground in a counter-attack ten days later. Haig was much criticized for the events of 1917; among his critics was Lloyd George, who supported the elevation of the Frenchman Ferdinand Foch to become Allied supreme commander on the Western Front in April 1918. After the October Revolution of 1917 the Russians withdrew from the war, although in April of that year the USA entered the conflict on the Allied side, bringing little military but much needed financial support. Haig played a significant role in the succession of victories, especially in August and September 1918, which forced the Germans to agree ARMISTICE terms on 10 November. The fighting stopped at 11 a.m. on 11 November – at the eleventh hour of the eleventh day of the eleventh month, which was preserved as a time of remembrance for the remainder of the century. A peace settlement was made with Germany in the treaty of VERSAILLES in 1919.

World War I was widely, though not universally, remembered in Britain for futility, the terrible death rate and poor military leadership – as a war of 'lions led by donkeys', in which brave foot soldiers were betrayed by incompetent generals. In reality, though, serious strategic mistakes were made that were as often the responsibility of civilian politicians as of military men; for example, the Dardanelles campaign was inspired by Winston CHURCHILL. British military leaders performed no worse than their peers in other armies, and all were coping with a revolution in weaponry and an imbalance between strong defensive and weaker offensive weaponry and tactics that persisted through the war and for which they were unprepared. Estimates of British war dead vary from 550,000 to 1,184,000. The historian J.M. Winter in *The Great War and the British People* (1985), after careful work, suggests 772,000 dead (11.76% of combatants) and 1,676,037 wounded (27.27%). Death rates were highest among officers, who went first into battle, and lowest among poorer manual workers, who were the section of the population most likely to be excused service on grounds of physical unfitness (*see* WORLD WAR I: HOME FRONT) or because they worked in essential war-related occupations, such as shipbuilding.

The war was not only costly in terms of human life. British government expenditure on defence was £77 million in 1913, and £2238 million in 1918. The national debt was £649.8 million in 1914, rising to £7434 million in 1919 – costs that the country continued to bear through the inter-war years.

FURTHER READING N. Ferguson, *The Pity of War* (1999); J. Keegan, *The First World War* (1999); H. Strachan, *The First World War, Vol. 1: To Arms* (2001).

World War II: home front. In World War II (1939–45) as in World War I the government took control of economic and social activities as it had not in peacetime. This time, however, owing to the experience of the previous war, the government was prepared in advance to take the necessary action at speed.

In some respects the government moved too fast. The initial expectations of heavy bombing did not immediately materialize (*see* BLITZ) and EVACUATION OF CHILDREN from cities and of routine cases from hospitals to make way for war casualties was premature. CONSCRIPTION was introduced immediately, initially of young men only, then of older men and women for noncombatant war work. The levels of physical fitness among service conscripts and volunteers were much higher than in the previous war, which testified to the decline in POVERTY, though it had not been eradicated, and it was found that levels of education among many servicemen were low. Such findings, and also discoveries of poverty during the war among the civilian population, especially among older people, led to demands for a WELFARE STATE and to the production and popularity of the BEVERIDGE Report.

The LABOUR FORCE was efficiently brought under government control by Ernest BEVIN as minister of labour from May 1940. RATIONING of food and other essential goods was also successfully introduced, being regarded as essential for maintaining civilian morale at a time when international trade was certain to be disrupted. Supplies of other essential goods, such as raw materials for industry, were also controlled, as were prices, in order to prevent the inflation experienced during World War I (*see also* UTILITY SCHEME). Once more the TRADE UNIONS cooperated with the war effort and sought, not wholly successfully, to prevent industrial action. Strikes continued during the war, some of them among women for EQUAL PAY, sometimes successfully. Again, women entered some occupations previously reserved for men as a result of war needs, though again this was temporary, for the duration of the war. Nevertheless, as in the previous war, some women made longer-term occupational gains, in particular as a result of the growth of white-collar employment (*see* LABOUR FORCE). As in World War I, standards of health among the civilian population improved, though more civilians this time experienced the war directly, as a result of the bombing. An estimated 60,000 British civilians were killed as a direct result of the war, as were about 35,000 merchant seamen.

It is sometimes argued that the stresses and privations of wartime lowered social barriers, especially after the reverse at DUNKIRK when all sections of society confronted possible defeat, leading to a greater willingness on the part of the better off to support measures designed to improve social welfare and to narrow social divisions. However, the evidence for this is, at best, mixed. The war does appear to have strengthened the determination of many people to seek to retain in peacetime the full employment and improved living standards experienced in the war, compared with the UNEMPLOYMENT and accompanying poverty of the 1930s. This determination helped to lead to a political transformation. The success of LABOUR PARTY ministers in the wartime coalition government also contributed to Labour's landslide victory in the general election that quickly followed the end of the European war in 1945. Though Winston CHURCHILL was much admired as a wartime leader, neither he nor the CONSERVATIVE PARTY, which he led, was trusted by a large section of the electorate to deliver prosperity in peacetime. **FURTHER READING** P. Addison, *The Road to 1945: British Politics and the Second World War* (1975, 1994); A. Calder, *The People's War: Britain 1939–45* (1969); H.L. Smith (ed.), *War and Social Change: British Society in the Second World War* (1986).

World War II: military. Britain declared war on Germany on 3 September 1939. The immediate cause was Germany's invasion of Poland on 1 September. In March 1939 the British government had pledged to defend Poland, ending its policy of APPEASEMENT of Nazi Germany; but Britain and its French ally could not save Poland from defeat and made little effort to do so. They imposed a blockade on Germany, but the latter could still obtain supplies from its then ally the USSR, and from neutral countries, including valuable iron ore from Sweden. Winston CHURCHILL, then first lord of the Admiralty in the Conservative-dominated NATIONAL GOVERNMENT, proposed to interrupt German supplies from Sweden by mining Norwegian waters, but he was pre-empted by Hitler's invasion of Denmark and Norway in April 1940. This brought to an end the so-called PHONEY WAR.

Then, from 10 May 1940, Hitler began an onslaught on the Low Countries and France, which led to the evacuation of the British army from DUNKIRK and other ports in May and June, and the fall of France. Churchill, who had replaced Neville CHAMBERLAIN as prime minister on 10 May, refused Hitler's offer to negotiate. The Germans began an aerial bombing campaign designed to control the skies over the Channel and to neutralize the Royal Navy prior to an invasion of Britain. The battle of BRITAIN ensued from July to October 1940 and foiled the invasion plan. This was followed by night-time bombing of Britain (the BLITZ) from October 1940 to May 1941. German submarine warfare, with assistance from surface raiders, seriously threatened British supplies until mid-1943 (*see* ATLANTIC, BATTLE OF THE). This threat was eventually defeated by the Ultra system for breaking coded German messages (*see* BLETCHLEY PARK), and by the use of RADAR and of convoys of merchant ships protected by armed naval vessels and aircraft.

Italy had entered the war on the side of the Germans just before the fall of France in June 1940. In 1940–1 the Italians were defeated by the British in Ethiopia, Libya and the Mediterranean. The Germans then started air attacks on the British base at MALTA and sent an expeditionary force under General Erwin Rommel to North Africa. This part of the world was of secondary importance to Hitler, who was more concerned to control northern, central and eastern Europe, but for Britain it was vital to protect its bases in GIBRALTAR, Malta, Cyprus, Palestine, Alexandria and Suez. But by this time the German–Soviet pact had been broken and in June 1941 Hitler invaded the USSR, thereby draining German resources away from the Mediterranean and the Atlantic.

Meanwhile, the United States was resisting British pressure to join the war, but President Franklin D. Roosevelt was leading a policy of helping Britain by all means short of entering the war, in particular providing finance and supplies. In March 1941 LEND-LEASE was introduced and the US navy attacked German submarines in defence of Lend-Lease convoys. Then the Japanese attacked Pearl Harbor on 7 December 1941, Hitler declared war on the United States and the Americans entered the war. The finance and supplies that the USA provided for the Allies were as vital a contribution as its military effort to the eventual victory.

Japan attacked the British EMPIRE in eastern Asia immediately after declaring war on the United States, aiming to replace Britain as the major imperial power in the region. It soon captured HONG KONG, MALAYA, most of BURMA and, most ignominiously for Britain, in February 1942 the great British naval base at SINGAPORE. Troops from the empire, especially from Australia and New Zealand, fought valiantly against Japan, while most British troops were heavily occupied in North Africa and then Europe. The war against Japan was left primarily to the United States.

By late 1942 and early 1943 the tide of war was turning everywhere. The USSR was victorious at Stalingrad and there were American victories in the Pacific. On the part of the British MONTGOMERY checked the Germans in North Africa at EL ALAMEIN, then forced Rommel to retreat. In November 1942 Anglo-American forces landed in western North Africa, attacking the Axis forces from the west until by May 1943 they had driven the Germans and Italians from North Africa. The US government was eager to invade France, but, in particular at a meeting with Roosevelt in Casablanca in January 1943, Churchill urged caution until they were better prepared. Britain preferred the easier option of attacking Italy, not least in order to open up the Mediterranean and the Suez Canal to Allied shipping, which was being forced to take the long route around southern Africa. British and American troops invaded Sicily in July 1943, which led to the fall of the Italian dictator Mussolini. Allied forces landed on the Italian mainland in September and the new Italian government agreed to an armistice. However, German forces poured into Italy, and the Allies were forced to fight their way slowly up the peninsula until the end of the war in Europe (*see also* ANZIO; MONTE CASSINO).

It was also agreed at Casablanca to continue the strategic bombing of enemy-occupied Europe, conducted by the United States by day, by the ROYAL AIR FORCE at night. Churchill wished to postpone an Allied landing in France until operations in the Mediterranean and on the Eastern Front, combined with strategic bombing, could inflict the maximum damage upon Germany. The United States and USSR, however, insisted on a cross-Channel attack in 1944. Churchill acquiesced at the Teheran conference in November–December 1943. By this stage British resources were becoming overstrained, while the United States and USSR were attaining full mobilization and were taking the leading roles in the war. The US general Dwight D. Eisenhower was appointed supreme commander for Operation Overlord, the Anglo-American landing in Normandy, in northwest France, which began on 6 June 1944 (D-DAY). Nevertheless, British and Canadian troops dominated three out of the five beaches on which the landings took place and British officers commanded all of Eisenhower's air, sea and land invasion forces.

After the break-out from Normandy in August 1944 Eisenhower took direct control of the land war in France. The British and Canadian forces, led by Montgomery, advanced at the north end of the line facing Germany, while the Americans, with the support of pro-Allied French forces, advanced along the rest of the front. Montgomery had been superseded by Eisenhower and conflict between the two did not assist the Allied advance. The Americans regarded Montgomery as too arrogant and slow-moving. Their critical view seemed to be justified when Montgomery failed to secure a bridgehead over the Rhine at ARNHEM in September 1944. The shock to the American forces when the Germans counter-attacked in the battle of the BULGE in December 1944 seemed to even the score, as Montgomery did not hesitate to point out. Montgomery's command was then extended.

The forward movement in Europe continued on both Eastern and Western fronts. In the west, Allied forces crossed the pre-war German frontier in early February 1945 and linked up with the Red

Army of the USSR on the Elbe on 28 April 1945. Germany formally capitulated at Rheims, in France, on 7 May 1945, with British forces in control of northwestern Germany.

Britain's contribution to the war in Asia had increased from 1944. In 1944 General SLIM led British and Commonwealth forces in the successful defence of INDIA. In spring 1945 Slim reconquered southern Burma. On 2 September, following the dropping of the first atomic bombs on Hiroshima and Nagasaki in Japan, Japan surrendered and the war was over. There had been about 300,000 deaths of British servicemen in the course of the war.

The financial costs of the war were immense and placed a long-term strain on the economy. Total government defence expenditure was £254 million in 1938, and £5125 million in 1944; the national debt stood at £7130 million in 1939, rising to £23,636 million in 1946.

FURTHER READING C. Barnett, *Engage the Enemy More Closely* (1990); P. Calvocoressi and G. Wint, *Total War* (1962); I. Dear and M.R.D. Foot (eds.), *The Oxford Companion to World War II* (2001); J. Ray, *The Second World War* (2000).

WRAC. *See* ARMY.

Y

Yalta, resort on the Black Sea coast of the Crimea, the setting for the second wartime meeting of Stalin, CHURCHILL and Roosevelt, 4–11 February 1945, to discuss arrangements to follow the end of WORLD WAR II. Roosevelt gained Stalin's agreement to enter the war against Japan and to support the establishment of the UNITED NATIONS. Churchill secured Soviet agreement to the eventual creation of French as well as British, Soviet and US zones of occupation in post-war Germany. There were also agreements about the boundaries of the Polish state. A 'Declaration on Liberated Europe' expressed the desire of the three leaders for democratic institutions in the lands formerly under German control. There was a de facto agreement on the post-war division of Europe between East and West. It was agreed, for example, that Greece and Italy should join the 'West', while Yugoslavia would be part of the Eastern bloc.

Yeats, W(illiam) B(utler) (1865–1939), Irish poet, ranked as one of the finest poets writing in English in the 20th century. Yeats was born in Dublin, the son of a portrait painter. The family soon moved to London and he attended the Godolphin School, Hammersmith. They returned to Dublin in 1881, where Yeats attended the High School, then studied drawing at the School of Art

for three years. At the same time he developed an interest in mystic religion and the supernatural, in which there was much interest among intellectuals at this time. He continued to be interested in spiritualism and occultism, as a member of Madame Blatavsky's Theosophical Society, 1887–90, then of the Hermetic Order of the Golden Dawn, 1890–1922. His first poems were published in 1885. In the following year, when his dramatic poem, *Mosada*, was published, he abandoned art in favour of literature.

In 1885 Yeats returned with his family to London, which remained his principal residence until 1919, although he also spent much time in Ireland during this period. He published a novella, *John Sherman and Dhoya* (1891), and edited *The Poems of William Blake* (1893), *The Works of William Blake* (with F.J. Ellis, 1893) and *Poems of Spenser* (1906). Though living in London, and of Protestant Anglo-Irish stock, he was very much an Irish nationalist. His first full volumes of poetry – *The Wanderings of Oisin and Other Poems* (1889) and *The Countess Kathleen and Various Legends and Lyrics* (1892) – were suffused with ancient Irish Celtic culture and allusions. He helped to found an Irish Literary Society in London in 1891 and another in Dublin in 1892. During the early 1890s he edited collections of Irish folklore, such as *The Celtic Twilight* (1893, expanded 1902), and literature. He had some success with three short-story collections published in 1897: *The Secret Rose, The Tables of the Law* and *The Adoration of the Magi*. He worked together with Lady Augusta Gregory to create an Irish national theatre, which was partly realized when his play *The Countess Cathleen* (1892) was performed in Dublin in 1899. An Irish amateur company was formed in 1902 and performed his *Cathleen ni Houlihan* in the same year. The Irish National Theatre Company was formed thereafter and, with generous patronage from Annie Horniman, an Englishwoman, acquired the Abbey Theatre in Dublin in 1904. During the first decade of the 20th century Yeats was very active in the management of the Abbey Theatre.

In London in 1889 Yeats met and fell in love with Maud Gonne (1866–1953), a beautiful and passionate Irish nationalist who lived in Paris and, unknown to Yeats, maintained until 1898 a secret liaison with a Frenchman. Yeats's frustrated pursuit of her inspired many poems in his early collections – *The Wanderings of Oisin, The Land of Heart's Desire* (1894), *The Wind Among the Reeds* (1899) and *The Shadowy Waters* (1900) – and some of his plays, including *On Baile's Strand* (1904) and *Deirdre* (1907). But in 1903 she married an exiled Irish nationalist, Major John McBride, though Yeats's courtship revived briefly in 1916 after McBride was executed for his role in the EASTER RISING.

The style of Yeats's poetry became sparser and more vigorous over time, adopting the rhythms of ordinary speech; in this he was cheered on by Ezra Pound, who became a close friend from 1909. The development of this new style was evident in *In the Seven Woods* (1903), *The Green Helmet and Other Poems* (1910, 1912), *Poems Written in Discouragement* (1913) and *Responsibilities* (1914). Looking back on those years, when he contributed to the rise of the MODERNISM in poetry, Yeats later said: 'In 1900 everybody got down off his stilts.' Yet his lifelong preference for rhyme and strict stanza forms set him apart from modernism and

he continued to admire a wide range of poetry and drama.

Yeats became disillusioned with Irish politics in 1912 and 1913, a disillusionment that is found, for example, in the poem 'September 1913', but the Easter Rising revived his faith in Irish nationalism, eloquently expressed in his poem 'Easter 1916'. In 1917 he proposed to Maud Gonne's daughter Iseult and was turned down. Later in the same year he married Georgie Hyde-Lees (1892–1968), 27 years his junior and obsessed with the occult. She attempted automatic writing on their honeymoon, an experience that profoundly affected his life and work. He believed that his wife's 'communicators' provided him with the symbolism described in his mystical prose work *The Vision* (1925) and many of his later poems. They had two children and lived in Ireland. In the civil war that followed the Anglo-Irish Treaty of 1921 (*see* IRELAND) Yeats was firmly on the side of the Irish Free State. In 1922 he took up permanent residence in Dublin and accepted a six-year appointment as a senator of the Irish Free State. In 1923 he was awarded the Nobel prize for literature. He continued to produce fine poetry and plays, written in a spare, colloquial, lyrical style, such as the collections *The Tower* (1928), *The Winding Stair* (1929, 1932) and *Words for Music Perhaps and Other Poems* (1932).

In 1924 Yeats was warned about his high blood pressure and told to reduce his public activities and avoid the Irish winter. (Thereafter he spent much time in the south of France, where he died.) Nevertheless he continued to be active in Dublin literary life and to write plays, such as translations of the Greek tragedies *King Oedipus* (1926) and *Oedipus at Colonus* (1927) and a play about spiritualism and the 18th-century Anglo-Irish writer Jonathan Swift, *The Words Upon the Window Pane* (1930). Yeats, who was no democrat, was unhappy about the Ireland that emerged in the 1930s and increasingly referred back to the social order of the 18th century and the former hegemony of the Anglo-Irish Protestant minority to which he belonged. He expressed these unpopular views in his essays *On the Boiler* (1939) and in plays such as *Purgatory* (1938). He carried on writing until his death. *Last Poems* was published in 1939, and contains his own epitaph: 'Cast a cold eye/On life, on death./Horseman, pass by!'

FURTHER READING R. Ellman, *Yeats: The Man and the Masks* (1979); R. Foster, *W.B. Yeats: The Apprentice Mage* (Vol. 1 of a biography, 1997).

Young Plan. *See* REPARATIONS.

youth. By the beginning of the 20th century 'youth' was widely viewed as a distinct stage of life, between about 14 and 21 years of age, that should be used for training and EDUCATION. While young people's lifestyles throughout the 20th century were affected by SOCIAL CLASS, gender and ethnic identity, elements of common experience facilitated the development of 'YOUTH CULTURES'.

At the turn of the century, increasing numbers of middle- and upper-class young people remained in full-time education throughout their teens, while working-class young people were in employment. Residing in the parental home and with no dependants, most young people had the time and money to enjoy some sort of LEISURE. Adults' concern over young people, in particular working-class lads, inspired the establishment of increasing numbers of youth movements, including the Boy Scouts, founded in 1908 (*see* BADEN-POWELL, ROBERT). Equivalent organizations for girls, providing training in femininity and domesticity, followed; the most popular was the Girl Guides (1912). WORLD WAR I led to a decline in apprenticeships for young male workers and an increase in employment opportunities for young female workers – trends that continued in the 1920s and 1930s (*see* LABOUR FORCE), and heightened a distinction between affluent but casually employed young workers and the older unemployed.

After WORLD WAR II the provision of universally free secondary schooling, the raising of the school-leaving age to 15 (1947; *see* EDUCATION)

and the expansion of higher education (*see* UNIVERSITIES) meant that youth was cemented in the national consciousness as a period of education. At the same time, CONSCRIPTION of young men into the armed forces, in the form of national service, continued after the war until the beginning of the 1960s. Full employment and the protection of apprenticeships in the post-war decades enabled young people to enjoy the consumer boom, asserting their cultural identity as teddy boys in the 1950s, or as mods or rockers in the early 1960s – groups defined by their distinctive clothing, accessories and tastes in music, and, in the case of mods and rockers, by violent antipathy towards each other. Youth culture's oppositional nature became explicitly political at times in the 1960s and 1970s, when young people participated in POPULAR PROTEST movements. The increasing homogeneity of youth in post-war Britain – which was furthered by the growth of comprehensive education in the 1960s and the raising of the school-leaving age to 16 in 1973 – was, however, halted by economic and political developments in the later 1970s and 1980s. Racism influenced some aspects of youth culture in the 1970s, youth UNEMPLOYMENT became widespread in the 1980s, and state benefits and grants for school leavers and students were reduced. Although youth employment increased in the 1990s, distinctions in the life experience of young people from different social groups remained, their common bond being dependence, on the family or the state, due to the economic insecurity of employment and education.

FURTHER READING A. Davies, *Leisure, Gender and Poverty: Working Class Culture in Salford and Manchester, 1900–39* (1992); B. Osgerby, *Youth in Britain since 1945* (1998).

youth culture. Evidence of 'youth culture' has been discerned in British society from the medieval period, but it is the 20th century with which a highly visible youth culture is most often associated. Youth culture became particularly prominent in the period following WORLD WAR II, although earlier manifestations, at least among the better off, included the 'flappers' of the 1920s jazz age.

The emergence of youth culture in its 20th-century form owes much to 19th-century legislation on education and child labour, but particularly in developments in psychology, which defined 'adolescence' as a distinct and unique stage in life between childhood and adulthood, associated with leisure and few responsibilities. With an accepted definition of youth in existence, it was the emergence of the cultural industries of cinema, broadcasting and popular music that set in place a commercial structure around which youth culture crystallized. This began to happen during the interwar period, although the Depression had a detrimental effect upon youth earnings and employment.

Youth subcultures had existed before World War II, but it is the 1950s that is most often perceived as the period that witnessed the emergence of youth culture. Indeed, many commentators have been more specific, and date the emergence of youth culture from the release of the US film *Rock Around the Clock*, with its rock-'n'-roll soundtrack, in 1956. The appearance of 'teddy boys' on British streets at the same time, with their unconventional yet uniform appearance, did indeed suggest that profound and, for some, frightening changes in British society were taking place. Establishment figures condemned teddy boys as indicators of a moral decline rooted in the mass-marketing of American culture, but these developments were part of broader shifts in post-war society.

The post-war 'baby boom' (*see* POPULATION) resulted in a sharp increase in the numbers of young people in Britain, while a rise in the school-leaving age to 15 in 1947 resulted in an extension of adolescence. Most importantly, increasing prosperity, full employment and greater opportunities to earn meant that youth, by the 1950s, had the means to express its identity through consumption. At the same time, burgeoning FASHION and entertainment industries were supplying products directly aimed at the youth market.

The 1950s was characterized by the emergence of a mainly working-class youth culture. The SIXTIES saw the expansion of this culture, and the further development of fashion and entertainment industries targeted specifically at the youth market (for example, commercial 'pirate' radio broadcasters such as Radio Caroline). New forms of youth 'cults' also continued to emerge. Allied to an expansion in higher education (*see* UNIVERSITIES), the manifestations of youth culture in the late 1960s tended to be more middle-class in origin. This was best exemplified by the hippie culture, which espoused a philosophy of 'peace and love' that was rooted in the needs and concerns of young people. By the 1960s youth culture was not only self-expressive, but also critical of mainstream society. One side of the youth culture of the late 1960s was its hedonism, involving indulgence in sex (*see* PERMISSIVE SOCIETY), drugs (*see* DRUG ADDICTION) and rock music, while another was an interest in Eastern mysticism as an alternative to the perceived materialism of adult society, both aspects manifesting themselves in 'happenings' and summer festivals. A third aspect of 1960s youth culture was more politically radical and found expression in protests against the Vietnam War (such as those outside the US embassy in Grosvenor Square in 1968) and student revolt (*see* POPULAR PROTEST).

The return of economic insecurity in the 1970s, accompanied by rising UNEMPLOYMENT, was reflected in more gritty forms of youth culture. The conflicts and harsh conditions of the inner-city environment spawned the working-class 'skinhead' movement, which was violent and racist in its philosophy, despite its appropriation of Caribbean music and fashion. The relationship between race and wider youth culture has also been ambiguous: on the one hand there is evidence that British youth is not exempt from the racist tendencies of wider British society; while on the other, British youth culture has been influenced by black (particularly African-American) forms of music and fashion.

The contrast between the realities of life for British youth and the lifestyles of many popular musicians led to the raucous, shocking punk rock of the later 1970s. Punk revitalized the fashion, music and design industries, and initiated the careers of creative individuals such as the fashion designer Vivienne Westwood and the filmmaker Derek Jarman. The 1980s saw the incorporation of youth cultural style into mainstream entertainment and fashion, while at the same time there were increasing tensions between youth and broader society. The collapse of youth employment during a series of economic recessions prompted the government to set up a number of much-criticized training schemes, such as the Youth Training Scheme, which replaced the Youth Opportunities Programme in 1981. Despite being hard hit by recession, the materialism of the 1980s was also expressed in the development of 'casual' subculture, with its enthusiasm for designer clothes and excessive consumption, especially of alcohol, resulting in media images of 'lager louts' rampaging through Britain. In the early 1990s there were violent confrontations between youth and police in deprived housing estates across the country, and in some less deprived locations, while the disaffection of an 'underclass' of youth was exemplified by the huge rise in car crime, especially 'joy-riding'.

By the late 1980s dance music was becoming the central element of youth culture, drawing its influence from the innovative 'house' music of Chicago gay clubs and the carnival atmosphere of the night clubs of Ibiza, a popular holiday destination for British youth. Impromptu parties held at disused warehouses began to attract more and more young people, and commercial party organizers became engaged in a battle to outwit police attempts to suppress their activities. As the parties became larger, their venues shifted to the countryside around large cities, particularly London, where such events were known as 'orbital raves' due to their proximity to the M25 orbital motorway around the capital.

In many ways the raves were similar to the open-air festivals that had originated in the 1960s and 1970s, particularly the annual event at Glastonbury in Somerset, which by the 1980s had begun to attract tens of thousands of mainly (but not exclusively) young people in search of 'alternative' culture. Another 1970s festival, the Stonehenge Free Festival, had by the mid-1980s become the focus for conflict between the authorities and the counter-culture.

Emerging from the 1970s free-festival circuit, the New Age travellers of the 1980s represented an amalgamation of 1960s hippie culture with the more gritty radicalism of punk. In 1985 a traveller convoy heading for the Stonehenge festival was halted at a police roadblock and subjected to a ferocious assault by riot police in what became known as the 'battle of the beanfield'. The event marked the beginning of a series of official attempts to outlaw the traveller subculture, which began to fuse with the rave culture of the early 1990s, culminating in the free week-long festival at Castlemorton in 1992. The government promised tough action in the face of media outrage and introduced in 1994 the Criminal Justice Act, which included the creation of a number of new criminal offences aimed directly at the rave and traveller counter-cultures.

By the end of the 20th century it was clear that the economic and social position of many young people in Britain was less secure than it had been fifty years earlier, and that youth tended to be associated in the public imagination with crime and delinquency. Young people were accused of disengagement from the concerns of mainstream society. Yet increasing numbers of them were in higher education (*see* UNIVERSITIES), most were working, and many were strongly committed to such issues as ENVIRONMENTALISM.

FURTHER READING B. Osgerby, *Youth in Britain Since 1945* (1998).

Ypres, medieval Flemish city around which the Allies held a massive salient throughout WORLD

WAR I. There were four battles of Ypres: (1) 12 October–11 November 1914, a German assault on British positions; (2) 22 April–24 May 1915, a second German assault, which again failed to break the British line despite the first use in warfare of poison gas; (3) 31 July–10 November 1917, a British, Canadian and French offensive, ending in the mud of PASSCHENDAELE; (4) 9–29 April 1918 (also known as the battle of the river Lys), an attempt by the Germans to encircle Ypres. There was further fighting around the Ypres salient in September 1918 as part of the general offensive that ended the war. Ypres never fell, although many of its medieval buildings were destroyed, and more than 500,000 British and EMPIRE troops were killed or seriously wounded in the battles around it.

FURTHER READING H. Strachan, *The First World War, Vol 1: To Arms* (2001).

Z

Zeppelin, a type of airship, created in Germany by Count Zeppelin. The first Zeppelin flight took place on 2 July 1900, and the airships were used by the Germans in WORLD WAR I. The first Zeppelin attack on England occurred on the night of 19/20 January 1915, when four airships crossed the North Sea, theoretically to bomb British military installations on the east coast. In reality, poor visibility, poor navigation and the impossibility of precision in bombing meant that most victims of Zeppelins, on this and later raids, were civilians. Only two bombs were dropped on the first raid and one man was killed, a bootmaker in his shop in Great Yarmouth. It was almost three months before the next raid. Systematic raids began in the spring and summer of 1915. On the night of 10/11 May the crew of one Zeppelin, which had been driven away by gunfire from the ground, dropped a card on Canvey Island, east of London reading: 'You English! We have come and will come again soon – kill or cure.' About ten people, including children, were killed in these raids. In total, in 51 raids, 556 people were killed and 1357 injured. The raids caused localized panic, but had little effect on the conduct of the war. Of the 80 Zeppelins built by the German navy between 1912 and 1917, 23 were shot down or destroyed on the ground and 31 were destroyed in accidents. By 1917 they were replaced by bomber aircraft.

Zimbabwe, the former British colony of Southern Rhodesia. The British colony of Rhodesia was established in the late 19th century following the acquisition of mining rights by Cecil Rhodes's British South Africa Company. European settlement followed, and in 1911 the colony was divided into Southern Rhodesia and Northern Rhodesia (now Zambia). After a referendum in 1922 Southern Rhodesia became a self-governing colony. Although the colony's constitution was in theory non-racial, voting rights were denied to most Africans, and legislation in the 1930s restricted African ownership of land and imposed a 'colour bar' on skilled and professional occupations.

In 1953 a Central African Federation of Southern Rhodesia, Northern Rhodesia and Nyasaland (Malawi) was established by the Conservative government in Britain as a way of encouraging more settlers and increased capital investment into the region. Undermined by African agitation within the northern states, the Federation collapsed in 1963. By the same time, African political ambitions in Southern Rhodesia had crystallized into two organizations, the Zimbabwe African People's Union (ZAPU) and the Zimbabwe African National Union (ZANU). The white government of Southern Rhodesia, meanwhile, came under the control of Ian Smith's (1919–) Rhodesian Front Party, and the Smith government proclaimed a unilateral declaration of independence (UDI) in 1965. The British government under Harold WILSON imposed sanctions against Rhodesia (as Southern Rhodesia was now known), which proved ineffective.

In response to UDI, ZANU and ZAPU launched a guerrilla war, which increased in intensity and effectiveness during the 1970s, particularly following the independence of neighbouring Mozambique in 1975. With ZANU and ZAPU allied in a new organization – the Patriotic Front – Ian Smith was forced to offer concessions to the nationalists. The failure of Smith's attempt to end the crisis led to a new round of negotiations, brokered by the British government, in 1979. The Lancaster House agreement of 1980 was followed by multiparty democratic elections, which brought ZAPU leader Robert Mugabe into power. The now formally independent state, renamed Zimbabwe, became a member of the COMMONWEALTH.

The years after the end of the independence war saw bitter and violent rivalry between ZANU and ZAPU, leading eventually to the amalgamation of the two parties into ZANU-PF in 1987. During the 1980s Zimbabwe took a leading role in coordinating the opposition of the 'front-line states' to the apartheid regime in SOUTH AFRICA, and remained a significant regional power into the 1990s. The question of land redistribution became an important domestic issue in the 1990s, with complaints that the process of redistribution was happening too slowly. In 2000 there were violent occupations of white-owned farms by organized supporters of Mugabe, who had become increasingly authoritarian. Economic problems associated with Zimbabwean involvement in the civil war in the Democratic Republic of Congo heightened domestic tensions, and at the end of the century opposition to Mugabe's government was increasing.

Zinoviev letter, a notorious document – purportedly of Soviet origin, but probably forged – that contributed to the defeat of the LABOUR PARTY in the GENERAL ELECTION of October 1924.

Following the Bolshevik Revolution of 1917 the Labour Party kept its distance from the USSR and from communism. However, the first Labour government opened diplomatic relations with the USSR early in 1924 and signed several treaties designed to improve trade and to reduce the USSR's international isolation. The prime minister, Ramsay MACDONALD, believed that it would do greater harm to international relations in the long run to boycott the USSR than to seek accommodation with it. The LIBERALS refused to agree the treaties and forced a general election in October 1924.

Four days before the election, on 25 October 1924, a letter was published in *The TIMES*, the *Daily Mail* and other papers that had apparently been intercepted by the Foreign Office. It purported to be from Grigori Zinoviev, president of the Comintern (the Soviet-dominated Third International), to the central committee of the COMMUNIST PARTY OF GREAT BRITAIN, urging them to promote revolution in Britain through acts of sedition, such as stirring up revolt in the armed forces. Following publication of the letter there was a virulent anti-Labour campaign in the press, in which Labour was undeservedly associated with revolution; this in turn contributed to the party's defeat in the election (although both the Labour and Conservative vote increased, while that of the Liberals collapsed). The Foreign Office believed that the letter was genuine, and certainly it was consistent with Comintern policy at that time. For their part, Labour believed that publication of the letter was a sign of Foreign Office hostility to the party. Over time, and after much controversy, historians came to believe that it was a fake.

Subject index

arts and media

Arts Council of Great Britain; Bloomsbury group; censorship; communications; Council for the Encouragement of Music and the Arts (CEMA); fashion; Festival of Britain; Institute of Contemporary Arts (ICA); modernism; national heritage; youth culture.

ARCHITECTURE

architecture; Mackintosh, Charles Rennie; country houses; National Trust.

CINEMA

film industry; Hitchcock, Alfred.

LITERATURE

Auden, W.H.; Bennett, Arnold; Bowen, Elizabeth; Childers, Erskine; Conrad, Joseph; Eliot, T.S.; Forster, E.M.; Galsworthy, John; Joyce, James; Lawrence, D.H.; Leavis, F.R.; Lessing, Doris; novels; Orwell, George; poetry; Russell, Bertrand; Sassoon, Siegfried; Spark, Muriel; Taylor, A.J.P.; Waugh, Evelyn; Wells, H.G.; Woolf, Virginia; Yeats, W.B.

MEDIA

Beaverbrook, Max Aitken, 1st Baron; British Broadcasting Corporation; *Manchester Guardian*; newspapers; Northcliffe, Alfred Harmsworth, 1st Viscount; Reith, John; *Times, The*.

MUSIC

Beatles, the; Britten, Benjamin; Elgar, Edward; music.

PERFORMING ARTS

ballet; drama; Entertainments National Service Association (ENSA); National Theatre; Royal Shakespeare Company; Shaw, George Bernard.

VISUAL ARTS

Bacon, Francis; Bell, Vanessa; BritArt; Camden Town Group; Clark, Kenneth; Epstein, Jacob; Euston Road School; Freud, Lucian; Frink, Elisabeth; Fry, Roger; Gill, Eric; Hamilton, Richard; Hepworth, Barbara; Hockney, David; John, Augustus; John, Gwen; Lowry, L.S.; Moore, Henry; Nicholson, Ben; Pasmore, Victor; Piper, John; Riley, Bridget; Sickert, Walter; Spencer, Stanley; Sutherland, Graham; visual arts.

Commonwealth and empire

Aden; Amritsar massacre; Anti-Apartheid Movement; Australia; Burma; Canada; Channel Islands; Commonwealth of Nations; Curzon, George Nathaniel; Cyprus; decolonization; empire; Falkland Islands; Gandhi, Mohandas Karamchand; Gibraltar; Halifax, 1st earl of; Hong Kong; imperial conferences; imperial preference; India; Isaacs, Rufus Daniel (Lord Reading); Kenya; Malaya/Malaysia; Malta; Middle East; Milner, Alfred; Mountbatten, Louis; New Zealand; Ottawa Conference; Palestine; Singapore; South Africa; Wavell, Archibald; West Indies; Zimbabwe.
See also foreign and international affairs; Ireland and Northern Ireland.

Chronology

1899

October: outbreak of BOER WAR

1900

February: Formation of LABOUR REPRESENTATION COMMITTEE

British take Pretoria and Johannesburg in BOER WAR

Conservative–Liberal Unionist coalition under Lord SALISBURY returned to power in 'khaki election'

LONDON GOVERNMENT Act

CONRAD's novel *Lord Jim*

ELGAR, *The Dream of Gerontius*

1901

January: Australian colonies unite as Commonwealth of AUSTRALIA

January: death of Queen Victoria; succeeded by EDWARD VII

B. Seebohm ROWNTREE publishes survey of POVERTY in York

TAFF VALE JUDGEMENT

1902

May: treaty of Vereeniging ends BOER WAR

BALFOUR succeeds Lord Salisbury as Conservative PM

Education Act establishes local education authorities (*see* EDUCATION)

Publication of Charles Booth's *Life and Labour of the People of London*, an important survey of POVERTY

Midwives Act licenses midwives and improves standards of midwifery

BENNETT's novel *Anna of the Five Towns*

CONRAD, *Heart of Darkness*

1903

Joseph CHAMBERLAIN proposes TARIFF REFORM

Formation of the SUFFRAGETTE organization, the Women's Social and Political Union, by Emmeline and Christabel PANKHURST

First 'Lib-Lab pact', between LIBERAL PARTY and LABOUR REPRESENTATION COMMITTEE

IRISH LAND ACT

Foundation of Workers' Educational Association (*see* ADULT EDUCATION)

NORTHCLIFFE launches *Daily Mirror*

SHAW, *Man and Superman*

1904

ENTENTE CORDIALE with France

Wireless Telegraphy Act (*see* CENSORSHIP)

CONRAD, *Nostromo*

J.M. Barrie, *Peter Pan*

1905

December: Conservative PM Arthur BALFOUR

resigns; CAMPBELL-BANNERMAN invited to form Liberal government

Formation of SINN FÉIN and ULSTER UNIONIST Council

Arrest of Christabel PANKHURST and Annie Kenney marks beginning of militant phase of SUFFRAGETTE movement

Unemployed Workmen Act allows local authorities to provide work for the unemployed

Aliens Act restricts IMMIGRATION

SHAW, *Major Barbara*

WELLS, *Kipps*

1906

Liberals win general election; Labour wins 29 seats

Formation of LABOUR PARTY

Trade Disputes Act overturns TAFF VALE JUDGE-MENT (*see also* TRADE UNIONS)

Free school meals introduced for needy children

Launch of HMS *DREADNOUGHT*

Street Betting Act bans GAMBLING on horse racing outside of racecourses

CONRAD, *The Secret Agent*

GALSWORTHY, *A Man of Property*, first novel in the *Forsyte Saga* (to 1922)

1907

Women permitted to stand for election in county and borough elections, and to serve as mayors

Medical inspections introduced in schools

Probation Act establishes national probation service

BADEN-POWELL founds Boy Scout movement

ENTENTE CORDIALE extended to include Russia, so becoming the Triple Entente

NEW ZEALAND achieves dominion status

J.M. Synge, *The Playboy of the Western World*

Delius, *Brigg Fair*

1908

April: Campbell-Bannerman resigns as PM due to ill health and is succeeded by ASQUITH

Introduction of means-tested OLD-AGE PENSIONS for a minority of people over 70

Children Act extends state responsibility for child welfare and establishes separate juvenile courts

Coal Mines Regulation Act sets maximum working day of 8 hours underground

Election of first woman mayor (in Aldeburgh, Suffolk)

Establishment of TERRITORIAL ARMY

Foundation of National Farmers' Union (*see* AGRICULTURE)

Ford Motor Company sells first Model T in Britain, imported from America

FORSTER, *A Room with a View*

Completion of MACKINTOSH's Glasgow School of Art

EPSTEIN's sculptures of naked male figures for the British Medical Association cause a scandal

1909

LLOYD GEORGE's 'People's Budget' rejected by HOUSE OF LORDS

Trade Boards Act establishes MINIMUM WAGE in some of the lowest-paid trades

Establishment of labour exchanges (*see* UNEM-PLOYMENT)

Reports of Royal Commission on the POOR LAWS and Relief of Distress

Housing and Town Planning Act (*see* TOWN AND COUNTRY PLANNING)

IRISH LAND ACT

WELLS, *Tono-Bungay*

Augustus JOHN, *The Smiling Woman*

First British performance of Ethel Smyth's opera *The Wreckers*

1910

February: Liberals under ASQUITH win general election

May: formation of Union of SOUTH AFRICA

May: death of EDWARD VII; succeeded by GEORGE V

November: TONYPANDY RIOTS

December: Liberals under ASQUITH win second general election of the year

Osborne judgement bans TRADE UNIONS from
funding political activity

BADEN-POWELL, with his sister Agnes, founds Girl
Guide movement

RUSSELL and Whitehead, *Principia Mathematica*
(to 1913)

FORSTER, *Howards End*

WELLS, *The History of Mr Polly*

FRY's first post-impressionist exhibition

1911

BALFOUR resigns as leader of the CONSERVATIVE
PARTY; succeeded by Bonar LAW

MACDONALD succeeds Keir HARDIE as chairman
of parliamentary LABOUR PARTY

Parliament Act restricts powers of HOUSE OF
LORDS

Payment of MPs introduced

Introduction of National Health and Unemployment Insurance (*see* WELFARE STATE)

Second OFFICIAL SECRETS ACT

AGADIR crisis

Two dockers shot dead by troops in Liverpool
during protests in support of dock and railway
strike

Emergence of CAMDEN TOWN GROUP of painters

1911–14

Wave of industrial unrest

1912

January: Captain Robert SCOTT and team reach
South Pole after Amundsen; all die on return
journey (March)

April: sinking of *TITANIC*

Irish HOME RULE bill introduced

CARSON organizes Ulster Volunteers to resist
HOME RULE for IRELAND

Establishment of British Board of Film Censors
(*see* CENSORSHIP)

Establishment of Royal Flying Corps, predecessor
of ROYAL AIR FORCE

WEBBS found FABIAN Research Department and
New Statesman

SHAW, *Pygmalion*

FRY's second post-impressionist exhibition

1912–13

MARCONI SCANDAL nearly ends LLOYD GEORGE's
career

1913

CAT AND MOUSE ACT

The SUFFRAGETTE Emily Davison throws herself
under the king's horse at the Derby

TRADE UNION Act reverses 1910 Osborne
judgement

ULSTER VOLUNTEER FORCE established

LAWRENCE, *Sons and Lovers*

EPSTEIN, *Rock Drill*, cubist sculpture (to 1914)

BELL and FRY set up Omega Workshop in
Bloomsbury

1914

Act disestablishing CHURCH OF ENGLAND in
Wales (becomes CHURCH IN WALES in 1920)

Government acquires over half the equity in the
strategically important Anglo-Persian Oil
Company

British Nationality and Status of Aliens Act further
restricts IMMIGRATION

Irish HOME RULE Act followed by CURRAGH
INCIDENT, in which army officers mutiny in
support of Ulster Unionists

WORLD WAR I

August: Britain declares war on Germany; British
Expeditionary Force dispatched to France and
Belgium; MACDONALD resigns as leader of
LABOUR PARTY in favour of Arthur HENDERSON;
DEFENCE OF THE REALM ACT gives government
wide-ranging emergency powers

September: first battle of the MARNE: Allies stop
German advance on Paris

October: first battle of Arras; first battle of YPRES
(to November)

November: Royal Navy squadron defeated at
battle of Coronel, in Pacific; beginning of
Mesopotamian campaign

December: German naval squadron defeated at

battle of Falkland Islands; German navy shells Scarborough and other towns on the eastern coast of England

JOYCE, *Dubliners*; *Portrait of the Artist as a Young Man* (to 1915)

YEATS, *Responsibilities*

Imagists begin publication of annual POETRY anthologies (to 1917)

Blast, Vorticist magazine edited by Wyndham Lewis, marks arrival of MODERNISM in Britain

Vaughan Williams, *The Lark Ascending*

1915

January: first ZEPPELIN raid on England

February: beginning of German SUBMARINE campaign; opening of Palestinian front

March: failure of DARDANELLES campaign

April: beginning of GALLIPOLI campaign; second battle of YPRES (to May)

May: outbreak of 'shell scandal' (*see* FRENCH, JOHN); ASQUITH forms coalition government with Conservatives; *Lusitania* sunk by German SUBMARINE; Italy joins Allies following secret treaty of LONDON (April)

June: LLOYD GEORGE becomes minister of munitions

July: Munitions of War Act (*see* WORLD WAR I: HOME FRONT; TRADE UNIONS)

October: Allies land at Salonika; Edith CAVELL executed by Germans

November: Allies withdraw from GALLIPOLI; CHURCHILL resigns as first lord of the Admiralty

December: FRENCH replaced by HAIG as commander of British forces on the Western Front

RENT STRIKES lead to statutory restrictions on rent and mortgage interest rises

Foundation of WOMEN'S INSTITUTES

Women's International Peace Conference at The Hague

LAWRENCE, *The Rainbow*

Rupert Brooke's posthumous war sonnets

John Buchan, *The Thirty-Nine Steps*

1916

January: Allies complete withdrawal from GALLIPOLI

February: CONSCRIPTION introduced following act of Parliament (January)

April: EASTER RISING in IRELAND

May–June: battle of JUTLAND

June: KITCHENER, the war minister, dies at sea

July–November: battle of the SOMME

August: execution of Irish nationalist Roger CASEMENT

December: ASQUITH ousted as PM; LLOYD GEORGE forms new coalition government

MINIMUM WAGE established for munitions workers

1917

March: British forces take Baghdad

April: USA joins Allies; Canadians take Vimy Ridge

June: British attack at Messines; 'Gotha' air raids on London begin

July: Arabs with T.E. LAWRENCE take Aqaba; GEORGE V changes family name to WINDSOR

July–November: third battle of YPRES, also known as PASSCHENDAELE

November: BALFOUR DECLARATION; battle of Cambrai witnesses first successful use of TANKS; Bolshevik Revolution in Russia

December: ALLENBY takes Jerusalem; beginning of British military rule in PALESTINE; armistice on Eastern Front following Russian Revolution

Industrial unrest, especially in engineering trade

Corn Production Act establishes MINIMUM WAGE for agricultural workers, and controls agricultural prices and rents (*see* AGRICULTURE)

Women's Army Auxiliary Corps established (*see* ARMY)

Family Endowment Society founded (*see* FAMILY ALLOWANCES)

1918

February: introduction of RATIONING of meat, butter and margarine

March: opening of German spring offensive on Western Front (to July)

April: formation of ROYAL AIR FORCE out of Royal Flying Corps and Royal Naval Air Service

July: Australians take Le Hamel, France; second battle of the MARNE marks collapse of German offensive; beginning of Anglo-French intervention in Russian Civil War

August: Allied Amiens offensive results in collapse of German 2nd Army; British intervention in Transcaucasia; POLICE strike in London

September: British breach Hindenburg Line; Megiddo offensive in Palestine; Allies sign armistice with Bulgaria

October: British and Arab forces take Damascus; Allies sign armistice with Turkey

November: Allies sign ARMISTICE with Austria-Hungary (3 November) and Germany (10 November); fighting on Western Front ends 11 November

REPRESENTATION OF THE PEOPLE ACT: all men over 21 and most women over 30 given right to vote

December: general election returns LLOYD GEORGE at head of coalition government; SINN FÉIN refuse to sit in Westminster and declare Irish independence in Dublin

Out-of-work donation introduced to support unemployed during demobilization

LABOUR PARTY produces new constitution, incorporating CLAUSE FOUR, and policy statement *Labour and the New Social Order*

Education Act raises school-leaving age to 14 (*see* EDUCATION)

Marie STOPES's *Married Love* and *Wise Parenthood*

Posthumous publication of Wilfred Owen's anti-war poetry

1918–19
INFLUENZA PANDEMIC

Widespread strikes (*see* TRADE UNIONS)

1919
January: opening of Paris Peace Conference

April: AMRITSAR MASSACRE

June: German High Seas Fleet scuttles at Scapa Flow, Orkney Islands; treaty of VERSAILLES

September: Allies sign treaty of St Germain with Austria

October: Allies complete withdrawal from northern Russia

November: Allies sign treaty of Neuilly with Bulgaria

SANKEY COMMISSION into COAL-MINING industry

Britain goes off GOLD STANDARD

Nancy ASTOR becomes first woman to sit in House of Commons

Women allowed to sit as MAGISTRATES

POLICE Act

Housing and Town Planning Act tightens up 1909 act (*see* TOWN AND COUNTRY PLANNING) and gives subsidies to local authorities and private builders for the construction of dwellings

Land Settlement Acts, and establishment of Forestry Commission (*see* LAND QUESTION)

Establishment of IRISH REPUBLICAN ARMY to fight war of independence against Britain in IRELAND

Aliens Act restricts IMMIGRATION

Ministry of Health established

National memorial to the war dead, the Cenotaph, unveiled in Whitehall, London

INDIA Act

KEYNES's *Economic Consequences of the Peace*

Alcock and Brown make first non-stop flight across Atlantic

ELGAR, cello concerto

1919–21
War of independence in IRELAND

1920
January: end of Paris Peace Conference; LEAGUE OF NATIONS comes into being

June: Allies sign treaty of Trianon with Hungary

August: Allies sign treaty of Sèvres with Turkey

November: Bloody Sunday (21 November; *see* BLACK AND TANS)

Unemployment Insurance Act extends unemployment insurance to all manual workers outside railways, agriculture and government service

Rent Act extends scope of rent control

Emergency Powers Act (*see* TRADE UNIONS)

CHURCH IN WALES comes into being following 1914 act disestablishing CHURCH OF ENGLAND in Wales

Formation of COMMUNIST PARTY OF GREAT BRITAIN

Agriculture Act confirms guaranteed prices to farmers (*see* AGRICULTURE)

Britain awarded mandate for PALESTINE by League of Nations

1921

March: Bonar LAW resigns from government and leadership of Conservative Party

April: Black Friday (23 April; *see* GENERAL STRIKE)

July: formation of British Legion (later the ROYAL BRITISH LEGION) out of a number of veterans' associations

December: Anglo-Irish treaty creates Irish Free State (*see* IRELAND)

Marie STOPES opens first BIRTH CONTROL clinic in Britain

RAILWAYS Act enforces consolidation of railway companies

ULSTER UNIONIST PARTY gains control of the Northern Ireland Parliament (until 1972)

Withdrawal of guaranteed prices to farmers, and abolition of MINIMUM WAGE for farm workers

CHURCH OF SCOTLAND Act

LAWRENCE, *Women in Love* (published in USA in 1920)

1922

August: assassination of Michael COLLINS

September–October: CHANAK CRISIS contributes to fall of LLOYD GEORGE coalition

October: Bonar LAW resumes leadership of Conservative Party and becomes PM, replacing the ousted Lloyd George

Formation of Transport and General Workers'

Union, with Ernest BEVIN as first general secretary

BRITISH BROADCASTING CORPORATION founded

ELIOT, *The Waste Land*

JOYCE, *Ulysses*

1922–3

First HUNGER MARCH

Civil war in IRELAND

1923

May: BALDWIN succeeds Bonar LAW as PM and leader of the Conservative Party

December: LABOUR wins more seats in general election than Liberals; Conservatives stay in power briefly as minority government

'GEDDES AXE' cuts government social expenditure

Reduction of rates (local taxes) on agricultural land

Women enabled to obtain DIVORCE on same grounds as men

IRISH LAND ACT

Treaty of Lausanne with Turkey, after Turkish Republic rejects 1920 treaty of Sèvres; UK gains CYPRUS

Sean O'Casey, *The Shadow of a Gunman*

First performance of WALTON's *Façade*, to words by Edith Sitwell

SHAW, *Saint Joan*

1924

January: Conservatives defeated in Commons over TARIFF REFORM; first LABOUR government formed, with Ramsay MACDONALD as PM

October: publication of ZINOVIEV LETTER

November: Conservatives return to power after October election, with BALDWIN as PM

Housing Act increases public subsidy for houses built for rent at controlled levels

Restoration of statutory regulation of wages in AGRICULTURE

Establishment of Central Electricity Generating Board as publicly owned corporation

Anglo-American Dawes Plan on German REPARATIONS

FORSTER, *A Passage to India*

1925

Britain returns to GOLD STANDARD

Pensionable age reduced to 65 (*see* OLD-AGE PENSIONS)

Introduction of widows' and orphans' pensions (*see* POOR LAW)

Foundation of Welsh National Party (later known as Plaid Cymru; *see* WALES)

LOCARNO PACT

Noël Coward, *Hay Fever*

1926

May: GENERAL STRIKE in support of miners' strike

ASQUITH resigns as leader of LIBERAL PARTY; succeeded by LLOYD GEORGE

Secretary of state appointed for SCOTLAND

ADOPTION Act

IMPERIAL CONFERENCE defines the 'white' dominions as 'autonomous communities within the British Empire, equal in status and freely associated as members of the British Commonwealth of Nations'

John Logie BAIRD demonstrates his TV system

Sean O'Casey, *The Plough and the Stars*

Hugh MacDiarmid, *A Drunk Man Looks at the Thistle*

Stanley SPENCER completes *Resurrection, Cookham*

1927

Trade Disputes and Trade Unions Act, aimed at reducing power of TRADE UNIONS (*see also* GENERAL STRIKE)

BRITISH BROADCASTING CORPORATION becomes a public corporation for the provision of public-service radio

WOOLF, *To the Lighthouse*

1928

EQUAL FRANCHISE ACT gives women vote on same basis as men, i.e. all those over 21 can vote

Foundation of National Party of SCOTLAND

First university ADULT EDUCATION department founded, at University College, Hull

FLEMING discovers penicillin

First showing in British cinemas of 'talking pictures'

LAWRENCE, *Lady Chatterley's Lover*, privately printed in Italy

YEATS, *The Tower*

WAUGH, *Decline and Fall*

1929

May: Labour wins a larger number of seats than any other party at general election; Ramsay MAC-DONALD becomes PM of minority government; Margaret BONDFIELD becomes first woman member of a British cabinet

September: establishment of MACMILLAN COMMITTEE ON FINANCE AND INDUSTRY

Wall Street Crash heralds GREAT CRASH

Local Government Act overhauls POOR LAW system

Second HUNGER MARCH

Abolition of rates (local taxes) on agricultural land

United Free Church rejoins CHURCH OF SCOTLAND

Young Plan on German REPARATIONS

WOOLF, *A Room of One's Own*

HITCHCOCK's first sound film, *Blackmail*

Eric GILL, stone reliefs for Broadcasting House

1930

Third HUNGER MARCH

Unification of BIRTH CONTROL societies (renamed Family Planning Association in 1939)

Britain stops making airships after destruction of R101

Noël Coward, *Private Lives*

1931

July: report of MAY COMMITTEE ON NATIONAL EXPENDITURE

August: international financial crisis (*see* GREAT CRASH) persuades Ramsay MACDONALD to form NATIONAL GOVERNMENT, which wins subsequent election

George LANSBURY becomes acting leader of LABOUR PARTY (formally appointed leader in 1932)

National Government adopts IMPERIAL PREFERENCE

Britain abandons GOLD STANDARD

Introduction of MEANS TEST

Statute of Westminster (*see* IMPERIAL CONFERENCES) grants legislative independence to 'white' dominions

INVERGORDON MUTINY

Japan invades Manchuria

WOOLF, *The Waves*

Walton's oratorio *Belshazzar's Feast*

1932

Abandonment of FREE TRADE leads SAMUEL and other Liberals to leave NATIONAL GOVERNMENT

INDEPENDENT LABOUR PARTY disassociates itself from LABOUR PARTY over latter's participation in NATIONAL GOVERNMENT

BRITISH UNION OF FASCISTS founded by Sir Oswald MOSLEY

Scottish Party founded (*see* SCOTLAND)

Town and Country Planning Act extends planning regulations to rural areas (*see* TOWN AND COUNTRY PLANNING)

Strands of METHODISM unite as Methodist Church

Mass trespass on Kinder Scout (*see* ENVIRONMENTALISM)

Fourth HUNGER MARCH

BRITISH BROADCASTING CORPORATION begins to broadcast to the empire; first royal Christmas broadcast

Lausanne Conference cancels German REPARATIONS

OTTAWA CONFERENCE

Atom split and neutron discovered at CAVENDISH LABORATORY, Cambridge

Aldous Huxley, *Brave New World*

Stanley SPENCER completes murals for the Sandham Memorial Chapel

1933

London transport comes into public ownership

Japan withdraws from LEAGUE OF NATIONS

Hitler comes to power in Germany

'New Deal' introduced in USA

Korda's film *The Private Lives of Henry VIII*

WELLS, *The Shape of Things to Come*

HEPWORTH, MOORE and NICHOLSON developing British abstract art

Arnos Grove station, one of Charles Holden's modernist designs for London Transport; Mendelsohn and Chermayeff's Bauhaus-style De La Warr Pavilion, Bexhill

1934

Government restores unemployment benefit rates to 1931 level

Special Areas Act introduces first regional economic policy

Fifth HUNGER MARCH

Formation of Scottish National Party (*see* SCOTLAND) out of National Party of Scotland and Scottish Party

1935

June: result of PEACE BALLOT

October: Italian invasion of Abyssinia (Ethiopia) provokes ABYSSINIAN CRISIS

November: BALDWIN wins general election, having succeeded MACDONALD as PM of NATIONAL GOVERNMENT

December: foreign secretary Samuel HOARE resigns following disclosure of HOARE–LAVAL PACT

ATTLEE succeeds LANSBURY as leader of the LABOUR PARTY

POPULAR FRONT against fascism advocated by COMMUNIST PARTY OF GREAT BRITAIN

GEORGE V's silver jubilee

Government of India Act (*see* INDIA)

Anglo-German naval treaty (*see* HOARE, SAMUEL)

ELIOT, *Murder in the Cathedral*

HITCHCOCK's film of *The 39 Steps*

Ben NICHOLSON, *White Relief*, notable for its uncompromising abstraction

Berthold Lubetkin's modernist Penguin Pool at London Zoo; Wallis Gilbert and Partners' art deco Hoover Factory in west London

1935–9

Policy of APPEASEMENT

1936

January: death of GEORGE V; succeeded by
EDWARD VIII

March: Hitler sends troops into Rhineland (*see*
LOCARNO PACT)

May: establishment of PEACE PLEDGE UNION

November–December: ABDICATION CRISIS;
Edward VIII abdicates 10 December; succeeded
by GEORGE VI

Formation of Rome–Berlin Axis and German-
Japanese Anti-Comintern Pact

Final HUNGER MARCH, including Jarrow
Crusaders

Formation of LEFT BOOK CLUB

Public Order Act, aimed at activities of BRITISH
UNION OF FASCISTS

BRITISH BROADCASTING CORPORATION
begins world's first regular TV broadcasting
service

KEYNES's *The General Theory of Employment,
Interest and Money*

Outbreak of SPANISH CIVIL WAR (to 1939)

Documentary film *Night Mail*, with words by
AUDEN and music by BRITTEN

1937

May: Neville CHAMBERLAIN succeeds Baldwin as
Conservative Party leader and as prime minister
of the NATIONAL GOVERNMENT; coronation
of GEORGE VI

Britain begins rearmament

Air-raid precautions introduced

Range of grounds for DIVORCE extended

Physical Training Act (*see* SPORT)

New constitution in IRELAND replaces Irish Free
State with 'sovereign state' of Eire

Japan mounts major invasion of China

ORWELL, *The Road to Wigan Pier*

J.R.R. Tolkien, *The Hobbit*

Establishment of EUSTON ROAD SCHOOL
of art

1938

February: EDEN resigns as foreign secretary over
appeasement of Italy; succeeded by HALIFAX

September: MUNICH AGREEMENT

CRIPPS and BEVAN expelled from Labour Party for
advocating POPULAR FRONT with communists

British open major naval base at SINGAPORE

Auxiliary Territorial Service (ATS) established for
women (*see* ARMY)

Formation of WOMEN'S ROYAL VOLUNTARY SERVICE

BRITISH BROADCASTING CORPORATION begins
foreign-language broadcasts

ORWELL, *Homage to Catalonia*

WAUGH, *Scoop*

Daphne du Maurier, *Rebecca*

1939

March: Hitler breaks MUNICH AGREEMENT by
invading rest of Czechoslovakia

May: CONSCRIPTION reintroduced

August: Nazi–Soviet pact

September: beginning of WORLD WAR II; Britain
and France declare war on Germany following
German invasion of Poland

October: Royal Navy battleship *Royal Oak* sunk in
Scapa Flow, Orkney Islands

December: battle of River Plate ends with scut-
tling of German battleship *Graf Spee*

Cotton industry forms cartel under the Cotton
Board (*see* TEXTILES)

Establishment of COUNCIL FOR THE ENCOUR-
AGEMENT OF MUSIC AND THE ARTS

JOYCE, *Finnegans Wake*

YEATS, *Last Poems*

1940

January: introduction of FOOD RATIONING

April: Germans overrun Denmark

May (10): Germany invades Low Countries;
Neville CHAMBERLAIN resigns as PM; replaced
by CHURCHILL, who forms coalition to replace
NATIONAL GOVERNMENT

May: formation of HOME GUARD

May–June: DUNKIRK evacuation

June: Norway surrenders to Germans; Italy declares war on Britain and attacks MALTA; French sign armistice with Germans; CHANNEL ISLANDS occupied

July: Italians invade British Somaliland

July–September: battle of BRITAIN

August: first RAF bombing raid on Berlin

September: beginning of the BLITZ; Italians advance into Egypt; Japan joins Axis

October: Hitler abandons plan to invade Britain; Italians invade Greece

November: British forces sent to Crete; CUNNINGHAM seriously damages Italian fleet at Taranto

December: British counterattack in Egypt

Qualifying age for women to receive OLD-AGE PENSIONS reduced to 60

Introduction of purchase tax

Graham Greene, *The Power and the Glory*

Henry MOORE begins his series of drawings of Londoners sheltering in underground stations during the Blitz; John PIPER, Graham SUTHER-LAND and Paul Nash also begin work as war artists

1941

January: British advance into Ethiopia, Eritrea and Italian Somaliland; capture of Tobruk

February: German forces under Rommel arrive in North Africa

March: LEND-LEASE Act; CUNNINGHAM defeats Italian fleet at Cape Matapan; British troops sent to Greece

April: Italians surrender in Ethiopia; Germans invade Yugoslavia and Greece; British troops withdrawn

May: German battleship *Bismarck* sunk, after sinking Royal Navy battleship *Hood*

June: British forces withdraw from Crete; German invasion of USSR

August: ATLANTIC CHARTER

December: USA joins Allies after Pearl Harbor (7 December); Japanese attack Malaya, BURMA, Borneo and Philippines, and capture HONG KONG

Test flight of Gloster Meteor, first jet fighter, designed by Frank Whittle

1942

January: Japanese invade Dutch East Indies, New Guinea and Solomon Islands

February: fall of SINGAPORE to Japanese

May: first RAF thousand-bomber raid on Germany; Philippines and Burma fall to Japanese

June: battle of Midway marks turning point in Pacific War

August: disastrous Dieppe raid involving troops from CANADA; civil disobedience campaign in INDIA

October–November: third, decisive battle of EL ALAMEIN; Allies land in northwest Africa

BEVERIDGE Report on establishing modern WELFARE STATE

Foundation of COMMON WEALTH PARTY

Completion of ELIOT's *Four Quartets*

1943

January: Casablanca Conference (CHURCHILL and Roosevelt)

February: German surrender at Stalingrad marks turning point on Eastern Front

May: Axis forces surrender in North Africa; German SUBMARINES withdrawn from Atlantic

July: Allied invasion of Sicily; Mussolini dismissed by king of Italy

September: Allied invasion of mainland Italy; Italy surrenders, but is occupied by German forces

November: Cairo Conference (CHURCHILL, Roosevelt and Chiang Kai-shek); Teheran Conference (CHURCHILL, Roosevelt and Stalin)

Powell and Pressburger's film *The Life and Times of Colonel Blimp*

1944

January: Allied landings at ANZIO, Italy

March–June: attempted Japanese invasion of Assam (eastern India) repelled

May: fall of strategic stronghold of MONTE CASSINO in Italy to Allies

June: fall of Rome to Allies (5 June); D-DAY landings in Normandy (6 June) begin Allied invasion of northwest Europe; first V-1 flying bombs fall on England

July: Allies land in the south of France; Bretton Woods Conference establishes International Monetary Fund and World Bank

August: Paris liberated

August–October: Dumbarton Oaks Conference sets out structure of UNITED NATIONS

September: beginning of V-2 missile attacks on England; battle of ARNHEM; British and Indian forces re-enter Burma

October: Allies retake Greece; British become involved in Greek civil war, opposing the communists

November: RAF sink German battleship *Tirpitz*

December: HOME GUARD disbanded; beginning of battle of the BULGE, German counteroffensive in the Ardennes (to January 1945)

Education Act raises school-leaving age to 15 (implemented 1947) and establishes free, compulsory secondary EDUCATION

Olivier's film of *Henry V*

BACON, *Three Studies at the Base of a Crucifixion*

1945

February: YALTA conference; Allied bombing of DRESDEN

March: Allies cross Rhine

May: unconditional surrender of all German forces; Allied victory in Europe

July: Potsdam Conference (Truman, CHURCHILL then ATTLEE, and Stalin) decides fate of postwar Germany and considers European reconstruction; LABOUR PARTY wins landslide in general election and Attlee becomes PM

August: atomic bombs dropped on Hiroshima and Nagasaki, leading to Japanese surrender and end of World War II

October: UNITED NATIONS comes into being

FAMILY ALLOWANCES Act

End of LEND-LEASE

First performance of BRITTEN's opera *Peter Grimes*

ORWELL, *Animal Farm*

WAUGH, *Brideshead Revisited*

RUSSELL, *A History of Western Philosophy*

1946

July: bread RATIONING introduced

Government decides to develop British atom bomb (*see* NUCLEAR WEAPONS)

NATIONALIZATION of BANK OF ENGLAND, COAL MINING, civil aviation and cable and wireless

NATIONAL HEALTH SERVICE Act; NHS comes into being in 1948

National Insurance Act and National Assistance Act (*see* WELFARE STATE)

Repeal of 1927 Trade Disputes and Trade Unions Act (*see* GENERAL STRIKE; TRADE UNIONS)

NEW TOWNS Act

Establishment of ARTS COUNCIL OF GREAT BRITAIN

Independence of Transjordan (British mandate since World War I) as Kingdom of Jordan

Dylan Thomas, *Deaths and Entrances*

Terence Rattigan, *The Winslow Boy*

David Lean's film of *Great Expectations*

1947

Economic crisis and fuel crisis; Britain hit by severest winter for over half a century

NATIONALIZATION of RAILWAYS, road transport and electricity industry

Development of British atomic bomb begins (*see* NUCLEAR WEAPONS); first British nuclear reactor built at Harwell

Following 1944 Education Act, school-leaving age raised to 15

TOWN AND COUNTRY PLANNING Act establishes 'green belts' and gives local authorities extensive powers

Britain signs up to GENERAL AGREEMENT ON TARIFFS AND TRADE

Failure of government-funded ground-nut scheme in Tanganyika

Independence of INDIA and Pakistan

Foundation of INSTITUTE OF CONTEMPORARY ARTS

1948

NATIONAL HEALTH SERVICE (NHS) comes into being

Non-means-tested OLD-AGE PENSIONS extended to whole population

National Assistance implemented following 1946 act

MARSHALL PLAN comes into effect

NATIONALIZATION of gas industry

REPRESENTATION OF THE PEOPLE ACT

British Nationality Act (*see* IMMIGRATION)

Abolition of trial of peers by peers

Olympic Games held in London

End of British mandate in PALESTINE; creation of state of Israel

WESTERN EUROPEAN UNION formed

Beginning of British military withdrawal from Egypt

Independence of Ceylon (Sri Lanka) and BURMA

Formation of Federation of MALAYA; beginning of 'Malayan Emergency' (until 1960)

Apartheid adopted as official policy in SOUTH AFRICA

Powell and Pressburger's film *The Red Shoes*

1948–9

BERLIN AIRLIFT

1949

Parliament Act further restricts powers of HOUSE OF LORDS

NATIONALIZATION of iron and STEEL INDUSTRY

Legal aid introduced

Pound devalued

Establishment of NATO

IRELAND leaves Commonwealth and becomes a republic

ORWELL, *Nineteen Eighty-Four*

Carol Reed's film *The Third Man*, with script by Graham Greene

Kind Hearts and Coronets, an early Ealing comedy

1950

February: LABOUR PARTY narrowly wins general election; ATTLEE remains as PM

Klaus Fuchs found guilty of passing atomic secrets to USSR

1950–3

British units fight with UN forces in KOREAN WAR

1951

April: BEVAN, WILSON and others resign from Labour government over charges for NHS dentures and spectacles, intended to help fund newly announced rearmament programme

May: Burgess and Maclean, two of the CAMBRIDGE SPIES, flee to Moscow

May–September: FESTIVAL OF BRITAIN

October: CONSERVATIVE PARTY narrowly wins general election; CHURCHILL becomes PM

Persia (Iran) nationalizes British oil interests

Anthony Powell publishes first in novel sequence *A Dance to the Music of Time* (to 1975)

John Wyndham, *The Day of the Triffids*

Lucian FREUD, *Interior at Paddington*

Frederick Gibberd's Royal Festival Hall

1952

February: death of GEORGE VI; succeeded by ELIZABETH II

October: test explosion of Britain's first atomic bomb (*see* NUCLEAR WEAPONS)

Conservatives reintroduce NHS prescription charges

British De Havilland Comet, world's first jet airliner, enters service

WAUGH, *Sword of Honour* trilogy (to 1961)

Tippett's opera *The Midsummer Marriage*

1953

May: British team succeed on Mount Everest; Edmund Hilary (New Zealand) and Tenzing Norgay (Nepal) reach summit

June: coronation of ELIZABETH II

Iron and STEEL INDUSTRY denationalized

End of food RATIONING

Over 300 die in North Sea floods

Major London smog (*see* CLEAN AIR ACT)

Central African Federation formed, consisting of Southern Rhodesia (ZIMBABWE), Northern Rhodesia (Zambia) and Nyasaland (Malawi)

Structure of DNA established at CAVENDISH LABORATORY, Cambridge

Ian Fleming, *Casino Royale*, first James Bond novel

Vaughan Williams, *Sinfonia Antarctica*

1954

Landlord and Tenant Act gives security of tenure to occupying tenants

EQUAL PAY established in public sector

Dylan Thomas, *Under Milk Wood*

William Golding, *Lord of the Flies*

SUTHERLAND, portrait of *Winston Churchill* (later destroyed by Lady Churchill)

1955

April: CHURCHILL resigns as PM; succeeded by EDEN

May: Conservatives win general election

December: GAITSKELL succeeds ATTLEE as leader of the LABOUR PARTY

Decision to develop British hydrogen bomb

Formation of WESTERN EUROPEAN UNION

First independent television broadcasts

London opening of Samuel Beckett's *Waiting for Godot*

1956

SUEZ CRISIS

CLEAN AIR ACT

Royal Navy diver Commander Crabb disappears during Soviet naval visit to Portsmouth

Soviet leaders Bulganin and Khrushchev visit Britain

Jo GRIMOND becomes leader of Liberal Party

Introduction of premium bonds (*see* GAMBLING)

John Osborne's play *Look Back in Anger* opens attack by 'Angry Young Men' on 'the establishment' (*see* DRAMA)

Foundation of Royal Ballet

Richard HAMILTON, *Just What Is It That Makes Today's Homes So Different, So Appealing?*, heralds arrival of British pop art

US film *Rock Around the Clock* introduces rock 'n' roll to Britain; emergence of teddy boys

1957

January: EDEN resigns as PM; succeeded by MACMILLAN

May: test explosion of first British hydrogen bomb

WOLFENDEN REPORT on sexual offences and prostitution recommends legalization of consensual homosexual sex between adults

Homicide Act restricts application of CAPITAL PUNISHMENT

Independence of MALAYA and Gold Coast (Ghana)

Establishment of EUROPEAN ECONOMIC COMMUNITY

British Trans-Antarctic Expedition

Elizabeth FRINK, *Wild Boar*, sculpture for Harlow New Town

1958

Formation of the CAMPAIGN FOR NUCLEAR DISARMAMENT

Introduction of life peerages (*see* HOUSE OF LORDS)

Race riots in Notting Hill (London) and Nottingham

Completion of Preston bypass, the first stretch of MOTORWAY in Britain

Establishment of WEST INDIES Federation

Harold Pinter, *The Birthday Party*

Iris Murdoch, *The Bell*

Graham Greene, *Our Man in Havana*

1959

October: Conservatives win general election and stay in power

Street Offences Act makes open soliciting on the street illegal but imposes no penalties on clients of prostitutes

Obscene Publications Act (*see* CENSORSHIP)

Hovercraft invented by British engineer, Christopher Cockerell

Completion of first section of M1 MOTORWAY

Driest summer in Britain for over 200 years

Independence of SINGAPORE

John Arden's *Serjeant Musgrave's Dance* first performed at the Royal Court Theatre

1960

Last conscripts begin National Service (finish service in 1962; *see* CONSCRIPTION)

Establishment of EUROPEAN FREE TRADE ASSOCIATION

Formation of ANTI-APARTHEID MOVEMENT

Lady Chatterley trial tests 1959 Obscene Publications Act (*see* CENSORSHIP)

Betting and Gaming Act legalizes betting shops, members' casinos and bingo clubs (*see* GAMBLING)

Cancellation of British Blue Streak missile project (*see* NUCLEAR WEAPONS)

Independence of CYPRUS, Nigeria and Malayan Federation, and end of Malayan Emergency (*see* MALAYA/MALAYSIA)

Karel Reisz's film version of Alan Sillitoe's *Saturday Night and Sunday Morning*

1961

Britain applies to join EUROPEAN ECONOMIC COMMUNITY

Establishment of NATIONAL ECONOMIC DEVELOPMENT COUNCIL

Introduction of BIRTH CONTROL pill

US military builds early-warning station at Fylingdales, Yorkshire

George Blake and others tried as Soviet spies

Independence of Tanganyika and Sierra Leone

Stage review *Beyond the Fringe* and magazine *Private Eye* mark the beginning of the satire movement

David Lean's film *Lawrence of Arabia*

Muriel SPARK, *The Prime of Miss Jean Brodie*

HOCKNEY, *We Two Boys Forever Clinging*, in his early pop art style

1962

July: MACMILLAN's 'night of the long knives': seven cabinet minister sacked

December: Nassau agreement with USA leads to Britain obtaining US Polaris missiles

End of National Service (*see* CONSCRIPTION)

Introduction of mandatory local authority grants for university students

Commonwealth Immigrants Act restricts IMMIGRATION from Commonwealth

First NEW TOWNS completed

British businessman, Greville Wynne, arrested in Hungary on charges of spying and taken to Soviet Union

Withdrawal of drug thalidomide after it causes deformities in babies

Royal College of Physicians announces link between smoking and health

Independence of Uganda, Jamaica, and Trinidad and Tobago

Dissolution of WEST INDIES Federation

LESSING, *The Golden Notebook*

That Was The Week That Was: BBC TV takes up satire

Dr No, first of the James Bond films

Completion of Basil Spence's new Coventry Cathedral; inside is SUTHERLAND's tapestry *Christ in Glory*; BRITTEN's *War Requiem* first performed at the new cathedral

Bridget RILEY developing op art

1963

January: Britain's application to join EUROPEAN ECONOMIC COMMUNITY vetoed by France

July: Nuclear Test Ban treaty

October: MACMILLAN resigns as PM following PROFUMO AFFAIR; succeeded by Sir Alec DOUGLAS-HOME

WILSON becomes leader of the Labour Party after death of GAITSKELL

Peerage Act (*see* HOUSE OF LORDS)

Kim Philby, the 'third man' of the CAMBRIDGE SPIES, flees to the USSR

Robbins Report advocates the expansion of higher education

Beeching Report leads to closure of many RAILWAY lines.

Great Train Robbery

Creation of NATIONAL THEATRE company

Independence of KENYA

Formation of Federation of MALAYSIA

Dissolution of Central African Federation of Southern Rhodesia (ZIMBABWE), Northern Rhodesia (Zambia) and Nyasaland (Malawi)

The BEATLES have three number-one records

John le Carré, *The Spy Who Came in from the Cold*

Joan Littlewood's Theatre Workshop production, *Oh, What a Lovely War!*

Joseph Losey's film *The Servant*, with screenplay by Harold Pinter

Barbara HEPWORTH, *Single Form*

1964

October: Labour wins general election with majority of 4 seats; WILSON becomes PM

Establishment of Welsh Office (*see* WALES) and Ministry of Technology

Violence between mods and rockers (*see* YOUTH CULTURE) in seaside resorts

Opening of Forth Road Bridge

Independence of Northern Rhodesia (Zambia), Nyasaland (Malawi) and MALTA

William Golding, *The Spire*

1965

Creation of Department of Economic Affairs and Prices and Incomes Board

First Race Relations Act and formation of Race Relations Board (*see* immigration)

Abolition of CAPITAL PUNISHMENT

Introduction of capital gains tax

Circular 10/65 requires local education authorities to reorganize secondary EDUCATION on comprehensive lines

Greater London Council replaces London County Council (*see* LONDON GOVERNMENT)

'Rediscovery' of POVERTY; foundation of Child Poverty Action Group

Decision to cut TERRITORIAL ARMY by 70,000 men

Sports Council established (*see* SPORT)

Establishment of COMMONWEALTH Secretariat

Independence of the Gambia

White government of Southern Rhodesia (ZIMBABWE) makes unilateral declaration of independence

Fighting breaks out between nationalists in ADEN and British forces; continues until British withdrawal in November 1967

Edward Bond's controversial play *Saved*

Joe Orton's *Loot*

1966

March: Labour wins general election with increased majority of 98 seats

October: ABERFAN disaster

Introduction of corporation tax

Plaid Cymru (*see* WALES) wins first seat in House of Commons in by-election

Failure of talks between WILSON and Rhodesian premier Ian Smith on HMS *Tiger*

Independence of Barbados, Guyana, Botswana and Lesotho

Colour TV transmissions begin in Britain

Tom Stoppard, *Rosencrantz and Guildenstern are Dead*

Harrison Birtwistle's opera *Punch and Judy*

1967

Britain's second application to join EUROPEAN ECONOMIC COMMUNITY vetoed, again by France

Appointment of first OMBUDSMAN

STEEL INDUSTRY renationalized

Jo GRIMOND resigns from leadership of Liberal Party; succeeded by Jeremy THORPE.

First Scottish National Party MP elected in by-election (*see* SCOTLAND)

Welsh Language Act (*see* WALES)

ABORTION becomes legal for the first time

Legalization of homosexual acts in private between consenting adults over the age of 21

Introduction of majority verdicts in criminal trials in England and Wales

Formation of NATIONAL FRONT

NORTHERN IRELAND Civil Rights Association founded

Foundation of WEST INDIES Federated States

GIBRALTAR votes to remain British

Britain withdraws from ADEN

HOCKNEY, *A Bigger Splash*

Completion of Frederick Gibberd's controversial Roman Catholic cathedral in Liverpool

The BEATLES' album *Sergeant Pepper's Lonely Hearts Club Band*

Hippy 'summer of love'

1968

Commonwealth Immigrants Act tightened up to restrict IMMIGRATION of Kenyan Asians

Enoch POWELL's 'Rivers of Blood' speech (*see* IMMIGRATION)

Race Relations Act

Trade Descriptions Act

Merger of Foreign and Commonwealth Offices

Fulton Report calls for overhaul of CIVIL SERVICE

Civil rights marches in NORTHERN IRELAND lead to sectarian violence

Bombings by extreme nationalists in WALES

Widespread student unrest; large anti-Vietnam War demonstration outside US embassy in Grosvenor Square, London

Collapse of Ronan Point tower block in east London prompts re-evaluation of high-rise HOUSING policy

Theatres Act abolishes CENSORSHIP of theatre

Nuclear non-proliferation treaty

Mauritius and Swaziland become independent

Arthur C. Clarke, *2001, A Space Odyssey*

1969

Voting age lowered to 18

In Place of Strife, white paper on industrial relations (*see* TRADE UNIONS)

Parliament votes for permanent abolition of CAPITAL PUNISHMENT

British troops sent to NORTHERN IRELAND; IRISH REPUBLICAN ARMY becomes active again; Terence O'NEILL resigns as Northern Ireland PM; succeeded by James Chichester-Clark; split between Official and Provisional wings of the IRISH REPUBLICAN ARMY and SINN FÉIN

More bombings by extreme nationalists in WALES

Introduction of 'no-fault' DIVORCE

Foundation of OPEN UNIVERSITY

First woman minister in CHURCH OF SCOTLAND

First flight of Concorde

Investiture of CHARLES as prince of Wales

John Fowles, *The French Lieutenant's Woman*

Peter Maxwell Davies, *Eight Songs for a Mad King*

1969–70

Protests against tour by South African rugby team by ANTI-APARTHEID MOVEMENT

1970

Expenditure on education exceeds that on defence for the first time

EQUAL PAY Act

Conservatives win June general election; Edward HEATH becomes prime minister; following month the new chancellor, Iain MACLEOD, dies in office

Formation of SOCIAL DEMOCRATIC AND LABOUR PARTY in NORTHERN IRELAND under leadership of Gerry FITT

First national conference of women's liberation movement

Rhodesia (now ZIMBABWE) declares itself a republic

Independence of Fiji, Tonga and Western Samoa

Ted Hughes, *Crow*

Germaine Greer, *The Female Eunuch*

Peter Brook's production of *A Midsummer Night's Dream* applies experimental approach to Shakespeare

1970–5

British forces involved in suppression of communist rebellion in Oman

1971

February: DECIMALIZATION of currency introduced.

Industrial Relations Act (*see* TRADE UNIONS)

Rolls-Royce company saved by government aid

Introduction of family income supplement (*see* FAMILY ALLOWANCES)

Discovery of oil and gas in North Sea (*see* NORTH SEA OIL)

Immigration Act further restricts Commonwealth IMMIGRATION

Abolition of free milk for schoolchildren

Withdrawal of British forces from Trucial States, which federate as United Arab Emirates

1972

January (30): BLOODY SUNDAY in Northern Ireland

March: suspension of NORTHERN IRELAND Parliament; direct rule from Westminster

Formation of Democratic Unionist Party, led by Ian PAISLEY

MINERS' STRIKE

Imposition of statutory incomes policy

Reorganization of LOCAL GOVERNMENT in England and Wales

1972–6

'COD WAR' with Iceland

1973

Britain joins European Community (*see* EUROPEAN ECONOMIC COMMUNITY)

Foundation of People's Party (later renamed Ecology Party, then Green Party; *see* ENVIRONMENTALISM)

Beginning of 'OIL SHOCK'

School-leaving age raised to 16

1973–4

MINERS' STRIKE leads to three-day week for industry and helps to bring down HEATH's Conservative government.

Graham Greene, *The Honorary Consul*

1974

January: power-sharing executive established in NORTHERN IRELAND; brought down by Protestant strike within five months

February: Labour under Harold WILSON forms minority government after general election

October: second general election of the year leaves Labour in power with small majority

November: Kilbrandon Report recommends separate assembly for SCOTLAND

Trade Union Act and Health and Safety at Work Act (*see* TRADE UNIONS)

First woman ordained to the Methodist ministry

Independence of Grenada

1975

Margaret THATCHER succeeds Edward HEATH as leader of Conservative Party

NORTH SEA OIL and gas comes on stream

Sex Discrimination Act (*see* EQUAL PAY); establishment of Equal Opportunities Commission

First Employment Protection Act

Referendum votes in favour of Britain's membership of European Community (*see* EUROPEAN ECONOMIC COMMUNITY)

BIRTH CONTROL available to all on NHS

Child Benefit Act (*see* FAMILY ALLOWANCES)

Introduction of earnings-related supplement to OLD-AGE PENSIONS

NATIONALIZATION of British Leyland

Reorganization of LOCAL GOVERNMENT in Scotland, establishing two-tier structure of regions and districts

Seamus Heaney, *North*

1976

March: Harold WILSON resigns as PM, and is succeeded by James CALLAGHAN

Labour Relations Act (*see* TRADE UNIONS)

Race Relations Act establishes Commission for Racial Equality (*see* IMMIGRATION)

Jeremy THORPE resigns as leader of Liberals; succeeded by David STEEL

Record hot summer; minister for drought appointed just before rain returns

Concorde enters regular service

Beginnings of punk rock

1977

Beginning of second 'Lib-Lab pact', in which Liberals keep Labour in power

Introduction of child-benefit payments (*see* FAMILY ALLOWANCES)

NATIONALIZATION of shipbuilding and ship-repairing industry; aircraft-manufacturing industry also nationalized (as British Aerospace)

Silver jubilee of ELIZABETH II

1978

Second Employment Protection Act

Ending of Lib-Lab pact

Independence of Dominica

Iris Murdoch, *The Sea, The Sea*

1978–9

'Winter of discontent': widespread TRADE UNION action in public sector against the CALLAGHAN government's wage restraints

1979

March: referendum for devolution for SCOTLAND fails to achieve sufficient majority; Scottish National Party MPs mount no-confidence vote in which CALLAGHAN government is defeated; Labour defeated by Conservatives in subsequent general election; Margaret THATCHER becomes PM

EUROPEAN MONETARY SYSTEM introduced

Anthony Blunt publicly revealed as the 'fourth man' of the CAMBRIDGE SPIES

MOUNTBATTEN assassinated by IRA

Independence of St Lucia and St Vincent

1980

UNEMPLOYMENT rises above 2 million for first time since 1938

Housing Act gives council tenants the right to buy their home

Government announces Polaris missiles to be replaced by Trident system (*see* NUCLEAR WEAPONS)

Michael FOOT succeeds CALLAGHAN as leader of the LABOUR PARTY; Denis HEALEY becomes deputy leader

Riots in Bristol

Independence of ZIMBABWE

1981

British Telecommunications separated from the Post Office

Privatization of Cable and Wireless and part of British Aerospace

Nationality Act

Employment Act outlaws secondary picketing in industrial disputes (*see* TRADE UNIONS)

Start of GREENHAM COMMON women's peace camp

Hunger strikes by IRA prisoners end in nine deaths

Riots in a number of inner-city areas

Formation of SOCIAL DEMOCRATIC PARTY

Marriage of CHARLES, PRINCE OF WALES, and Lady DIANA Spencer

Independence of Antigua and Barbuda

Salman Rushdie, *Midnight's Children*

1982

April–June: Falklands War (see FALKLAND ISLANDS)

UNEMPLOYMENT rises above 3 million for first time since 1933

CANADA Act

Second commercial TV channel, Channel 4, begins broadcasting

1983

June: Conservatives win general election; Neil KINNOCK succeeds Michael FOOT as leader of the Labour Party; David OWEN succeeds Roy JENKINS as leader of the SOCIAL DEMOCRATIC PARTY

Gerry ADAMS becomes president of SINN FÉIN

Independence of St Kitts and Nevis

Peter Greenaway's film *The Draughtsman's Contract*

1984

March: beginning of MINERS' STRIKE

October: IRA bomb attack on THATCHER government at Brighton hotel

November: privatization of British Telecommunications

Divorce allowed after one year of marriage

1985

March: MINERS' STRIKE ends in defeat for miners and closure of many mines

LOCAL GOVERNMENT Act leads to abolition of Greater London Council in 1986 (*see* LONDON GOVERNMENT)

Anglo-Irish agreement (*see* IRELAND; NORTHERN IRELAND)

Riots in Handsworth (Birmingham) and Tottenham (London)

'Battle of the beanfield': police stop traveller convoy reaching Stonehenge festival (*see* YOUTH CULTURE)

Stephen Frears's film *My Beautiful Laundrette*

1986

January: resignation of defence secretary Michael Heseltine over Westland affair (*see* THATCHER, MARGARET)

First ever peacetime deficit in balance of trade in manufacturing

Abolition of Greater London Council (*see* LONDON GOVERNMENT)

British Gas privatized

BIG BANG in the City of London

Richard Rogers's hi-tech Lloyd's of London building (*see* ARCHITECTURE)

Derek Jarman's film *Caravaggio*

1987

June: Conservatives win general election

October (19): 'Black Monday' sees dramatic crash in share prices

November: eleven people die in IRA attack on Remembrance Day parade in Enniskillen

David OWEN resigns as leader of SOCIAL DEMOCRATIC PARTY after it votes to enter merger negotiations with LIBERAL PARTY

20:50 Richard Wilson (*see* VISUAL ARTS)

1988

March: members of both parties vote to merge LIBERAL PARTY and SOCIAL DEMOCRATIC PARTY as 'Social and Liberal Democrats'; David STEEL retires as leader; succeeded by Paddy ASHDOWN

September: Margaret THATCHER's anti-European Bruges speech

Family income supplement replaced by family credit (*see* FAMILY ALLOWANCES)

IMMIGRATION Act further restricts rights of relatives and dependants to settle in Britain

EDUCATION Reform Act introduces National Curriculum and opting out of local education authority control

Privatization of British STEEL Corporation

Foundation of CHARTER 88

1989

COMMUNITY CHARGE ('poll tax') implemented in Scotland

Third OFFICIAL SECRETS ACT

Social and Liberal Democrats renamed 'Liberal Democrats' (*see* LIBERAL PARTY)

Iranian leader Ayatollah Khomeini pronounces fatwa (death sentence) on Salman Rushdie for blasphemy in his novel *The Satanic Verses* (pub. 1988)

1990

COMMUNITY CHARGE ('poll tax') implemented in England and Wales; POPULAR PROTEST against it in central London turns into riot

David TRIMBLE becomes leader of Ulster Unionist Party

Geoffrey HOWE's resignation speech (November) precipitates downfall of Margaret THATCHER; succeeded as PM by John MAJOR

British Nationality (Hong Kong) Act prevents all but a small (and wealthy) minority of HONG KONG holders of British passports from settling in Britain

1991

January–February: GULF WAR

IRA mortar attack on Downing Street fails to inflict injuries

Electricity industry privatized

Abolition of NATIONAL ECONOMIC DEVELOP-MENT COUNCIL

1992

February: treaty of MAASTRICHT on formation of EUROPEAN UNION (1993)

April: Conservatives under John MAJOR returned to power in general election; subsequently Neil KINNOCK resigns from leadership of Labour Party; succeeded by John SMITH

June: First British troops sent to Bosnia as part of UN mission

September (17): 'Black Wednesday': Britain forced to devalue pound and withdraw from European Exchange Rate Mechanism

Separation of CHARLES, PRINCE OF WALES, and DIANA, PRINCESS OF WALES

Many polytechnics begin to convert into universities

1993

EUROPEAN UNION succeeds European Community

Government announces plans to privatize railways

COMMUNITY CHARGE ('poll tax') replaced by 'council tax'

Downing Street declaration on NORTHERN IRELAND

Murder of Stephen LAWRENCE

1994

Death of John SMITH; succeeded by Tony BLAIR as leader of the Labour Party

Criminal Justice Act includes provisions targeted at rave and traveller counter-cultures (*see* YOUTH CULTURE)

Trident NUCLEAR WEAPON system comes into use with ROYAL NAVY

Two-tier LOCAL GOVERNMENT in Scotland and Wales replaced by unitary authorities

IRA and Protestant paramilitaries call ceasefire in NORTHERN IRELAND

Start of National Lottery (*see* GAMBLING)

1995

Labour Party abandons original wording of CLAUSE FOUR of its constitution

John MAJOR defeats John Redwood in ballot for Conservative Party leadership

1996

January: IRA ends ceasefire with bombing in London Docklands; Manchester city centre destroyed later in year

Divorce of CHARLES, PRINCE OF WALES, and DIANA, PRINCESS OF WALES

1997

May: LABOUR PARTY achieves landslide victory in general election; Tony BLAIR becomes PM and Gordon BROWN chancellor; subsequently William HAGUE replaces John MAJOR as leader of the Conservative Party; government hands control over interest rates to committee of BANK OF ENGLAND

July: IRA calls ceasefire, allowing participation of SINN FÉIN in NORTHERN IRELAND peace talks

July: HONG KONG reverts to Chinese rule, marking symbolic end to the British EMPIRE

August: DIANA, PRINCESS OF WALES, killed in car crash

'Sensation' exhibition of BRITART at Royal Academy

1998

April: Good Friday agreement in NORTHERN IRELAND

August: dissident Republicans set of bomb in Omagh, NORTHERN IRELAND, killing 29 people

Referendums in SCOTLAND and WALES come out in favour of devolution (*see also* HOME RULE)

1999

Introduction of national MINIMUM WAGE

Publication of MacPherson Report into Stephen LAWRENCE murder

Elections for new Scottish Parliament and Welsh Assembly (*see* SCOTLAND; WALES)

Number of hereditary peers allowed to participate in work of HOUSE OF LORDS reduced to 92

Paddy ASHDOWN succeeded as leader of Liberal Democrats (*see* LIBERAL PARTY) by Charles Kennedy

British forces participate in NATO KOSOVO campaign

AUSTRALIA votes in referendum to keep British monarch as head of state

2000

May: new London-wide authority elected, with Ken Livingstone separately elected as mayor (*see* LONDON GOVERNMENT)

June: LABOUR PARTY wins general election with a second landslide majority

General reading

A dictionary of this kind necessarily focuses upon the trees and this brings with it a danger that the reader might lose sight of the wood. What follows is a list of overviews of broad aspects of British history in the twentieth century, which are not referred to elsewhere in the volume, but which might assist readers to place the entries on specific topics in a wider context. They all include suggestions for further, specialized reading.

Clarke, P., *Hope and Glory. Britain, 1900–1990* (1996) is an excellent synthesis and overview.

Harrison, B., *Peaceable Kingdom : Stability and Change in Modern Britain* (1985) usefully surveys a slightly shorter span of the century but also discusses the late nineteenth-century roots of twentieth-century processes.

Reynolds, D., *Britannia Overruled: British Policy and World Power in the Twentieth Century* (2nd edn, 2000) is an excellent, succinct overview of Britain's international relations.

Three volumes in the Penguin Social History of Britain series that cover the century and are readable and insightful:

Harris, J., *Private Lives, Public Spirit: A Social History of Britain 1870–1914* (1993).

Stevenson, J., *British Society, 1914–45* (1984).

Marwick, A., *British Society since 1945* (2nd edn, 1990).

Pollard, S., *The Development of the British Economy 1914–1990* (4th edn, 1992) provides a clear and accessible overview on the economy, as, coming up closer to end of the century, does R. Middleton, *The British Economy Since 1945* (2000).

Indispensable compendia of information are:

Butler, D., and G. Butler, *Twentieth Century British Political Facts* (2000) provides information about politics and government administration, though it also contains useful statistics on the economy, the press and religion.

Halsey, A.H. and J. Webb (eds.), *Twentieth Century British Social Trends* (2000) combines statistical tables with analytical essays on major features of British society and the economy, including demography, social class and social mobility, education, health, immigration, urbanization, housing, crime and punishment, leisure and religion.

Maps are useful aids.

Overy, R. (ed.), *The Times Atlas of the 20th century* (1996) is very helpful.